MW00748819

80386/80486 Assembly Language Programming

80386/80486 Assembly Language Programming

Penn Brumm
Don Brumm

Windcrest®/McGraw-Hill

NOTICES

Turbo™   Borland International
Intel™   Intel Corp.
IBM®   International Business Machines Corp.
Microsoft®   Microsoft Corp.
MS™
MS-DOS™

FIRST EDITION
FIRST PRINTING

© 1993 by **Windcrest Books**, an imprint of TAB Books.
TAB Books is a division of McGraw-Hill, Inc.
The name "Windcrest" is a registered trademark of TAB Books.

Printed in the United States of America. All rights reserved. The publisher takes no
responsibility for the use of any of the materials or methods described in this book,
nor for the products thereof.

Library of Congress Cataloging-in-Publication Data

Brumm, Penn.
     80386/80486 Assembly language programming / by Penn Brumm and Don
Brumm.
       p.   cm.
    Includes bibliographical references and index.
    ISBN 0-8306-4099-1 (hard)   ISBN 0-8306-4100-9 (paper)
     1. Intel 80386 (Microprocessor)—Programming.   2. Intel 80486
(Microprocessor)—Programming.   3. Assembler language (Computer
program language)   I. Brumm, Don.   II. Title.
QA76.8.I2928B77   1992
005.265—dc20   92-14590
                                           CIP

Acquisitions Editor: Roland S. Phelps
Editor: Alan H. Danis
Director of Production: Katherine G. Brown
Book Design: Jaclyn J. Boone   WP1

Contents

APPENDICES

Introduction

Software needs are increasing dramatically, but the number of people available to supply that demand is increasing at a much slower rate. U.S. Department of Defense figures show that qualified software personnel increases at a 4 percent annual rate, while their average productivity increases at about the same rate. Demand—the number of jobs that could be filled—is increasing at 12 percent per year. This is where you come in.

In addition to a relative dearth of people to do the work, the percentage of total system life-cycle costs assigned to software has risen steadily over the past 30 years. Software costs were less than 20 percent of total life-cycle costs in 1955. By 1985, software costs exceeded 80 percent, and between 1985 and 1990, the total cost for software doubled. Costs will double again before the turn of the century.

Intended audience

This book can help you get to where you want to be when you're trying to write assembly code to solve a problem. We have included some topics as background material in case you're experienced in one area but not another. We don't expect you to be expert in everything. In case you don't have time to key in all the routines you'll find in this book, you can obtain a disk that contains them from the publisher.

It is assumed that you have done some assembly language programming using MS-DOS (a recent version or a look-alike). It is also assumed that you understand how assembly language works. If you code some clever routines, we would like to hear from you. Write to us in care of Windcrest (McGraw-Hill). Also write to us if you find errors, as they can creep into the best of code.

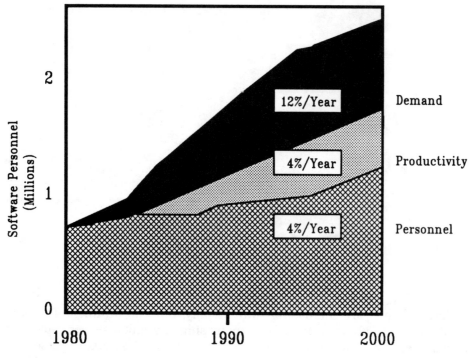

I-1 Growth of programmer demand, productivity, and personnel.

There are many operating systems for the IBM Personal Computer and its clones, but this book concentrates on Microsoft's MS-DOS, level 5.0 and higher. The programs, procedures, and shorter routines were written on an 80486-based computer with MS-DOS 5.0 using Borland's Turbo Assembler 2.0 (TASM). The 1991 release of TASM contains a bug if you use the CMXCHG instruction. Evidently, Borland designers used the Intel documentation and coded the hex instruction of 0F A6 and 0F A7 instead of the data sheet that shows the correct notation of 0F B0 and 0F B1. We contacted Borland, so later releases of TASM will contain the correct hex notation.

Together, Don and I have a combined 55 years in the technical side of data processing. We both got started with IBM mainframe systems in the 1960s, not discovering the fascinating world of owning our own microcomputers until the mid-1970s. We've been part of a team that programmed an IBM mainframe operating system from scratch, written compilers, done network programming, and been systems engineers. Don stayed in systems software programming, and I finally opted for management (Product Support, Quality Assurance, Software Development, and Engineering Test Development). We now own (and use extensively) five microcomputers, two of which (an 80386-based and an 80486-based) were used for this book; the 80386 was used for the word processing, while the

80486 was used for coding. We have four printers, from a dot-matrix, to a daisy wheel, to a laser printer.

Book contents

Chapter 1 gives you a background on systems design, going into structured design, database design, program coding, testing, maintenance, and debugging. Chapter 2 covers general programming tips and methods to make MS-DOS work for you. We like to be productive as soon as possible, so we included a working program skeleton. You can use the skeleton to try out some of the things you find in this book. Simply insert the code in the right places in the skeleton, then assemble, link, and run. Included also in chapter 2 are tips on how to assemble and link your code. You'll be introduced to functions and MS-DOS interrupts that make your programming life a lot easier.

Chapter 3 addresses the 80486, with programming notes and tips that we found when we first began programming with Intel's processor. Traps you can easily fall into when you work with memory, descriptors, registers, tasks, privilege, protection, and test and debug are covered.

Starting with chapter 4, we provide background and toolkit programs, a mix of complete programs, and working procedures and pieces you can add as integral parts of whatever programs you write. Chapter 5 covers masked and unmasked exceptions—80486 processor interrupts—with toolkit programs.

Chapter 6 covers bit and string manipulation and shifts. We show you how to convert uppercase to lowercase and vice versa and also how to allocate from a bitmap. The string operations are standard, general ones you need for programs, such as finding one string within another.

Chapter 7 goes into 16- and 32-bit code conversion, with background information on 80486 data handling. The toolkit programs convert hex to binary, binary to hex, ASCII to EBCDIC, EBCDIC to ASCII, and BCD to ASCII and back. You'll learn how to go from single to double precision and back. In case you're an IBM EBCDIC-based person, we included a procedure, FLIPS, that changes the System/370 data storage method to an Intel data storage method (which, by the way, are logically incompatible and confusing the first time you run into the differences).

Chapter 8 discusses input/output, beginning with background on the 80486 I/O. The toolkit programs show you how to handle input editing, reading input character-by-character, writing output character-by-character, and reading and writing from files. Toolkit procedures show you how to create and close a file and perform EOF handling. Also shown is how to check for existing and nonexisting files and to count characters in files.

Algorithms are covered in chapter 9 along with background information on the various subjects. The toolkit programs include binary search, two different sorts, buffer handling, and encrypting/decrypting. Chapter 10 starts you on graphics, with bit shifting, and the design of a character

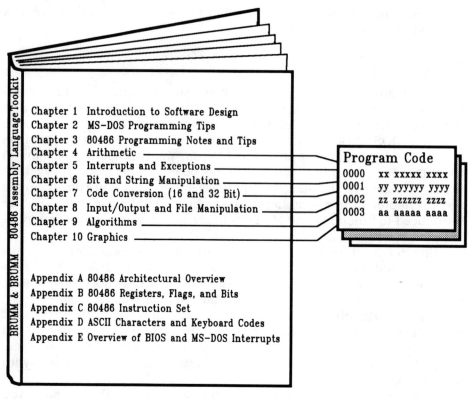

I-2 Location of toolkit code.

set. Elementary graphics are demonstrated with screen clearing, cursor positioning, line smoothing, point plotting, line drawing, and filling a rectangular area. Of interest, one of the programs shows how to get into graphics mode and do direct I/O to a graphics controller chip.

There are five appendices. Appendix A covers an overview of the 80486 architecture. Appendix B describes 80486 registers in detail, showing the various flags and bits you'll use once you get familiar with what the 80486 offers. Included are the Floating-Point Unit (FPU) registers, the System Flags Register (EFLAGS), the Control Register (CR0), Test Registers TR6 and TR7, Selector flags, segment descriptor flags, and an alphabetic listing of 80486 registers, flags, and bits.

Appendix C is an overview on the 80486 full instruction set. If you want a more complete discussion on either the architecture or the instruction set, read TAB's *80486: A Programming and Design Handbook*.

Appendix D contains an ASCII to decimal to hex to binary translation, with an illustration of the box graphics. Appendix E gives a thorough overview of the BIOS and MS-DOS interrupts, one of the most thorough that appears anywhere. At the back of the book, you'll find a complete glossary, in case the meaning of a word or phrase eludes you.

Assembly language

For some of the procedures included in this book to be useful, they must be combined with other routines to form complete programs. This can be done by including them when you link edit or by copying the code into your main-line program. We recommend that you divide your code into procedures and assemble and link each (to check for assembly errors) before you combine them into one large program. You cut down on the number of hard-to-find bugs this way.

Assembly language is the fastest and most powerful programming language, providing you with the same type of control a stick-shift transmission does compared to an automatic transmission. Even for experienced people, however, assembly language can be time-consuming, especially when you have to write routines to perform specific tasks that you do over and over. You keep thinking you'll build a library of routines, but you're busy and that task stays on a back burner. The aim of this book is to make it easy for you to incorporate fast, efficient 80486 assembly language routines into your programs. And don't worry about building a library. It's here for you.

1
Introduction to software design

When I first saw Cannery Row, my head was just high enough for me to see out the backseat window of a Hudson Hornet. We pulled into town, Dad driving past the sand dunes and scrub juniper of Fort Ord and along the crumbling docks of a Monterey, little changed from its brawling Spanish-grant, state capitol days.

Dad drove the Hudson slowly so we kids could savor the town John Steinbeck made famous. The air stank of dead fish and iodine, of dust catching at the back of the throat, of a whiff of unwashed sweat. Adobe buildings with red tiled roofs stood next to aging gray-dun wood buildings with slanting porches. Along the seashore, rusty corrugated iron walls of abandoned canneries flaked quietly in the salty air.

Mom stared straight ahead as Dad drove us past a ramshackle house with a two-chair porch. A lady wearing a nubby red pullover rocked languidly under the morning light—odd she wasn't dressed this near noontime. She waved. Dad cleared his throat, the back of his neck a sudden red to match the lady's robe. I lifted a hand just before we turned the corner for which the lady rewarded me with a thrown kiss.

For me, assembly language contains the same kind of mystique as the years-gone Monterey. Yet, assembly language is the basic mechanism, the cogs and wheels that makes machines run and programmers are the ones who build those internal parts. And, yes, there's a silent glamour to the ownership of this skill.

Programmers act as the link between a problem (or process to be computerized) and its successful solution on a computer. As programmers, you share in the definition and specification of the problem itself, as well as the design and coding of algorithms to be used in its solution.

After being assigned the problem, you define the scope of the problem, design the detail structure of the implementation, select the most suitable programming language, write and debug the necessary programs, and provide clear and complete documentation for both the user and other programmers who later might need to modify your program(s). To do this in the best way possible, you structure the programs to make them efficient, to make them usable, to document them, and to test them for errors.

Structured design

Structured design means the design of both the components of a system and the interrelationship between those components. Structured design has a significant effect on programming and program maintainability; a structured program's elements and their interdependencies can be graphed on a structure chart and quickly understood. The quicker the grasp, the shorter the startup time for new programmers.

Well-structured programs have five traits. First, the total program easily divides into modules arranged in a structure that defines their logical relationships. That is, A links to B, which links to C, and so on. Second, execution flows from module to module in easy-to-understand schemes, where control always enters the module at one unique point and always exits at another unique point. After each subroutine call, control always returns to the calling module or program. The third property of a structured program is that each program variable serves only one purpose, and the scope and limit of the variable is controlled and clear. For example, a variable called Index might be used as a step value in a loop or as a condition flag. Fourth, error processing follows normal program control (except in the case of unrecoverable errors). And finally, each module is documented to explain its function, data requirements, how it is invoked, and what it invokes. Figure 1-1 gives an overview of structured design. Now let's look at each aspect in more detail:

- Divide each program into independent pieces, called modules. A *module* is a self-contained unit whose code is physically and logically separate from the code of any other module in the program.
- Limit independent program pieces to fewer than 100 instructions. This number isn't "set in concrete" but is used to help you concentrate on keeping modules small enough to handle.
- Relate the modules to one another in a hierarchical manner. That is, each lower level in the structure represents a more detailed function.
- Begin each module with a common block that explains its function, the values passed to it, the values returned, what modules call this one, and what modules this one calls. See the programs included in this book for examples of this point.
- Avoid unnecessary labels. Also, don't use labels as comments.
- Make all variable and module names meaningful. The names

should suggest the function they perform and their purpose in the program.

- Begin variable names, ones that belong to the same table or to the same module, with the same prefix.
- Limit the scope of a branch statement to the module in which it occurs.
- Avoid obscure (tricky) code.

In Structured Design:

* Keep module size small.
* Design top-down.
* Document internally.
* Use labels sparingly.
* Make variable names meaningful.
* Limit branches to within modules.
* Keep code simple and straightforward.

1-1 Structured design overview.

Structured techniques also provide some basic project management assistance. Project status information can be attached to the graphic descriptions (the basic blocks in the graphic chart). Managers can then see the status for use in status reporting. If you're managing your own job, at any point in the development cycle you can tell, at a glance, just how far into the job you are.

Efficiency

Once you have the basic structuring concepts in mind, then tackle simple efficiency techniques. *Efficiency* is the extent to which a program performs its intended function without wasting machine resources such as memory, storage, channel capacity, and execution time.

Efficiency is important—but not when taken to extremes. Some programmers spend so much time being certain that they use the fewest possible lines of code that they lose sight of the fact that the program should be easy to use and maintain. Some things to keep in mind are:

- Modularize the program into logical pieces, e.g., keep I/O in one section, error handling in another, and so on.
- Use only a small subset of the program's pages at any point during execution, which aids in the efficient use of memory.
- Eliminate all unused labels and expressions, to take full advantage of compiler and assembler optimization. If it's not used, don't put it in.
- Isolate exception routines and error-handling routines in separate modules. Because errors are out of the mainstream of processing, don't clutter the main line of code with their presence.
- Process outside a loop all code that does not need to be processed within the loop.

- Use integer arithmetic whenever possible, instead of floating-point.
- Avoid mixed data types in arithmetic or logical operations whenever possible to eliminate unnecessary data conversions.
- Align program variables in storage.
- Avoid nonstandard subroutine and/or function calls.
- In a complex logical condition, test the most likely True condition first.
- Use the most efficient data type for subscripts.

Program usability

Usability is difficult to define and to measure in quantitative fashion. End users see usability in ways that depend on their experience, how frequently they use a system, their ideas of human factoring, how critical the system is to getting a task done, and exactly how the software interacts with them. Programmers define *usability* as the ease of maintenance/enhancement/bug-fixing. Program managers often see it as how many lines of correct code can be written within a time limit. No matter what criteria are used, making programs more usable is very effective, even if the programmer is the intended final user.

Generally speaking, a usable program minimizes confusion, is easy to operate/run, and is tolerant of user errors and changing needs. Usability, simply, is the extent to which a program is convenient, practical, and easy to use. The following is a usability checklist with which to measure your programs.

- Is there a Help feature for every function and available on request?
- Is a correct, complete explanation of each command and/or operating mode available on request?
- Can the user learn the program without human assistance?
- Does the program allow interruption of a task and is it able to restart or resume at logical points?
- Does the program allow the user to cancel it, without harmful side effects?
- Does the program have detailed, understandable prompting for input and processes, such as starting a printer?
- Are the error messages understandable? Are there suggestions as how to correct the errors?
- Are all input formats, requirements, and restrictions clearly explained?
- Does the program do the "housekeeping" such as deleting temporary files?
- Can the program handle typing errors?
- Can the program accept reduced input when actions are to be repeated?
- Can commands be abbreviated?

- Does the program edit/validate input data?
- Does the program allow the user to extend the commands?
- Does the program allow an experienced user to work with a faster version, such as abbreviated commands, default values, and so on?
- Are there audit trails so that users and programmers can figure out what went wrong?

If a program is used over a long period of time, it's best to make it easy to use. Human memory is tricky—people forget just that tiny detail that makes a program work correctly instead of incorrectly.

Documentation

Well-documented programs are easier to work with than undocumented programs. The key is that a program should be its own documentation. This section describes "documentation" as that needed by programmers. Not addressed is user documentation, external manuals, and operations documentation.

Program documentation describes the program components and data, what the program does, plus why and how the program works as it does. The two types of documentation are internal and external.

External documentation is the written assumptions you make before you write code, the hard-copy program listings, and the typed description of inputs, outputs, and the processes of the program(s). This external documentation is separate from source code. If the program is well-structured, often the programmer allows external documentation to lapse behind the internal.

Internal documentation is those "remarks" that appear in the actual program source code, the well-defined variables, and the module headers. This is the documentation that doesn't get lost when you need it most. And it is the most accurate documentation about the program. Take a look at the internal documentation on each of the toolkit programs included in this book. No matter if you type in the code or copy it from the available diskette, the comments ensure that you'll know what the code does, and how it does it.

Creating databases

After deciding the major structure of your program(s), next define any databases you'll need. A *database* is an integrated source of data that is accessed and controlled by a database management system. Figure 1-2 shows an overview of a database management system. Databases are used to store information that users need for future processing, so design and structure your databases just as carefully as you do your programs. Before you design a new database, however, find out if the user already has something that can be used: Can part of an existing one and part of another be used? If not, then design a new one.

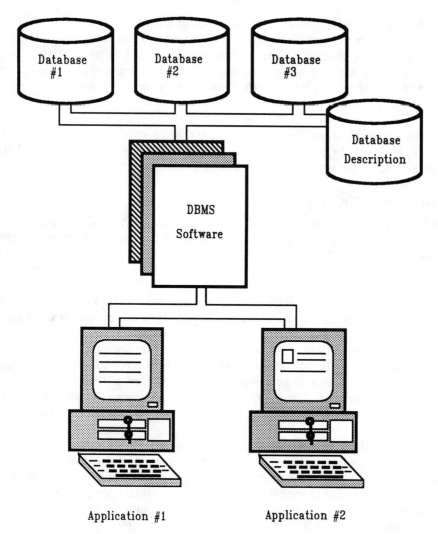

1-2 Overview of a database management system.

First, determine what files are needed in the database, by finding out what information the user needs. Ensure that each file contains the key fields needed for the end-user output(s). Define where data should be stored, e.g., floppy or hard disk, and determine how often it will be updated.

Finally, decide what software and database backup plans should be set in place. For instance, will the user back it up each time it is used, or once a week, or when? Then, after the basic design, you begin your detail design:

- First, cluster the fields into groups (records), each of which forms the basis for detailed handling. Decide if new records will be created from the ones the user puts in. Are there edit or other controls that each input record must be compared to?

- Second, check each input field. Can it be simplified in its handling and storage? Be sure that each field has a specific name, specific use, and specific storage. Are there dependencies among fields? Or among different records? For instance, in a check balancing and recording system, should space be left for checks that have not yet returned, or should the program only capture those that have returned?
- Third, should space be left for future growth? If so, how much— 20%, 50%? Does the user have any idea how the data has historically increased and/or decreased? Are there calendar year-ends or fiscal year-ends that will create data which must be stored for the remainder of the year? At this point, sketch a quick chart (such as Fig. 1-3) that lists the fields of the various databases, flagging the key field of each database which ties that series of records to all other databases.

Database 1 Valid Users	Database 2 Account Record
Account Number First Name Second Name	*Account Number* Balance

Database 3 Name and Address	Database 4 Payment Record
Account Number Name Address City State Zip	*Account Number* January Payment February Payment . . December Payment

1-3 Data dependencies. Here, four databases are tied together with one field, the Account Number. Four different programs can update the databases, or any number at the convenience/design of the programmer.

Interrupt handling: transfers, subroutines, and macros

After you've defined the program structure and the databases, you next decide how the pieces interact. They do this by the main procedure allowing interrupts, calling subroutines, or invoking macros.

When activated, most modules begin execution at the beginning, at the first executable statement. Once the interrupt occurs, processor control transfers to the process that asked for the interrupt. A jump is made out of the current executing sequence with the condition that control eventually be returned to the execution sequence from which the jump was made. The jump can be either conditional or unconditional.

A *conditional transfer* always refers to a target location explicitly (by name, address, or other identifier). Once the interrupt has been handled, control returns to the original module. A return always transfers to the location of an instruction in the sequence associated with the most recently conditioned transfer for which a return has not yet been made. In this way, the pattern of conditional transfers and returns always defines a fully nested set of activations. Figure 1-4 shows how the logic appears in a block diagram of transfers and returns. This system is hierarchical because the conditioned transfer sets up its origin as a sequence having control over the target sequence.

Line 1 – Program Initialization
Line 2
Line 3 – Calls Subroutine 1

    Subroutine 1 – Entry Point

    Subroutine Process

    Subroutine 1 – Exit (to Line 4)

Line 4

Line 5 – Calls Subroutine 2

    Subroutine 2 – Entry Point

    Subroutine – Calls Subroutine 3

        Subroutine 3 – Entry Point

        Subroutine Process

        Subroutine 3 – Exit (to Subroutine 2 Process)

    Subroutine Process

    Subroutine 2 – Exit (to Line 6)

Line 6

Line 7 – Program Termination

1-4 A nested set of jumps/activities.

The *unconditional transfer* carries no tacit condition of return. This transfer sets up a new control stream, activating the module as a parallel or coordination process.

A *subroutine* is a module activated at execution time by a conditioned transfer. Subroutines, as a general rule, can accept arguments and cannot be executed by themselves as stand-alone code. Historically, subroutines were called "closed routines" or "off-line subroutines" to differentiate them from a separate process called a macro.

A *macro* is a module whose body is effectively copied in-line during translation (for example, compilation or assembly) as the result of being invoked by name. The process of copying in-line is called *expansion*. A macro is expanded as a result of being invoked. Translation of the macro into the target can happen before, during, or after expansion, although the current trend prefers translation after expansion.

Termination processing

We've seen how interrupts can transfer control to a second set of code, call a subroutine, or invoke a macro. Once the program has finished its required work, it's time to terminate. When terminating, the software should "clean up" before exiting, in either a normal exit or an unexpected exit which causes (or should cause) a dump. This clean-up includes closing of files, elimination of temporary files, and doing final input/output (I/O) to clear all buffers.

Writing a program

Now that you have the design concepts in mind, it's time to specify the handling of individual programs.

Concept/framework definition

The first step is to define the basic assumptions. For instance, you'll write the program on (and for) a microcomputer that has a certain number of diskette drives, a hard disk, and perhaps a tape backup. That computer has a set number of bytes of memory for the program and can display to a screen and write out to a printer. List those assumptions.

For example, your target system might have: (1) an 80486 processor; (2) 4 megabytes (4Mb) of memory; (3) a high-density micro disk drive with 1.44Mb and an 80Mb hard disk; (4) Hewlett-Packard LaserJet parallel printer; (5) Microsoft MS-DOS 5.0; (6) a VGA monitor with 24 lines, each of 80 characters; and (7) Borland's Turbo Assembler, level 2.0 (TASM).

Your software assumptions might be: (1) data will be in standard character strings (A–Z, a–z), numbers (0–9), and certain special characters (period or decimal point, comma, and dollar sign); (2) no number will be larger than can be stored in a double word; and (3) the instruction set is the 80486.

The second step is to list the specific objectives, remembering that most problems arise from a design that's too limited or one that's incomplete. Good system design avoids excessive complexity—so don't be afraid to simplify, simplify, simplify. The objective here is to decide on the pieces that fit together into a complete software program which solves the current needs, while staying flexible for future requirements. Most programs evolve in a natural process as changes come along—that's part of software life.

For now, decide what inputs will come in, what outputs will be needed, and how the inputs will get to the outputs. For instance, in a checkbook balancing program, the user might type in a series of numeric digits (their bank check numbers), and a dollar amount. The program reads from the keyboard, stores the check numbers into an array, keeps a running total of the dollar amounts, and prints a single-line item to the printer. There might be constants to include in the program, such as a bank charge if the balance falls below a certain amount. At the end of the program, the user might wish a printed balance. That balance should be saved, so the program needs to write the check numbers and the running balance to permanent storage.

The third step in the overall design is to divide those objectives into blocks that flow in a sequential manner. The result is an overall flowchart as shown in Fig. 1-5.

Fourth, define what algorithms are needed. That is, are there certain routines that will be used again and again, such as date verification? An *algorithm* is a finite series of steps that performs a single task. A result is reached with relatively few instructions; often a single algorithm is a subroutine (or handled as one).

When the main program calls the subroutine, control passes temporarily to that subroutine and should be passed back when the subroutine ends. Data can be handed to the subroutine by passing parameters, or the subroutine can be written so that it "knows" where the data will be. This last design decision is how most of the procedures in this book are written.

The technique where data is transferred to a subroutine and the subroutine computation results are transferred back to the main routine are called calling sequence and exit sequence. The main routine has a calling sequence that stores data in registers or specific memory locations before the call to the subroutine. At the end of the subroutine, data is also stored in registers or specific memory locations before returning to the main program or the calling routine.

Once to this step, review the toolkit programs that are included in this book. There will be a lot of already written code that can be simply "plugged in" to your program, before you have to write any new code. This plug-in shortens your development time because you don't have to reinvent

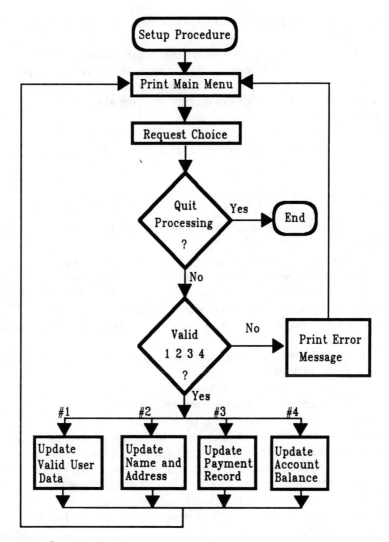

1-5   Overview flowchart.

what's already invented and tested. Once you write the final program, you must test it.

Program testing

Testability is defined as the ease with which program correctness can be demonstrated. Testability is an important program property when building high-quality software packages. In many software shops, the test process consumes approximately half of the development budget. And rightfully so, when the test dollars are spent in prevention rather than "fix it after release."

The cost of correcting errors in the analysis and design phases of development is only a small fraction of the costs incurred by later correction. In fact, the cost of error correction at the actual-use phase can be 100 times more than the cost of correction during system analysis. Testing reduces these costs.

Testing a program involves selecting a set of test cases and executing the program with each case. Selecting those test cases is guided by the following:

- Each program instruction and each path should be executed at least once.
- The more heavily used paths should be tested much more thoroughly.
- All modules should be tested individually before they are combined. Then the paths between the modules should be tested.
- Test the program(s)/system as a whole, as the parts might add up to something other than what was originally designed.
- Testing should proceed from the most simple case to the most complex.
- Tests should include normal processing cases, extreme cases, and all error conditions.

Most errors that occur in software are attributable to the earliest phases: analysis and design. A study done in 1980 by TRW showed that 64% of software errors arose from the analysis and design phase, as shown in Fig. 1-6. Only 30% of those errors were being detected before the software was delivered for acceptance testing. On the other hand, 75% of coding (36% of total errors) were detected before delivery, which illustrates the importance of testing during early development stages.

Reliability is a measure of the absence of errors. What we're talking about here is a measure of your ability to demonstrate the absence of those errors. The simpler the program, the easier it is to demonstrate its correctness. Simplicity in this case means that the program is modular and well-structured.

Software maintenance

Modifying existing programs is the most basic maintenance function and perhaps the most challenging of all programming activities. Not only must you make certain that the new logic is correct, but also that the program continues to perform its functions correctly. Undesired side effects can result from even the most innocent-seeming program changes. These side effects cause loss of development time (until the causes are isolated

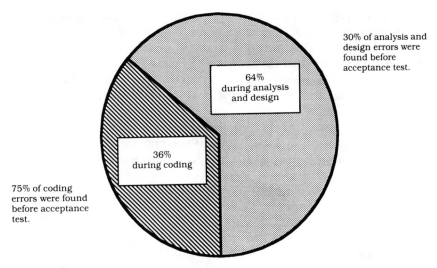

30% of analysis and design errors were found before acceptance test.

64% during analysis and design

36% during coding

75% of coding errors were found before acceptance test.

1-6   Errors found in software.

and fixed), so careful consideration is the first criterion of maintenance. A common quote is, "Think before you act."

Maintenance programmers fix bugs in existing programs and add new functions to those programs. If your task is to correct an error, first locate the error and then determine how to change the program. If your task is to enhance the program, you'll develop new logic and write new code.

Use a top-down approach for designing and making program changes. First, review the program and check the interfaces, variables, and the database. Second, isolate the areas that need to be changed. Third, study the change areas carefully and then check the logic on how the changes will be inserted. Finally, desk-check all pathways to see that old procedures continue to work correctly and new ones perform as designed. Only then do you actually begin to code the changes.

Some maintenance guidelines that have evolved over a cumulative 55 years of programming are:

- Always make a backup copy before beginning any changes, any whatsoever.
- Read the code to be sure of the overall flow before making even one-line changes.
- Change only what is necessary. Getting carried away (to make it prettier, sharper, more compact) can open Pandora's box. Don't "fix" what isn't broken.
- Do not attempt to share program variables that already exist, if you're not absolutely sure how each one is used, each time it's used.
- Write in some error-checking around the changes. That is, put in

some debugging code (perhaps print lines) and do some testing before considering the change final. Remove the error-checking once the change is proven correct.

- Consider what effect the change has on the overall processing of the program. Does the sort really have to be here? Or could it wait until later, so that the user doesn't have to sit and wait between input screens.
- Update the program documentation. Each time a change is made, type in (in the remarks area) what the change actually does.
- Use structured concepts. If a new subroutine is needed, be sure that the subroutine fits with the rest of the code in both format, idea, and physical placement.

Debugging

Once the program is written, it's time to debug it. As discussed under program testing, finding errors before they get to acceptance testing (whether formal or informal) significantly reduces software cost.

Debugging means finding errors. Those errors come from the programmer either incorrectly understanding the original design or, more often, from a human error in remembering flags, semaphores, logic flow, or using incorrect code statements.

How well programmers find errors depends on the individuals. Often, programmers have difficulty because they make invalid assumptions and their conjectures become prematurely fixed, which blinds them to other possibilities. Programmers often use the following as debugging aids:

- Source code listing.
- Output listing (assembly or compiler output listing).
- Statement trace.
- Debug software that "steps through" programs with debug traps or displays.
- Clues from compilers or assemblers, such as error messages.

Program errors are more likely to occur in larger, highly complex programs. A systematic approach allows programmers to find those errors more quickly. The following is a guideline for quick debugging:

- First, exclude the most unlikely sources of the error. In the search for errors, go from the most likely to the least likely.
- Isolate one error at a time and stick to that error until it is located and fixed. Only then move on to the next. If a second error is located during the search for the first, note its location and return there once the first one is fixed.
- Study actual output and compare it to samples of expected output.
- Check the data handled by the program. Often the input data is

either incorrect (and not discovered during input editing) or was not included in the original design as potential data.
- Keep track of where the errors occur in the program as errors tend to "clump." This can aid in predicting where future errors will occur.

When searching for an error, don't dismiss the possibility that its cause might be an error in the original design. Note: If you can prove that a machine error occurred, treasure it—they are more rare than raw diamonds in the sands of silicon valley.

Software aids

There are catastrophic errors from which it is difficult to recover. Sooner or later in your software design cycle, you're going to run into them. They generally group in the area of "human error while under pressure," such as erasing a file when you didn't mean to. Some software exists to help you with this, and one software designer, Peter Norton, deserves the reputation he's earned.

The Norton Utilities are a set of programs that supplement the MS-DOS operating system and help you use your computer more effectively. Norton realized that people become involved in what they're doing (programming) and often make a mistake that sets them back hours if not days.

If your computer is one of the IBM family, or closely compatible, the Norton Utilities will work just fine. To use the programs, you must be running with a version of MS-DOS at 2.0 or higher. Finally, to get the best use of the programs, you need to be familiar with DOS. Chapter 2 helps with that.

2
MS-DOS programming tips

There are many operating systems for the IBM Personal Computer and its look-alike clones. This book concentrates on MS-DOS at level 5.0 and higher. The software in this book was written on an 80486-based IBM-compatible clone with MS-DOS 5.0 and Borland's TASM.

The 1991 release of TASM contains a bug if you use the CMXCHG instruction. Evidently, Borland designers used the Intel documentation and coded the hex instruction of 0F A6 and 0F A7 instead of the data sheet, which shows the correct notation of 0F B0 and 0F B1. We contacted Borland with this information, and later releases of TASM will contain the correct hex notation.

This chapter gives you general MS-DOS programming tips, discusses a few of the more useful MS-DOS interrupts, and gives you some easy MS-DOS bypasses for common problems. We thought you might want to get your show on the road as soon as possible, so we included a skeleton assembly language program in which you can insert code you want to write and test.

OS/2 uses system CALLs instead of INTs. Just as with MS-DOS, you move function numbers into registers; instead of issuing an INT *n* (where *n* is the hex function number), however, you do a CALL to LOC_50h. For an example, Fig. 2-1 shows how to get the time with each type of call. The MS-DOS interrupt and function number used in the example is described later in this chapter and more fully in appendix E.

Throughout the examples, you'll see how to code the routines using MS-DOS. Note that the numbers used throughout this book are in hexadecimal, unless specifically stated that they are in decimal; for example, Interrupt 21 hex is shown as INT 21, not INT 21h (only in the book—in the program listings, they're shown with the "h" because both TASM and Turbo default to decimal representation).

For MS-DOS

```
        MOV     AH,2CH      ; 2C is the Get Time function
        INT     21h         ; Issue the Interrupt
```

For OS/2

```
        MOV     AH,2CH      ; 2C is the Get Time function
        CALL    LOC__50h
```

2-1   Get__Time program.

Definitions

Let's look at some basic MS-DOS and system terms and concepts you'll run into when you program on an IBM system or look-alike clone.

BIOS   The Basic I/O System, or BIOS, is the (usually) ROM-based code that interfaces with MS-DOS to process I/O inside your computer. BIOS is examined below, and BIOS interrupts are detailed in appendix E.

DEBUG   In capital letters, this is the Debug.com program that usually comes with your MS-DOS disk. It's a utility program that allows you to troubleshoot your programs. With DEBUG, you can load files and sectors, edit them, and write changes to memory or register locations. Borland's Turbo Debug and MicroSoft's CodeView are both significant expansions over DEBUG.

file handle   Starting with MS-DOS 2.0, file handles were introduced to manipulate files instead of using the more cumbersome File Control Blocks (FCBs). To keep track of a file, all you need is its file handle, a 16-bit word that you move from register to register as required. A keyboard and a printer are considered files for purposes of using handles. If you want to refer to a file, move its handle into whatever register INT 21 requires. File handles 0–4 are predefined, as shown in Table 2-1, so use 5 or above for your programs.

MASM   The Microsoft Macro Assembler (MASM) is a software package that translates a copy of your source files into .obj files (for input to a

Table 2-1   Preassigned file handles.

Handle	Assigned meaning
0	Standard Input Device (Usually a keyboard)
1	Standard Output Device (Usually a screen)
2	Standard Error Output Device
3	Standard Auxiliary Device (AUX)
4	Standard Printer Device (PRN)

linker) and .lst files (so you can scan and/or print the result of the assembly). TASM is Borland's equivalent and is used to assemble the programs in this book.

microcode A list of small program steps and a set of control functions performed by the instruction decoding and executing logic of a computer system. It is code that is below the level of assembly language; that is, closer to the machine.

pseudo-OP Pseudo-ops are commands coded with source code and are for the assembler only. There are many pseudo-ops available; among them are ASSUME, in which you tell the assembler how registers will be set; ENDS, which tells where the segment ends; and the PROC and ENDP pair, which tells where procedures start and end.

System overview

MS-DOS consists of three components: a Boot record, which is the system initialization; a BIOS interface; and the MS-DOS program, which is generally stored as Command.com). See Fig. 2-2. The Boot record is read into memory when you do either a power-on or a system reset (Ctrl+Alt+Del). Boot is read into memory and given control. It then checks the directory to ensure that the first records are your MS-DOS controls. It reads initialization code that determines equipment status, resets the system, initializes the attached devices, and sets the low-numbered interrupt vectors. This initialization code is overlaid later by data areas and the command processor.

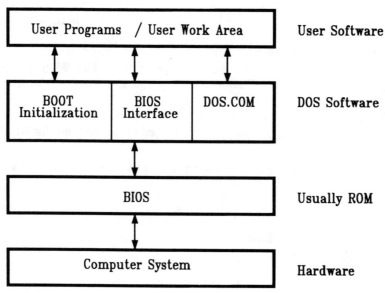

2-2 System overview.

Next, Boot initializes its internal working tables, determines the correct memory locations for file allocation tables (FATs), the directory, and the data buffers. It initializes interrupt vectors (for interrupts 20–27) and loads Command.com. Finally, it passes control to Command.com.

Command.com consists of three separate parts. One portion contains the code to process certain critical interrupts, with overlay areas to handle others. A second portion controls startup and also contains the Autoexec-.bat file processor setup routine. The third part is a command processor: one duty of this processor is to provide the prompt, e.g., C>.

MS-DOS provides a number of functions available to user programs through the issuance of a set of interrupt codes and function calls: interrupts 20–27, each with subfunctions. These interrupts access BIOS entry point interrupts. BIOS and MS-DOS interrupts are discussed in two separate sections later in the chapter and more fully in appendix E.

A skeleton program

Assembly language instructions divide into four fields:

[*label:*]
mnemonic
[*operand*]
[*; comment*]

Of these, you must include only the mnemonic. The brackets indicate that the other fields are optional. For mnemonics that require operands, of course, those operands are not optional. Fields are entered anywhere on a line (separated by a space or a tab), but it makes program reading easier if you use some standard spacing throughout your programs. Many of the programmer-helpful edit packages (such as Borland's Turbo Editor) insert spaces for you.

The skeleton program shown in Fig. 2-3 gives you the "must-haves" to assemble source programs correctly. The first line (PAGE) tells the assembler how many lines you want to appear on a page and how wide those lines are. The second line (.386) tells the assembler that you are including 80386 instructions and requests the assembler to build 80386 displacements. (For the 80486 programs, using TASM, we've used the simplified segment directives: a MODEL statement, a .486 statement, a .DATA for the data, a .CODE for the code, and an END.)

The instruction set for each successive member of the Intel 8086 through the 80486 family contains the preceding set(s). This means that the 80486 full set includes all the instructions developed for the 8086, 80186, 80286, and 80386. See appendix C for the 80486 instruction set descriptions.

The next three lines of the skeleton program set up a stack segment with 100 bytes. You need this area for working space. The next line (CODE) shows where the actual code begins, with parameters making the code

```
            PAGE        55,132
            .486
STACKT      SEGMENT     'STACK' STACK
            DW          100 DUP(?)
STACKT      ENDS
CODE        SEGMENT     PARA 'CODE' PUBLIC USE16
            ASSUME      CS:CODE, DS:CODE, SS:CODE
; Purpose:  [Here you enter your overall documentation]
;                  [Note that each comment begins with a ";"]
;
; Inputs:
;
; Process:
;
; Outputs:
;
NAME:       MOV         AX,CS
            MOV         DS,AX
            JMP         BEGINHERE
[Define your variables and constants here]
BEGINHERE:

                 [Enter your code here]
ENDHERE:
            MOV         AH,4Ch        ; Standard Ending
            INT         21h
CODE        ENDS
            END         NAME
```

2-3 Skeleton program.

public and instructing the assembler to use 16-bit registers. The ASSUME line initializes three segment-pointer registers for use within the program.

The next block section generally is left out of lazy programmers' work—and they regret it only a few months later when they have to debug their own work. We've included extensive internal documentation in all the programs, procedures, and modules in this book.

The NAME is where you put the name of your program, each with a unique name. The two MOV lines set data into your segment-pointer registers and initializes them. The jump (JMP) gets the working program around the variable definition that is done during assembly. Define your variables and/or initialize storage. DB defines one or more bytes. DW defines 2-byte words and DD defines 4-byte words (doublewords).

The BEGINHERE: line is the start of your working code. You can use any unique label for this. Then insert your code. The ENDHERE: label is simply an easy place to remember that you are terminating your program. We used the INT 21 Function 4C exit that terminates and turns control back to the parent process (usually MS-DOS) with an optional, 1-byte return code. The standard functions are defined below and more fully in appendix E. You need two final lines: CODE ENDS and END *name*, where *name* is the same as your program NAME that you chose at the beginning.

You'll see this skeleton around most of the working programs in this book. It's easy to test the BIOS and MS-DOS functions and interrupts by inserting them in this skeleton program code, assembling them, and then linking them. Once you get handy with that, you can try things out within minutes.

Assembling programs

For the assembly tip in this section, it's assumed that you have your editors, assemblers, and linkers on drive C in a directory called ASM. Your assembly language program also is assumed to be in the same directory. Two commas and a semicolon at the end of the command says that you want to use the same base name (in this case, Program_Name) for both your .obj and .lst files.

After a clean assembly (see Fig. 2-4 for the command format), you get a file called Program_Name.obj and one called Program_Name.lst. You now need to link the object file(s) before you can run Program_Name. To do this, at the system MS-DOS prompt enter LINK (for MicroSoft's linker to TLINK for Borland's) and *Program_Name* (see Fig. 2-5). Answer with a carriage return (Enter) to all the link prompts or enter a semicolon (;) after *Program_Name* to tell the linker that you want to default to the standard entries.

2-4 Macro assembling command, where Program_Name is the name of your program.

C: TASM *Program_Name*,,;

2-5 Link edit command, where Program_Name is the .OBJ file you wish to link.

C:> TLINK *Program_Name*

The linker looks for Program_Name.obj in your default directory. Your output will be Program_Name.exe. Your program can now be run by entering *Program_Name*, as shown in Fig. 2-6. In the assembly or the link steps, you can allow the assembler and linker to prompt you for output file names. If you want to direct the output to other directories or rename the .obj, .exe, or .lst files, you can enter the path names and/or different file names at the prompts.

C:> *Program_Name*

2-6 Program execution command, where Program_Name is the .EXE program you want to run.

Library management

In the long run, it is best if you keep your working routines in subdirectories as modules that can be assembled and linked with new code. If you don't have a hard disk, divide your disk on drive B into subdirectories. We suggest putting your source code in one library (subdirectory), your object in another, and your executable code in a third. Be sure to back-up these libraries on a regular basis.

You'll have enough to think about when you're programming—here at the start, divide your working modules logically. For instance, keep all your arithmetic modules in a directory called MATH. Keep your graphics in one called GRAPHICS, and so on.

Routines and variables that are in one module and are called/used from/in another must be declared PUBLIC within their own assembly language module. Also, they must be defined as EXTRN (external) in the file that contains the code that calls them. If you don't declare them this way, you'll get a list of errors when you try to assemble your main-line program—the assembler assumes you forgot to write them as part of your main program.

Each external reference gives the name of the routine that isn't physically present in your main code and assigns a type to it. The linker needs this type to determine the proper machine code for referencing the external routine. Since your routines will probably be in their own separate code segments, they'll be called far and require far CALLs in machine language.

Common MS-DOS operations

Viewing ASCII files in DOS

For this tip, let's assume you are at the MS-DOS prompt (usually C> for a hard disk and A> for a floppy disk drive) and you want to use the MS-DOS command Type to view a file. The file scrolls too fast for you to read easily. You can use Ctrl+S to stop the scrolling momentarily, but you can also use the More.com filter. Load the More.com file into the same directory as the file you want to view (or you can use the Path command to point to the directory where More.com is located). Then type the command in as shown in Fig. 2-7.

2-7 Viewing ASCII files, where FILENAME.TXT is the file you want to view.

C> TYPE *FILENAME.TXT* | MORE

The Type command filters through More.com and displays the text file one page at a time. The message —MORE— displays at the bottom of your screen. Press any key to advance the display to the next page. For larger programs, you may want to use the DOS 5.0 Edit command.

Merging files

Current versions of MS-DOS don't include a merge command, but it is possible to combine files by using the MS-DOS Copy command. For instance, assume you have two files, named File1 and File2. You can append the second to the first, as shown in Fig. 2-8.

If you don't name a target file (in the example, *1NEWFILE*), the first file in the list (in the example, FILE1) will be replaced by a new file that contains both.

2-8 Merging files in MS-DOS, where NEWFILE is the target file for the combined FILE1 and FILE2.

C> COPY FILE1+FILE2 *NEWFILE*

Printing files without saving them

You can type documentation at the MS-DOS prompt and print it out by using the Copy command. At the C> prompt (or A> if you're using a floppy disk drive), type the entry as shown in Fig. 2-9.

```
C> COPY CON PRN
```

2-9 Printing a file without having to save it, where CON is your console and PRN is your printer.

The PRN after COPY.CON directs all the information you type to the printer. The file will not be printed until you finish typing and end the file by entering Ctrl + Z (appears as ^Z on your screen). You'll get a response on the screen of 1 file(s) copied. Neither the COPY CON.PRN command nor Ctrl + Z prints on your printer. Also, because MS-DOS is not a word processor, it doesn't have word wrap; therefore, type your information exactly as you want it to print.

Printing the screen

When working interactively with MS-DOS, you can hold down the Shift key and press the PrtSc key (with some systems, you press only PrtSc) to send the information on the screen to the printer. MS-DOS uses Interrupt 5 for this purpose, so you can use the PrtSc operation from within a program by issuing the command INT 5. You can prevent a user from doing a PrtSc by pointing Int 5 to a return instruction. Program Inthndlr in chapter 5 shows how to intercept BIOS or MS-DOS interrupts.

BIOS interrupts

The ROM-resident BIOS provides device-level control of the major I/O devices in the system unit. BIOS routines allow you to perform block-level (diskette and cassette) or character-level (keyboard, printer, and video communications) I/O operations without concern for device addresses and operating characteristics. BIOS also insulates you from the hardware, which allows new devices to be added to the system unit while retaining the BIOS level interface to the device. In this way, your programs are transparent to hardware modifications and enhancements.

Access to BIOS is through interrupts. Each BIOS entry point has its own interrupt vector (address), summarized in Table 2-2 and detailed in

Table 2-2   BIOS interrupt vectors.

Interrupt number (in hex)	Function name
5	Print Screen
8	Time of Day
9	Keyboard Scan Code
10	Video
11	Equipment Check
12	Memory Size
13	DIskette Service
14	Communications (Serial Transfer)
15	Cassette and TopView
16	Keyboard character
17	Printer
18	Cassette BASIC /ROM BASIC
19	Bootstrap
1A	Time of Day
1B	Keyboard Break
1C	Timer Tick

appendix E. Most BIOS interrupts require parameters, although some do not (for instance, the memory-size BIOS interrupt INT 12) and all parameters passed to and from BIOS go through registers. When BIOS has several possible operations, the AH register is used on input to indicate your desired operation. As a general rule, BIOS preserves all registers except AX and various flags. Other registers are modified on return only if they return a value or error condition to your program.

ROM BIOS uses the memory region from 400 to 4FF hex (see Fig. 2-10), which includes the addresses for serial and parallel ports, the equipment list (devices and internal equipment installed on your computer at the time of the last power-up or reset), and the size of working memory.

You can't alter ROM BIOS, but you might want to alter what happens when interrupts are issued. For instance, you might want to interchange two keyboard keys. You do this by changing the interrupt vector for keyboard servicing. Then you check each input key to see if it is one you want to change. If so, change it and then branch to the regular ROM BIOS keyboard routine to complete the operation.

If you want to disable an interrupt, change the vector so that it points to a Return statement in the ROM BIOS. BIOS Interrupt 10 (Video Services) and its various subfunctions are explained in detail in chapter 10, which deals with graphics.

Starting Address

00000	BIOS Interrupt Vectors
00080	Available Interrupt Vectors
00400	BIOS Data Area
00500	User Read/Write Memory
A0000	Reserved for Devices
F4000	User Read Only Memory
F6000	On PCs, BASIC Interpreter
FE000	BIOS Program Area

2-10 BIOS memory map.

Let's use one of the BIOS interrupts to show how this works. In the example in Fig. 2-11, we want to find out what mode the screen is in. The function requests call MS-DOS routines to manage system resources. When MS-DOS takes control after a function call, it switches to an internal stack. Registers not used to return information (except AX) are preserved. The calling program's stack must be large enough to accommodate the interrupt system—at least 128 bytes in addition to other needs.

MS-DOS interrupts

You can use MS-DOS interrupts (20–27) to gain entry to useful operations that MS-DOS reserves for its own use. MS-DOS maintains the table of interrupt routine vectors (addresses) in locations 80–FC; most of the interrupts have been superseded by function requests in Interrupt 21. Table 2-3 lists the MS-DOS reserved interrupts, which are detailed in appendix E.

```
@SCREEN__MODE          MACRO
              ; This Macro determines the screen mode
              ;
              ; Register AH holds the function of 0F hex.
2-11  SCREEN__MODE      ;  The mode number is returned in AL.
      macro.              ;

              MOV    AH,0Fh      ; Read the mode
              INT    10h
              ENDM
```

Interrupt 20: Program termination

To terminate your COM-format programs, use Interrupt 20 and control is returned to MS-DOS, or the parent process. All open files are closed, the disk cache is cleaned, and all file buffers are flushed to disk. The CS register must contain the segment address of the Program Segment Prefix before you call this interrupt.

It is important to close all files that have changed in length before issuing this interrupt. The file's new length is not recorded correctly in the directory if you do not close it first. (*Tip:* The most useful way to automatically close all files and finish cleanly is to load AH with 4C and issue INT 21 or CALL LOC__50.)

Table 2-3   MS-DOS reserved interrupts.

Interrupt vector (in hex)	Function
20	Program Terminate
21	General DOS Functions
22	Terminate Address
23	CONTROL—BREAK Exit
24	Fatal Error Vector
25	Absolute Disk Read
26	Absolute Disk Write
27	Program Terminate, fix in storage

Table 2-4   Interrupt 21 vectors.

Description	Function (in hex)	Description	Function (in hex)
Allocate Memory	48	Display String	09
Auxiliary Input	03	Duplicate a File Handle	45
Auxiliary Output	04	File Size	23
Buffered Keyboard Input	0A	Find Match File	4E
Change Attributes	43	Flush Buffer, Read Keyboard	0C
Change Current Directory	3B	Force A Duplicate of a Handle	46
Check Keyboard Status	0B	Free Allocated Memory	49
Close a File Handle	3	Get Date	2A
Close a File	10	Get Disk Free Space	36
CONTROL-C Check	33	Get Disk Transfer Address	2F
Create A File	3C	Get MS-DOS Version Number	30
Create File	16	Get Interrupt Vector	35
Create New Program Segment	26	Get Time	2C
Create Sub-Directory	39	Get/Set Date/Time of File	57
Current Disk	19	I/O Control for Devices	44
Delete a Directory Entry	41	Keep Process	31
Delete File	13	Load and Execute a Program	4B
Direct Console Input	07	Modify Allocated Memory Blocks	4A
Direct Console I/O	06	Move a Directory Entry	56
Display Character	02	Move a File Pointer	42
Reserved	18	Reset Disk	0D
Reserved	1B-20	Return Country-Dependent Info	38
Reserved	32	Return Current Setting of Verify	54
Reserved	34	Return Text of Current Directory	47
Reserved	37	Return the Return Code of a Child	4D
Reserved	50-53	Search for First Entry	11
Reserved	55	Search for Next Entry	12
Open a File	3D	Select Disk	0E
Open File	0F	Sequential Read	14
Parse File Name	29	Sequential Write	15
Print Character	05	Set Date	2B
Random Block Read	27	Set Disk Transfer Address	1A
Random Block Write	28	Set Relative Record	24
Random Read	21	Set Time	2D
Random Write	22		25

Description	Function (in hex)	Description	Function (in hex)
		Set Vector	2E
Read from File/Device	3F	Set/Reset Verify Flag	4F
Read Keyboard	08	Step Through Directory, Matching Files	4C
Read Keyboard and Echo	01	Terminate A Process	00
Remove a Directory Entry	3A	Terminate Program	40
Rename File	17	Write to File or Device	

Interrupt 21: General MS-DOS functions

Interrupt 21 has several useful functions that are summarized in Table 2-4. To use this interrupt, place the appropriate function number in register AH, then issue INT 21. Eleven of the functions are described in the following sections. They'll give you an idea of how useful Interrupt 21 is. For more detail and the remainder of the Interrupt 21 functions, see appendix E.

Function 1 Read/display keyboard character. If you want your program to halt until a key is pressed, use this function. See Fig. 2-12 for an example. Set the AH register to 1 and execute INT 21. The input character returns in register AL, if it is ASCII. If the character is extended ASCII, AL contains a value of 0, which means that this function must be repeated to get the extended code.

```
STNDINE    PROC
           MOV    AH,1     ; Standard Input with Echo
           INT    21h      ; Issue Interrupt
           RET             ; Code ends, return
STNDINE    ENDP
CODE       ENDS
           END
```

2-12 Standard input with echo.

If the second value is less than 84, it represents the scan code of the pressed key. For example, the user may press the F1 key. The value you'll receive is a 3B, since the scan code for F1 is 3B. See appendix D for ASCII characters and the IBM PC keyboard scan codes.

Function 2 Write character to video screen. This function is useful for writing one or two characters (especially special characters) to the screen. It gets the characters from the DL register. (Function 9 writes longer character strings but it cannot write a special character—the dollar sign $— since it uses $ as the delimiter to terminate strings.)

Use Function 2 in conjunction with Function 8, which reads characters from the keyboard but does not display them. See an example of Function 2 in Fig. 2-13. We used Function 2 to display the contents of a memory input buffer in the program Buffer (see chapter 9).

If you read in the backspace key, you will move the cursor to the left but will not erase the character from the screen.

The macro in Fig. 2-13 loads into DX the location of a buffer already allocated in memory. The dummy parameter, *PCHAR?*, indicates that there is input expected. If no parameter is input to the macro, it will display whatever contents are already in register DL. You can ask it to print whatever is in AL, by using *AL* as an input parameter. The macro sets up a call to INT 21 Function 2.

```
@DISPL_CHAR    MACRO   PCHAR?

        ; Display input character on screen
        ; You can use this macro to:
        ;   @DISPL_CHAR 'x'    to display a character on the screen
        ;                          where x is that character
        ;   @DISPL_CHAR AL    to display contents of AL register
        ;   @DISPL_CHAR        to display a value in DL
        ;
            IFNB    <PCHAR?>
            PUSH    DX
            MOV     DL,PCHAR?
            ENDIF
            MOV     AH,2
            INT     21H
            IFNB    <PCHAR?>
            POP     DX
            ENDIF
            ENDM
```

2-13 Displaying a single character.

Function 3 Read from serial port. Function 3 reads a byte from the standard auxiliary input, AUX or COM1. Store a 3 in the AH register and issue Interrupt 21. The character read is returned in AL. See examples in Fig. 2-12 and Fig. 2-13 on how to use this.

Function 4 Write to serial port. This function sends whatever byte is in register DL to the auxiliary port, AUX or COM1. Store a 4 in register AH and issue INT 21. See examples of function use in Fig. 2-12 and Fig. 2-13.

Function 5 Write to printer port. This function sends the character in register DL to the standard printer port, PRN or LPT1. Store a 5 in the AH register and issue INT 21. See examples of function use in Fig. 2-12 and Fig. 2-13 on how functions work.

Function 6   Direct keyboard input and video output. This function does both input and output. The AL register receives the input and the DL register contains the output character. Ask for input by storing FF in the DL register. Store a 6 in register AH and issue INT 21. On return from the function, the zero flag is set (ZF = 1) if no character is ready. If ZF = 0, then a character was read into AL. If DL contains any other value but FF, that character is sent to the standard output device.

   This function does not wait for an input character. Also, the character is not automatically displayed on the screen. See examples of function use in Fig. 2-12 and Fig. 2-13.

Function 7   Read keyboard character without echo or break detection. Function 7 waits for a keyboard character. If an ASCII character (number, letter, or control character) was entered, the ASCII value returns in AL. This function does not display the character and Ctrl + Break does not terminate it. (Compare this function with Function 8.)

   IBM graphic-style characters can be entered by holding down the Alt key and typing the decimal value with the keypad numbers. The number is in AL. If an extended character such as a function key or Alt combination is entered, a 0 is stored in AL, and Function 7 must be called a second time to find out what other character was entered. See appendix E for the extended ASCII characters. See examples in Fig. 2-12 and Fig. 2-13 on how to use functions.

Function 8   Read keyboard character without echo but with break detection. Function 8 is like Function 1; it waits for a character to be keyed in and terminates when Ctrl + Break is pressed. The input character is not displayed and the Tab is not expanded. To use Function 8, store an 8 in the AH register and issue Int 21.

Function 9   Display a string of characters. To use Function 9, store a string of characters in memory somewhere and terminate it with $. This means that $ cannot be part of the string. The function does not automatically send the cursor to the start of the next line after the string is printed. To do this, append 0Dh (carriage return) and 0Ah (line feed) to the line, just before $. There are many programs in this book that do this. For example, see CAP_IT in chapter 6. (If you need to print a dollar sign, use Function 2 to print that character.) Store the address of the string in the DS:DX register. Store 9 in AH and issue INT 21 as shown in Fig. 2-14.

Function 0A   Buffered keyboard input. Before you can use this function, you need to set up a buffer in memory. Add two auxiliary bytes at the beginning of the buffer. Set the first to the maximum length of text that can be stored in the buffer; the second holds the number of characters your user enters. Store the value of the first byte. MS-DOS stores the second after the input has been read, but does not include the carriage return in the count of input characters. So set the buffer size 3-bytes higher than you'll need. For an example of setting up a buffer and storing the bytes, see

Program

```
;   Note that a carriage return is 0Dh, and a line feed
;   is 0Ah.  The two hex characters are placed at the
;   beginning of the string to print.
;   They could also be placed at the end, such as in the
;   EXAMPLE below.
        .
        .
EXAMPLE    DB    ' This is another example.',0Ah,0Dh,'$'
PRINT—STR  DB    0Dh,0Ah,'This is the string to print.$'
        .
        .
           LEA    DX,PRINT—STR    ; Point to String
           MOV    AH,9            ; String—print Function
           INT    21h
        .
        .
```

2-14   Displaying a string of characters.

program Strsrch in chapter 6 and Buffer in chapter 9. If you have debug software, run Strsrch through it and watch how the buffer contents change.

All the characters typed by the user are entered into this buffer and the control keys are available for use, such as Insert, Delete, and the cursor control keys. When the user presses the carriage return (Enter) key, the entire line goes from the keyboard buffer to the input buffer.

To use Function 0A, store in DS:DX the pointer to the first auxiliary byte (the byte that defines the maximum buffer size), which is located 2 bytes in front of the text. Store 0A in register AH and issue Interrupt 21. Figure 2-15 shows how to use this function.

Program
```
    :
INPUT—STR  DB    23 DUP (?)
    :
           MOV    INPUT—STR,20    ; Maximum allowed on input
           LEA    DX,INPUT—STR    ; Point to string for input
           MOV    AH,0Ah          ; Buffered keyboard input function
           INT    21h
```
2-15   Buffered keyboard input example.

Function 0B Keyboard status. There may be times when you do not want to wait for character input. You can avoid waiting by using Int 21 Function 0B to check the keyboard status. Store a 0B in the AH register and execute INT 21. On return, register AL contains a value if a character is waiting; it holds a 0 if no key has been pressed. Function 0B does not read the character. You must use Function 1, 7, or 8 for that.

Interrupt 21 error return codes

Interrupt 21 error return codes. Many system calls return values in a register that specify whether or not the operation succeeded. Your program can handle error conditions by checking the register that contains the error code (AX) and taking appropriate action. Table 2-5 lists the error codes.

Because newer versions of MS-DOS allow extended error handling, we included a procedure (Exterror—see chapter 5 for a description and listing).

Table 2-5   Error return codes.

Code	Meaning
1	Invalid Function Number
2	File Not Found
3	Path Not Found
4	Too Many Open Files
5	Access Denied
6	Invalid File Handle
7	Memory Control Blocks Destroyed
8	Insufficient Memory
9	Invalid Memory Block Address
10	Invalid Environment
11	Invalid Format
12	Invalid Access Code
13	Invalid Data
14	(Not Used)
15	Invalid Drive Specified
16	Attempted to Remove Current Directory
17	Not Same Device
18	No More Files

This procedure allows you to access additional information on errors, a great help during program debugging.

Interrupt 23: Intercept Ctrl + Break

Users generally stop program execution by holding the Ctrl key and pressing Break (Ctrl+C often does the same thing). These keystrokes cause a branch to Interrupt 23 and then to an MS-DOS routine to stop the program.

You can keep users from interrupting a program (or enhance what happens when they do) by changing the Interrupt 23 so that it branches into your program. Then, when your user hits what is thought to be a Break key, you take control. When you've finished, you might want the new value to remain in effect until the system is shut off, or you might want to restore the original value before the program finishes. With Interrupt 23, MS-DOS always restores the original value when the current program finishes.

Common DOS file name extensions

The Microsoft system programs and language products commonly use the following file name extensions. They're included here so you'll know what they are if/when they appear in any of your libraries.

Extension	Description
.@@@	Backup ID file
.asc	ASCII text file
.asm	MASM uses this for assembly language source code
.bak	Backup file
.bat	Batch file containing MS-DOS commands
.bin	Binary file
.cod	Object listing file
.com	Executable program file
.crf	MASM cross-reference file
.dat	Data file
.doc	Documentation or document file
.drv	Driver file
.err	Error file
.exe	Executable program file
.fnt	Font file
.hex	Intel hexadecimal format file
.hlp	Help file
.inc	Include file
.lib	Library file
.map	Address map file

.mod	Module file
.obj	Relocatable object module
.ovl	Overlay file
.qlb	Library file, Microsoft Quick products
.ref	Cross-reference listing file
.scr	Script file
.sym	Symbol file
.sys	System file or device driver
.tmp	Temporary file
.txt	Text file or Windows Notepad file

3
80486 programming notes and tips

In general, software developed for one generation of the Intel microprocessor family works without alteration on the next higher (more modern) level. This chapter lists various facts you need to remember when you program or design around the 80486.

First, we address the current software/hardware environment with a list of guidelines for software developers. The chapter then reviews certain aspects of programming for the 80486 that can cause problems. Although the operating systems being offered by the major companies often force the use of USE16 in programs (which limits the effectiveness of the 80486), there are some very nice items programmers can use.

The greatest thing the 80486 does is provide large segments, which virtually eliminates 64K segment-limit headaches. The fact that there isn't an operating system (among the very popular operating systems) that supports the large model is an irritant. A large model provides easy array indexing and makes very good use of the 80486 instructions. As shown by many of the programs in this book, you can make use of the extended addressing features as long as you're careful about overflows of 64K words. You can use SIB *byte* for indexing, which is a real pleasure to use because it provides a high-level language for indexing. You don't have to load values, multiply them by the appropriate other values, and load into registers. The instruction does it for you.

The addition of another byte in the jump instructions, which allows the use of a 16-bit displacement instead of the 8-bit, gives a much wider range of displacement addresses. It eases a lot of programming problems of jumping only certain bytes ahead or behind.

Other useful instructions are the bit test instructions that do bitmap operations, such as handling the Task State Segment (TSS). See appendix

A for a discussion of this segment. Even with the limitations of current operating systems, the 80486 is a very powerful and capable processor.

With MS-DOS in real mode and OS/2 in protected mode, providing only a 16-bit address capability, the 80486 runs as effectively as a fast 80286. This limits 32-bit addressing, which, in our opinion, is the most significant 80486 capability.

The additional instructions are useful, but they do things that can be done some other way. You can get around the addressing (which we show in the array routines in chapter 9) but running in protected mode, programs are more expensive in machine cycles to run. In addition to the overhead and keeping track of where you are, there are descriptors that impose the overhead of having to load them—where what you'd like to do is load the descriptor to your array, mush around in the array, and never have to load the descriptor again.

There are DOS versions available that do provide 32-bit addressing. UNIX for the 80486 runs normally in the USE32 mode. In fact, we've heard very good things about it.

Terminology

First, let's look at some 80486 definitions. You will find more complete descriptions of the terms in appendix A.

base address   In 80486 terms, the physical address of the start of a segment.

cache flush   An operation that marks all cache lines as invalid. The 80486 has instructions for flushing both internal and external caches.

cache line   The smallest unit of storage that can be allocated in a cache. The 80486 has a line size of 128 bits.

cache miss   A request for access to memory that requires actually reading main memory.

code segment   An address space that contains instructions; an executable segment.

control word   A 16-bit FPU register that a user can set, to determine the modes of computation the FPU will use and the exception interrupts that will be enabled.

descriptor   Descriptors are data structures used to define the characteristics of a program element. For example, descriptors might describe a data record, a segment, or a task.

double extended   IEEE Std. 754 term for the FPU's extended format, with more exponent and significand bits than the double format and an explicit integer bit in the significand.

extended cache   A cache memory provided outside of the processor chip. The 80486 has instructions and page-table entry bits that are used to control external caches from software.

flag   A flag is an indicator whose state is used to inform a later section of a program that a condition has occurred. The condition is identified with the flag and designated by the state of the flag; that is, the flag is either set (ON = 1) or not set (OFF = 0).

Floating-Point Unit (FPU)   The part of the 80486 that contains the floating-point registers and performs the operations required by floating-point instructions.

gate   A gate is a logic design that allows only certain processes to pass through it. The 80486 provides protection for control transfers among executable segments at differing privilege levels by use of gate descriptors, of which there are four: call gates, trap gates, interrupt gates, and task gates.

Instruction Pointer (IP)   A register that contains the offset of the instruction currently being executed. A selector for the segment containing this instruction is stored in the CS register. In the 80486, the EIP (an extended instruction pointer) is a 32-bit register that contains the offset address of the next sequential instruction to be executed. The low-order 16 bits of the EIP are the IP.

internal cache   A cache memory on the processor chip. The 80486 has 8K of internal cache memory.

I/O Permissions Bit Map   The mechanism that allows the 80486 to selectively trap references to specific I/O addresses. The Permissions Bit Map resides in the Task State Segment (TSS). The map is a bit vector and its size and location in the TSS are variable. The 80486 locates the map by means of the I/O Map Base field in the fixed portion of the TSS.

linear address space   An address indicates the location of a register, a particular place in storage, or some other data source or destination. In the 80486, the memory's linear address space runs from byte 0 to 4Gb. A linear address points to a particular byte within this space.

logical address   First, there is no conceptual parallel from linear address space to the space used by logical addressing. A logical address consists of a selector and offset. The selector points to some segment descriptor (part of which is that segment's linear base address). The offset tells how far into the segment the required byte is. In the programs in this book, you see notations like DS:DX that often point to a memory buffer. What this notation means is that the contents of the DX register [DX] point to bytes at an offset from the data segment [DS] beginning.

physical address   The address that actually selects the memory where a required byte is located. In the 80486, linear and physical addresses differ only when paging is in effect.

segment   Beginning with the 8086, Intel introduced the concept of segments, which were defined as units of contiguous (adjacent) address space. In the 8086, this space had a maximum of 64K (65536 bytes). In the 80486, that limitation no longer applies. You can now view segments as one-dimensional subspaces, each with some specified length up to 4Gb.

task   A task is a basic, unique function of a program or system. It can be one instance of the execution of a program.

Task State Segment (TSS)   A TSS is a data structure delineated and pointed to by a descriptor, wherein the interrupted state of a task is stored each time the task is interrupted. Systems software creates TSSs and places the initial information in them, such as correct stack pointers for interrupt handlers. TSSs are described in detail in appendix A.

paging Paging refers to a procedure that transmits the consecutive bytes called a page between locations, such as between disk storage and memory. A paging function simplifies the operating system swapping algorithms because it provides a uniform mechanism for managing the physical structure of memory.

Software guidelines

Applications designed for the 8086/8088 execute transparently in the 80486's virtual-8086 mode. Virtual environments bridge existing applications to new microprocessor systems and provide upward compatibility while offering the new environment enhanced functions and performance. Remember that performance of applications executed in virtual-8086 mode tends to be lower than in real mode in the same processor. This occurs because an operating system intervenes to handle interrupts and emulate certain instructions.

To this intervention time is added the execution time of the code that saves and restores machine state and emulates the instruction. The primary impact is in interrupt-intensive programs because straight code tends to execute unimpeded in virtual-8086 mode.

Until an operating system is designed specifically for the 80486, certain guidelines should be kept in mind when developing a software product that is intended to run on 80486 systems; those guidelines are summarized in Fig. 3-1.

Guidelines Overview

* The 80486 is faster so don't depend on real-time events as with earlier chips. Use a timing source independent of the 80486.
* Avoid defining any bits that are Intel-reserved.
* If writing for an entire chip family (8086 thru 80486), write for 8086. 80486 instruction set is a superset of all previous generations.
* Values in various registers are different on the earlier microprocessors. Load values explicitly.
* Only use instruction Opcodes that are explicitly defined.

3-1 Software guidelines overview.

- The 80486 tends to execute specific code sequences significantly faster than earlier processors. Any code that interacts with real-time events or that depends on its execution time to perform its function should use a timing source independent of the 80486 clock speed.

- Routines written to run specifically on an 80486 system should be insensitive to the state of the Protection Enable (PE) bit in the Machine Status Word (MSW) of CR0. Setting PE causes the processor to begin executing in protected mode. The visibility of the PE bit via the Store Machine Status Word (SMSW) instruction might cause problems for code that attempts to act differently based on whether the 80486 is executing in real or protected mode.
- Avoid any implicit or explicit use of register bits, flags, or data structures that are declared undefined or reserved for future Intel development.
- If the software is intended to run on various levels of processors (8086/8088, 80286 or 80486), write to the lowest common denominator, which is the 8086/8088.
- The value of various registers and flags after reset is different on different processors. Do not depend on the power-on state of a particular processor. A program should explicitly load the required values.
- Do not use instruction opcodes that are not explicitly documented in Intel literature. An opcode that is not part of the supported instruction set may be defined differently in a later generation, even if it seemed to have a function in the earlier processor.

Programming for the 80486

The 80486 is compatible with applications developed for earlier Intel processors while providing a full, 32-bit-large linear address programming environment. There are several issues to keep in mind when programming specifically for the 80486 environment that might not be clear from the documentation and which are covered in the following sections.

Program instructions

The 80286 implements the bus lock function differently than the 80486. Programs that use forms of memory locking specific to the 80286 may not execute correctly when transported to a specific program on the 80486.

LOCK can be used only with certain 80486 instructions (as shown in Fig. 3-2) when they modify memory. An undefined opcode exception results from using LOCK before any other instruction.

1. One-operand arithmetic and logical: INC, DEC, NOT, and NEG.
2. Two-operand arithmetic and logical: ADD, ADC, SBB, SUB, AND, OR, and XOR.
3. Exchange: XCHG.
4. Bit test and change: BTS, BTR, BTC.

The LOCK prefix and its corresponding output signal should only be used to prevent other bus masters from interrupting a data movement

LOCK works *only* with:

3-2 LOCK limits.

BT, BTC, BTR, BTS	Memory, Reg/Imm
ADD, OR, ADC, SBB, AND, SUB, XOR .	Memory, Reg/Imm
DEC, INC, NEG, NOT	Memory
XCHG	Reg/Memory or Memory/Reg

operation. A locked instruction is guaranteed to lock only the areas of memory specifically defined by the destination operand. Typical 8086 and 80286 configurations lock the entire physical memory space. With the 80486, the defined area of memory is guaranteed to be locked against access by a processor executing a locked instruction on exactly the same memory area; that is, only with an operand with identical starting address and identical length.

The 80486 allows a CALL or JMP directly to another segment only if one of the following rules is satisfied: (1) the conforming bit of the target code-segment descriptor is set and the DPL of the target is less than or equal to the CPL; or (2) the DPL of the target is equal to the CPL. Most code segments are not conforming. For these segments, control can be transferred without a gate only to executable segments at the same privilege level. To transfer control to numerically smaller privilege levels, the CALL instruction is used with call gate descriptors. The JMP instruction may never transfer control to a nonconforming segment whose DPL does not equal CPL.

Only CALL instructions can use gates to transfer to lower numeric privilege levels. A gate can be used by a JMP instruction only to transfer to an executable segment with the same privilege level, or to a conforming segment.

The Bit Scan Forward (BSF) instruction scans a word or doubleword for a one bit and stores the index of the first set bit into a register. The bit string being scanned can be in either a register or in memory. ZF is set if the entire word is 0; that is, no set bits are found. ZF is cleared if a one bit is found. Note: If no set bit is found, the value of the destination register is undefined.

With the Unsigned Integer Divide (DIV) instruction, non-integer quotients are truncated to integers toward zero. The remainder is always less than the divisor. For unsigned byte division, the largest quotient is 255; for unsigned word division, it is 65,535. For unsigned doubleword division, it is $(2^{32} - 1)$. For shift instructions such as SAL, Carry Flag (CF) always contains the value of the last bit shifted out of the destination operand. In a single-bit shift, Overflow Flag (OF) is set if the value of the high-order (the sign) bit was changed by the operation. If the sign bit was not changed, OF is cleared. After a multi-bit shift, OF is always undefined.

The difference between TEST (Logical Compare) and AND is that

TEST does not alter the destination operand. TEST differs from Bit Test (BT) in that TEST tests the value of multiple bits in one operation, whereas BT tests a single bit.

Memory

Physical address formation in real-address mode: Unlike the 8086, when calculating the effective address, the 80486's resulting linear address can have up to 21 significant bits. There is a possibility of a carry when the base address is added to the effective address. On the 8086, the carry bit is truncated. On the 80486, the carry bit is stored in bit position 20 of the linear address. See Fig. 3-3 for an overview of how the 80486 maps a linear address to a physical address.

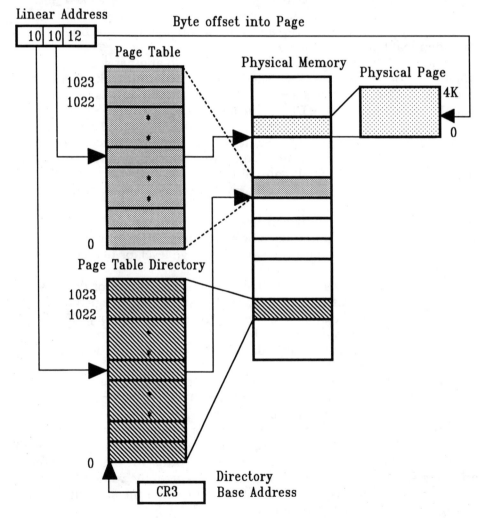

3-3 Linear to physical address mapping.

Unlike the 8086 and the 80286, 32-bit effective addresses can be generated via the address-size prefix. However, the value of a 32-bit address in real mode cannot exceed 65,536, or it will cause an exception.

With the 80286, any base and offset combination that addresses beyond 16Mb wraps around to the first megabyte of the 80286 address space. Because the 80486 has greater physical address space, any such address falls into the 17th megabyte. In the event that any software depends on this anomaly, the same effect can be simulated on the 80486 by using paging to map the first 64K of the 17th megabyte of logical address to physical addresses in the first megabyte.

For maximum flexibility in a data structure's efficient memory use, words are not required to be aligned at even-numbered addresses. Also, doublewords do not have to be aligned at addresses evenly divisible by four. When using a system with a 32-bit bus, however, actual transfers of data between processor and memory take place in units of doublewords that begin at addresses evenly divisible by four. The misaligned words cause an increase in the number of memory cycles to fetch data, thus decreasing performance.

It might be expedient to turn off the 80486 segmentation when the 80486 is used to execute software designed for special architectures that do not have segments. The processor does not have a specific mode to disable segmentation. However, the same effect is achieved by initially loading the segment registers with selectors for descriptors that encompass the entire 32-bit linear address space. Once the descriptors are loaded, the segment registers are not changed. The 80486 instructions' 32-bit offsets address the entire linear-address space.

In a write cycle (with 8-bit I/O devices), if BE3# and/or BE2# but not BE1# or BE0#, the write data on the top half of the data bus is duplicated on the bottom half. If the addresses of two devices differ only in the values of BE3#–BE0# (that is, the addresses lie within the same doubleword boundaries), BE3#–BE0# must be decoded to provide a chip select signal that prevents a write to one device from erroneously performing a write to the other. This chip select can be generated using an address decoder PAL device or TTL logic.

Descriptors

Because the 80486 uses the contents of the reserved word (the last word) of every descriptor, 80286 programs that place values in this word might not execute correctly on the 80486. See Fig. 3-4 for the format of segment descriptors.

Code that manages space in descriptor tables often use an invalid value in the access-rights field of descriptor-table entries to identify unused entries. Access rights values of 80h and 00h remain invalid on the 80486. Other values that might have been invalid for the 80286 might now be valid for the 80486 because of new descriptor types.

Descriptor Used for Special System Segments

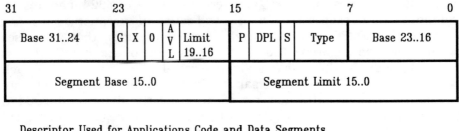

| 31 | 23 | 15 | 7 | 0 |

| Base 31..24 | G | X | 0 | A V L | Limit 19..16 | P | DPL | S | Type | Base 23..16 |

| Segment Base 15..0 | Segment Limit 15..0 |

Descriptor Used for Applications Code and Data Segments

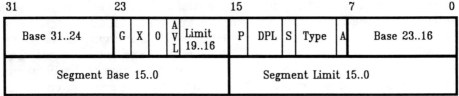

| 31 | 23 | 15 | 7 | 0 |

| Base 31..24 | G | X | 0 | A V L | Limit 19..16 | P | DPL | S | Type | A | Base 23..16 |

| Segment Base 15..0 | Segment Limit 15..0 |

3-4 General Segment Descriptor format.

To tell the difference between an 80286-type descriptor and an 80486-type descriptor, the processor checks the upper word. If the word is zero, then the descriptor is an 80286-type. An executable segment whose descriptor has the conforming bit (bit 10) set is called a *conforming segment*. The conforming segment allows procedures to be shared that might be called from differing privilege levels but should execute at the privilege level of the calling procedure. When control is transferred to a conforming segment, the CPL does not change. This is the only case when CPL can be unequal to the DPL of the currently executable segment.

Registers

Certain bits in various registers are shown as either reserved or undefined. When using registers with these bits, treat the bits as truly undefined. Do not depend on the states of any undefined bits when testing the values of defined register bits. Mask out the undefined ones. Do not depend on the states of any undefined bits when storing them in memory or in another register, or on the ability of these bits to retain information. When loading registers, always load the undefined or reserved bits as zeros or unchanged from their values as stored.

The VM bit of the EFLAGS register can be set only two ways: by the IRET instruction in protected mode, only if the current privilege level is zero; and by task switches at any privilege level.

The low-order 16 bits of the CR0 register is the 80286 Machine Status Word and can be addressed separately as the MSW. See Fig. 3-5 for the format of Control Register Zero (CR0).

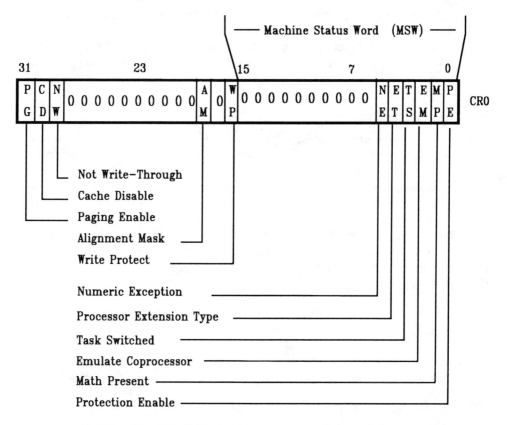

Note: Zero bits indicate Intel reserved. Do not define.

3-5 Control Register Zero (CR0) with MSW. (Zero entries indicate Intel-reserved bits; do not define.)

Tasks

The only way to leave real-address mode is to deliberately switch to protected mode. The 80486 enters protected mode when a MOV to CR0 instruction sets the PE bit in CR0. A TSS can reside anywhere in the linear address space. The single caution is when the TSS spans a page boundary. In this case, the 80486 raises an exception if it encounters the not-present page while reading the TSS during a task switch.

To prevent this, allocate the TSS so that it does not cross a page boundary or ensure that both pages are either both present or not present at the time of a task switch. In the latter case, if both pages are not present, the page-fault handler makes both pages present before restarting the instruction that caused the page default. Tasks are not reentrant. The B-bit on the TSS descriptor allows the processor to detect an attempt to switch to a task that is already busy. In the TSS descriptor, the LIMIT defines the size of the segment. This LIMIT must contain a value of 103 or higher. An attempt to switch to a task whose LIMIT is less than 103 causes an exception.

Every task switch sets the TS bit in the MSW (in CR0). The TS bit signals that the context of a numeric coprocessor might not correspond to the current 80486 task.

Privilege and protection

The privilege level at which execution restarts in an incoming task is not restricted in any way by the privilege level of an outgoing task. When paging is enabled, the processor first checks segment protection and then evaluates page protection. If the 80486 detects a protection violation at either level, it cancels the requested operation and generates a protection exception.

The processor examines type information (in segment descriptors) on two sets of occasions. The first is when a selector of a descriptor is loaded into a segment register. Certain segment registers can contain only fixed descriptor types, such as:

- Only selectors of writable data segments can be loaded into SS.
- The CS register can be loaded only with a selector of an executable segment.
- Selectors of executable segments (that are not readable) cannot be loaded into data-segment registers.

The second class of occasion is when an instruction implicitly or explicitly refers to a segment register. Some segments can be used by instructions only in certain ways, such as:

- Unless the readable bit is set, no instruction can read an executable segment.
- Unless the writable bit is set, no instruction can write into a data segment.
- No instruction can write into an executable segment.

To combine page and segment protection, it is possible to define a large enough data segment that has some subunits that are read-only and other subunits that are read-write. If you do, the page directory or page table entries for the read-only subunits would have the User/Supervisor (U/S) and the Read/Write (R/W) bits set to $x0$. This indicates that there are no write rights for all the pages described by that directory entry or for the individual pages.

This technique could be useful in a UNIX-like system to define a large data segment, part of which is read-only (for shared data or ROMed constants). This would enable the system to define a flat data space as one large segment, use flat pointers to address within this space, and yet be able to protect shared data, supervisor areas, and shared files mapped into virtual space.

Code segments can hold constants, but cannot be written to. There are three methods of reading data in code segments:

1. Use a CS override prefix to read a readable, executable segment whose selector is already loaded in the CS register.
2. Load a data-segment register with a selector or a nonconforming, readable, executable segment.
3. Load a data-segment register with a selector of a conforming, readable, executable segment.

Case 1 is always valid because the DPL of the code segment in CS is, by definition, equal to CPL. Case 2 uses the same rules as for access to data segments. Case 3 is always valid because the privilege level of a segment whose conforming bit is set is effectively the same as CPL, regardless of its DPL.

Testing and debugging

Since the first entry of the Global Descriptor Table (GDT) is not used by the processor, a selector that has both an index and a table indicator of zero can be used as a null selector. This process does not cause an exception when a segment register (other than CS or SS) is loaded with a null selector. The process will cause an exception when the segment register is used to access memory. This feature is useful for initializing unused segment registers so as to trap accidental references.

The Translation Lookaside Buffer (TLB) is a cache used for translating linear addresses to physical addresses. Figure 3-6 shows the general structure of the TLB. Note that the TLB testing mechanism is unique to the 80486 and might not be continued in the same way in future processors. Software that uses this mechanism as it currently is implemented might be incompatible with future processors.

The complement of the Dirty, User, and Writable bits in Test Register 6 (TR6) are provided to force a hit or miss for TLB lookups. A lookup operation with a bit and its complement both low is forced to be a miss. If both bits are high, a hit is forced. A write operation is always performed when a bit and its complement have opposite values.

It is important not to write the same linear address to more than one TLB entry. Otherwise, hit information returned during a TLB lookup operation is undefined. To look up or read a TLB entry:

1. Move a doubleword that contains the appropriate linear address and attributes to TR6. Be sure C = 1 for lookup.
2. Store TR7. If the HT bit in TR7 is 1, then other values reveal the TLB contents. If HT = 0, then the other values are undefined. See Fig. 3-7 for TR6 and TR7 formats.

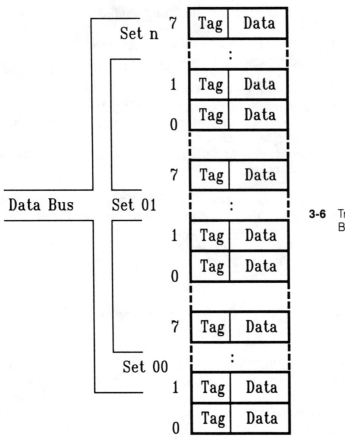

3-6 Translation Lookaside Buffer (TLB) structure.

3. For testing purposes, the V bit acts as another bit of address. The V bit for a lookup request should be set, so that uninitialized tags do not match. Lookups with V = 0 are unpredictable if any tags are uninitialized.

To write a TLB entry, do the following:

1. Move a doubleword that contains the desired physical address, HT, and REP values to TR7. HT must contain a 1, and REP must point to the associative block in which to place the entry.
2. Move a doubleword that contains the appropriate linear address and values for V, D, U, and W to TR6. Be sure C = 0 for write command.
3. Be careful not to write duplicate tags because the results are undefined.

31			11		7		4		0	
Physical Address			PLD	PWT	L R U	0 0	PL	REP	0 0	TR7
Linear Address			V	D D#	U U#	W W#	0 0 0 0		C	TR6

TR7   PCD   = Page–level Cache Disable
       PWT   = Page–level Write–Through
       LRU   = Used in pseudo–LRU Cache Replacement
                    Algorithm

       PL   = Lookup was a HIT=1, MISS=0
       REP   = Block where tag was found, if HT=1,
                    Undefined if HT=0.

TR6   V   = Valid bit
       D/D#   = Dirty bit
       U/U#   = User bit
       W/W#   = Read/Write bit
       C   = Command bit

Note: Zeros represent Intel reserved bits. Do not define.

3-7   Test Registers TR6 and TR7. (Zero entries indicate Intel-reserved bits; do not define.)

4
Arithmetic

Computers were designed as fast arithmetic engines that solve a variety of problems. In most computers, a single number occupies a single memory unit, usually labeled as *word*. Such word-length numbers are called *single precision*, in contrast to double-precision numbers. Double-precision numbers occupy two words (doublewords or dwords) and are used when you require additional accuracy.

Programmers work with numbers that are powers of two. Table 4-1 shows the numeric abbreviations, the powers of two, and decimal values. A given number can be stored as fixed-point, floating-point, or binary-coded decimal (BCD). In fixed-point, the binary point (the *decimal* or *radix point*) is assumed to be at a fixed place, such as at the left end of the number. The mechanics of fixed-point arithmetic are essentially those of ordinary binary arithmetic, given the restriction that negative numbers are usually stored and manipulated in some complement form.

The major snare in fixed-point addition and subtraction is the phenomenon known as *overflow*. Because not only the two operands but also the result in addition and subtraction must be less than 1 in magnitude, a result greater than this will not be handled correctly. Overflow occurs when the high-order numeric bit has a carry-out into the sign bit. Normally, the system indicates this by setting an internal switch that the programmer can test.

Hardware that stored and manipulated numbers in fixed-point form was the only type available in early computers. Unfortunately, handling them and doing arithmetic with them created major problems. For instance, how could numbers with magnitudes of 1 or greater be handled? More significantly, how could numbers be handled whose implicit decimal points were in different positions? How could they be added, subtracted, divided, or multiplied?

Table 4-1   Numeric abbreviations.

Programmer notation	Power of two	Decimal value
1K	2^{10}	1024
4K	2^{12}	4096
16K	2^{14}	16,384
32K	2^{15}	32,768
64K	2^{16}	65,536
2G	2^{31}	2,147,483,648
4G	2^{32}	4,294,967,296

To do arithmetic, programs shift the contents of the words, bit by bit, relative to the others. The process of such shifting and the associated problem of choosing the location of the implicit binary point for numbers before they are stored is called *scaling*. The difficulty of scaling for all but the simplest computations led to the introduction of floating-point hardware capabilities.

As with other processors, the 80486 supports the basic unsigned number data in byte (8-bit), word (16-bit), and dword (32-bit) lengths. Figure 4-1 shows these types. The most significant bit (MSB) of unsigned

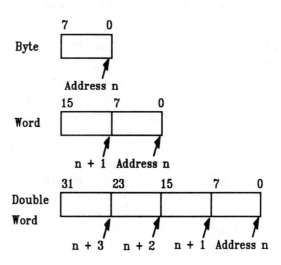

4-1 80486 basic data types, shown as it appears in registers (not as it appears in memory).

numbers is bit 7 for bytes, 15 for words, and 31 for dwords. By extension, the least significant bit (LSB) is at 0 for all types.

A sign is a binary indicator of the position of the size (magnitude) of a number, relative to zero. Sign magnitude in computer numbers has a bit that represents the sign—0 if positive and 1 if negative. The remainder of the bits give the absolute value of the number.

Exponents use biased numbers for expressing values of floating-point exponents. Biases are 127, 1023, and 16,383 for short, long, and temporary real formats. Biased numbers ease numeric comparisons (e.g., greater than or less than) and are computed by taking the initial positive or negative number and adding a bias value to it. This bias makes sure that the most positive number allowable becomes the largest value of the representation and the most negative number becomes zero.

Two's complement represents signed integers. The 80486 supports both two's complement and unsigned data. In two's complement, the simple binary adder used for unsigned numbers also adds two numbers in two's complement format with no additional transformations. Two's complement is formed by computing the one's complement of the number and adding 1 to the result. (A one's complement number is computed by inverting every bit, including the MSB.) The MSB of the byte, word, or dword is the sign bit. MSB = 1 shows a negative number and MSB = 0 indicates a positive number.

In binary arithmetic, the product of two bits is 1 if and only if both bits are 1. In adding two bits, the sum is 1 if and only if one but not both summands have the value of 1; the carry bit is 1 if and only if both summands have the value 1. Thus we compute the sum bit by using the logical inequivalence (the exclusive OR) operation and the carry bit by using the logical conjunction (the AND) operation. Since the negative of an integer is normally represented by a complementary bit pattern (two's complement), arithmetic negation is accomplished by logical negation (or Boolean complementation) and adding one to form the two's complement.

Binary addition and subtraction

The rules of binary addition are the same as for decimal values. In decimal, adding a 9 and a 1 results in a 10. We call this value ten, but it really is this: We've exceeded the count for the units position and this is the base number in the units position and a carry to the tens position. The same occurs in binary addition. Adding 1 and 1 results in a zero in that position with a 1 carried to the left. The rules of binary addition are shown in Fig. 4-2.

Computers don't subtract, so you have to do some fancy footwork to make them appear to (if you choose not to use the SUB instruction). Of the two numbers you want to work with, the first (that appears on top) is called the *minuend*. The second (that appears underneath) is called the *subtrahend*. To get a correct answer, take the two's complement of the subtrahend and add it to the minuend. Figure 4-3 shows how this is done.

Rule 1: ZERO plus ZERO equals ZERO
Rule 2: ZERO plus ONE equals ONE
Rule 3: ONE plus ONE   equals ZERO, with a
                       carry to the left

Rule 1:	Rule 2:	Rule 3:
0	0	1
+ 0	+ 1	+ 1
0	1	10

4-2 Rules of binary addition.

Examples:

BINARY	DECIMAL	BINARY	DECIMAL
0011	3	1001	9
+ 0111	+ 7	+0101	+ 5
1010	10	1110	14

Rule: Take the two's complement of the
      subtrahend and add to the
      minuend

Regular	BINARY	DECIMAL	
	S		S=Sign
Minuend	0 1010	10	
Subtrahend	0 0111	7	

4-3 Rules of binary subtraction.

The Two's complement is taken by
inverting all bits and adding 1 to the low bit

	S		
Minuend	0	1010	10
Subtrahend	1	1001	−7
	C	0011	3

Binary addition and subtraction are cumbersome for humans once you get into numbers of any size. Thus, designers came up with binary coded decimal, which is easy for humans and more difficult for computers.

Binary coded decimal (BCD)

Binary coded decimal (BCD) is a system of number representation where each decimal digit is represented by a combination of four binary digits (bits), as shown in Fig. 4-4. The largest single digit in BCD is 9 decimal, or 1001 binary.

Binary	Decimal
0000	0
0001	1
0010	2
0011	3
0100	4
0101	5
0110	6
0111	7
1000	8
1001	9

4-4 Binary Coded Decimal (BCD) representation.

Convert 3571 to BCD

Digit	3	5	7	1
Binary	0011	0101	0111	0001

BCD arithmetic is accurate because there is no limit to the size of the operands and the decimal point can be repositioned easily. The BCD system is based on the fact that each of the decimal digits 0 through 9 can be held conveniently in a single, 4-bit nibble (half-byte). One format, called *packed BCD*, uses the two nibbles of a byte to represent two decimal digits. *Unpacked BCD* ignores the upper half of a byte and uses the lower nibble to hold a decimal digit.

BCD arithmetic involves conversion overhead before and after each operation. Packed BCD requires that two digits be packed into a series of bytes before the operation and then unpacked into ASCII representation in order to display them. Unpacked BCD is simpler because the ASCII digits

0 through 9 start out in the correct format; for example, the low nibble of the ASCII character 6 is a binary 6 (see appendix D for additional numeric translations).

A 64-bit addition/subtraction program

BIN64ADD (Program 4-1 at the end of this chapter) provides a 64-bit binary add and subtract. The numbers are considered to be 63-bits long, with the high-order bit being a sign (negative numbers are kept in two's complement form). BIN64ADD uses the 32-bit integer form of the 80486.

DS:SI points to one number and DS:DI points to the other. For subtraction, the minuend is the number at DS:SI and the subtrahend is at DS:DI. The arithmetic result is stored at DS:BX. The condition codes are returned exactly as if a simple add or subtract had been done. Zero, Carry, Sign, and Overflow flags are all returned, depending on the result of the add or subtract.

Packed decimal routines

A BCD driver program

DRIVEBCD (Program 4-2 at the end of the chapter) drives the BCD routines. It allows you to enter numbers and converts them to BCD. The standard BCD convention used in the routines is 8-bytes long, which is 14 BCD digits with one byte taken for the sign. The routines are easily extensible to use some bits of the sign byte for a floating decimal. The BCD routines make use of the 80486 extended register set.

The BCD routines avoid creating the anomaly of a negative zero by testing the number to determine if it is zero and forcing the sign byte to reflect the result of the test.

BCD pack and unpack programs

BCD pack and unpack programs, or BCDUNPK, (Program 4-3) accepts a signed BCD number with the form

    SSddddddddddddddd

where SS is the sign byte and the 7 pairs of dds are the BCD digits. BCDUNPK creates, as output, an ASCIIZ string in the form:

    []NNNNNNNNNNNNNNNN \ 0

The ASCIIZ string might have a leading minus sign if the BCD number was negative. At least a single zero will be produced and the number will be terminated with a null (hex 00).

DS:BX points to the BCD number coming in and ES:DI points to the ASCII string. The number pointed to by BX will first have its sign transferred to the output string if it is negative. Leading zero digits are bypassed until the final digit, which is converted and output as are all digits after the first non-zero. The resulting ASCII string is then terminated with a null, which makes it an ASCIIZ string.

BCDPACK (Program 4-4) does the reverse. It produces a signed BCD number in the form:

SSdddddddddddddd

where SS is the sign byte and the 7 pairs of dds are the BCD digits, from an ASCII string in the form of

[+/−]NNNNNNNNNNNNNN

The ASCII string can have a leading plus or minus sign. Up to 14 ASCII digits will be packed. Within the 14-digit limit, packing stops at the first non-digit.

DS:BX points to the BCD number and DS:SI points to the ASCII string. The number pointed to by BX is first cleared to zero. If the ASCII string has a leading minus, the sign will be tentatively set minus. The string will be examined from left to right to determine its numeric length. It will then be packed, right to left, into the target BCD number. An invalid numeric terminates the scan of the source number. The Zero Flag (ZF) is set if the result of the pack was zero. At the end of the procedure, SI points to the character beyond the converted number. The area pointed to by BX contains the packed number.

Signed test of a BCD number

Signed test of a BCD number, or BCDTST, (Program 4-5) provides a signed test of a BCD number in the form:

SSdddddddddddddd

where SS is the sign byte (bit 7 is on for minus, off for plus) and the 7 pairs of dds make up a 14-digit packed BCD number. BCDTST uses the 80486 expanded register set, so the routine ends up being half the size it would be if it were written for an 80286-based system (or earlier generation of chip).

DS:BX points to the BCD number. The number is tested for zero. If it is, the sign is forced to zero and a zero condition code is returned. Otherwise, the sign is set according to the value of the number's sign. Register AL contains a 1, 0, or + 1, depending on the result of the comparison. The Zero Flag (ZF) and the Sign Flag (SF) are also set, depending on the results of the comparison.

Signed comparison of BCD numbers

A signed comparison of BCD numbers, or BCDCMP, (Program 4-6) performs a signed comparison of BCD numbers in the form:

SSdddddddddddddd

where SS is the sign byte (bit 7 on for minus, off for plus) and the 7 pairs of dds make up a 14-digit packed BCD number. If the signs of the two numbers being compared are the same, the numbers are compared. If the signs are different, the numbers cannot be the same, so the one with the negative sign is taken to be the lower number. If both numbers are negative, the smaller absolute value is determined to be closer to zero, so is therefore greater.

BCD shift left and shift right

BCD shift left and shift right, or BCDSHL, (Program 4-7) provides a BCD left shift of an accumulator (double-precision) or a standard BCD value. The reason for shifting an accumulator is to allow scaling before a division. If working with an implied decimal point, you can scale it left to provide decimals in the quotient.

The number of digits shifted can be from zero to the size of the input number. AL contains the size code of the value to be shifted, with zero indicating a standard number. Non-zero indicates a double-precision accumulator. AH contains the number of digits to shift and BX contains the address of the field to shift.

The size code is replaced with the size of the number in bytes (less one) for use in computing the rightmost byte address. It is also used to select a comparand for the check of the shift amount; an oversized shift (more than 13 digits for this example) results in zero and a zero condition code is set. If an odd number of digits is requested, the number is shifted left one digit. The shift amount is divided by two and the number is moved left. If a non-zero digit was shifted out of the number, the Carry Flag (CF) is set to indicate the loss of significance.

BCDSHR (Program 4-8) provides a BCD right shift of an accumulator (double-precision) or a standard BCD value. The reason for the shifting of an accumulator is to allow for scaling after a multiplication. If working with an implied decimal point, you can scale it back to get rid of the unwanted decimals.

The number of digits shifted can be from zero to the size of the input number. AL contains the size code of the value to be shifted. Zero indicates a standard number. Non-zero indicates a double-precision accumulator. AH contains the number of digits to shift. BX contains the address of the field to shift.

The size code is replaced with the size of the number in bytes (less one) for use in computing the rightmost byte address. It is also used to select a comparand for the check of the shift amount; an oversized shift (more than 13 digits for this example) results in zero and a zero condition code is set. If an odd number of digits is requested, the number is shifted right one digit. The shift amount is divided by two and the number is moved right, with zeros filling the vacated positions.

BCD arithmetic programs

Addition and subtraction

BCD adding and subtracting are combined into one procedure, BCDADD (Program 4-9). This is done because the two arithmetic functions differ only in that the sign of the subtrahend is inverted for subtraction.

Stack space is reserved as a work area for computing the result. If the signs of the two numbers are the same, the result is computed directly by addition and receives the same sign. If the signs differ, the number with the smaller absolute value is subtracted from the larger and the result receives the sign of the larger. If the result is zero, the sign is forced to positive. If an overflow occurs, the Carry Flag will be set.

Multiplication

BCD multiplication, BCDMPY (Program 4-10), provides signed multiplication for BCD numbers in the form:

SSdddddddddddddd

where SS is the sign byte (bit 7 is on for minus, off for plus) and the 7 pairs of dds make up a 14-digit packed BCD number, packed two digits per byte. The product is placed in the 16-byte accumulator specified by DS:BX. If the accumulator overlaps either the multiplier or the multiplicand, the results are undefined.

DS:SI points to one BCD number and DS:DI points to the other. DS:BX points to the accumulator where the product is formed. The sign of the product is computed and set, and the accumulator is cleared to zero. The algorithm used to form the product is an adaptation of a simple manual multiplication.

The product is formed by selecting each digit of the multiplier from right to left and performing a right-to-left, digit-by-digit multiplication, adding the result to the accumulator. Because there are two decimal digits in each byte, we have four variants of the multiply. That is, if we are multiplying 76 by 34, we have to multiply 6 by 4, getting a product of 24. We then multiply 70 by 4 and add that partial product (280) to the 24 to get 304. We then multiply 6 by 30 to get 180 as a partial product which, when added, gives 484. Finally, we multiply 70 by 30 to get the partial product 2100 which we add to our previous sum, to get the final result of 2584.

Division

BCD division, BCDDIV (Program 4-11), provides a signed division of an accumulator, a 16-byte product:

SSxxddddddddddddddddddddddddddddddddd

In this case, xx is filler to force the sign to the left-most byte of the high-order word by a BCD number:

536-4444
WAREHOUSE "HOTLINE"
OR THE
PHONE ANY STORE

TRY US
to special order
that elusive title.

NEW AND RECENT
P/B RELEASES

MYSTERY
FAN?

Black Bond Books

ique of repeated subtraction to form the quo-
r from the left digits of the dividend until the
g the number of times it was subtracted and
e value, then shift right one nibble. This cre-
e upper half of the double-wide accumulator
e lower portion.

D number which is the divisor and DS:BX
mulator). Division by zero is checked. In the
y Flag is set and no quotient or remainder is

Program 4-1

Microsoft (R)

```
                                  55,132

0000                        para 'CODE' PUBLIC USE16
                            CS:code, DS:code, SS:code

                      DD
          llowing procedure provides a 64 bit binary add
          btract.  The numbers are considered to be 63 bits
          ith the high order bit being a sign.  Negative
          s are kept in 2's compliment form.
          s the 32 bit integer form of the 80386.


          points to one number, DS:DI points to the other.
          ubtraction the minuend is the number at DS:SI, the
          ahend is at DS:DI.  (i.e. DS:BX=DS:SI-DS:DI)
          points to the location for the sum (or difference).

          dd entry point preserves EAX and EDX and loads them
          the number at DS:DI.  The subtract entry does the
          and in addition takes the 2's compliment of the
          r.  The number at DS:SI is then added and the result
          red at DS:BX.

          ithmetic result is stored at DS:BX.  The condition
;         s returned exactly as if a simple add or subtract had
;         been done.  Zero, carry, sign, and overflow are all
;         returned.
;
                            PUBLIC  Bin64add
;
                   Bin64add PROC
0000    66| 52              push    EDX                 ; Save entry registers
0002    66| 50              push    EAX
0004    66| 8B 05           mov     EAX,DWORD PTR[DI+0]  ; Load low 32
0007    66| 8B 55 04        mov     EDX,DWORD PTR[DI+4]  ; and high 32.
000B    EB 18 90            jmp     goaddem             ; Go do addition.
;
; Entry point for subtract.
;
```

Program 4-1 Continued.

```
                                   PUBLIC  Bin64sub
                           Bin64sub:
000E
000E   66| 52                      push    EDX               ; Save entry registers
0010   66| 50                      push    EAX
0012   66| 8B 05                   mov     EAX,DWORD PTR[DI+0] ; Load low 32
0015   66| 8B 55 04                mov     EDX,DWORD PTR[DI+4] ; and high 32.
0019   66| F7 D0                   not     EAX               ; Get the one's compliment.
001C   66| F7 D2                   not     EDX
001F   66| 40                      inc     EAX               ; Add one for two's compliment
0021   66| 83 D2 00                adc     EDX,0             ; propagate the carry if any.
                           ;
                           ; The routines are the same from here out.
                           ;
0025                       goaddem:
0025   66| 03 04                   add     EAX,DWORD PTR[SI+0] ; Add the low 32 bits
0028   66| 89 07                   mov     DWORD PTR[BX+0],EAX ; and store the result.
002B   9F                          lahf                      ; Preserve the condition code.
002C   8A C4                       mov     AL,AH             ; In AL.
002E   66| 13 54 04                adc     EDX,DWORD PTR[SI+4] ; Include carry in the high 32.
0032   66| 89 57 04                mov     DWORD PTR[BX+4],EDX ; Store the result.
0036   9F                          lahf                      ; Get the condition code.
0037   B6 00                       mov     DH,0              ; assume no overflow
0039   0F 81 003F R                jno     didnt             ; and skip if it didn't
003D   B6 80                       mov     DH,080h           ; set to cause one otherwise.
003F                       didnt:
                           ;
                           ; We need to combine the condition codes from the two adds as follows:
                           ; Sign and carry from the high order add, aux-carry and parity from
                           ; the low order add, and zero is set only if on in both.
                           ;
003F   B2 40                       mov     DL,01000000b      ; mask to preserve zero flag.
0041   22 D4                       and     DL,AH
0043   22 D0                       and     DL,AL             ; Zero is set if on in both.
                           ;           AH high AL low    cc from add of
                           ;           szxaxpxcszxaxpxc  bits
0045   25 AB3E                      and     AX,1010101100111110b ;
0048   0A E0                       or      AH,AL             ; Combine low half flags and high
004A   0A E2                       or      AH,DL             ; With zero if necessary.
004C   02 F6                       add     DH,DH             ; Reset overflow if needed then
004E   9E                          sahf                      ; set the combined other flags.
004F   66| 58                      pop     EAX               ; Restore the entry registers
0051   66| 5A                      pop     EDX
0053   C3                          ret                       ; and return.
0054                       Bin64add  ENDP
0054                       code      ENDS
                                     END
```

Program 4-2 DRIVEBCD

```
Microsoft (R) Macro Assembler Version 5.00



                                   PAGE    55,132
                                   .386


                           ;
                           ; Name:   DRIVEBCD
                           ;
                           ; Purpose: This program demonstrates the BCD package.
                           ;
                           ; Inputs:  We prompt for three numbers to be entered: A first number,
                           ;          a second number, and a number to divide.
                           ;
```

```
;   Process:  The program loops requesting the first number (we end if an
;             empty line is entered), and a second number.  We then add
;             the numbers and display the result, subtract the numbers
;             and display the result, multiply the numbers and display
;             the result.  We then prompt for a third number and divide
;             it by the second.  We display the resulting quotient and
;             remainder.  We then shift the quotient left 5 and right 3
;             displaying the results.  We shift the product left 4 and
;             right 2 displaying the results.  We test number 1 and
;             display the result.  We compare number 2 to number 1 and
;             display the result.  We then loop.
;
;   Outputs:  All output is displayed as the result of the above tests.
;
;
;   Declare the routines we are going to use
;
                        EXTRN   BCDPACK:NEAR
                        EXTRN   BCDUNPK:NEAR
                        EXTRN   BCDSUB:NEAR
                        EXTRN   BCDADD:NEAR
                        EXTRN   BCDMPY:NEAR
                        EXTRN   BCDDIV:NEAR
                        EXTRN   BCDCMP:NEAR
                        EXTRN   BCDTST:NEAR
                        EXTRN   BCDSHL:NEAR
                        EXTRN   BCDSHR:NEAR

0000                    stack   SEGMENT para 'STACK' STACK
0000  0100[             dq      256 DUP(?)
      ?????????????????
      ?
                   ]

0800                    stack   ENDS
0000                    data    SEGMENT para
0000  0100[             string  db      256 DUP(?)          ; String scratch area
      ??
                   ]

0100  0008[             bcdno1  db      8 DUP(?)            ; First BCD number
      ??
                   ]

0108  0008[             bcdno2  db      8 DUP(?)            ; Second BCD number
      ??
                   ]

0110  0010[             bcdacum db      16 DUP(?)           ; Accumulator
      ??
                   ]

0120  0010[             bcdacum1 db     16 DUP(?)           ; Accumulator 2
      ??
                   ]

0130  80 00 00 00 00 00 00    minus1  db      128,0,0,0,0,0,0,1   ; minus one
      01
0138  00 00 00 00 00 00 00    zero    db      0,0,0,0,0,0,0,0     ; and zero
      00
0140  00 00 00 00 00 00 00    plus1   db      0,0,0,0,0,0,0,1     ; plus one
      01
0148  0A 0A 0A 0D 45 6E 74    query1  db      10,10,10,13,"Enter first number: $"
      65 72 20 66 69 72 73
      74 20 6E 75 6D 62 65
      72 3A 20 24
0161  0A 0D 45 6E 74 65 72    query2  db      10,13,"Enter second number: $"
      20 73 65 63 6F 6E 64
      20 6E 75 6D 62 65 72
      3A 20 24
```

```
0179  0A 0D 45 6E 74 65 72    query3    db      10,13,"Enter a number to divide: $"
      20 61 20 6E 75 6D 62
      65 72 20 74 6F 20 64
      69 76 69 64 65 3A 20
      24
0196  53 75 6D 20 20 20 3D    output1   db      "Sum  = $"
      20 24
019F  44 69 66 66 20 20 3D    output2   db      "Diff = $"
      20 24
01A8  50 72 6F 64 20 20 3D              db      "Prod = $"
      20 24
01B1  51 75 6F 74 20 20 3D              db      "Quot = $"
      20 24
01BA  52 65 6D 20 20 20 3D              db      "Rem  = $"
      20 24
01C3  53 68 6C 20 35 20 3D              db      "Shl 5 = $"
      20 24
01CC  53 68 72 20 33 20 3D              db      "Shr 3 = $"
      20 24
01D5  53 68 6C 20 34 20 3D              db      "Shl 4 = $"
      20 24
01DE  53 68 72 20 32 20 3D              db      "Shr 2 = $"
      20 24
01E7  54 73 74 20 31 20 3D              db      "Tst 1 = $"
      20 24
01F0  43 6D 70 31 3A 32 3D              db      "Cmp1:2= $"
      20 24
01F9  0000                    nxtdisp   dw      0                  ; output pointer
01FB                          data      ENDS
0000                          code      SEGMENT  para 'CODE' USE16 PUBLIC
                                        ASSUME   CS:code, DS:data
                              ;
                              ; Set up the environment
                              ;
0000                          Begin:
0000  B8 ---- R                         mov      AX,data           ; Get data segment pointer
0003  8E D8                             mov      DS,AX             ; into DS,
0005  8E C0                             mov      ES,AX             ; and ES.
0007  2B F6                             sub      SI,SI             ; Clear indices
0009  2B FF                             sub      DI,DI
000B                          nextnum:
000B  8D 16 0196 R                      lea      DX,output1        ; Set output pointer
000F  89 16 01F9 R                      mov      nxtdisp,DX        ; initially for add.
0013  8D 16 0148 R                      lea      DX,query1         ; ask for it
0017  E8 0110 R                         call     getinp            ; get first number
001A  0B C9                             or       CX,CX             ; Is it null
001C  0F 84 00FD R                      jz       Exit              ; If null - quit
0020  8B F3                             mov      SI,BX             ; Point to string,
0022  8D 1E 0100 R                      lea      BX,bcdno1         ; number, and
0026  E8 0000 E                         call     bcdpack           ; convert it.
0029                          getsecnd:
0029  8D 16 0161 R                      lea      DX,query2         ; ask for it
002D  E8 0110 R                         call     getinp            ; get first number
0030  E3 F7                             jcxz     getsecnd          ; If null - try again
0032  8B F3                             mov      SI,BX             ; Point to string,
0034  8D 1E 0108 R                      lea      BX,bcdno2         ; number, and
0038  E8 0000 E                         call     bcdpack           ; convert it.
                              ;
                              ; Add them and display the result
                              ;
003B  8D 1E 0110 R                      lea      BX,bcdacum        ; Point to result
003F  8D 36 0100 R                      lea      SI,bcdno1         ; first number,
0043  8D 3E 0108 R                      lea      DI,bcdno2         ; second number,
0047  E8 0000 E                         call     bcdadd            ; and add them.
004A  E8 0137 R                         call     display           ; Put out a line.
                              ;
```

```
                         ; Subtract them and display the result
                         ;
004D  E8 0000 E                  call     bcdsub          ; subtract them
0050  E8 0137 R                  call     display         ; Put out a line

                         ; Multiply them and display the result
                         ;
0053  8D 1E 0120 R               lea      BX,bcdacum1      ; Use alt accum
0057  E8 0000 E                  call     bcdmpy          ; multiply them
005A  A0 0120 R                  mov      AL,bcdacum1      ; Get sign
005D  8D 1E 0128 R               lea      BX,bcdacum1+8    ; point to it.
0061  88 07                      mov      BYTE PTR [BX],AL ; Position the sign.
0063  E8 0137 R                  call     display         ; display it

                         ; Get a number for the dividend
                         ;
0066                     getdiv:
0066  8D 16 0179 R               lea      DX,query3        ; ask for it
006A  E8 0110 R                  call     getinp          ; get first dividend
006D  E3 F7                      jcxz     getdiv          ; If null - try again
006F  8B F3                      mov      SI,BX           ; Point to string,
0071  8D 1E 0118 R               lea      BX,bcdacum+8     ; number, and
0075  E8 0000 E                  call     bcdpack         ; convert it.
0078  66| 2B C0                  sub      EAX,EAX         ; Get leading zeros
007B  66| A3 0114 R              mov      DWORD PTR bcdacum+4,EAX ; force leading zeros
007F  86 06 0118 R               xchg     AL,bcdacum+8    ; Get sign and clear old
0083  66| A3 0110 R              mov      DWORD PTR bcdacum,EAX ; force leading zeros

                         ; Divide by the second number and display both quotient and remainder.
                         ;
0087  8D 1E 0110 R               lea      BX,bcdacum       ; Point to accum
008B  8D 36 0108 R               lea      SI,bcdno2        ; second number,
008F  E8 0000 E                  call     bcddiv          ; and divide
0092  E8 0137 R                  call     display         ; display the quotient
0095  8D 1E 0118 R               lea      BX,bcdacum+8
0099  E8 0137 R                  call     display          ; and remainder.

                         ; Shift the quotient as a number and display it.
                         ;
009C  8D 1E 0110 R               lea      BX,bcdacum       ; Quotient
00A0  B0 00                      mov      AL,0            ; as a number
00A2  B4 05                      mov      AH,5            ; shift count
00A4  E8 0000 E                  call     bcdshl          ; and shift it left 5
00A7  E8 0137 R                  call     display         ; and display the number

                         ; Shift it back three and display it.
                         ;
00AA  8D 1E 0110 R               lea      BX,bcdacum       ; Quotient
00AE  B0 00                      mov      AL,0            ; as a number
00B0  B4 03                      mov      AH,3            ; shift count
00B2  E8 0000 E                  call     bcdshr          ; and shift it right 3
00B5  E8 0137 R                  call     display         ; and display the number

                         ; Shift the product and display it as an accumulator.
                         ;
00B8  8D 1E 0120 R               lea      BX,bcdacum1      ; Product
00BC  B0 01                      mov      AL,1            ; as an accum
00BE  B4 04                      mov      AH,4            ; shift count
00C0  E8 0000 E                  call     bcdshl          ; and shift it left 4
00C3  8D 1E 0128 R               lea      BX,bcdacum1+8    ; shift for number display
00C7  E8 0137 R                  call     display         ; and display the number
00CA  8D 1E 0120 R               lea      BX,bcdacum1      ; Product
00CE  B0 01                      mov      AL,1            ; as an accum
00D0  B4 02                      mov      AH,2            ; shift count
00D2  E8 0000 E                  call     bcdshr          ; and shift it right 2
00D5  8D 1E 0128 R               lea      BX,bcdacum1+8    ; shift for number display
00D9  E8 0137 R                  call     display         ; and display the number
                         ;
```

Program 4-2 Continued.

```
                                 ; Test the first number and display the result
                                 ;
00DC  8D 1E 0100 R                   lea     BX,bcdno1          ; point to number
00E0  E8 0000 E                      call    bcdtst             ; check it
00E3  E8 0103 R                      call    pzmpoint           ; Get value pointer
00E6  E8 0137 R                      call    display            ; Display the result
                                 ;
                                 ; Compare number2 to number1 and display the result.
                                 ;
00E9  8D 3E 0108 R                   lea     DI,bcdno2          ; point to comparand 2
00ED  8D 36 0100 R                   lea     SI,bcdno1          ; point to comparand 1
00F1  E8 0000 E                      call    bcdcmp             ; compare them
00F4  E8 0103 R                      call    pzmpoint           ; Get value pointer
00F7  E8 0137 R                      call    display            ; Display the result
                                 ;
                                 ; Get another set of test values and repeat.
                                 ;
00FA  E9 000B R                       jmp     nextnum
00FD                            Exit:
00FD  B0 00                           mov     AL,0               ; Set return code
00FF  B4 4C                           mov     AH,04ch            ; Set good-by
0101  CD 21                           int     21h                ; Return to the system

                                 ;
                                 ; Point to a -1, 0, or +1 based on AL  (preserve flags too)
                                 ;
0103                            pzmpoint    PROC
0103  9C                                pushf                     ; save flags
0104  98                                cbw                       ; get a word index
0105  C1 E0 03                          shl     AX,3              ; times 8
0108  8D 1E 0138 R                      lea     BX,zero           ; Point to the number
010C  03 D8                             add     BX,AX             ; matching the return code
010E  9D                                popf
010F  C3                                ret
0110                            pzmpoint    ENDP
                                 ;
                                 ; Read a string in response to a prompt
                                 ; The prompt must be in DX.  The string will be returned in string.
                                 ; The length of string is returned in CX.
                                 ; BX points to the start of the string.
                                 ;
0110                            getinp      PROC
0110  50                                push    AX                ; Save registers
0111  56                                push    SI
0112  B4 09                             mov     AH,9              ; and dos request
0114  CD 21                             int     21h               ; put out the string
0116  8D 16 0000 R                      lea     DX,string         ; point to input area
011A  C6 06 0000 R FE                   mov     string,254        ; Set max length in
011F  B4 0A                             mov     AH,10             ; Ask for read of string
0121  CD 21                             int     21h               ; from DOS.
0123  8D 1E 0002 R                      lea     BX,string+2       ; Point to just read data
0127  8A 0E 0001 R                      mov     CL,string+1       ; Get length read
012B  B5 00                             mov     CH,0              ; as a word.
012D  8B F1                             mov     SI,CX             ; Set length
012F  C6 84 0002 R 00                   mov     string+2[SI],0    ; and make an asciiz string.
0134  5E                                pop     SI
0135  58                                pop     AX                ; Restore registers
0136  C3                                ret                       ; and return.
0137                            getinp      ENDP

                                 ;
                                 ; Display the number pointed to by BX.
                                 ;
0137                            display     PROC
0137  60                                pusha                     ; Save registers
```

64   Arithmetic

```
0138  B8 0D0A                          mov    AX,0d0ah        ; Set c/r lf
013B  A3 0000 R                        mov    WORD PTR string,AX ; into output
013E  66| B8 534F435A                  mov    EAX,'SOCZ'      ; All on
0144  66| A3 0002 R                    mov    DWORD PTR string+2,EAX ; into output
0148  B8 2420                          mov    AX,'$ '         ; Stopper
014B  A3 0006 R                        mov    WORD PTR string+6,AX ; into output
014E  0F 84 0155 R                     jz     nonzer
0152  A2 0002 R                        mov    BYTE PTR string+2,AL ; If flag not set - blank it
0155                          nonzer:
0155  0F 82 015C R                     jc     noncry
0159  A2 0003 R                        mov    BYTE PTR string+3,AL ; If flag not set - blank it
015C                          noncry:
015C  0F 80 0163 R                     jo     nonovf
0160  A2 0004 R                        mov    BYTE PTR string+4,AL ; If flag not set - blank it
0163                          nonovf:
0163  0F 88 016A R                     js     nonsgn
0167  A2 0005 R                        mov    BYTE PTR string+5,AL ; If flag not set - blank it
016A                          nonsgn:
016A  8D 16 0000 R                     lea    DX,string       ; Point to output
016E  B4 09                            mov    AH,9            ; set dos code.
0170  CD 21                            int    21h             ; Write it
0172  8B 16 01F9 R                     mov    DX,nxtdisp      ; Get output type
0176  CD 21                            int    21h             ; Put it out
0178  83 C2 09                         add    DX,output2-output1 ; step it
017B  89 16 01F9 R                     mov    nxtdisp,DX      ; and save it
017F  8D 3E 0000 R                     lea    DI,string       ; output pointer
0183  E8 0000 E                        call   bcdunpk         ;
0186  C6 85 0000 R 24                  mov    string[DI],'$'  ; set ender
018B  8D 16 0000 R                     lea    DX,string       ; Point to it
018F  B4 09                            mov    AH,9            ; set print
0191  CD 21                            int    21h             ; and do it.

0193  61                               popa                   ; Restore registers
0194  C3                               ret                    ; and return
0195                          display  ENDP

0195                          code     ENDS
                                       END    Begin
```

Program 4-3 BCDUNPK

Microsoft (R) Macro Assembler Version 5.00

```
                             PAGE      55,132
                             .386
0000                code     SEGMENT   para 'CODE' PUBLIC USE16
                             ASSUME    CS:code, DS:code, SS:code

                    ; Name:    BCDUNPK
                    ;
                    ; Purpose: The following procedure accepts a signed BCD number in
                    ;          the 'standard' form of SSddddddddddddd and creates an
                    ;          ASCIIZ string of the form [-]NNNNNNNNNNNNNN\0.
                    ;          Where SS is the sign byte (bit 7 is on for minus, off for
                    ;          plus) and the 7 pairs of dd's make up a 14 digit packed BCD
                    ;          number.  The ascii string may have a leading minus sign if
                    ;          the bcd number was negative.  At least a single zero will
                    ;          be produced.  The number will be terminated with a null.
                    ;
                    ;
                    ; Inputs:  DS:BX points to the BCD number ES:DI points to the ascii
                    ;          string.
                    ;
                    ; Process: The number pointed to by BX will first have its sign
```

```
                               ;        transferred to the output string if it is negative.  Leading
                               ;        zero digits are bypassed until the final digit which is
                               ;        converted and output as are all digits after the first
                               ;        non-zero.  The resulting ascii string is then terminated
                               ;        with a null.
                               ;
                               ; Output:  The ascii representation of the number will be placed into
                               ;          ES:DI and DI will point to the null following the number.
                               ;
                               ;
                               ;
                               ;
                                        PUBLIC  Bcdunpk
                                        PUBLIC  Bcdunpka
                               ;
0000              Bcdunpk      PROC
0000  50                       push     AX                    ; Save work registers
0001  51                       push     CX
0002  B9 0007                  mov      CX,7                  ; Set count of pairs.
0005  EB 06 90                 jmp      setsi
0008              Bcdunpka:
0008  50                       push     AX                    ; Save work registers
0009  51                       push     CX
000A  B9 000F                  mov      CX,15                 ; Set count of pairs.
000D              setsi:
000D  56                       push     SI
000E  BE 0001                  mov      SI,1                  ; Set source index

0011  FC                       cld                            ; Set direction to up.
0012  F6 07 80                 test     BYTE PTR[BX+0],080h   ; is the number negative?
0015  0F 84 001C R             jz       leadzero              ; no - skip
0019  B0 2D                    mov      AL,'-'                ; Get minus sign
001B  AA                       stosb                          ; into number.

001C              leadzero:
001C  8A 00                    mov      AL,BYTE PTR[BX+SI]    ; Get pair of digits
001E  46                       inc      SI                    ; Point to next
001F  0A C0                    or       AL,AL                 ; check it
0021  0F 85 0028 R             jnz      leadzero1             ; A digit! Go check high/low.
0025  E2 F5                    loop     leadzero              ; Check all pairs.
                               ;
                               ; The number was zero - just plug a zero and a null and exit.
                               ;
0027  41                       inc      CX                    ; We want to stop below too.
0028              leadzero1:
0028  A8 F0                    test     AL,0f0h               ; Is high nibble zero?
002A  0F 84 0040 R             jz       highzero              ; Yes just store low.
002E  EB 04 90                 jmp      highdig               ; No go do both
0031              moredigs:
0031  8A 00                    mov      AL,BYTE PTR[BX+SI]    ; Get pair of digits
0033  46                       inc      SI                    ; Point to next
0034              highdig:
0034  8A E0                    mov      AH,AL                 ; Copy to save low nibble
0036  C0 E8 04                 shr      AL,4                  ; Get a digit from the high
0039  0C 30                    or       AL,'0'                ; Put proper zone in.
003B  AA                       stosb                          ; Then store digit.
003C  8A C4                    mov      AL,AH                 ; Get low digit in AL.
003E  24 0F                    and      AL,00fh               ; Clear high nibble
0040              highzero:
0040  0C 30                    or       AL,'0'                ; Set the zone
0042  AA                       stosb                          ; and place the digit
0043  E2 EC                    loop     moredigs              ; Go do all the rest.
                               ;
                               ; All digit pairs have been translated
                               ;
0045  B0 00                    mov      AL,0                  ; Get a null
0047  AA                       stosb                          ; use it to follow the number
```

```
0048  5E                          pop      SI               ; Restore registers
0049  59                          pop      CX
004A  58                          pop      AX
004B  C3                          ret                       ; and return.
004C              Bcdunpk  ENDP
004C              code     ENDS
                           END
```

Program 4-4   BCDPACK

Microsoft (R) Macro Assembler Version 5.00

```
                              PAGE     55,132
                              .386
0000              code     SEGMENT  para 'CODE' PUBLIC USE16
                           ASSUME   CS:code, DS:code, SS:code

                  ; Name:    BCDPACK
                  ;
                  ; Purpose: The following procedure produces a signed BCD number in
                  ;          the 'standard' form of SSdddddddddddddd from an ascii
                  ;          string of the form [+/-]NNNNNNNNNNNNNN.
                  ;          Where SS is the sign byte (bit 7 is on for minus, off for
                  ;          plus) and the 7 pairs of dd's make up a 14 digit packed BCD
                  ;          number.  The ascii string may have a leading plus or minus
                  ;          sign.  Up to 14 ascii digits will be packed.  Within the 14
                  ;          digit limit, packing stops at the first non digit.
                  ;
                  ;
                  ; Inputs:  DS:BX points to the BCD number DS:SI points to the ascii
                  ;          string.
                  ;
                  ; Process: The number pointed to by BX is cleared to zero. If the
                  ;          ASCII string has a leading -, the sign will be tentatively
                  ;          set minus.  The string will be examined left to right to
                  ;          determine its numeric length.  It will then be packed,
                  ;          right to left into the target BCD number.  An invalid
                  ;          numeric terminates the scan of the source number.
                  ;
                  ; Output:  The zero flag will be set if the result of the pack was
                  ;          zero.
                  ;          SI will point to the character beyond the converted number.
                  ;          The area pointed to by BX will contain the packed number.
                  ;
                  ;
                  ;
                              PUBLIC   Bcdpack
                  ;
0000              Bcdpack  PROC
0000  66| 50                      push     EAX              ; Save work registers
0002  51                          push     CX
0003  57                          push     DI

0004  66| 2B C0                   sub      EAX,EAX          ; Get a double word of zero.
0007  66| 89 07                   mov      DWORD PTR[BX+0],EAX ; Load the first half
000A  66| 89 47 04                mov      DWORD PTR[BX+4],EAX ; and the second half.
000E  80 3C 2B                    cmp      BYTE PTR[SI],'+' ; Leading plus?
0011  0F 84 001F R                jz       leadplus         ; If so - just skip it
0015  80 3C 2D                    cmp      BYTE PTR[SI],'-' ; Negative number?
0018  0F 85 0020 R                jnz      notminus         ; no - skip
001C  C6 07 80                    mov      BYTE PTR[BX+0],080h ; set number negative
001F              leadplus:
001F  46                          inc      SI               ; and skip the sign.
0020              notminus:
0020  B9 000E                     mov      CX,14            ; Set maximum number of digits
0023  FC                          cld                       ; and set direction up.
```

Program 4-4 Continued.

```
0024                             chknbr:
0024  AC                                 lodsb                           ; Get a byte from the string.
0025  34 30                              xor     AL,'0'                  ; Check if it is a number
0027  3C 09                              cmp     AL,9                    ;
0029  0F 87 0030 R                       ja      endnbr                  ; if >9 we are done.
002D  E2 F5                              loop    chknbr                  ; try next one
002F  46                                 inc     SI                      ; Pretend we went too far.
0030                             endnbr:
0030  4E                                 dec     SI                      ; Point to stopper byte.
0031  56                                 push    SI                      ; Save location of next char.
0032  4E                                 dec     SI                      ; Point to last digit
0033  B8 000E                            mov     AX,14                   ; Prepare to get number of
0036  2B C1                              sub     AX,CX                   ; digits in the string.
0038  8B C8                              mov     CX,AX                   ; Set in count position.
003A  E3 1E                              jcxz    donenbr                 ; If none - get out
003C  BF 0007                            mov     DI,7                    ; Get right-hand index to dest.
003F  FD                                 std                             ; Work right to left
0040                             nextpair:
0040  AC                                 lodsb                           ; Get a digit
0041  E2 07                              loop    havetop                 ; If it has a top half - get it
0043  24 0F                              and     AL,0fh                  ; set top half zero.
0045  88 01                              mov     BYTE PTR[BX+DI],AL      ; Put into number
0047  EB 11 90                           jmp     donenbr                 ; and exit.
004A                             havetop:
004A  8A E0                              mov     AH,AL                   ; Save AL for
004C  AC                                 lodsb                           ; load of high order digit.
004D  25 0F0F                            and     AX,0f0fh                ; Isolate digits
0050  C0 E0 04                           shl     AL,4                    ; Position high as high,
0053  0A C4                              or      AL,AH                   ; and combine into AL.
0055  88 01                              mov     BYTE PTR[BX+DI],AL      ; Put into number
0057  4F                                 dec     DI                      ; point to next digit
0058  E2 E6                              loop    nextpair                ; Go do another pair
005A                             donenbr:
005A  5E                                 pop     SI                      ; Restore pointer to next char.
005B  66| 8B 07                          mov     EAX,[BX+0]              ; Get top word
005E  B0 00                              mov     AL,0                    ; less sign
0060  66| 0B 47 04                       or      EAX,[BX+4]              ; Combine with the low word
0064  0F 85 006A R                       jnz     donenbr0                ; Go
0068  88 07                              mov     BYTE PTR[BX+0],AL       ; Plug sign with zero.
006A                             donenbr0:
006A  5F                                 pop     DI                      ; Restore registers
006B  59                                 pop     CX
006C  66| 58                             pop     EAX
006E  C3                                 ret                             ; and return.
006F                             Bcdpack  ENDP
006F                             code     ENDS
                                          END
```

Program 4-5 BCDTST

Microsoft (R) Macro Assembler Version 5.00

```
                                 PAGE    55,132
                                 .386
0000                     code    SEGMENT para 'CODE' PUBLIC USE16
                                 ASSUME  CS:code, DS:code, SS:code

                         ; Name:   BCDTST
                         ;
                         ; Purpose: The following procedure provides a signed test of a
                         ;          BCD number in the 'standard' form of SSdddddddddddddd.
                         ;          Where SS is the sign byte (bit 7 is on for minus, off for
```

```
                              ;    plus) and the 7 pairs of dd's make up a 14 digit packed
                              ;    BCD number.
                              ;
                              ;
                              ;  Inputs:  DS:BX points to the BCD number.
                              ;
                              ;  Process: The number pointed to by BX is tested for zero. If it is,
                              ;           the sign is forced to zero and a zero cc is returned.
                              ;           Otherwise, the sign is set according to the value of the
                              ;           number's sign.
                              ;
                              ;
                              ;
                              ;  Output:  Register AL will contain -1, 0, +1 depending on the result
                              ;           of the comparison.
                              ;           The zero and sign flags will also be set.
                              ;
                              ;
                                        PUBLIC  Bcdtst
                              ;
0000                          Bcdtst    PROC
0000 66| 50                             push    EAX                   ; Save work register
0002 80 27 80                           and     BYTE PTR[BX+0],080h   ; Force good sign byte
0005 66| 8B 07                          mov     EAX,DWORD PTR[BX+0]   ; Load the first half
0008 B0 00                              mov     AL,0                  ; Clear the sign byte
000A 66| 0B 47 04                       or      EAX,DWORD PTR[BX+4]   ; Combine with second half
000E 66| 58                             pop     EAX                   ; restore entry register
0010 B0 00                              mov     AL,0                  ; set for zero
0012 0F 85 0017 R                       jnz     notyet                ; Return zero
0016 C3                                 ret
0017                          notyet:
0017 F6 07 80                           test    BYTE PTR[BX+0],080h   ; check the sign
001A 0F 85 0021 R                       jnz     minus                 ; it is negative
001E FE C0                              inc     AL                    ; set AL and cc
0020 C3                                 ret
0021                          minus:
0021 FE C8                              dec     AL                    ; Set AL and cc
0023 C3                                 ret                           ; and return.
0024                          Bcdtst    ENDP
0024                          code      ENDS
                                        END
```

Program 4-6 BCDCMP

```
                                 .386
0000                          code    SEGMENT  para 'CODE' PUBLIC USE16
                                      ASSUME   CS:code, DS:code, SS:code
                              ;
                              ;  Name:    BCDCMP
                              ;
                              ;  Purpose: The following procedure provides signed comparison
                              ;           of BCD numbers in the 'standard' form of
                              ;           SSddddddddddddd.  Where SS is the sign byte (bit 7 is on
                              ;           for minus, off for plus) and the 7 pairs of dd's make up a
                              ;           14 digit packed BCD number.
                              ;
                              ;  Inputs:  DS:SI points to one BCD number, DS:DI points to the other.
                              ;
                              ;  Process: The number pointed to by SI is compared to the number
                              ;           pointed to by DI.  (Conceptually the number (DI) is
                              ;           subtracted from the number (SI).)  The comparison is
                              ;           performed to determine relative magnitude and the
                              ;           result is adjusted depending on the signs of the numbers.
                              ;
                              ;  Output:  Register AL will contain -1, 0, +1 depending on the result
                              ;           of the comparison (SI)<(DI), (SI)=(DI), (SI)>(DI).  The
                              ;           zero and sign flags will also be set.
                              ;
```

Program 4-6 Continued.

```
                                  PUBLIC  Bcdcmp
                            ;
0000                        Bcdcmp  PROC
0000  51                            push    CX              ; Save entry registers
0001  56                            push    SI
0002  57                            push    DI
0003  06                            push    ES
0004  8C D9                         mov     CX,DS
0006  8E C1                         mov     ES,CX

0008  FC                            cld                     ; Set direction for compare.
0009  8A 24                         mov     AH,BYTE PTR [SI] ; Get the sign of SI's number
000B  8A 05                         mov     AL,BYTE PTR [DI] ; and the sign of DI's number
000D  25 8080                       and     AX,08080h       ; Isolate the signs.
0010  OF 84 001C R                  jz      bothpos         ; Both numbers are positive.
0014  3A C4                         cmp     AL,AH           ; Are the signs the same?
0016  OF 85 0029 R                  jne     signset         ; Are both are negative?
001A  87 F7                         xchg    SI,DI           ; Reverse the compare if so.
001C                        bothpos:
001C  B9 0007                       mov     CX,7            ; Set count to compare.
001F  46                            inc     SI
0020  47                            inc     DI
0021  F3/ A6                        repz cmpsb              ; and compare magnitudes.
0023  B0 00                         mov     AL,0            ; Set for equal
0025  OF 84 0031 R                  je      done            ; and get out if they were.

0029                        signset:
0029  B0 01                         mov     AL,1            ; Set (SI)>(DI)
002B  OF 87 0031 R                  ja      done            ; Get out if true.
002F  B0 FF                         mov     AL,0ffh         ; Set (SI)<(DI)
0031                        done:

0031  07                            pop     ES              ; Restore the entry registers
0032  5F                            pop     DI
0033  5E                            pop     SI
0034  59                            pop     CX
0035  C3                            ret                     ; and return.
0036                        Bcdcmp  ENDP
0036                        code    ENDS
                                    END
```

Program 4-7 BCDSHL

Microsoft (R) Macro Assembler Version 5.00

```
                            PAGE    55,132
                            .386
0000                code    SEGMENT para 'CODE' PUBLIC USE16
                            ASSUME  CS:code, DS:code, SS:code


                    ; Name:   BCDSHL
                    ;
                    ; Purpose: The following procedure provides a BCD left shift of
                    ;          an accumulator (double precision) or a standard BCD
                    ;          value.  The number of digits shifted can be from zero
                    ;          to the size of the input number.
                    ;
                    ;
                    ; Inputs:  AL contains the size code of the value to be shifted.
                    ;          Zero indicates a standard number.  Non zero indicates
                    ;          a double precision accumulator.
```

```
;               AH contains the number of digits to shift.
;               BX contains the address of the field to shift.
;
; Process: The size code is replaced with the size of the number in
;               bytes less one (for use in computing the rightmost byte
;               address).  It is also used to select a comparand for the
;               check of the shift amount (an oversized shift results in
;               zero).
;
;               The shift amount is divided by two and the number is
;               moved left the required number of bytes.  The overlaid
;               bytes are checked for zero and if not, the fact is
;               remembered so that carry can be set.  Remaining bytes to
;               the right are zeroed.
;
;               If an odd number of digits was requested, the number is
;               shifted left one digit.  The leftmost bcd digit is also
;               checked for zero to allow setting of carry.
;
; Output: The number is shifted left the desired number of digits.
;               If the result is zero, a zero condition code is set.
;               If a non-zero digit was shifted out of the number,
;               carry is set to indicate the loss of significance.
;
;

                PUBLIC  Bcdshl
```

```
0000                    Bcdshl    PROC
0000  66| 52                      push    EDX                     ; Save entry registers
0002  51                          push    CX
0003  53                          push    BX
0004  66| 50                      push    EAX
0006  56                          push    SI
0007  57                          push    DI
0008  06                          push    ES
0009  8C DA                       mov     DX,DS                   ; Set ES to DS
000B  8E C2                       mov     ES,DX
000D  B9 000D                     mov     CX,13                   ; set max digits for non-zero
0010  0A C0                       or      AL,AL                   ; Accumulator size
0012  B0 07                       mov     AL,7                    ; Assume not
0014  0F 84 0020 R                jz      notaccum                ; Good guess
0018  B0 0E                       mov     AL,14                   ; Need 14 digit pairs
001A  B1 1B                       mov     CL,27                   ; and more digits for non zero.
001C  C6 47 01 00                 mov     BYTE PTR [BX+1],0       ; Force extra digit to zero.
0020                    notaccum:
0020  B6 00                       mov     DH,0                    ; Set flag for no carry
0022  80 27 80                    and     BYTE PTR [BX],080h      ; Clear all but the sign bit
0025  3A E1                       cmp     AH,CL                   ; Shift to zero?
0027  0F 8F 00BD R                jg      zeroit                  ; if so - clear the field
002B  8A D4                       mov     DL,AH                   ; copy the amount to shift
;
; Shift the even digit pairs if any.
;
002D  D0 EC                       shr     AH,1                    ; Get the number of pairs
002F  0F 84 0054 R                jz      oddshiftq               ; If no pairs - check if odd.
0033  50                          push    AX                      ; Save size value
0034  8B FB                       mov     DI,BX                   ;
0036  8A CC                       mov     CL,AH                   ; Get bytes to check
0038  47                          inc     DI                      ; Point to leftmost destination
0039  3C 07                       cmp     AL,7                    ; If number - ok
003B  0F 84 0040 R                jz      notaccum1               ;
003F  47                          inc     DI                      ; Need to skip top accum byte
0040                    notaccum1:
0040  8B F7                       mov     SI,DI                   ; Get leftmost byte for check
;
; Check overlaid digit pairs for zero (remember the result in DH).
```

```
                                   ;
0042                               checkzer:
0042  0A 34                                or      DH,BYTE PTR [SI]    ; Combine to check significance
                                                                       ; loss
0044  46                                   inc     SI                  ; Shift to next source
0045  E2 FB                                loop    checkzer            ; and check all overlaid bytes
                                   ;
                                   ; Now we can overlay the leftmost digit pairs with the remainder of
                                   ; the original number.
                                   ;
0047  8A C8                                mov     CL,AL               ; Get count of bytes to process
0049  2A CC                                sub     CL,AH               ; less number checked.
004B  F3/ A4                               rep movsb                   ; Close over those checked.
                                   ;
                                   ; Fill the remainder with zeros.
                                   ;
004D  8A CC                                mov     CL,AH               ; Get count to set zero.
004F  B0 00                                mov     AL,0                ; Get the zero value
0051  F3/ AA                               rep stosb                   ; and fill zeros to the right.
0053  58                                   pop     AX                  ; Restore size value
                                   ;
                                   ; Now take care of any odd shift necessary.
                                   ;
0054                               oddshiftq:
0054  F6 C2 01                             test    DL,1                ; Was the amount to shift odd?
0057  0F 84 0089 R                         jz      shiftx              ; No - skip odd shift
005B  50                                   push    AX                  ; Save digit count
                                   ;
                                   ; Shift the odd digit
                                   ;
005C  8A C8                                mov     CL,AL               ; Set count to shift
005E  2A CC                                sub     CL,AH               ; (bytes less zeros filled)
0060  8B F3                                mov     SI,BX               ; Point SI to leftmost pair
0062  46                                   inc     SI
0063  3C 07                                cmp     AL,7                ; Is it a number?
0065  0F 84 006A R                         jz      number              ; Yes - we are set
0069  46                                   inc     SI                  ; Accumulators have an extra
006A                               number:
006A  8B FE                                mov     DI,SI               ; Set destination too
006C  FC                                   cld                         ; Set direction to up.
006D  8A 04                                mov     AL, BYTE PTR [SI]   ; Get value of top pair
006F  24 F0                                and     AL,0f0h             ; Get the digit lost
0071  0A F0                                or      DH,AL               ; and save for significance
                                                                       ; loss check
0073                               shift1:
0073  8A 24                                mov     AH, BYTE PTR [SI]   ; Get a byte into AH
0075  E2 08                                loop    shift2              ; Skip special handling of last
                                   ;
                                   ; Last pair of digits cannot fetch the next pair (it doesn't exist);
                                   ; We need to fill a zero to the right.
                                   ;
0077  C0 E4 04                             shl     AH,4                ; Fill zeros on right
007A  88 25                                mov     BYTE PTR [DI],AH    ; and put down in place.
007C  EB 0A 90                             jmp     shift3              ; we are done.
007F                               shift2:
007F  46                                   inc     SI                  ; point source to next pair
0080  8A 04                                mov     AL, BYTE PTR [SI]   ; and get for top nibble
0082  C1 E8 04                             shr     AX,4                ; Shift right one nibble
0085  AA                                   stosb                       ; Put shifted byte back
0086  EB EB                                jmp     shift1              ; and do next one
0088                               shift3:
0088  58                                   pop     AX                  ; Restore digit count
                                   ;
                                   ; The shift is completed - check if result is zero and set cc and sign
                                   ;
```

```
0089                          shiftx:
0089  52                          push     DX             ; Save significance loss
008A  8A C8                      mov      CL,AL          ; Set size in CX
008C  C0 E9 02                   shr      CL,2           ; Divide by word size (4)
008F  8B F3                      mov      SI,BX          ; Set start
0091  66| AD                     lodsd                   ; Get first word
0093  B0 00                      mov      AL,0           ; less the sign byte
0095  66| 8B D0                  mov      EDX,EAX        ; set into accumulator.
0098                          shiftx0:
0098  66| AD                     lodsd                   ; Get the next double word
009A  66| 0B D0                  or       EDX,EAX        ; combine and set z/nz
009D  E2 F9                      loop     shiftx0        ; do for 1 or 3 more dwords
009F  0F 85 00A6 R               jnz      shiftx1        ; Done if non zero
00A3  C6 07 00                   mov      BYTE PTR [BX],0 ; force sign to positive
00A6                          shiftx1:
00A6  0F 94 C0                   setz     AL             ; Put a 1 in AL if zero result
00A9  5A                         pop      DX             ; Restore significance loss
00AA  0A F6                      or       DH,DH          ; check if we lost significance
00AC  0F 84 00B1 R               jz       shiftx2        ; If not carry is off from or.
00B0  F9                         stc                     ; Force it on.
00B1                          shiftx2:
00B1  FE C8                      dec      AL             ; Reset zero flag from setz.
00B3  07                         pop      ES             ; Restore the entry registers
00B4  5F                         pop      DI
00B5  5E                         pop      SI
00B6  66| 58                     pop      EAX
00B8  5B                         pop      BX
00B9  59                         pop      CX
00BA  66| 5A                     pop      EDX
00BC  C3                         ret                     ; and return.
                                ;
                                ; The shift would result in zeros - clear the result.  First we must
                                ; check if we would loose significance.
                                ;
00BD                          zeroit:
00BD  50                         push     AX             ; Save sizes
00BE  8A C8                      mov      CL,AL          ; Set size in CX
00C0  C0 E9 02                   shr      CL,2           ; Divide by word size (4)
00C3  8B F3                      mov      SI,BX          ; Set start
00C5  66| AD                     lodsd                   ; Get first word
00C7  B0 00                      mov      AL,0           ; less the sign byte
00C9  66| 8B D0                  mov      EDX,EAX        ; set into accumulator.
00CC                          zerock0:
00CC  66| AD                     lodsd                   ; Get the next double word
00CE  66| 0B D0                  or       EDX,EAX        ; combine and set z/nz
00D1  E2 F9                      loop     zerock0        ; do for 1 or 3 more dwords
00D3  0F 95 C6                   setnz    DH             ; Done with significance check
00D6  58                         pop      AX
                                ;
                                ; DH is set if we lost significance so we can clear the field.
                                ;
00D7  50                         push     AX             ; Re-save sizes
00D8  8B FB                      mov      DI,BX          ; Set destination,
00DA  8A C8                      mov      CL,AL          ; and count,
00DC  C1 E9 02                   shr      CX,2           ; divide by word size
00DF  41                         inc      CX             ; include sign word.
00E0  66| 2B C0                  sub      EAX,EAX        ; Get a double zero
00E3  FC                         cld                     ; Set direction up
00E4  F3/ 66| AB                 rep stosd               ; Fill with zeros
00E7  58                         pop      AX             ; Restore sizes
00E8  EB 9F                      jmp      shiftx         ; exit (cc is set)
00EA                          Bcdshl  ENDP
00EA                          code    ENDS
                                      END
```

Program 4-8 BCDSHR

Microsoft (R) Macro Assembler Version 5.00

```
                              PAGE      55,132
                              .386
0000                  code    SEGMENT   para 'CODE' PUBLIC USE16
                              ASSUME    CS:code, DS:code, SS:code

                      ;
                      ; Name:    BCDSHR
                      ;
                      ; Purpose: The following procedure provides a BCD right shift of
                      ;          an accumulator (double precision) or a standard BCD
                      ;          value.  The number of digits shifted can be from zero
                      ;          to the size of the input number.
                      ;
                      ;
                      ; Inputs:  AL contains the size code of the value to be shifted.
                      ;          Zero indicates a standard number.  Non zero indicates
                      ;          a double precision accumulator.
                      ;          AH contains the number of digits to shift.
                      ;          BX contains the address of the field to shift.
                      ;
                      ; Process: The size code is replaced with the size of the number in
                      ;          bytes less one (for use in computing the rightmost byte
                      ;          address).  It is also used to select a comparand for the
                      ;          check of the shift amount (an oversized shift results in
                      ;          zero).
                      ;
                      ;          If an odd number of digits is requested, the number is
                      ;          shifted right one digit.
                      ;
                      ;          The shift amount is divided by two and the number is
                      ;          moved right
                      ;
                      ; Output:  The number is shifted right the desired number of digits.
                      ;          If the result is zero, a zero condition code is set.
                      ;
                      ;
                      ;

                              PUBLIC  Bcdshr

0000                  Bcdshr  PROC
0000  66| 52                  push    EDX                     ; Save entry registers
0002  51                      push    CX
0003  53                      push    BX
0004  66| 50                  push    EAX
0006  56                      push    SI
0007  57                      push    DI
0008  06                      push    ES
0009  8C DA                   mov     DX,DS                   ; Set ES to DS
000B  8E C2                   mov     ES,DX
000D  B9 000D                 mov     CX,13                   ; set max digits for non-zero
                                                              ; (note that this clears CH)
0010  0A C0                   or      AL,AL                   ; Accumulator size
0012  B0 07                   mov     AL,7                    ; Assume not
0014  0F 84 0020 R            jz      notaccum                ; Good guess
0018  B0 0F                   mov     AL,15                   ; Need 14 digit pairs of 15
001A  B1 1B                   mov     CL,27                   ; and more digits for non zero.
001C  C6 47 01 00             mov     BYTE PTR [BX+1],0       ; Force extra digit to zero.
0020                  notaccum:
0020  80 27 80                and     BYTE PTR [BX],080h      ; Clear all but the sign bit
0023  3A E1                   cmp     AH,CL                   ; Shift to zero?
```

```
0025   0F 87 008B R                  ja      zeroit          ; if so - clear the field
0029   8A D4                         mov     DL,AH           ; copy the amount to shift
                                 ;
                                 ; Shift the even digit pairs if any.
                                 ;
002B   FD                            std                     ; Set decrement
002C   D0 EC                         shr     AH,1            ; Any pairs to shift?
002E   0F 84 0048 R                  jz      oddshift        ; No - go check for odd shift
0032   50                            push    AX              ; Save digit count
0033   8B FB                         mov     DI,BX           ;
0035   8A C8                         mov     CL,AL           ; Get bytes to rightmost
0037   03 F9                         add     DI,CX           ; Get destination rightmost
0039   8B F3                         mov     SI,BX           ;
003B   2A CC                         sub     CL,AH           ; Get bytes to rightmost source
003D   03 F1                         add     SI,CX           ; and rightmost source.
003F   F3/ A4                        rep movsb               ; Now shift pairs
0041   8A CC                         mov     CL,AH           ; Get count to set zero
0043   B0 00                         mov     AL,0            ; and a zero to set
0045   F3/ AA                        rep stosb               : Clear each pair.
0047   58                            pop     AX              ; Restore size value
                                 ;
                                 ; Shift the odd digit
                                 ;
0048                             oddshift:
0048   F6 C2 01                      test    DL,1            ; Is there an odd digit?
004B   0F 84 0064 R                  jz      shiftx          ; No, we are done.
004F   50                            push    AX              ; save lengths
0050   8A C8                         mov     CL,AL           ; Set count to rightmost.
0052   8B F3                         mov     SI,BX           ; Point SI to Rightmost pair
0054   03 F1                         add     SI,CX           ;
0056   8B FE                         mov     DI,SI           ; Set destination too
                                                             ; Direction is down.
0058   2A CC                         sub     CL,AH           ; Take out the pairs we zeroed.
005A                             shift1:
005A   AC                            lodsb                   ; Get a byte into AL
005B   8A 24                         mov     AH, BYTE PTR [SI] ; Get the next byte to the left
005D   C1 E8 04                      shr     AX,4            ; Shift right one nibble
0060   AA                            stosb                   ; Put shifted byte back
0061   E2 F7                         loop    shift1          ; and do next one
0063   58                            pop     AX              ; Restore digit count
                                 ;
                                 ; The shift is completed - check if result is zero and set cc and sign
                                 ;
0064                             shiftx:
0064   FC                            cld                     ; Set direction up
0065   8A C8                         mov     CL,AL           ; Set size in CX
0067   C0 E9 02                      shr     CL,2            ; Divide by word size (4)
006A   8B F3                         mov     SI,BX           ; Set start
006C   66| AD                        lodsd                   ; Get first word
006E   B0 00                         mov     AL,0            ; less the sign byte
0070   66| 8B D0                     mov     EDX,EAX         ; set into accumulator.
0073                             shiftx0:
0073   66| AD                        lodsd                   ; Get the next double word
0075   66| 0B D0                     or      EDX,EAX         ; combine and set z/nz
0078   E2 F9                         loop    shiftx0         ; do for 1 or 3 more dwords
007A   0F 85 0081 R                  jnz     shiftx1         ; Done if non zero
007E   C6 07 00                      mov     BYTE PTR [BX],0 ; force sign to positive
0081                             shiftx1:
0081   07                            pop     ES              ; Restore the entry registers
0082   5F                            pop     DI
0083   5E                            pop     SI
0084   66| 58                        pop     EAX
0086   5B                            pop     BX
0087   59                            pop     CX
0088   66| 5A                        pop     EDX
008A   C3                            ret                     ; and return.
                                 ;
                                 ; The shift would result in zeros - clear the result, and set cc z.
```

```
                                    ;
008B                                zeroit:
008B  8B FB                                 mov     DI,BX           ; Set destination,
008D  8A C8                                 mov     CL,AL           ; and count,
008F  C0 E9 02                              shr     CL,2            ; divided by 4.
0092  FE C1                                 inc     CL              ; plus 1.
0094  B5 00                                 mov     CH,0            ; Set CX by zeroing upper half
0096  66| 2B C0                             sub     EAX,EAX         ; Get a double zero
0099  FC                                    cld                     ; Set direction up
009A  F3/ 66| AB                            rep stosd
009D  EB E2                                 jmp     shiftx1         ; exit (cc is set)
009F                           Bcdshr       ENDP
009F                           code         ENDS
                                            END
```

Program 4-9 BCDADD

Microsoft (R) Macro Assembler Version 5.00

```
                              PAGE      55,132
                              .386
0000                 code     SEGMENT   para 'CODE' PUBLIC USE16
                              ASSUME    CS:code, DS:code, SS:code

               ; Name:    BCDADD
               ;
               ; Purpose: The following procedures provides signed addition and
               ;          subtraction of BCD numbers in the 'standard' form of
               ;          SSddddddddddddddd.  Where SS is the sign byte (bit 7 is on
               ;          for minus, off for plus) and the 7 pairs of dd's make up
               ;          a 14 digit packed BCD number.
               ;
               ;
               ; Inputs:  DS:SI points to one BCD number, DS:DI points to the other.
               ;          DS:BX points to the area for the sum (BX may be the same
               ;          as SI or DI).
               ;
               ; Process: The entry points, bcdadd and bcdsub differ as entry points
               ;          in bcdsub's inversion of the sign of the second number.
               ;          Both then use the common routine addsub to compute the
               ;          sum or difference.
               ;
               ;          Stack space is reserved as a work area for computing the
               ;          result.  If the signs of the two numbers are the same, the
               ;          result is computed directly by addition and receives the
               ;          same sign.  If the signs differ, the number with the
               ;          smaller absolute value is subtracted from the larger and
               ;          the result receives the sign of the larger.  (If the result
               ;          is zero, the sign is forced to positive (0)).
               ;
               ;          The result is copied from the work area to the desired
               ;          location.  If an overflow occurred carry will be set on
               ;          exit, otherwise reset.
               ;
               ; Output:  The sum or difference of the two numbers will be returned
               ;          in the area indicated.  Carry will be on if the result
               ;          overflowed.
               ;
                              PUBLIC  Bcdadd
```

```
                          PUBLIC    Bcdsub
                      ;
0000              Bcdadd    PROC
0000   66| 50               push      EAX               ; Save AX for sign use.
0002   8A 05                mov       AL, BYTE PTR [DI]  ; Get sign of 'b'.
0004   0F 8A 000E R         jp        saverest
0008              Bcdsub:
0008   66| 50               push      EAX               ; Save AX for sign use.
000A   8A 05                mov       AL, BYTE PTR [DI]  ; Get sign of 'b'
000C   34 80                xor       AL,080h           ; and flip it for subtract.

000E              saverest:
000E   52                   push      DX                ; Save entry registers
000F   51                   push      CX
0010   53                   push      BX
0011   56                   push      SI
0012   57                   push      DI
0013   06                   push      ES
0014   8C D9                mov       CX,DS
0016   8E C1                mov       ES,CX
0018   C8 0008 00           enter     8,0               ; Reserve 8 byte work area
                      ;
                      ; First check for signs the same.
                      ;
001C   8A 24                mov       AH, BYTE PTR [SI]  ; Get sign byte of 'a',

001E   32 C4                xor       AL,AH             ; Check if they are the same.
0020   24 80                and       AL,080h           ; (remove all but the sign.)
0022   0F 84 0058 R         jz        samesign          ; They were the same!
                      ;
                      ; We will find the one with the largest magnitude and then subtract
                      ; the other one from it.  The sign will be taken from the larger
                      ; number.
                      ;
0026   53                   push      BX                ; Save result pointer
0027   B9 0007              mov       CX,7              ; Get loop count
002A   8B D6                mov       DX,SI             ; Save number pointers
002C   8B DF                mov       BX,DI
002E   46                   inc       SI
002F   47                   inc       DI                ; and step over sign byte
0030   FC                   cld                         ; Set to increment
0031   F3/ A6               repz cmpsb                   ; locate larger (or equal)
0033   0F 83 0039 R         jnb       dilower           ; SI has larger.
0037   87 D3                xchg      DX,BX             ; Flip the pointers.
0039              dilower:
0039   8B F2                mov       SI,DX             ; Restore pointer to larger
003B   8B FB                mov       DI,BX             ; and smaller.
003D   B9 0007              mov       CX,7              ; Prepare to point to
                                                        ; rightmost.
0040   03 F1                add       SI,CX             ; do so for 'a'
0042   03 F9                add       DI,CX             ; and 'b'.
0044   FD                   std                         ; Set direction for auto dec.
0045   F8                   clc                         ; and clear carry
0046              subtloop:
0046   AC                   lodsb                       ; get a byte (2 digits) of 'a'.
0047   1A 05                sbb       AL, BYTE PTR [DI]  ; subtract 'b' & carry from it.
0049   2F                   das                         ; Decimal adjust the result.
004A   4F                   dec       DI                ; Position to next byte and
004B   88 46 00             mov       BYTE PTR [BP+0],AL ; store result temporarily.
004E   4D                   dec       BP                ; Step target pointer.
004F   E2 F5                loop      subtloop          ; Subtract all seven pairs
0051   AC                   lodsb                       ; get the sign of the larger
0052   24 80                and       AL,080h           ; with any garbage removed.
0054   5B                   pop       BX                ; Restore target pointer
0055   EB 1B 90             jmp       setreslt          ; and go set the result.
```

Program 4-9 Continued.

```
0058                              samesign:
0058  B9 0007                         mov     CX,7                      ; Prepare to point to
                                                                        ; rightmost
005B  03 F1                           add     SI,CX                     ; do so for 'a'
005D  03 F9                           add     DI,CX                     ; and 'b'.
005F  FD                              std                               ; Set direction for auto dec.
0060  80 E4 80                        and     AH,080h                   ; Get sign isolated. (clears
                                                                        ; carry)

0063                              samesloop:
0063  AC                              lodsb                             ; get a byte (2 digits) of 'a'.
0064  12 05                           adc     AL, BYTE PTR [DI]         ; add 'b' and carry to it.
0066  27                              daa                               ; Decimal adjust the result.
0067  4F                              dec     DI                        ; Position to next byte and
0068  88 46 00                        mov     BYTE PTR [BP+0],AL        ; store result temporarily.
006B  4D                              dec     BP                        ; Step target pointer.
006C  E2 F5                           loop    samesloop                 ; Add all seven pairs
006E  8A C4                           mov     AL,AH                     ; position the sign.
0070  14 00                           adc     AL,0                      ; Add carry from high digit.

0072                              setreslt:
0072  53                              push    BX                        ; Save output pointer
0073  88 07                           mov     BYTE PTR [BX],AL          ; store sign
0075  43                              inc     BX                        ; and step pointer.
0076  B9 0007                         mov     CX,7                      ; Get loop count.
0079  45                              inc     BP                        ; point to digit pair
007A                              nextreslt:
007A  8A 46 00                        mov     AL, BYTE PTR [BP+0]       ; Get digits
007D  88 07                           mov     BYTE PTR [BX],AL          ; into target
007F  45                              inc     BP
0080  43                              inc     BX                        ; Adjust pointers
0081  E2 F7                           loop    nextreslt                 ; and move next result.
0083  4D                              dec     BP                        ; Correct for one too far.
0084  5B                              pop     BX                        ; Get output pointer
0085  66| 8B 07                       mov     EAX,DWORD PTR[BX]         ; Check the result for
0088  B0 00                           mov     AL,0                      ; zero except for the sign.
008A  66| 0B 47 04                    or      EAX,DWORD PTR[BX+4]       ; Check for a zero result.
008E  0F 85 0094 R                    jnz     exit                      ; Leave sign alone if not.
0092  88 07                           mov     BYTE PTR [BX],AL          ; Avoid -0.
0094                              exit:

0094  C9                              leave                             ; Restore the entry registers
0095  07                              pop     ES
0096  5F                              pop     DI
0097  5E                              pop     SI
0098  5B                              pop     BX
0099  59                              pop     CX
009A  5A                              pop     DX
009B  66| 58                          pop     EAX
009D  F6 07 0F                        test    BYTE PTR [BX],0fh         ; check if an overflow occurred,
00A0  0F 84 00A5 R                    jz      nooflow                   ; if not - skip (carry is off)
00A4  F9                              stc                               ; set of carry on
00A5                              nooflow:
00A5  C3                              ret                               ; and return.
00A6                   Bcdadd       ENDP
00A6                   code         ENDS
                                    END
```

Program 4-10 BCDMPY

Microsoft (R) Macro Assembler Version 5.00

PAGE   55,132
.386

78   Arithmetic

```
0000                    code    SEGMENT    para 'CODE' PUBLIC USE16
                        ASSUME     CS:code, DS:code, SS:code
                ;
                ; Name:    BCDMPY
                ;
                ; Purpose: The following procedure provides signed multiplication for
                ;          BCD numbers in the 'standard' form of SSddddddddddddddd.
                ;          Where SS is the sign byte (bit 7 is on for minus, off for
                ;          plus) and the 7 pairs of dd's make up a 14 digit packed BCD
                ;          number.  (Packed two digits per byte.)
                ;
                ;          The product is placed in the 16 byte accumulator specified
                ;          by DS:BX.  If the accumulator overlaps either the multiplier
                ;          or the multiplicand the results are undefined.
                ;
                ; Inputs:  DS:SI points to one BCD number, DS:DI points to the other.
                ;          DS:BX points to the accumulator where the product is formed.
                ;
                ; Process: The sign of the product is computed and set and the
                ;          accumulator is cleared to zero.  The algorithm used to form
                ;          the product is an adaptation of simple manual
                ;          multiplication.  The product is formed by selecting each
                ;          digit of the multiplier from right to left and performing a
                ;          right to left digit by digit multiplication, adding the
                ;          result to the accumulator.
                ;
                ;          Because there are two decimal digits in each byte, we have
                ;          four variants of the multiply.  (assume 76 * 34, we
                ;          multiply 6 by 4, getting a product of 24.  We then multiply
                ;          70 by 4 and add that partial product (280) to 24 to get 304.
                ;          We then multiply 6 by 30 to get 180 as a partial product
                ;          which gives us 484.  Finally, we multiply 70 by 30 to get
                ;          the partial product 2100 which we add to our product to get
                ;          the final result of 2584.)  The aam instruction assumes the
                ;          product was formed from two bcd digits so we adjust our
                ;          point of addition into the product.
                ;
                ; Output:  The product will be returned in the accumulator as a signed
                ;          double precision value.
                ;
                            PUBLIC Bcdmpy
                ;
0000            Bcdmpy      PROC
0000  06                    push    ES
0001  52                    push    DX                      ; Save entry registers
0002  51                    push    CX
0003  53                    push    BX
0004  50                    push    AX
0005  56                    push    SI
0006  57                    push    DI
                ;
                ; clear the accumulator and set its sign
                ;
0007  8A 04                 mov     AL,[SI]                 ; Get multiplier sign byte
0009  32 05                 xor     AL,[DI]                 ; Combine with multiplicand's
000B  25 0080               and     AX,00080h               ; Isolate the sign
000E  8C D9                 mov     CX,DS                   ; Get DS
0010  8E C1                 mov     ES,CX                   ; into ES,
0012  FC                    cld                             ; set direction to incr,
0013  87 FB                 xchg    DI,BX                   ; and prepare to clear accum.
0015  AB                    stosw                           ; Set sign value and 00
0016  8A C4                 mov     AL,AH                   ; Get word of zeros,
0018  B9 0007               mov     CX,7                    ; the count to clear and
001B  F3/ AB                rep stosw                       ; clear words 1 - 7
001D  87 FB                 xchg    DI,BX                   ; Get DI back again.
001F  4B                    dec     BX                      ; Point to rightmost accum loc.
                ;
                ; point to the rightmost byte of each of the other fields.
```

Program 4-10 Continued.

```
                                   ;
0020  B9 0007                      mov     CX,7                ; Get count of bytes.
0023  03 F1                        add     SI,CX               ; Multiplier and
0025  03 F9                        add     DI,CX               ; Multiplicand

                                   ;
                                   ; Begin the bytewise selection of multiplier digits
                                   ;
0027                       nextmpyr:
0027  51                           push    CX                  ; Save byte count remaining.
0028  8A 14                        mov     DL, BYTE PTR [SI]   ; Load a pair of digits.
002A  8A F2                        mov     DH,DL               ; Save the top digit
002C  80 E2 0F                     and     DL,0fh              ; Isolate the low digit
002F  0F 84 0096 R                 jz      dohigh              ; If zero - go do high digit.
0033  53                           push    BX                  ; Save BX for high digit
0034  57                           push    DI                  ; Save right hand m'p'cand ptr.
0035  B9 0007                      mov     CX,7                ; Get count of digit pairs

                                   ;
                                   ; This section multiplies the right nibble of the multiplicand by the
                                   ; right nibble of the multiplier and adds the result to the right
                                   ; nibble of the accumulator.  i.e.   z := z + x * y
                                   ;                        ss dd dd dd dd dd dd dx    Multiplicand
                                   ;                        ss dd dd dd dd dd dd dy    Multiplier
                                   ;        ss dd dd dd dd dd dd dd dd dd dd dd dd dz  Product
                                   ;
0038                       nextmpcnd:
0038  8A 05                        mov     AL, BYTE PTR [DI]   ; Get digit pair
003A  24 0F                        and     AL,0fh              ; Isolate right one.
003C  0F 84 005E R                 jz      donert              ; If zero - do leftmost.
0040  F6 E2                        mul     DL                  ; Multiply
0042  D4 0A                        aam                         ; adjust product and get
0044  C0 E4 04                     shl     AH,4                ; high digit positioned
0047  0A C4                        or      AL,AH               ; for bcd combination with low.
0049  02 07                        add     AL, BYTE PTR [BX]   ; add to product.
004B  27                           daa                         ; Adjust back to bcd
004C  88 07                        mov     BYTE PTR [BX],AL    ; and put it back
004E  0F 83 005E R                 jnc     donert              ; Done if no carry to propagate
0052  53                           push    BX                  ; Save product pointer
0053                       undonert:
0053  4B                           dec     BX                  ; step to next pair
0054  B0 00                        mov     AL,0                ; We just need to propagate cy.
0056  12 07                        adc     AL, BYTE PTR [BX]   ; add to product.
0058  27                           daa                         ; Adjust back to bcd
0059  88 07                        mov     BYTE PTR [BX],AL    ; and put it back
005B  72 F6                        jc      undonert            ; If no more carry - done.
005D  5B                           pop     BX                  ; Restore product pointer
005E                       donert:
                                   ;
                                   ; This section multiplies the left nibble of the multiplicand by the
                                   ; right nibble of the multiplier and adds the result to the left
                                   ; nibble of the accumulator.  i.e.   z := z + x * y
                                   ;                        ss dd dd dd dd dd dd xd    Multiplicand
                                   ;                        ss dd dd dd dd dd dd dy    Multiplier
                                   ;        ss dd dd dd dd dd dd dd dd dd dd dd dd zd  Product
                                   ;
005E  8A 05                        mov     AL, BYTE PTR [DI]   ; Get digit pair
0060  24 F0                        and     AL,0F0h             ; isolate leftmost digit
0062  0F 84 0090 R                 jz      donelft             ; If zero - pair is done.
0066  C0 E8 04                     shr     AL,4                ; Get it into low nibble
0069  F6 E2                        mul     DL                  ; Multiply
006B  D4 0A                        aam                         ; adjust partial product
006D  C0 E0 04                     shl     AL,4                ; and get it positioned for
0070  02 07                        add     AL, BYTE PTR [BX]   ; add to product.
0072  27                           daa                         ; Adjust back to bcd
0073  88 07                        mov     BYTE PTR [BX],AL    ; and put it back
0075  4B                           dec     BX                  ; Point to next pair
```

80   Arithmetic

```
0076  8A 07                    mov    AL, BYTE PTR [BX]    ; load it
0078  12 C4                    adc    AL,AH                ; add the upper nibble + carry
007A  27                       daa                         ; adjust to bcd pair
007B  88 07                    mov    BYTE PTR [BX],AL     ; and put it back
007D  0F 83 0091 R             jnc    donelft0             ; Done if no carry to propagat
0081  53                       push   BX                   ; Save product pointer
0082              undonelft:
0082  4B                       dec    BX                   ; step to next pair
0083  B0 00                    mov    AL,0                 ; We need to propagate carry.
0085  12 07                    adc    AL, BYTE PTR [BX]    ; add to product.
0087  27                       daa                         ; Adjust back to bcd
0088  88 07                    mov    BYTE PTR [BX],AL     ; and put it back
008A  72 F6                    jc     undonelft            ; If carry to propagate, do it
008C  5B                       pop    BX                   ; Restore product pointer
008D  EB 02 90                 jmp    donelft0             ; (Already at next higher.)
0090              donelft:
0090  4B                       dec    BX                   ; Next higher product digits
0091              donelft0:
0091  4F                       dec    DI                   ; and multiplicand digits
0092  E2 A4                    loop   nextmpcnd            ; To do all 7 pairs.
0094  5F                       pop    DI                   ; Get multiplicand right hand.
0095  5B                       pop    BX                   ; Get product byte pointer.
                    ;
                    ; Process the next (left) multiplier digit.  This process is similar
                    ; to the above but the point of addition into the product is shifted
                    ; left one nibble.  Thus the above routine is reversed.  Note that
                    ; the point at which we begin adding to the product has shifted by a
                    ; nibble.
                    ;
                    ;
                    ;
                    ; This section multiplies the right nibble of the multiplicand by the
                    ; left nibble of the multiplier and adds the result to the left
                    ; nibble of the accumulator.   i.e.   z := z + x * y
                    ;                              ss dd dd dd dd dd dd dx   Multiplicand
                    ;                              ss dd dd dd dd dd dd yd   Multiplier
                    ;    ss dd dd dd dd dd dd dd dd dd dd dd dd dd dd zd   Product
                    ;
0096              dohigh:
0096  80 E6 F0                 and    DH,0f0h              ; isolate the high digit
0099  0F 84 0103 R             jz     donehigh             ; Exit if zero - no mpy needed.
009D  C0 EE 04                 shr    DH,4                 ; Position the high digit
00A0  57                       push   DI                   ; Save right hand multiplicand
00A1  53                       push   BX                   ; Save BX for next pair
                                                            ; pointer.
00A2  B9 0007                  mov    CX,7                 ; Get count of digit pairs
00A5              nextmpcnd2:
00A5  8A 05                    mov    AL, BYTE PTR [DI]    ; Get digit pair
00A7  24 0F                    and    AL,0fh               ; Isolate right one.
00A9  0F 84 00D4 R             jz     dolef2               ; If zero - do leftmost.
00AD  F6 E6                    mul    DH                   ; Multiply
00AF  D4 0A                    aam                         ; adjust partial product
00B1  C0 E0 04                 shl    AL,4                 ; and get positioned for
00B4  02 07                    add    AL, BYTE PTR [BX]    ; add to product.
00B6  27                       daa                         ; Adjust back to bcd
00B7  88 07                    mov    BYTE PTR [BX],AL     ; and put it back
00B9  4B                       dec    BX                   ; Point to next pair
00BA  8A 07                    mov    AL, BYTE PTR [BX]    ; load it
00BC  12 C4                    adc    AL,AH                ; add the upper nibble + carry
00BE  27                       daa                         ; adjust to bcd pair
00BF  88 07                    mov    BYTE PTR [BX],AL     ; and put it back
00C1  0F 83 00D5 R             jnc    donert20             ; Done if no carry to propagate
00C5  53                       push   BX                   ; Save product pointer
00C6              undonert2:
00C6  4B                       dec    BX                   ; step to next pair
00C7  B0 00                    mov    AL,0                 ; Just need to propagate carry.
00C9  12 07                    adc    AL, BYTE PTR [BX]    ; add to product.
```

```
00CB   27                          daa                           ; Adjust back to bcd
00CC   88 07                       mov      BYTE PTR [BX],AL      ; and put it back
00CE   72 F6                       jc       undonert2            ; Done if no carry.
00D0   5B                          pop      BX                   ; Restore product pointer
00D1   EB 02 90                    jmp      donert20             ; Skip product ptr adjust

00D4                       dolef2:
                           ;
                           ; This section multiplies the left nibble of the multiplicand by the
                           ; left nibble of the multiplier and adds the result to the right
                           ; nibble of the accumulator.   i.e.   z := z + x * y
                           ;                                ss dd dd dd dd dd dd xd   Multiplicand
                           ;                                ss dd dd dd dd dd dd yd   Multiplier
                           ;     ss dd dd dd dd dd dd dd dd dd dd dd dd dz dd   Product
                           ;
00D4   4B                          dec      BX                   ; Next higher product digits
00D5                       donert20:
00D5   8A 05                       mov      AL, BYTE PTR [DI]     ; Get digit pair
00D7   24 F0                       and      AL,0f0h              ; isolate leftmost digit
00D9   OF 84 00FE R                jz       donelf2              ; If zero - done with pair.
00DD   C0 E8 04                    shr      AL,4                 ; Get it into low nibble
00E0   F6 E6                       mul      DH                   ; Multiply,
00E2   D4 0A                       aam                           ; adjust partial product,
00E4   C0 E4 04                    shl      AH,4                 ; and get digit positioned
00E7   0A C4                       or       AL,AH                ; for bcd combination with low.
00E9   02 07                       add      AL, BYTE PTR [BX]     ; add into product.
00EB   27                          daa                           ; Adjust back to bcd
00EC   88 07                       mov      BYTE PTR [BX],AL      ; and put it back
00EE   OF 83 00FE R                jnc      donelf2              ; If no carry - done
00F2   53                          push     BX                   ; Save product pointer
00F3                       undonelf2:
00F3   4B                          dec      BX                   ; step to next pair
00F4   B0 00                       mov      AL,0                 ; Just need to propagate carry.
00F6   12 07                       adc      AL, BYTE PTR [BX]     ; add to product.
00F8   27                          daa                           ; Adjust back to bcd
00F9   88 07                       mov      BYTE PTR [BX],AL      ; and put it back
00FB   72 F6                       jc       undonelf2            ; If carry to propagate do it.
00FD   5B                          pop      BX                   ; Restore product pointer
00FE                       donelf2:
                                                                 ; We have the next product ptr.
                                                                 ; and multiplicand digits
00FE   4F                          dec      DI                   ; to do all 7 pairs.
00FF   E2 A4                       loop     nextmpcnd2
0101   5B                          pop      BX                   ; Restore product pointer and
0102   5F                          pop      DI                   ; right-hand multiplicand digit.
                           ;
                           ; The point at which we want to begin adding to our product is now
                           ; two digits to the left (one byte).  BX needs to be adjusted to
                           ; reflect this.
                           ;
0103                       donehigh:
0103   59                          pop      CX                   ; Restore outer loop count
0104   49                          dec      CX                   ; subtract one from pair count
0105   OF 84 010E R                jz       mpydone              ; If zero - skip the adjustment
0109   4B                          dec      BX                   ; to product formation
010A   4E                          dec      SI                   ; next multiplier and go
010B   E9 0027 R                   jmp      nextmpyr             ; to do seven pairs.

010E                       mpydone:
010E   5F                          pop      DI                   ; Restore the entry registers
010F   5E                          pop      SI
0110   58                          pop      AX
0111   5B                          pop      BX
0112   59                          pop      CX
0113   5A                          pop      DX
0114   07                          pop      ES
0115   C3                          ret                           ; and return.
```

```
0116                    Bcdmpy    ENDP
0116                    code      ENDS
                                  END
```

Program 4-11 BCDDIV

Microsoft (R) Macro Assembler Version 5.00

```
                              PAGE      55,132
                              .386
0000                    code  SEGMENT   para 'CODE' PUBLIC USE16
                              ASSUME    CS:code, DS:code, SS:code

                        ; Name:     BCDDIV
                        ;
                        ; Purpose: The following procedure provides signed division of an
                        ;           accumulator (16 byte product
                        ;           SSxxddddddddddddddddddddddddddddddd)
                        ;           by a BCD number in the 'standard' form of SSddddddddddddddd.
                        ;           Where SS is the sign byte (bit 7 is on for minus, off for
                        ;           plus) and the 7 pairs of dd's make up a 14 digit packed BCD
                        ;           number.
                        ;
                        ;
                        ; Inputs:   DS:SI points to the BCD number which is the divisor, DS:BX
                        ;           points to the dividend (accumulator).
                        ;
                        ; Process: The number pointed to by BX is divided by the number
                        ;           pointed to by SI.  The algorithm uses repeated subtraction
                        ;           to generate each quotient digit (Subtract, if the result is
                        ;           not negative add one to the quotient digit and repeat.
                        ;           Otherwise, add back, preserve the quotient digit and shift
                        ;           the point of subtraction one digit right.)  This is appliec
                        ;           twice per byte (once for each packed digit), then a pair of
                        ;           quotient digits are stored.  When the quotient has been
                        ;           formed, the sign of the dividend is placed in the
                        ;           remainder's sign position.  The sign of the quotient is
                        ;           computed from the signs of the divisor and dividend.
                        ;
                        ; Output:   The quotient is returned in the leftmost 8 bytes of the
                        ;           accumulator.  The remainder is returned in the right 8
                        ;           bytes.  (i.e. SSqqqqqqqqqqqqqqSSrrrrrrrrrrrrrr replaces
                        ;           the dividend.)
                        ;
                        ;           In the case of an overflow, carry will be set - this
                        ;           includes division by zero.  In this case, no quotient or
                        ;           remainder is formed.
                        ;
                        ;
                        ;           PUBLIC    Bcddiv
                        ;
0000                    Bcddiv    PROC
0000   66| 50                     push      EAX                 ; Save entry registers
0002   53                         push      BX
0003   51                         push      CX
0004   52                         push      DX
0005   56                         push      SI
0006   57                         push      DI
0007   06                         push      ES
0008   8C D9                      mov       CX,DS
000A   8E C1                      mov       ES,CX
000C   C8 0020 00                 enter     32,0                ; Get some work space.
                        ;
                        ; We will copy the divisor into our work space twice.  Shifted left
```

```
                                          ; one nibble and standard without sign.
                                          ;
0010  8A 24                       mov     AH,BYTE PTR[SI]     ; Get the sign
0012  80 E4 80                    and     AH,080h             ; isolated to the bit
0015  88 66 F1                    mov     BYTE PTR[BP-15],AH  ; in our work area.
                                          ;
                                          ; The first copy checks for division by zero
                                          ;
0018  BF FFF9                     mov     DI,-7               ; index for shifted number
001B  56                          push    SI                  ; Save number's index

                                          ;
                                          ; Shift left one nibble
                                          ;
001C  B6 00                       mov     DH,0                ; Clear for div by zero check
001E  B9 0007                     mov     CX,7                ; Set count to shift
0021  FC                          cld                         ; Set direction to up.
0022  B4 00                       mov     AH,0                ; Get leading zero
0024                      shift2:
0024  46                          inc     SI                  ; point source to next pair
0025  8A 04                       mov     AL, BYTE PTR [SI]   ; and get for top nibble
0027  C1 E8 04                    shr     AX,4                ; Shift right one nibble
002A  88 03                       mov     BYTE PTR [BP+DI],AL ; Put shifted byte back
002C  47                          inc     DI
002D  8A 24                       mov     AH, BYTE PTR [SI]   ; Get a byte into AH
002F  0A F4                       or      DH,AH               ; For zero check
0031  E2 F1                       loop    shift2              ; Skip special handling of
                                                              ; last pair
                                          ;
                                          ; Last pair of digits cannot fetch the next pair (it doesn't exist);
                                          ; We need to fill a zero to the right.
                                          ;
0033  C0 E4 04                    shl     AH,4                ; Fill zeros on right
0036  88 23                       mov     BYTE PTR [BP+DI],AH ; and put down in place.
0038  5E                          pop     SI                  ; Restore index to number
0039  0A F6                       or      DH,DH               ; Divide by zero?
003B  0F 84 0102 R                jz      zerodiv             ; Yes - error.
                                          ;
                                          ; Now copy the unshifted number over.
                                          ;
003F  46                          inc     SI                  ; Step over sign.
0040  BF FFF2                     mov     DI,-14              ; Set start of unshifted no.
0043  B1 07                       mov     CL,7                ; Get count of digits
0045                      copyno:
0045  8A 04                       mov     AL, BYTE PTR[SI]    ;
0047  88 03                       mov     BYTE PTR [BP+DI],AL ; Copy a digit pair.
0049  46                          inc     SI
004A  47                          inc     DI                  ; Step the pointers
004B  E2 F8                       loop    copyno              ; and do all digit pairs.
                                          ;
                                          ; Begin the division process.  We use repeated subtraction in each
                                          ; digit position.  This involves two subtract loops, the first to
                                          ; create the high nibble subtracts the shifted divisor, the second
                                          ; which creates the low nibble subtracts the original divisor.
                                          ;
                                          ;
004D  BF 0009                     mov     DI,9                ; Set beginning displacement
0050                      highsub:
0050  66| 2B C0                   sub     EAX,EAX             ; Initialize quotient pair
0053                      highsub0:
0053  57                          push    DI                  ; Save displacement into
                                                              ; divisor.
0054  BE 0000                     mov     SI,0                ; Set right digit pair.
0057  B9 0008                     mov     CX,8                ; Set count of digits.
```

```
005A  F8                          clc                              ; and clear carry for first
                                                                   ; subtract.
005B                  highsub1:
005B  8A 01                       mov    AL, BYTE PTR[BX+DI]       ; Get digit pair
005D  1A 02                       sbb    AL, BYTE PTR[BP+SI]       ; Subtract with any borrow
                                                                   ; needed.
005F  2F                          das                              ; adjust to bcd.
0060  88 01                       mov    BYTE PTR[BX+DI],AL        ; and put it back
0062  4F                          dec    DI                        ; Point to next dividend pair
0063  4E                          dec    SI                        ; and divisor pair
0064  E2 F5                       loop   highsub1                  ; Do all pairs.
0066  5F                          pop    DI                        ; Restore dividend displacement
0067  0F 82 0073 R                jc     highadd                   ; We went minus - pass is done.
006B  66| 05 00001000             add    EAX,01000h                ; Add to high nibble and note
                                                                   ; overflow from byte.
0071  EB E0                       jmp    highsub0                  ; Go subtract again.
                      ;
                      ; We need to add back having gone too far.
                      ;
0073                  highadd:
0073  57                          push   DI                        ; Save displacement
0074  BE 0000                     mov    SI,0                      ; Point to right digit pair
0077  B9 0008                     mov    CX,8                      ; Set count to add back
007A  F8                          clc                              ; Clear carry for first add.
007B                  highadd0:
007B  8A 01                       mov    AL, BYTE PTR[BX+DI]       ; Get pair,
007D  12 02                       adc    AL, BYTE PTR[BP+SI]       ; add back,
007F  27                          daa                              ; adjust to bcd,
0080  88 01                       mov    BYTE PTR[BX+DI],AL        ; and set result back.
0082  4F                          dec    DI
0083  4E                          dec    SI                        ; Adjust pointers and
0084  E2 F5                       loop   highadd0                  ; do all 8 digits.
0086  5F                          pop    DI                        ; Restore displacement
                      ;
                      ; Check for overflow (quotient digit > 9)
                      ;
0087  66| 3D 000090FF             cmp    EAX,090ffh                ; Did we overflow (first
                                                                   ; time only)?
008D  0F 87 0102 R                ja     zerodiv                   ; If so - same as zero divide.
                      ;
                      ; Subtract the unshifted number from the same displacement.
                      ;
0091                  lowsub:
0091  57                          push   DI                        ; Save displacement
0092  BE FFF8                     mov    SI,-8                     ; Set right digit pair,
0095  B9 0007                     mov    CX,7                      ; count of digits, and
0098  F8                          clc                              ; clear carry for first sbb.
0099                  lowsub0:
0099  8A 01                       mov    AL, BYTE PTR[BX+DI]       ; Get digit pair
009B  1A 02                       sbb    AL, BYTE PTR[BP+SI]       ; Subtract with borrow needed.
009D  2F                          das                              ; adjust to bcd.
009E  88 01                       mov    BYTE PTR[BX+DI],AL        ; and put it back
00A0  4F                          dec    DI                        ; Point to next dividend pair
00A1  4E                          dec    SI                        ; and divisor pair
00A2  E2 F5                       loop   lowsub0                   ; Do all pairs.
00A4  5F                          pop    DI                        ; Restore dividend displacement
00A5  0F 82 00AD R                jc     lowadd                    ; We went minus - pass is done.
00A9  FE C4                       inc    AH                        ; Add to low nibble.
00AB  EB E4                       jmp    lowsub                    ; Go subtract again.
                      ;
                      ; We need to add back having gone too far.
                      ;
00AD                  lowadd:
00AD  57                          push   DI                        ; Save displacement
00AE  BE FFF8                     mov    SI,-8                     ; Point to right digit pair
00B1  B9 0007                     mov    CX,7                      ; Set count to add back
00B4  F8                          clc                              ; Clear carry for first add.
```

Program 4-11 Continued.

```
00B5                    lowadd0:
00B5  8A 01                     mov     AL, BYTE PTR[BX+DI]  ; Get pair,
00B7  12 02                     adc     AL, BYTE PTR[BP+SI]  ; add back,
00B9  27                        daa                         ; adjust to bcd,
00BA  88 01                     mov     BYTE PTR[BX+DI],AL   ; and set result back.
00BC  4F                        dec     DI
00BD  4E                        dec     SI                  ; Adjust pointers and
00BE  E2 F5                     loop    lowadd0             ; do all 8 digits.
00C0  5F                        pop     DI                  ; Restore displacement
                        ;
                        ; Store the pair of quotient digits which we have produced.
                        ;
00C1  8B F7                     mov     SI,DI               ; Copy displacement into accum
00C3  83 EE 08                  sub     SI,8                ; Back up by number size
00C6  88 20                     mov     BYTE PTR[BX+SI],AH  ; and store digit pair.
00C8  47                        inc     DI                  ; Need to do the next pair
00C9  83 FF 10                  cmp     DI,16               ; Check if we are done
00CC  7C 82                     jl      highsub             ; loop to do all pairs.
                        ;
                        ; We have generated the quotient, the remainder is in the low 8
                        ; bytes of the accumulator.
                        ; We need to set the signs for each number.  The remainder keeps
                        ; the sign of the original dividend (if it isn't zero) and the
                        ; quotient is positive if the dividend and divisor signs were the
                        ; same (or if it is zero) and negative otherwise.
                        ;
00CE  8A 07                     mov     AL,BYTE PTR[BX+0]   ; Get dividend sign
00D0  88 47 08                  mov     BYTE PTR[BX+8],AL   ; Into remainder.
00D3  32 46 F1                  xor     AL,BYTE PTR[BP-15]  ; Combine with divisor sign
00D6  88 07                     mov     BYTE PTR[BX+0],AL   ; to make the quotient's sign.
                        ;
                        ; Check for the zero cases.
                        ;
00D8  66| 8B 07                 mov     EAX,DWORD PTR[BX+0] ; Get first 4 bytes
00DB  B0 00                     mov     AL,0                ; (without sign)
00DD  66| 0B 47 04             or      EAX,DWORD PTR[BX+4] ; and combine with low 4.
00E1  0F 85 00E7 R              jnz     quotnz              ; If not zero - skip
00E5  88 07                     mov     BYTE PTR[BX+0],AL   ; plug of zero sign
00E7                    quotnz:
00E7  66| 8B 47 08             mov     EAX,DWORD PTR[BX+8] ; Get first 4 bytes
00EB  B0 00                     mov     AL,0                ; (without sign)
00ED  66| 0B 47 0C             or      EAX,DWORD PTR[BX+12]; and combine with low 4.
00F1  0F 85 00F8 R              jnz     remdrnz             ; If not zero - skip
00F5  88 47 08                  mov     BYTE PTR[BX+8],AL   ; plug of zero sign
00F8                    remdrnz:

00F8                    divexit:
00F8  C9                        leave                       ; Return work space
00F9  07                        pop     ES                  ; Restore the entry registers
00FA  5F                        pop     DI
00FB  5E                        pop     SI
00FC  5A                        pop     DX
00FD  59                        pop     CX
00FE  5B                        pop     BX
00FF  66| 58                    pop     EAX
0101  C3                        ret                         ; and return.
                        ;
                        ; Zero divide or overflow.
                        ;
0102                    zerodiv:
0102  F9                        stc                         ; set carry
0103  EB F3                     jmp     divexit             ; and get out
0105                    Bcddiv  ENDP
0105                    code    ENDS
                                END
```

5

Interrupts and exceptions

To process an interrupt means to stop a current sequence and pay attention to another request that might occur at any normally unpredictable time. Interrupts enable processors to respond to these requests in a controlled manner through code called *interrupt handlers*. For example, unpredictable incidents might be:

- Signals generated by an error condition, such as an array subscript that goes beyond the bounds of the array.
- Signals sent by an external device, such as a storage device responding that the requested data has been found and is ready for use.
- A user signaling the end of a typed message (with a carriage return) that requires analysis and response.

Interrupts often have no relation to the instruction executing when the interrupt is received. The interrupt calls an interrupt handler and control is turned over to that program or subroutine. Figure 5-1 gives a general overview of how a program interrupts and transfers control. First, the processor stores the current condition of the executing program and then changes the flow of program control to link to (and execute) that subroutine. The interrupt handler processes its code and, if appropriate, the original program is restarted at the point where the interrupt came in. To do this, the interrupt handler executes an IRET instruction.

The 80486 has both hardware- and software-generated interrupts that alter the programmed execution. A hardware-generated interrupt occurs in response to an active input on one of the two 80486 interrupt inputs: NMI, which is nonmaskable, or INTR, which is maskable. A software-gen-

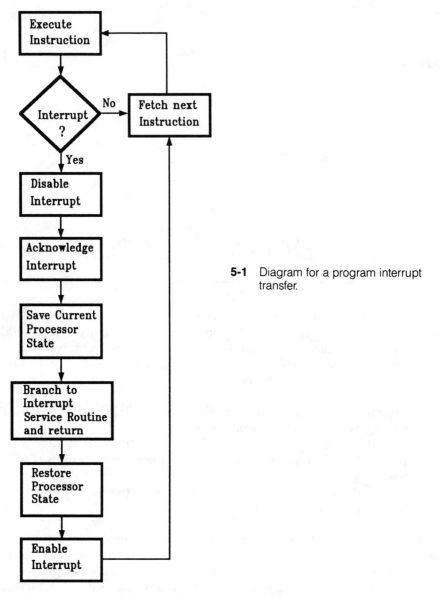

5-1 Diagram for a program interrupt transfer.

erated interrupt occurs in response to an INT instruction or an exception (a software condition that requires servicing). Table 5-1 gives valid 80486 interrupt and exception ID assignments.

Exceptions are unusual or invalid conditions detected during instruction execution. The key difference between an interrupt and an exception is that exceptions are noted by the processor and directly associated with the interrupted instruction, while interrupts are not. For example, the software interrupt instruction INT *n* is classified as an exception rather than interrupt because its execution causes the interrupt.

Table 5-1 Interrupt and exception ID assignments.

Identifier	Description
0	Divide error
1	Debug exception
2	Nonmaskable interrupt
3	Breakpoint
4	INTO-detected overflow
5	BOUNDS range exceeded
6	Invalid opcode
7	Device not available
8	Double fault
9	(RESERVED)
10	Invalid TSS
11	Segment not present
12	Stack fault
13	General protection
14	Page fault
15	(RESERVED)
16	Floating-point error
17	Alignment check
18–31	(RESERVED)
32–255	Available for maskable interrupts

Exceptions are divided into faults, traps, or aborts. A *fault* is an exception that is reported at the instruction boundary before the instruction in which the exception was detected. The 80486 reports the fault in such a way that the instruction can be restarted, such as after a fault handler processes the fault.

A *trap* is reported at the instruction boundary immediately after the instruction in which the 80486 detected the exception; the instruction cannot be restarted.

An *abort* is the most serious of the three exceptions; it does not always report the location of the instruction causing the exception and does not always allow restart of the program that caused the exceptions. Aborts report severe errors, such as hardware errors and illegal values in system tables.

BIOS and MS-DOS interrupts

BIOS and MS-DOS interrupts were introduced in chapter 2, and are detailed in appendix E. In this chapter, we look at working with them. BIOS vectors are located at the beginning of memory and are followed by the MS-DOS interrupt vectors. Each vector uses 4 bytes, so a quick calculation of the location of interrupt n is $n*4$. Therefore, the INT 10 vector is located at location 0000:0040.

One of the programs in this chapter, Inthndlr, allows you to intercept an MS-DOS or BIOS interrupt and replace it with one of your own. You replace the BIOS or MS-DOS interrupt vector with a vector that points to your routine by using Function 25 of INT 21. Remember to change the vector back before ending your program.

Masked and unmasked exceptions

A *mask* is a machine word that specifies which part(s) of another machine word is to be operated on. Masking is a technique for sensing specific binary conditions and ignoring others. It is typically accomplished by placing zeros in bit positions of no interest and ones in bit positions to be sensed.

Certain conditions and flags cause the 80486 to ignore interrupts and debug exceptions. In these cases, the 80486 holds the interrupts pending and discards the debug exceptions:

- If the Resume Flag (RF) bit in the EFLAGS register is 1, debug faults (but not traps) are masked.
- If the Interrupt Enable Flag (IF) bit in EFLAGS is zero, INTR interrupts are masked.
- If the Set Interrupt Flag (STI) instruction executes with IF = 0, INTR interrupts are masked until after the next instruction.
- A POP or MOV instruction (with the SS register as the destination) masks interrupts and debug exceptions until after the next instruction.
- After reporting an NMI, further NMIs are masked until an IRET instruction executes.

80486 interrupts

The 80486 handles both interrupts and exceptions between instructions. Instructions, such as repeated string instructions, are built so that they update both pointer and count registers. Thus, they handle interrupts after each repeat step, which provides good interrupt response while ensuring that the string instruction can be resumed.

Table 5-1 shows that each interrupt and exception has an identification or vector number. The vector number selects the handler for a particular interrupt or exception from the interrupt descriptor table. Exceptions have preassigned vector numbers that range from 0 to 31. While you can assign your own numbers (from 0 to 255) to your interrupts and exceptions, it's best if you stick to the range of 32 to 255. The 80486 recognizes certain defined error codes, which are described briefly as:

Interrupt 0: Divide error   The divide error occurs during an unsigned divide (DIV) or signed divide (IDIV) instruction when the divisor is zero.

Interrupt 1: Debug exceptions   The 80486 generates this interrupt for five general conditions:

1. Task-switch breakpoint trap.
2. General detect fault.
3. Data address breakpoint trap.
4. Instruction address breakpoint fault.
5. Single-step trap.

Interrupt 2: Nonmaskable interrupt

Interrupt 3: Breakpoint   INT 3 (Call to Interrupt Procedure) causes this trap. INT 3 is 1-byte long, which makes it easy to replace an opcode in an executable segment with the breakpoint opcode. The saved CS:EIP (Code Segment, Instruction Pointer) points to the byte following the breakpoint.

Interrupt 4: Overflow   When the 80486 executes a Call to Interrupt Procedure for Overflow (INTO) and the Overflow (OF) flag is set, this interrupt is triggered. Both signed and unsigned arithmetic use the same arithmetic instructions. Since the 80486 cannot judge which is meant, it does not cause overflow exceptions automatically, so it sets the OF flag when the results would be out of range.

Interrupt 5: Bounds check   While executing a Check Array Index Against Bounds (BOUNDS) instruction, if the 80486 finds that the operand is greater than the limit, the processor signals this fault. Software can also use BOUND to check a signed array index against signed limits that are defined in a block of memory.

Interrupt 6: Invalid opcode   This fault occurs if an invalid opcode is found by the execution unit. That exception is not detected until the processor attempts to execute the invalid opcode. That is, pre-fetching the invalid opcode does not trigger this interrupt. Also, no error code is pushed on the stack. Another problem can cause this exception. If the type of operand is invalid for a given opcode, the fault is triggered. For example, an interrupt will occur if a Load Full Pointer into ES Register (LES) uses a register source operand. Figure 5-2 shows a list of undefined opcodes that are reserved by Intel. Note that these opcodes do not generate interrupt 6.

Interrupt 7: Device not available   This exception occurs in either one of two conditions: (1) the processor executes a WAIT instruction or an ESC (Escape, the signal used with the 80386 indicating that this is a coprocessor instruction) and the Task Switched (TS) bits of Control Register Zero (CR0) is set; or (2) the 80486 finds an ESC instruction and the Emulate (EM) bit of CR0 is set.

On the 80386 and 80486, the MP bit in the CR0 register is used with the TS bit to see if WAIT instructions should generate exceptions. Always set the MP bit when using the 80486.

Single Byte	82
	D6
	F1
Double Byte	0F 07
	0F 10
	0F 11
	0F 12
	0F 13
	F6 XX
	F7 XX
	C0 XX
	C1 XX
	D0 XX
	D1 XX
	D2 XX
	D3 XX

5-2 Undefined opcodes, Intel reserved.

Interrupt 8: Double fault The 80486 generally handles exceptions serially. If it cannot, it signals a double-fault condition. To be able to determine if the error is a double-fault condition, the 80486 divides exceptions into three classes: benign exceptions, contributory exceptions, and page faults. These are shown in Table 5-2.

The 80486 always pushes an error code of zero onto the stack of the double-fault handler. The faulting instruction cannot be restarted. If another exception occurs while the processor is attempting to handle a double fault, the processor shuts down.

Interrupt 9: Intel reserved

Interrupt 10: Invalid task state segment (TSS) An attempt to switch to an invalid TSS causes this exception. Eleven conditions can cause a TSS to be considered invalid and Table 5-3 lists the conditions. An error code is pushed onto the stack to help identify which cause it is. The External

Table 5-2   Three classes of double faults.

Class	Identification	Description
	1	Debug exceptions
	2	NMI
Benign	3	Breakpoint
exceptions	4	Overflow
	5	Bounds check
	6	Invalid opcode
	7	Device not available
	16	Floating-point error
	0	Divide error
	10	Invalid TSS
Contributory	11	Segment not present
exceptions	12	Stack fault
	13	General protection
Page fault	14	Page fault

Table 5-3   Conditions invalidating a TSS.

Error code	Conditions
TSS segment	TSS segment limit less than 67h.
LDT segment	Invalid LDT or LDT not present.
Stack segment	Stack segment selector exceeds descriptor table limit.
Stack segment	Stack segment is not writable.
Stack segment	Stack segment DPL not compatible with CPL.
Stack segment	Stack segment selector RPL not compatible with CPL
Code segment	Code segment selector exceeds descriptor table limit.
Code segment	Code segment is not executable.
Code segment	Nonconforming code segment DPL not equal to CPL.
Code segment	Conforming code segment DPL greater than CPL.
Data segment	Data segment selector exceeds descriptor table limit.
Data segment	Data segment not readable.

(EXT) bit indicates if the exception was caused by a condition outside the control of the program, such as an external interrupt via a task gate that triggered the switch to an invalid TSS. To ensure a correct TSS to process this condition, the exception handler must be a task call via a task gate.

Interrupt 11: Segment not present   This exception occurs when the 80486 finds that the Present (P) bit of a descriptor is zero. This fault is restartable.

The exception handler makes the segment present and returns. The interrupted program then resumes execution. Generally, an operating system uses this exception to implement virtual memory at the segment level.

Interrupt 12: Stack exception   Interrupt 12 occurs in either of two conditions. The first is if the 80486 attempts to load the SS register with a descriptor that is marked as not-present but is otherwise valid. This might occur in an interlevel CALL, an interlevel return, in a task switch, an LSS instruction, or a MOV or POP instruction to SS.

The second Interrupt 12 exception condition is any operation that refers to the SS register and has a limit violation. This includes stack-oriented instructions such as ENTER, LEAVE, POP, and PUSH. It also includes other memory references that imply use of the SS register. An instruction that causes this interrupt is restartable in all cases. The return pointer pushed onto the exception handler's stack points to the instruction to be restarted.

Interrupt 13: General protection exception   This exception is the catch-all. All protection violations that do not cause another exception cause a general exception. The following are sample causes:

1. Writing into a read-only data segment or into a code segment.
2. Switching to a busy task.
3. Violating privilege rules.
4. Exceeding segment limit when using CS, DS, ES, FS, or GS.
5. Loading the CR0 register with a set paging enabled (PG) bit and a clear protection disabled (PE).
6. Transferring control to a segment that is not executable.
7. Reading from an execute-only code segment.
8. Accessing memory using the DS, ES, FS, or GS register when it contains a null selector.

Interrupt 14: Page fault   Interrupt 14 occurs when paging is enabled (PG = 1) and the processor finds one of the two following conditions when translating a linear address to a physical address. The first is when the current procedure does not have enough privilege to access the indicated page; the second is when the page-table entry or page-directory that is needed for the address translation has a zero in its P bit.

Interrupt 15: Reserved for future Intel use

Interrupt 16: Floating-point error   A floating-point error occurs when there is an error generated using floating-point arithmetic. Interrupt 16 occurs only if the numeric exception (NE) bit in the CR0 register is set.

Interrupt 17: Alignment check   This fault occurs when access is made to unaligned operands; for example, this could be when there is a word stored at an odd-byte address, or a doubleword stored at an address that is not an integer multiple of four.

See Table 5-4 for a summary of these interrupt exceptions.

Table 5-4   Exception summary.

Number	Description	Return to faulting instruction	Caused by
0	Divide error	Yes	DIV, IDIV
0	Debug exceptions	Yes	Any
3	Breakpoint	No	INT3 Instruction
4	Overflow	No	INTO
5	Bounds check	Yes	BOUND
6	Invalid opcode	Yes	Reserved opcodes
7	Device not available	Yes	ESC, WAIT
8	Double fault	Yes	Any instruction
10	Invalid TSS	Yes	JMP, CALL, IRET interrupt
11	Segment not present	Yes	Any instruction which changes segments
12	Stack fault	Yes	Stack operations
13	General protection	Yes	Any memory reference or code fetch
14	Page fault	Yes	Any memory reference or code fetch
16	Floating-point error	No	ESC, WAIT
17	Alignment check	Yes	Any data reference
0–255	Two-byte SW interrupt	No	Int n

Interrupt and error code handling

BIOS and MS-DOS interrupt vectors are located in low memory. You can use MS-DOS interrupts to locate the vectors if you want to see how MS-DOS handles the interrupts (by unassembling the code with a debug package). You also can change how the interrupts are handled by intercepting the calls and replacing the interrupt handlers with ones you have written.

Intercepting BIOS/DOS interrupts

In INTHNDLR (Program 5-1), we replace PrtSc (INT 5) with a handler for the BOUND interrupt. Although the example is simple, it illustrates the approved method for replacing interrupt vectors. The early operating system designers for the PC used reserved but unused BIOS interrupt vectors, which is why there is overlap and confusion today.

One way to invalidate an interrupt is to use INT 21 Function 35 and get the interrupt vector into DX. Subtract one byte and you run into the IRET of the previous interrupt. If you substitute the new address as the vector of the interrupt you intercept, nothing happens. The interrupt simply returns.

A Read/Write error message program

Program 5-2, ERRORMSG, is a simple-minded example showing how to index into an error table. It links with another procedure CODEHXTB (described and listed in chapter 7), which converts hexadecimal input to binary. For the purpose of this example, ERRORMSG reads in a number from the keyboard and then looks up that message in the error table. In practice, you will want to pass ERRORMSG a number in an array and have ERRORMSG look up that passed parameter. To link, you enter:

LINK ERR__MSG + CODEHXTB,,,;

or, using the library on the available diskette:

LINK ERR__MSG,,,LIBRARY;

Because we entered only four sample messages into the error table in the program, type a number between 1 and 4. The program checks and will not accept any other number. If ERRORMSG were to be part of a final program, you would test for the limits of input so that your user could not receive unexpected output.

Extended error messages

The extended error codes returned by INT 21 Function 59 correspond to error values that are returned in AX by various MS-DOS functions (level 3.0 and later) that set the Carry Flag = 1. If a function call results in an error, INT 21 Function 59 returns meaningful information—but only if it is the next call to MS-DOS, after the one that received the error. Any other intervening call to another MS-DOS function, whether explicit or indirect, causes the error value for the unsuccessful function to be lost. We hard-coded the error messages into the procedure EXTERROR (Program 5-3) and used the return values in the various registers to index into the messages.

To use INT 21 Function 59, store 59 in AH, a hex 0 (00) in BX and issue INT 21. Unlike many MS-DOS functions, this function modifies registers, so we do a PUSHA in the beginning to save the registers and a POPA at the end to restore them. Function 59 returns the extended error code in AX, the error class in BH, a suggested action in BL, and the location of the error in CH.

Program 5-1 INTHNDLR

Microsoft (R) Macro Assembler Version 5.00

```
                               PAGE     55,132
                               .386
                       ;
                       ; Name: INTHNDLR
                       ;
                       ; Purpose: This program shown an example of intercepting an
                       ;          interrupt and replacing it with one specially written.
                       ;          The intercepted interrupt could just as well be an MS-DOS
                       ;          interrupt.  We replace interrupt 5 (print screen) with
                       ;          a handler for the bound interrupt.
                       ;
                       ; Inputs:  The program itself embodies a simple game of guessing the
                       ;          bounds.  All input is prompted for.
                       ;
                       ; Process: The program preserves the original value of the interrupt
                       ;          vector for the INT 5h handler.  It then sets its interrupt
                       ;          handler vector in DS:DX and requests MS-DOS to replace the
                       ;          vector.  The program then prompts for guesses and using the
                       ;          bound instruction checks whether the guesses are in bounds.
                       ;          Messages are produced for high, low and in bounds.
                       ;          The game is over when both upper and lower bounds are
                       ;          found.
                       ;
                       ; Outputs: All outputs are displayed.
                       ;
                       ; Note:    The program demonstrates techniques for swapping interrupt
                       ;          vectors.
                       ;
                       ;
                       ;
                       ; Declare the routines we are going to use
                       ;
                               EXTRN   CODEASB:PROC
                               EXTRN   CODEBAS:PROC

                       ; Define a range of values for our bound test
                       ;
=-000D                 lowval   EQU     -13
= 0002                 valid    EQU     2
= 0017                 hival    EQU     23

0000                   stack    SEGMENT para 'STACK' STACK
0000  0100[            dq       256 DUP(?)
      ??????????????????
      ?
                  ]

0800                   stack    ENDS

0000                   data     SEGMENT para
0000  0000 0000        int5save dw      0,0                  ; Will save it here

0004  FFF3 0017        okbound  dw      lowval,hival         ; target for our bound check
0008  00               fndlow   db      0
0009  00               fndhi    db      0
000A  0100[            string   db      256 DUP(?)           ; String scratch area
      ??
                  ]
```

```
010A   0A 0D 59 6F 75 20 67        rules     db        10,13,"You get to find the lowest and highest"
       65 74 20 74 6F 20 66
       69 6E 64 20 74 68 65
       20 6C 6F 77 65 73 74
       20 61 6E 64 20 68 69
       67 68 65 73 74
0132   20 76 61 6C 69 64 20                  db        " valid array bounds."
       61 72 72 61 79 20 62
       6F 75 6E 64 73 2E
0146   0A 0D 20 49 66 20 79                  db        10,13," If you get tired, a null entry will exit.$"
       6F 75 20 67 65 74 20
       74 69 72 65 64 2C 20
       61 20 6E 75 6C 6C 20
       65 6E 74 72 79 20 77
       69 6C 6C 20 65 78 69
       74 2E 24

0173   0A 0D 49 74 20 69 73        itisin    db        10,13,"It is in.$"
       20 69 6E 2E 24
017F   0A 0A 0D 45 6E 74 65        query     db        10,10,13,"Enter a number to test: $"
       72 20 61 20 6E 75 6D
       62 65 72 20 74 6F 20
       74 65 73 74 3A 20 24
019B   0A 0D 59 6F 75 20 67        gotlow    db        10,13,"You got the low value!$"
       6F 74 20 74 68 65 20
       6C 6F 77 20 76 61 6C
       75 65 21 24
01B4   0A 0D 59 6F 75 20 67        gothigh   db        10,13,"You got the high value!$"
       6F 74 20 74 68 65 20
       68 69 67 68 20 76 61
       6C 75 65 21 24

01CE                               data      ENDS
0000                               code      SEGMENT para 'CODE' USE16 PUBLIC
                                             ASSUME  CS:code, DS:data
                                   ;
                                   ; Set up the environment
                                   ;
0000                               Begin:
0000   B8 ---- R                             mov       AX,data           ; Get data segment pointer
0003   8E D8                                 mov       DS,AX             ; into DS,
                                   ;
                                   ; Get int 5's current handler and save it.
                                   ;
0005   B8 3505                               mov       AX,3505h          ; Set both AH and AL
0008   CD 21                                 int       21h
000A   8C 06 0000 R                          mov       int5save,ES       ; save segment
000E   89 1E 0002 R                          mov       int5save+2,BX     ; and offset
0012   8D 16 0095 R                          lea       DX,ibound         ; Point DX to the routine
0016   8C C9                                 mov       CX,CS             ; Get the CS value
0018   8C DB                                 mov       BX,DS             ; Save our DS
001A   8E D9                                 mov       DS,CX             ; set segment for move
001C   B8 2505                               mov       AX,2505h          ; Set int code
001F   CD 21                                 int       21h               ; and put our handler in
0021   8E DB                                 mov       DS,BX             ; restore DS
0023   8D 16 010A R                          lea       DX,rules          ; point to our simple rules
0027   B4 09                                 mov       AH,9
0029   CD 21                                 int       21h
002B                               getnbr:
002B   8D 16 017F R                          lea       DX,query          ; get a number
002F   E8 009B R                             call      getinp
0032   E3 52                                 jcxz      Exit              ; got tired
0034   8B F3                                 mov       SI,BX             ; Set input pointer
0036   E8 0000 E                             call      Codeasb           ; Do the convert
0039   72 F0                                 jc        getnbr            ; Go get a good one
003B   BB 0001                               mov       BX,1              ; Set the good signal
003E   62 06 0004 R                          bound     AX,DWORD PTR okbound ; Do the bound instruction
```

```
0042   0B DB                or     BX,BX              ; was it valid?
0044   74 E5                jz     getnbr             ; no - try again
0046   50                   push   AX                 ; Save the number
0047   8D 16 0173 R         lea    DX,itisin          ; Point to the ok msg
004B   B4 09                mov    AH,9
004D   CD 21                int    21h                ; and put it out
004F   58                   pop    AX
0050   3D FFF3              cmp    AX,lowval          ; is it the low
0053   0F 84 0073 R         jz     foundlow           ; yes
0057   3D 0017              cmp    AX,hival           ; is it the high?
005A   75 CF                jnz    getnbr             ; no
005C   FE 06 0009 R         inc    fndhi              ; set non zero
0060   8D 16 01B4 R         lea    DX,gothigh
0064   B4 09                mov    AH,9
0066   CD 21                int    21h                ; write message
0068   A0 0008 R            mov    AL,fndlow          ; both found?
006B   0A C0                or     AL,AL              ;
006D   0F 85 0086 R         jnz    Exit
0071   EB B8                jmp    getnbr             ; nope
0073           foundlow:
0073   FE 06 0008 R         inc    fndlow             ; set non zero
0077   8D 16 019B R         lea    DX,gotlow
007B   B4 09                mov    AH,9
007D   CD 21                int    21h                ; write message
007F   A0 0009 R            mov    AL,fndhi           ; both found?
0082   0A C0                or     AL,AL              ;
0084   74 A5                jz     getnbr


0086           Exit:
0086   C5 16 0000 R         lds    DX,DWORD PTR int5save ; point to original
008A   B8 2505              mov    AX,2505h           ; Set the code and int no.
008D   CD 21                int    21h
008F   B0 00                mov    AL,0               ; Set return code
0091   B4 4C                mov    AH,04ch            ; Set good-by
0093   CD 21                int    21h                ; Return to the system
               ;
               ;  Interrupt 5 handler.
               ;       This is a simplified handler for the bound interrupt.
               ;       It corrects the value in AX to an in-bound value and
               ;       clears BX to indicate the error.  It then returns.
               ;

0095           ibound:
0095   2B DB                sub    BX,BX              ; clear the flag register
0097   B8 0002              mov    AX,valid           ; Set a valid value
009A   CF                   iret                      ; and return
               ;
               ; Read a string in response to a prompt
               ; The prompt must be in DX.  The string will be returned in string.
               ;
009B           getinp PROC
009B   50                   push   AX                 ; Save registers
009C   56                   push   SI
009D   B4 09                mov    AH,9               ; and dos request
009F   CD 21                int    21h                ; put out the string
00A1   8D 16 000A R         lea    DX,string          ; point to input area
00A5   C6 06 000A R FE      mov    string,254         ; Set max length in
00AA   B4 0A                mov    AH,10              ; Ask for read of string
00AC   CD 21                int    21h                ; from DOS.
00AE   8D 1E 000C R         lea    BX,string+2        ; Point to just read data
00B2   8A 0E 000B R         mov    CL,string+1        ; Get length read
00B6   B5 00                mov    CH,0               ; as a word.
00B8   8B F1                mov    SI,CX              ; Set length
00BA   C6 84 000C R 00      mov    string+2[SI],0     ; and make an asciiz string.
00BF   5E                   pop    SI
```

Program 5-1 Continued.

```
00C0  58                              pop     AX              ; Restore registers
00C1  C3                              ret                     ; and return.
00C2                    getinp        ENDP

00C2                    code          ENDS
                                      END     Begin
```

Program 5-2 ERRORMSG

Microsoft (R) Macro Assembler Version 5.00

```
                              PAGE    55,132
                              .386
                      ;
                      ; Declare the external procedure used to change hex to binary
                      ;
                              EXTRN   CODEHXTB:PROC
                      ;
0000                  STACK   SEGMENT 'STACK' STACK
0000  0064[                   DW      100 DUP(?)
      ????
                   ]

00C8                  STACK   ENDS
0000                  CODE    SEGMENT para 'CODE' PUBLIC USE16
                              ASSUME  CS:CODE, DS:CODE, SS:STACK
                      ;
                      ; Name: ERRORMSG
                      ;
                      ; Purpose:      This program has a table of error messages.  It uses
                      ;               messages of the same length, to ease the indexing into
                      ;               the table.  Note that each messages ends with a "$"
                      ;               which is not printed.  Function 9 of INT 21 uses the
                      ;               "$" as an end of text symbol.  Also "0Dh" is a
                      ;               carriage return and "0Ah" is a line feed.
                      ;
                      ; Inputs:       The hex error number is read into AH,AL (AX).  This
                      ;               program then calls CODEHXTB, which converts hex to
                      ;               binary of whatever value is in AX.  If only a single
                      ;               digit is passed to CODEHXTB, then AH must be set to
                      ;               "30".  CODEHXTB is described in Chapter 7, Code
                      ;               Conversion of the "80386 Assembly Language Toolkit"
                      ;               from TAB Books Inc.
                      ;
                      ; Process:      DX points to the address of the beginning of the
                      ;               error table.  The error number is the index into the
                      ;               table.  Once the message is found, it prints on the
                      ;               screen.
                      ;
                      ; Outputs:      A printed message on the screen.
                      ;
                      ; NOTE:         For the purposes of this example, a number is read in
                      ;               from the keyboard.
                      ;
0000                  ERRORMSG:
0000  8C C8                   MOV     AX,CS           ; Prepare to set DS
0002  8E D8                   MOV     DS,AX           ;    and set it.
0004  E9 009E R               JMP     BEGINHERE
                      ;
0007  0028[          INPUTSTR DB      40 DUP(?)
      ??
                   ]
002F  54 79 70 65 20 61 20  QUERY   DB      'Type a number 0-3 $'
      6E 75 6D 62 65 72 20
      30 2D 33 20 24
```

```
0042   55 6E 61 62 6C 65 20      MESSAGES          DB          'Unable to open file.',0Dh,0Ah,'$'
       74 6F 20 6F 70 65 6E
       20 66 69 6C 65 2E 0D
       0A 24
0059   46 69 6C 65 20 64 6F                        DB          'File does not exist.',0Dh,0Ah,'$'
       65 73 20 6E 6F 74 20
       65 78 69 73 74 2E 0D
       0A 24
0070   49 6E 76 61 6C 69 64                        DB          'Invalid file name.  ',0Dh,0Ah,'$'
       20 66 69 6C 65 20 6E
       61 6D 65 2E 20 20 0D
       0A 24
0087   44 61 74 61 20 6E 6F                        DB          'Data not found.     ',0Dh,0Ah,'$'
       74 20 66 6F 75 6E 64
       2E 20 20 20 20 20 0D
       0A 24
009E                            BEGINHERE:
009E   8D 16 002F R                               LEA         DX,QUERY          ; Print the prompt
00A2   B4 09                                      MOV         AH,9h
00A4   CD 21                                      INT         21h
00A6   8D 16 0007 R                               LEA         DX,INPUTSTR       ; Point to input buffer
00AA   C6 06 0007 R 25                            MOV         INPUTSTR,37       ; This max to read in
00AF   B4 0A                                      MOV         AH,0Ah            ; Get ready to read in a value
00B1   CD 21                                      INT         21h
00B3   A0 0009 R                                  MOV         AL,INPUTSTR+2     ; Get the digit into AL
00B6   B4 30                                      MOV         AH,30h            ; Since only 1 input digit
                                ;
                                ; Turn the hex into binary
                                ;
00B8   E8 0000 E                                  CALL        CODEHXTB
                                ;
                                ; Now point to table entry
                                ;
00BB   3D 0003                                    CMP         AX,3              ; Check value
00BE   77 DE                                      JA          BEGINHERE         ; If bad try again
00C0   8D 16 0042 R                               LEA         DX,MESSAGES       ; Load in Table entry point
00C4   B1 17                                      MOV         CL,23             ; Each message is 23 bytes
00C6   F6 E1                                      MUL         CL                ; CL X AL = Result in AL
00C8   03 D0                                      ADD         DX,AX             ; Add this result to entry
00CA   B4 09                                      MOV         AH,9h             ; Get ready to print
00CC   CD 21                                      INT         21h
                                ;
                                ; End of Program - Wrap-Up
                                ;
00CE                            ENDHERE:
00CE   B4 4C                                      MOV         AH,4Ch            ; Standard Ending
00D0   CD 21                                      INT         21h
00D2                            CODE              ENDS
                                                  END         ERRORMSG
```

Program 5-3   EXTERROR

Microsoft (R) Macro Assembler Version 5.00

```
                                               PAGE      55,132
                                               .386
0000                            STACK          SEGMENT 'STACK' STACK
0000   00C8[                                   DW        200 DUP(?)
       ????
                          ]

0190                            STACK          ENDS
0000                            CODE           SEGMENT para 'CODE' PUBLIC USE16
                                               ASSUME  CS:CODE, DS:CODE, SS:STACK
                                ;
```

```
                              ; Name:          EXTERROR
                              ;
                              ; Purpose:       This program reads the error code and gives an
                              ;                extended code, with additional information in other
                              ;                registers.  These extended error codes are especially
                              ;                helpful when attempting to create new files or to
                              ;                modify existing ones.
                              ;
                              ;                The extended error codes returned by INT 21 Function 59
                              ;                correspond to the error values returned in AX by
                              ;                functions in MS-DOS, versions 2.0 and later, that set
                              ;                the Carry Flag=1.
                              ;
                              ; Inputs:        Store 59 in AH, 00 in BX and issue INT 21h.
                              ;
                              ; Process:       INT 21 Function 59 modifies registers CL, DX, SI,
                              ;                DI, ES and DS.  These registers must be preserved
                              ;                prior to invoking Function 59, if their contents are
                              ;                needed for later processing.
                              ;
                              ; Outputs:       AX = extended error code.
                              ;                BX = Error class and action
                              ;                     BH = Error class
                              ;                     BL = Suggested Action
                              ;                CH = Location of Error
                              ;
                                              PUBLIC  EXTERROR
0000                          EXTERROR        PROC
0000  E9 1379 R                               JMP     BEGINHERE
                              ;
0003  0A 0D 20 45 52 52 4F    HEADER          DB      0Ah,0Dh,' ERROR FOUND$'
      52 20 46 4F 55 4E 44
      24
0012  0A 0D 20 45 72 72 6F    CODES           DB      0Ah,0Dh,' Error code:     $'
      72 20 63 6F 64 65 3A
      20 20 20 20 20 20 20
      24
0028  0A 0D 20 45 72 72 6F    CLASS           DB      0Ah,0Dh,' Error class:    $'
      72 20 63 6C 61 73 73
      3A 20 20 20 20 20 20
      24
003E  0A 0D 20 53 75 67 67    ACTION          DB      0Ah,0Dh,' Suggested action: $'
      65 73 74 65 64 20 61
      63 74 69 6F 6E 3A 20
      24
0054  0A 0D 20 4C 6F 63 61    LOCATION        DB      0Ah,0Dh,' Location:       $'
      74 69 6F 6E 3A 20 20
      20 20 20 20 20 20 20
      24
006A  0A 0D 24                CR_LF           DB      0Ah,0Dh,'$'
                              ;
                              ; AX Error Codes
006D  4E 6F 20 65 72 72 6F    AX00            DB      'No error encountered           $'
      72 20 65 6E 63 6F 75
      6E 74 65 72 65 64 20
      20 20 20 20 20 20 20
      20 20 20 20 20 20 20
      20 20 20 20 20 20 24
0097  49 6E 76 61 6C 69 64    AX01            DB      'Invalid function number        $'
      20 66 75 6E 63 74 69
      6F 6E 20 6E 75 6D 62
      65 72 20 20 20 20 20
      20 20 20 20 20 20 20
      20 20 20 20 20 20 24
00C1  46 69 6C 65 20 6E 6F    AX02            DB      'File not found                 $'
      74 20 66 6F 75 6E 64
```

```
        20 20 20 20 20 20 20
        20 20 20 20 20 20 20
        20 20 20 20 20 20 20
        20 20 20 20 20 20 24
00EB    50 61 74 68 20 6E 6F    AX03    DB    'Path not found                    $'
        74 20 66 6F 75 6E 64
        20 20 20 20 20 20 20
        20 20 20 20 20 20 20
        20 20 20 20 20 20 20
        20 20 20 20 20 20 24
0115    54 6F 6F 20 6D 61 6E    AX04    DB    'Too many files open, no handles available$'
        79 20 66 69 6C 65 73
        20 6F 70 65 6E 2C 20
        6E 6F 20 68 61 6E 64
        6C 65 73 20 61 76 61
        69 6C 61 62 6C 65 24
013F    41 63 63 65 73 73 20    AX05    DB    'Access denied                     $'
        64 65 6E 69 65 64 20
        20 20 20 20 20 20 20
        20 20 20 20 20 20 20
        20 20 20 20 20 20 20
        20 20 20 20 20 20 24
0169    49 6E 76 61 6C 69 64    AX06    DB    'Invalid handle                    $'
        20 68 61 6E 64 6C 65
        20 20 20 20 20 20 20
        20 20 20 20 20 20 20
        20 20 20 20 20 20 20
        20 20 20 20 20 20 24
0193    4D 65 6D 6F 72 79 20    AX07    DB    'Memory control blocks destroyed   $'
        63 6F 6E 74 72 6F 6C
        20 62 6C 6F 63 6B 73
        20 64 65 73 74 72 6F
        79 65 64 20 20 20 20
        20 20 20 20 20 20 24
01BD    49 6E 73 75 66 66 69    AX08    DB    'Insufficient memory               $'
        63 69 65 6E 74 20 6D
        65 6D 6F 72 79 20 20
        20 20 20 20 20 20 20
        20 20 20 20 20 20 20
        20 20 20 20 20 20 24
01E7    49 6E 76 61 6C 69 64    AX09    DB    'Invalid memory-block address      $'
        20 6D 65 6D 6F 72 79
        2D 62 6C 6F 63 6B 20
        61 64 64 72 65 73 73
        20 20 20 20 20 20 20
        20 20 20 20 20 20 24
0211    49 6E 76 61 6C 69 64    AX0A    DB    'Invalid environment               $'
        20 65 6E 76 69 72 6F
        6E 6D 65 6E 74 20 20
        20 20 20 20 20 20 20
        20 20 20 20 20 20 20
        20 20 20 20 20 20 24
023B    49 6E 76 61 6C 69 64    AX0B    DB    'Invalid format                    $'
        20 66 6F 72 6D 61 74
        20 20 20 20 20 20 20
        20 20 20 20 20 20 20
        20 20 20 20 20 20 20
        20 20 20 20 20 20 24
0265    49 6E 76 61 6C 69 64    AX0C    DB    'Invalid access code               $'
        20 61 63 63 65 73 73
        20 63 6F 64 65 20 20
        20 20 20 20 20 20 20
        20 20 20 20 20 20 20
        20 20 20 20 20 20 24
028F    49 6E 76 61 6C 69 64    AX0D    DB    'Invalid data                      $'
        20 64 61 74 61 20 20
        20 20 20 20 20 20 20
        20 20 20 20 20 20 20
```

Program 5-3 Continued.

```
      20 20 20 20 20 20 20
      20 20 20 20 20 20 24
02B9  52 65 73 65 72 76 65     AX0E    DB      'Reserved                              $'
      64 20 20 20 20 20 20
      20 20 20 20 20 20 20
      20 20 20 20 20 20 20
      20 20 20 20 20 20 20
      20 20 20 20 20 20 24
02E3  49 6E 76 61 6C 69 64     AX0F    DB      'Invalid disk drive                    $'
      20 64 69 73 6B 20 64
      72 69 76 65 20 20 20
      20 20 20 20 20 20 20
      20 20 20 20 20 20 20
      20 20 20 20 20 20 24
030D  41 74 74 65 6D 70 74     AX10    DB      'Attempt to remove current directory   $'
      20 74 6F 20 72 65 6D
      6F 76 65 20 63 75 72
      72 65 6E 74 20 64 69
      72 65 63 74 6F 72 79
      20 20 20 20 20 20 24
0337  44 65 76 69 63 65 20     AX11    DB      'Device not the same                   $'
      6E 6F 74 20 74 68 65
      20 73 61 6D 65 20 20
      20 20 20 20 20 20 20
      20 20 20 20 20 20 20
      20 20 20 20 20 20 24
0361  4E 6F 20 6D 6F 72 65     AX12    DB      'No more files                         $'
      20 66 69 6C 65 73 20
      20 20 20 20 20 20 20
      20 20 20 20 20 20 20
      20 20 20 20 20 20 20
      20 20 20 20 20 20 24
038B  57 72 6F 74 65 2D 70     AX13    DB      'Wrote-protected disk                  $'
      72 6F 74 65 63 74 65
      64 20 64 69 73 6B 20
      20 20 20 20 20 20 20
      20 20 20 20 20 20 20
      20 20 20 20 20 20 24
03B5  55 6E 6B 6E 6F 77 6E     AX14    DB      'Unknown unit                          $'
      20 75 6E 69 74 20 20
      20 20 20 20 20 20 20
      20 20 20 20 20 20 20
      20 20 20 20 20 20 20
      20 20 20 20 20 20 24
03DF  44 72 69 76 65 20 6E     AX15    DB      'Drive not ready                       $'
      6F 74 20 72 65 61 64
      79 20 20 20 20 20 20
      20 20 20 20 20 20 20
      20 20 20 20 20 20 20
      20 20 20 20 20 20 24
0409  49 6E 76 61 6C 69 64     AX16    DB      'Invalid command                       $'
      20 63 6F 6D 6D 61 6E
      64 20 20 20 20 20 20
      20 20 20 20 20 20 20
      20 20 20 20 20 20 20
      20 20 20 20 20 20 24
0433  44 61 74 61 20 65 72     AX17    DB      'Data error based on CRC               $'
      72 6F 72 20 62 61 73
      65 64 20 6F 6E 20 43
      52 43 20 20 20 20 20
      20 20 20 20 20 20 20
      20 20 20 20 20 20 24
045D  4C 65 6E 67 74 68 20     AX18    DB      'Length of request structure invalid   $'
      6F 66 20 72 65 71 75
      65 73 74 20 73 74 72
      75 63 74 75 72 65 20
```

```
        69 6E 76 61 6C 69 64
        20 20 20 20 20 20 24
0487    53 65 65 6B 20 65 72    AX19    DB      'Seek error                         $'
        72 6F 72 20 20 20 20
        20 20 20 20 20 20 20
        20 20 20 20 20 20 20
        20 20 20 20 20 20 20
        20 20 20 20 20 20 24
04B1    4E 6F 6E 2D 4D 53 2D    AX1A    DB      'Non-MS-DOS disk                    $'
        44 4F 53 20 64 69 73
        6B 20 20 20 20 20 20
        20 20 20 20 20 20 20
        20 20 20 20 20 20 20
        20 20 20 20 20 20 24
04DB    53 65 63 74 6F 72 20    AX1B    DB      'Sector not found                   $'
        6E 6F 74 20 66 6F 75
        6E 64 20 20 20 20 20
        20 20 20 20 20 20 20
        20 20 20 20 20 20 20
        20 20 20 20 20 20 24
0505    50 72 69 6E 74 65 72    AX1C    DB      'Printer out of paper               $'
        20 6F 75 74 20 6F 66
        20 70 61 70 65 72 20
        20 20 20 20 20 20 20
        20 20 20 20 20 20 20
        20 20 20 20 20 20 24
052F    57 72 69 74 65 20 66    AX1D    DB      'Write fault                        $'
        61 75 6C 74 20 20 20
        20 20 20 20 20 20 20
        20 20 20 20 20 20 20
        20 20 20 20 20 20 20
        20 20 20 20 20 20 24
0559    52 65 61 64 20 66 61    AX1E    DB      'Read fault                         $'
        75 6C 74 20 20 20 20
        20 20 20 20 20 20 20
        20 20 20 20 20 20 20
        20 20 20 20 20 20 20
        20 20 20 20 20 20 24
0583    47 65 6E 65 72 61 6C    AX1F    DB      'General failure                    $'
        20 66 61 69 6C 75 72
        65 20 20 20 20 20 20
        20 20 20 20 20 20 20
        20 20 20 20 20 20 20
        20 20 20 20 20 20 24
05AD    53 68 61 72 69 6E 67    AX20    DB      'Sharing violation                  $'
        20 76 69 6F 6C 61 74
        69 6F 6E 20 20 20 20
        20 20 20 20 20 20 20
        20 20 20 20 20 20 20
        20 20 20 20 20 20 24
05D7    4C 6F 63 6B 20 76 69    AX21    DB      'Lock violation                     $'
        6F 6C 61 74 69 6F 6E
        20 20 20 20 20 20 20
        20 20 20 20 20 20 20
        20 20 20 20 20 20 20
        20 20 20 20 20 20 24
0601    49 6E 76 61 6C 69 64    AX22    DB      'Invalid disk change                $'
        20 64 69 73 6B 20 63
        68 61 6E 67 65 20 20
        20 20 20 20 20 20 20
        20 20 20 20 20 20 20
        20 20 20 20 20 20 24
062B    46 69 6C 65 20 43 6F    AX23    DB      'File Control Block unavailable     $'
        6E 74 72 6F 6C 20 42
        6C 6F 63 6B 20 75 6E
        61 76 61 69 6C 61 62
        6C 65 20 20 20 20 20
        20 20 20 20 20 20 24
```

```
0655   53 68 61 72 69 6E 67    AX24    DB      'Sharing buffer exceeded                       $'
       20 62 75 66 66 65 72
       20 65 78 63 65 65 64
       65 64 20 20 20 20 20
       20 20 20 20 20 20 20
       20 20 20 20 20 20 24
067F   52 65 73 65 72 76 65    AX25    DB      'Reserved                                      $'
       64 20 20 20 20 20 20
       20 20 20 20 20 20 20
       20 20 20 20 20 20 20
       20 20 20 20 20 20 20
       20 20 20 20 20 20 24
06A9   52 65 73 65 72 76 65    AX26    DB      'Reserved                                      $'
       64 20 20 20 20 20 20
       20 20 20 20 20 20 20
       20 20 20 20 20 20 20
       20 20 20 20 20 20 20
       20 20 20 20 20 20 24
06D3   52 65 73 65 72 76 65    AX27    DB      'Reserved                                      $'
       64 20 20 20 20 20 20
       20 20 20 20 20 20 20
       20 20 20 20 20 20 20
       20 20 20 20 20 20 20
       20 20 20 20 20 20 24
06FD   52 65 73 65 72 76 65    AX28    DB      'Reserved                                      $'
       64 20 20 20 20 20 20
       20 20 20 20 20 20 20
       20 20 20 20 20 20 20
       20 20 20 20 20 20 20
       20 20 20 20 20 20 24
0727   52 65 73 65 72 76 65    AX29    DB      'Reserved                                      $'
       64 20 20 20 20 20 20
       20 20 20 20 20 20 20
       20 20 20 20 20 20 20
       20 20 20 20 20 20 20
       20 20 20 20 20 20 24
0751   52 65 73 65 72 76 65    AX2A    DB      'Reserved                                      $'
       64 20 20 20 20 20 20
       20 20 20 20 20 20 20
       20 20 20 20 20 20 20
       20 20 20 20 20 20 20
       20 20 20 20 20 20 24
077B   52 65 73 65 72 76 65    AX2B    DB      'Reserved                                      $'
       64 20 20 20 20 20 20
       20 20 20 20 20 20 20
       20 20 20 20 20 20 20
       20 20 20 20 20 20 20
       20 20 20 20 20 20 24
07A5   52 65 73 65 72 76 65    AX2C    DB      'Reserved                                      $'
       64 20 20 20 20 20 20
       20 20 20 20 20 20 20
       20 20 20 20 20 20 20
       20 20 20 20 20 20 20
       20 20 20 20 20 20 24
07CF   52 65 73 65 72 76 65    AX2D    DB      'Reserved                                      $'
       64 20 20 20 20 20 20
       20 20 20 20 20 20 20 20
       20 20 20 20 20 20 20
       20 20 20 20 20 20 20
       20 20 20 20 20 20 24
07F9   52 65 73 65 72 76 65    AX2E    DB      'Reserved                                      $'
       64 20 20 20 20 20 20
       20 20 20 20 20 20 20
       20 20 20 20 20 20 20
       20 20 20 20 20 20 20
       20 20 20 20 20 20 24
```

```
0823    52 65 73 65 72 76 65    AX2F    DB      'Reserved                                $'
        64 20 20 20 20 20 20
        20 20 20 20 20 20 20
        20 20 20 20 20 20 20
        20 20 20 20 20 20 20
        20 20 20 20 20 20 24
084D    52 65 73 65 72 76 65    AX30    DB      'Reserved                                $'
        64 20 20 20 20 20 20
        20 20 20 20 20 20 20
        20 20 20 20 20 20 20
        20 20 20 20 20 20 20
        20 20 20 20 20 20 24
0877    52 65 73 65 72 76 65    AX31    DB      'Reserved                                $'
        64 20 20 20 20 20 20
        20 20 20 20 20 20 20
        20 20 20 20 20 20 20
        20 20 20 20 20 20 20
        20 20 20 20 20 20 24
08A1    55 6E 73 75 70 70 6F    AX32    DB      'Unsupported network request             $'
        72 74 65 64 20 6E 65
        74 77 6F 72 6B 20 72
        65 71 75 65 73 74 20
        20 20 20 20 20 20 20
        20 20 20 20 20 20 24
08CB    52 65 6D 6F 74 65 20    AX33    DB      'Remote machine not listening            $'
        6D 61 63 68 69 6E 65
        20 6E 6F 74 20 6C 69
        73 74 65 6E 69 6E 67
        20 20 20 20 20 20 20
        20 20 20 20 20 20 24
08F5    44 75 70 6C 69 63 61    AX34    DB      'Duplicate name on network               $'
        74 65 20 6E 61 6D 65
        20 6F 6E 20 6E 65 74
        77 6F 72 6B 20 20 20
        20 20 20 20 20 20 20
        20 20 20 20 20 20 24
091F    4E 65 74 77 6F 72 6B    AX35    DB      'Network name not found                  $'
        20 6E 61 6D 65 20 6E
        6F 74 20 66 6F 75 6E
        64 20 20 20 20 20 20
        20 20 20 20 20 20 20
        20 20 20 20 20 20 24
0949    4E 65 74 77 6F 72 6B    AX36    DB      'Network busy                            $'
        20 62 75 73 79 20 20
        20 20 20 20 20 20 20
        20 20 20 20 20 20 20
        20 20 20 20 20 20 20
        20 20 20 20 20 20 24
0973    44 65 76 69 63 65 20    AX37    DB      'Device no longer exists on network      $'
        6E 6F 20 6C 6F 6E 67
        65 72 20 65 78 69 73
        74 73 20 6F 6E 20 6E
        65 74 77 6F 72 6B 20
        20 20 20 20 20 20 24
099D    4E 65 74 20 42 49 4F    AX38    DB      'Net BIOS command limit exceeded         $'
        53 20 63 6F 6D 6D 61
        6E 64 20 6C 69 6D 69
        74 20 65 78 63 65 65
        64 65 64 20 20 20 20
        20 20 20 20 20 20 24
09C7    45 72 72 6F 72 20 69    AX39    DB      'Error in network adapter hardware       $'
        6E 20 6E 65 74 77 6F
        72 6B 20 61 64 61 70
        74 65 72 20 68 61 72
        64 77 61 72 65 20 20
        20 20 20 20 20 20 24
09F1    49 6E 63 6F 72 72 65    AX3A    DB      'Incorrect response from network         $'
        63 74 20 72 65 73 70
```

Program 5-3 Continued.

```
        6F 6E 73 65 20 66 72
        6F 6D 20 6E 65 74 77
        6F 72 6B 20 20 20 20
        20 20 20 20 20 20 24
0A1B    55 6E 65 78 70 65 63    AX3B    DB    'Unexpected network error                $'
        74 65 64 20 6E 65 74
        77 6F 72 6B 20 65 72
        72 6F 72 20 20 20 20
        20 20 20 20 20 20 20
        20 20 20 20 20 20 24
0A45    52 65 6D 6F 74 65 20    AX3C    DB    'Remote adapt incompatible               $'
        61 64 61 70 74 20 69
        6E 63 6F 6D 70 61 74
        69 62 6C 65 20 20 20
        20 20 20 20 20 20 20
        20 20 20 20 20 20 24
0A6F    50 72 69 6E 74 20 71    AX3D    DB    'Print queue full                        $'
        75 65 75 65 20 66 75
        6C 6C 20 20 20 20 20
        20 20 20 20 20 20 20
        20 20 20 20 20 20 20
        20 20 20 20 20 20 24
0A99    51 75 65 75 65 20 6E    AX3E    DB    'Queue not full                          $'
        6F 74 20 66 75 6C 6C
        20 20 20 20 20 20 20
        20 20 20 20 20 20 20
        20 20 20 20 20 20 20
        20 20 20 20 20 20 24
0AC3    4E 6F 74 20 65 6E 6F    AX3F    DB    'Not enough room for print file          $'
        75 67 68 20 72 6F 6F
        6D 20 66 6F 72 20 70
        72 69 6E 74 20 66 69
        6C 65 20 20 20 20 20
        20 20 20 20 20 20 24
0AED    4E 65 74 77 6F 72 6B    AX40    DB    'Network name deleted                    $'
        20 6E 61 6D 65 20 64
        65 6C 65 74 65 64 20
        20 20 20 20 20 20 20
        20 20 20 20 20 20 20
        20 20 20 20 20 20 24
0B17    41 63 63 65 73 73 20    AX41    DB    'Access denied                           $'
        64 65 6E 69 65 64 20
        20 20 20 20 20 20 20
        20 20 20 20 20 20 20
        20 20 20 20 20 20 20
        20 20 20 20 20 20 24
0B41    49 6E 63 6F 72 72 65    AX42    DB    'Incorrect network device type           $'
        63 74 20 6E 65 74 77
        6F 72 6B 20 64 65 76
        69 63 65 20 74 79 70
        65 20 20 20 20 20 20
        20 20 20 20 20 20 24
0B6B    4E 65 74 77 6F 72 6B    AX43    DB    'Network name not found                  $'
        20 6E 61 6D 65 20 6E
        6F 74 20 66 6F 75 6E
        64 20 20 20 20 20 20
        20 20 20 20 20 20 20
        20 20 20 20 20 20 24
0B95    4E 65 74 77 6F 72 6B    AX44    DB    'Network name limit exceeded             $'
        20 6E 61 6D 65 20 6C
        69 6D 69 74 20 65 78
        63 65 65 64 65 64 20
        20 20 20 20 20 20 20
        20 20 20 20 20 20 24
0BBF    4E 65 74 20 42 49 4F    AX45    DB    'Net BIOS session limit exceeded         $'
        53 20 73 65 73 73 69
```

```
              6F 6E 20 6C 69 6D 69
              74 20 65 78 63 65 65
              64 65 64 20 20 20 20
              20 20 20 20 20 20 24
    0BE9      54 65 6D 70 6F 72 61      AX46    DB    'Temporary pause                        $'
              72 79 20 70 61 75 73
              65 20 20 20 20 20 20
              20 20 20 20 20 20 20
              20 20 20 20 20 20 20
              20 20 20 20 20 20 24
    0C13      4E 65 74 77 6F 72 6B      AX47    DB    'Network request not accepted           $'
              20 72 65 71 75 65 73
              74 20 6E 6F 74 20 61
              63 63 65 70 74 65 64
              20 20 20 20 20 20 20
              20 20 20 20 20 20 24
    0C3D      50 72 69 6E 74 20 6F      AX48    DB    'Print or disk redirection paused       $'
              72 20 64 69 73 6B 20
              72 65 64 69 72 65 63
              74 69 6F 6E 20 70 61
              75 73 65 64 20 20 20
              20 20 20 20 20 20 24
    0C67      52 65 73 65 72 76 65      AX49    DB    'Reserved                               $'
              64 20 20 20 20 20 20
              20 20 20 20 20 20 20
              20 20 20 20 20 20 20
              20 20 20 20 20 20 20
              20 20 20 20 20 20 24
    0C91      52 65 73 65 72 76 65      AX4A    DB    'Reserved                               $'
              64 20 20 20 20 20 20
              20 20 20 20 20 20 20
              20 20 20 20 20 20 20
              20 20 20 20 20 20 20
              20 20 20 20 20 20 24
    0CBB      52 65 73 65 72 76 65      AX4B    DB    'Reserved                               $'
              64 20 20 20 20 20 20
              20 20 20 20 20 20 20
              20 20 20 20 20 20 20
              20 20 20 20 20 20 20
              20 20 20 20 20 20 24
    0CE5      52 65 73 65 72 76 65      AX4C    DB    'Reserved                               $'
              64 20 20 20 20 20 20
              20 20 20 20 20 20 20
              20 20 20 20 20 20 20
              20 20 20 20 20 20 20
              20 20 20 20 20 20 24
    0D0F      52 65 73 65 72 76 65      AX4D    DB    'Reserved                               $'
              64 20 20 20 20 20 20
              20 20 20 20 20 20 20
              20 20 20 20 20 20 20
              20 20 20 20 20 20 20
              20 20 20 20 20 20 24
    0D39      52 65 73 65 72 76 65      AX4E    DB    'Reserved                               $'
              64 20 20 20 20 20 20
              20 20 20 20 20 20 20
              20 20 20 20 20 20 20
              20 20 20 20 20 20 20
              20 20 20 20 20 20 24
    0D63      52 65 73 65 72 76 65      AX4F    DB    'Reserved                               $'
              64 20 20 20 20 20 20
              20 20 20 20 20 20 20
              20 20 20 20 20 20 20
              20 20 20 20 20 20 20
              20 20 20 20 20 20 24
    0D8D      46 69 6C 65 20 61 6C      AX50    DB    'File already exists                    $'
              72 65 61 64 79 20 65
              78 69 73 74 73 20 20
              20 20 20 20 20 20 20
```

```
          20 20 20 20 20 20 20
          20 20 20 20 20 20 24
0DB7      52 65 73 65 72 76 65    AX51    DB      'Reserved                                        $'
          64 20 20 20 20 20 20
          20 20 20 20 20 20 20
          20 20 20 20 20 20 20
          20 20 20 20 20 20 20
          20 20 20 20 20 20 24
0DE1      43 61 6E 6E 6F 74 20    AX52    DB      'Cannot make directory                           $'
          6D 61 6B 65 20 64 69
          72 65 63 74 6F 72 79
          20 20 20 20 20 20 20
          20 20 20 20 20 20 20
          20 20 20 20 20 20 24
0E0B      46 61 69 6C 75 72 65    AX53    DB      'Failure on Interrupt 24h (Critical Error)$'
          20 6F 6E 20 49 6E 74
          65 72 72 75 70 74 20
          32 34 68 20 28 43 72
          69 74 69 63 61 6C 20
          45 72 72 6F 72 29 24
0E35      4F 75 74 20 6F 66 20    AX54    DB      'Out of structures                               $'
          73 74 72 75 63 74 75
          72 65 73 20 20 20 20
          20 20 20 20 20 20 20
          20 20 20 20 20 20 20
          20 20 20 20 20 20 24
0E5F      41 6C 72 65 61 64 79    AX55    DB      'Already assigned                                $'
          20 61 73 73 69 67 6E
          65 64 20 20 20 20 20
          20 20 20 20 20 20 20
          20 20 20 20 20 20 20
          20 20 20 20 20 20 24
0E89      49 6E 76 61 6C 69 64    AX56    DB      'Invalid password                                $'
          20 70 61 73 73 77 6F
          72 64 20 20 20 20 20
          20 20 20 20 20 20 20
          20 20 20 20 20 20 20
          20 20 20 20 20 20 24
0EB3      49 6E 76 61 6C 69 64    AX57    DB      'Invalid parameter                               $'
          20 70 61 72 61 6D 65
          74 65 72 20 20 20 20
          20 20 20 20 20 20 20
          20 20 20 20 20 20 20
          20 20 20 20 20 20 24
0EDD      4E 65 74 20 77 72 69    AX58    DB      'Net write fault                                 $'
          74 65 20 66 61 75 6C
          74 20 20 20 20 20 20
          20 20 20 20 20 20 20
          20 20 20 20 20 20 20
          20 20 20 20 20 20 24

                                  ;
                                  ; BH = Error Class
                                  ;
0F07      4F 75 74 20 6F 66 20    BH01    DB      'Out of resource (such as storage)               $'
          72 65 73 6F 75 72 63
          65 20 28 73 75 63 68
          20 61 73 20 73 74 6F
          72 61 67 65 29 20 20
          20 20 20 20 20 20 20
          20 20 20 20 20 20 20
          24
0F39      54 65 6D 70 6F 72 61    BH02    DB      'Temporary situation, will end, not an error     $'
          72 79 20 73 69 74 75
          61 74 69 6F 6E 2C 20
          77 69 6C 6C 20 65 6E
          64 2C 20 6E 6F 74 20
```

```
           61 6E 20 65 72 72 6F
           72 20 20 20 20 20 20
           24
    0F6B   41 75 74 68 6F 72 69    BH03    DB     'Authorization problem                          $'
           7A 61 74 69 6F 6E 20
           70 72 6F 62 6C 65 6D
           20 20 20 20 20 20 20
           20 20 20 20 20 20 20
           20 20 20 20 20 20 20
           20 20 20 20 20 20 20
           24
    0F9D   49 6E 74 65 72 6E 61    BH04    DB     'Internal error in system hardware              $'
           6C 20 65 72 72 6F 72
           20 69 6E 20 73 79 73
           74 65 6D 20 68 61 72
           64 77 61 72 65 20 20
           20 20 20 20 20 20 20
           20 20 20 20 20 20 20
           24
    0FCF   48 61 72 64 77 61 72    BH05    DB     'Hardware failure                               $'
           65 20 66 61 69 6C 75
           72 65 20 20 20 20 20
           20 20 20 20 20 20 20
           20 20 20 20 20 20 20
           20 20 20 20 20 20 20
           20 20 20 20 20 20 20
           24
    1001   53 79 73 74 65 6D 20    BH06    DB     'System software failure, not active process fault$'
           73 6F 66 74 77 61 72
           65 20 66 61 69 6C 75
           72 65 2C 20 6E 6F 74
           20 61 63 74 69 76 65
           20 70 72 6F 63 65 73
           73 20 66 61 75 6C 74
           24
    1033   41 70 70 6C 69 63 61    BH07    DB     'Application program error                      $'
           74 69 6F 6E 20 70 72
           6F 67 72 61 6D 20 65
           72 72 6F 72 20 20 20
           20 20 20 20 20 20 20
           20 20 20 20 20 20 20
           20 20 20 20 20 20 20
           24
    1065   46 69 6C 65 20 6F 72    BH08    DB     'File or item not found                         $'
           20 69 74 65 6D 20 6E
           6F 74 20 66 6F 75 6E
           64 20 20 20 20 20 20
           20 20 20 20 20 20 20
           20 20 20 20 20 20 20
           20 20 20 20 20 20 20
           24
    1097   46 69 6C 65 2F 69 74    BH09    DB     'File/item an invalid format/type or unsuitable $'
           65 6D 20 61 6E 20 69
           6E 76 61 6C 69 64 20
           66 6F 72 6D 61 74 2F
           74 79 70 65 20 6F 72
           20 75 6E 73 75 69 74
           61 62 6C 65 20 20 20
           24
    10C9   46 69 6C 65 20 6F 72    BH0A    DB     'File or item interlocked                       $'
           20 69 74 65 6D 20 69
           6E 74 65 72 6C 6F 63
           6B 65 64 20 20 20 20
           20 20 20 20 20 20 20
           20 20 20 20 20 20 20
           20 20 20 20 20 20 20
           24
    10FB   44 72 69 76 65 20 68    BH0B    DB 'Drive has wrong disk or storage medium problem   $'
```

Program 5-3 Continued.

```
         61 73 20 77 72 6F 6E
         67 20 64 69 73 6B 20
         6F 72 20 73 74 6F 72
         61 67 65 20 6D 65 64
         69 75 6D 20 70 72 6F
         62 6C 65 6D 20 20 20
         24
112D     41 6C 72 65 61 64 79   BH0C    DB  'Already exists                              $'
         20 65 78 69 73 74 73
         20 20 20 20 20 20 20
         20 20 20 20 20 20 20
         20 20 20 20 20 20 20
         20 20 20 20 20 20 20
         20 20 20 20 20 20 20
         24
115F     55 6E 6B 6E 6F 77 6E   BH0D    DB  'Unknown                                     $'
         20 20 20 20 20 20 20
         20 20 20 20 20 20 20
         20 20 20 20 20 20 20
         20 20 20 20 20 20 20
         20 20 20 20 20 20 20
         20 20 20 20 20 20 20
         24

                                 ;
                                 ; BL = Suggested action
                                 ;
1191     52 65 74 72 79 20 62   BL01    DB  'Retry before prompting user to Abort or Ignore
         65 66 6F 72 65 20 70
         72 6F 6D 70 74 69 6E
         67 20 75 73 65 72 20
         74 6F 20 41 62 6F 72
         74 20 6F 72 20 49 67
         6E 6F 72 65 20 20 20
         20 20 20 20 20 20 20
         20 20 24
11CC     52 65 74 72 79 20 77   BL02    DB  'Retry with pause before prompt to user to Abort or Ignore $'
         69 74 68 20 70 61 75
         73 65 20 62 65 66 6F
         72 65 20 70 72 6F 6D
         70 74 20 74 6F 20 75
         73 65 72 20 74 6F 20
         41 62 6F 72 74 20 6F
         72 20 49 67 6E 6F 72
         65 20 24
1207     50 72 6F 6D 70 74 20   BL03    DB  'Prompt user to enter corrected information           $'
         75 73 65 72 20 74 6F
         20 65 6E 74 65 72 20
         63 6F 72 72 65 63 74
         65 64 20 69 6E 66 6F
         72 6D 61 74 69 6F 6E
         20 20 20 20 20 20 20
         20 20 20 20 20 20 20
         20 20 24
1242     43 6C 65 61 6E 20 75   BL04    DB  'Clean up and exit the application              $'
         70 20 61 6E 64 20 65
         78 69 74 20 74 68 65
         20 61 70 70 6C 69 63
         61 74 69 6F 6E 20 20
         20 20 20 20 20 20 20
         20 20 20 20 20 20 20
         20 20 20 20 20 20 20
         20 20 24
127D     45 78 69 74 20 69 6D   BL05    DB  'Exit immediately without cleanup               $'
         6D 65 64 69 61 74 65
```

```
        6C 79 20 77 69 74 68
        6F 75 74 20 63 6C 65
        61 6E 75 70 20 20 20
        20 20 20 20 20 20 20
        20 20 20 20 20 20 20
        20 20 20 20 20 20 20
        20 20 24
12B8    49 67 6E 6F 72 65 20  BL06    DB      'Ignore - informational error                              $'
        2D 20 69 6E 66 6F 72
        6D 61 74 69 6F 6E 61
        6C 20 65 72 72 6F 72
        20 20 20 20 20 20 20
        20 20 20 20 20 20 20
        20 20 20 20 20 20 20
        20 20 20 20 20 20 20
        20 20 24
12F3    50 72 6F 6D 70 74 20  BL07    DB      'Prompt user to correct error (like change disk) then retry$'
        75 73 65 72 20 74 6F
        20 63 6F 72 72 65 63
        74 20 65 72 72 6F 72
        20 28 6C 69 6B 65 20
        63 68 61 6E 67 65 20
        64 69 73 6B 29 20 74
        68 65 6E 20 72 65 74
        72 79 24
                              ;
                              ; CH = Location of error
                              ;
132E    55 6E 6B 6E 6F 77 6E  CH01    DB      'Unknown      $'
        20 20 20 20 20 20 20
        24
133D    42 6C 6F 63 6B 20 64  CH02    DB      'Block device $'
        65 76 69 63 65 20 20
        24
134C    4E 65 74 77 6F 72 6B  CH03    DB      'Network      $'
        20 20 20 20 20 20 20
        24
135B    53 65 72 69 61 6C 20  CH04    DB      'Serial device $'
        64 65 76 69 63 65 20
        24
136A    4D 65 6D 6F 72 79 20  CH05    DB      'Memory related$'
        72 65 6C 61 74 65 64
        24
                              ;
                              ;
1379                         BEGINHERE:
1379    60                            PUSHA                    ; Save all registers
137A    8D 16 006A R                  LEA     DX,CR_LF         ; Space error away
137E    B4 09                         MOV     AH,9
1380    CD 21                         INT     21h
                              ;
1382    8D 16 0003 R                  LEA     DX,HEADER
1386    B4 09                         MOV     AH,9
1388    CD 21                         INT     21h
                              ;
138A    8D 16 0012 R                  LEA     DX,CODES
138E    B4 09                         MOV     AH,9
1390    CD 21                         INT     21h
                              ;
1392    BB 0000                       MOV     BX,00            ; Zero out BX
1395    B4 59                         MOV     AH,59h
1397    CD 21                         INT     21h
                              ;
                              ; Print the AX message
                              ;   AX = Extended error code
                              ;
```

```
1399  87 CD                XCHG    CX,BP          ; Save CX (the error location)
139B  2B C9                SUB     CX,CX          ; Use CX for multiplication
139D  B1 2A                MOV     CL,42          ; Each AX message is 42 bytes
139F  F7 E1                MUL     CX             ; Mul AX x CX, result in AX
13A1  8D 16 006D R         LEA     DX,AX00        ; Point to beginning of AX messages
13A5  03 D0                ADD     DX,AX          ; Point at correct message
13A7  B4 09                MOV     AH,9           ; Now print AX message
13A9  CD 21                INT     21h
                           ;
                           ; Print the BH Error Class message
                           ;   BH = Error class
                           ;
13AB  8D 16 0028 R         LEA     DX,CLASS       ; Print the "prefix"
13AF  B4 09                MOV     AH,9
13B1  CD 21                INT     21h
                           ;
13B3  2B C0                SUB     AX,AX
13B5  8A C7                MOV     AL,BH          ; Error class
13B7  2B C9                SUB     CX,CX          ; Use CX for multiplication
13B9  B1 32                MOV     CL,50          ; Each BH message is 50 bytes
13BB  F7 E1                MUL     CX             ; Mul AX x CX, result in AX
13BD  8D 16 0F07 R         LEA     DX,BH01        ; Point to beginning of BH messages
13C1  03 D0                ADD     DX,AX          ; Point at correct message
13C3  83 EA 32             SUB     DX,50          ; Correct position
13C6  B4 09                MOV     AH,9           ; Now print AX message
13C8  CD 21                INT     21h
                           ;
                           ; Print the BL Suggested Action message
                           ;   BL = Suggested action
                           ;
13CA  8D 16 003E R         LEA     DX,ACTION      ; Print the "prefix"
13CE  B4 09                MOV     AH,9
13D0  CD 21                INT     21h
                           ;
13D2  2B C0                SUB     AX,AX
13D4  8A C3                MOV     AL,BL          ; Suggested Action
13D6  2B C9                SUB     CX,CX          ; Use CX for multiplication
13D8  B1 3B                MOV     CL,59          ; Each BL message is 59 bytes
13DA  F7 E1                MUL     CX             ; Mul AX x CX, result in AX
13DC  8D 16 1191 R         LEA     DX,BL01        ; Point to beginning of BL messages
13E0  03 D0                ADD     DX,AX          ; Point at correct message
13E2  83 EA 3B             SUB     DX,59
13E5  B4 09                MOV     AH,9           ; Now print AX message
13E7  CD 21                INT     21h
                           ;
                           ; Print the CX Location message
                           ;   CH = Location of error
                           ;
13E9  8D 16 0054 R         LEA     DX,LOCATION    ; Print the "prefix"
13ED  B4 09                MOV     AH,9
13EF  CD 21                INT     21h
                           ;
13F1  87 CD                XCHG    CX,BP          ; Retrieve the location
13F3  2B C0                SUB     AX,AX
13F5  8A C5                MOV     AL,CH          ; Location
13F7  2B C9                SUB     CX,CX          ; Use CX for multiplication
13F9  B1 0F                MOV     CL,15          ; Each CH message is 15 bytes
13FB  F7 E1                MUL     CX             ; Mul AX x CL, result in AX
13FD  8D 16 132E R         LEA     DX,CH01        ; Point to beginning of CH messages
1401  03 D0                ADD     DX,AX          ; Point at correct message
1403  83 EA 0F             SUB     DX,15          ; Correct position
1406  B4 09                MOV     AH,9           ; Now print AX message
1408  CD 21                INT     21h
                           ;
                           ;
```

```
140A   8D 16 006A R                    LEA     DX,CR_LF        ; Space errors
140E   B4 09                           MOV     AH,9
1410   CD 21                           INT     21h
                              ;
1412   61                              POPA                    ; Retrieve all registers
1413   C3                              RET
1414                 EXTERROR          ENDP
1414                 CODE              ENDS
                                       END
```

6
Bit and string manipulation

Bit manipulation is important for system control, such as for modifying bitmaps and semaphores. For example, each bit in a bitmap can represent a pixel—each dot on the display—and you might want to turn the bits on and off. You might also need to know the status of a bit that keeps track of whether an overflow has occurred. That bit is called a signal flag or semaphore. When you use a semaphore, the bit is either set (ON = 1) when busy or reset (OFF = 0) when free.

Register bytes, words, and doublewords are actually templates for other objects, each with its own meaning. Each bit in the register can have a separate meaning, such as each bit in the EFLAGS register (see appendix B for a detailed format of EFLAGS). The 80486 accesses each individual bit: reads it, writes it, or tests it.

80486 bit manipulation instructions

Simply, the 80486 bit manipulation instructions manipulate bit patterns within registers and memory locations. The instructions divide into three groups: logical, shift, and rotate.

Logical bit manipulation

Logical instructions follow rules of Boolean logic. That is, each bit of an operand is operated on with its corresponding bit in the second operand without consideration of other bit positions. To use this logic, assembly language uses the AND, OR, XOR, NOT, and TEST instructions. See Fig. 6-1 for an overview of the results of these instructions.

	AND	OR	XOR	NOT	TEST
Operand 1	1010	1010	1010	1010	1010
Operand 2	0111	1100	1110		0111
Result	0010	1110	0100	0101	1010
Flags Modified	SF ZF PF	SF ZF PF	SF ZF PF	SF ZF PF	SF ZF PF
Flags Reset	OF CF	OF CF	OF CF	OF CF	OF CF

CF   Carry Flag—Set on high-order bit carry or borrow.

PF   Parity Flag—Set if low-order 8 bits of result contain an even number of 1 bits; cleared otherwise.

AF   Adjust Flag—Set on carry from or borrow to the low order 4 bits of AL; cleared otherwise.

ZF   Zero Flag—Set if result is 0; cleared otherwise.

SF   Sign Flag—Set if high-order bit of result is 0 = positive, 1 = negative.

OF   Overflow Flag—Set if result is too large a positive number or too small a negative number (excluding the sign-bit) to fit in the destination operand; cleared otherwise.

6-1   Overview of AND, OR, XOR, NOT, and TEST.

Any bit ANDed with 0 is set to 0, while any bit ANDed with 1 retains its original value. OR, on the other hand, is used to force specific bits to 1. The OR instruction checks bits in each position of the operands. If either or both bits are 1, OR forces the destination to be a 1. The exclusive-OR (XOR) also checks each bit position of the operands. XOR sets a 1 in the destination operand for every bit position in which the operands differ. Where one operand has a 0 and the other has a 1, XOR sets a 1 in the destination; it sets 0 if they are the same.

NOT reverses the setting of each bit in a register or memory location. It effectively does a one's complement. However, NOT has no effect on the flags. TEST does an AND of its operands but only changes the flags, not the contents of the operands.

Bit scanning

Instructions such as Bit Scan Forward (BSF) and Bit Scan Reverse (BSR) work only on 16-bit or 32-bit registers. They cannot be used on memory operands or 8-bit registers. The source register (the first operand in the instruction) contains the value to be scanned. The destination register is set to the number of the position of the first or last set bit. See Fig. 6-2 for bit scanning examples.

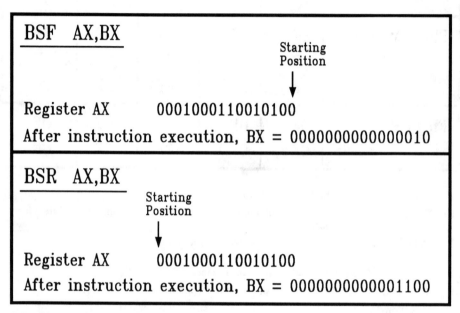

6-2 Bit scanning examples.

BSF scans the bits of the source register starting with the 0 bit (the rightmost bit) and works toward the most significant bit (MSB), the left-most bit. BSR works just the opposite; it scans the bits in the source register starting with the MSB and going toward the 0 bit.

Shift and rotate

The shift and rotate instructions have been with the Intel family of chips since the 8086. Bits can be moved left (toward the most significant bit, MSB) or right (toward 0). Values that shift off the end go into the Carry Flag (CF). See Fig. 6-3 for examples of how shifts and rotates move in and out of CF.

The shift instructions move the bits whatever number of positions you tell them to. The last bit in the direction of the shift "falls off" (actually it goes into CF). The first bit is then filled with 0 or with the value of the preceding first bit. Rotate moves bits in a circle. The specified number of

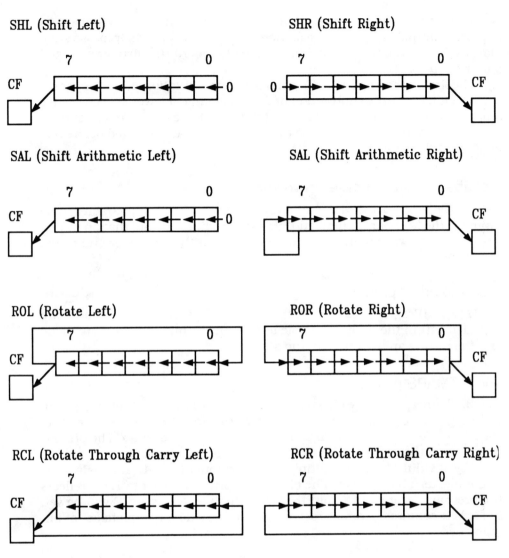

6-3 Examples of shifts and rotates, using the Carry Flag (CF).

places move to the right or left as you code. For each bit rotated, the last bit in the direction of the rotate moves into the first bit position at the other end of the operand. See appendix C for a complete description of each instruction used in the 80486.

Bit manipulation programs

Bitmaps are often used to store information about a set of items that can be mapped to integers, e.g., the sectors on a disk. If done, the in-use state of each sector would be recorded in a bitmap (1 = available, 0 = in-use). As another example, 4K pages of real memory can also have their in-use state mapped by a bitmap. A second bitmap could record the dirty or changed bit for the page.

The first program, CAP_IT, is not a bit manipulation program per se, because it is a simple subtraction of 20h to change a lowercase character into an uppercase character. The program does logically fit here, however, because no matter how simplistic the case, the bits are changed before displaying on the screen.

Alphabetic character case conversion

CAP-IT (Program 6-1 at the end of the chapter) asks for a character to be input via the keyboard. Then it does a simple edit to be sure that an uppercase character was entered. It subtracts 20 from the character and prints the result.

A bitmap driver program

BITMAPDV (Program 6-2) drives the BITMAPS procedure. All inputs are provided within the program. Basic tests of the bitmap routines are made and the results are reported on the screen.

The BITMAPS procedure

The BITMAPS procedure (Program 6-3) provides a means of setting a bit in a bitmap that corresponds to the number provided. AX has the number of the bit to be set, changed from 0 to 1. BX points at the bitmap. The process is to convert the number into a doubleword (dword) displacement into the map by dividing by 32, multiplying the quotient by 4, and using the remainder as a bit number. The bit in the word is then set to 1. CF reflects the previous setting of the bit; that is, if the bit was zero, CF will be set. BITMAPS contains several procedures that provide a complete set of bitmap operations:

- BITMAPR provides a means of clearing a bit in a bitmap that corresponds to the number provided. AX has the number of the bit to be reset (changed from 1 to 0). BX points to the bitmap. The process is to convert the number into a doubleword displacement into the map by dividing by 32, multiplying the quotient by 4, and using the remainder as a bit number. The bit in the word is then set to 0. Carry reflects the previous setting of the bit.
- BITMAPT provides a means of testing a bit in a bitmap that corresponds to the number provided. AX has the number of the bit to be tested and BX points to the bitmap. The process is to convert the number into a doubleword displacement into the map by dividing by 32, multiplying the quotient by 4, and using the remainder as a

bit number. The bit in the word is then tested. CF reflects the setting of the bit.

- BITMAPL provides a means of locating the first 1 bit in a bitmap. BX points to the bitmap and CX has the number of doublewords in the map. The process is to scan the bitmap for a doubleword which is non-zero. The word is then scanned for the first 1 bit. A bit number is returned as doubleword number * 32, plus the bit number.

Note: Doublewords are numbered from zero. If the bit is located, its number will be in AX and Carry will be reset (CF = 0). If the map is empty, AX is undefined and Carry is set (CF = 1).

Manipulating EFLAGS bits

EFLAGSCH (Program 6-4) demonstrates the bit test and complement instruction. EFLAGSCH captures the bit flags in the EFLAGS register and allows a change. EFLAGSCH prints a menu of items to be changed and prints EFLAGS before the change. The flag to change is entered via the keyboard. It is estimated that this program in its current form will not work under OS/2 in protected mode. You could cause it to get the lower 16 bits, called FLAGS, which would work in protected mode.

String manipulation

The word *string* generally refers to a sequence of characters. The usage is analogous to physical objects strung together, one after another, such as a string of beads. As we look at them, strings are typically written from left to right. Thus, XYZ is a string of three characters, the first being X and the last being Z. In principle, strings may be arbitrarily any length, but there are always restrictions in practice.

Two strings joined together form another string that is the result of the joining. Appending (one way to join strings) one string to another is called *concatenation*. A *null string* contains no characters and is important because it is the identity with respect to concatenation. Note that concatenating the null string onto a second string does not change either string. A sequence of consecutive characters within a string is a *substring*. Thus, MAC is a substring of MACRO, but MC is not.

Almost all computer input and output consists of strings, including programs and data. One important aspect of strings is the characters they may contain. This is determined by the character set of the computer on which the string is represented. Character sets differ in specific characters, the number of characters they contain, and the order in which they are arranged. (Most common are ASCII and EBCDIC.)

Characters arranged in order of their internal numerical representation are said to be in *collating sequence* or *lexical order*. For letters, this order corresponds to ordinary alphabetical order. Note that in ASCII the digits come before the letters, while in EBCDIC the converse is true. The lexical order extends to strings, which allows strings to be compared lexically (for their relative alphabetical order). This comparison is the basis for string sorting.

To sort strings, the leftmost character in the string is the most significant one for the purposes of determining lexical order; the next character is the second most important, and so on. Characters, digits, and special characters all can be sorted.

A *graphic* is the printed representation of a character, and one character set can differ widely from another character set in their individual printed representations, especially of special characters. The character sets sometimes vary for other characters, depending on the printer or printing device and the representation chosen (generally several character sets are built into laser printers as internal fonts). Not all characters have graphics, the blank for example. In addition, there are characters that perform control functions, such as Line Feed and Tab, which affect the behavior of the output device.

String operations

There were no generally agreed-upon string operations when string processing was first developed. However, four operations have now achieved general acceptance: concatenation, identification of substrings, pattern matching, and transformation of strings to replace identified substrings by other strings.

Concatenation is the process of appending one string to another to produce a longer string. The result of concatenating the string XYZ to ABC is the string ABCXYZ. This operation is the natural extension of the idea of a string as a sequence of characters. Substring is a string within another string, where DEF is a substring of CDEFGH. *Pattern matching* is the most important and far-reaching string operation. It is the process of examining a string to locate substrings or to determine if a string has certain properties. Transformation typically is accomplished in conjunction with pattern matching and uses the results of matching to effect a replacement of substrings. Figure 6-4 shows examples of these four generic types of string operations.

80486 string instructions

80486 string instructions operate on blocks of consecutive bytes or words in memory. These strings can consist of either text characters or numeric values and can be up to 4Gb long (using ECX). There are seven types of 80486 string instructions: input, output, compare, scan, load, move, and store.

After the string instruction operates, the pointer moves either higher or lower in memory. Its direction is set by use of the Direction Flag (DF) in

Operation	Logical Instruction	Result
Concatenation (Appending)	Concatenate 1,2	AAAA000AXXXX
Substring	Place 2 inside 1 beginning with position 3	AAXXXXAA000A
Pattern Matching	Find String 3 inside String 1	AAAA000A ↑ Position 5
Transformation	Find String 3 inside String 1 and replace with 3 bytes of String 2	AAAA000A ↑ Find it at Position 5 Then make it into: AAAAXXXA

Where: String 1 = AAAA000A
String 2 = XXXX
String 3 = 000

6-4   Generic string manipulation examples.

EFLAGS, which is set by using the Set Direction Flag (STD) or Clear Direction Flag (CLD) instructions. If DF=0, the pointer increases (moves upward to the next element). IF DF=1, it decreases (moves downward to the previous element). See Fig. 6-5 and Fig. 6-6 for examples of direction and repetition.

String search routines

String instructions can operate on a series of elements. To do this, use the repeat prefix (REP). The 80486 then repeats the instruction based on a count you move into the CX register. On each iteration of the string instruction, the 80486 decrements the count by one. There are two additional aids in the REP prefix. They involve the Zero Flag (ZF), but can be used only with Scan String (SCAS) and Compare String (CMPS). Repeat

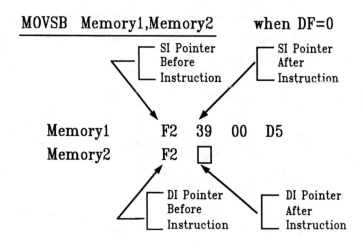

MOVSB Memory1,Memory2   when DF=0

Memory1   F2   39   00   D5
Memory2   F2   ☐

SI Pointer Before Instruction

SI Pointer After Instruction

DI Pointer Before Instruction

DI Pointer After Instruction

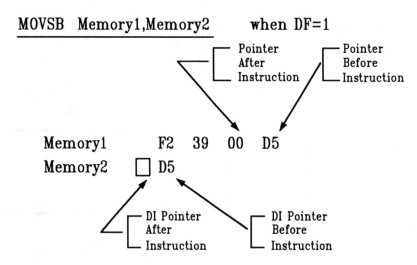

MOVSB Memory1,Memory2   when DF=1

Memory1   F2   39   00   D5
Memory2   ☐   D5

Pointer After Instruction

Pointer Before Instruction

DI Pointer After Instruction

DI Pointer Before Instruction

6-5 Examples of a string move with the Direction Flag (DF) set.

While Not Equal (REPNE) repeats the instruction as long as ZF is 0 and CX is not 0. Repeat While Equal (REPE) repeats as long as ZF is 1 and CX is not 0.

Searching for substrings

Searching for substrings, STRSRCH (Program 6-5), searches for the first occurrence of a specified substring within another given string. If the substring is found, the starting location (byte) returns in register DX.

A target string of some length is offered and its length in bytes determined. A second string is specified, with its length. The strings are checked for simple validity—was anything entered in each and was the

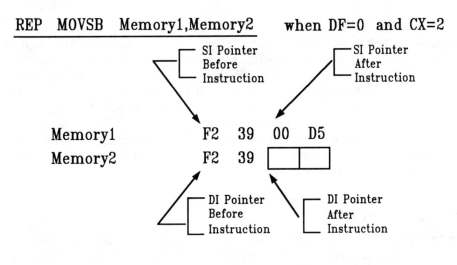

REP MOVSB Memory1,Memory2   when DF=0 and CX=2

SI Pointer Before Instruction

SI Pointer After Instruction

Memory1   F2 39 00 D5
Memory2   F2 39 ☐☐

DI Pointer Before Instruction

DI Pointer After Instruction

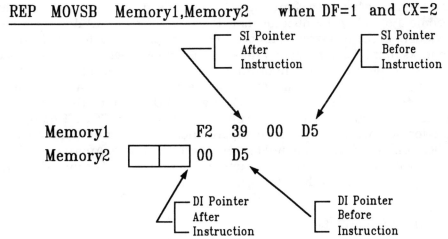

REP MOVSB Memory1,Memory2   when DF=1 and CX=2

SI Pointer After Instruction

SI Pointer Before Instruction

Memory1   F2 39 00 D5
Memory2   ☐☐ 00 D5

DI Pointer After Instruction

DI Pointer Before Instruction

6-6 Example of a string move with direction set and the REP prefix used.

search string longer than the target string? If the strings pass, go to search. If not, an error message is written, DX set to 0, and the program ended. To print the byte, the external procedure CODEBAS is called. (See chapter 7 for a description of CODEBAS.) CODEBAS turns binary characters into printable ASCII.

Inserting substrings

Inserting substrings, STRINSRT (Program 6-6), asks for a target string to be input from the keyboard. Then it asks for a second string to insert into the target and the position in the target string in which to insert the second string. Notice the compactness of the code that does the actual insert—no more than 14 instructions.

Working with strings

Working with strings, STRWORKS (Program 6-7), demonstrates the shell-sort algorithm, as demonstrated in the procedure SHELLSRT (described in chapter 9). It requests a series of variable-length alphabetic words (not to be confused with computer memory words) until the user inputs a null string (carriage return). STRWORKS forces them to an ASCIIZ strings and puts them into preallocated memory area, one right after another, and builds an array of displacements. After the null entry is entered, the array of displacements are passed to SHELLSRT. The strings are sorted and, once finished, printed out in sequence.

Comparing two strings

Comparing two strings, STRZCOMP (Program 6-8), compares two ASCIIZ strings and returns the resulting condition code flags. ASCIIZ (with its hex 00 terminating byte) is a common string form used by C programs and has become a standard because of that. Because STRZCOMP doesn't know the length of the two strings, it does a compare on each byte and, if equal, it checks that it hasn't reached the terminator. Otherwise, it terminates if the two strings are equivalent down to some point and one string is longer, the longer string will be considered the greater in the comparison.

DS:SI contains the address of String1. ES:DI contains the address of String2. The comparison is String1 minus String2. STRZCOMP compares byte for byte with each equal compare checked for a null (end-of-string indicator). An unequal or a null terminates the compare. Appropriate flags are set with the result of the subtraction of String2 from String1. Only the flags are set, with no other change.

Determining string length

Determining string length, STRZLNG (Program 6-9), finds the length of an ASCIIZ string. ES:DI points to the string to examine and CX has the maximum length to examine. The registers are set for a repeated SCASB. The length of the string is scanned, excluding the null (hex 00) that ends the string. On return, AX has the count of bytes in the string, excluding the null. Carry is reset if the null was found. Otherwise, Carry is set to 1 and AX is returned equal to the input CX value.

String parsing routines

Parsing is the process by which the phrases in a string of characters are associated with the component names of the grammar that generated the string. Parsing is the heart of the compilation process of source programs in a high-level language into machine language. The compiler must take the string of characters written by the programmer and associate appropriate substrings of characters with the syntactic components of the high-level language in order to determine the structure of the given program so that it can be translated into machine code.

Parsing is also important when editing input from a keyboard and to fill in the blanks; that is, to separate pieces of input and assign them to variables or fields which the program needs to process data.

In the program shown in this section, the procedure parses input text into a token that it returns to the driver. We decided to run parsing from a driver to allow you to enter a string of characters, special characters, blanks, and so on, from a keyboard and watch the output. The parsing routine uses punctuation and blanks to recognize the division between tokens. Note that if you enter a $, the parser quits scanning. This is because INT 21 Function 9 is used to read in the keyboard input; this function recognizes $ as the end of a string.

A parsing driver

PARSEDRV (Program 6-10) provides a test for the parser, PARSING, and an example of its use. The program prompts for a line to be parsed and reads the input from the keyboard. The input is passed to PARSING until an end-of-data token is returned. Each token is displayed as it is returned. At end-of-data, another line of input is requested. If a null line (Enter only is pressed) comes in, the program terminates.

A string parsing program

PARSING (Program 6-11) is an example of how you might want to write a parser. PARSING parses input text into tokens and returns them to the driving process. It demonstrates many of the standard operations in a parsing routine: skips leading spaces, checks for end of text string, identifies the types of input (numeric, alphabetic), and so on.

If a number is encountered, PARSING verifies that the following non-space, non-punctuation is also a number. It repeats until a proper end is detected and returns the number token. If an unknown character is encountered, it scans until a space or punctuation is detected to identify the unknown token's size and return as an unknown. If the non-blank is a capital letter, PARSING potentially identifies the token as a capitalized word. If lowercase, it potentially identifies the token as a lowercase word. In either alphabetic case, check the following characters for either lowercase letters or a proper ending (spaces or punctuation). If a non-space is a punctuation mark, PARSING returns the proper token type.

PARSING reads the string of characters in the input string that the DRIVER passes to it. It divides the input string into tokens and prints them back with a code that identifies it as:

Cwd	Capitalized word
Lwd	Lowercase word

Nbr	Number
Per	Period
Com	Comma
Exc	Exclamation point
Qmk	Question mark
Unk	Unknown

Program 6-1 CAP__IT

Microsoft (R) Macro Assembler Version 5.00

```
                                    PAGE    55,132
                                    .386
0000                        STACK   SEGMENT 'STACK' STACK
0000   0064[                        DW      100 DUP(?)
         ????
                        ]

00C8                        STACK   ENDS
0000                        CODE    SEGMENT para 'CODE' PUBLIC
                                    ASSUME  CS:CODE, DS:CODE, SS:STACK
                            ;
                            ; Name:      CAP_IT
                            ;
                            ; Purpose:   This program reads in a character from the keyboard
                            ;            and, if it is a lower case character, converts it to
                            ;            upper case.
                            ;
                            ; Inputs:    A character from the keyboard.
                            ;
                            ; Process:   Since the ASCII representation of a lower-case character
                            ;            is 20h greater than a capital letter, the character is
                            ;            read in, checked to see that it is an alphabetic character
                            ;            between "a" and "z", then 20h is subtracted from it and
                            ;            it is printed.
                            ;
                            ; Outputs:   Error message if a non-lowercase alpha character is typed.
                            ;            If the input character is lower case alphabetic character,
                            ;            it's capitalized and printed back to the screen.
                            ;
0000                        CAP_IT:
0000   66| 8C C8                    MOV     AX,CS           ; Prepare to set DS
0003   66| 8E D8                    MOV     DS,AX           ;   and set it.
0006   E9 0000008B R                JMP     BEGINHERE
                            ;
000B   20 2D 20 4E 6F 74 20 NOT_ALPHA   DB      ' - Not a lower-case alpha character.',0Ah,0Dh,'$'
       61 20 6C 6F 77 65 72
       2D 63 61 73 65 20 61
       6C 70 68 61 20 63 68
       61 72 61 63 74 65 72
       2E 0A 0D 24
0032   20 20 20 20 20 20 20 NOT_2ND     DB                          Re-enter.',0Ah,0Dh,'$'
       20 20 20 20 20 20 20
       20 20 20 20 20 20 20
       20 20 20 52 65 2D 65
       6E 74 65 72 2E 0A 0D
       24
0056   45 6E 74 65 72 20 61 PROMPT      DB      'Enter a character > $'
       20 63 68 61 72 61 63
       74 65 72 20 3E 20 24
006B   54 68 65 20 63 61 70 CAPS        DB      'The capitalized character = $'
       69 74 61 6C 69 7A 65 64
```

128   Bit and string manipulation

```
       64 20 63 68 61 72 61
       63 74 65 72 20 3D 20
       24
0088   0A 0D 24              CR_LF        DB      0Ah,0Dh,'$'
                             ;
008B                        BEGINHERE:
008B   8D 15 00000056 R                  LEA     DX,PROMPT      ; Print prompt
0091   B4 09                             MOV     AH,9
0093   CD 21                             INT     21h
0095   B4 01                             MOV     AH,1           ; Read in the character
0097   CD 21                             INT     21h
                             ;
0099   3C 60                             CMP     AL,60h         ; See what input char was
009B   0F 8E 000000CC R                  JLE     OOPS           ; Less than an "a"?
00A1   3C 7B                             CMP     AL,7Bh         ; Past a "z"?
00A3   0F 8D 000000CC R                  JGE     OOPS
                             ;
00A9   2C 20                             SUB     AL,20h         ; Lower case, so subtract to upper
00AB   8A C8                             MOV     CL,AL          ; Save character
                             ;
                             ;          Go to new line on screen
                             ;
00AD   8D 15 00000088 R                  LEA     DX,CR_LF       ; Carriage Ret/Line Feed
00B3   B4 09                             MOV     AH,9
00B5   CD 21                             INT     21h
00B7   8D 15 0000006B R                  LEA     DX,CAPS        ; Print message
00BD   B4 09                             MOV     AH,9
00BF   CD 21                             INT     21h
                             ;
00C1   8A D1                             MOV     DL,CL          ; Move char to DL & Print
00C3   B4 02                             MOV     AH,2
00C5   CD 21                             INT     21h
00C7   EB 17 90 90 90                    JMP     ENDHERE
                             ;
00CC                        OOPS:
00CC   8D 15 0000000B R                  LEA     DX,NOT_ALPHA ; Print error and go get char
00D2   B4 09                             MOV     AH,9
00D4   CD 21                             INT     21h
00D6   8D 15 00000032 R                  LEA     DX,NOT_2ND
00DC   CD 21                             INT     21h
00DE   EB AB                             JMP     BEGINHERE
                             ;
00E0                        ENDHERE:
00E0   B4 4C                             MOV     AH,4Ch         ; Standard Ending
00E2   CD 21                             INT     21h
00E4                        CODE         ENDS
                                         END     CAP_IT
```

Program 6-2 BITMAPDV

Microsoft (R) Macro Assembler Version 5.00

```
                        PAGE    55,132
                        .386
                ;
                ; Name:    BITMAPDV
                ;
                ; Purpose: This program exercises the bitmap routines.
                ;
                ; Inputs:  All inputs are provided within the program.
                ;
                ; Process: Basic tests of the bitmap routines are made and the results
                ;          are reported on the screen.
                ;
```

```
                              ; Outputs: The only outputs are to the screen.
                              ;
                              ;
                              ; Declare the routines we are going to use
                              ;
                                      EXTRN    BITMAPS:PROC       ; Set bit
                                      EXTRN    BITMAPR:PROC       ; Reset bit
                                      EXTRN    BITMAPT:PROC       ; Test bit
                                      EXTRN    BITMAPL:PROC       ; Locate bit

0000                          stack   SEGMENT para 'STACK' STACK
0000  0100[                           dq       256 DUP(?)
      ???????????????
      ?
                    ]

0800                          stack   ENDS
0000                          data    SEGMENT para
0000  000A[                   empty   dd       10 DUP(0)
      00000000
                    ]

0028  000A[                   full    dd       10 DUP(-1)
      FFFFFFFF
                    ]

0050  0100[                   string  db       256 DUP(?)           ; String scratch area
      ??
                    ]

0150  0A 0D 45 6D 70 74 79    emptyms db       10,13,"Empty detected.$"
      20 64 65 74 65 63 74
      65 64 2E 24
0162  0A 0D 46 75 6C 6C 20    fullms  db       10,13,"Full returned bit 0.$"
      72 65 74 75 72 6E 65
      64 20 62 69 74 20 30
      2E 24
0179  0A 0D 4C 61 73 74 20    lastm1  db       10,13,"Last bit was on.$"
      62 69 74 20 77 61 73
      20 6F 6E 2E 24
018C  0A 0D 4C 61 73 74 20    lastm2  db       10,13,"Last bit was off.$"
      62 69 74 20 77 61 73
      20 6F 66 66 2E 24
01A0  0A 0A 0A 0D 45 20 52    errom   db       10,10,10,13,"E R R O R $"
      20 52 20 4F 20 52 20
      24
01AF  0A 0A 0D 41 20 4C 20    lastm3  db       10,10,13,"A L L   O K ! ! $"
      4C 20 20 20 4F 20 4B
      20 21 20 21 20 24
01C3                          data    ENDS
0000                          code    SEGMENT para 'CODE' USE16 PUBLIC
                                      ASSUME  CS:code, DS:data
                              ;
                              ; Set up the environment
                              ;
0000                          Begin:
0000  B8 ---- R                       mov      AX,data              ; Get data segment pointer
0003  8E D8                           mov      DS,AX                ; into DS,
0005  8E C0                           mov      ES,AX                ; and ES.
0007  2B F6                           sub      SI,SI                ; Clear indices
0009  2B FF                           sub      DI,DI
                              ;
                              ; Locate bit in empty map
                              ;
000B  B9 000A                         mov      CX,10                ; Set count
```

```
000E   8D 1E 0000 R              lea     BX,empty        ; map pointer
0012   E8 0000 E                 call    Bitmapl         ; Try a locate
0015   0F 83 00A8 R              jnc     fullerr         ; Should be empty
0019   8D 16 0150 R              lea     DX,emptyms      ; point to message
001D   B4 09                     mov     AH,9
001F   CD 21                     int     21h             ; and write it

                            ;
                            ; locate bit in full map
                            ;
0021   8D 1E 0028 R              lea     BX,full         ; use full map
0025   E8 0000 E                 call    Bitmapl         ; Try a locate
0028   0F 82 00A8 R              jc      fullerr         ; error if not found
002C   0B C0                     or      AX,AX           ; was proper bit found
002E   0F 85 00A8 R              jnz     fullerr
0032   8D 16 0162 R              lea     DX,fullms       ; Point to message
0036   B4 09                     mov     AH,9
0038   CD 21                     int     21h             ; and write it

                            ;
                            ; reset last bit
                            ;
003A   B8 013F                   mov     AX,320-1        ; number of last bit
003D   E8 0000 E                 call    Bitmapr         ; Go reset it
0040   0F 83 00A8 R              jnc     fullerr         ; If it was off - bad
0044   8D 16 0179 R              lea     DX,lastm1       ; Point to message
0048   B4 09                     mov     AH,9
004A   CD 21                     int     21h             ; and write it

                            ;
                            ; now set it again
                            ;
004C   B8 013F                   mov     AX,320-1        ; Number of last bit
004F   E8 0000 E                 call    Bitmaps         ; Go set it
0052   0F 82 00A8 R              jc      fullerr         ; If bad - out
0056   8D 16 018C R              lea     DX,lastm2       ; Point to message
005A   B4 09                     mov     AH,9
005C   CD 21                     int     21h             ; and write it

                            ;
                            ; Test last bit in full
                            ;
005E   B8 013F                   mov     AX,320-1        ; number of last bit
0061   E8 0000 E                 call    Bitmapt         ; Go test it
0064   0F 83 00A8 R              jnc     fullerr         ; If it was off - bad
0068   8D 16 0179 R              lea     DX,lastm1       ; Point to message
006C   B4 09                     mov     AH,9
006E   CD 21                     int     21h             ; and write it

                            ;
                            ; now test it in the empty
                            ;
0070   8D 1E 0000 R              lea     BX,empty        ; Point to the empty
0074   B8 013F                   mov     AX,320-1        ; Number of last bit
0077   E8 0000 E                 call    Bitmapt         ; Go set it
007A   0F 82 00A8 R              jc      fullerr         ; If bad - out
007E   8D 16 018C R              lea     DX,lastm2       ; Point to message
0082   B4 09                     mov     AH,9
0084   CD 21                     int     21h             ; and write it
0086   8D 1E 0028 R              lea     BX,full         ; point back to full

                            ;
                            ; copy full to empty
                            ;
                            fullcopy:
008A
008A   B9 000A                   mov     CX,10           ; Count of words
008D   8D 1E 0028 R              lea     BX,full         ; Bitmap
0091   E8 0000 E                 call    Bitmapl         ; Find a bit
0094   0F 82 00B3 R              jc      fulldone        ; When empty we are done
0098   E8 0000 E                 call    Bitmapr         ; Clear the bit
009B   0F 83 00A8 R              jnc     fullerr         ; error if not on for clear
009F   8D 1E 0000 R              lea     BX,empty        ; Point to empty
00A3   E8 0000 E                 call    Bitmaps         ; copy bit into it
00A6   73 E2                     jnc     fullcopy        ; As long as it was off - ok
```

```
00A8                                    fullerr:
00A8    8D 16 01A0 R                            lea     DX,errom          ; Set error message
00AC    B4 09                                   mov     AH,9
00AE    CD 21                                   int     21h
00B0    EB 24 90                                jmp     Exit
00B3                                    fulldone:
00B3    66| 2B C0                               sub     EAX,EAX           ; Set comparand
00B6    8D 3E 0028 R                            lea     DI,full           ; check all off in full
00BA    B9 000A                                 mov     CX,10
00BD    F3/ AE                                  repe scasb                ; Check
00BF    75 E7                                   jne     fullerr           ; Error if not empty
00C1    66| 48                                  dec     EAX               ; Get all ones
00C3    8D 3E 0000 R                            lea     DI,empty          ; Should be full now
00C7    B9 000A                                 mov     CX,10
00CA    F3/ AE                                  repe scasb                ; Check
00CC    75 DA                                   jne     fullerr           ; Error if not full

00CE    8D 16 01AF R                            lea     DX,lastm3         ; Point to message
00D2    B4 09                                   mov     AH,9
00D4    CD 21                                   int     21h               ; and write it
00D6                                    Exit:
00D6    B0 00                                   mov     AL,0              ; Set return code
00D8    B4 4C                                   mov     AH,04ch           ; Set good-by
00DA    CD 21                                   int     21h               ; Return to the system
                                        ;
                                        ; Read a string in response to a prompt
                                        ; The prompt must be in DX.  The string will be returned in string.
                                        ;
00DC                                    getinp  PROC
00DC    50                                      push    AX                ; Save registers
00DD    56                                      push    SI
00DE    B4 09                                   mov     AH,9              ; and dos request
00E0    CD 21                                   int     21h               ; put out the string
00E2    8D 16 0050 R                            lea     DX,string         ; point to input area
00E6    C6 06 0050 R FE                         mov     string,254        ; Set max length in
00EB    B4 0A                                   mov     AH,10             ; Ask for read of string
00ED    CD 21                                   int     21h               ; from DOS.
00EF    8D 1E 0052 R                            lea     BX,string+2       ; Point to just read data
00F3    8A 0E 0051 R                            mov     CL,string+1       ; Get length read
00F7    B5 00                                   mov     CH,0              ; as a word.
00F9    8B F1                                   mov     SI,CX             ; Set length
00FB    C6 84 0052 R 00                         mov     string+2[SI],0    ; and make an asciiz string.
0100    5E                                      pop     SI
0101    58                                      pop     AX                ; Restore registers
0102    C3                                      ret                       ; and return.
0103                                    getinp  ENDP

0103                                    code    ENDS
                                                END     Begin
```

Program 6-3 BITMAPS

Microsoft (R) Macro Assembler Version 5.00

```
                                        PAGE      55,132
                                        .386
0000                                    code    SEGMENT   para 'CODE' USE16 PUBLIC
                                                ASSUME    CS:code, DS:code, SS:code
                                        ;
                                        ; Name:    BITMAPS
                                        ;
                                        ; Purpose: The following procedure provides a means of setting a bit
                                        ;          in a bitmap which corresponds to the number provided.
```

```
;  Inputs:   AX has the number of the bit to be set (changed from 0 to
;            1).
;            BX points to the bitmap.
;
;  Process: The process is to convert the number into a double word
;            displacement into the map by dividing by 32, multiplying
;            the quotient by 4 and using the remainder as a bit number.
;            The bit in the word is then set to 1.
;
;  Output:  The carry flag reflects the previous setting of the bit.
;            i.e. if the bit was zero, the carry flag will be set.
;
;
;
```

			PUBLIC	Bitmaps	; Make the name usable
0000		Bitmaps	PROC		
0000	66| 51		push	ECX	; Save entry registers
0002	53		push	BX	
0003	50		push	AX	
0004	66| 2B C9		sub	ECX,ECX	; clear bit register
0007	8A C8		mov	CL,AL	; copy bit number
0009	80 E1 1F		and	CL,31	; clear garbage
000C	24 E0		and	AL,0e0h	; and bit number from AX
000E	C1 E8 03		shr	AX,3	; Get proper word index
0011	03 D8		add	BX,AX	; point to the word
0013	66| 0F AB 0F		bts	[BX],ECX	; Reset the bit
0017	58		pop	AX	; Restore the entry registers
0018	5B		pop	BX	
0019	66| 59		pop	ECX	
001B	C3		ret		; and return.
001C		Bitmaps	ENDP		

```
;  Name:    BITMAPR
;
;  Purpose: The following procedure provides a means of clearing a bit
;            in a bitmap which corresponds to the number provided.
;
;  Inputs:   AX has the number of the bit to be reset (changed from 1 to
;            0).
;            BX points to the bitmap.
;
;  Process: The process is to convert the number into a double word
;            displacement into the map by dividing by 32, multiplying
;            the quotient by 4 and using the remainder as a bit number.
;            The bit in the word is then set to 0.
;
;  Output:  The carry flag reflects the previous setting of the bit.
;            i.e. if the bit was carry, the zero flag will be set.
;
;
;
```

			PUBLIC	Bitmapr	; Make the name usable
001C		Bitmapr	PROC		
001C	66| 51		push	ECX	; Save entry registers
001E	53		push	BX	
001F	50		push	AX	
0020	66| 2B C9		sub	ECX,ECX	; clear bit register
0023	8A C8		mov	CL,AL	; copy bit number
0025	80 E1 1F		and	CL,31	; clear garbage
0028	24 E0		and	AL,0e0h	; and bit number from AX
002A	C1 E8 03		shr	AX,3	; Get proper word index
002D	03 D8		add	BX,AX	; point to the word
002F	66| 0F B3 0F		btr	[BX],ECX	; Reset the bit
0033	58		pop	AX	; Restore the entry registers

String parsing routines   133

```
0034  5B                          pop     BX
0035  66| 59                      pop     ECX
0037  C3                          ret                             ; and return.
0038                    Bitmapr   ENDP


                      ;
                      ; Name:    BITMAPT
                      ;
                      ; Purpose: The following procedure provides a means of testing a bit
                      ;          in a bitmap which corresponds to the number provided.
                      ;
                      ; Inputs:  AX has the number of the bit to be tested.
                      ;          BX points to the bitmap.
                      ;
                      ; Process: The process is to convert the number into a double word
                      ;          displacement into the map by dividing by 32, multiplying
                      ;          the quotient by 4 and using the remainder as a bit number.
                      ;          The bit in the word is then tested.
                      ;
                      ; Output:  The carry flag reflects the setting of the bit.
                      ;          i.e. if the bit was carry, the zero flag will be set.
                      ;
                      ;
                      ;
                                PUBLIC  Bitmapt                 ; Make the name usable
0038                  Bitmapt   PROC
0038  66| 51                    push    ECX                     ; Save entry registers
003A  53                        push    BX
003B  50                        push    AX
003C  66| 2B C9                 sub     ECX,ECX                 ; clear bit register
003F  8A C8                     mov     CL,AL                   ; copy bit number
0041  80 E1 1F                  and     CL,31                   ; clear garbage
0044  24 E0                     and     AL,0e0h                 ; and bit number from AX
0046  C1 E8 03                  shr     AX,3                    ; Get proper word index
0049  03 D8                     add     BX,AX                   ; point to the word
004B  66| 0F A3 0F              bt      [BX],ECX                ; Test the bit
004F  58                        pop     AX                      ; Restore the entry registers
0050  5B                        pop     BX
0051  66| 59                    pop     ECX
0053  C3                        ret                             ; and return.
0054                  Bitmapt   ENDP


                      ;
                      ; Name:    BITMAPL
                      ;
                      ; Purpose: The following procedure provides a means of locating the
                      ;          first one bit in a bitmap.
                      ;
                      ; Inputs:  BX points to the bitmap.
                      ;          CX has the number of double words in the map.
                      ;
                      ; Process: The process is to scan the bitmap for a double word which
                      ;          is non zero.  The word is then scanned for the first one
                      ;          bit.  A bit number is returned as double word number * 32
                      ;          plus the bit number.  (double words are numbered from
                      ;          zero.)
                      ;
                      ; Output:  If a bit is located, its number will be in AX and carry
                      ;          will be reset.  If the map is empty, AX is undefined and
                      ;          carry is set.
                      ;
```

```
                              ;
                              ;
                              PUBLIC  Bitmapl              ; Make the name usable
0054                  Bitmapl  PROC
0054  06                       push    ES                 ; Save entry registers
0055  57                       push    DI
0056  51                       push    CX
0057  53                       push    BX
0058  51                       push    CX                 ; save count again
0059  66| 2B C0                sub     EAX,EAX            ; Get comparand
005C  8C DF                    mov     DI,DS              ; Get DS into
005E  8E C7                    mov     ES,DI              ; ES
0060  8B FB                    mov     DI,BX              ; and map into DI
0062  F3/ 66| AF               repe scasd                 ; look for non zero dword
0065  5B                       pop     BX                 ; get original count in BX
0066  0F 84 007F R             jz      errorl             ; Map is empty
006A  83 EF 04                 sub     DI,4               ; point to the word
006D  2B D9                    sub     BX,CX              ; Get its word number +1
006F  4B                       dec     BX
0070  66| 0F BC 05             bsf     EAX,DWORD PTR [DI] ; Get the bit number
0074  C1 E3 05                 shl     BX,5               ; Word number times 32
0077  03 C3                    add     AX,BX              ; Plus bit number
0079  F8                       clc                        ; clear carry
007A                  exitl:
007A  5B                       pop     BX                 ; Restore the entry registers
007B  59                       pop     CX
007C  5F                       pop     DI
007D  07                       pop     ES
007E  C3                       ret                        ; and return.
007F                  errorl:
007F  F9                       stc                        ; Return with carry set
0080  EB F8                    jmp     exitl
0082                  Bitmapl  ENDP
0082                  code     ENDS
                               END
```

Program 6-4 EFLAGSCH

Microsoft (R) Macro Assembler Version 5.00

```
                              PAGE    55,132
                              .386
0000                  STACK   SEGMENT 'STACK' STACK
0000  0064[                   DW      100 DUP(?)
         ????
                      ]

00C8                  STACK   ENDS
0000                  CODE    SEGMENT para 'CODE' PUBLIC USE16
                              ASSUME  CS:CODE, DS:CODE, SS:STACK
                      ;
                      ; Name:    EFLAGSCH
                      ;
                      ; Purpose: This routine captures the bit flags in EFLAGS and
                      ;          allows a change.  The flag to change is entered via
                      ;          the keyboard.
                      ;
                      ; Inputs:  Enter the flag to be changed, the choice coming from a
                      ;          menu printed at the beginning.  EFLAGS is printed as it
                      ;          is prior to the change.
                      ;
                      ; Process: The EFLAGS register is captured and then we loop getting
                      ;          the number of a bit to change and changing the bit until
                      ;          a null line is entered.  At this time, we place the new
                      ;          value into EFLAGS.
```

```
                                ;
                                ; Outputs: EFLAGS is printed after the change.
                                ;
                                        EXTRN   CODEASB:PROC
0000                            EFLAGSCH:
0000  8C C8                             MOV     AX,CS           ; Prepare to set DS
0002  8E D8                             MOV     DS,AX           ;   and set it.
0004  E9 02ED R                         JMP     BEGINHERE
                                ;
0007  0100[                     string  db      256 DUP(?)              ;
         ??
              ]

0107  0A 0D 45 46 4C 41 47      BEFORE  DB      0Ah,0Dh,'EFLAGS before change: $'
      53 20 62 65 66 6F 72
      65 20 63 68 61 6E 67
      65 3A 20 24
0120  0A 0D 45 46 4C 41 47      AFTER   DB      0Ah,0Dh,'EFLAGS after change:  $'
      53 20 61 66 74 65 72
      20 63 68 61 6E 67 65
      3A 20 20 24
0139  0A 0D 45 46 4C 41 47      MENU    DB      0Ah,0Dh,'EFLAGS bits: '
      53 20 62 69 74 73 3A
      20
0148  0A 0D 31 37 2E 20 20              DB      0Ah,0Dh,'17.  VM = Virtual 8086 Mode '
      56 4D 20 3D 20 56 69
      72 74 75 61 6C 20 38
      30 38 36 20 4D 6F 64
      65 20
0166  0A 0D 31 36 2E 20 20              DB      0Ah,0Dh,'16.  RF = Resume Flag '
      52 46 20 3D 20 52 65
      73 75 6D 65 20 46 6C
      61 67 20
017E  0A 0D 31 34 2E 20 20              DB      0Ah,0Dh,'14.  NT = Nested Task Flag'
      4E 54 20 3D 20 4E 65
      73 74 65 64 20 54 61
      73 6B 20 46 6C 61 67
019A  0A 0D 31 33 2E 20 20              DB      0Ah,0Dh,'13.  IOPL = I/O Privilege Level'
      49 4F 50 4C 20 3D 20
      49 2F 4F 20 50 72 69
      76 69 6C 65 67 65 20
      4C 65 76 65 6C
01BB  0A 0D 31 31 2E 20 20              DB      0Ah,0Dh,'11.  OF = Overflow'
      4F 46 20 3D 20 4F 76
      65 72 66 6C 6F 77
01CF  0A 0D 31 30 2E 20 20              DB      0Ah,0Dh,'10.  DF = Direction Flag'
      44 46 20 3D 20 44 69
      72 65 63 74 69 6F 6E
      20 46 6C 61 67
01E9  0A 0D 20 39 2E 20 20              DB      0Ah,0Dh,' 9.  IF = Interrupt Enable Flag'
      49 46 20 3D 20 49 6E
      74 65 72 72 75 70 74
      20 45 6E 61 62 6C 65
      20 46 6C 61 67
020A  0A 0D 20 38 2E 20 20              DB      0Ah,0Dh,' 8.  TF = Trap Flag'
      54 46 20 3D 20 54 72
      61 70 20 46 6C 61 67
021F  0A 0D 20 37 2E 20 20              DB      0Ah,0Dh,' 7.  SF = Sign Flag'
      53 46 20 3D 20 53 69
      67 6E 20 46 6C 61 67
0234  0A 0D 20 36 2E 20 20              DB      0Ah,0Dh,' 6.  ZF = Zero Flag'
      5A 46 20 3D 20 5A 65
      72 6F 20 46 6C 61 67
0249  0A 0D 20 34 2E 20 20              DB      0Ah,0Dh,' 4.  AF = Auxiliary Carry Flag'
      41 46 20 3D 20 41 75
```

```
      78 69 6C 69 61 72 79
      20 43 61 72 72 79 20
      46 6C 61 67
0269  0A 0D 20 32 2E 20 20                  DB      0Ah,0Dh,' 2.  PF = Parity Flag'
      50 46 20 3D 20 50 61
      72 69 74 79 20 46 6C
      61 67
0280  0A 0D 20 30 2E 20 20                  DB      0Ah,0Dh,' 0.  CF = Carry Flag'
      43 46 20 3D 20 43 61
      72 72 79 20 46 6C 61
      67
                                       ;
0296  0A 0D 20 4E 6F 74 65   NOTE         DB      0Ah,0Dh,' Note: unlisted bits are reserved.$'
      3A 20 75 6E 6C 69 73
      74 65 64 20 62 69 74
      73 20 61 72 65 20 72
      65 73 65 72 76 65 64
      2E 24
02BB  0A 0D 24               CR_LF        DB      0Ah,0Dh,'$'
02BE  0A 0D 45 6E 74 65 72   PROMPT       DB      0Ah,0Dh,'Enter the bit number of the flag to'
      20 74 68 65 20 62 69
      74 20 6E 75 6D 62 65
      72 20 6F 66 20 74 68
      65 20 66 6C 61 67 20
      74 6F
02E3  20 63 68 61 6E 67 65                  DB      ' change: $'
      3A 20 24
                             ;
                             BEGINHERE:
02ED
02ED  66| 9C                              pushfd                  ; Get EFLAGS
02EF  66| 5B                              pop     EBX             ; locally
02F1                         showflags:
02F1  8D 16 0107 R                        lea     DX,before       ; Set message
02F5  B4 09                               mov     AH,9
02F7  CD 21                               int     21h             ; and display it
02F9  E8 0331 R                           call    outbits         ; followed by the bits
02FC  8D 16 0139 R                        lea     DX,menu         ; Point to menu
0300  B4 09                               mov     AH,9
0302  CD 21                               int     21h             ; and write it
0304                         getnbr:
0304  8D 16 02BE R                        lea     DX,prompt       ;
0308  E8 034A R                           call    getinp          ; Get bit to change
030B  E3 0F                               jcxz    donechg         ; If null entered -
030D  E8 0000 E                           call    Codeasb         ; Convert the bit number
0310  66| 83 F8 1F                        cmp     EAX,31          ; check bit number
0314  77 EE                               ja      getnbr          ; If bad - try again.
                             ;
                             ; Note how easy the bit gets flipped!
                             ;
0316  66| 0F BB C3                        btc     EBX,EAX         ; change the bit
031A  EB D5                               jmp     showflags       ; loop
031C                         donechg:
031C  8D 16 0120 R                        lea     DX,after        ; message
0320  B4 09                               mov     AH,9
0322  CD 21                               int     21h             ; out followed by
0324  E8 0331 R                           call    outbits         ; bits
0327  66| 53                              push    EBX             ; Stack the flags
0329  66| 9D                              popfd                   ; and set them

032B                         ENDHERE:
032B  2A C0                               sub     AL,AL           ; Set return code 0
032D  B4 4C                               MOV     AH,4Ch          ; Standard Ending
032F  CD 21                               INT     21h
                             ;
                             ; Display the bits of EBX as they are set.
                             ;
0331                         outbits   PROC
0331  66| 53                              push    EBX             ; Don't destroy the bits
```

Program 6-4 Continued.

```
0333  B4 02                          mov    AH,2                ; We do a character at a time
0335  B9 0020                        mov    CX,32               ; Full register worth
0338                       onebit:
0338  B2 31                          mov    DL,'1'              ; Assume bit is 1
033A  66| D1 E3                      shl    EBX,1               ; check it
033D  0F 82 0343 R                   jc     isaone              ; We were right
0341  FE CA                          dec    DL                  ; Set it zero
0343                       isaone:
0343  CD 21                          int    21h                 ; put the bit out.
0345  E2 F1                          loop   onebit              ; Do all 32
0347  66| 5B                         pop    EBX                 ; Restore our bits
0349  C3                             ret                        ; and return
034A                       outbits   ENDP


                           ;
                           ; Read a string in response to a prompt
                           ; The prompt must be in DX.  The string will be returned in string.
                           ;
034A                       getinp    PROC
034A  50                             push   AX                  ; Save registers
034B  B4 09                          mov    AH,9                ; and dos request
034D  CD 21                          int    21h                 ; put out the string
034F  8D 16 0007 R                   lea    DX,string           ; point to input area
0353  C6 06 0007 R FE                mov    string,254          ; Set max length in
0358  B4 0A                          mov    AH,10               ; Ask for read of string
035A  CD 21                          int    21h                 ; from DOS.
035C  8D 36 0009 R                   lea    SI,string+2         ; Point to just read data
0360  8A 0E 0008 R                   mov    CL,string+1         ; Get length read
0364  B5 00                          mov    CH,0                ; as a word.
0366  03 F1                          add    SI,CX               ; Set length
0368  C6 04 00                       mov    BYTE PTR [SI],0     ; and make an asciiz string.
036B  2B F1                          sub    SI,CX
036D  58                             pop    AX                  ; Restore registers
036E  C3                             ret                        ; and return.
036F                       getinp    ENDP

036F                       CODE      ENDS
                                     END    EFLAGSCH
```

Program 6-5 STRSRCH

Microsoft (R) Macro Assembler Version 5.00

```
                                     PAGE    55,132
                                     .386
                                     EXTRN   CODEBAS:PROC
0000                       STACK     SEGMENT 'STACK' STACK
0000  0064[                          DW      100 DUP(?)
        ????
                       ]

00C8                       STACK     ENDS
0000                       CODE      SEGMENT para 'CODE' PUBLIC
                                     ASSUME  CS:CODE, DS:CODE, SS:STACK
                           ;
                           ; Name:    STRSRCH
                           ;
                           ; Purpose:          This program searches for the first occurrence of a
                           ;          specified substring within another given string.  If
                           ;          the substring is found, the starting location (byte)
                           ;          returns in register DX.
                           ;
```

```
                    ; Inputs:    A string is specified.  The search string is also
                    ;            specified.
                    ;
                    ; Process:   A target string of some length is offered.  Its length
                    ;            in bytes is determined.  Then a second string is
                    ;            specified, with its length.  The strings are checked
                    ;            for simple validity: was anything entered in each and
                    ;            was the SEARCH string longer than the TARGET string. If
                    ;            the strings pass, go to search.     If not, an error message
                    ;            is written, DX set to 0, and the program ended.
                    ;
                    ;            To print the byte, the external procedure CODEBAS
                    ;            is called.  CODEBAS turns binary characters into
                    ;            printable ASCII for 80286-based computers.  The program
                    ;            is described in Chapter 7 of the "80386 Assembly
                    ;            Language Toolkit" from TAB Books.
                    ;
                    ; Outputs:   If the substring is found, its offset in bytes is
                    ;            in DX.  If it is not found, DX=0.
                    ;
0000                STRSRCH:
0000  66| 8C C8              MOV       AX,CS              ; Prepare to set DS
0003  66| 8E D8              MOV       DS,AX              ;   and set it.
0006  66| 8E C0              MOV       ES,AX              ; Also set ES
0009  E9 000001CF R          JMP       BEGINHERE
                    ;
000E  0064[              TARGET_STR DB      100 DUP(?)
         ??
                 ]

0072  0064[              SEARCH_STR DB      100 DUP(?)
         ??
                 ]

00D6  49 6E 70 75 74 20 74    PROMPT      DB      'Input the Target string>$'
      68 65 20 54 61 72 67
      65 74 20 73 74 72 69
      6E 67 3E 24
00EF  0A 0D 49 6E 70 75 74  PROMPT1     DB      0Ah,0Dh,'Input the Search string>$'
      20 74 68 65 20 53 65
      61 72 63 68 20 73 74
      72 69 6E 67 3E 24
010A  0A 0D 54 68 65 20 53  TOO_LONG    DB      0Ah,0Dh,'The Search string is longer than the Target
      65 61 72 63 68 20 73                         string.$'
      74 72 69 6E 67 20 69
      73 20 6C 6F 6E 67 65
      72 20 74 68 61 6E 20
      74 68 65 20 54 61 72
      67 65 74 20 73 74 72
      69 6E 67 2E 24
0140  0A 0D 54 68 65 20 54  EMPTY       DB      0Ah,0Dh,'The Target string is empty.$'
      61 72 67 65 74 20 73
      74 72 69 6E 67 20 69
      73 20 65 6D 70 74 79
      2E 24
015E  0A 0D 54 68 65 20 53  EMPTY1      DB      0Ah,0Dh,'The Search string is empty.$'
      65 61 72 63 68 20 73
      74 72 69 6E 67 20 69
      73 20 65 6D 70 74 79
      2E 24
017C  0A 0D 54 68 65 20 53  NOT_HERE    DB      0Ah,0Dh,'The Search string is not in the Target
      65 61 72 63 68 20 73                         string.',0Ah,0Dh,'$'
      74 72 69 6E 67 20 69
      73 20 6E 6F 74 20 69
      6E 20 74 68 65 20 54
      61 72 67 65 74 20 73
      74 72 69 6E 67 2E 0A
      0D 24
```

Program 6-5 Continued.

```
01AF   0A 0D 4D 61 74 63 68      IS_HERE     DB      0Ah,0Dh,'Match found.  Starts in byte $'
       20 66 6F 75 6E 64 2E
       20 20 53 74 61 72 74
       73 20 69 6E 20 62 79
       74 65 20 24

01CF                             ;
                                 BEGINHERE:
                                 ;
                                 ; Get the strings from the keyboard.  They go into a keyboard buffer
                                 ;       which has two bytes at the beginning of the buffer.  The first
                                 ;       byte is your statement of the maximum number allowed in the
                                 ;       buffer.   The second byte is MS-DOS's count of how many bytes
                                 ;       were ACTUALLY entered.  The character string begins at byte
                                 ;       2 (counting from 0), or the third byte of the buffer.
                                 ;

01CF   66| 2B DB                     SUB     BX,BX                ; Be sure count variables are
01D2   66| 2B C9                     SUB     CX,CX                ;    zero
01D5   C6 05 0000000E R 62          MOV     TARGET_STR,98        ; Maximum entry
01DC   8D 15 000000D6 R             LEA     DX,PROMPT
01E2   B4 09                        MOV     AH,9
01E4   CD 21                        INT     21h
01E6   8D 15 0000000E R             LEA     DX,TARGET_STR        ; Point to input buffer
01EC   B4 0A                        MOV     AH,0Ah               ; Get ready to read in
01EE   CD 21                        INT     21h
01F0   8A 0D 0000000F R             MOV     CL,TARGET_STR+1 ; The number actually read in
01F6   8A F9                        MOV     BH,CL                ; Save it in BH
                                 ;
01F8   C6 05 00000072 R 62          MOV     SEARCH_STR,98        ; Maximum entry
01FF   8D 15 000000EF R             LEA     DX,PROMPT1
0205   B4 09                        MOV     AH,9
0207   CD 21                        INT     21h
0209   8D 15 00000072 R             LEA     DX,SEARCH_STR
020F   B4 0A                        MOV     AH,0Ah
0211   CD 21                        INT     21h
0213   8A 1D 00000073 R             MOV     BL,SEARCH_STR+1      ; The number of bytes read in
                                 ;
                                 ; Check validity of strings
                                 ;
0219   0A FF                        OR      BH,BH                ; Is target string empty?
021B   0F 84 000002C5 R             JZ      MSG1                 ; Give msg if so
0221   0A DB                        OR      BL,BL                ; Is substring empty?
0223   0F 84 000002D0 R             JZ      MSG2                 ; Message if so
0229   3A DF                        CMP     BL,BH                ; Is substring too large?
022B   0F 87 000002DB R             JA      MSG3                 ; If so - message
0231   FE CB                        DEC     BL                   ; Since we look for the first
                                                                 ; byte, then scan for the rest
                                                                 ; we only need length -1.
                                 ;
0233   FC                           CLD                          ; Increment after scan

0234   8D 3D 00000010 R             LEA     DI,TARGET_STR+2      ; Point to one to find it in
                                 ;
                                 ;    Scan for match
                                 ;       The target of SCANSB is in AL.  REPNE uses the count
                                 ;       in CX and decrements CX at each pass.
                                 ;
023A                             SEARCH1:
023A   8D 35 00000074 R             LEA     SI,SEARCH_STR+2      ; Point to string to find
0240   67| 8A 04                    MOV     AL,[SI]              ; Scan target
0243   F2/ AE                       REPNE SCASB
0245   0F 85 000002B2 R             JNE     NOT_FOUND            ; If no match at all
                                 ;
                                 ;    Got a match on first character
                                 ;
```

```
024B   3A CB                         CMP    CL,BL              ; Enough left in target?
024D   0F 82 000002B2 R             JB     NOT_FOUND          ; If not - don't look.
0253   66| 8B EF                    MOV    BP,DI              ; Save offset of next
0256   66| 8B D1                    MOV    DX,CX              ; and count remaining.
                                ;
                                ;     DI points at target (current location)
                                ;     SI at search (current location)
                                ;
0259   8A CB                        MOV    CL,BL              ; Is next n chars = ?
025B   66| 46                       INC    SI                 ; Go to next value in Search
025D   66| E3 18                    JCXZ   FOUND              ; If only one byte - found
0260   F3/ A6                       REPZ CMPSB                 ; Compare two strings
0262   0F 84 00000278 R            JE     FOUND              ; If = for count - got it.
                                ;
                                ; Otherwise, found a non-match, so resume our scansb at the location
                                ; and with the count we saved.
                                ;
0268   66| 8B FD                    MOV    DI,BP              ; Offset where to start looking
026B   66| 8B CA                    MOV    CX,DX              ; and count remaining.
026E   3A CB                        CMP    CL,BL              ; Count remaining > search-1
0270   0F 86 000002B2 R            JNA    NOT_FOUND          ; No - not there.
0276   EB C2                        JMP    SEARCH1
                                ;
                                ;
0278                           FOUND:
0278   2A FA                        SUB    BH,DL              ; Loc = count - count remaining
027A   8D 15 000001AF R            LEA    DX,IS_HERE
0280   B4 09                        MOV    AH,9
0282   CD 21                        INT    21h
0284   8A C7                        MOV    AL,BH              ; Get offset
0286   B4 00                        MOV    AH,0               ; As a word
0288   98                           CWDE                      ; (double)
0289   E8 00000000 E                CALL   CODEBAS            ; DI=pointer to converted data
028E   67| 8A 15                    MOV    DL,BYTE PTR [DI]   ; VALUE that DI points to
0291   B4 02                        MOV    AH,2               ; Print that value
0293   CD 21                        INT    21h
0295   67| 8A 55 01                 MOV    DL,BYTE PTR [DI+1] ; Another digit?
0299   80 FA 30                     CMP    DL,30h             ; Less than zero?
029C   0F 8C 000002EA R            JL     ENDHERE
02A2   80 FA 39                     CMP    DL,39h             ; Greater than 9 ?
02A5   0F 87 000002EA R            JA     ENDHERE
02AB   CD 21                        INT    21h                ; Otherwise print it
02AD   EB 3B 90 90 90               JMP    ENDHERE
02B2                           NOT_FOUND:
02B2   8D 15 0000017C R            LEA    DX,NOT_HERE
02B8   66| BE 0000                  MOV    SI,0
02BC   B4 09                        MOV    AH,9
02BE   CD 21                        INT    21h
02C0   EB 28 90 90 90               JMP    ENDHERE
                                ;
                                ;
                                ; Error messages
                                ;
02C5                           MSG1:
02C5   8D 15 00000140 R            LEA    DX,EMPTY           ; Target is empty
02CB   EB 14 90 90 90               JMP    MSG99
02D0                           MSG2:
02D0   8D 15 0000015E R            LEA    DX,EMPTY1          ; Substring is empty
02D6   EB 09 90 90 90               JMP    MSG99
02DB                           MSG3:
02DB   8D 15 0000010A R            LEA    DX,TOO_LONG        ; Print error and exit
02E1                           MSG99:
02E1   B4 09                        MOV    AH,9
02E3   CD 21                        INT    21h
02E5   EB 03 90 90 90               JMP    ENDHERE
                                ;
                                ;
```

```
02EA                                ENDHERE:
02EA  B4 4C                                        MOV     AH,4Ch              ; Standard Ending
02EC  CD 21                                        INT     21h
02EE                                CODE            ENDS
                                                    END     STRSRCH
```

Program 6-6 STRINSRT

Microsoft (R) Macro Assembler Version 5.00

```
                                                   PAGE     55,132
                                                   .386
0000                                STACK          SEGMENT 'STACK' STACK
0000  0064[                                        DW       100 DUP(?)
        ????
                          ]

00C8                                STACK          ENDS
0000                                CODE           SEGMENT para 'CODE' PUBLIC USE16
                                                   ASSUME  CS:CODE, DS:CODE, SS:STACK
                                    ;
                                    ; Name:    STRINSRT
                                    ;
                                    ; Purpose: This program inserts a source string into a
                                    ;          specified place in a target string.  Both
                                    ;          strings are input via the keyboard.
                                    ;
                                    ; Inputs:  The Target string and the Insert strings both are
                                    ;          keyed into the program.  The place to insert is also.
                                    ;
                                    ; Process: We prompt for and read the target string, the string to
                                    ;          insert and the location (0 to the end of the target) to
                                    ;          insert the string.  We then form the new string by
                                    ;          copying the leading bytes of the target (if any), the
                                    ;          insert string, and any remaining bytes of the target.
                                    ;
                                    ; Outputs: After the run, the resulting string is displayed.
                                    ;          The beginning byte where the insertion was done is
                                    ;          given.  Also, the new length of the resulting string
                                    ;          is given.
                                    ;
                                                   EXTRN    CODEBAS:PROC
                                                   EXTRN    CODEASB:PROC
0000                                STRINSRT:
0000  8C C8                                        MOV      AX,CS              ; Prepare to set DS
0002  8E D8                                        MOV      DS,AX              ;   and set it.
0004  8E C0                                        MOV      ES,AX              ;   (ES too)
0006  E9 0257 R                                    JMP      BEGINHERE
                                    ;
0009  0A 0A 0D 41 6E 20 65          PROMPT         DB       10,10,13,'An empty target string ends the program.'
      6D 70 74 79 20 74 61
      72 67 65 74 20 73 74
      72 69 6E 67 20 65 6E
      64 73 20 74 68 65 20
      70 72 6F 67 72 61 6D
      2E
0034  0A 0D 45 6E 74 65 72                         DB       10,13,'Enter the Target String: $'
      20 74 68 65 20 54 61
      72 67 65 74 20 53 74
      72 69 6E 67 3A 20 24
0050  0A 0D 45 6E 74 65 72          PROMPT1        DB       10,13,'Enter the Insert String: $'
      20 74 68 65 20 49 6E
      73 65 72 74 20 53 74
      72 69 6E 67 3A 20 24
006C  0A 0D 45 6E 74 65 72          PROMPT2        DB       10,13,'Enter the position to insert after: $'
      20 74 68 65 20 70 6F
```

```
                 73 69 74 69 6F 6E 20
                 74 6F 20 69 6E 73 65
                 72 74 20 61 66 74 65
                 72 3A 20 24
0093  0A 0D 54 68 65 20 74        NEW_LENGTH DB        0Ah,0Dh,'The total length is: $'
                 6F 74 61 6C 20 6C 65
                 6E 67 74 68 20 69 73
                 3A 20 24
00AB  0064[                       TARGET     DB        100 DUP(?)
         ??
                         ]

010F  0064[                       INSERT     DB        100 DUP(?)
         ??
                         ]

0173  0A 0D 54 68 65 20 72        RESULTM    DB        0Ah,0Dh,'The resulting string is:',10,13
                 65 73 75 6C 74 69 6E
                 67 20 73 74 72 69 6E
                 67 20 69 73 3A 0A 0D
018F  00C8[                       RESULT     DB        200 DUP(?)
         ??
                         ]

                                  ;
0257                              BEGINHERE:
0257  8D 1E 00AB R                           LEA       BX,TARGET      ; Point to input buffer
025B  8D 16 0009 R                           LEA       DX,PROMPT       ; and prompt
025F  E8 02EF R                              CALL      GETIN          ; Do prompt and get input
0262  0B C9                                  OR        CX,CX          ; was a target entered?
0264  0F 85 026B R                           JNZ       ASKAGAIN       ; yes.
0268  E9 02EB R                              JMP       ENDHERE        ; Quit on a null
026B                              ASKAGAIN:
026B  8D 1E 010F R                           LEA       BX,INSERT      ; Point to input buffer
026F  8D 16 0050 R                           LEA       DX,PROMPT1      ; prompt, and
0273  E8 02EF R                              CALL      GETIN          ; get input.
0276  E3 F3                                  JCXZ      ASKAGAIN       ; null insert not allowed.
0278                              GETNUMB:
0278  8D 16 006C R                           LEA       DX,PROMPT2      ; Point to prompt,
027C  8D 1E 018F R                           LEA       BX,RESULT      ; input buffer, and
0280  E8 02EF R                              CALL      GETIN          ; get number.
0283  E3 F3                                  JCXZ      GETNUMB        ; (required)
0285  8D 36 0191 R                           LEA       SI,RESULT+2    ; Set the number pointer.
0289  E8 0000 E                              CALL      CODEASB        ; Convert the number.
028C  72 EA                                  JC        GETNUMB        ; Overflow?
028E  0B C0                                  OR        AX,AX          ; how about negative
0290  78 E6                                  JS        GETNUMB        ; Try again on minus.
0292  8A 0E 00AC R                           MOV       CL,TARGET+1    ; Get target size.
0296  3B C1                                  CMP       AX,CX          ; In or at end is ok.
0298  7F DE                                  JG        GETNUMB        ; beyond is not!
029A  8D 3E 018F R                           LEA       DI,RESULT      ; Point at result.
029E  8D 36 00AD R                           LEA       SI,TARGET+2    ; Target string to move.
02A2  2B C8                                  SUB       CX,AX          ; Get size left.
02A4  91                                     XCHG      AX,CX          ; Count to move in CX.
02A5  E3 02                                  JCXZ      DOINSERT       ; If insert in front - ok
02A7  F3/ A4                                 REP MOVSB                ; Move first part of string
02A9                              DOINSERT:
02A9  56                                     PUSH      SI             ; Save loc in target
02AA  8D 36 0111 R                           LEA       SI,INSERT+2    ; Set string to insert.
02AE  8A 0E 0110 R                           MOV       CL,INSERT+1    ; and its length.
02B2  F3/ A4                                 REP MOVSB                ; Move insert
02B4  5E                                     POP       SI             ; Get target back.
02B5  8B C8                                  MOV       CX,AX          ; and remaining length
02B7  E3 02                                  JCXZ      MOVDONE        ; if none _ done.
02B9  F3/ A4                                 REP MOVSB                ; Put rest of target out
02BB                              MOVDONE:
02BB  C6 05 24                               MOV       BYTE PTR [DI],'$'  ; Follow with stopper.
02BE  A0 00AC R                              MOV       AL,TARGET+1    ; Get length of target,
```

Program 6-6 Continued.

```
02C1  8A 0E 0110 R            MOV    CL,INSERT+1            ; and length of insert.
02C5  03 C1                   ADD    AX,CX                  ; add to get total length.
02C7  8D 3E 00AB R            LEA    DI,TARGET              ; Convert area
02CB  E8 0000 E               CALL   CODEBAS                ; get length as ASCII
02CE  8D 16 0173 R            LEA    DX,RESULTM             ; point to results
02D2  B4 09                   MOV    AH,9                   ;
02D4  CD 21                   INT    21h                    ; and print them.
02D6  8D 16 0093 R            LEA    DX,NEW_LENGTH          ;
02DA  CD 21                   INT    21h                    ;
02DC  B4 02                   MOV    AH,2                   ; Number follows
02DE              PRTNUMB:
02DE  8A 15                   MOV    DL,BYTE PTR[DI]        ; Get a digit
02E0  0A D2                   OR     DL,DL                  ; if zero _ done
02E2  0F 84 0257 R            JZ     BEGINHERE              ; Let it be done again!
02E6  CD 21                   INT    21h
02E8  47                      INC    DI
02E9  EB F3                   JMP    PRTNUMB                ; Do all digits

02EB              ENDHERE:
02EB  B4 4C                   MOV    AH,4Ch          ; Standard Ending
02ED  CD 21                   INT    21h
02EF              GETIN   PROC
02EF  B4 09                   MOV    AH,9                   ; Set write
02F1  CD 21                   INT    21h                    ; of prompt
02F3  8B D3                   MOV    DX,BX                  ; point to input buffer
02F5  C6 07 62                MOV    BYTE PTR[BX],98        ; set max length.
02F8  B4 0A                   MOV    AH,10                  ; Set read to buffer
02FA  CD 21                   INT    21h                    ; and read it.
02FC  8A 4F 01                MOV    CL,BYTE PTR [BX+1]     ; get length
02FF  2A ED                   SUB    CH,CH                  ; as a word in CX
0301  C3                      RET                           ; Return
0302              GETIN   ENDP
0302              CODE    ENDS
                          END    STRINSRT
```

Program 6-7 STRWORKS

Microsoft (R) Macro Assembler Version 5.00

```
                          PAGE    55,132
                          .386

;
; Name:        STRWORKS
;
; Purpose: This program does several things:
;                 1.  Sets up an ordered list of ASCIIZ strings
;                 2.  Requests an input string
;                 3.  Finds the position within the ordered list
;                 4.  Inserts the new string
;
; Inputs:  A series of variable length alphabetic words are typed
;          in, until a word of null length (a carriage return).
;          Then a Source word is entered.
;
; Process: We loop, requesting strings be entered until an empty
;          line is entered.  Each string is copied into a string
;          area and its displacement is saved in the array 'ordered'
;          (We check for and also stop if we run out of either array
;          space or string space.)
;          We call the shell sort routine to sort the strings and
;          print the ordered result.
;
; Outputs: The ordered list is displayed, with the Source word
```

```
                          ;              in its correct position.

                          EXTRN   SHELLSRT:PROC

0000                      stack      SEGMENT para 'STACK' STACK
0000  0100[               dq         256 DUP(?)
          ???????????????
          ?
                  ]

0800                      stack      ENDS
0000                      data       SEGMENT para
0000  0100[               string     db         256 DUP(?)              ; String scratch area
          ??
                  ]

0100  0A 0A 0D 45 6E 74 65     query      db         10,10,13,"Enter the next string: $"
      72 20 74 68 65 20 6E
      65 78 74 20 73 74 72
      69 6E 67 3A 20 24
011B  0A 0A 0D 41 72 72 61     toomany    db         10,10,13,"Array space is full!$"
      79 20 73 70 61 63 65
      20 69 73 20 66 75 6C
      6C 21 24
0133  0A 0A 0D 53 74 72 69     toobig     db         10,10,13,"String storage space is full!$"
      6E 67 20 73 74 6F 72
      61 67 65 20 73 70 61
      63 65 20 69 73 20 66
      75 6C 6C 21 24
0154  0A 0A 0D 54 68 65 20     heading    db         10,10,13,"The ordered list is:",10,"$"
      6F 72 64 65 72 65 64
      20 6C 69 73 74 20 69
      73 3A 0A 24

                          ;
                          ; The following contains the array of displacements into the string
                          ;    area.  If the number of strings grows beyond the size of the
                          ;    array, it may be necessary to increase not only the size but
                          ;    the method of storage
                          ;
= 0200                    maxnbr     EQU        512
016D  90                  ALIGN      2
016E  0200[               ordered    dw         maxnbr DUP(?)           ; ordered string displacements
          ????
                  ]

                          ;
                          ; String storage area - Once placed here, the strings are not moved
                          ; again.  Only their displacements are manipulated.
                          ;
056E  1400[               strarea    db         maxnbr*10 DUP(?)
          ??
                  ]

= 196E                    strend     EQU        $
196E  0000                count      dw         0                      ; count of strings
1970  056E                nextstrp   dw         strarea-data           ; displacement into string area
1972                      data       ENDS
0000                      code       SEGMENT para 'CODE' USE16 PUBLIC
                          ASSUME  CS:code, DS:data
                          ;
                          ;
0000                      STRWORKS:
0000  B8 ---- R           mov        AX,data                ; Prepare to set DS
0003  8E D8               mov        DS,AX                  ;   and set it.
0005  8E C0               mov        ES,AX                  ;   (ES too)
0007  8B 36 1970 R        mov        SI,nextstrp            ; Set first SI
000B  8D 1E 016E R        lea        BX,ordered             ; Set pointer to array
                          ;
```

Program 6-7 Continued.

```
                          ; Loop getting words (or strings) until a null string is entered or
                          ; we run out of string storage space.
                          ;
000F                      nextstr:
000F  8D 16 0100 R                 lea     DX,query          ; Point to message
0013  E8 008C R                    call    getinp            ; Get a word,string or a null
0016  E3 3D                        jcxz    endinp            ; Null ends our loop
0018  41                           inc     CX                ; Include the zero in the move
0019  8B C1                        mov     AX,CX             ; Copy string length
001B  03 C6                        add     AX,SI             ; Add the starting loc
001D  8D 3E 196E R                 lea     DI,strend         ; Get the last +1 loc
0021  3B C7                        cmp     AX,DI             ; is there room?
0023  0F 83 004D R                 jnb     outroom           ; No - do message
0027  8D 3E 0002 R                 lea     DI,string+2       ; Point to string location
002B  89 37                        mov     WORD PTR[BX],SI   ; Save the destination displ.
002D  83 C3 02                     add     BX,2              ; Point to the next area.
0030  87 F7                        xchg    SI,DI             ; Flip source and destination
0032  F3/ A4                       rep movsb                 ; put string in position.
0034  8B F7                        mov     SI,DI             ; Get pointer back
0036  FF 06 196E R                 inc     count             ; Add to the count
003A  81 3E 196E R 0200            cmp     count,maxnbr      ; At the max?
0040  75 CD                        jne     nextstr           ; No - get another.
0042  8D 16 011B R                 lea     DX,toomany        ; Point to the message
0046  B4 09                        mov     AH,9
0048  CD 21                        int     21h               ; and put it out
004A  EB 09 90                     jmp     endinp            ; go sort
004D                      outroom:
004D  8D 16 0133 R                 lea     DX,toobig         ; set message
0051  B4 09                        mov     AH,9
0053  CD 21                        int     21h               ; and put it out
0055                      endinp:
0055  8B 0E 196E R                 mov     CX,count          ; Get count in CX
0059  8D 1E 016E R                 lea     BX,ordered        ; Point to the array of displ.
005D  E8 0000 E                    call    Shellsrt          ; Order them
0060  8D 16 0154 R                 lea     DX,heading        ; Put out the heading
0064  B4 09                        mov     AH,9
0066  CD 21                        int     21h
0068  B4 02                        mov     AH,2              ; Set code for rest
006A                      display:
006A  B2 0A                        mov     DL,10             ; l/f
006C  CD 21                        int     21h
006E  B2 0D                        mov     DL,13             ; cr
0070  CD 21                        int     21h
0072  8B 37                        mov     SI,WORD PTR[BX]   ; get string pointer
0074                      outstr:
0074  AC                           lodsb                     ; Get byte in AL
0075  0A C0                        or      AL,AL             ; check it
0077  0F 84 0081 R                 jz      donestr           ; zero is done
007B  8A D0                        mov     DL,AL             ; position it
007D  CD 21                        int     21h               ; put it out
007F  EB F3                        jmp     outstr            ; and get next
0081                      donestr:
0081  83 C3 02                     add     BX,2              ; Step string pointer.
0084  E2 E4                        loop    display           ; and do till done


0086                      endhere:
0086  2A C0                        sub     AL,AL             ; Return ok
0088  B4 4C                        mov     AH,4Ch            ; Standard Ending
008A  CD 21                        int     21h
                          ;
                          ; Read a string in response to a prompt
                          ; The prompt must be in DX.  The string will be returned in string.
                          ;
008C                      getinp  PROC
008C  50                           push    AX                ; Save registers
```

```
008D  56                              push    SI
008E  B4 09                           mov     AH,9              ; and dos request
0090  CD 21                           int     21h               ; put out the string
0092  8D 16 0000 R                    lea     DX,string         ; point to input area
0096  C6 06 0000 R FE                 mov     string,254        ; Set max length in
009B  B4 0A                           mov     AH,10             ; Ask for read of string
009D  CD 21                           int     21h               ; from DOS.
009F  8A 0E 0001 R                    mov     CL,string+1       ; Get length read
00A3  B5 00                           mov     CH,0              ; as a word.
00A5  8B F1                           mov     SI,CX             ; Set length
00A7  C6 84 0002 R 00                 mov     string+2[SI],0    ; and make an asciiz string.
00AC  5E                              pop     SI
00AD  58                              pop     AX                ; Restore registers
00AE  C3                              ret                       ; and return.
00AF                      getinp      ENDP

00AF                      CODE        ENDS
                                      END     STRWORKS
```

Program 6-8 STRZCOMP

Microsoft (R) Macro Assembler Version 5.00

```
                                      PAGE    55,132
                                      .386
0000                      code        SEGMENT para 'CODE' PUBLIC USE16
                                      ASSUME  CS:code, DS:code, SS:code

                          ; Name:    STRZCOMP
                          ;
                          ; Purpose: The following procedure compares two ASCIIZ strings
                          ;          and returns the resulting condition code flags.
                          ;
                          ;
                          ; Inputs:  DS:SI contains the address of string 1.
                          ;          ES:DI contains the address of string 2.
                          ;          (The comparison is string 1 - string 2.)
                          ;
                          ; Process: A byte by byte comparison is performed with each equal
                          ;          compare checked for a null (end of string indicator).
                          ;          An unequal or a null terminates the compare.
                          ;
                          ; Output:  The flags are set with the result of the subtraction
                          ;          of string 2 from string 1 (only the flags are set no
                          ;          other changes are returned).
                          ;
                          ; Note:    No procedure for fixed length strings is provided - see
                          ;          the text (repe cmpsb is used - no proc is needed).
                          ;
                                      PUBLIC  Strzcomp
                          ;
0000                      Strzcomp    PROC
0000  56                              push    SI                ; Save entry registers
0001  57                              push    DI
0002  50                              push    AX
0003                      cmpnext:
0003  AC                              lodsb                     ; Get string 1 byte in AL
0004  AE                              scasb                     ; Compare to string 2 byte
0005  0F 85 000D R                    jne     cmpdone           ; Not equal - done
0009  3C 00                           cmp     AL,0              ; Equal at end of string?
000B  75 F6                           jne     cmpnext           ; Not yet!
000D                      cmpdone:
000D  58                              pop     AX                ; Restore the entry registers
000E  5F                              pop     DI
000F  5E                              pop     SI
```

Program 6-8 Continued.

```
0010 C3                              ret                      ; and return.
0011                    Strzcomp     ENDP
0011                    code         ENDS
                                     END
```


Program 6-9 STRZLNG

Microsoft (R) Macro Assembler Version 5.00


```
                                PAGE      55,132
                                .386
        0000                    code    SEGMENT   para 'CODE' PUBLIC USE16
                                        ASSUME    CS:code, DS:code, SS:code
                                ;
                                ; Name:    STRZLNG
                                ;
                                ;
                                ; Purpose: The following procedure scans an ASCIIZ string and
                                ;          returns its length.
                                ;
                                ;
                                ; Inputs:  ES:DI has the address of the string to examine.
                                ;          CX has the maximum length to examine.
                                ;
                                ; Process: We set the registers for a repeated scasb and do it.
                                ;          Compute the length excluding the null and return it.
                                ;
                                ; Output:  AX has the count of bytes in the string (excluding the
                                ;          terminating null).  Carry is reset if the null was found,
                                ;          otherwise carry is set and AX is returned equal to the
                                ;          input CX value.
                                ;
                                        PUBLIC  Strzlng
                                ;
        0000                    Strzlng PROC
        0000 57                         push    DI              ; Save entry registers
        0001 51                         push    CX              ; Save CX twice for length
        0002 51                         push    CX              ; computation.
        0003 2B C0                      sub     AX,AX           ; Clear AX (AL for scan)
        0005 0B C9                      or      CX,CX           ; is CX zero
        0007 0F 84 001A R               jz      outbad          ; Exit if none to scan
        000B FC                         cld                     ; Scan low to high
        000C F2/ AE                     repne scasb             ; Condition for terminating
                                                                ; scan is a null.
        000E 0F 85 001A R               jne     outbad          ; If count ran out - die
        0012 41                         inc     CX              ; Don't include the terminator
        0013 58                         pop     AX              ; Get saved length
        0014 2B C1                      sub     AX,CX           ; and the count processed.
        0016 F8                         clc                     ; Ensure carry is reset
        0017 59                         pop     CX
        0018 5F                         pop     DI              ; Restore registers
        0019 C3                         ret                     ; and return with length.
        001A                    outbad:
        001A F9                         stc                     ; Indicate an error
        001B 58                         pop     AX
        001C 59                         pop     CX
        001D 5F                         pop     DI              ; Restore registers
        001E C3                         ret                     ; and return AX=CX.
        001F                    Strzlng ENDP
        001F                    code    ENDS
                                        END
```

Microsoft (R) Macro Assembler Version 5.00

```
                              PAGE      55,132
                              .386

                          ; Name:    PARSEDRV
                          ;
                          ; Purpose: The following program provides a simple test for the
                          ;          sample parser PARSING.
                          ;
                          ;
                          ; Inputs:  The program prompts for a line to be parsed and reads
                          ;          the input.
                          ;
                          ; Process: The input is passed to the parsing routine until the
                          ;          end of data token is returned.  Each token is displayed
                          ;          as it is returned.  At end of data, another line of input
                          ;          is requested.  If a null line (enter only) is input, the
                          ;          program terminates.
                          ;
                          ; Output:  The output is the displayed tokens.
                          ;
                          ;
                          ; Declare the routine we are going to use
                          ;
                              EXTRN     PARSING:PROC

0000                      stack   SEGMENT   para 'STACK' STACK
0000  0100[                       dq        256 DUP(?)
        ??????????????????
        ?
                 ]

0800                      stack   ENDS
0000                      data    SEGMENT   para
0000  0100[               string  db        256 DUP(?)        ; String scratch area
        ??
                 ]

0100  0100[               outwork db        256 DUP(?)        ; Output work area
        ??
                 ]

0200  0D 0A 45 6E 74 65 72 query   db        13,10,"Enter a string to parse: $"
      20 61 20 73 74 72 69
      6E 67 20 74 6F 20 70
      61 72 73 65 3A 20 24
021C  0D 0A 54 6F 6B 65 6E sayret  db        13,10,"Token="
      3D
0224  0004[               rettokt db        4 DUP(?)          ; Type of token
        ??
                 ]

0228  73 74 72 69 6E 67 3D         db        "string=",34      ; ending quote by 34
      22
0230  0080[               rettokv db        128 DUP(?)        ; Lots of room for the token
        ??
                 ]

0280  24                           db        "$"              ; Ender just in case
02B1  55 6E 6B 20         tokent  db        "Unk "           ; Type zero
02B5  43 77 64 20                  db        "Cwd "           ; 1
```

```
02B9  4C 77 64 20              db      "Lwd "           ; 2
02BD  4E 62 72 20              db      "Nbr "           ; 3
02C1  50 20 2E 20              db      "P . "           ; 4
02C5  50 20 2C 20              db      "P , "           ; 5
02C9  50 20 21 20              db      "P ! "           ; 6
02CD  50 20 3F 20              db      "P ? "           ; 7
02D1                    data    ENDS
                        ;
                        ;
                        ; Standard equates for token types
                        ;
= 0001                  tokencwd  EQU   1               ; Capitalized word
= 0002                  tokenlwd  EQU   2               ; Lower-Case word
= 0003                  tokennbr  EQU   3               ; Number
= 0004                  tokenper  EQU   4               ; Period
= 0005                  tokencom  EQU   5               ; Comma
= 0006                  tokenexc  EQU   6               ; Exclamation point
= 0007                  tokenqmk  EQU   7               ; Question mark
= 0000                  tokenunk  EQU   0               ; Unknown type
= 00FF                  tokeneod  EQU   255             ; End of data
                        ;


0000                    code    SEGMENT   para 'CODE' USE16 PUBLIC
                                ASSUME    CS:code, DS:data
                        ;
                        ; Set up the environment
                        ;
0000                    Begin:
0000  B8 ---- R                 mov     AX,data          ; Get data segment pointer
0003  8E D8                     mov     DS,AX            ; into DS,
0005  8E C0                     mov     ES,AX            ; and ES.
0007  2B F6                     sub     SI,SI            ; Clear indices
0009  2B FF                     sub     DI,DI
                        ;
                        ; Parse a line entered from the keyboard and repeat until a null
                        ; line is entered.
                        ;
000B                    getparse:
000B  E8 0049 R                 call    getinp           ; Get a line in
000E  E3 33                     jcxz    endit            ; if empty - exit.
                        ;
                        ; Loop thru the parse routine until an end of data is returned.
                        ;
0010                    nexttoken:
0010  E8 0000 E                 call    parsing          ; Go isolate token
0013  3C FF                     cmp     AL,tokeneod      ; End of data?
0015  74 F4                     jz      getparse         ; Need more data if so
                        ;
                        ; Put out the data which was returned.
                        ;
0017  53                        push    BX
0018  51                        push    CX               ; Save next pointers
0019  98                        cbw                      ; Get token number
001A  66| 98                    cwde                     ; as double word index.
001C  67| 66| 8B 0485 0000      mov     EAX,DWORD PTR tokent[EAX*4] ; Get into register
      02B1 R
0025  66| A3 0224 R             mov     DWORD PTR rettokt,EAX ; and into message.
0029  8B CA                     mov     CX,DX            ; Set the length
002B  8D 3E 0230 R              lea     DI,rettokv       ; and destination.
002F  F3/ A4                    rep movsb                ; then move token,
0031  B0 22                     mov     AL,34            ; ending quote,
0033  AA                        stosb                    ;
0034  B0 24                     mov     AL,'$'           ; and stopper.
0036  AA                        stosb
0037  B4 09                     mov     AH,9             ; Set code,
```

```
0039   8D 16 021C R            lea      DX,sayret        ; text pointer,
003D   CD 21                   int      21h              ; and do the message.
003F   59                      pop      CX
0040   5B                      pop      BX               ; Restore our registers and
0041   EB CD                   jmp      nexttoken        ; try for next token


0043            endit:
0043   B0 00                   mov      AL,0             ; Set return code
0045   B4 4C                   mov      AH,04ch          ; Set good-by
0047   CD 21                   int      21h              ; Return to the system
                        ;
                        ; Read a string in response to a prompt
                        ;
0049            getinp   PROC
0049   52                      push     DX               ; Save registers
004A   50                      push     AX
004B   56                      push     SI
004C   8D 16 0200 R            lea      DX,query         ; Set output prompt
0050   B4 09                   mov      AH,9             ; and dos request
0052   CD 21                   int      21h              ; put out the string
0054   8D 16 0000 R            lea      DX,string        ; point to input area
0058   C6 06 0000 R FE         mov      string,254       ; Set max length in
005D   B4 0A                   mov      AH,10            ; Ask for read of string
005F   CD 21                   int      21h              ; from DOS.
0061   8D 1E 0002 R            lea      BX,string+2      ; Point to just read data
0065   8A 0E 0001 R            mov      CL,string+1      ; Get length read
0069   B5 00                   mov      CH,0             ; as a word.
006B   8B F1                   mov      SI,CX            ; Set length
006D   C6 84 0002 R 00         mov      string+2[SI],0   ; and make an asciiz string.
0072   5E                      pop      SI
0073   58                      pop      AX
0074   5A                      pop      DX               ; Restore registers
0075   C3                      ret                       ; and return.
0076            getinp   ENDP

0076            code     ENDS
                         END     Begin
```

Program 6-11 PARSING

Microsoft (R) Macro Assembler Version 5.00

```
                        PAGE     55,132
                        .386
0000            code     SEGMENT  para 'CODE' USE16 PUBLIC
                         ASSUME   CS:code, DS:code, SS:code
                        ;
                        ; Name:    PARSING
                        ;
                        ; Purpose: The following procedure parses input text into a token
                        ;          which it returns to the driving process.
                        ;
                        ;
                        ; Inputs:  DS:BX points to the next text to parse.  CX has the
                        ;          length of text remaining.  If CX is zero, end of data
                        ;          is returned.
                        ;
                        ; Process: Leading spaces are skipped. If we ran out of data, return
                        ;          end of data.  Examine the non-blank we located.
                        ;
```

```
;                  If it's a number, verify that the following non-space, non-
;                  punctuation is also a number.  Repeat until a proper end
;                  is detected and return the number token.  If an unknown
;                  is detected, scan until a space or punctuation is detected
;                  to identify the unknown token's size and return an unknown.
;
;                  If it's a capital letter, potentially identify the token as
;                  a capitalized word.
;                  If it's a lower-case letter, potentially identify the token
;                  as a lower-case word.
;                  In either case, check the following for either lower-case
;                  letters or a proper ending (space or punctuation).  Treat
;                  an unknown token the same as above.
;
;                  Otherwise check if the non-space is a punctuation mark
;                  and if so return the proper token type.  Otherwise, treat
;                  the unknown token as above.
;
; Output:          AL will contain the type of token detected.  SI will point
;                  to the start of the token and DX will contain its length.
;                  BX will point to the character which stopped the scan and
;                  CX will contain the count of characters remaining.
;
;
;
; Standard equates for token types
;
```

= 0001	tokencwd	EQU	1		; Capitalized word
= 0002	tokenlwd	EQU	2		; Lower-Case word
= 0003	tokennbr	EQU	3		; Number
= 0004	tokenper	EQU	4		; Period
= 0005	tokencom	EQU	5		; Comma
= 0006	tokenexc	EQU	6		; Exclamation point
= 0007	tokenqmk	EQU	7		; Question mark
= 0000	tokenunk	EQU	0		; Unknown type
= 00FF	tokeneod	EQU	255		; End of data

```
                ;
                          PUBLIC    Parsing
                ;
0000            Parsing   PROC
0000  06                  push      ES              ; Save entry registers
0001  E3 32               jcxz      enddata         ; If no more data - say so
                ;
                ; Skip all leading spaces
                ;
0003  8C D8               mov       AX,DS           ; Set up for scan
0005  8E C0               mov       ES,AX           ; ES
0007  8B FB               mov       DI,BX           ; and DI
0009  FC                  cld                       ; Go up scanning
000A  B0 20               mov       AL,' '          ; for non space.
000C  F3/ AE              repe scasb                ; skip all leading spaces.
000E  0F 84 0035 R        jz        enddata         ; End of data if all spaces.
0012  41                  inc       CX              ; Add overage back
                ;
                ; Identify the kind of token found.  Our repe took us one too far.
                ; We need to back the pointer up one and ultimately count this byte
                ; out of CX.  We need to delay counting the byte until after we
                ; determine the type in order to handle single byte tokens at the
                ; end of the input.
                ;
                ; We change ES here to allow its use in checkend where it could be
                ; set multiple times.  (Protected mode checking makes segment
                ; register setting more expensive. 18 clocks.)
                ;
0013  8C CE               mov       SI,CS           ; Prepare for check ending
0015  8E C6               mov       ES,SI           ; Set ES
```

```
0017  8B F7                       mov     SI,DI             ; Need to check each byte
0019  4E                          dec     SI                ; Point to token start.
001A  56                          push    SI                ; Save the start.
001B  AC                          lodsb                     ; Get a byte (step SI).
001C  34 30                       xor     AL,'0'            ;
001E  3C 09                       cmp     AL,9              ; Is it a number
0020  0F 87 0048 R                ja      checkalph         ; No - go check for alpha
0024  EB 0A 90                    jmp     numbere           ; Yes, go count char found
                              ;
                              ; We have either a number or an unknown
                              ;
0027                          number:
0027  AC                          lodsb                     ; Get the next byte
0028  34 30                       xor     AL,'0'            ; Check if a number
002A  3C 09                       cmp     AL,9              ; Is it
002C  0F 87 0039 R                ja      numbend           ; No - check proper endings.
0030                          numbere:
0030  E2 F5                       loop    number            ; go check the next
                              ;
                              ; We ended on a valid number.
                              ;
0032  EB 0F 90                    jmp     goodnum           ; We are OK.
                              ;
                              ; End of data - return token type saying so
                              ;
0035                          enddata:
0035  B0 FF                       mov     AL,tokeneod       ; Set token type
0037  07                          pop     ES                ; restore register
0038  C3                          ret                       ; and exit.
                              ;
                              ; We had a number up to this byte - if it is punctuation or a space
                              ; the number is valid.  Otherwise we have an unknown.
                              ;
0039                          numbend:
0039  4E                          dec     SI                ; We went one too far!
003A  34 30                       xor     AL,'0'            ; Put it back as it was.
003C  E8 00AE R                   call    checkend          ; Is it an ending
003F  0F 85 0095 R                jne     unklook           ; Bad so scan to a good one.
                              ;
                              ; Our token is a number
                              ;
0043                          goodnum:
0043  B0 03                       mov     AL,tokennbr       ; Set the type
0045  EB 5E 90                    jmp     outtoken          ; Build token for return.
                              ;
                              ; We may have a lower-case or capitalized word.
                              ;
0048                          checkalph:
0048  34 30                       xor     AL,'0'            ; Fix char again.
004A  B4 01                       mov     AH,tokencwd       ; Assume it is.
004C  3C 41                       cmp     AL,'A'            ; Check if it is a cap
004E  0F 82 0066 R                jb      checkpunct        ; No - go check punctuation.
0052  3C 5A                       cmp     AL,'Z'            ; Is it a cap
0054  0F 86 0082 R                jna     checkworde        ; Yes - it may be a word!
0058  B4 02                       mov     AH,tokenlwd       ; Assume a lower-case word.
005A  3C 61                       cmp     AL,'a'            ; Check if it is a lower
                              ;                             Note: in case we add punct-
005C  0F 82 0066 R                jb      checkpunct        ; uation we go check here.
0060  3C 7A                       cmp     AL,'z'            ; Is it a-z?
0062  0F 86 0082 R                jna     checkworde        ; yes -
                              ;
                              ; It may be punctuation
                              ;
0066                          checkpunct:
0066  E8 00AE R                   call    checkend          ; Check for punctuation ending.
0069  0F 85 009D R                jne     unknown           ; If not - go find some.
                              ;
                              ; We need to adjust the count for the single byte processed.
```

```
                                       ;
006D  49                               dec     CX              ; So count this out.
006E  B0 03                            mov     AL,tokenper-1   ; Set the amount to add
0070  02 C4                            add     AL,AH           ; and add to get token type.
0072  EB 31 90                         jmp     outtoken        ; Go build token pointers.
                                       ;
                                       ; Check for more lower-case alpha with a proper ending.
                                       ;
0075                          checkword:
0075  AC                               lodsb                   ; Get the next byte
0076  3C 61                            cmp     AL,'a'          ; Is it a
0078  0F 82 0089 R                     jb      wordendq        ; If low - can't be
007C  3C 7A                            cmp     AL,'z'          ; thru z?
007E  0F 87 0089 R                     ja      wordendq        ; if high - is isn't
0082                          checkworde:
0082  E2 F1                            loop    checkword       ; If another - check it
0084  8A C4                            mov     AL,AH           ; Set the token type and
0086  EB 1D 90                         jmp     outtoken        ; go build pointers.
                                       ;
                                       ; A word has ended - check for proper ending.
                                       ;
0089                          wordendq:
0089  4E                               dec     SI              ; We went too far by 1.
008A  50                               push    AX              ; Save our possible token type
008B  E8 00AE R                        call    checkend        ; check for proper ending.
008E  58                               pop     AX              ; Restore token type
008F  8A C4                            mov     AL,AH           ; into proper register
0091  0F 84 00A5 R                     je      outtoken        ; If proper ending - done.
                                       ;
                                       ; Scan forward to a proper ending
                                       ;
0095                          unklook:
0095  AC                               lodsb                   ; Get the next byte
0096  E8 00AE R                        call    checkend        ; Is it a good ending?
0099  0F 84 00A2 R                     je      unknowne        ; It is - get out
009D                          unknown:
009D  E2 F6                            loop    unklook         ; Count it and if more - check
009F  EB 02 90                         jmp     outunknown
00A2                          unknowne:
00A2  4E                               dec     SI              ; Back up to punctuation
00A3                          outunknown:
00A3  B0 00                            mov     AL,tokenunk     ; Set type as unknown
                                       ;
                                       ; Build the token pointer and length for return.
                                       ;
00A5                          outtoken:
00A5  8B DE                            mov     BX,SI           ; Set next char pointer.
00A7  5E                               pop     SI              ; Get start
00A8  8B D3                            mov     DX,BX           ; Set next into length.
00AA  2B D6                            sub     DX,SI           ; Get the length=next-start
00AC  07                               pop     ES              ; Restore ES
00AD  C3                               ret                     ; and return.
00AE                          checkend        PROC
                                       ;
                                       ; Check if the byte in AL is one of our delimiters.  If it is, we exit
                                       ; with AH set to the remaining count from CX and the zero flag set.
                                       ; Otherwise, the zero flag is not set on exit.
                                       ;
                                       ;
00AE  51                               push    CX              ; Save current count left
00AF  8D 3E 00BD R                     lea     DI,CS:punct     ; Point to the proper endings
00B3  B9 0005 90                       mov     CX,punctct      ; Set the proper count.
                                       ;
                                       ; The following is a good way to test for set inclusion.  AL (AX or
                                       ; EAX) is tested against all CX items until a match is found.  The
                                       ; number of clocks (5+8n) is small enough to make even moderate
```

```
                               ; size lists efficient.  Of course, large lists are more efficiently
                               ; searched with a non-linear technique such as a binary search or
                               ; hashing.
                               ;
00B7  F2/ AE                          repne scasb                 ; Check if any of the endings.
00B9  8A E1                           mov    AH,CL                ; Save residual
00BB  59                              pop    CX                   ; Restore count left
00BC  C3                              ret

00BD                           checkend  ENDP

00BD  3F 21 2C 2E 20           punct     db      '?!,. '          ; Proper endings
= 0005                         punctct   EQU     $-punct

00C2                           Parsing   ENDP
00C2                           code      ENDS
                                         END
```

7

Code conversion

Conversion is the process of changing information from one form to another. Often, you have little control over the form of input, and you must convert numbers from one base to another or character sets from one to another, in order to better handle a process within a program. A second need for conversion comes when the hardware or software, or both, of the host system cannot easily handle a particular input set.

80486 data handling

The processor views memory as if it were a sequential array of bytes. Think of it as beginning from your left hand, moving to your right hand, and continuing to the right for as many bytes as are built into your system. However, the bits within the bytes are counted (or positioned) from right to left, as shown in Fig. 7-1. The byte address starts at the left with zero and moves to the right. In Fig. 7-1, the byte for "40" is stored in memory storage location zero (0), yet the least significant bit (LSB) is on the right and the most significant bit (MSB) is on the left.

The 80486 moves data from memory one byte at a time into specified registers. The registers begin their counting from the right. So, the 80486 stores it from the first byte in the right-hand slot (the AL byte register in the example). The second byte goes in the second slot (the AH register in the example). Therefore, if you look at a dump of a location in memory, it probably will not look like a dump of a register that holds the same data.

80486 data types

The 80486 operates on signed and unsigned integers, binary coded decimals (BCD)—both packed and unpacked, floating-points, bits, and strings.

Memory is viewed from the processor as if it were a sequential array of bytes.

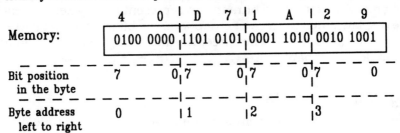

Memory:

| 4 | 0 | D | 7 | 1 | A | 2 | 9 |

0100 0000 | 1101 0101 | 0001 1010 | 0010 1001

Bit position in the byte: 7 0 7 0 7 0 7 0

Byte address left to right: 0 | 1 | 2 | 3

Example 1: Move a memory byte "40" to a byte register, AL, the low order byte of AX. The 80386 moves memory byte 0, the "40".

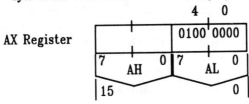

AX Register

Example 2: Move a word to a word register AX. When memory word "40 D7" is moved to AX, the 80386 moves "40" to AL (low order byte of AX). Then the "D7" is moved to AH (high order byte of AX). Memory byte 0 is moved first ("40"). Memory byte 1 is moved second ("D7").

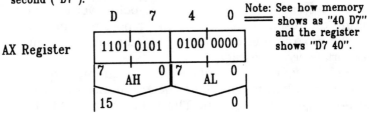

AX Register

Note: See how memory shows as "40 D7" and the register shows "D7 40".

Example 3: Move a double word (dword) to the EAX register. Again, memory moves one byte at a time, going from AL to AH and then to the byte 3 and 4 of EAX.

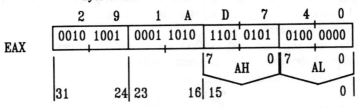

EAX

7-1 Storage examples of memory and registers.

The 80486 uses 8-bit bytes, 16-bit words, and 32-bit doublewords (dwords). The 80486 processor supports seven data types: word integer, short integer, long integer, BCD, short real, long real, and temporary real.

The 80486 supports bit manipulation, from a single bit to bit string up to 2^{32} bits in length. Bit manipulation is important for use in bitmaps and as semaphores. For example, a bitmap can represent each pixel, i.e., each dot on the display. When used as semaphore, the bit is either set (ON = 1) when busy or reset (OFF = 0) when free. Bit and string manipulation are discussed in detail in chapter 6.

Floating-point numbers

Floating-point numbers allow computations where the magnitude of the numbers is very large, larger than can be handled with fixed-point numbers (except with great difficulty). Floating-point representation of numbers corresponds to what is usually called scientific notation; that is, each number is represented as the product of a normal number with a decimal point and an integral power of the radix. For example, the number 57.2233 is expressed in scientific notation as 0.57223×10^2, with the 0.57223 being called the *fractional* part and the 2 the *exponent* part. This notation is called floating-point in computer arithmetic because the radix point of the entire number is not fixed but can float, depending on the value of the exponent.

The most difficult operations in floating-point arithmetic are addition and subtraction. Overflow can occur in all floating-point operations when the magnitude of the result exceeds the capacity of the floating-point number system. The result of floating-point overflow is handled either by making the result the largest number possible and setting an indicator that the programmer can test, or by stopping the computation with an appropriate error message.

Underflow, which results from the attempt to produce a nonzero result too small in magnitude to be accommodated, can also result from any floating-point operation. The usual response is to generate a zero result. Often, an indicator is set that you can check with your program code.

Floating-point multiplication and division require only performing the appropriate action on the fractional parts, rounding the results, adding (for multiplication) or subtracting (for division) the exponents, and then normalizing if necessary.

Real numbers are represented as floating-point numbers. Their formats are composed of significand, exponent, and sign. Table 7-1 shows the bits used for the real formats and the general format of real numbers.

The sign of the number is a sign bit, at the MSB location. If the sign = 0, the number is positive; if sign = 1, it is negative. The significand hold the significant bits of the number, often called the mantissa. To show maximum precision, the results of arithmetic computations are normalized, i.e., numbers have their exponents adjusted so that the most significant bit of the binary significand is 1. The binary point is then to the right of this 1. The correct normalized result of the number 1 is 1.0×10^0. Note that an exponent of zero means the value of one.

Table 7-1   Real-number data format.

Data Type	Total Bits	Significand	Exponent	Sign
Short	32	23	8	1
Long	64	52	11	1
Temporary	80	64	15	1

General Format

Sign	Exponent	Significand

The exponent field holds the power of two needed to scale the significand to get the final result. The exponent is stored in biased form to ease numerical comparisons.

Conversion routines

The conversion routines in Programs 7-1 through 7-15 at the end of the chapter are meant to ease your programming to convert number representation. We included a driver so you can test the routines and see how they are called and implemented before you use or modify them.

A code conversion driver program

A code conversion driver program, CODEDRV (Program 7-1), drives the various code conversion routines in this book. This provides both a test for the conversion routines themselves and a working example of the calling sequences. Input is typed at the keyboard in response to prompts. The input is passed through the conversion routines, first converting from the ASCII to either binary or EBCDIC. The reverse conversion is then done and the output displayed. Output should equal input. The reverse conversion results are displayed.

Hex to binary and back

Hexadecimal representation is a condensed visual representation where each hex digit (0–9, A–F) represents a 4-bit value. Because a byte is 8 bits, it can be represented visually by two hex digits, which is the most compact representation that also allows easy mental conversion to bit form. A pair of hex digits is converted into a binary byte. The left hex digit becomes the most significant nibble (4 bits). The right hex digit becomes the least significant nibble.

CODEHXTB (Program 7-2) converts a displayable hexadecimal number into its binary equivalent. It accepts two ASCII hex digits and returns a byte. Each input nibble is converted and, at the same time, edited to ensure that the presented value is 0 – 9 or A – F (or a – f). An error causes a set Carry Flag and an immediate return.

After subtracting the character 0 (hex 30), it ANDs bit 5 off (which would be on for a lowercase character). This allows it to treat all alphabetic character inputs (the A – F of hex notation) without special handling of case. This AND replaces a comparison, a branch, and special handling with a single instruction.

Binary numbers generally are too clumsy for easy use. The base-16 hexadecimal (hex) numbering system evolved as the most convenient one for assembly language programming largely for two reasons: first, conversions are easily done between hex and binary; and second, programmers are more accustomed to the digits 0 – 9 and A – F.

CODEBTHX (Program 7-3) provides a single-byte conversion from binary to displayable hexadecimal. The calling program passes the byte to be converted in AL. CODEBTHX converts the left nibble of AL and returns it in AH, then converts the right nibble and returns it in AL. The BUFFER program (described and listed in chapter 9) calls CODEBTHX to display a memory register.

ASCII to EBCDIC and back

Bytes are units of information that consist of 8 bits. In addition to carrying numeric entities, bytes also represent alphabetic and special characters. The American Standard Code for Information Interchange (ASCII) is an assignment of a numeric value to each digit, letter, and special character. ASCII also has control codes, such as Carriage Return, that carry special information. (See appendix D for the full ASCII character set.)

On the other hand, Binary-Coded Decimal Interchange Code (BCDIC) developed because alphabetic data could not be represented in any combination of 4 bits (see chapter 4 for more information). To get around this, BCD was expanded by the addition of two extra bits, called B and A bits, which were used extensively in second-generation computers. The A and B bits were used to record the zone portion of alphabetic data as coded in the standard (Hollerith) punched card. Figure 7-2 shows where they were placed.

When third-generation computers came along, the 6-bit BCDIC was discarded for an 8-bit coding scheme—Extended Binary-Coded Decimal Interchange Code (EBCDIC)—that allowed both uppercase and lowercase alphabetic characters, as well as many of the special characters. Two ver-

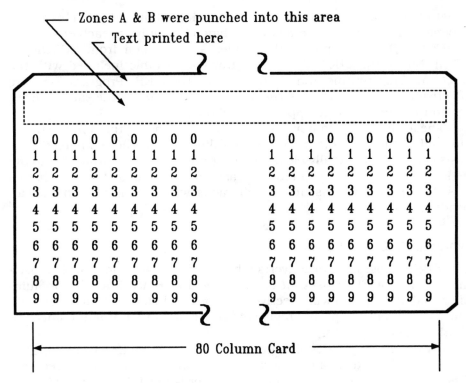

7-2 Standard punched card format.

sions of the 8-bit code were devised: EBCDIC and ASCII. In each, two sets of 4-bit codes were used, with each 4-bit set being coded with the "8-4-2-1" scheme. ASCII became the industry standard for data exchange between computers. In the 1960s, IBM adopted 8-bit EBCDIC for their System/360 mainframes, while much of the remainder of the industry adopted ASCII. Today, ASCII is used on most microcomputers.

CODEASB (Program 7-7) converts an ASCII numeric string to its doubleword binary equivalent. Because the end number is a doubleword, CODEASB uses the 80486 extended register set. This routine is useful in pulling multiple numbers out of a long string when the numbers are separated by commas or by spaces. You could intersperse this routine with scanning of text, for instance.

The procedure scans the string to get the count of digits. The technique of the routine is new: CODEASB fetches decimal digit pairs from left to right. The prior result is multiplied by 100 and the new pair is converted to binary and added to the prior result. Each pair in the source is processed. If an odd number of digits is presented, the first digit is processed alone before going on to the pairs.

It turns out that the 8086 through 80486 ASCII Adjust for Division (AAD) will take a pair of digits and do the combination and multiplication to get them into a range from 0 to 99 in a single binary byte. This is less expensive in terms of machine cycles than a multiply for each character.

CODEEBAS (Program 7-4) provides a conversion from EBCDIC to ASCII. Notice the EBCDIC to ASCII translation table included with the program. This routine and its partner, CODEASEB (Program 7-5), are effectively the same. The instructions used in both are the same, except the conversion is done in opposite directions.

The technique of combining error bits and leaving them in the translate table if the value did not translate validly to EBCDIC is interesting. It costs very little to initially clear a register and OR each character into the register, but at the end you have an easy method to detect "bad" characters. The character translates to a character with the high bit on and can be identified.

Binary to ASCII and back

CODEBAS (Program 7-6) converts a binary doubleword to an ASCII decimal string. CODEBAS uses the fact that the 80486 ASCII Adjust for Multiply (AAM) instruction will effectively perform a divide by 10 and separate the two digits in the proper registers. This results in a program check to eliminate leading zeros.

EAX contains the doubleword to be converted and ES:DI contains the pointer to a 12-byte area for the converted data. The sign is captured and, if negative, the absolute value of the number is used. Next, we divide the number by 100. The two-decimal digit remainder is converted and stored in the target string from right to left. The procedure is repeated until the quotient is zero. We chose this technique of repeated division because it is easily expandable to larger binary numbers, as well as for its simplicity. CODEASB (Program 7-7) converts in the other direction.

A floating-point routine driver program

A floating-point routine driver program, FPDRIVE (Program 7-8), exercises the floating-point conversion routines. You are prompted for a floating-point number, which must be in the form:

$(-)d*.d*e(-)d*$

where $(-)$ is an optional minus sign, $d*$ is one or more numeric digits, the decimal "." is a required decimal, and e is a required start-of-exponent signal; e can be either uppercase or lowercase. Inputting a null (pressing Enter) ends the program.

The floating-point number is converted to an IEEE long floating-point number; an error causes a re-prompt. The floating-point number is then converted to ASCII and displayed in hexadecimal, converted to IBM format, displayed in hex, converted to IEEE format and displayed in hex again. The number is then converted to short floating-point form, displayed in hex, converted to long form, displayed in hex and converted to ASCII and displayed again. The program then loops back to the original user prompt for input.

Single to double precision and back

Single to double precision and back, FPLONGTS (Program 7-9), converts an IEEE format long floating-point number to an IEEE short format floating-point number. Intel provides both a short floating-point and a long floating-point, and you might need to convert from one to the other. IEEE long format has an 11-digit binary exponent biased by 1023. It appears in memory reversed from its form in registers. IEEE short format has 8 bits of exponent biased by 127 and a 23-bit fraction. Conversion from long to short can either overflow or underflow the short exponent. An overflow returns a short infinity, while an underflow returns a short zero. In either case, the Carry Flag is set upon return.

DS:SI points to an IEEE format long floating-point number in memory, which is assumed to be a normalized number. The exponent is unbiased and checked for overflow or underflow and, if found, the Carry Flag is set. Otherwise, the exponent is biased as a short number and the fraction truncated to 23 bits and combined with the new exponent and sign. The converted number is returned in EAX.

FPSTLONG (Program 7-10) does the opposite. This conversion is simpler. It's a matter of rebiasing the exponent and adding some zeros at the end of the number. Conversion from short to long can neither overflow nor underflow the long exponent. Zero and short infinity must be checked for and preserved. Infinity is recognized and the Carry Flag set on return. The converted number is returned in EAX:EDX.

IEEE to IBM double precision and back

FPIBMEEE (Program 7-11) provides a conversion of an IBM-format long floating-point number to an IEEE long-format floating-point number. The IBM/370 format is hexadecimal-based and appears in memory in the same form as it does in registers. The IEEE format is binary-based and, on the 80486, appears reversed in memory from its form in registers.

IEEE format appears to have 4 bits less precision than IBM format, but the average precision of IBM format is 54.5 bits because it is hexadecimal. The hidden bit in front of the fraction of the IEEE format extends its precision to 53 bits. The conversion routines ignore this discrepancy. The IBM format's exponent base (16) provides a maximum value of $2^{(64 \times 4)}$ or 2^{256}. The IEEE format provides a maximum of 2^{1023}. Therefore, there is no problem converting from IBM to IEEE.

DS:SI points to an IBM-format long floating-point number in memory. This is assumed to be a normalized number. It is in IBM order as it would be if read from a network, IBM file, or magnetic tape. The number is reversed into 80486 format. The exponent is then converted from IBM to IEEE base in signed form. The fraction is then renormalized from IBM to IEEE form and shifted right to make room for the biased exponent and sign. The exponent is then biased by 1023, the sign appended, and the resulting 12 bits are combined with the fraction. The result is stored over the original number.

FPIEEEBM (Program 7-12) does the reverse. Both routines use 80486 instructions (double shift left and right, for example), which eases the conversion in addition to using the large 80486 registers.

Note: When going from IBM to IEEE, you can't overflow. However, when going from IEEE to IBM, you can overflow and underflow because there are more positions in the exponent of IEEE numbers. As an implementation decision, if you underflow, the routine returns zero; if you overflow, it provides the maximum IBM floating-point number. If either occurs, the Carry Flag is set.

IEEE long float to ASCII and back

In floating-point numbers, the binary point is allowed to float. A portion of the data shows the location of the binary point and the rest specifies the significant data bits. This allows you to extend the representable range of numbers while providing you with precision over the entire range. The 80486 FPU supports the IEEE floating-point standard.

FPLFPASC (Program 7-13) converts from an Intel IEEE-format long floating-point number to an ASCII representation of a floating-point number. The technique used is a binary search of exponents to reduce the number of floating-point multiplication to be done (divides are avoided wherever possible). We scaled exponents to an appropriate power and multiplied by ten. Then, we multiplied by 100 and ASCII Adjusted after Multiplication (AAM) to convert to character. This cut the number of machine cycles in half, over a multiply by 10.

IEEE long format has an 11-digit binary exponent biased by 1023. It appears in memory reversed from its form in registers. An ASCII representation is a string in the form:

[–]digit.digitsE[–]digits

where [–] indicates an optional minus sign; digit is an ASCII digit preceding the decimal point (.); digits is one or more ASCII digits following the decimal point; and E begins the exponent.

Conversion to ASCII of a valid long floating-point number is always possible. Infinity is checked for and is returned as 9.9E999 or – 9.9E999, depending on the number's sign. Zero is returned as 0.0E0. Zero and infinity are returned for exponents of 00000000000 and 11111111111, respectively. The fraction is not checked in either case (ignoring NaNs).

EAX:EDX contains the long floating-point number. BX is assumed to point to a string area of (at least) 25 bytes. The sign is transferred to the output and the number is replaced by its absolute value if it is negative. The decimal exponent is then created by scaling the number to a value between 1.0 and 10.0. The digit is extracted, converted to ASCII, and placed in the output followed by a decimal point.

FPASCLFP (Program 7-14) does the opposite conversion. Both routines make extensive use of the 80486 extended register set.

Conversion might overflow or underflow, which results in a zero or infinity, depending on whether you underflowed or overflowed. FPASCLFP converts the digits into a quadword, binary number, and then counts digits beyond to convert to the proper exponent value. Then FPASCLFP converts the exponent and combines the two to form the number. The final exponent is formed by using a binary search.

IBM System/370 to Intel and back

FLIPS (Program 7-15) provides data conversions for a word, a doubleword, and a quadword from mainframe style (such as used on IBM mainframes) to the Intel style. Intel stores the register's low-order byte to low-order address and high-order byte to high-order address. In memory, then, it makes the bytes look "reversed" on a byte basis. Mainframes generally store bytes exactly as they appear in registers.

If you're getting data from a mainframe, either through a communications line or on magnetic tape, that data will be in the mainframe order. Before you can work with it on a system based on an Intel microprocessor, you have to flip it around to make it usable.

The 80486 instruction BSWAP implements this program in a single instruction, for 2 to 4 bytes. FLIP486 (Program 7-16) contains the entry points and uses the BSWAP instruction. FLIPS is also provided for those still waiting for their 80486 computer.

FLIPDRV (Program 7-17) drives the flip routines. It provides both a test for the routines themselves and a working example of the calling sequences.

Program 7-1 CODEDRV
Microsoft (R) Macro Assembler Version 5.00

```
                              PAGE    55,132
                              .386
              ;
              ; Name:    CODEDRV
              ;
              ; Purpose: This program drives the various code conversion routines.
              ;          This provides both a test for the routines themselves and
              ;          a working example of the calling sequences.
              ;
              ; Inputs:  Input is typed at the keyboard in response to prompts.
              ;
              ; Process: The input is passed through the conversion routines, first
              ;          converting from the ASCII to either binary or EBCDIC.  The
```

```
;                    reverse conversion is then done and the output displayed.
;
; Outputs: The reverse conversion results are displayed for
;          inspection.
;
; Declare the routines we are going to use
;
                EXTRN   CODEEBAS:PROC
                EXTRN   CODEASEB:PROC
                EXTRN   CODEASB:PROC
                EXTRN   CODEBAS:PROC
                EXTRN   CODEHXTB:PROC
                EXTRN   CODEBTHX:PROC

0000            stack       SEGMENT para 'STACK' STACK
0000  0100[                 dq      256 DUP(?)
      ???????????????????
      ?
                 ]

0800            stack       ENDS
0000            data        SEGMENT para
0000  00000000  number      dd      0
0004  0100[     string1     db      256 DUP(?)          ; String scratch area
      ??
                 ]

0104  0100[     string2     db      256 DUP(?)          ; Second scratch area
      ??
                 ]

0204  0A 0D     string3p    db      10,13
0206  0100[     string3     db      256 DUP(?)          ; Third scratch area
      ??
                 ]

0306  0A 0D 49 6E 76 61 6C  badhexm     db      10,13,"Invalid hex entered.$"
      69 64 20 68 65 78 20
      65 6E 74 65 72 65 64
      2E 24
031D  0A 0D 4E 75 6D 62 65  oflowmsg    db      10,13,"Number overflows extended register.$"
      72 20 6F 76 65 72 66
      6C 6F 77 73 20 65 78
      74 65 6E 64 65 64 20
      72 65 67 69 73 74 65
      72 2E 24
0343  0A 0D 43 6F 6E 76 65  numbert     db      10,13,"Converted to: $"
      72 74 65 64 20 74 6F
      3A 20 24
0354  0A 0A 0D 45 6E 74 65  query1      db      10,10,13,"Enter a string to convert: $"
      72 20 61 20 73 74 72
      69 6E 67 20 74 6F 20
      63 6F 6E 76 65 72 74
      3A 20 24
0373  0A 0A 0D 45 6E 74 65  query2      db      10,10,13,"Enter a number to convert: $"
      72 20 61 20 6E 75 6D
      62 65 72 20 74 6F 20
      63 6F 6E 76 65 72 74
      3A 20 24
0392  0A 0A 0D 45 6E 74 65  query3      db      10,10,13,"Enter a string of hex digits "
      72 20 61 20 73 74 72
      69 6E 67 20 6F 66 20
      68 65 78 20 64 69 67
      69 74 73 20
03B2  74 6F 20 63 6F 6E 76              db      "to convert: $"
      65 72 74 3A 20 24
```

```
03BF                    data        ENDS
0000                    code        SEGMENT para 'CODE' USE16 PUBLIC
                                    ASSUME  CS:code, DS:data
                        ;
                        ; Set up the environment
                        ;
0000                    Begin:
0000  B8 ---- R                     mov     AX,data             ; Get data segment pointer
0003  8E D8                         mov     DS,AX               ; into DS,
0005  8E C0                         mov     ES,AX               ; and ES.
0007  2B F6                         sub     SI,SI               ; Clear indices
0009  2B FF                         sub     DI,DI
                        ;
                        ; First convert ascii to ebcdic and back
                        ;
000B                    nexttry:
000B  8D 16 0354 R                  lea     DX,query1           ; Get a string to convert
000F  E8 00D2 R                     call    getinp              ;
0012  0B C9                         or      CX,CX               ; Was any entered?
0014  0F 84 00CC R                  jz      Exit                ; No - simple exit
0018  8D 36 0006 R                  lea     SI,string1+2        ; Source string
001C  8D 3E 0104 R                  lea     DI,string2          ; destination string
0020  51                           push    CX                  ; Save CX
0021  E8 0000 E                     call    Codeaseb            ; Make ebcdic
0024  8D 36 0104 R                  lea     SI,string2          ; Set ebcdic source
0028  8D 3E 0206 R                  lea     DI,string3          ; and ascii destination
002C  59                           pop     CX                  ; length
002D  51                           push    CX                  ; save it
002E  E8 0000 E                     call    Codeebas            ; back to ascii
0031  5B                           pop     BX                  ; Get length back
0032  C6 87 0206 R 24               mov     string3[BX],'$'     ; Set stopper
0037  8D 16 0204 R                  lea     DX,string3p         ; Point to lf/cr
003B  B4 09                         mov     AH,9                ; Set code for DOS
003D  CD 21                         int     21h                 ; and put it out.
                        ;
                        ; Do ascii to binary and back
                        ;
003F  8D 16 0373 R                  lea     DX,query2           ; Point to number query.
0043  E8 00D2 R                     call    getinp              ; read a number to convert
0046  8D 36 0006 R                  lea     SI,string1+2        ; Point to string entered.
004A  E8 0000 E                     call    Codeasb             ; Convert it to binary.
004D  0F 82 00C2 R                  jc      oflomsg             ; If too large - do message
0051  66| A3 0000 R                 mov     number,EAX          ; Save the number
0055  8D 3E 0104 R                  lea     DI,string2          ; Point to output string.
0059  E8 0000 E                     call    Codebas             ; Convert it back.
005C  8D 16 0343 R                  lea     DX,numbert          ; Point to text
0060  B4 09                         mov     AH,9
0062  CD 21                         int     21h                 ; and write it
0064  B4 02                         mov     AH,2                ; Set code for single byte
0066                    numbout:
0066  8A 15                         mov     DL,BYTE PTR [DI]    ; Get a byte
0068  0A D2                         or      DL,DL               ; test for stopper
006A  0F 84 0073 R                  jz      numbout0            ; done
006E  CD 21                         int     21h
0070  47                           inc     DI                  ; Point to next
0071  EB F3                         jmp     numbout             ; Do the next.
0073                    numbout0:
                        ;
                        ; Do hex to binary and back
                        ;
0073  8D 16 0392 R                  lea     DX,query3           ; Request the data
0077  E8 00D2 R                     call    getinp              ; in the string1 area.
007A  D1 E9                         shr     CX,1                ; Get number of pairs.
007C  E3 F5                         jcxz    numbout0            ; require one.
007E  8D 36 0006 R                  lea     SI,string1+2        ; Point to the input data
0082  8D 3E 0104 R                  lea     DI,string2          ; and to the output.
0086  51                           push    CX                  ; Save the count
0087  FC                           cld                         ; Set direction up.
```

Program 7-1 Continued.

```
0088                            nexthex:
0088   8A 24                                mov     AH,BYTE PTR[SI]      ; Get the high byte
008A   46                                   inc     SI
008B   AC                                   lodsb                        ; and the low
008C   E8 0000 E                            call    Codehxtb             ; Convert them
008F   0F 82 00B6 R                         jc      badhex               ; If an error - quit
0093   AA                                   stosb                        ; Store the converted byte.
0094   E2 F2                                loop    nexthex              ; Back for the next pair.
0096   59                                   pop     CX                   ; Restore the pair count
0097   8D 36 0104 R                         lea     SI,string2           ; Set the binary pointer
009B   8D 3E 0206 R                         lea     DI,string3           ; and the display pointer
009F                            nextbin:
009F   AC                                   lodsb                        ; Get a byte
00A0   E8 0000 E                            call    codebthx             ; convert it to display form
00A3   86 C4                                xchg    AL,AH                ; Flip the bytes
00A5   AB                                   stosw                        ; and put them down
00A6   E2 F7                                loop    nextbin              ; do all pairs
00A8   C6 05 24                             mov     BYTE PTR[DI],'$'     ; Terminate the string
00AB   8D 16 0204 R                         lea     DX,string3p          ; put it out
00AF   B4 09                                mov     AH,9                 ;
00B1   CD 21                                int     21h
00B3   E9 000B R                            jmp     nexttry              ; Go try again
00B6                            badhex:
00B6   59                                   pop     CX                   ; clear the stack
00B7   8D 16 0306 R                         lea     DX,badhexm           ; Point to the message
00BB   B4 09                                mov     AH,9                 ; Set code
00BD   CD 21                                int     21h                  ; display it
00BF   E9 000B R                            jmp     nexttry              ; and loop
00C2                            oflomsg:
00C2   8D 16 031D R                         lea     DX,oflowmsg          ; Set message
00C6   B4 09                                mov     AH,9
00C8   CD 21                                int     21h                  ; put it out
00CA   EB A7                                jmp     numbout0             ; continue
00CC                            Exit:
00CC   B0 00                                mov     AL,0                 ; Set return code
00CE   B4 4C                                mov     AH,04ch              ; Set good-by
00D0   CD 21                                int     21h                  ; Return to the system
                               ;
                               ; Read a string in response to a prompt
                               ; The prompt must be in DX.  The string will be returned in string.
                               ;
00D2                            getinp    PROC
00D2   50                                   push    AX                   ; Save registers
00D3   56                                   push    SI
00D4   B4 09                                mov     AH,9                 ; and dos request
00D6   CD 21                                int     21h                  ; put out the string
00D8   8D 16 0004 R                         lea     DX,string1           ; point to input area
00DC   C6 06 0004 R FE                      mov     string1,254          ; Set max length in
00E1   B4 0A                                mov     AH,10                ; Ask for read of string
00E3   CD 21                                int     21h                  ; from DOS.
00E5   8D 1E 0006 R                         lea     BX,string1+2         ; Point to just read data
00E9   8A 0E 0005 R                         mov     CL,string1+1         ; Get length read
00ED   B5 00                                mov     CH,0                 ; as a word.
00EF   8B F1                                mov     SI,CX                ; Set length
00F1   C6 84 0006 R 00                      mov     string1+2[SI],0      ; and make an asciiz string.
00F6   5E                                   pop     SI
00F7   58                                   pop     AX                   ; Restore registers
00F8   C3                                   ret                          ; and return.
00F9                            getinp    ENDP

00F9   :                        code      ENDS
                                          END     Begin
```

Program 7-2 CODEHXTB

Microsoft (R) Macro Assembler Version 5.00

```
                                    PAGE      55,132
                                    .386
0000                        code    SEGMENT   para 'CODE' PUBLIC USE16
                                    ASSUME    CS:code, DS:code, SS:code
                            ;
                            ; Name:     Codehxtb
                            ;
                            ; Purpose: The following procedure provides conversion from
                            ;          hexadecimal representation into binary.
                            ;
                            ;
                            ; Inputs:   AH has the hex value for the left nibble.
                            ;           AL has the hex value for the right nibble.
                            ;
                            ; Process: Each nibble is converted and at the same time edited to
                            ;          ensure that the presented value is 0-9 or A-F (a-f).
                            ;          An error causes carry to be set and an immediate return.
                            ;
                            ;          The high nibble value is shifted left 4 bits and combined
                            ;          with the low nibble in AL, carry is reset and we return.
                            ;
                            ; Output:   AL has the binary value if the hex values were valid.
                            ;           Carry is reset.
                            ;
                            ;           If the hex values are in error, AL is undefined and
                            ;           Carry is set.
                            ;
                            ;
                                    PUBLIC    Codehxtb                ; Make name known.
                            ;
0000                        Codehxtb PROC
0000  80 EC 30                      sub       AH,'0'                  ; Convert the high nibble
0003  0F 88 0040 R                  js        badhex                  ; Negative is bad
0007  80 FC 09                      cmp       AH,9                    ; Was it 0-9?
000A  0F 86 001F R                  jna       gothi                   ; Yes, High is converted.
000E  80 E4 DF                      and       AH,0dfh                 ; Make lower into upper case.
0011  80 EC 07                      sub       AH,'a'-'9'              ; Must have been A-F
0014  0F 88 0040 R                  js        badhex                  ; No - was between 9 and A
0018  80 FC 0F                      cmp       AH,15                   ; Check if valid.
001B  0F 87 0040 R                  ja        badhex                  ; Above is bad!
001F                        gothi:
001F  2C 30                         sub       AL,'0'                  ; Convert the low nibble
0021  0F 88 0040 R                  js        badhex                  ; Negative is bad
0025  3C 09                         cmp       AL,9                    ; Was it 0-9?
0027  0F 86 0039 R                  jna       gotlo                   ; Yes, low is converted.
002B  24 DF                         and       AL,0dfh                 ; Make lower into upper case.
002D  2C 07                         sub       AL,'a'-'9'              ; Must have been A-F
002F  0F 88 0040 R                  js        badhex                  ; No - was between 9 and A
0033  3C 0F                         cmp       AL,15                   ; Check if valid.
0035  0F 87 0040 R                  ja        badhex                  ; Above is bad!
0039                        gotlo:
0039  C0 E4 04                      shl       AH,4                    ; Position high nibble
003C  02 C4                         add       AL,AH                   ; Combine with low
003E  F8                            clc                               ; Clear the carry flag
003F  C3                            ret                               ; and return.
0040                        badhex:
0040  F9                            stc                               ; Set the carry flag
0041  C3                            ret                               ; and return.
0042                        Codehxtb ENDP
0042                        code    ENDS
                                    END
```

Program 7-3 CODEBTHX
Microsoft (R) Macro Assembler Version 5.00

```
                                PAGE        55,132
                                .386
0000                    code    SEGMENT     para 'CODE' PUBLIC USE16
                                ASSUME      CS:code, DS:code, SS:code

                        ; Name:    CODEBTHX
                        ;
                        ; Purpose: The following procedure provides a single byte conversion
                        ;          from binary to displayable hexadecimal (base 16).
                        ;
                        ; Inputs:  The byte to be converted is passed in AL.
                        ;
                        ; Process: The left nibble is converted into AH.
                        ;          The right nibble is converted into AL.
                        ;
                        ; Output:  The converted data is returned in AH and AL.
                        ;
                                PUBLIC  Codebthx
                        ;
0000                    Codebthx    PROC
0000  8A E0                     mov     AH,AL           ; Copy the byte and
0002  C0 EC 04                  shr     AH,4            ; isolate the left nibble.
0005  24 0F                     and     AL,15           ; Isolate the right nibble.
0007  80 C4 30                  add     AH,'0'          ; Add the zone for 0-9
000A  80 FC 39                  cmp     AH,'9'          ; Is it above 9?
000D  0F 86 0014 R              jna     highok          ; If not - we are ok.
0011  80 C4 07                  add     AH,'a'-'9'      ; Shift to A-F.
0014                    highok:
0014  04 30                     add     AL,'0'          ; We do the same for the low 4.
0016  3C 39                     cmp     AL,'9'          ; Is it ok?
0018  0F 86 001E R              jna     lowisok         ; Yes, skip
001C  04 07                     add     AL,'a'-'9'      ; shift to A-F
001E                    lowisok:
001E  C3                        ret                     ; and return.
001F                    Codebthx    ENDP
001F                    code    ENDS
                                END
```

Program 7-4 CODEEBAS
Microsoft (R) Macro Assembler Version 5.00

```
                                PAGE        55,132
                                .386
0000                    code    SEGMENT     para 'CODE' PUBLIC USE16
                                ASSUME      CS:code, DS:code, SS:code

                        ; Name:    CODEEBAS
                        ;
                        ; Purpose: The following procedure provides a conversion from
                        ;          EBCDIC (the code used by the IBM 370 mainframes) to
                        ;          ASCII.
                        ;
                        ; Inputs:  CX has the count of bytes to translate.
                        ;          DS:SI points to the EBCDIC source to translate.
                        ;          ES:DI points to the destination ASCII data.
                        ;
                        ; Process: The routine simply loops loading, translating, flagging any
                        ;          untranslatable data, and storing the result for CX bytes.
                        ;
```

```
;   Output:  The area pointed to by ES:DI will have CX bytes of
;            ASCII data as translated from DS:SI.
;            If any of the data presented has no ASCII representation
;            carry will be set on exit, otherwise carry is reset.
;
;   Notes:   There are other considerations if general data is to be
;            transferred from 370 class machines.  The 370 orders bytes
;            in memory the same as it does in registers.  This requires
;            that binary data be re-arranged in order to make it usable.
;            i.e. A two byte integer (370 halfword) appears in memory as
;                 AH,AL.  An 8086 word appears as AL,AH.
;            The 370 does not use IEEE format floating point so floating
;            point numbers must be converted.
;
;                PUBLIC Codeebas
;
0000            Codeebas    PROC
0000  E3 1C                 jcxz     getout          ; If count is zero - exit
0002  57                    push     DI              ; Save entry registers
0003  56                    push     SI
0004  51                    push     CX
0005  53                    push     BX
0006  50                    push     AX
0007  2A E4                 sub      AH,AH           ; Indicate no error.
0009  8D 1E 0020 R          lea      BX,CS:toasc     ; Get translate table offset
000D  FC                    cld                      ; Ensure direction is 'up'.
000E            ebasnxt:
000E  AC                    lodsb                    ; Get a byte to translate
000F  2E: D7                xlat     CS:[BX]         ; Translate the byte.
0011  0A E0                 or       AH,AL           ; Combine for check later.
0013  AA                    stosb                    ; Place the result
0014  E2 F8                 loop     ebasnxt         ; Do CX bytes
0016  D0 E4                 shl      AH,1            ; Was there an error?
0018  58                    pop      AX              ; Restore the entry registers
0019  5B                    pop      BX
001A  59                    pop      CX
001B  5E                    pop      SI
001C  5F                    pop      DI
001D  C3                    ret                      ; return.
001E            getout:
001E  F8                    clc                      ; indicate no error
001F  C3                    ret                      ; and return.
```

```
;
; EBCDIC to ASCII translation table
;        Note that extended ASCII is not included in the table.
;        EBCDIC values with no corresponding ASCII translate to
;        values with bit 7 set.  This allows easy detection.
;        If your application defines translations beyond the ASCII
;        character set, this table may be filled in and the error
;        check in the translate routine removed or changed.
;
;        Also note that the full ASCII graphic set is not defined
;        in the EBCDIC graphics.  Where possible, the IBM U.S.
;        standard bit pattern assignments were used.  [ and ] are
;        taken from the 120 graphic print chain.  ^ is taken from
;        the not character.
;
;
```

```
0020  00 01 02 03 84 09 86  toasc   db      000h,001h,002h,003h,084h,009h,086h,07Fh
      7F
;                            0x   NUL  SOH  STX  ETX  SEL   HT  RNL  DEL
0028  88 89 8A 0B 0C 0D 0E          db      088h,089h,08Ah,00Bh,00Ch,00Dh,00Eh,00Fh
      0F
;                                 GE  SPS  RPT   VT   FF   CR   SO   SI
0030  10 11 12 13 84 85 08          db      010h,011h,012h,013h,084h,085h,008h,087h
      87
```

```
0038   18 19 8A 8B 8C 1D 1E        ;            DLE  DC1 DC2 DC3 RES  NL   BS   POC
       1F                          db  1x   018h,019h,08Ah,08Bh,08Ch,01Dh,01Eh,01Fh

0040   80 81 1C 83 84 0A 17        ;            CAN  EM  UBS  CU1 IFS  IGS  IRS  IUS
       1B                          db       080h,081h,01Ch,083h,084h,00Ah,017h,01Bh

0048   88 89 8A 8B 8C 05 06        ;       2x   DS  SOS  FS  WUS  BYP  LF  ETB  ESC
       07                          db       088h,089h,08Ah,08Bh,08Ch,005h,006h,007h

0050   80 81 16 83 84 85 86        ;            SA  SFE  SM  CSP  MFA  ENQ  ACK  BEL
       04                          db       080h,081h,016h,083h,084h,085h,086h,004h

0058   88 89 8A 8B 14 15 8E        ;       3x  -?-  -?-  SYN  IR   PP  TRN  NBS  EOT
       1A                          db       088h,089h,08Ah,08Bh,014h,015h,08Eh,01Ah

0060   20 81 82 83 84 85 86        ;            SBS  IT  RFF  CU3  DC4  NAK  -?-  SUB
       87                          db       020h,081h,082h,083h,084h,085h,086h,087h

0068   88 89 8A 2E 3C 28 2B        ;       4x  -?-  -?-  -?-  -?-  -?-  -?-  -?-  -?-
       8F                          db       088h,089h,08Ah,02Eh,03Ch,028h,02Bh,08Fh

0070   26 81 82 83 84 85 86        ;            -?-  -?-  -?-   .    <    (    +   -?-
       87                          db       026h,081h,082h,083h,084h,085h,086h,087h

0078   88 89 21 24 2A 29 3B        ;       5x   &   -?-  -?-  -?-  -?-  -?-  -?-  -?-
       5E                          db       088h,089h,021h,024h,02Ah,029h,03Bh,05Eh

0080   2D 2F 82 83 84 85 86        ;            -?-  -?-   !    $    *    )    ;    ¬
       87                          db       02Dh,02Fh,082h,083h,084h,085h,086h,087h

0088   88 89 7C 2C 25 5F 3E        ;       6x   -    /   -?-  -?-  -?-  -?-  -?-  -?-
       3F                          db       088h,089h,07Ch,02Ch,025h,05Fh,03Eh,03Fh

0090   80 81 82 83 84 85 86        ;            -?-  -?-   |   -?-   ,    %    >    ?
       87                          db       080h,081h,082h,083h,084h,085h,086h,087h

0098   88 60 3A 23 40 27 3D        ;       7x  -?-  -?-  -?-  -?-  -?-  -?-  -?-  -?-
       22                          db       088h,060h,03Ah,023h,040h,027h,03Dh,022h

00A0   80 61 62 63 64 65 66        ;            -?-   `    :    #    @    '    =    "
       67                          db       080h,061h,062h,063h,064h,065h,066h,067h

00A8   68 69 8A 8B 8C 8D 8E        ;       8x  -?-   a    b    c    d    e    f    g
       8F                          db       068h,069h,08Ah,08Bh,08Ch,08Dh,08Eh,08Fh

00B0   80 6A 6B 6C 6D 6E 6F        ;            h    i   -?-  -?-  -?-  -?-  -?-  -?-
       70                          db       080h,06Ah,06Bh,06Ch,06Dh,06Eh,06Fh,070h

00B8   71 72 8A 8B 8C 8D 8E        ;       9x  -?-   j    k    l    m    n    o    p
       8F                          db       071h,072h,08Ah,08Bh,08Ch,08Dh,08Eh,08Fh

00C0   80 7E 73 74 75 76 77        ;            q    r   -?-  -?-  -?-  -?-  -?-  -?-
       78                          db       080h,07Eh,073h,074h,075h,076h,077h,078h

00C8   79 7A 8A 8B 8C 5B 8E        ;       Ax  -?-   ~    s    t    u    v    w    x
       8F                          db       079h,07Ah,08Ah,08Bh,08Ch,05Bh,08Eh,08Fh

00D0   80 81 82 83 84 85 86        ;            y    z   -?-  -?-  -?-   [   -?-  -?-
       87                          db       080h,081h,082h,083h,084h,085h,086h,087h

00D8   88 89 8A 8B 8C 5D 8E        ;       Bx  -?-  -?-  -?-  -?-  -?-   ]   -?-  -?-
       8F                          db       088h,089h,08Ah,08Bh,08Ch,05Dh,08Eh,08Fh

00E0   7B 41 42 43 44 45 46        ;            -?-   ]   -?-  -?-  -?-  -?-  -?-  -?-
       47                          db       07Bh,041h,042h,043h,044h,045h,046h,047h
```

```
                                    ;              Cx      {    A    B    C    D    E    F    G
00E8  48 49 8A 8B 8C 8D 8E                  db     048h,049h,08Ah,08Bh,08Ch,08Dh,08Eh,08Fh
      8F
                                    ;                   H    I   -?-  -?-  -?-  -?-  -?-  -?-
00F0  7D 4A 4B 4C 4D 4E 4F                  db     07Dh,04Ah,04Bh,04Ch,04Dh,04Eh,04Fh,050h
      50
                                    ;              Dx      )    J    K    L    M    N    O    P
00F8  51 52 8A 8B 8C 8D 8E                  db     051h,052h,08Ah,08Bh,08Ch,08Dh,08Eh,08Fh
      8F
                                    ;                   Q    R   -?-  -?-  -?-  -?-  -?-  -?-
0100  5C 81 53 54 55 56 57                  db     05Ch,081h,053h,054h,055h,056h,057h,058h
      58
                                    ;              Ex      \   -?-   S    T    U    V    W    X
0108  59 5A 8A 8B 8C 8D 8E                  db     059h,05Ah,08Ah,08Bh,08Ch,08Dh,08Eh,08Fh
      8F
                                    ;                   Y    Z   -?-  -?-  -?-  -?-  -?-  -?-
0110  30 31 32 33 34 35 36                  db     030h,031h,032h,033h,034h,035h,036h,037h
      37
                                    ;              Fx      0    1    2    3    4    5    6    7
0118  38 39 8A 8B 8C 8D 8E                  db     038h,039h,08Ah,08Bh,08Ch,08Dh,08Eh,08Fh
      8F
                                    ;                   8    9   -?-  -?-  -?-  -?-  -?-  -?-
0120                                Codeebas  ENDP
0120                                code      ENDS
                                              END
```

Program 7-5 CODEASEB

Microsoft (R) Macro Assembler Version 5.00

```
                                    PAGE      55,132
                                    .386
0000                       code     SEGMENT   para 'CODE' PUBLIC USE16
                                    ASSUME    CS:code, DS:code, SS:code

                           ; Name:    CODEASEB
                           ;
                           ; Purpose: The following procedure provides a conversion from ASCII
                           ;          to EBCDIC (the code used by the IBM 370 mainframes).
                           ;
                           ;
                           ; Inputs:  CX has the count of bytes to translate.
                           ;          DS:SI points to the source to translate.
                           ;          ES:DI points to the destination EBCDIC data.
                           ;
                           ;
                           ; Process: The routine simply loops loading, masking, translating and
                           ;          storing the result for CX bytes.
                           ;
                           ; Output:  The area pointed to by ES:DI will have CX bytes of
                           ;          EBCDIC data as translated from DS:SI.
                           ;
                           ; Notes:   There are other considerations if general data is to be
                           ;          transferred to 370 class machines.  The 370 orders bytes
                           ;          in memory the same as it does in registers.  This requires
                           ;          that binary data be re-arranged in order to make it usable.
                           ;          i.e. A two byte integer (word) appears in memory as AL,AH
                           ;               a 370 halfword would appear as AH,AL.
                           ;          The 370 does not use IEEE format floating point so floating
                           ;          point numbers must be converted.
                           ;
                           ;          PUBLIC  Codeaseb
                           ;
0000                       Codeaseb  PROC
0000  E3 19                          jcxz    getout            ; If count is zero - exit
```

```
0002   57                        push    DI                          ; Save entry registers
0003   56                        push    SI
0004   51                        push    CX
0005   53                        push    BX
0006   50                        push    AX
0007   B4 7F                     mov     AH,7Fh                      ; Set the mask for ASCII
0009   8D 1E 001C R              lea     BX,CS:ascto                 ; Get translate table offset
000D   FC                        cld                                 ; Ensure direction is 'up'.
000E           asebnxt:
000E   AC                        lodsb                               ; Get a byte to translate
000F   22 C4                     and     AL,AH                       ; Don't allow extended bit.
0011   2E: D7                    xlat    CS:[BX]                     ; Translate the byte.
0013   AA                        stosb                               ; Place the result
0014   E2 F8                     loop    asebnxt                     ; Do CX bytes
0016   58                        pop     AX                          ; Restore the entry registers
0017   5B                        pop     BX
0018   59                        pop     CX
0019   5E                        pop     SI
001A   5F                        pop     DI
001B           getout:
001B   C3                        ret                                 ; and return.
                        ;
                        ; ASCII to EBCDIC translation table
                        ;       Note that extended ASCII is not included in the table.
                        ;       If your application defines translations beyond the ASCII
                        ;       character set, this table may be extended and the masking
                        ;       in the translate routine removed.
                        ;
                        ;       Also note that the ASCII graphics are not all defined in
                        ;       the EBCDIC graphic set.  The IBM standard U.S. bit patterns
                        ;       conflict with the bit patterns used for their 120 graphic
                        ;       character print trains.  The translate table uses the IBM
                        ;       standard except for [ and ] which only appear in the 120
                        ;       graphic set.  ^ is translated as the not sign.
                        ;
                        ;
001C   00 01 02 03 37 2D 2E      ascto   db      000h,001h,002h,003h,037h,02Dh,02Eh,02Fh
       2F
                        ;               NUL  SOH  STX  ETX  EOT  ENQ  ACK  BEL
0024   16 05 25 0B 0C 0D 0E              db      016h,005h,025h,00Bh,00Ch,00Dh,00Eh,00Fh
       0F
                        ;                BS  TAB   LF   VT   FF   CR   SO   SI
002C   10 11 12 13 3C 3D 32              db      010h,011h,012h,013h,03Ch,03Dh,032h,026h
       26
                        ;               DLE  DC1  DC2  DC3  DC4  NAK  SYN  ETB
0034   18 19 3F 27 22 1D 1E              db      018h,019h,03Fh,027h,022h,01Dh,01Eh,01Fh
       1F
                        ;               CAN   EM  SUB  ESC   FS   GS   RS   US
003C   40 5A 7F 7B 5B 6C 50              db      040h,05Ah,07Fh,07Bh,05Bh,06Ch,050h,07Dh
       7D
                        ;                     !    "    #    $    %    &    '
0044   4D 5D 5C 4E 6B 60 4B              db      04Dh,05Dh,05Ch,04Eh,06Bh,060h,04Bh,061h
       61
                        ;                (    )    *    +    ,    -    .    /
004C   F0 F1 F2 F3 F4 F5 F6              db      0F0h,0F1h,0F2h,0F3h,0F4h,0F5h,0F6h,07Fh
       F7
                        ;                0    1    2    3    4    5    6    7
0054   F8 F9 7A 5E 4C 7E 6E              db      0F8h,0F9h,07Ah,05Eh,04Ch,07Eh,06Eh,06Fh
       6F
                        ;                8    9    :    ;    <    =    >    ?
005C   7C C1 C2 C3 C4 C5 C6              db      07Ch,0C1h,0C2h,0C3h,0C4h,0C5h,0C6h,0C7h
       C7
                        ;                @    A    B    C    D    E    F    G
0064   C8 C9 D1 D2 D3 D4 D5              db      0C8h,0C9h,0D1h,0D2h,0D3h,0D4h,0D5h,0D6h
       D6
```

```
                                       ;            H   I   J   K   L   M   N   O
006C  D7 D8 D9 E2 E3 E4 E5                db        0D7h,0D8h,0D9h,0E2h,0E3h,0E4h,0E5h,0E6h
      E6
                                       ;            P   Q   R   S   T   U   V   W
0074  E7 E8 E9 AD E0 BD 5F                db        0E7h,0E8h,0E9h,0ADh,0E0h,0BDh,05Fh,06Dh
      6D
                                       ;            X   Y   Z   [   \   ]   ^   _
007C  79 81 82 83 84 85 86                db        079h,081h,082h,083h,084h,085h,086h,087h
      87
                                       ;            `   a   b   c   d   e   f   g
0084  88 89 91 92 93 94 95                db        088h,089h,091h,092h,093h,094h,095h,096h
      96
                                       ;            h   i   j   k   l   m   n   o
008C  97 98 99 A2 A3 A4 A5                db        097h,098h,099h,0A2h,0A3h,0A4h,0A5h,0A6h
      A6
                                       ;            p   q   r   s   t   u   v   w
0094  A7 A8 A9 C0 6A D0 A1                db        0A7h,0A8h,0A9h,0C0h,06Ah,0D0h,0A1h,007h
      07
                                       ;            x   y   z   {   |   }   ~   DEL
009C                                     Codeaseb   ENDP
009C                                     code       ENDS
                                                    END
```

Program 7-6 CODEBAS

```
                               PAGE       55,132
                               .386
0000                  code     SEGMENT    para 'CODE' PUBLIC USE16
                               ASSUME     CS:code, DS:code, SS:code
                      ;
                      ; Name:    CODEBAS
                      ;
                      ; Purpose: The following converts a binary double word to an ASCII
                      ;          decimal string.
                      ;
                      ;
                      ;
                      ; Inputs:  EAX contain the double word to be converted.
                      ;          ES:DI contains the pointer to a 12 byte area for the
                      ;               converted data.
                      ;
                      ; Process: The sign is 'captured' and if negative, the absolute
                      ;          value is used.  The conversion divides the number by 100.
                      ;          The 2 decimal digit remainder is converted and stored in
                      ;          the target string from right to left.
                      ;          The preceding is repeated until the quotient is zero.
                      ;          If there is a leading zero, it is removed from the string.
                      ;          (A zero value converts to a single ASCII zero.)
                      ;
                      ; Output:  ES:DI point to the first byte of the ASCIIZ string
                      ;          containing the converted value.
                      ;
                      ;
                      ; Notes:   The technique of repeated division is essentially a brute
                      ;          force method.  It was chosen because it is easily
                      ;          expandable to larger binary numbers as well as for its
                      ;          simplicity.
                      ;
                                PUBLIC  Codebas
                      ;
0000                  Codebas   PROC
0000   66| 52                   push    EDX                 ; Save entry registers
0002   66| 51                   push    ECX
0004   66| 50                   push    EAX
0006   66| 0B C0                or      EAX,EAX             ; check the sign.
0009   0F 89 0012 R             jns     positive            ; If positive, no problem.
```

```
000D  66| F7 D0                 not    EAX                          ; Get the inverted number
0010  66| 40                    inc    EAX                          ; plus one.
0012                  positive:
0012  FD                        std                                 ; We create digits from right
0013  83 C7 0B                  add    DI,11                        ; to left.
0016  26: C6 45 01 00           mov    BYTE PTR ES:1[DI],0          ; Set ASCIIZ terminator.
001B  66| B9 00000064           mov    ECX,100                      ; and the divisor.
0021  66| 2B D2                 sub    EDX,EDX                      ; prepare to do division
0024                  divdh:
0024  66| F7 F1                 div    ECX                          ; Divide by 100
0027  66| 92                    xchg   EDX,EAX                      ; Flip quotient and remainder.
                      ;
                      ;   The remainder is the next 2 digits of the number.
                      ;
0029  D4 0A                     aam                                 ; We expand the two digits,
002B  0D 3030                   or     AX,'00'                      ; put zones on them,
002E  AA                        stosb
002F  8A C4                     mov    AL,AH
0031  AA                        stosb                               ; and store the pair.
0032  66| 2B C0                 sub    EAX,EAX                      ; Clear our working register
0035  66| 92                    xchg   EAX,EDX                      ; Get quotient for division.
0037  66| 0B C0                 or     EAX,EAX                      ; Is there more left?
003A  75 E8                     jnz    divdh                        ; Yes - go do it
003C  26: 80 7D 01 30           cmp    BYTE PTR ES:1[DI],'0'        ; Leading zero?
0041  0F 85 0046 R              jne    nolead0                      ; No, don't
0045  47                        inc    DI                           ; back up over it.
0046                  nolead0:
0046  66| 58                    pop    EAX                          ; Get number back,
0048  66| 0B C0                 or     EAX,EAX                      ; check its sign, and
004B  0F 89 0054 R              jns    positive2                    ; skip if positive.
004F  26: C6 05 2D              mov    BYTE PTR ES:[DI],'-'         ; Set sign
0053  4F                        dec    DI                           ; and make room for it.
0054                  positive2:
0054  47                        inc    DI                           ; Point to first digit.
0055  66| 59                    pop    ECX
0057  66| 5A                    pop    EDX
0059  C3                        ret                                 ; and return.
005A                  Codebas   ENDP
005A                  code      ENDS
                                END
```

Program 7-7 CODEASB

```
                                PAGE      55,132
                                .386
0000                  code      SEGMENT   para 'CODE' USE16 PUBLIC
                                ASSUME    CS:code, DS:code, SS:code

                      ; Name:    CODEASB
                      ;
                      ; Purpose: The following procedure converts an ASCII numeric string
                      ;          to a double word binary equivalent.
                      ;
                      ;
                      ;
                      ; Inputs:  SI points to the string which is to be converted.  It is
                      ;          edited to ensure it is valid data.
                      ;          CX has the count of ASCII characters which may exceed the
                      ;          count of digits.
                      ;
                      ; Process: The procedure scans the string to get the count of digits.
                      ;          The procedure fetches decimal digit pairs from left to
                      ;          right.  The prior result is multiplied by 100, the new pair
                      ;          is converted to binary and added to to the prior result.
                      ;          Each pair in the source is processed.  (If an odd number of
                      ;          digits are presented, the first digit is processed alone.)
```

```
                              ;
                              ; Output:   If the conversion is without overflow, carry is reset and
                              ;              EAX contains the result.
                              ;           If the conversion overflows, carry is set and EAX is
                              ;              undefined.
                              ;           If no digits are valid, the result is zero in EAX.
                              ;           SI points to the digit following the last character
                              ;              converted and
                              ;           CX contains the remaining count.
                              ;
                              ;
                                     PUBLIC  Codeasb
                              ;
0000                 Codeasb   PROC
0000  66| 53                   push    EBX             ; Save work registers
0002  66| 52                   push    EDX
0004  57                       push    DI
0005  56                       push    SI              ; Save first character pointer
0006  66| 2B DB                sub     EBX,EBX         ; Clear the result
0009  66| 2B C0                sub     EAX,EAX         ; and rest of EAX.
000C  FC                       cld                     ; Force direction to up.
000D  80 3C 2D                 cmp     BYTE PTR[SI],'-' ; Negative?
0010  0F 84 001B R             je      signed          ; Yes
0014  80 3C 2B                 cmp     BYTE PTR[SI],'+' ; Positive
0017  0F 85 001D R             jne     unsigned        ; No - skip
001B                 signed:
001B  46                       inc     SI              ; step over of sign.
001C  49                       dec     CX              ; and counting it
001D                 unsigned:
001D  56                       push    SI              ; Save for conversion pass
001E  8B F9                    mov     DI,CX           ; Save char count.
0020  BA 0930                  mov     DX,0930h        ; set '0' in DL and 9 in DH.
0023  E3 0B                    jcxz    numdone         ;
0025                 numscan:
0025  AC                       lodsb                   ; Get a possible digit
0026  32 C2                    xor     AL,DL           ;
0028  3A C6                    cmp     AL,DH           ; Check if it is a digit.
002A  0F 87 0030 R             ja      numdone         ; get out if not
002E  E2 F5                    loop    numscan         ; try another digit.
0030                 numdone:
0030  5E                       pop     SI              ; Restore for conversion pass
0031  87 CF                    xchg    CX,DI           ; Set original count
0033  2B CF                    sub     CX,DI           ; and get digit count
0035  F6 C1 01                 test    CL,1            ; Is the count odd?
0038  0F 84 0041 R             jz      cxeven          ; No, skip
003C  AC                       lodsb                   ; the load of the first byte
003D  24 0F                    and     AL,15           ; as a binary value.
003F  8A D8                    mov     BL,AL           ; We have a starting value.
0041                 cxeven:
0041  D1 E9                    shr     CX,1            ; divide the count by 2
0043  0F 84 0077 R             jz      outgood         ; If the result is zero - out.
0047  66| 55                   push    EBP             ;
0049  66| BD 00000064          mov     EBP,100         ; Get multiplier in a register
004F                 dopair:
004F  AD                       lodsw                   ; Get pair of bytes (reversed)
0050  86 C4                    xchg    AL,AH           ; back in proper order
0052  25 0F0F                  and     AX,0F0Fh        ; clear zones
0055  D5 0A                    aad                     ; convert pair to binary.
0057  66| 93                   xchg    EAX,EBX         ; Position accum for mpy
0059  66| F7 E5                mul     EBP             ; and make room for digits.
005C  66| 0B D2                or      EDX,EDX         ; Check if overflow
005F  0F 85 008E R             jnz     outoflo         ; Out if it did
0063  66| 0B C0                or      EAX,EAX         ; Check overflow into sign.
0066  0F 88 008E R             js      outoflo         ; Out if it did
006A  66| 03 C3                add     EAX,EBX         ; Add new pair in.
006D  0F 80 008E R             jo      outoflo         ; exit if overflow occurred
0071  66| 93                   xchg    EAX,EBX         ; Put registers back
```

Program 7-7 Continued.

```
0073 E2 DA                              loop     dopair          ; Do each pair
0075 66| 5D                             pop      EBP             ; Restore EBP
0077                          outgood:                           ; Go back
0077 66| 88 C3                          mov      EAX,EBX         ; with number in EAX.
007A 8B CF                              mov      CX,DI           ; Remaining count in CX
007C 5B                                 pop      BX              ; Restore the sign pointer.
007D 80 3F 2D                           cmp      BYTE PTR [BX],'-' ; Was a minus entered?
0080 0F 85 0087 R                       jne      positive        ; nope
0084 66| F7 D8                          neg      EAX             ; Force it minus
0087                          positive:
0087 F8                                 clc                      ; Clear carry (neg could set)
0088 5F                                 pop      DI              ; Restore the entry registers
0089 66| 5A                             pop      EDX
008B 66| 5B                             pop      EBX
008D C3                                 ret                      ; and return.
008E                          outoflo:
008E 66| 5D                             pop      EBP             ; Restore work register.
0090 F9                                 stc                      ; Set error then
0091 5F                                 pop      DI              ; Clear sign pointer
0092 5F                                 pop      DI              ; Restore the entry registers
0093 66| 5A                             pop      EDX
0095 66| 5B                             pop      EBX
0097 C3                                 ret                      ; and return.
0098                          Codeasb  ENDP
0098                          code     ENDS
                                       END
```

Program 7-8 FPDRIVE

Microsoft (R) Macro Assembler Version 5.00

```
                              PAGE    55,132
                              .386
                    ;
                    ; Name:    FPDRIVE
                    ;
                    ; Purpose: This program exercises the floating point conversion
                    ;          routines.
                    ;
                    ; Inputs:  The user is prompted for a floating point number.
                    ;          The number must be of the form (-)d*.d*e(-)d* where
                    ;          (-) is an optional minus sign, d* is one or more numeric
                    ;          digits, . is a required decimal and e is a required start
                    ;          of exponent signal.  e may be either upper or lower case.
                    ;
                    ; Process: The user is prompted for a floating-point number.  A null
                    ;          terminates the program.  The floating-point number will be
                    ;          converted to an IEEE long floating-point number, an error
                    ;          causes a reprompt.  The floating-point number is then
                    ;          converted to ASCII and displayed.  It is displayed in
                    ;          hexadecimal, converted to IBM format, displayed in
                    ;          hexadecimal, converted to IEEE format and displayed in
                    ;          hexadecimal again.  The number is then converted to short
                    ;          form, displayed in hexadecimal, converted to long form,
                    ;          displayed in hexadecimal and converted to ASCII and
                    ;          displayed again.  The program then loops.
                    ;
                    ; Outputs: The output is the displayed results of each conversion.
                    ;
                    ;
                    ; Declare the routines we are going to use
                    ;
```

```
                              ;
                              ; Declare those routines we are going to use
                              ;
                              EXTRN    Fpasclfp:PROC
                              EXTRN    Fplfpasc:PROC
                              EXTRN    Fpieeebm:PROC
                              EXTRN    Fpibmeee:PROC
                              EXTRN    Fplongts:PROC
                              EXTRN    Fpstlong:PROC
                              EXTRN    Codebthx:PROC

0000                 stack        SEGMENT para 'STACK' STACK
0000  0100[                      dq       256 DUP(?)
      ??????????????????
      ?
                     ]

0800                 stack        ENDS
0000                 data         SEGMENT para
0000  0100[          string       db       256 DUP(?)            ; String scratch area
      ??
                     ]

0100  0100[          string2      db       256 DUP(?)
      ??
                     ]

0200  0A 0D 24       lfcr         db       10,13,'$'             ; linefeed and carriage return
0203  0A 0D 45 6E 74 65 72  query db       10,13,"Enter a floating point number: $"
      20 61 20 66 6C 6F 61
      74 69 6E 67 20 70 6F
      69 6E 74 20 6E 75 6D
      62 65 72 3A 20 24
0225  9A99993E                    dd       3.0e-1
0229  333333333333D33F            dq       3.0e-1
0231                 data         ENDS
0000                 code         SEGMENT para 'CODE' USE16 PUBLIC
                                  ASSUME CS:code, DS:data
                     ;
                     ; Set up the environment
                     ;
0000                 Begin:
0000  B8 ---- R                   mov      AX,data               ; Get data segment pointer
0003  8E D8                       mov      DS,AX                 ; into DS,
0005  8E C0                       mov      ES,AX                 ; and ES.
0007  2B F6                       sub      SI,SI                 ; Clear indices
0009  2B FF                       sub      DI,DI
000B                 cvtloop:
000B  8D 16 0203 R                lea      DX,query              ; point to query
000F  E8 00CB R                   call     getinp                ; Get a number
0012  8D 16 0200 R                lea      DX,lfcr               ; space down
0016  B4 09                       mov      AH,9                  ;
0018  CD 21                       int      21h
001A  E3 5E                       jcxz     Exit                  ; A null ends the program
001C  8B F3                       mov      SI,BX                 ; Point to the number
001E  E8 0000 E                   call     fpasclfp              ; convert it
0021  72 E8                       jc       cvtloop               ; If error get another
0023  66| A3 0100 R               mov      DWORD PTR string2,EAX ; set low half
0027  66| 89 16 0104 R            mov      DWORD PTR string2+4,EDX ; set high half
002C  E8 00A6 R                   call     cvtprt                ; convert it and print
002F  E8 0080 R                   call     hexprt2               ; dump it in hex
0032  8D 36 0100 R                lea      SI,string2            ; Point to it
0036  E8 0000 E                   call     Fpieeebm              ; convert to IBM format
0039  E8 0080 R                   call     hexprt2               ; dump it
003C  E8 0000 E                   call     Fpibmeee              ; re-convert it
003F  E8 0080 R                   call     hexprt2               ; dump it
0042  66| A1 0100 R               mov      EAX,DWORD PTR string2 ; Prepare to print
0046  66| 8B 16 0104 R            mov      EDX,DWORD PTR string2+4
004B  E8 00A6 R                   call     cvtprt                ; convert it again
```

```
004E   E8 0000 E                   call     Fplongts           ; Get as short
0051   66| 8B D0                   mov      EDX,EAX            ; Set number as 'high'
0054   66| 2B C0                   sub      EAX,EAX            ; Clear low half
0057   66| A3 0100 R               mov      DWORD PTR string2,EAX ; set low half
005B   66| 89 16 0104 R            mov      DWORD PTR string2+4,EDX ; set high half
0060   E8 0080 R                   call     hexprt2            ; dump it
0063   66| 8B C2                   mov      EAX,EDX            ; Set short to cvt
0066   E8 0000 E                   call     Fpstlong           ; convert to long
0069   66| A3 0100 R               mov      DWORD PTR string2,EAX ; set low half
006D   66| 89 16 0104 R            mov      DWORD PTR string2+4,EDX ; set high half
0072   E8 0080 R                   call     hexprt2            ; dump it
0075   E8 00A6 R                   call     cvtprt             ; convert it again
0078   EB 91                       jmp      cvtloop            ; Go get another number

007A                      Exit:
007A   B0 00                       mov      AL,0               ; Set return code
007C   B4 4C                       mov      AH,04ch            ; Set good-by
007E   CD 21                       int      21h                ; Return to the system
                          ;
                          ; display the 8 byte string2 area in hex
                          ;
0080                      hexprt2    PROC
0080   66| 60                      pushad
0082   8D 36 0100 R                lea      SI,string2         ; point to string
0086   B9 0008                     mov      CX,8               ; Want 8 bytes
0089                      hexstrl:
0089   AC                          lodsb                       ; get a byte
008A   E8 0000 E                   call     Codebthx           ; Convert them
008D   8B D0                       mov      DX,AX              ; save them
008F   86 F2                       xchg     DH,DL              ; print left first
0091   B4 02                       mov      AH,2               ; set dos code
0093   CD 21                       int      21h                ; print it
0095   8A D6                       mov      DL,DH              ; Do right byte
0097   CD 21                       int      21h
0099   E2 EE                       loop     hexstrl            ; loop to do all 8
009B   B4 09                       mov      AH,9               ;
009D   8D 16 0200 R                lea      DX,lfcr            ; point to lf/cr
00A1   CD 21                       int      21h                ; put it out
00A3   66| 61                      popad
00A5   C3                          ret
00A6                      hexprt2    ENDP


                          ;
                          ; convert the long float in EAX:EDX to a string and display it.
                          ;
00A6                      cvtprt     PROC
00A6   66| 60                      pushad                      ; save the registers
00A8   8D 1E 0000 R                lea      BX,string          ; Point to string work
00AC   E8 0000 E                   call     Fplfpasc           ; Convert to string
00AF   8B D9                       mov      BX,CX
00B1   C6 87 0000 R 0D             mov      string[BX],13
00B6   C6 87 0001 R 0A             mov      string[BX+1],10    ; c/r lf
00BB   C6 87 0002 R 24             mov      string[BX+2],'$'   ; and dos stopper
00C0   8D 16 0000 R                lea      DX,string          ; point to string
00C4   B4 09                       mov      AH,9               ; Request print
00C6   CD 21                       int      21h                ;
00C8   66| 61                      popad
00CA   C3                          ret
00CB                      cvtprt     ENDP
                          ;
                          ; Read a string in response to a prompt
                          ; The prompt must be in DX.  The string will be returned in string.
                          ;
00CB                      getinp     PROC
00CB   50                          push     AX                 ; Save registers
00CC   56                          push     SI
```

```
00CD   B4 09                           mov      AH,9            ; and dos request
00CF   CD 21                           int      21h             ; put out the string
00D1   8D 16 0000 R                    lea      DX,string       ; point to input area
00D5   C6 06 0000 R FE                 mov      string,254      ; Set max length in
00DA   B4 CA                           mov      AH,10           ; Ask for read of string
00DC   CD 21                           int      21h             ; from DOS.
00DE   8D 1E 0002 R                    lea      BX,string+2     ; Point to just read data
00E2   8A 0E 0001 R                    mov      CL,string+1     ; Get length read
00E6   B5 00                           mov      CH,0            ; as a word.
00E8   8B F1                           mov      SI,CX           ; Set length
00EA   C6 84 0002 R 00                 mov      string+2[SI],0  ; and make an asciiz string.
00EF   5E                              pop      SI
00F0   58                              pop      AX              ; Restore registers
00F1   C3                              ret                      ; and return.
00F2                     getinp        ENDP

00F2                     code          ENDS
                                       END      Begi
```

Program 7-9 FPLONGTS

```
                                PAGE        55,132
                                .386
0000                    code    SEGMENT     para 'CODE' PUBLIC USE16
                                ASSUME      CS:code, DS:code, SS:code
                        ;
                        ; Name:      FPLONGTS
                        ;
                        ; Purpose: The following procedure provides a conversion of an IEEE
                        ;          format long floating point number to an IEEE short format
                        ;          floating point number.
                        ;          IEEE long format has an 11 digit binary exponent biased by
                        ;          1023.  It appears in memory reversed from its form in
                        ;          registers. i.e.
                        ;    bbbbcccc9999aaaa77778888555566663333444411112222eeee0000seeeeeeee
                        ;       0       1       2       3       4       5       6       7
                        ;
                        ;          IEEE short format has 8 bits of exponent biased by 127,
                        ;          a 23 bit fraction and appears in memory as:
                        ;          3444455512222333e0000111seeeeeee
                        ;          0       1       2       3
                        ;
                        ;          Conversion from long to short can either overflow or
                        ;          underflow the short exponent.  An overflow will return a
                        ;          short infinity while an underflow will return a short zero.
                        ;          In either case the carry flag will be set at return.
                        ;
                        ;
                        ; Inputs:  DS:SI points to an IEEE format long floating point number
                        ;          in memory.  (This is assumed to be a normalized number.)
                        ;
                        ; Process: The exponent is unbiased and checked for over or underflow.
                        ;          If either occurs, infinity or zero is returned with carry
                        ;          set.  Otherwise, the exponent is biased as a short number,
                        ;          the fraction is truncated to 23 bits, and combined with the
                        ;          new exponent and sign.
                        ;
                        ; Output:  The converted number is returned in EAX.  Carry is set if
                        ;          over or underflow occurred and reset otherwise.
                        ;
                        ;
                                PUBLIC  Fplongts
                        ;
0000                    Fplongts PROC
0000   66| 52                   push    EDX             ; Save entry registers
0002   66| 53                   push    EBX
0004   66| 2B C0                sub     EAX,EAX         ; Clear short number
```

Program 7-9 Continued.

```
                                    ;
                                    ; Get the biased exponent.
                                    ;
0007  8B 5C 06               mov     BX,WORD PTR [SI+6]  ; Get seeeeeeeeeee1111
000A  8B D3                  mov     DX,BX              ; preserve sign.
000C  C1 EB 04               shr     BX,4               ; then 0000seeeeeeeeeee
000F  81 E3 07FF             and     BX,07ffh           ; and  00000eeeeeeeeeee
0013  0F 84 0058 R           jz      alldone            ; Get out if zero.
0017  81 EB 03FF             sub     BX,1023            ; Unbias the exponent.
001B  83 C3 7F               add     BX,127             ; Re-bias as short.
001E  83 FB 01               cmp     BX,1               ; check for short underflow.
0021  0F 8C 005D R           jl      setcyz             ; If so - exit with a zero+cy
0025  8A E6                  mov     AH,DH              ; Copy sign to return reg.
0027  0D 7F80                or      AX,07f80h          ; Set signed short infinity.
002A  66| C1 E0 10           shl     EAX,16             ; Position exponent and sign.
002E  81 FB 00FE             cmp     BX,254             ; check to max exponent.
0032  0F 8F 0058 R           jg      alldone            ; and get out if >= to max.
                                    ;
                                    ; Position as short exponent and get the sign back
                                    ;
0036  C1 E3 07               shl     BX,7               ; position exponent.
0039  81 E2 8000             and     DX,08000h          ; Isolate the sign
003D  0B DA                  or      BX,DX              ; and combine with exponent.
003F  66| C1 E3 10           shl     EBX,16             ; Position for short fraction.
                                    ;
                                    ; Prepare to get the fraction into position.
                                    ;
0043  66| 8B 44 04           mov     EAX,DWORD PTR [SI+4] ; Load high 32 bits
0047  66| 8B 14              mov     EDX,DWORD PTR [SI]   ; and low 32 bits.
004A  66| 0F A4 D0 03        shld    EAX,EDX,3          ; Keep 23 fraction bits.
004F  66| 25 007FFFFF        and     EAX,007fffffh      ; Clear top 9 to
0055  66| 0B C3              or      EAX,EBX            ; combine with sign + exponent.
                                                        ; (also clears carry flag)
                                    ;
                                    ;
                                    ; and exit
                                    ;
0058                         alldone:
0058  66| 5B                 pop     EBX                ; Restore the entry registers
005A  66| 5A                 pop     EDX
005C  C3                     ret                        ; and return.
005D                         setcyz:
005D  0A C0                  or      AL,AL              ; Force a zero
005F  F9                     stc                        ; and a carry
0060  EB F6                  jmp     alldone            ; and exit
0062                         Fplongts ENDP
0062                         code    ENDS
                                     END
```

Program 7-10 FPSTLONG

Microsoft (R) Macro Assembler Version 5.00

```
                             PAGE    55,132
                             .386
0000                 code    SEGMENT para 'CODE' PUBLIC USE16
                             ASSUME  CS:code, DS:code, SS:code

                     ; Name:   FPSTLONG
                     ;
                     ; Purpose: The following procedure provides a conversion of an IEEE
                     ;          format short floating point number to an IEEE long format
                     ;          floating point number.
                     ;          IEEE long format has an 11 digit binary exponent biased by
                     ;          1023.  It appears in memory reversed from its form in
```

```
                        ; registers. i.e.
                        ; bbbbcccc9999aaaa777788885555666633334444111122eeee0000seeeeeeee
                        ;  0       1       2       3       4       5       6       7
                        ;
                        ;       IEEE short format has 8 bits of exponent biased by 127, a
                        ;       23 bit fraction and appears in memory as:
                        ;       3444455512222333e0000111seeeeeee
                        ;       0       1       2       3
                        ;
                        ;       Conversion from short to long can neither overflow nor
                        ;       underflow the long exponent.  Zero and short infinity must
                        ;       be checked for and preserved.  Infinity will be recognized
                        ;       and carry set on its return.
                        ;
                        ; Inputs: EAX contains an IEEE format short floating point number.
                        ;       (This is assumed to be a normalized number.)
                        ;
                        ; Process: The exponent is unbiased and checked for zero or infinity.
                        ;       If zero, return is made with a long zero.
                        ;       Infinity is converted to long infinity and returned with
                        ;       carry set.  Otherwise, the exponent is biased as a long
                        ;       number, the fraction's 23 bits are extended with zeros and
                        ;       combined with the new exponent and sign.
                        ;
                        ; Output: The converted number is returned in EAX:EDX.  Carry is set
                        ;       if infinity is returned and reset otherwise.
                        ;
                        ;
                                PUBLIC  Fpstlong
                        ;
0000                    Fpstlong PROC
0000    66| 53                  push    EBX                 ; Save work register.
0002    66| 2B D2               sub     EDX,EDX             ; Clear rest of long number.
0005    66| 92                  xchg    EAX,EDX             ; Position high to EDX.
                        ;
                        ; Get the biased exponent.
                        ;
0007    66| 8B DA               mov     EBX,EDX             ; Copy number
000A    66| C1 EB 17            shr     EBX,23              ; Get 0000000seeeeeeee
000E    81 E3 00FF              and     BX,0ffh             ; isolate exponent
0012    0F 84 0039 R           jz      alldone             ; If zero - we are done.
0016    81 FB 00FF             cmp     BX,0ffh             ; Check if infinity
001A    0F 84 003C R           jz      infinity            ; If so - return such.
001E    81 C3 0380             add     BX,1023-127         ; get new bias.
0022    66| 0F AC D0 03        shrd    EAX,EDX,3           ; Shift the fraction into EAX
0027    66| C1 FA 03           sar     EDX,3               ; make room for long exponent
002B    66| C1 E3 14           shl     EBX,20              ; Get 0eeeeeeeeeee0000 in high
002F    66| 81 E2 800FFFFF     and     EDX,0800fffffh      ; save sign and clear for
0036    66| 0B D3              or      EDX,EBX             ; insert of exponent.
                        ;                                    (also clears carry flag)
                        ;
                        ; and exit
                        ;
0039                    alldone:
0039    66| 5B                 pop     EBX                 ; Restore the entry registers
003B    C3                     ret                         ; and return.
                        ;
                        ; Form long infinity over short
                        ;
003C                    infinity:
003C    66| 81 E2 80000000     and     EDX,080000000h      ; Preserve sign of infinity
0043    66| 81 CA 7FF00000     or      EDX,07ff00000h      ; make long infinity
004A    F9                     stc                         ; Set carry flag
004B    EB EC                  jmp     alldone             ; and exit.
004D                    Fpstlong ENDP
004D                    code    ENDS
                                END
```

Microsoft (R) Macro Assembler Version 5.00

```
                              PAGE      55,132
                              .386
0000                  code    SEGMENT   para 'CODE' PUBLIC USE16
                              ASSUME    CS:code, DS:code, SS:code

              ; Name:    FPIBMEEE
              ;
              ; Purpose: The following procedure provides a conversion of an IBM
              ;          format long floating point number to an IEEE long format
              ;          floating point number.  The IBM 370 format is hexadecimal
              ;          based and appears in memory in the same form as it does in
              ;          registers.  i.e.
              ;          seeeeeee00001111222233334444555566667777888899999aaaabbbbccccdddd
              ;          0       1       2       3       4       5       6       7
              ;          IEEE format is binary based and on the 80386 appears
              ;          reversed in memory from its form in registers. i.e.
              ;          bbbbcccc9999aaaa777788885555666633334444411112222eeee0000seeeeeee
              ;          0       1       2       3       4       5       6       7
              ;
              ;          IEEE format appears to have 4 bits less precision than IBM
              ;          format but the average precision of IBM format is 54.5 bits
              ;          because it is hexadecimal.  The hidden bit in front of the
              ;          fraction of the IEEE format extends its precision to 53
              ;          bits.
              ;
              ;          The conversion routines ignore this discrepancy.
              ;
              ;          The IBM format's exponent base (16) provides a maximum
              ;          value of 2**(64*4) or 2**(256).  The IEEE format provides a
              ;          maximum of 2**(1023).  Therefore, there is no problem
              ;          converting from IBM to IEEE.
              ;
              ;
              ;
              ; Inputs:  DS:SI points to an IBM format long floating point number in
              ;          memory.  (This is assumed to be a normalized number.)  It
              ;          is in IBM order as it would be if read from a network or
              ;          file.
              ;
              ; Process: The number is reversed into 80386 format.  The exponent is
              ;          then converted from IBM to IEEE base in signed form.  The
              ;          fraction is then re-normalized from IBM to IEEE form.  It
              ;          is then shifted right to make room for the biased exponent
              ;          and sign.  The exponent is then biased by 1023, the sign is
              ;          appended, and the resulting 12 bits are combined with the
              ;          fraction.  The result is stored over the original number.
              ;
              ; Output:  The converted number replaces the input number.
              ;
              ;
              ; Note:    This requires the procedure flip8 from the file FLIPS.
              ;
                              EXTRN     Flip8:NEAR
                              PUBLIC    Fpibmeee
              ;
0000          Fpibmeee  PROC
0000  66| 52                  push      EDX               ; Save entry registers
0002  66| 53                  push      EBX
0004  66| 50                  push      EAX

              ;
```

```
                            ; Get number re-ordered to 80386 order.
                            ;
0006  66| 8B 04             mov     EAX,DWORD PTR [SI]  ; Get
                            ;                                 44445555222233330000111seeeeeee
0009  8A D8                 mov     BL,AL                ; Save exponent and sign.
000B  66| 8B 54 04          mov     EDX,DWORD PTR [SI+4] ; and
                            ;                                 ccccddddaaaabbbb8888999966667777
000F  E8 0000 E             call    Flip8                ; convert to
                            ;                           EDX  seeeeeee000011112222333344445555
                            ;                           EAX  6666777788889999aaaabbbbccccdddd
0012  66| 81 E2 00FFFFFF    and     EDX,00ffffffh        ; Clear out seeeeeee
0019  0F 85 0024 R          jnz     havenbr              ; Fraction is non zero
001D  66| 0B C0             or      EAX,EAX              ; Have we got one?
0020  0F 84 006D R          jz      alldone              ; If zero, we're done.
0024                havenbr:
                            ;
                            ; Left adjust the fraction's leftmost hex digit
                            ;
0024  66| 0F A4 C2 08       shld    EDX,EAX,8            ; Get bits shifted to high
0029  66| C1 E0 08          shl     EAX,8                ; complete shift in low.


                            ;
                            ; Re-scale the exponent.
                            ;
002D  83 E3 7F              and     BX,07fh              ; and clear out the sign.
0030  83 EB 40              sub     BX,040h              ; Get as signed, unbiased number.
0033  C1 E3 02              shl     BX,2                 ; Multiply by 4 to get binary exp.
                            ;                              (2**4)**x=2**(4*x)
                            ;
                            ; Adjust normalization from hexadecimal to IEEE binary.
                            ;        (IBM uses 0.x, IEEE uses 1.b and hides the 1)
                            ;
0036                normq:
0036  4B                    dec     BX                   ; Count out the shift.
0037  66| 0F A4 C2 01       shld    EDX,EAX,1            ; Shift one bit left
003C  0F 82 0045 R          jc      normal               ; Done if normalized
0040  66| D1 E0             shl     EAX,1                ; Adjust the lower bits.
0043  EB F1                 jmp     normq                ; Go check if normalized
0045                normal:
0045  66| D1 E0             shl     EAX,1                ; Complete the shift of the fraction.


                            ;
                            ; Re-bias the exponent to IEEE (add 1023) and insert the sign.
                            ;
0048  81 C3 03FF            add     BX,1023              ; Add bias amount
004C  F6 04 80              test    BYTE PTR [SI],080H   ; Check the original sign.
004F  0F 84 0056 R          jz      positive             ; If ok as is skip the
0053  80 CF 08              or      BH,08h               ; set of the sign minus.
0056                positive:
                            ;
                            ; Make room for the exponent and sign.
                            ;
0056  66| 0F AC D0 0C       shrd    EAX,EDX,12           ; From low of EDX to EAX
005B  66| C1 EA 0C          shr     EDX,12               ; then make room in EDX.
005F  66| C1 E3 14          shl     EBX,20               ; Position the exponent and sign
0063  66| 0B D3             or      EDX,EBX              ; and combine with the fraction.
                            ;
                            ; The conversion is done.
                            ;
0066  66| 89 54 04          mov     DWORD PTR [SI+4],EDX ; Put number's high 32 down
006A  66| 89 04             mov     DWORD PTR [SI],EAX   ; and the low 32

006D                alldone:
006D  66| 58                pop     EAX                  ; Restore the entry registers
006F  66| 5B                pop     EBX
0071  66| 5A                pop     EDX
0073  C3                    ret                          ; and return.
0074                Fpibmeee  ENDP
0074                code      ENDS
                              END
```

```
                              PAGE      55,132
                              .386
0000                  code    SEGMENT   para 'CODE' PUBLIC USE16
                              ASSUME    CS:code, DS:code, SS:code

                      ;
                      ; Name:    FPIEEEBM
                      ;
                      ; Purpose: The following procedure provides a conversion of an IEEE
                      ;          format long floating point number to an IBM long format
                      ;          floating point number.  The IBM 370 format is hexadecimal
                      ;          based and appears in memory in the same form as it does in
                      ;          registers.  i.e.
                      ;   seeeeeee000011112222333344445555666677778888999 9aaaabbbbccccdddd
                      ;   0         1         2         3         4         5         6       7
                      ;          IEEE format is binary based and on the 80386 appears
                      ;          reversed in memory from its form in registers. i.e.
                      ;   bbbbcccc9999aaaa88887777666655554444333322221111eeee0000seeeeeee
                      ;   0         1         2         3         4         5         6       7
                      ;
                      ;          IEEE format has 10 bits of exponent while IBM format has
                      ;          only 8 (reduced to 6 because IBM uses hexadecimal).
                      ;          Therefore, while the IBM format can hold the IEEE fraction
                      ;          (including the hidden 1. bit) an exponent overflow or
                      ;          underflow could occur.
                      ;
                      ;          The conversion routine represents an underflow as zero and
                      ;          an overflow as the maximum possible number.  If either
                      ;          occurs, the routine returns with carry set (otherwise carry
                      ;          is reset).
                      ;
                      ; Inputs:  DS:SI points to an IEEE format long floating point number
                      ;          in memory.  (This is assumed to be a normalized number.)
                      ;
                      ; Process: The exponent is unbiased and the fraction is converted to
                      ;          0.1 format.  The exponent is checked for zero and an IBM
                      ;          format zero is returned if it is.  The exponent is checked
                      ;          for underflow and if so, zero and carry are returned.  The
                      ;          exponent is then checked for overflow and if so, a maximum
                      ;          value IBM number is returned with carry set.  A convertible
                      ;          number has its exponent converted to a base 16 exponent by
                      ;          shifting right two bits.  The fraction is adjusted to
                      ;          hexadecimal by shifting right for the count given by the
                      ;          two bits shifted out of the exponent.  The exponent is
                      ;          then biased by 64, the sign is appended and the resulting
                      ;          number is stored in reverse form as expected by an IBM 370.
                      ;          Carry is cleared and the routine returns.
                      ;
                      ; Output:  The converted number replaces the input number.  Carry is
                      ;          set if over or underflow occurred and reset otherwise.
                      ;
                              PUBLIC    Fpieeebm
                              EXTRN     Flip8:PROC
                      ;
0000                  Fpieeebm  PROC
0000  66| 52                    push      EDX                  ; Save entry registers
0002  66| 51                    push      ECX
0004  66| 53                    push      EBX
0006  66| 50                    push      EAX


                      ;
                      ; Get number in 80386 order.
                      ;
0008  66| 8B 04                 mov       EAX,DWORD PTR [SI]   ; Get low order 32
000B  66| 8B 54 04              mov       EDX,DWORD PTR [SI+4] ; and the high.
000F  8B 5C 06                  mov       BX,WORD PTR [SI+6]   ; Get seeeeeeeeeee0000
```

```
0012  66| 0F A4 C2 0B          shld    EDX,EAX,11        ; Position fraction to bits 62
0017  66| C1 E0 0B             shl     EAX,11            ; through 11
001B  66| 0F BA EA 1F          bts     EDX,31            ; Set hidden one bit.
                               ;
                               ; The fraction is now left adjusted in EAX:EDX
                               ;
0020  2B C9                    sub     CX,CX             ; Assume ok conversion.
0022  C1 EB 04                 shr     BX,4              ; Position biased exponent
0025  81 E3 07FF               and     BX,07ffh          ; isolate it
0029  0F 84 0043 R             jz      iszero            ; and exit if zero.
002D  81 EB 03FF               sub     BX,03ffh          ; remove the bias
0031  43                       inc     BX                ; add one for the right shift.
                               ;
                               ; Check for exponent overflow.
                               ;
0032  81 FB 00FF               cmp     BX,255            ; check to maximum positive
0036  0F 8F 004C R .           jg      overflow          ; out if overflow.
003A  81 FB FEFD               cmp     BX,-259           ; check for minimum negative
003E  0F 8D 005C R             jnl     neither           ; continue if it converts.
0042  49                       dec     CX                ; Flag as underflow
0043                   iszero:
0043  66| 2B C0                sub     EAX,EAX           ; Zero the completed
0046  66| 2B D2                sub     EDX,EDX           ; 8 byte float number
0049  EB 43 90                 jmp     setit             ; and go put it down.
004C                   overflow:
004C  49                       dec     CX                ; Flag as overflow
004D  66| BA 7FFFFFFF          mov     EDX,7fffffffh     ; Set maximum exponent,
0053  66| B8 FFFFFFFF          mov     EAX,-1            ; and a fraction of
0059  EB 33 90                 jmp     setit             ; all one bits.
005C                   neither:
005C  8A CB                    mov     CL,BL             ; Get low two
005E  80 E1 03                 and     CL,3              ; exponent bits as shift count.
0061  80 E9 04                 sub     CL,4
0064  F6 D9                    neg     CL
0066  66| 0F AD D0             shrd    EAX,EDX,CL        ; Shift fraction to
006A  66| D3 EA                shr     EDX,CL            ; hexadecimal normalization.
006D  C1 FB 02                 sar     BX,2              ; Divide exponent by 4
0070  83 C3 41                 add     BX,64+1           ; and add IBM bias amount.
                                                         ; +1 for point position.
0073  80 E3 7F                 and     BL,07fh           ; Clear sign bit and
0076  8A 4C 07                 mov     CL,BYTE PTR [SI+7] ; Get the sign of the fraction
0079  80 E1 80                 and     CL,080h           ; isolate it and
007C  0A D9                    or      BL,CL             ; Set if negative.
007E  66| C1 E3 18             shl     EBX,24            ; Position new exponent & sign
0082  66| 0F AC D0 08          shrd    EAX,EDX,8         ; make room for it
0087  66| C1 EA 08             shr     EDX,8             ; in EDX
008B  66| 0B D3                or      EDX,EBX           ; and combine them
                               ;
                               ; Re-order the bytes as we store them into IBM order.
                               ;
008E                   setit:
008E  E8 0000 E                call    Flip8             ; Reorder the bytes
0091  66| 89 04                mov     DWORD PTR [SI],EAX ; Put them down
0094  66| 89 54 04             mov     DWORD PTR [SI+4],EDX ;
                               ;
                               ; Set carry if needed
                               ;
0098  D0 E5                    shl     CH,1              ; Shift sign into carry.
                               ;
                               ; and exit
                               ;
009A  66| 58                   pop     EAX               ; Restore the entry registers
009C  66| 5B                   pop     EBX
009E  66| 59                   pop     ECX
00A0  66| 5A                   pop     EDX
00A2  C3                       ret                       ; and return.
00A3                   Fpieeebm  ENDP
00A3                   code      ENDS
                                 END
```

Program 7-13 FPLFPASC

Microsoft (R) Macro Assembler Version 5.00

```
0000
                              PAGE      55,132
                              .386
                              .287
                    code      SEGMENT   para 'CODE' USE16 PUBLIC
                              ASSUME    CS:code, DS:code, SS:code
                    ;
                    ; Name:   FPLFPASC
                    ;
                    ; Purpose: The following procedure provides a conversion from an IEEE
                    ;          format long floating point number to an ASCII
                    ;          representation of a floating point number. IEEE long format
                    ;          has an 11 digit binary exponent biased by 1023.  It appears
                    ;          in memory reversed from its form in registers. i.e.
                    ;    bbbbcccc9999aaaa77778888555566663333444411112222eeee0000seeeeeee
                    ;          0       1       2       3       4       5       6       7
                    ;
                    ;          An ASCII representation is a string of the form:
                    ;          [-]digit.digitsE[-]digits  Where:
                    ;          [-] indicates an optional minus sign,
                    ;          digit is an ASCII digit preceding the decimal point (.),
                    ;          digits is one or more ASCII digits following the decimal
                    ;          point, the E which begins the exponent or the minus sign if
                    ;          the exponent is negative.
                    ;
                    ;          Some possible values are: 0.0E0 for zero, -1.0E0 for -1,
                    ;          -2.345E-3 for -.002345.
                    ;
                    ;          Conversion to ASCII of a valid long floating point number
                    ;          is always possible.  Infinity is checked for and is
                    ;          returned as 9.9E999 or -9.9E999 depending on the number's
                    ;          sign.  Zero is returned as 0.0E0.
                    ;          Zero and infinity are returned for exponents of 00000000000
                    ;          and 11111111111 respectively.  The fraction is not checked
                    ;          in either case.
                    ;
                    ; Inputs: EAX:EDX contains the long floating point number.  BX is
                    ;          assumed to point to a string area of at least 25 bytes.
                    ;
                    ; Process: The number is checked for infinity or zero and if either,
                    ;          is detected, the appropriate values are returned.
                    ;          The sign is transferred to the output and the number is
                    ;          replaced by its absolute value if it was negative.
                    ;          The decimal exponent is then created by scaling the number
                    ;          to a value between 1.0 and 10.0.  The digit is extracted,
                    ;          converted to ASCII and placed in the output followed by a
                    ;          decimal point.
                    ;
                    ;          We then enter the following loop:
                    ;          The integer portion is subtracted from our scaled number.
                    ;          The result is checked for zero and if it is we exit this
                    ;          loop.  Otherwise the result is multiplied by 100.  The
                    ;          result is a new integer portion in the range 100>i>=0
                    ;          which is extracted, converted to ASCII and placed in the
                    ;          output. If our fraction is 15 digits long we exit the loop.
                    ;
                    ;          If the fraction is 15 digits long, we round it to 14 digits
                    ;          by adding 1 to the 14th digit if digit 15 is 5 or more. If
                    ;          the result is over 9 we 'eat' the digit and propagate the
                    ;          carry to the next digit to the left for as many digits as
                    ;          necessary.
                    ;
```

```
;   Output:   The converted number is returned memory as an ASCIIZ string
;             in the area pointed to by DS:BX.  The length of the string
;             is returned in CX.  All other registers are preserved.
;
;
;
=                         fpnohi    EQU       SS:DWORD PTR[BP-4]      ; High part of float
=                         fpnolo    EQU       SS:DWORD PTR[BP-8]      ; Low part of float
=                         fpnumb    EQU       SS:QWORD PTR[BP-8]      ; Complete number
=                         fpcntl    EQU       SS:WORD PTR[BP-12]      ; Save area for control flags
;
                                    PUBLIC    Fplfpasc
;
                          Fplfpasc  PROC
0000                                enter     16,0                   ; Get work space
0000  C8 0010 00                    mov       fpnchi,EDX             ; Store the number.
0004  66| 89 56 FC                  mov       fpnolo,EAX
0008  66| 89 46 F8                  push      DI                     ; Save work registers.
000C  57                            push      SI
000D  56                            push      EDX
000E  66| 52                        push      EAX
0010  66| 50                        sub       DI,DI                  ; Clear index registers
0012  2B FF                         sub       SI,SI
0014  2B F6                         and       EDX,07ff00000h         ; isolate binary exponent
0016  66| 81 E2 7FF00000            jz        outzero                ; Exit if zero.
001D  0F 84 0045 R
;
;  Infinity may be positive or negative as may the number.
;
0021  66| 0F BA 76 FC 1F            btr       fpnohi,31              ; Check sign of number
0027  0F 83 002F R                  jnc       positive               ; Positive
002B  C6 07 2D                      mov       BYTE PTR [BX+0],'-'     ; Negative
002E  46                            inc       SI                     ; count the sign.
002F                       positive:
002F  66| 81 FA 7FF00000            cmp       EDX,07ff00000h         ; Check if infinity
0036  0F 85 0059 R                  jnz       number                 ; No - need to convert.
003A  B9 0007 90                    mov       CX,infsize             ; Set count of bytes.
003E  8D 3E 0262 R                  lea       DI,infinity            ; and address.
0042  EB 09 90                      jmp       moveit                 ; go copy infinity.
0045                       outzero:
0045  B9 0005 90                    mov       CX,zersize             ; set count of bytes.
0049  8D 3E 0269 R                  lea       DI,zero                ; and address
004D                       moveit:
004D  2E: 8A 05                     mov       AL,BYTE PTR CS:[DI]     ; Get a byte
0050  88 00                         mov       BYTE PTR [BX+SI],AL    ; and put it down
0052  46                            inc       SI                     ; step indices
0053  47                            inc       DI
0054  E2 F7                         loop      moveit                 ; and copy constant.
0056  E9 01A3 R                     jmp       exit                   ; Then get out
;
;  A number needs to be converted.
;
;  First we scale the number to the range 1.0<=n<10.0
;
                          number:
0059                                finit                            ; Reset the box.
0059  9B DB E3                      fnstcw    fpcntl                 ; Preserve control flag state.
005C  D9 7E F4                      mov       AX,fpcntl              ; changing only the round
005F  8B 46 F4                      or        AX,0000110000000000b   ; Set rounding to truncate
0062  0D 0C00                       mov       fpcntl,AX              ; Put back in memory and
0065  89 46 F4                      fldcw     fpcntl                 ; cause truncation not rounding
0068  9B D9 6E F4                   push      SI                     ; Save possible sign.
006C  56                            mov       DI,8*8                 ; Set index of powers
006D  BF 0040                       mov       SI,8*2
0070  BE 0010                       sub       EDX,EDX                ; Clear accum of powers stepped
0073  66| 2B D2                     fld       fpnumb                 ; Set number into unit.
0076  DD 46 F8
```

```
0079   2E: DC 16 0200 R              fcom    CS:conof1           ; Check to 1.0
007E   9B DF E0                      fstsw   AX                  ; Get results into AX
0081   9E                            sahf                        ; and then into flags.
0082   0F 82 00AA R                  jb      mustgoup            ; If ST low - need to scale up
                               ;
                               ; We need to scale down
                               ;
0086                          nextdown:
0086   2E: DC 95 01B0 R              fcom    CS:pospower[DI]     ; Check to positive power
008B   9B DF E0                      fstsw   AX                  ; of ten.
008E   9E                            sahf
008F   0F 82 009F R                  jb      below               ; If we are under, leave alone.
0093   2E: DD 85 0208 R              fld     CS:negpower[DI]     ; Bring it down a step
0098   DE C9                         fmul
009A   2E: 03 94 0250 R              add     DX,CS:valpower[SI]  ; Add the power we stepped.
009F                          below:
009F   83 EE 02                      sub     SI,2
00A2   83 EF 08                      sub     DI,8                ; Try next lower
00A5   79 DF                         jns     nextdown            ; Go try it
00A7   EB 35 90                      jmp     convert             ; Done - go convert the number.
                               ;
                               ; We need to scale up
                               ;
00AA                          mustgoup:
00AA   2E: DC 95 0208 R              fcom    CS:negpower[DI]     ; Check to next negative power
00AF   9B DF E0                      fstsw   AX                  ; of ten.
00B2   9E                            sahf
00B3   0F 87 00C3 R                  ja      above               ; If not lower - leave alone.
00B7   2E: DD 85 01B0 R              fld     CS:pospower[DI]     ; Bring it up a step
00BC   DE C9                         fmul
00BE   2E: 2B 94 0250 R              sub     DX,CS:valpower[SI]  ; Down the power we stepped.
00C3                          above:
00C3   83 EF 08                      sub     DI,8                ; Try next higher
00C6   83 EE 02                      sub     SI,2
00C9   79 DF                         jns     mustgoup            ; Go try it
                               ;
                               ; The above can leave us with a value less than 1 - check if it did.
                               ;
00CB   2E: DC 16 0200 R              fcom    CS:conof1           ; Check to 1.0
00D0   9B DF E0                      fstsw   AX                  ; Get results into AX
00D3   9E                            sahf                        ; and then into flags.
00D4   0F 83 00DE R                  jnb     convert             ; If ST isn't low - skip
00D8   2E: DC 0E 01B0 R              fmul    CS:conof10          ; Get leading digit non zero
00DD   4A                            dec     DX                  ; and account for it.
                               ;
                               ; Now convert the first digit, place it in the output followed by a
                               ; decimal point.  If the fraction is zero a zero is placed after the
                               ; decimal and we are done.
                               ;
00DE                          convert:
00DE   5E                            pop     SI                  ; Get output pointer back.
00DF   DD D1                         fst     ST(1)               ; Copy the number from ST.
00E1   DF 18                         fistp   WORD PTR[BX+SI]     ; Put word in user's area
00E3   DF 00                         fild    WORD PTR[BX+SI]     ; and get the integer back.
00E5   80 08 30                      or      BYTE PTR[BX+SI],'0' ; Put the zone on it
00E8   46                            inc     SI                  ; point to the point position
00E9   C6 00 2E                      mov     BYTE PTR[BX+SI],'.' ; and put it there
00EC   46                            inc     SI                  ; Point to next position.
00ED                          hundreds:
00ED   DE E9                         fsub                        ; Subtract integer ST=ST(1)-ST
00EF   2E: DC 0E 01B8 R              fmul    CS:con100           ; Fraction times 100
00F4   DD D1                         fst     ST(1)               ; Save a copy.
00F6   DF 5F 18                      fistp   WORD PTR[BX+24]     ; Copy integer to memory
00F9   DF 47 18                      fild    WORD PTR[BX+24]     ; and back on stack.
00FC   8B 47 18                      mov     AX,WORD PTR[BX+24]  ; Get into AX in order to
```

```
00FF  D4 0A                        aam                        ; spread to two digits,
0101  0D 3030                      or      AX,'00'            ; and place zones on them.
0104  86 E0                        xchg    AH,AL              ; Reverse them
0106  89 00                        mov     WORD PTR[BX+SI],AX ; and store them
0108  83 C6 02                     add     SI,2               ; Step the destination
010B  83 FE 10                     cmp     SI,16              ; Did we fill last part
010E  0F 83 0126 R                 jnb     donefull           ; Yes, check for rounding.
0112  D8 D1                        fcom                       ; Was this the last pair?
                                                              ; i.e. would ST(1)-ST be <= 0?
0114  9B DF E0                     fstsw   AX                 ; Get the resulting condition
0117  9E                           sahf                       ; code into the flags.
                                                              ; Exit if it would. (C0=0)
0118  72 D3                        jc      hundreds           ; Go do more digits.

                            ;
                            ; All digits of the number have been converted.
                            ;
011A  80 78 FF 30                  cmp     BYTE PTR[BX+SI-1],'0' ; Was a zero the last digit?
011E  0F 85 016E R                 jnz     doexponent         ; No, leave it alone, but
0122  4E                           dec     SI                 ; overlay it otherwise.
0123  EB 3B 90                     jmp     trail0s            ; Go get rid of others.

                            ;
                            ; The fraction filled all digits of the output -
                            ; round it up if ST+.5-ST(1)<=0
                            ;
0126                        donefull:
0126  2E: DC 06 01F8 R             fadd    CS:point5          ; Add the rounding value.
012B  D8 D1                        fcom                       ; Check if we need to round.
012D  9B DF E0                     fstsw   AX                 ; Get condition code
0130  9E                           sahf                       ; into the flags
0131  0F 87 0160 R                 ja      trail0s            ; If no rounding needed - out.
0135                        donefull0:
0135  4E                           dec     SI                 ; Need to round up
0136  80 38 2E                     cmp     BYTE PTR[BX+SI],'.' ; At decimal point?
0139  0F 84 0148 R                 je      moveptq            ; We may have to move it
013D  FE 00                        inc     BYTE PTR[BX+SI]    ; So do it.
013F  80 38 39                     cmp     BYTE PTR[BX+SI],'9' ; Do we have a carry?
0142  77 F1                        ja      donefull0          ; Yes. propagate it.
0144  46                           inc     SI                 ; No. leave it.
0145  EB 19 90                     jmp     trail0s            ; Go do trailing zeros

                            ;
                            ; The rounding went into the decimal point.
                            ;
0148                        moveptq:
0148  4E                           dec     SI                 ; Get leading digit
0149  80 38 39                     cmp     BYTE PTR[BX+SI],'9' ; Need to adjust exponent?
014C  0F 85 0154 R                 jne     moveptq1           ; We may have to move it
0150  C6 00 30                     mov     BYTE PTR[BX+SI],'0' ; We do - and make 1.0
0153  42                           inc     DX                 ; Add one to exponent.
0154                        moveptq1:
0154  FE 00                        inc     BYTE PTR[BX+SI]    ; Step the digit
0156  83 C6 02                     add     SI,2               ; point to trailing zero
0159  C6 00 30                     mov     BYTE PTR[BX+SI],'0' ; fill it in
015C  46                           inc     SI                 ; Get next position
015D  EB 0F 90                     jmp     doexponent         ; Go do exponent

                            ;
                            ; Eliminate any trailing zeros
                            ;
0160                        trail0s:
0160  83 FE 03                     cmp     SI,3               ; Check where we are
0163  0F 86 016E R                 jna     doexponent         ; if just x.x - leave it
0167  4E                           dec     SI
0168  80 38 30                     cmp     BYTE PTR[BX+SI],'0' ; Trailing zero
016B  74 F3                        je      trail0s            ; Yes - get rid of most
016D  46                           inc     SI

                            ;
                            ; We only need to convert the power of ten
                            ;
```

```
016E                          doexponent:
016E  9B DB E3                        finit                               ; Leave the box neutral.
0171  C6 00 45                        mov     BYTE PTR[BX+SI],'E'  ; Set exponent indicator
0174  46                              inc     SI
0175  2B C0                           sub     AX,AX                       ; Clear leading digit
0177  0B D2                           or      DX,DX                       ; Check sign
0179  0F 89 0183 R                    jns     posexpon            ; and if it is positive - skip
017D  C6 00 2D                        mov     BYTE PTR[BX+SI],'-'  ; setting exponent sign.
0180  46                              inc     SI                          ; leave room
0181  F7 DA                           neg     DX                          ; force positive
0183                          posexpon:
0183  83 EA 64                        sub     DX,100                      ; Back out the hundreds
0186  0F 88 018D R                    js      backin                      ; too far - back it in
018A  40                              inc     AX                          ; Add the digit.
018B  EB F6                           jmp     posexpon                    ; Go do another
018D                          backin:
018D  83 C2 64                        add     DX,100                      ; Put it back
0190  0C 30                           or      AL,'0'                      ; set zone
0192  88 00                           mov     BYTE PTR[BX+SI],AL  ; and put digit out
0194  8B C2                           mov     AX,DX                       ; position low two
0196  D4 0A                           aam                                 ; and convert them
0198  0D 3030                         or      AX,'00'                     ; to ASCII digits
019B  86 E0                           xchg    AH,AL                       ; reverse them
019D  89 40 01                        mov     WORD PTR[BX+SI+1],AX ; and store them.
01A0  83 C6 03                        add     SI,3                        ; count them

01A3                          exit:
01A3  C6 00 00                        mov     BYTE PTR [BX+SI],0   ; Follow with a null
01A6  8B CE                           mov     CX,SI                       ; set the count of bytes.
01A8  66| 58                          pop     EAX                         ; Restore work registers
01AA  66| 5A                          pop     EDX
01AC  5E                              pop     SI
01AD  5F                              pop     DI
01AE  C9                              leave
01AF  C3                              ret                                 ; and return.
                              ;
                              ; Power of ten conversion - positive and negative to |511|
                              ;
                                      ALIGN   4

01B0  0000000000002440        pospower   dq      1.0E+001             ; Positive powers of ten
=                             conot10    equ     pospower
01B8  0000000000005940        con100     dq      1.0E+002
01C0  000000000088C340                   dq      1.0E+004
01C8  0000000084D79741                   dq      1.0E+008
01D0  0080E03779C34143                   dq      1.0E+016
01D8  176E05B5B5B89346                   dq      1.0E+032
01E0  F5F93FE9034F384D                   dq      1.0E+064
01E8  321D30F94877825A                   dq      1.0E+128
01F0  3CBF737FDD4F1575                   dq      1.0E+256
01F8  000000000000E03F        point5     dq      5.0E-001             ; .5
0200  000000000000F03F        conof1     dq      1.0
0208  9A9999999999B93F        negpower   dq      1.0E-001             ; Negative powers of ten
0210  7B14AE47E17A843F                   dq      1.0E-002
0218  2D431CEBE2361A3F                   dq      1.0E-004
0220  3A8C30E28E79453E                   dq      1.0E-008
0228  BC89D897B2D29C3C                   dq      1.0E-016
0230  33A7A8D523F64939                   dq      1.0E-032
0238  3DA7F444FD0FA532                   dq      ` 0E-064
0240  9D978CCF08BA5B25                   dq      ,.0E-128
0248  436FAC642806C80A                   dq      1.0E-256
0250  0001                    valpower   dw      1                    ; Table of powers stepped
0252  0002                               dw      2
0254  0004                               dw      4
0256  0008                               dw      8
0258  0010                               dw      16
```

```
025A  0020                              dw      32
025C  0040                              dw      64
025E  0080                              dw      128
0260  0100                              dw      256
                                ;
                                ; Easy conversions
                                ;
0262  39 2E 39 45 39 39 39      infinity  db    '9.9E999'
 = 0007                         infsize   equ   $-infinity
0269  30 2E 30 45 30            zero      db    '0.0E0'
 = 0005                         zersize   equ   $-zero


026E                           Fplfpasc  ENDP
026E                           code      ENDS
                                         END
```

Program 7-14 FPASCLFP

Microsoft (R) Macro Assembler Version 5.00

```
                                PAGE      55,132
                                .386
                                .287
0000                   code     SEGMENT   para 'CODE' USE16 PUBLIC
                                ASSUME    CS:code, DS:code, SS:code

                       ; Name:    FPASCLFP
                       ;
                       ; Purpose: The following procedure provides a conversion to an IEEE
                       ;          format long floating point number from an ASCII
                       ;          representation of a floating point number.
                       ;          IEEE long format has an 11 digit binary exponent biased by
                       ;          1023. It appears in memory reversed from its form in
                       ;          registers. i.e.
                       ;          bbbbcccc9999aaaa777788885555666633334444111122222eeee0000seeeeeee
                       ;          0       1       2       3       4       5       6       7
                       ;
                       ;          An ASCII representation is a string of the form:
                       ;          [+/-] [digits].[digits][E[+/-]digits] where [+/-] indicates
                       ;          an optional sign of either + or -, [digits] indicates
                       ;          possible required digits (0 - 9), a required decimal point (.)
                       ;          potentially followed by digits and an optional exponent
                       ;          which if present must be E followed by an optional sign and
                       ;          1 to 3 digits.  Possible numbers are:
                       ;          5.,  -., (or .  both giving the same as 0.0), -5.3E-2 etc.
                       ;          The numbers are ASCII strings in memory.
                       ;
                       ;          Conversion from ASCII to long can either underflow or
                       ;          overflow the long exponent.  Zero and infinity are returned
                       ;          respectively and flagged with a carry.
                       ;
                       ; Inputs:  DS:SI point to the ASCII string, CX has its maximum length.
                       ;
                       ; Process: The string is parsed from left to right with possible
                       ;          leading spaces ignored.  The sign is assumed + if omitted.
                       ;          Digits are converted into a quadword integer.  Digits to
                       ;          the right of the decimal also are counted in the exponent.
                       ;          The exponent is converted and added to the count of digits
                       ;          to the right of the decimal point.
                       ;
                       ;          The quadword integer is converted to a long floating point
                       ;          number.  (If zero we are done.)  The exponent is created
                       ;          as 64-the number of leading zero bits in the quadword.
                       ;          The resulting floating point number is further scaled by
```

```
                          ;
                          ;             the power of ten given in the decimal exponent.
                          ;
                          ;             A malformed number is returned as zero with carry set.
                          ;             i.e. -5E (no decimal) 55a (invalid digit) would both
                          ;             be returned as zero.
                          ;
                          ; Output:    The converted number is returned in EAX:EDX.  Carry is set
                          ;            if infinity is returned and reset otherwise.  SI points
                          ;            beyond the last digit converted and CX has the remaining
                          ;            length.
                          ;
                          ;
                          ;
                          ;
=                         fpnohi    EQU    SS:DWORD PTR[BP-4]   ; High part of float
=                         fpnolo    EQU    SS:DWORD PTR[BP-8]   ; Low part of float
=                         fpnumb    EQU    SS:QWORD PTR[BP-8]   ; Complete number
                          ;
                                    PUBLIC  Fpasclfp
                          ;
0000                      Fpasclfp  PROC
0000  C8 0010 00                    enter   16,0                ; Get work space
0004  66| 53                        push    EBX                 ; Save work registers.
0006  57                            push    DI
0007  E3 59                         jcxz    badnum              ; If no digits - exit
0009  06                            push    ES
000A  8C DB                         mov     BX,DS
000C  8E C3                         mov     ES,BX
000E  8B FE                         mov     DI,SI
0010  66| 2B DB                     sub     EBX,EBX             ; Clear first part of long
0013  66| 2B D2                     sub     EDX,EDX             ; Clear rest of long number.
0016  66| 0F B7 C9                  movzx   ECX,CX              ; Clear sign indicator
001A  FC                            cld                         ; Force direction to up.

                          ;
                          ; Strip leading blanks
                          ;
001B  B0 20                         mov     AL,' '              ; Set space as skip
001D  F3/ AE                        repe scasb                  ;
001F  4F                            dec     DI                  ; Point back to non-space.
0020  41                            inc     CX                  ; back count up too
0021  8B F7                         mov     SI,DI               ; Use SI for lodsb
0023  07                            pop     ES                  ; Restore ES
0024  E3 3C                         jcxz    badnum              ; If all spaces - exit
0026  2B FF                         sub     DI,DI               ; Clear exponent digit count
0028  AC                            lodsb                       ; Get the non blank and step SI
0029  34 30                         xor     AL,'0'              ; Check if sign omitted
002B  3C 09                         cmp     AL,9                ; Is it a digit?
002D  0F 86 0059 R                  jna     isdigit             ; Yes - start number
0031  3C 1E                         cmp     AL,'.' XOR '0'      ; Is it a period?
0033  0F 84 0072 R                  jz      decpoint            ; Yes - Number may be valid
0037  3C 1D                         cmp     AL,'-' XOR '0'      ; Is it a minus
0039  0F 85 0045 R                  jnz     checkpl             ; No - maybe a plus?
003D  66| 0F BA E9 1F               bts     ECX,31              ; Remember in high bit of ECX.
0042  EB 07 90                      jmp     sign                ; Yes - skip the sign.
0045                      checkpl:
0045  3C 1B                         cmp     AL,'+' XOR '0'      ; Is it a plus sign
0047  0F 85 0062 R                  jnz     badnum              ; If not - error
004B                      sign:
004B  49                            dec     CX                  ; Count the character
004C  0F 84 0062 R                  jz      badnum              ; Can't end with sign!
                          ;
                          ; Collect leading digits
                          ;
0050                      digitq:
```

```
0050   AC                           lodsb                    ; Get the next byte and step SI
0051   34 30                        xor     AL,'0'           ; Check if it is a digit
0053   3C 09                        cmp     AL,9             ; Is it a digit?
0055   0F 87 006E R                 ja      decptq           ; No - leading digits are gone
0059                        isdigit:
0059   E8 0240 R                    call    accumd           ; accumulate leading digits.
005C   0F 82 0088 R                 jc      skiprest         ; for 64 bits max.
0060   E2 EE                        loop    digitq           ; Count it and try next
                                                                  No decimal point!
                                 ;
                                 ;
                                 ; An error in the number's format was encountered.  Exit with an
                                 ; error.
                                 ;
0062                        badnum:
0062   5F                           pop     DI               ; Restore work registers
0063   66| 5B                       pop     EBX
0065   66| 2B C0                    sub     EAX,EAX          ; Clear the number
0068   66| 2B D2                    sub     EDX,EDX
006B   F9                           stc                      ; Set carry on and
006C   C9                           leave
006D   C3                           ret                      ; return.
                                 ;
                                 ; We must encounter a decimal point now.
                                 ;
006E                        decptq:
006E   3C 1E                        cmp     AL,'.' XOR '0'   ; Is it a decimal point?
0070   75 F0                        jnz     badnum           ; If not - too bad.
0072                        decpoint:
0072   AC                           lodsb                    ; Get the next byte and step SI
0073   34 30                        xor     AL,'0'           ; Check for digit
0075   3C 09                        cmp     AL,9             ; Is it?
0077   0F 87 00A3 R                 ja      checke           ; If not - it must be exponent
007B   E8 0240 R                    call    accumd           ; accumulate another digit
007E   0F 82 0097 R                 jc      skiprestp        ; No more will fit!
0082   4F                           dec     DI               ; Reduce exponent by a power
                                                             ; of 10.
0083   E2 ED                        loop    decpoint         ; Get more digits
0085   E9 0110 R                    jmp     scandone         ; If no more - done
                                 ;
                                 ; Precision has been exceeded but we have significant digits of
                                 ; the number.  We skip digits to the decimal point, counting
                                 ; places into the exponent.
                                 ;
0088                        skiprest:
0088   49                           dec     CX               ; Count the digit out
0089   74 D7                        jz      badnum           ; All digits and no decimal!
008B   47                           inc     DI               ; Add to exponent count
008C   AC                           lodsb                    ; get next byte
008D   34 30                        xor     AL,'0'           ; Check for another digit
008F   3C 09                        cmp     AL,9             ; Is it?
0091   76 F5                        jna     skiprest         ; Yes - go count for exponent
                                 ;
                                 ; We must have a decimal point here or we will bomb out.
                                 ;
0093   3C 1E                        cmp     AL,'.' XOR '0'   ; Is it?
0095   75 CB                        jnz     badnum           ; No - too bad
                                 ;
                                 ; Now we skip unusable fraction digits.  An exponent may be present
                                 ; so we must look for it but we don't require one.
                                 ;
0097                        skiprestp:
0097   49                           dec     CX               ; Count the digit out
0098   0F 84 0110 R                 jz      scandone         ; If no more - scan is done.
009C   AC                           lodsb                    ; Get next digit
009D   34 30                        xor     AL,'0'           ; Check if it is
009F   3C 09                        cmp     AL,9             ;
00A1   76 F4                        jna     skiprestp        ; loop if so
                                 ;
```

```
                              ; We now expect an exponent - E (or e) followed by an optionally
                              ; signed number.
                              ;
00A3                          checke:
00A3   3C 55                          cmp     AL,'e' XOR '0'     ; Is it lower case
00A5   0F 84 00AD R                   jz      havee              ; Yes - go get exponent.
00A9   3C 75                          cmp     AL,'E' XOR '0'     ; Is it upper case?
00AB   75 B5                          jnz     badnum             ; No - It is bad.
00AD                          havee:
00AD   49                             dec     CX                 ; Count out the E
00AE   74 B2                          jz      badnum             ; error if no number after.
00B0   AC                             lodsb                      ; Get next character.
00B1   3C 2D                          cmp     AL,'-'             ; Is it minus?
00B3   0F 85 00BF R                   jnz     posexpon           ; no - check further
00B7   66| 0F BA E9 1E                bts     ECX,30             ; remember it was minus
00BC   EB 07 90                       jmp     getexpd            ;
00BF                          posexpon:
00BF   3C 2B                          cmp     AL,'+'             ; Is it plus?
00C1   0F 85 00C9 R                   jnz     expond             ; No - must be digit.
00C5                          getexpd:
00C5   49                             dec     CX                 ; Count the exponent's sign
00C6   74 9A                          jz      badnum             ; Just a sign is an error.
00C8   AC                             lodsb                      ; Get next byte
                              ;
                              ; We now collect the exponent digits.
                              ;
00C9                          expond:
00C9   3C 30                          cmp     AL,'0'             ; Check if under zero
00CB   72 95                          jb      badnum             ; if so - bad
00CD   3C 39                          cmp     AL,'9'             ; is it over 9
00CF   77 91                          ja      badnum             ; if so - bad
00D1   66| 52                         push    EDX                ; Save accumed number
00D3   66| 53                         push    EBX
00D5   66| 2B DB                      sub     EBX,EBX            ; Clear for accum of exponent
00D8   66| 2B D2                      sub     EDX,EDX
00DB   EB 09 90                       jmp     expond1            ; Digit is loaded
00DE                          expond2:
00DE   66| 5B                         pop     EBX                ; Clean up the stack
00E0   66| 5A                         pop     EDX
00E2   E9 0062 R                      jmp     badnum             ; and report the error
00E5                          expond0:
00E5   AC                             lodsb                      ; Get the next digit (if any)
00E6                          expond1:
00E6   34 30                          xor     AL,'0'             ; check if digit
00E8   3C 09                          cmp     AL,9               ;
00EA   0F 87 00F5 R                   ja      expond3            ; We have trailing other data
00EE   E8 0240 R                      call    accumd             ; accumulate digit
00F1   72 EB                          jc      expond2            ; Too many exponent digits.
00F3   E2 F0                          loop    expond0            ; Go try another.
00F5                          expond3:
                              ;
                              ; EBX has the power of ten - Need to feed in the sign and combine
                              ; with the value in DI.
                              ;
00F5   66| 81 FB 000001FF             cmp     EBX,511            ; check if exponent too big.
00FC   77 E0                          ja      expond2            ; If so - number is malformed.
00FE   66| 0F BA E1 1E                bt      ECX,30             ; check if exponent negative.
0103   0F 83 010A R                   jnc     expplus            ; If not - EBX is ok as is.
0107   66| F7 DB                      neg     EBX                ; Get 2's compliment
010A                          expplus:
010A   03 FB                          add     DI,BX              ; Get the exponent into DI
010C   66| 5B                         pop     EBX                ; Restore the 64 bit number
010E   66| 5A                         pop     EDX
                              ;
                              ; The exponent (as a power of ten) is now in DI, and the 64 bit
                              ; number is in EDX:EBX.  CX has the remaining count of characters.
```

```
                                         ; SI points to the character after the last number digit.
                                         ;
0110                            scandone:
0110  51                                push     CX                       ; Save character count and
0111  56                                push     SI                       ; pointer for work registers.
                                         ;
                                         ; First we normalize the 64 bit number.  Doing this we create a binary
                                         ; exponent in the range of 0 to 63.  Then we form a long floating
                                         ; point by combining the exponent and the fraction.  Finally we need
                                         ; to apply the proper power of ten to the result.
0112  66| 0B D2                          or       EDX,EDX                  ; Is the top dword occupied?
0115  0F 84 012F R                       jz       topzero                  ; No, exponent range is 0 - 31.
0119  66| 0F BD C2                       bsr      EAX,EDX                  ; Get bit number of highest on.
011D  B9 0020                            mov      CX,32                    ; 32-(bit#) is the shift amount
0120  2B C8                              sub      CX,AX                    ; in CX.
0122  05 0020                            add      AX,32                    ; 32+(bit#) is exponent in AX.
0125  66| 0F A5 DA                       shld     EDX,EBX,CL               ; Adjust to get top bit out
0129  66| D3 E3                          shl      EBX,CL                   ; and fill zeros to right.
012C  EB 17 90                           jmp      makefp                   ; and go make the number
012F                            topzero:
012F  66| 0B D3                          or       EDX,EBX                  ; Shift 32 bits
0132  0F 84 01A5 R                       jz       outzero                  ; If zero - done - totally!
0136  66| 2B DB                          sub      EBX,EBX                  ; Fill 32 zero bits to right.
0139  66| 0F BD C2                       bsr      EAX,EDX                  ; Get bit number of highest on.
                                         ;                                   It is the exponent!
013D  B9 0020                            mov      CX,32                    ; 32-bit number is shift amount
0140  2B C8                              sub      CX,AX                    ; in CX.
0142  66| D3 E2                          shl      EDX,CL                   ; Do the shift.
                                         ;
                                         ; We have the sign, exponent, and the fraction; now put them together.
                                         ;
0145                            makefp:
0145  66| 0F AC D3 0C                    shrd     EBX,EDX,12               ; push bits into right part
014A  66| C1 EA 0C                       shr      EDX,12                   ; and zeros into left part
014E  05 03FF                            add      AX,1023                  ; Bias the exponent,
0151  66| C1 E0 14                       shl      EAX,20                   ; position it,
0155  66| 0B D0                          or       EDX,EAX                  ; and combine with number.
0158  66| 0F BA E1 1F                    bt       ECX,31                   ; Do we want minus?
015D  0F 83 0166 R                       jnc      makefp1                  ; No - We are done.
0161  66| 0F BA EA 1F                    bts      EDX,31                   ; Yes - set the sign minus.
0166                            makefp1:
0166  66| 89 56 FC                       mov      fpnohi,EDX               ; Put number into work memory
016A  66| 89 5E F8                       mov      fpnolo,EBX               ; (both halves)
                                         ;
                                         ; The power of ten is the only thing left to handle.
                                         ;
016E  0B FF                              or       DI,DI                    ; Check the exponent
0170  0F 84 01A8 R                       jz       alldone                  ; If zero - we are done.
0174  8D 1E 01B0 R                       lea      BX,CS:pospower           ; Assume positive.
0178  0F 89 0187 R                       jns      itispos                  ; It is.
017C  81 C3 0048                         add      BX,negpower-pospower     ; shift to negative exponents
0180  8B C7                              mov      AX,DI                    ; Get exponent's
0182  BF 0000                            mov      DI,0                     ;
0185  2B F8                              sub      DI,AX                    ; absolute value.
0187                            itispos:
0187  DD 46 F8                           fld      fpnumb                   ; Get the number
018A                            nextpowr:
018A  D1 EF                              shr      DI,1                     ; shift a bit out of exponent
018C  0F 83 0193 R                       jnc      skipmpy                  ; If not a one - don't mpy
0190  2E: DC 0F                          fmul     QWORD PTR CS:[BX+0]      ; multiply by power of ten
0193                            skipmpy:
0193  83 C3 08                           add      BX,8                     ; Step power pointer
0196  0B FF                              or       DI,DI                    ; Check if done
0198  75 F0                              jnz      nextpowr                 ; if not - do again
019A  DD 56 F8                           fst      fpnumb                   ; Get the number from the unit.
019D  66| 8B 56 FC                       mov      EDX,fpnohi               ; Get number from work memory
01A1  66| 8B 5E F8                       mov      EBX,fpnolo               ; (both halves)
01A5                            outzero:
```

```
01A5  66| 8B C3                        mov      EAX,EBX           ; Position number as EAX:EDX

01A8                       alldone:
01A8  5E                               pop      SI                ; Restore work registers
01A9  59                               pop      CX
01AA  5F                               pop      DI
01AB  66| 5B                           pop      EBX               ; Restore the entry registers
01AD  C9                               leave
01AE  C3                               ret                        ; and return.
                           ;
                           ; Power of ten conversion - positive and negative to |511|
                           ;
01AF  90                               ALIGN    4
01B0  0000000000002440     pospower    dq       1.0E+001
01B8  0000000000005940                 dq       1.0E+002
01C0  000000000088C340                 dq       1.0E+004
01C8  0000000084D79741                 dq       1.0E+008
01D0  0080E03779C34143                 dq       1.0E+016
01D8  176E05B5B5B89346                 dq       1.0E+032
01E0  F5F93FE9034F384D                 dq       1.0E+064
01E8  321D30F94877825A                 dq       1.0E+128
01F0  3CBF737FDD4F1575                 dq       1.0E+256
01F8  9A9999999999B93F     negpower    dq       1.0E-001
0200  7B14AE47E17A843F                 dq       1.0E-002
0208  2D431CEBE2361A3F                 dq       1.0E-004
0210  3A8C30E28E79453E                 dq       1.0E-008
0218  BC89D897B2D29C3C                 dq       1.0E-016
0220  33A7A8D523F64939                 dq       1.0E-032
0228  3DA7F444FD0FA532                 dq       1.0E-064
0230  9D978CCF08BA5B25                 dq       1.0E-128
0238  436FAC642806C80A                 dq       1.0E-256
                           ;
                           ; Accumulate another digit into our 64 bit number
                           ;
                           ; The 64 bit number is accumulated in EBX:EDX, the new digit is passed
                           ; in AL (the rest of EAX is assumed to be zero).  If the digit can be
                           ; accommodated, it is, and return is made with carry reset.  Otherwise,
                           ; carry is set and EBX:EDX is returned unchanged.
                           ;
0240                       accumd      PROC     NEAR
0240  66| 51                           push     ECX               ; Save work register
0242  66| 53                           push     EBX               ; Save the low 32 bits.
0244  66| 52                           push     EDX               ; Save high 32 bits

0246  66| 50                           push     EAX               ; Save the digit
0248  66| 52                           push     EDX               ; Save high 32 bits
024A  66| 8B C3                        mov      EAX,EBX           ; Get low 32 bits in EAX
024D  66| B9 0000000A                  mov      ECX,10            ; Get the multiplier
0253  66| F7 E1                        mul      ECX               ; multiply low 32 bits
0256  66| 8B D8                        mov      EBX,EAX           ; save low 32 bits of product
0259  66| 58                           pop      EAX               ; Get high 32 bits of number
025B  66| 52                           push     EDX               ; Save overflow from low mpy
025D  66| F7 E1                        mul      ECX               ; multiply high 32 bits by 10
0260  66| 0B D2                        or       EDX,EDX           ; if we overflow beyond 64 bits
0263  66| 5A                           pop      EDX               ; Possible overflow of low
0265  0F 85 0288 R                     jnz      toobig            ; We must quit.
0269  66| 03 D0                        add      EDX,EAX           ; add result of the high mpy
026C  0F 82 0288 R                     jc       toobig            ; If it carried - we must quit.
0270  66| 58                           pop      EAX               ; Restore the new digit
0272  66| 83 E0 0F                     and      EAX,0fh           ; Clear all but digit
0276  66| 03 D8                        add      EBX,EAX           ; and add it to low 32 bits.
0279  66| 83 D2 00                     adc      EDX,0             ; Propagate the possible carry
027D  0F 82 028B R                     jc       toobig1           ; If carry out of top 32, quit.
0281  66| 59                           pop      ECX               ; The new number is OK
0283  66| 59                           pop      ECX               ; so we don't need the old one.
0285  66| 59                           pop      ECX               ; Finally, restore the work reg
0287  C3                               ret                        ; and return (carry is off).
```

```
0288                        toobig:
0288    F9                          stc                         ; Set the carry flag
0289    66| 58                      pop      EAX                ; Clear stack of digit
028B                        toobig1:
028B    66| 5A                      pop      EDX                ; Get old high 32
028D    66| 5B                      pop      EBX                ; and low 32.
028F    66| 59                      pop      ECX                ; Restore work register
0291    C3                          ret                         ; and return (carry is set)
0292                        accumd   ENDP

0292                        Fpasclfp ENDP
0292                        code     ENDS
                                     END
```

Program 7-15   FLIPS

```
1                                              .386
2       0000                code     SEGMENT    para 'CODE' USE16 PUBLIC
3                                    ASSUME     CS:code, DS:code, SS:code
4                           ; Name:    FLIPS  (Flip2, Flip4, and Flip8)
5                           ;
6                           ; Purpose: The following procedures provide data conversions for
7                           ;          a word (for completeness), a double word and a quadword
8                           ;          from Intel ordering to its reverse (or visa-versa).
9                           ;
10                          ; Inputs:  AX has the word to be flipped.
11                          ;
12                          ; Process: AL and AH are exchanged.
13                          ;
14                          ; Output:  AX has the reversed word.
15                          ;
16                          ;
17                          ;
18                                    PUBLIC   Flip2               ; Make the name usable
19      0000                Flip2    PROC
20      0000  86 C4                  xchg     AL,AH               ; Reverse the byte order
21      0002  C3                     ret                          ; and return.
22      0003                Flip2    ENDP
23      0003  C3                     ret                          ; then return.
24
25                          ;
26                          ;
27                          ; Inputs:  EAX:EDX has the 64 bit quadword to reorder
28                          ;             (memory 7654 3210)
29                          ;          Loaded as:   mov  EAX,qword
30                          ;                        mov  EDX,qword+4
31                          ;
32                          ; Process: see below
33                          ;
34                          ; Output:  EAX:EDX has the reversed quadword.
35                          ;          To store as:  mov   qword,EAX
36                          ;                         mov   qword+4,EDX
37                          ;             (memory 0123 4567)
```

Program 7-15 Continued.

```
38                              ;
39                              ;
40                              ;
41                                              PUBLIC  Flip8              ; Make the name usable
42     0004                     Flip8   PROC
43                              ;                                  EAX  EDX
44                              ;                                   HL   HL
45                              ;                              Assume:   4567 0123
46     0004  E8 0002                    call    Flip4              ; get 7654 0123
47     0007  66| 92                     xchg    EDX,EAX            ;     0123 7654
48                                                                 ;     3210 7654
49                              ;
50                              ;
51                              ; Inputs:  EAX has the 32 bit double word to reorder.
52                              ;
53                              ; Process: see below
54                              ;
55                              ; Output:  EAX has the reversed word.
56                              ;
57                              ;
58                              ;
59                                              PUBLIC  Flip4              ; Make the name usable
60     0009                     Flip4:
61                              ;                              Assume:    0123
62     0009  86 C4                      xchg    AL,AH              ; get 0132
63     000B  66| C1 C0 10               rol     EAX,16             ;     3201
64     000F  86 C4                      xchg    AL,AH              ;     3210
65
66     0011  C3                         ret                        ; and return.
67     0012                     Flip8   ENDP
68     0012                     code    ENDS
69                                      END
```

Symbol Name	Type	Value	Cref (defined at #)
??DATE	Text	"02/29/92"	
??FILENAME	Text	"flips "	
??TIME	Text	"08:03:28"	
??VERSION	Number	0202	
aCPU	Text	0D0FH	#1
aCURSEG	Text	CODE	#2
aFILENAME	Text	FLIPS	
aWORDSIZE	Text	2	#1 #2
FLIP2	Near	CODE:0000	18 #19
FLIP4	Near	CODE:0009	46 59 #60
FLIP8	Near	CODE:0004	41 #42

Groups & Segments	Bit Size Align	Combine Class	Cref (defined at #)
CODE	16 0012 Para	Public CODE	#2 3 3 3

Program 7-16 FLIP486

```
 1
 2
 3                                        .486
 4    0000                    code    SEGMENT    para 'CODE' USE16 PUBLIC
 5                                    ASSUME     CS:code, DS:code, SS:code
 6                            ;
 7                            ; Name:    FLIPS   (Flip2, Flip4, and Flip8)
 8                            ;
 9                            ; Purpose: The following procedures provide data conversions for
10                            ;          a word (for completeness), a double word and a quadword
11                            ;          from Intel ordering to its reverse (or visa-versa).
12                            ;
13                            ; Inputs:  AX has the word to be flipped.
14                            ;
15                            ; Process: AL and AH are exchanged.
16                            ;
17                            ; Output:  AX has the reversed word.
18                            ;
19                            ;
20                            ;
21                                    PUBLIC  Flip2               ; Make the name usable
22    0000                    Flip2   PROC
23    0000  86 C4                     xchg    AL,AH               ; Reverse the byte order
24    0002  C3                        ret                         ; and return.
25    0003                    Flip2   ENDP
26                            ;
27                            ;
28                            ; Inputs:  EAX has the 32 bit double word to reorder.
29                            ;
30                            ; Process: The process is complete in the new 80486 instruction BSWAP.
31                            ;          This entry is included to allow minimal changes to programs
32                            ;          which use the 80386 version of this package.
33                            ;
34                            ; Output:  EAX has the reversed word.
35                            ;
36                            ;
37                            ;
38                                    PUBLIC  Flip4               ; Make the name usable
39    0003                    Flip4   PROC
40                            ;                                   Assume:    0123
41    0003  66| 0F C8                 bswap   EAX                 ; get 3210
42    0006  C3                        ret                         ; then return.
43    0007                    Flip4   ENDP
44                            ;
45                            ;
46                            ; Inputs:  EAX:EDX has the 64 bit quadword to reorder
47                            ;                  (qword  db 0,1,2,3,4,5,6,7)
```

```
48                              ;           Loaded as:   mov  EAX,qword
49                              ;                         mov  EDX,qword+4
50                              ;
51                              ; Process: see below
52                              ;
53                              ; Output: EAX:EDX has the reversed quadword.
54                              ;         To store as:   mov   qword,EAX
55                              ;                         mov   qword+4,EDX
56                              ;        (qword   db 7,6,5,4,3,2,1,0)
57                              ;
58                              ;
59                                      PUBLIC  Flip8            ; Make the name usable
60      0007                    Flip8   PROC
61                              ;                                      EAX: EDX
62                              ;                                       HL   HL
63                              ;                              Assume:  3210 7654
64      0007  66| 0F C8                 bswap   EAX         ;   0123 7654
65      000A  66| 0F CA                 bswap   EDX         ;   0123 4567
66      000D  66| 92                    xchg    EAX,EDX     ;   4567 0123
67      000F  C3                        ret                 ; and return.
68      0010                    Flip8   ENDP
69      0010                    code    ENDS
70                              END
```

Symbol Name	Type	Value	Cref (defined at #)		
??DATE	Text	"02/29/92"			
??FILENAME	Text	"flip486 "			
??TIME	Text	"09:03:03"			
??VERSION	Number	0202			
@CPU	Text	0D1FH	#3		
@CURSEG	Text	CODE	#4		
@FILENAME	Text	FLIP486			
@WORDSIZE	Text	2	#3	#4	
FLIP2	Near	CODE:0000	21	#22	
FLIP4	Near	CODE:0003	38	#39	
FLIP8	Near	CODE:0007	59	#60	

Groups & Segments	Bit	Size	Align	Combine	Class	Cref (defined at #)			
CODE	16	0010	Para	Public	CODE	#4	5	5	5

Program 7-17 FLIPDRV

```
 1                                              .386
 2                                    ;
 3                                    ; Name:    FLIPDRV
 4                                    ;
 5                                    ; Purpose: This program drives the flip routines.
 6                                    ;          This provides both a test for the routines themselves and
 7                                    ;          a working example of the calling sequences.
 8                                    ;
 9                                    ; Inputs:  Input is typed at the keyboard in response to a prompt
10                                    ;          (8 characters are requested and used.  Fewer than 8 will
11                                    ;          bypass the 8 wide flip, fewer than 4 will bypass the 4 wide
12                                    ;          flip and fewer than 2 terminate the program.)
13                                    ;
14                                    ;
15                                    ; Process: The input is passed through the flip routines, first through
16                                    ;          flip8, next through flip 4 and finally through flip2.  Each
17                                    ;          flipped output is displayed then the prompt is repeated.
18                                    ;
19                                    ; Outputs: The flipped data are displayed for inspection.
20
21
22      0000                          stackt    SEGMENT para 'STACK' STACK USE16
23      0000  0100*               +             dq      256 DUP(?)
24            (??????????????????)
25      0800                          stackt    ENDS
26
27      0000                          data      SEGMENT para USE16
28      0000  0100*(??)               string1   db      256 DUP(?)              ; String scratch area
29      0100  0A 0D 45 6E 74 65 72+   prompt    db      10,13,"Enter up to 8 characters to be flipped - $"
30            20 75 70 20 74 6F 20+
31            38 20 63 68 61 72 61+
32            63 74 65 72 73 20 74+
33            6F 20 62 65 20 66 6C+
34            69 70 70 65 64 20 2D+
35            20 24
36      012C  0A 0D 46 6C 69 70 20+   msgf8     db      10,13,"Flip 8 results are '"
37            38 20 72 65 73 75 6C+
38            74 73 20 61 72 65 20+
39            27
40      0142  02*(????????)           outf8     dd      2 DUP(?)
41      014A  0A 0D 24                          db      10,13,"$"
42      014D  0A 0D 46 6C 69 70 20+   msgf4     db      10,13,"Flip 4 results are '"
43            34 20 72 65 73 75 6C+
44            74 73 20 61 72 65 20+
45            27
46      0163  01*(????????)           outf4     dd      1 DUP(?)
47      0167  0A 0D 24                          db      10,13,"$"
```

Program 7-17 Continued.

```
48    016A  0A 0D 46 6C 69 70 20+   msgf2     db      10,13,"Flip 2 results are '"
49          32 20 72 65 73 75 6C+
50          74 73 20 61 72 65 20+
51          27
52    0180  01*(????)              outf2     dw      1 DUP(?)
53    0182  0A 0D 24                         db      10,13,"$"
54    0185                         data      ENDS
55    0000                         code      SEGMENT para 'CODE' USE16 PUBLIC
56
57                            ;
58                            ; Declare the routines we are going to use
59                            ;
60                                        EXTRN   Flip8:PROC
61                                        EXTRN   Flip4:PROC
62                                        EXTRN   Flip2:PROC
63
64                                        ASSUME  CS:code, DS:data
65                            ;
66                            ; Set up the environment
67                            ;
68    0000                   Begin:
69    0000  B8 0000s                     mov     AX,data            ; Get data segment pointer
70    0003  8E D8                        mov     DS,AX              ; into DS,
71    0005  8E C0                        mov     ES,AX              ; and ES.
72    0007  2B F6                        sub     SI,SI              ; Clear indices
73    0009  2B FF                        sub     DI,DI
74                            ;
75                            ; First get the string to flip
76                            ;
77    000B                   nexttry:
78    000B  BA 0100r                     lea     DX,prompt          ; Get a string to convert
79    000E  E8 0059                      call    getinp             ;
80    0011  0B C9                        or      CX,CX              ; Was any entered?
81    0013  74 4F                        jz      SHORT Exit         ; No - simple exit
82    0015  83 F9 08                     cmp     CX,8               ; 8 bytes entered?
83    0018  72 1C                        jb      SHORT try4         ; No - skip 8 byte flip
84    001A  66| A1 0002r                 mov     EAX,DWORD PTR string1+2 ; load first 4 bytes
85    001E  66| 8B 16 0006r              mov     EDX,DWORD PTR string1+6 ; then next 4
86    0023  E8 0000e                     call    Flip8              ; Perform transform
87    0026  66| A3 0142r                 mov     outf8,EAX          ; Plug first 4
88    002A  66| 89 16 0146r              mov     outf8+4,EDX        ; Plug next 4
89
90    002F  BA 012Cr                     lea     DX,msgf8           ; Set message
91    0032  B4 09                        mov     AH,9
92    0034  CD 21                        int     21h                ; put it out
93    0036                   try4:
94    0036  83 F9 04                     cmp     CX,4               ; 4 bytes entered?
```

```
95    0039  72 12              jb     SHORT try2           ; No - skip 4 byte flip
96    003B  66| A1 0002r        mov    EAX,DWORD PTR string1+2 ; load 4 bytes
97    003F  E8 0000e           call   Flip4                ; Perform transform
98    0042  66| A3 0163r        mov    outf4,EAX            ; Plug 4
99
100   0046  BA 014Dr           lea    DX,msgf4             ; Set message
101   0049  B4 09              mov    AH,9
102   004B  CD 21              int    21h                  ; put it out
103   004D             try2:
104   004D  83 F9 02           cmp    CX,2                 ; At least 2?
105   0050  72 12              jb     SHORT Exit           ; No - exit
106   0052  A1 0002r           mov    AX,WORD PTR string1+2 ; load 2 bytes
107   0055  E8 0000e           call   Flip2                ; Perform transform
108   0058  A3 0180r           mov    outf2,AX             ; Plug 2
109
110
111   005B  BA 016Ar           lea    DX,msgf2             ; Set message
112   005E  B4 09              mov    AH,9
113   0060  CD 21              int    21h                  ; put it out
114   0062  EB A7              jmp    nexttry              ; continue
115   0064             Exit:
116   0064  B0 00              mov    AL,0                 ; Set return code
117   0066  B4 4C              mov    AH,04ch              ; Set good-by
118   0068  CD 21              int    21h                  ; Return to the system
119                   ;
120                   ; Read a string in response to a prompt
121                   ; The prompt must be in DX.  The string will be returned in string.
122                   ;
123   006A             getinp  PROC
124   006A  50                 push   AX                   ; Save registers
125   006B  56                 push   SI
126   006C  B4 09              mov    AH,9                 ; and dos request
127   006E  CD 21              int    21h                  ; put out the string
128   0070  BA 0000r           lea    DX,string1           ; point to input area
129   0073  C6 06 0000r FE      mov    string1,254          ; Set max length in
130   0078  B4 0A              mov    AH,10                ; Ask for read of string
131   007A  CD 21              int    21h                  ; from DOS.
132   007C  BB 0002r           lea    BX,string1+2         ; Point to just read data
133   007F  8A 0E 0001r         mov    CL,string1+1         ; Get length read
134   0083  B5 00              mov    CH,0                 ; as a word.
135   0085  8B F1              mov    SI,CX                ; Set length
136   0087  C6 84 0002r 00      mov    string1+2[SI],0      ; and make an asciiz string.
137   008C  5E                 pop    SI
138   008D  58                 pop    AX                   ; Restore registers
139   008E  C3                 ret                         ; and return.
140   008F             getinp  ENDP
141
142   008F             code    ENDS
143                            END    Begin
```

Program 7-17 Continued.

Symbol Name	Type	Value	Cref (defined at #)
??DATE	Text	"02/29/92"	
??FILENAME	Text	"flipdrv "	
??TIME	Text	"08:44:26"	
??VERSION	Number	0202	
@CPU	Text	0D0FH	#1
@CURSEG	Text	CODE	#22 #27 #55
@FILENAME	Text	FLIPDRV	
@WORDSIZE	Text	2	#1 #22 #27 #55
BEGIN	Near	CODE:0000	#68 143
EXIT	Near	CODE:0064	81 105 #115
FLIP2	Near	CODE:---- Extern	#62 107
FLIP4	Near	CODE:---- Extern	#61 97
FLIP8	Near	CODE:---- Extern	#60 86
GETINP	Near	CODE:006A	79 #123
MSGF2	Byte	DATA:016A	#48 111
MSGF4	Byte	DATA:014D	#42 100
MSGF8	Byte	DATA:012C	#36 90
NEXTTRY	Near	CODE:000B	#77 114
OUTF2	Word	DATA:0180	#52 108
OUTF4	Dword	DATA:0163	#46 98
OUTF8	Dword	DATA:0142	#40 87 88
PROMPT	Byte	DATA:0100	#29 78
STRING1	Byte	DATA:0000	#28 84 85 96 106 128 129 132 133 136
TRY2	Near	CODE:004D	95 #103
TRY4	Near	CODE:0036	83 #93

Groups & Segments	Bit	Size	Align	Combine	Class	Cref (defined at #)
CODE	16	008F	Para	Public	CODE	#55 64
DATA	16	0185	Para	none		#27 64 69
STACKT	16	0800	Para	Stack	STACK	#22

8

Input/output and file manipulation

The primary reason for the initial development (and later growth) of operating systems concerns the handling of input and output (I/O) operations. Simply, a computer takes in information, "crunches" it, and sends it back out. Input is the translation of incoming information into useful formats suitable for storage and future handling. That handling could be within a program, for display on a screen, or storage within a data file. Output is the reverse process, generally going to a disk, screen, or printer.

Responsibility for processor-level I/O operations moved from the programmer to the operating system for several reasons. First, the construction of code for handling I/O deserves its reputation for being one of the more demanding and contrary aspects of programming. By not forcing everyone to savor the intricate I/O, programming became accessible to a greater number of people. Second, a common set of I/O routines executed by all system facilities and user programs saves duplicated effort, storage, and development dollars. In addition, carefully debugged routines provide a measure of protection against destruction of important data files caused by incomplete knowledge of what the system really needed that particular flag for.

Standard input/output

By *standard input* and *standard output*, we understand the transfer of data to (or from) a computer from (or to) an external agent, generally a human operator. Input might originate at a keyboard and output might go to a display screen. In any case, its characteristics are that it is readable and typically consists of a sequence of characters. This readability condition is responsible for another complication incurred in most I/O operations. Apart from the actual data transfer, I/O also involves a trans-formation of representation. For example, numbers represented (inter-nally in the computer) in binary form need to be transformed into readable, decimal notation.

The most common handling of input data is to edit it to a previously known standard. For example, when requesting a date input, you put lim-its on the year, such as no earlier than 1900 or later than 2000. You restrict months to numbers from 1 to 12; days from 1 to 31; and so on.

Text editing implies a "reasonability check," e.g., allowing only char-acters between A and Z (in addition to the lowercase equivalents), digits 0 through 9, and special characters (decimal point, dollar sign, parentheses, and percent).

I/O goes between your fingertips and some storage medium. The most common storage are hard drives and diskettes, which have their own for-mats for you to remember.

Disk organization

Disks are divided into *tracks*, with an equal number of bytes available on each track for storage. There are 40 tracks on normal, double-density floppy diskettes. Hard disks also have tracks; however, the hard disk is composed of a number of parallel hard disks with a read/write head per surface. These heads move in and out together on a single actuator, so they use the concept of cylinders. As Fig. 8-1 shows, a *cylinder* is simply a convenient idea: all tracks a certain distance (radius) from the center are thought of as a logical unit. Hard disks use cylinders to minimize read/write head movement, which gives you faster I/O seek times. When data is stored on a hard disk, the storage algorithm uses all the tracks (up and down) on a cylinder before moving over to a new cylinder.

Sectors

Tracks divide into 512-byte *sectors* under most MS-DOS formats. Sectors are grouped into *clusters* and MS-DOS keeps track of clusters individually, each as one entry in the File Allocation Table (FAT), which keeps a record of which clusters are used and which are free. The number of sectors in a cluster varies from disk format to disk format. Double-sided diskettes have two sectors to a cluster, while high-density diskettes have only one sector to a cluster. File clusters can be scattered all over the disk, matching the available space. The FAT chains them so that your program can read from the beginning of your data to the end. Because files might be broken up into pieces for efficient disk storage, some size limitation had to be made for minimal space, and that limit is 1024 bytes.

The first sector of a double-sided diskette contains the boot record, stored on logical sector 0. The next two pairs of sectors (1–2 and 3–4) each contain a copy of the FAT. DOS maintains two copies to compare each

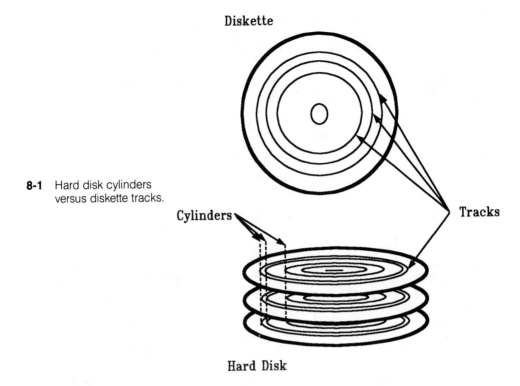

8-1 Hard disk cylinders versus diskette tracks.

for correctness; if the FAT goes bad, your data becomes garbage. Next come the directories, which occupy seven sectors and fills logical sectors 5–11 on every double-sided, nine-sector disk.

If you've loaded Command.com onto your formatted diskette, the file Ibmbio.com (the disk interface to BIOS) starts right after the directory. Next comes Ibmdos.com; then begins the actual data area (your files).

Directories

Directory entries are 32-bytes long and, on a double-sided diskette, there are seven sectors of directory. This means that there are 112 directory entries possible; this is calculated by multiplying the 7 sectors by 512 bytes per sector, and then dividing by 32 bytes per entry.

The first 8 directory bytes (0–7) contain the file's name, and the next three bytes (8–10) hold the file's extension. Byte 11 has the file's attribute (normal, read-only, hidden, system, subdirectory, and the archive bit). Bytes 12–21 are reserved for future use while bytes 22–25 contain the time of day the file was created, calculated as follows:

$$\text{TIME} = (seconds/2) + 2^5 \times (minutes) + 2^{11} \times (hours)$$

Bytes 24-25 contain the date, calculated by:

$$DATE = (days) + 2^5 \times (months) + 2^9 \times (year - 1980)$$

If you dumped the directory entry for Autoexec.bat, you'd see the directory entry as shown in Fig. 8-2.

Byte	0	1	2	3	4	5	6	7
0	A	U	T	O	E	X	E	C
8	B	A	T	File Attrib	Reserved			
16	Reserved					Time file created or updated		
24	Date file created or updated		Starting Cluster		File size in bytes			
					Low Order		High Order	

8-2 Autoexec.bat directory entry.

Bytes 26-27 contain the file's starting cluster number, and (28-31) contain the file size, which is the only place MS-DOS keeps accurate track of the file's size. Bytes 26 and 27 tell you where the first 1024 bytes of your file are located. Bytes 26-31 are useful in case you accidentally delete a file. You can use a debugger to modify the entries to recreate your file, but only if you haven't used any of the chained clusters in another file: remember, when you released those clusters back to the FAT, MS-DOS thought that it could use them for storage.

80486 input/output

The 80486 processor supports 8-, 16-, and 32-bit input/output (I/O) devices; I/O can be mapped either onto the 4Gb physical memory address space using general-purpose operand manipulation instructions, or onto the 64K I/O address space using specific I/O instructions. I/O mapping and memory mapping differ in three major ways as follows:

- Memory mapping offers more flexibility in protection than I/O mapping does because memory-mapped devices are protected by memory management and protection features.

- The address decoding necessary to generate chip select for I/O-mapped devices is generally simpler than for memory-mapped devices. I/O-mapped devices reside in the 64K I/O space of the 80486, while memory-mapped devices reside in much larger memory space that makes use of more address lines, the 4Gb.
- Memory-mapped devices can be accessed using any 80486 instruction, which allows for efficient coding of I/O-to-memory, memory-to-I/O, and I/O-to-I/O transfers. I/O-mapped devices can be accessed through four instructions: IN, INS, OUT, and OUTS. All I/O transfers are done via the AL (8-bit), AX (16-bit), or EAX (32-bit) registers. See Fig. 8-3 for the general layout of EAX. The first 256 bytes of I/O space are directly addressable, and the entire 64K I/O space is indirectly addressable through the DX register.

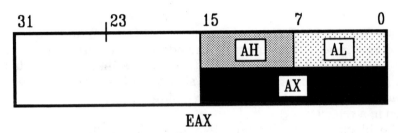

8-3 General layout of the EAX register.

The 80486 has a separate I/O address space distinct from physical memory, which can be used to address the I/O ports that are used for external 16-bit devices. This I/O address space is made up of 2^{16} (64K) individually addressable 8-bit ports. Any even-numbered consecutive 8-bit port can be treated as a 16-bit port, and any doubleword-addressed consecutive 8-bit port can be treated as a 32-bit port. This means that the total I/O address space accommodates the following. Figure 8-4 illustrates these divisions of the I/O address space.

Ports (in bits)	Quantity	Numbered
8	64K	0, 1, 2, . . . , 65535
16	32K	0, 2, 4, . . . , 65534
32	16K	0, 4, 8, . . . , 65532

I/O instructions

The 80486 I/O instructions give access to the processor's I/O ports for data transfer to and from peripheral devices. Instructions that directly use

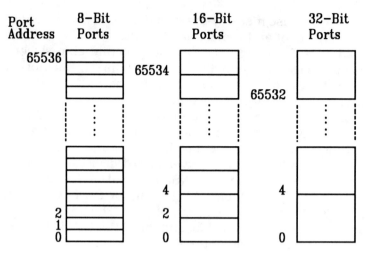

8-4 I/O address spaces.

addresses in the 80486's I/O space are IN, INS, OUT, and OUTS. These instructions have, as one operand, the address of a port in the I/O space. There are two classes of I/O instructions: those that transfer strings of items located in memory (known as *string I/O instructions* or *block I/O instructions*) and those that transfer a single byte, word, or doubleword located in a register.

The block I/O instructions, INS and OUTS, move blocks of data between I/O ports and memory space. These instructions use the DX register to specify the address of a port in the I/O address space. INS uses ES:DI to specify the memory space in which to input; OUTS uses DS:SI.

The IN and OUT instructions move data between I/O ports and the AL register for 8-bit I/O, AX for 16-bit I/O, and EAX for 32-bit I/O. IN and OUT addresses I/O ports either directly (with the addresses of one of up to 256 port addresses coded in the instruction) or indirectly (using the DX register to one of up to 64K port addresses). See appendix C for a complete alphabetic list of 80486 instructions.

I/O privilege

At privilege level 0, all I/O instructions are allowed. Instructions that deal with I/O not only need to be restricted, they need to be executed by procedures that execute at privilege levels other than zero. To allow this, the 80486 uses two bits of the EFLAGS register to store the I/O Privilege Level (IOPL), which defines the privilege level needed to execute I/O-related instructions.

In protected mode, IOPL offers protection by allowing a task to access I/O devices that are flagged accessible in the task's I/O Bitmap, or by preventing a task from accessing any I/O device. In virtual-8086 mode (V86),

31	23	16	15	7	0	

Bits 31–16	Bits 15–0	Offset
I/O Permission Bitmap Base	0 0 0 0 0 0 0 0 0 0 0 0 0 0 0 T	64
0 0 0 0 0 0 0 0 0 0 0 0 0 0 0 0	Local Descriptor Table (LDT)	
0 0 0 0 0 0 0 0 0 0 0 0 0 0 0 0	GS	
0 0 0 0 0 0 0 0 0 0 0 0 0 0 0 0	FS	
0 0 0 0 0 0 0 0 0 0 0 0 0 0 0 0	DS	
0 0 0 0 0 0 0 0 0 0 0 0 0 0 0 0	SS	
0 0 0 0 0 0 0 0 0 0 0 0 0 0 0 0	CS	
0 0 0 0 0 0 0 0 0 0 0 0 0 0 0 0	ES	48
EDI		
ESI		
EBP		
ESP		
EBX		
EDX		
ECX		2C
EAX		
EFLAGS		
EIP		
(Reserved)		
0 0 0 0 0 0 0 0 0 0 0 0 0 0 0 0	SS2	18
ESP2		
0 0 0 0 0 0 0 0 0 0 0 0 0 0 0 0	SS1	
ESP1		0C
0 0 0 0 0 0 0 0 0 0 0 0 0 0 0 0	SS0	
ESP0		
0 0 0 0 0 0 0 0 0 0 0 0 0 0 0 0	Back Link to Previous TSS	0

8-5 TSS with I/O Permission Bitmap. (Zero entries indicate Intel reserved bits; do not define.)

the I/O Permission Bitmap is not checked. The I/O Permission Bitmap is the controlling factor in whether or not I/O is allowed. See Fig. 8-5 and Fig. 8-6 to see where the bitmap is stored in the TSS.

The TSS consists of three parts: the Intel-defined minimum, an operating-system-defined extension, and the I/O bitmap itself. I/O protection is

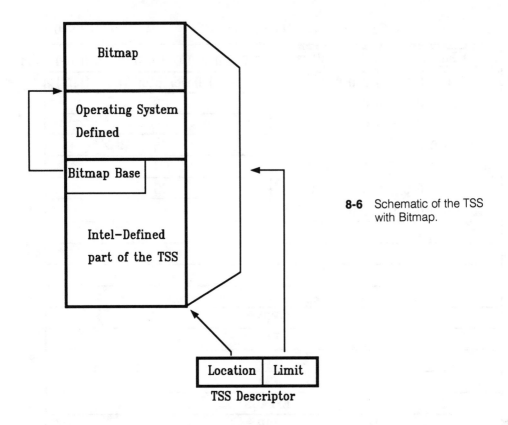

8-6 Schematic of the TSS with Bitmap.

provided in two ways: the I/O Permission Bitmap in the TSS defines the right to use ports in the I/O address space, and the IOPL flag in the EFLAGS register defines the right to use I/O-related instructions. See appendix B for a detailed description of the EFLAGS format. These mechanisms work in protected mode only, which includes the virtual-8086 mode. They do not work in real mode. In real mode, any procedure executes I/O instructions and any I/O port can be addressed by any of those instructions.

The 80486 selectively traps references to specific I/O addresses. The mechanism that allows this trapping is the I/O Permission Bitmap in the TSS. The bitmap is a bit vector and its size and location in the TSS are variable. The 80486 locates the bitmap by means of the 16-bit I/O Map Base field in the fixed portion of the TSS, which contains the offset to the beginning of the bitmap. The upper limit of the bitmap is the same as the limit of the TSS segment. Because the bitmap is in the TSS, different tasks can have different bitmaps. Thus, the operating system can allocate ports to a task by changing the I/O Permission Bitmap in the task's TSS.

Each bit in the bitmap corresponds to an I/O port byte address. For instance, the bit for port 41 is found at I/O Bitmap Base+5, bit offset 1.

The 80486 tests all bits that correspond to the I/O addresses spanned by an I/O operation. That is, a doubleword operation will test four bits that correspond to four adjacent byte addressees. If any tested bit is set, the 80486 signals a general protection exception. If all tested bits are zero, the I/O operation proceeds.

Each task in the system has its own unique copy of the EFLAGS register. Therefore, each task can have a different IOPL. A task can change the IOPL only with a POPF instruction. Such changes are privileged. No procedure can alter IOPL in EFLAGS unless the procedure is executing at privilege level zero.

An input editing program

As time goes on, you'll probably be writing your own I/O routines. If you haven't done this in the past, you might want to practice using the routines that follow. Try them out as they appear, running a dump program that steps through them one at a time so you can see the various register, flag, and memory changes. Then customize them into the shape you need for your programming.

There are two very common input/output routines that most programs contain—editing input, and handling carriage returns and line feeds. Editing input tends to lie in the area of verifying numbers and alphabetic characters. Whether the numbers are single or multiple digits, the individual numbers are limited to the 0–9 range. Alphabetic characters are almost as straightforward. They must be in the range of uppercase A–Z, or lowercase a–z. Alphabetic characters can be part of character strings that are divided by blanks or special characters, such as a slash (/), or punctuation, such as a semicolon (;).

IOEDIT (Program 8-1) shows how to handle input buffers and to edit single digits. More complex editing is an extension of the simple methods shown.

In MS-DOS, an input buffer contains the input data and two auxiliary bytes. You supply the first byte, a count of the maximum number of characters allowed before MS-DOS beeps and disallows more entry. MS-DOS uses the second byte to indicate the actual number of characters entered. An input buffer might look like the example in Fig. 8-7. Notice that the counts and digits are displayed in hex (although they are actually stored as binary), and that the amount actually entered is less than the maximum allowable.

IOEDIT uses an input buffer called INPUT_STR. In the data initialization area, INPUT_STR is established to be 4-bytes long and initialized. Later, a hex 4 is moved into the first byte. Then the index into the buffer is moved two bytes (from byte 0 to byte 2) because actual input goes into byte 2.

The carriage return (0D) is captured on input, but MS-DOS does not count that character as part of the count in byte 1. If you're working with an ASCIIZ string (which, by definition, must end in hex 00), you would

Program Code

```
        *
        *
INPUT_STR   DB    6 DUP (?)
        *
        *

        MOV     INPUT_STR,4     ; Maximum count into string
        LEA     DX,INPUT_STR    ; Move pointer to buffer into DX
        ADD     DX,2            ; Skip auxiliary bytes
        MOV     AH,0Ah          ; Buffered keyboard input function
        INT     21h

        *
        *
```

Assume the entered data is two digits: 1 and 4
After entry, the buffer would appear like:

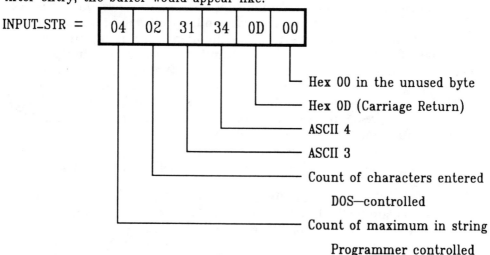

INPUT_STR = | 04 | 02 | 31 | 34 | 0D | 00 |

Hex 00 in the unused byte

Hex 0D (Carriage Return)

ASCII 4

ASCII 3

Count of characters entered

DOS—controlled

Count of maximum in string

Programmer controlled

8-7 Input Buffer with auxiliary bytes.

take the count from byte 1, add 2 to it, and replace that byte with hex 00. That byte is the 0D. Note that the 0D is shown in Fig. 8-7. If you're not working with ASCIIZ strings, you might not care that the 0D remains in the string, as we didn't in IOEDIT.

Figure 8-8 shows three lines of code from IOEDIT, which we believe merit your attention. (We've never seen them coded anywhere else.) They make the decision as to whether or not a character is numeric into a very few lines of code. You move a byte from the input buffer into a byte register,

Assume INPUT_STR is an input buffer that has a character entered into byte 2. Byte 0 and 1 are auxiliary bytes for an input buffer.

```
MOV    CL,BYTE PTR INPUT_STR[2]
XOR    CL,30h
CMP    CL,9h
```

8-8 Easy method to determine if a character is numeric.

exclusive-or (XOR) it against 30 hex (which is an ASCII zero), and then compare (CMP) the result against a 9 hex. A value greater than 9 is non-numeric.

File manipulation

A *file* is a collection of data stored on some external storage device (such as a magnetic disk) for use at a future time. Files have structures that determine how the records in the file are organized.

Structure subdivides into logical structure and physical structure. The logical structure of a file is the user's view of the file. A file declaration that appears in a program is basically a logical structure specification, and generally involves defining the attribute(s) of the record type(s) and possibly specifying a relationship (e.g., an ordering relationship) on the record occurrences.

Physical structure, on the other hand, is associated with how a file is organized physically on the storage medium on which it resides. This organization normally involves pointers, indexes, and how the records are laid out on the external storage device. Note the differences between logical and physical structure shown in Fig. 8-9.

You access files in various ways. The most common access method is sequential because computer files were first stored on inherently sequential storage media such as magnetic tape. To access a record in a sequential file, the earlier records must be passed over (read and ignored).

A second, more-widely used access method is random (direct) access of records. With direct access, any record in a file can be retrieved without looking first at the records that precede it. Techniques for implementing direct access generally involve some method for translating a key that identifies the record sought into the absolute or relative address of the corresponding record on the device on which it is stored. This translation is normally done by an index (or indexes) or a key-to-address transformation function (called a *hashing function*) that computes the address of the record from the key (or keys). See chapter 9 for information on hashing.

Logical File Format:

Title:	Dr.
First Name:	Elizabeth
Last Name:	Doe
Street Address:	111 Main Street
City:	Anytown
State:	California
Zip:	95117
Telephone:	(408) 555-1212

Physical File Format:

Text Representation:

ASCII Representation:

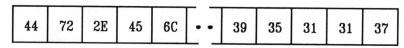

8-9 Differences between logical and physical file structures.

Checking, renaming, and deleting a file

IOWORKS (Program 8-2) performs several functions. It deletes an existing file, renames an existing file, and checks for the file's existence. It uses Interrupt 21 Function 41 to delete a file, Interrupt 21 Function 56 to rename a file, and Interrupt 21 Function 4E to find a file. A Disk Transfer Area (DTA) is established when a file is found. Inside the DTA is the file size (see Fig. 8-10).

If an error is found, this program uses EXTERROR (described and listed in chapter 5) to determine the extended error and to print error messages. EXTERROR uses Interrupt 21 Function 59, which returns an extended error code, an error class and action, plus the location of the error.

You'll probably notice that most of the programs in this book have positive responses to users. This is a human engineering feature often left out (because its not thought of) by many programmers. Users request an action, which computer goes and does. The user knows the computer is performing a task because the disk read light comes on. When the task is finished, the user sees the system prompt. What happened? Either the user has faith that the task was completed, or checks some other way.

Bytes	Contents
0–20	Reserved
21	Found Attribute
22–23	File's Time
24–25	File's Date
26–27	File's Size, Low word
28–29	File's Size, High word
30–42	Name and Extension *

8-10 DTA layout. Note that there is no drive or library name (e.g., no path name).

When you are programming, rather than leave a user guessing, display a message that states the conclusion of a "transparent" action.

Opening and reading an existing file

You must open a file (use INT 21 Function 3D) to read from it. First, store the attribute into AX. The attribute is how you want to access the file (0=read, 1=write, 2=read/write). Store the pointer to the ASCIIZ file name (an ASCII string that ends in hex 00) into DS:DX and issue the open. The file handle returns in AX. Because the other file-handle functions use BX for the file name, move the handle into BX immediately.

When the file is opened, the Read/Write pointer points to the first byte. After each read, the pointer moves to the first byte past the end of the read. To read in bytes, set up a memory buffer with two auxiliary bytes at the front of the buffer. Set the first byte (byte 0) with the maximum number of bytes in the buffer (counting the carriage return). DOS sets the second byte (byte 1) as how many were actually entered. However, DOS does not count the carriage return in the bytes read, although the 0Dh is in the buffer. The actual bytes you want to read (or write with INT 21 Function 3F) go into bytes 2 through n, where n is the end of the memory buffer.

Figure 8-11 shows a dump of an actual memory buffer used in IOREAD (Program 8-3). The memory buffer holds the ASCIIZ string of the file name that IOREAD requested. The dump first sets a breakpoint (BP) in the IOREAD program; the location was determined from the assembly listing of the program. The file name is asked for and the program goes on. It stops at the breakpoint and displays the current register contents.

Next, a display of bytes at the memory buffer location (taken from the assembled listing of the program) shows how the buffer appears in memory. Byte zero is 1E, which shows that a total of 30 bytes could be read in. Byte one shows an 11, which says that 17 bytes actually were read in. A

```
C:\ASM>SYMDEB IOREAD.EXE
Microsoft (R) Symbolic Debug Utility  Version 4.00
Copyright (C) Microsoft Corp 1984, 1985.  All rights reserved.

Processor is [80286]
-BP 03D3
-G
AX=0A0D  BX=0000  CX=0013  DX=0041  SP=00C8  BP=0000  SI=0013  DI=0000
DS=15D7  ES=15BA  SS=15CA  CS=15D7  IP=03D3    NV UP EI PL NZ NA PO NC
15D7:03D3 8D161900        LEA     DX,[0019]                    ;BR0 DS:0019=0D0A
-DB 0041 0055
15D7:0040       1E 11 43 3A 5C 41 53-4D 5C 49 4F 52 45 41 44    ..C:\ASM\IOREAD
15D7:0050  2E 41 53 4D 00 00                                    .ASM..
-DA 0041 0055
15D7:0041  ..C:\ASM\IOREAD.ASM..
-Q

C:\ASM>
```

8-11 Dump of memory buffer, showing auxiliary bytes.

count of C:\ASM\IOREAD.ASM shows 17 bytes. The carriage return does not appear because the program has already overwritten the 0D with 00 (see the IOREAD program listing), because we needed an ASCIIZ string. Finally, an ASCII dump was taken to show how you can read the file using ASCII dumps.

If there is an error in the file read, the Carry Flag is set to 1. Then you examine AX, where the error code was returned. If CF=0, the read was successful.

IOREAD was run, to read from an assembly language source file, IOREAD.ASM, in the C:\ASM\ path. A hex dump (using the Norton Utilities) of IOREAD.ASM, in Fig. 8-12, shows the first bytes of the program. Compare that with Fig. 8-13, the IOREAD run. As you can see, some of the ASCII characters in the file do not print. You can attack this difference several ways.

For example, you could (1) change IOREAD to print binary equivalents of the non-printable ASCII characters, (2) use a utility program to see the actual non-printable characters and decide if you need to know them, or (3) change IOREAD to print periods (.) for non-printable characters.

Creating, writing, and closing a file

Creating a file used to be a difficult problem. Today it is much easier, thanks to file handles. Program 8-4, IOWRITE, illustrates the process. You

```
09504147 45093535 2C313332 0D0A092E 3238360D 0A094558 PAGE    55,132
         .286
     EX|
54524E09 434F4445 41534232 3A50524F 430D0A53 5441434B TRN        CODEASB2:PROC
STACK|
09534547 4D454E54 20275354 41434B27 20535441 434B0D0A SEGMENT 'STACK' STACK

09445709 31303020 44555028 3F290D0A 53544143 4B09454E DW       100 DUP(?)
STACK   EN|
44530D0A 434F4445 09534547 4D454E54 09706172 61202743 DS
CODE     SEGMENT para 'C|
4F444527 20505542 4C49430D 0A094153 53554D45 0943533A ODE' PUBLIC
        ASSUME  CS:|
434F4445 2C204453 3A434F44 452C2053 533A5354 41434B0D CODE, DS:CODE, SS:STACK
0A3B0D0A 3B204E61 6D653A09 09494F52 4541440D 0A3B0D0A
                                                      ;
; Name:        IOREAD
;
;
3B205075 72706F73 653A2009 54686973 2070726F 63656475 ; Purpose:  This procedu|
72652072 65616473 20627974 65732066 726F6D20 61206669 re reads bytes from a fi|
6C652E0D 0A3B0D0A 3B20496E 70757473 3A202009 41534349 le.
;
; Inputs:     ASCI|
49204669 6C652069 73207370 65636966 69656420 28647269 I File is specified (dri|
76655C70 6174685C 66696C65 6E616D65 292C2061 6C6F6E67 ve\path\filename), along|
200D0A3B 09097769 74682074 6865206E 756D6265 7220666F
            with the number of|
20627974 65732074 6F207265 61642066 726F6D20 74686520 bytes to read from the |
66696C65 2E202054 6865200D 0A3B0909 66696C65 20636861 file.  The
;                                             file cha|
72616374 65727320 61726520 6C696D69 74656420 746F2061 racters are limited to a|
206D6178 696D756D 206F6620 33302E20 20497420 63616E20  maximum of 30.  It can|
0D0A3B09 09626520 616E7920 6E756D62 65722079 6F752077
            be any number you w|
616E7420 746F2073 70656369 66792C20 7768656E 20796F75 ant to specify, when you|
20636861 6E676520 69740D0A 3B090974 6F20796F 75722063 change it
;                  to your c|
6F64652E 0D0A3B0D                                      ode.
;                         Press Enter for help        |
```

8-12 Hex dump of IOREAD.ASM.

create an ASCIIZ string (an ASCII string that ends with a hex 00) with the file name, and point to it with DS:DX. Then you decide which file attribute you want (0 = normal, 01 = read-only, 02 = hidden file, 04 = system file, 08 = volume label, 10 = subdirectory, and 20 = archive) and store that value in CX. Then use INT 21 Function 5B. If the create is successful, the Carry Flag = 0 and the file handle returns in AX. If unsuccessful, CF = 1 and AX holds the extended error code.

To get additional information about the error, use Interrupt 21 Function 59, which returns a great deal of information in various registers. (For a list of extended error codes, see EXTERROR in chapter 6, a procedure that contains the codes and explains their use.)

```
C:\ASM>IOREAD
Read which file? C:\ASM\IOREAD.ASM
How many bytes? 15
Read from file:   PAGE  55,132

C:\ASM>
```

8-13 IOREAD run, reading the IOREAD.ASM file.

```
C:\ASM>DIR A:

 Volume in drive A is TESTIT
 Directory of  A:\

File not found

C:\ASM>IOWRITE

Write to which file? A:THISFILE
Enter the bytes? These are the entered bytes.
Closing the file.

C:\ASM>TYPE A:THISFILE
These are the entered bytes.
C:\ASM>DIR A:

 Volume in drive A is TESTIT
 Directory of  A:\

THISFILE            28   2-17-88   3:57p
        1 File(s)    361472 bytes free

C:\ASM>
```

8-14 IOWRITE sample run.

To open the file after creation, use Interrupt 21 Function 3D, which requires the same ASCIIZ file name. Store the access code (0 = read, 1 = write, and 2 = read/write) in AL. After the interrupt, AL holds the file handle or an error code if the Carry Flag is set. To write to the file, use the file handle and Interrupt 21 Function 40. If the write is successful, CF = 0 and AX has the number of bytes written. If unsuccessful, CF = 1 and AX holds the error code.

When you finish writing to a file, you must close the file (use INT 21 Function 3E). If you don't close the file, the disk directory is incorrect and the file almost useless. Furthermore, INT 21 Function 3E releases the assigned handle so that it can be reused for the next file-handle operation. It isn't a requirement to close files that were opened for reading only, because they did not change length; however, closing them releases the file handle. See Fig. 8-14 for a sample run of IOWRITE.

Before the sample run, a diskette was formatted and a directory taken to show an empty disk. Then IOWRITE ran, requesting a path/file name be entered. Next it prompted for the bytes to write to the file. Once the bytes were written and the file closed, a message displayed on the screen. The next step in the sample run was to use the DOS command TYPE to show the contents of A:Thisfile. The contents were identical to what had been entered from the keyboard. Next, a DIR was requested which showed that Thisfile now exists and contains data. As you can see, the date and time of the file update was automatically stored in the directory.

Setting up the memory buffer for the file name is discussed in the section on IOREAD. The same process is used with IOWRITE. Then IOWRITE asks for input from the keyboard to be written to the file. Once the data has been written to the file, the file is closed using INT 21 Function 3E.

Program 8-1   IOEDIT

Microsoft (R) Macro Assembler Version 5.00

```
                                    PAGE    55,132
                                    .386
        0000                STACK   SEGMENT 'STACK' STACK
        0000  0064 [        DW      100 DUP(?)
              ????
                        ]

        00C8                STACK   ENDS
        0000                CODE    SEGMENT para 'CODE' PUBLIC USE16
                                    ASSUME  CS:CODE, DS:CODE, SS:STACK
                            ;
                            ; Name:       IOEDIT
                            ;
                            ; Purpose:    This program uses an input buffer to edit numeric and
                            ;             alpha characters.  It also shows how to set up and
                            ;             print Carriage Return/Line Feed.  To print CR/LF, the
                            ;             hex characters (0A=Line Feed, 0D=Carriage Return) are
                            ;             placed in a character string which ends with a "$",
                            ;             so that Interrupt 21 Function 9A can print it.
                            ;
```

Program 8-1 Continued.

```
                                        ;                   On input, the 0D (carriage return) is kept in the input
                                        ;                   string by DOS.  If the program worked with the entire
                                        ;                   string, the 0D would have to be figured into the program
                                        ;                   logic.
                                        ;
                                        ; Inputs:           A single digit number or alpha character is requested.
                                        ;                   It is entered via keyboard into a buffered input area.
                                        ;                   Only a single character is entered.  Additional numbers
                                        ;                   could be requested and CODEASB (convert ASCII to Binary)
                                        ;                   called to convert the larger number for verification.
                                        ;                   The alpha characters could be checked one at a time by
                                        ;                   stepping through the input string.
                                        ;
                                        ; Process:          First the entered character is checked to see if it is
                                        ;                   a number. If so, it is checked to see that it is between
                                        ;                   0 and 9.  For purposes of this example, negative numbers
                                        ;                   are ignored.  If it's alpha, its checked to see if it is
                                        ;                   between A-Z or a-z.
                                        ;
                                        ; Outputs:          Messages with the results of each action.  Note that
                                        ;                   carriage return and line feed are the first two characters
                                        ;                   of each output line.
                                        ;
0000                                    IOEDIT:
0000  8C C8                                     MOV       AX,CS          ; Prepare to set DS
0002  8E D8                                     MOV       DS,AX          ;    and set it.
0004  E9 00E7 R                                 JMP       BEGINHERE
                                        ;
0007  0A 0D 20 45 6E 74 65     PROMPT           DB        0Ah,0Dh,' Enter a number or character > $'
      72 20 61 20 6E 75 6D
      62 65 72 20 6F 72 20
      63 68 61 72 61 63 74
      65 72 20 3E 20 24
0029  0A 0D 24                 CR_LF            DB        0Ah,0Dh,'$'
002C  0004[                    INPUT_STR        DB        4 DUP(?)
         ??
                        ]

0030  0A 0D 20 54 68 69 73     ERR_NUM          DB        0Ah,0Dh,' This number is not a positive 0-9.$'
      20 6E 75 6D 62 65 72
      20 69 73 20 6E 6F 74
      20 61 20 70 6F 73 69
      74 69 76 65 20 30 2D
      39 2E 24
0056  0A 0D 20 54 68 69 73     ERR_CHAR         DB        0Ah,0Dh,' This is not an alphabetic character.$'
      20 69 73 20 6E 6F 74
      20 61 6E 20 61 6C 70
      68 61 62 65 74 69 63
      20 63 68 61 72 61 63
      74 65 72 2E 24
007E  0A 0D 20 54 68 69 73     NUM_FOUND        DB        0Ah,0Dh,' This is a positive number 0-9.$'
      20 69 73 20 61 20 70
      6F 73 69 74 69 76 65
      20 6E 75 6D 62 65 72
      20 30 2D 39 2E 24
00A0  0A 0D 20 54 68 69 73     CHAR_FOUND       DB        0Ah,0Dh,' This is a lower-case character.$'
      20 69 73 20 61 20 6C
      6F 77 65 72 2D 63 61
      73 65 20 63 68 61 72
      61 63 74 65 72 2E 24
00C3  0A 0D 20 54 68 69 73     CHAR1_FOUND      DB        0Ah,0Dh,' This is an upper-case character.$'
      20 69 73 20 61 6E 20
      75 70 70 65 72 2D 63
      61 73 65 20 63 68 61
      72 61 63 74 65 72 2E
      24
```

```
00E7                                    BEGINHERE:
00E7  8D 16 0007 R                              LEA     DX,PROMPT          ; Print the request for input
00EB  B4 09                                     MOV     AH,9
00ED  CD 21                                     INT     21h

00EF  C6 06 002C R 04                           MOV     INPUT_STR,4        ; Max number of chars in string
00F4  8D 16 002C R                              LEA     DX,INPUT_STR       ; Input Buffer
00F8  B4 0A                                     MOV     AH,0Ah
00FA  CD 21                                     INT     21h                ; Buffered keyboard input
                                        ;
                                        ; Now edit the input.
                                        ;
00FC  2B C9                                     SUB     CX,CX              ; Be sure CX is empty
00FE  8D 36 002C R                              LEA     SI,INPUT_STR       ; Point to input buffer
0102  83 C6 02                                  ADD     SI,2               ; Skip the auxiliary bytes
                                        ;
                                        ;  See if it is a number - no matter how many are entered, only one
                                        ;      is checked, for this example.  See Prolog for other ways to
                                        ;      check multiple digits.
                                        ;
0105  8A 0E 002E R                              MOV     CL,BYTE PTR INPUT_STR[2]
0109  80 F1 30                                  XOR     CL,30h
010C  80 F9 09                                  CMP     CL,9               ; Is this a number?
010F  0F 86 0116 R                              JBE     EDIT0
0113  EB 2F 90                                  JMP     CHAR0              ; Go see if it is a character
0116                                    EDIT0:
0116  0B C0                                     OR      AX,AX              ; Is the number negative?
0118  0F 89 011F R                              JNS     EDIT2              ; If it is, it's called an error
011C  EB 0C 90                                  JMP     ERR0               ;   and a new request is made
011F                                    EDIT2:
011F  8D 16 007E R                              LEA     DX,NUM_FOUND       ; Print message
0123  B4 09                                     MOV     AH,9
0125  CD 21                                     INT     21h
0127  EB 55 90                                  JMP     ENDHERE

                                        ;
                                        ; Input error - neither positive number or character
                                        ;
012A                                    ERR0:
012A  8D 16 0030 R                              LEA     DX,ERR_NUM         ; Error message
012E  EB 05 90                                  JMP     ERR2
0131                                    ERR1:
0131  8D 16 0056 R                              LEA     DX,ERR_CHAR
0135                                    ERR2:
0135  B4 09                                     MOV     AH,9
0137  CD 21                                     INT     21h
0139  8D 16 0029 R                              LEA     DX,CR_LF           ; Space up a line
013D  B4 09                                     MOV     AH,9
013F  CD 21                                     INT     21h
0141  EB 3B 90                                  JMP     ENDHERE            ; Go get next entry

                                        ;
                                        ; Was it an alphabetic character - A single character is checked.  See
                                        ;       the Prolog for ways to check more than one character.
                                        ;
0144                                    CHAR0:
0144  2B C9                                     SUB     CX,CX              ; Zero out CX
0146  8A 0E 002E R                              MOV     CL,BYTE PTR INPUT_STR[2]
014A  80 F9 41                                  CMP     CL,41h             ; Capital Letter?
014D  0F 8D 0153 R                              JGE     CHAR1
0151  EB DE                                     JMP     ERR1               ; No, less than "A"
0153                                    CHAR1:
0153  80 F9 5A                                  CMP     CL,5Ah             ; Is this <= a "Z" ?
0156  0F 8D 0161 R                              JGE     CHAR3              ; Go see if it's a small letter
015A  8D 16 00C3 R                              LEA     DX,CHAR1_FOUND
015E  EB 17 90                                  JMP     CHAR5              ; It's upper case, go print message
0161                                    CHAR3:
0161  80 F9 61                                  CMP     CL,61h             ; Lower case letter?
0164  0F 8D 016A R                              JGE     CHAR4
```

Program 8-1 Continued.

```
0168  EB C7                               JMP     ERR1
016A                      CHAR4:
016A  80 F9 7A                            CMP     CL,7Ah           ; Is this <= "z" ?
016D  8D 16 00A0 R                        LEA     DX,CHAR_FOUND    ; Print message
0171  0F 8E 0177 R                        JLE     CHAR5            ; Yes, go print message
0175  EB BA                               JMP     ERR1             ; Not alpha character
0177                      CHAR5:
0177  B4 09                               MOV     AH,9
0179  CD 21                               INT     21h
017B  EB 01 90                            JMP     ENDHERE
                          ;
                          ;
017E                      ENDHERE:
017E  8D 16 0029 R                        LEA     DX,CR_LF         ; Space up one line
0182  B4 09                               MOV     AH,9
0184  CD 21                               INT     21h
                          ;
0186  B4 4C                               MOV     AH,4Ch           ; Standard Ending
0188  CD 21                               INT     21h
018A                      CODE            ENDS
                                          END     IOEDIT
```

Program 8-2 IOWORKS

```
Microsoft (R) Macro Assembler Version 5.00


                              PAGE    55,132
                              .386
                              EXTRN   CODEBAS:PROC
                              EXTRN   EXTERROR:PROC
                              EXTRN   CODEASB:PROC
0000                  STACK   SEGMENT 'STACK' STACK
0000  00C8[                   DW      200 DUP(?)
        ????
                      ]

0190                  STACK   ENDS
0000                  CODE    SEGMENT para 'CODE' PUBLIC USE16
                              ASSUME  CS:CODE, DS:CODE, SS:STACK
                      ;
                      ; Name:        IOWORKS
                      ;
                      ; Purpose:     This program performs several functions:
                      ;              1. Delete a file
                      ;              2. Rename a file
                      ;              3. Checking for Existing/non-existing files
                      ;
                      ;              To see how to create a file, see IOWRITE
                      ;                      open a file, see IOREAD
                      ;                      Read from a file, see IOREAD
                      ;                      Write to a file, see IOWRITE
                      ;                      Close a file, see IOWRITE
                      ;              All these programs are documented in Chapter 8
                      ;              of "80386 Assembly Language Toolkit."  They are also
                      ;              available on disk from TAB Books.
                      ;
                      ; Inputs:      File names are requested.  They are entered via
                      ;              keyboard.
                      ;
                      ; Process:     1. Delete a file:   INT 21 Function 41
                      ;              2. Rename a file:   INT 21 Function 56
                      ;              3. Find first file: INT 21 Function 4E
                      ;                      Once the file is found, file size is printed.
                      ;                      A Disk Transfer Area (DTA) is set up.
```

```
                              ;
                              ;      If any of the processes find an error, they go to
                              ;      an error location that calls EXTERROR, a procedure
                              ;      that finds the extended error code and associated
                              ;      messages to aid debug.  See Chapter 5 of "80386
                              ;      Assembly Language Toolkit" for a description of all
                              ;      the processes of EXTERROR.
                              ;
                              ;      To find the file, a DTA needs to be established.  Once
                              ;      it is, and the file is found, then you can find the file
                              ;      size.  Use CODEBAS to convert the binary size to printable
                              ;      ASCII.
                              ;
                              ; Outputs:          Messages with the results of each action.
                              ;
0000                         IOWORKS:
0000  8C C8                            MOV     AX,CS             ; Prepare to set DS
0002  8E D8                            MOV     DS,AX             ;   and set it.
0004  8E C0                            MOV     ES,AX
0006  E9 01F7 R                        JMP     BEGINHERE
                              ;
0009  0A 0D 20 43 68 6F 6F   MENU      DB      0Ah,0Dh,' Choose a number: $'
      73 65 20 61 20 6E 75
      6D 62 65 72 3A 20 24
001E  0A 0D 20 31 2E 20 44             DB      0Ah,0Dh,' 1. Delete a file $'
      65 6C 65 74 65 20 61
      20 66 69 6C 65 20 24
0033  0A 0D 20 32 2E 20 52             DB      0Ah,0Dh,' 2. Rename a file $'
      65 6E 61 6D 65 20 61
      20 66 69 6C 65 20 24
0048  0A 0D 20 33 2E 20 46             DB      0Ah,0Dh,' 3. Find a file   $'
      69 6E 64 20 61 20 66
      69 6C 65 20 20 20 24
005D  0A 0D 20 30 2E 20 54             DB      0Ah,0Dh,' 0. To end       $'
      6F 20 65 6E 64 20 20
      20 20 20 20 20 20 24
                              ;
0072  0A 0D 20 45 6E 74 65   PROMPT    DB      0Ah,0Dh,' Enter a number > $'
      72 20 61 20 6E 75 6D
      62 65 72 20 3E 20 24
0087  0A 0D 20 45 6E 74 65   PROMPT1   DB      0Ah,0Dh,' Enter new name > $'
      72 20 6E 65 77 20 6E
      61 6D 65 20 3E 20 24
009C  0A 0D 20 45 6E 74 65   PROMPT2   DB      0Ah,0Dh,' Enter file name> $'
      72 20 66 69 6C 65 20
      6E 61 6D 65 3E 20 24
00B1  0A 0D 20 49 6E 63 6F   ERR1      DB      0Ah,0Dh,' Incorrect. Re-enter.$'
      72 72 65 63 74 2E 20
      52 65 2D 65 6E 74 65
      72 2E 24
00C9  0A 0D 24               CR_LF     DB      0Ah,0Dh,'$'
00CC  000A[                  INPUT_STR DB      10 DUP(?)
        ??
                        ]

00D6  0024[                  FILE_NAME DB      36 DUP(?)
        ??
                        ]

00FA  0024[                  NEWFILE   DB      36 DUP(?)
        ??
                        ]

011E  0A 0D 20 54 68 65 20   SUCCESS   DB      0Ah,0Dh,' The process was successful.$'
      70 72 6F 63 65 73 73
      20 77 61 73 20 73 75
      63 63 65 73 73 66 75
      6C 2E 24
```

Program 8-2 Continued.

```
013D  0A 0D 20 46 6F 75 6E     FILESIZE      DB       0Ah,0Dh,' Found it.  Its size in bytes is : $'
      64 20 69 74 2E 20 20
      49 74 73 20 73 69 7A
      65 20 69 6E 20 62 79
      74 65 73 20 69 73 20
      3A 20 24
0163  0014[                    SIZE1         DB       20 DUP(?)
        ??
                        ]

0177  0080[                    DTA_AREA      DB       128 DUP(?)
        ??
                        ]

                           ;
01F7                       BEGINHERE:
01F7  B9 0005                              MOV      CX,5           ; Number of menu items to print
01FA  8D 16 0009 R                         LEA      DX,MENU
01FE  B4 09                                MOV      AH,9
0200                       MENUPRT:
0200  CD 21                                INT      21h
0202  83 C2 15                             ADD      DX,21          ; Each prompt is 21 bytes long
0205  E2 F9                                LOOP     MENUPRT
0207                       MENUPRT1:
0207  8D 16 00C9 R                         LEA      DX,CR_LF       ; Space down a line
020B  B4 09                                MOV      AH,9
020D  CD 21                                INT      21h
020F  8D 16 0072 R                         LEA      DX,PROMPT
0213  B4 09                                MOV      AH,9
0215  CD 21                                INT      21h
                           ;
0217  C6 06 00CC R 0A                      MCV      INPUT_STR,10   ; Max number of chars in string
021C  8D 16 00CC R                         LEA      DX,INPUT_STR   ; Input Buffer
0220  B4 0A                                MOV      AH,0Ah
0222  CD 21                                INT      21h            ; Buffered keyboard input
                           ; Now edit the input.  First CALL CODEASB to turn the entered ASCII
                           ;      number into a binary number.
                           ;      SI - points to the string to be converted
                           ;      CX - the count of characters
                           ;      If successful, Carry Flag = 0 and AX holds the returned number
                           ;      If not, Carry Flag = 1
                           ;
0224  2B C9                                SUB      CX,CX          ; Be sure CX is empty
0226  8A 0E 00CD R                         MOV      CL,INPUT_STR[1] ; The count of characters entered
022A  8D 36 00CC R                         LEA      SI,INPUT_STR
022E  83 C6 02                             ADD      SI,2           ; Now points to char string
                           ;
                           ;  See if it is a number before calling CODEASB
                           ;
0231  8A 0E 00CE R                         MOV      CL,BYTE PTR INPUT_STR[2]
0235  80 F1 30                             XOR      CL,30h
0238  80 F9 09                             CMP      CL,9           ; Is this a number?
023B  0F 86 0242 R                         JBE      EDIT0
023F  EB 29 90                             JMP      ERR0
0242                       EDIT0:
0242  E8 0000 E                            CALL     CODEASB
0245  0F 83 024C R                         JNC      EDIT1          ; Carry Flag set?
0249  EB 1F 90                             JMP      ERR0
024C                       EDIT1:
024C  0B C0                                OR       AX,AX          ; Is the number negative?
024E  0F 89 0255 R                         JNS      EDIT2
0252  EB 16 90                             JMP      ERR0
0255                       EDIT2:
0255  2B C9                                SUB      CX,CX          ; Zero out CX
0257  8A C8                                MOV      CL,AL          ; AL holds the number in binary
```

```
0259   80 F9 00                        CMP    CL,0            ; End?
025C   0F 8F 0263 R                    JG     EDIT3
0260   E9 035E R                       JMP    ENDHERE
0263                   EDIT3:
0263   80 F9 04                        CMP    CL,4            ; Too high?
0266   0F 8C 027D R                    JL     GETFILE
                       ;
                       ; Input error
                       ;
026A                   ERRO:
026A   8D 16 00B1 R                    LEA    DX,ERR1         ; Error message
026E   B4 09                           MOV    AH,9
0270   CD 21                           INT    21h
0272   8D 16 00C9 R                    LEA    DX,CR_LF        ; Space up a line
0276   B4 09                           MOV    AH,9
0278   CD 21                           INT    21h
027A   E9 01F7 R                       JMP    BEGINHERE       ; Go get next entry
                       ;
027D                   GETFILE:
027D   8D 16 009C R                    LEA    DX,PROMPT2      ; Ask for file name
0281   B4 09                           MOV    AH,9
0283   CD 21                           INT    21h
0285   C6 06 00D6 R 24                 MOV    FILE_NAME,36    ; Max chars to enter
028A   8D 16 00D6 R                    LEA    DX,FILE_NAME
028E   B4 0A                           MOV    AH,0Ah          ; Buffered keyboard entry
0290   CD 21                           INT    21h
0292   83 C2 02                        ADD    DX,2            ; Point at path/file
0295   2B C0                           SUB    AX,AX           ; Zero out AX
0297   A0 00D7 R                       MOV    AL,[FILE_NAME+1] ; Count of actually entered bytes
029A   04 02                           ADD    AL,2            ; Find position after last char
029C   8B F0                           MOV    SI,AX           ; Move count to an index register
029E   C6 84 00D6 R 00                 MOV    FILE_NAME[SI],00 ; Make into ASCIIZ string
                       ;
                       ; Delete a file
                       ;     INT 21 Function 41
                       ;     DS:DX = segment:offset of ASCIIZ file name
                       ;     If successful, Carry Flag = 0
                       ;     unsuccessful, Carry Flag = 1 and AX has error
                       ;
02A3   80 F9 01                        CMP    CL,1            ; Delete a file choice ?
02A6   0F 8F 02BF R                    JG     RENAME
02AA   2B C0                           SUB    AX,AX
02AC   B4 41                           MOV    AH,41h          ; Delete file from directory
02AE   CD 21                           INT    21h
02B0   0F 82 0358 R                    JC     ERROR_MSG
02B4   8D 16 011E R                    LEA    DX,SUCCESS      ; Give positive results
02B8   B4 09                           MOV    AH,9
02BA   CD 21                           INT    21h
02BC   E9 035E R                       JMP    ENDHERE
                       ;
                       ; Rename a file
                       ;     INT 21 Function 56
                       ;     DS:DX = segment:offset of ASCIIZ file name
                       ;     ES:DI = segment:offset of new ASCIIZ pathname for file
                       ;
02BF                   RENAME:
02BF   80 F9 02                        CMP    CL,2            ; Rename a file choice ?
02C2   0F 8F 0304 R                    JG     CHECK
02C6   87 D5                           XCHG   DX,BP           ; Save pointer to old name
02C8   8D 16 0087 R                    LEA    DX,PROMPT1      ; Ask for new name
02CC   B4 09                           MOV    AH,9
02CE   CD 21                           INT    21h
02D0   C6 06 00FA R 24                 MOV    NEWFILE,36      ; Max chars to be entered
02D5   8D 16 00FA R                    LEA    DX,NEWFILE      ; Point to new file name
02D9   B4 0A                           MOV    AH,0Ah          ; Buffered keyboard input
02DB   CD 21                           INT    21h
02DD   2B C0                           SUB    AX,AX           ; Zero out AX
02DF   A0 00FB R                       MOV    AL,[NEWFILE+1]  ; How many chars entered
```

```
02E2   04 02                        ADD      AL,2              ; Find position after last char
02E4   8B F0                        MOV      SI,AX             ; Move count to index register
02E6   C6 84 00FA R 00              MOV      NEWFILE[SI],00    ; Make new name into ASCIIZ str
02EB   8D 3E 00FC R                 LEA      DI,NEWFILE+2      ; Point to new name
02EF   87 D5                        XCHG     DX,BP             ; Retrieve pointer to old name
02F1   B4 56                        MOV      AH,56h            ; Rename function
02F3   CD 21                        INT      21h
02F5   0F 82 0358 R                 JC       ERROR_MSG         ; Was there an error?
02F9   8D 16 C11E R                 LEA      DX,SUCCESS        ; Give positive results
02FD   B4 09                        MOV      AH,9
02FF   CD 21                        INT      21h
0301   EB 5B 90                     JMP      ENDHERE
                                ;
                                ;
                                ; Check for existing file name
                                ;       INT 21 Function 4E
                                ;       DS:DX = segment:offset of ASCIIZ filename
                                ;       CX = attribute word (0=normal file, 1=read only, 2=hidden,
                                ;            4=system, 8=volume label, 10=subdirectory, and
                                ;            20=archive)  For a multipurpose procedure/program,
                                ;            request this from the user.  0 Used for this example.
                                ;
                                ;       If successful, Carry Flag=0, and DTA holds:
                                ;            Offset   length   Value
                                ;            00       21       MS-DOS reserved
                                ;            15       1        file attribute
                                ;            16       2        Time of last write
                                ;            18       2        Date of last write
                                ;            1A       2        Low word of file size
                                ;            1C       2        High word of file size
                                ;            1E       13       Filename & extension in ASCIIZ
                                ;
                                ;       If unsuccessful, Carry Flag = 1, AX has error code
                                ;
0304                            CHECK:
0304   80 F9 03                     CMP      CL,3              ; File size choice?
0307   0F 8F 0358 R                 JG       ERROR_MSG
                                ; Set up DTA area
030B   8D 16 0177 R                 LEA      DX,DTA_AREA
030F   B4 1A                        MOV      AH,1Ah            ; Set the DTA address
0311   CD 21                        INT      21h
                                ;
                                ; Get the file attributes.  Attribute returns in CX
                                ;       DS:DX points to file name
                                ;
0313   8D 16 00D6 R                 LEA      DX,FILE_NAME
0317   83 C2 02                     ADD      DX,2
031A   B4 43                        MOV      AH,43h            ; Get attributes function
031C   B0 00                        MOV      AL,00
031E   CD 21                        INT      21h               ; Return attrib in CX
                                ;
0320   B4 4E                        MOV      AH,4Eh            ; Check for file
0322   CD 21                        INT      21h
0324   0F 82 0358 R                 JC       ERROR_MSG         ; Was there an error?
                                ;
                                ; Print file size.  CALL CODEBAS : AX word to be converted
                                ;                                  DI char string returned
                                ;
0328   8D 16 013D R                 LEA      DX,FILESIZE       ; Print file size header
032C   B4 09                        MOV      AH,9
032E   CD 21                        INT      21h
                                ;
0330   A1 0191 R                    MOV      AX,WORD PTR [DTA_AREA+1Ah] ; Get word
0333   66| 98                       CWDE                       ; As a double
0335   8D 3E 0163 R                 LEA      DI,SIZE1          ; The pointer to string
0339   E8 0000 E                    CALL     CODEBAS           ; Convert to ASCII
```

```
033C  2B D2                          SUB     DX,DX           ; Be sure DX is empty to start
033E                        SIZEPRT:
033E  8A 15                           MOV     DL,BYTE PTR [DI]
0340  0A D2                           OR      DL,DL           ; Is this byte a hex 00 ?
0342  0F 84 034D R                    JE      MSG
0346  B4 02                           MOV     AH,2
0348  CD 21                           INT     21h
034A  47                              INC     DI
034B  EB F1                           JMP     SIZEPRT
034D                        MSG:
034D  8D 16 011E R                    LEA     DX,SUCCESS      ; Give positive results
0351  B4 09                           MOV     AH,9
0353  CD 21                           INT     21h
0355  EB 07 90                        JMP     ENDHERE
                            ;
                            ;
                            ; If any of the processes find an error, they come to this section
                            ; which calls EXTERROR, to determine the extended error and the
                            ; messages to help pinpoint the problem.
                            ;
0358                        ERROR_MSG:
0358  E8 0000 E                       CALL    EXTERROR
035B  EB 01 90                        JMP     ENDHERE
                            ;
035E                        ENDHERE:
035E  8D 16 00C9 R                    LEA     DX,CR_LF        ; Space up one line
0362  B4 09                           MOV     AH,9
0364  CD 21                           INT     21h
                            ;
0366  B4 4C                           MOV     AH,4Ch          ; Standard Ending
0368  CD 21                           INT     21h
036A                        CODE        ENDS
                                        END     IOWORKS
```

Program 8-3 IOREAD

Microsoft (R) Macro Assembler Version 5.00

```
                                    PAGE    55,132
                                    .386
                                    EXTRN   CODEASB:PROC
0000                        STACK   SEGMENT 'STACK' STACK
0000  0064[                         DW      100 DUP(?)
        ????
                    ]

00C8                        STACK   ENDS
0000                        CODE    SEGMENT para 'CODE' PUBLIC USE16
                                    ASSUME  CS:CODE, DS:CODE, SS:STACK
                            ;
                            ; Name:       IOREAD
                            ;
                            ; Purpose:    This procedure reads bytes from a file.
                            ;
                            ; Inputs:     ASCII File is specified (drive\path\filename), along
                            ;             with the number of bytes to read from the file.  The
                            ;             file characters are limited to a maximum of 30.  It can
                            ;             be any number you want to specify, when you change it
                            ;             to your code.
                            ;
                            ;             For purposes of this example, the bytes to be read
                            ;             are limited to a 40 characters.  This eliminates having
                            ;             format the screen printout.
                            ;
                            ; Process:    INT 21 Function 3D is used to open the file.  This
```

```
                              ;                      function requires the ASCIIZ filename to be in DS:DX.
                              ;                      AL is the Access code (0=reading, 1=writing, 3=both
                              ;                      reading and writing).  If open is successful, AX
                              ;                      contains the file handle.  If not, AL has an error
                              ;                      code.  For error codes, see Appendix 6 of "80386
                              ;                      Assembly Language Toolkit."
                              ;
                              ;                      Once the bytes are read, the file is closed using INT
                              ;                      21 Function 3E.  BX holds the valid file handle.  If
                              ;                      an unsuccessful close, AL=6 which says invalid handle.
                              ;
                              ; Outputs:             The bytes read are displayed.
                              ;
0000                          IOREAD:
0000 8C C8                                 MOV      AX,CS        ; Prepare to set DS
0002 8E D8                                 MOV      DS,AX        ;   and set it.
0004 E9 03AE R                             JMP      BEGINHERE
                              ;
0007 52 65 61 64 20 77 68     PROMPT       DB       'Read which file? $'
     69 63 68 20 66 69 6C
     65 3F 20 24
0019 0A 0D 48 6F 77 20 6D     PROMPT1      DB       0Ah,0Dh,'How many bytes? $'
     61 6E 79 20 62 79 74
     65 73 3F 20 24
002C 0A 0D 52 65 61 64 20     HEADER       DB       0Ah,0Dh,'Read from file:    $'
     66 72 6F 6D 20 66 69
     6C 65 3A 20 20 20 24
0041 0020[                    FILE_NAME    DB       32 DUP(?)
        ??
                      ]

0061 0020[                    BYTE_NO      DB       32 DUP(?)
        ??
                      ]

0081 0028[                    INPUT_STR    DB       40 DUP(?)
        ??
                      ]

00A9 0A 0D 24                 CR_LF        DB       0Ah,0Dh,'$'
00AC 0A 0D 20 45 52 52 4F     ERROR_MSG    DB       0Ah,0Dh,' ERROR - $'
     52 20 2D 20 24
00B8 0A 0D 20 49 6E 76 61     INVALID_NO   DB       0Ah,0Dh,' Invalid Number entered.$'
     6C 69 64 20 4E 75 6D
     62 65 72 20 65 6E 74
     65 72 65 64 2E 24
                              ;
                              ; Error Return Codes
                              ;
00D3 20 46 75 6E 63 74 69     ERROR1       DB       ' Function number not valid.                    $'
     6F 6E 20 6E 75 6D 62
     65 72 20 6E 6F 74 20
     76 61 6C 69 64 2E 20
     20 20 20 20 20 20 20
     20 20 20 20 20 20 20
     24
00FE 20 46 69 6C 65 20 6E     ERROR2       DB       ' File not found.                               $'
     6F 74 20 66 6F 75 6E
     64 2E 20 20 20 20 20
     20 20 20 20 20 20 20
     20 20 20 20 20 20 20
     20 20 20 20 20 20 20
     24
0129 20 49 6E 76 61 6C 69     ERROR3       DB       ' Invalid path.                                 $'
     64 20 70 61 74 68 2E
     20 20 20 20 20 20 20
```

```
          20 20 20 20 20 20 20
          20 20 20 20 20 20 20
          20 20 20 20 20 20 20
          24
0154      20 54 6F 6F 20 6D 61    ERROR4      DB      ' Too many files open at the same time.      $'
          6E 79 20 66 69 6C 65
          73 20 6F 70 65 6E 20
          61 74 20 74 68 65 20
          73 61 6D 65 20 74 69
          6D 65 2E 20 20 20 20
          24
017F      20 41 63 63 65 73 73    ERROR5      DB      ' Access is denied.                          $'
          20 69 73 20 64 65 6E
          69 65 64 2E 20 20 20
          20 20 20 20 20 20 20
          20 20 20 20 20 20 20
          20 20 20 20 20 20 20
          24
01AA      20 46 69 6C 65 20 68    ERROR6      DB      ' File handle is invalid.                    $'
          61 6E 64 6C 65 20 69
          73 20 69 6E 76 61 6C
          69 64 2E 20 20 20 20
          20 20 20 20 20 20 20
          20 20 20 20 20 20 20
          24
01D5      20 4D 65 6D 6F 72 79    ERROR7      DB      ' Memory control blocks destroyed.           $'
          20 63 6F 6E 74 72 6F
          6C 20 62 6C 6F 63 6B
          73 20 64 65 73 74 72
          6F 79 65 64 2E 20 20
          20 20 20 20 20 20 20
          24
0200      20 4E 6F 74 20 65 6E    ERROR8      DB      ' Not enough memory.                         $'
          6F 75 67 68 20 6D 65
          6D 6F 72 79 2E 20 20
          20 20 20 20 20 20 20
          20 20 20 20 20 20 20
          20 20 20 20 20 20 20
          24
022B      20 4D 65 6D 6F 72 79    ERROR9      DB      ' Memory block address is invalid.           $'
          20 62 6C 6F 63 6B 20
          61 64 64 72 65 73 73
          20 69 73 20 69 6E 76
          61 6C 69 64 2E 20 20
          20 20 20 20 20 20 20
          24
0256      20 45 6E 76 69 72 6F    ERROR10     DB      ' Environment String is invalid.             $'
          6E 6D 65 6E 74 20 53
          74 72 69 6E 67 20 69
          73 20 69 6E 76 61 6C
          69 64 2E 20 20 20 20
          20 20 20 20 20 20 20
          24
0281      20 46 6F 72 6D 61 74    ERROR11     DB      ' Format invalid.                            $'
          20 69 6E 76 61 6C 69
          64 2E 20 20 20 20 20
          20 20 20 20 20 20 20
          20 20 20 20 20 20 20
          20 20 20 20 20 20 20
          24
02AC      20 41 63 63 65 73 73    ERROR12     DB      ' Access code invalid.                       $'
          20 63 6F 64 65 20 69
          6E 76 61 6C 69 64 2E
          20 20 20 20 20 20 20
          20 20 20 20 20 20 20
          20 20 20 20 20 20 20
          24
02D7      20 44 61 74 61 20 69    ERROR13     DB      ' Data invalid.                              $'
```

```
           6E 76 61 6C 69 64 2E
           20 20 20 20 20 20 20
           20 20 20 20 20 20 20
           20 20 20 20 20 20 20
           20 20 20 20 20 20 20
           24
0302       20 49 6E 76 61 6C 69    ERROR15     DB          ' Invalid drive specified.                    $'
           64 20 64 72 69 76 65
           20 73 70 65 63 69 66
           69 65 64 2E 20 20 20
           20 20 20 20 20 20 20
           20 20 20 20 20 20 20
           24
032D       20 41 74 74 65 6D 70    ERROR16     DB          ' Attempt made to remove current directory.$'
           74 20 6D 61 64 65 20
           74 6F 20 72 65 6D 6F
           76 65 20 63 75 72 72
           65 6E 74 20 64 69 72
           65 63 74 6F 72 79 2E
           24
0358       20 4E 6F 74 20 73 61    ERROR17     DB          ' Not same device.                            $'
           6D 65 20 64 65 76 69
           63 65 2E 20 20 20 20
           20 20 20 20 20 20 20
           20 20 20 20 20 20 20
           20 20 20 20 20 20 20
           24
0383       20 4E 6F 20 6D 6F 72    ERROR18     DB          ' No more files found.                        $'
           65 20 66 69 6C 65 73
           20 66 6F 75 6E 64 2E
           20 20 20 20 20 20 20
           20 20 20 20 20 20 20
           20 20 20 20 20 20 20
           24
                                   ;
03AE                               BEGINHERE:
03AE       8D 16 0007 R                        LEA         DX,PROMPT         ; Print the file prompt
03B2       B4 09                               MOV         AH,9
03B4       CD 21                               INT         21h
03B6       C6 06 0041 R 1E                     MOV         FILE_NAME,30      ; Max characters in input
03BB       8D 16 0041 R                        LEA         DX,FILE_NAME      ; Get file name/path (if any)
03BF       B4 0A                               MOV         AH,0Ah
03C1       CD 21                               INT         21h
03C3       8A 0E 0042 R                        MOV         CL,[FILE_NAME+1] ; How many bytes read in
03C7       80 C1 02                            ADD         CL,2              ; Find position after last char
03CA       B5 00                               MOV         CH,00
03CC       8B F1                               MOV         SI,CX             ; Move to index register
03CE       C6 84 0041 R 00                     MOV         FILE_NAME[SI],00 ; Make into ASCIIZ string
                                   ;
03D3       8D 16 0019 R                        LEA         DX,PROMPT1        ; Now read how many bytes
03D7       B4 09                               MOV         AH,9
03D9       CD 21                               INT         21h
03DB       C6 06 0061 R 26                     MOV         BYTE_NO,38
03E0       8D 16 0061 R                        LEA         DX,BYTE_NO
03E4       B4 0A                               MOV         AH,0Ah            ; Read in digit(s)
03E6       CD 21                               INT         21h
                                   ;
                                   ;   Convert to a binary number
                                   ;   SI points to the string which is to be converted
                                   ;   CX has the count of ASCII characters
                                   ;   If CALL is Successful, Carry Flag = 0
                                   ;                          AX has result
                                   ;   If not successful,     Carry Flag = 1
                                   ;                          AX = 0
                                   ;
03E8       2B C9                               SUB         CX,CX
```

```
03EA  8A 0E 0062 R                        MOV      CL,BYTE_NO[1]      ; Number of bytes read in
03EE  8D 36 0063 R                        LEA      SI,BYTE_NO[2]      ; The character string
03F2  E8 0000 E                           CALL     CODEASB
                                  ;
03F5  2B C9                               SUB      CX,CX              ; Zero CX
03F7  A2 0061 R                           MOV      BYTE_NO,AL         ; Save the Number
03FA  0F 82 0407 R                        JC       INVALID            ; Was Carry Flag Set?
03FE  80 3E 0061 R 00                     CMP      BYTE_NO,0          ; Was a zero entered?
0403  0F 85 0412 R                        JNE      OPENO
0407                      INVALID:
0407  8D 16 00B8 R                        LEA      DX,INVALID_NO      ; Error on entry
040B  B4 09                               MOV      AH,9
040D  CD 21                               INT      21h
040F  EB 6A 90                            JMP      ENDHERE
                                  ;
                                  ; Open file
                                  ;       DX = ASCIIZ string with file name
                                  ;       AL = File attribute (0=read only, 1=write only,
                                  ;                             2=read/write)
                                  ;            Successful read, AX = File handle
                                  ;            Unsuccessful read, AX = Error Code and CF=1
                                  ;
0412                      OPENO:
0412  8D 16 0043 R                        LEA      DX,FILE_NAME+2     ; The file/path
0416  B0 00                               MOV      AL,0               ; Read file only
0418  B4 3D                               MOV      AH,3Dh
041A  CD 21                               INT      21h
041C  8B F8                               MOV      DI,AX              ; Save file handle
                                  ;
                                  ;       Check for errors
                                  ;       If there's an error, Carry Flag is set and error number in AL
                                  ;
041E                      ERROR_HERE:
041E  0F 83 0448 R                        JNC      READO
0422  95                                  XCHG     AX,BP              ; Save error number
0423  8D 16 00A9 R                        LEA      DX,CR_LF           ; Carriage Return/Line Feed
0427  B4 09                               MOV      AH,9
0429  CD 21                               INT      21h
042B  8D 16 00AC R                        LEA      DX,ERROR_MSG       ; Print that there is an error
042F  B4 09                               MOV      AH,9
0431  CD 21                               INT      21h
0433  95                                  XCHG     AX,BP              ; Get error number back
0434  8D 16 00D3 R                        LEA      DX,ERROR1          ; Print which error was found
0438  B1 2B                               MOV      CL,43              ; Each error is 43 bytes
043A  F6 E1                               MUL      CL                 ; CL x AX = Result in AL
043C  2D 002B                             SUB      AX,43              ; Back up to correct position
043F  03 D0                               ADD      DX,AX              ; Index into error messages
0441  B4 09                               MOV      AH,9
0443  CD 21                               INT      21h
0445  EB 34 90                            JMP      ENDHERE
                                  ;
                                  ; Read from file
                                  ;       DI = File Handle, Moved into BX
                                  ;       BYTE_NO = Number of bytes to read from file
                                  ;               Successful read, AX has Number actually read
                                  ;               Unsuccessful read, AX has error number
                                  ;
0448                      READO:
0448  8B DF                               MOV      BX,DI              ; File handle
044A  8D 16 0081 R                        LEA      DX,INPUT_STR
044E  8A 0E 0061 R                        MOV      CL,BYTE_NO         ; Number of bytes to read
0452  B4 3F                               MOV      AH,3Fh             ; Read function number
0454  CD 21                               INT      21h
0456  8B C8                               MOV      CX,AX              ; Number actually read
                                  ;
                                  ; If an error on read Carry Flag is set
                                  ;
0458  0F 83 0466 R                        JNC      DISPLAYO
```

Program 8-3 Continued.

```
045C  3D 0005                              CMP     AX,5
045F  74 BD                                JE      ERROR_HERE
0461  3D 0006                              CMP     AX,6
0464  74 B8                                JE      ERROR_HERE

                        ; Display the bytes read
                        ;       CX has the number of bytes, so use CX as loop index
                        ;       INPUT_STR is the buffer with the characters read from
                        ;              the ASCII file
                        ;
0466                    DISPLAY0:
0466  8D 16 002C R                         LEA     DX,HEADER        ; Output header
046A  B4 09                                MOV     AH,9
046C  CD 21                                INT     21h
046E  2B F6                                SUB     SI,SI            ; Initialize index
0470                    SHOW0:
0470  46                                   INC     SI               ; Index into INPUT_STR
0471  8A 94 0081 R                         MOV     DL,INPUT_STR[SI] ; Load character into DX
0475  B4 02                                MOV     AH,2             ; Print the character
0477  CD 21                                INT     21h
0479  E0 F5                                LOOPNZ  SHOW0
                        ;
                        ;
047B                    ENDHERE:
047B  B4 4C                                MOV     AH,4Ch           ; Standard Ending
047D  CD 21                                INT     21h
047F                    CODE    ENDS
                                END     IOREAD
```

Program 8-4 IOWRITE

Microsoft (R) Macro Assembler Version 5.00

```
                                PAGE    55,132
                                .386
                                EXTRN   EXTERROR:PROC
0000                    STACK   SEGMENT 'STACK' STACK
0000  00C8[                     DW      200 DUP(?)
        ????
                    ]

0190                    STACK   ENDS
0000                    CODE    SEGMENT para 'CODE' PUBLIC USE16
                                ASSUME  CS:CODE, DS:CODE, SS:STACK
                        ;
                        ; Name:      IOWRITE
                        ;
                        ; Purpose:   This procedure creates a file, then writes bytes
                        ;            to that file, and then closes the file.
                        ;
                        ; Inputs:    An ASCII File is specified (drive\path\filename).
                        ;            For purposes of this example, the path/file characters
                        ;            are limited to a maximum of 30.  It can be any number
                        ;            you want to specify, when you change it to your code.
                        ;
                        ;            Also, for purposes of this example, the bytes to be
                        ;            written are limited to 40 characters.  Again this was
                        ;            arbitrary for the purposes of an example.
                        ;
                        ;            This program calls EXTERROR to process errors. EXTERROR
                        ;            contains the extended error codes and uses INT 21
                        ;            Function 59 to get them.  After INT 21 Function 59
                        ;            is issued, AX holds the extended error code, BH holds
```

```
;                                   the error class, BL holds the suggested action, and
;                                   CH holds the location of the error.  See EXTERROR in
;                                   Chapter 5 of the "80386 Assembly Language Toolkit"
;                                   for further information.
;
; Process:                          INT 21 Function 5B creates a file handle, with DS:DX
;                                   pointing to the ASCIIZ string with path/file name, and
;                                   CX pointing to the file attribute (0=normal file, 1=read
;                                   only, 2=hidden file, 4=system file, 8=volume label,
;                                   10=subdirectory, and 20=archive).  Note that if the
;                                   file already exists, INT 21 Function 5B will return with
;                                   an error message.  Use INT 21 Function 59 to get what
;                                   the extended error message is.  EXTERROR gets the error
;                                   and prints explanatory messages.
;
;                                   INT 21 Function 3D is used to open the file.  This
;                                   function requires the ASCIIZ filename to be in DS:DX.
;                                   AL is the Access code(0=read only, 1=write only, and
;                                   2=read/write).  If open is successful, AX
;                                   contains the file handle.  If not, AL has an error
;                                   code.  For error codes, see Appendix 6 of "80386
;                                   Assembly Language Toolkit."  Also, codes are in
;                                   EXTERROR.
;
;                                   INT 21 40 is used to write the bytes to the file.  Once
;                                   they are written the read/write pointer is automatically
;                                   updated so that the next write goes to the byte that
;                                   follows the end of the previous write.
;
;                                   Once the bytes are written, the file is closed using INT
;                                   21 Function 3E.  BX holds the valid file handle.  If
;                                   an unsuccessful close, AL=6 which says invalid handle.
;
; Outputs:                          A File Closed message is displayed on the screen.
;
; Note:                             INT 21 Function 5B will abort with a "File already
;                                   exists if the file has been ERASED from the disk (when a
;                                   file is erased the first character is overwritten but
;                                   INT 21 Function 5B still "finds" the file.
;
0000                                IOWRITE:
0000  8C C8                                     MOV     AX,CS         ; Prepare to set DS
0002  8E D8                                     MOV     DS,AX         ;   and set it.
0004  E9 00B4 R                                 JMP     BEGINHERE
                                    ;
0007  0A 0D 57 72 69 74 65         PROMPT      DB      0Ah,0Dh,'Write to which file? $'
      20 74 6F 20 77 68 69
      63 68 20 66 69 6C 65
      3F 20 24
001F  0A 0D 45 6E 74 65 72         PROMPT1     DB      0Ah,0Dh,'Enter the bytes? $'
      20 74 68 65 20 62 79
      74 65 73 3F 20 24
0033  0A 0D 43 6C 6F 73 69         CLOSEFILE   DB      0Ah,0Dh,'Closing the file.$'
      6E 67 20 74 68 65 20
      66 69 6C 65 2E 24
0047  0020[                        FILE_NAME   DB      32 DUP(?)
         ??
                            ]

0067  0020[                        BYTE_NO     DB      32 DUP(?)
         ??
                            ]

0087  002A[                        INPUT_STR   DB      42 DUP(?)
         ??
                            ]

00B1  0A 0D 24                     CR_LF       DB      0Ah,0Dh,'$'
```

Program 8-4 Continued.

```
                                       ;
00B4                                   BEGINHERE:
00B4  8D 16 0007 R                           LEA     DX,PROMPT        ; Print the file prompt
00B8  B4 09                                  MOV     AH,9
00BA  CD 21                                  INT     21h
00BC  C6 06 0047 R 1E                        MOV     FILE_NAME,30     ; Max characters in input
00C1  8D 16 0047 R                           LEA     DX,FILE_NAME     ; Get file name/path (if any)
00C5  B4 0A                                  MOV     AH,0Ah
00C7  CD 21                                  INT     21h
00C9  8A 0E 0048 R                           MOV     CL,[FILE_NAME+1] ; How many bytes read in
00CD  80 C1 02                               ADD     CL,2             ; Find position after last char
00D0  B5 00                                  MOV     CH,00
00D2  8B F1                                  MOV     SI,CX            ; Move count to index register
00D4  C6 84 0047 R 00                        MOV     FILE_NAME[SI],00 ; Make into ASCIIZ string
                                       ;
00D9  8D 16 001F R                           LEA     DX,PROMPT1       ; Request input
00DD  B4 09                                  MOV     AH,9
00DF  CD 21                                  INT     21h
00E1  C6 06 0087 R 26                        MOV     INPUT_STR,38     ; Max 38 characters
00E6  8D 16 0087 R                           LEA     DX,INPUT_STR
00EA  B4 0A                                  MOV     AH,0Ah           ; Read in data
00EC  CD 21                                  INT     21h
                                       ;
                                       ; Create a File Handle, Create a new file
                                       ;        Note: If file already exists, its length is set to 0
                                       ;              at the end of this routine
                                       ;        DS:DX holds the pointer to path/file name
                                       ;        CX = file attribute (see prolog information)
                                       ;        On return, if Carry Flag = 0, successful and AX holds handle
                                       ;                   if Carry Flag = 1, unsuccessful, AX=error code
                                       ;
00EE  8D 16 0047 R                           LEA     DX,FILE_NAME     ; Load pointer to file name
00F2  83 C2 02                               ADD     DX,2             ; Skip auxiliary bytes
00F5  B9 0000                                MOV     CX,0             ; Normal file
00F8  B4 5B                                  MOV     AH,5Bh           ; Create handle
00FA  CD 21                                  INT     21h
00FC  0F 83 0106 R                           JNC     OPEN0            ; Was Carry Flag set?
                                       ;
                                       ; Error while trying to create a file
                                       ;
0100  E8 0000 E                              CALL    EXTERROR         ; Get error code & print messages
0103  EB 4F 90                               JMP     ENDHERE

                                       ; Open file
                                       ;     DX = ASCIIZ string with file name
                                       ;     AL = File attribute (0=read only, 1=write only,
                                       ;                2=read/write)
                                       ;          Successful read, AX = File handle
                                       ;          Unsuccessful read, AX = Error Code and CF=1
                                       ;
0106                                   OPEN0:
0106  8D 16 0049 R                           LEA     DX,FILE_NAME+2 ; The file/path
010A  B0 02                                  MOV     AL,2           ; Read/write file
010C  B4 3D                                  MOV     AH,3Dh
010E  CD 21                                  INT     21h
0110  8B F8                                  MOV     DI,AX          ; Save file handle
                                       ;
                                       ;        Check for errors
                                       ;        If there's an error, Carry Flag is set and error number
                                       ;                returned in AL
                                       ;
0112  0F 83 011C R                           JNC     WRITE0
0116  E8 0000 E                              CALL    EXTERROR       ; Get error & print messages
0119  EB 39 90                               JMP     ENDHERE
                                       ;
                                       ; Write to file
```

```
                    ;          DI = File Handle, Moved into BX
                    ;          CX = Number of bytes to write (from 2nd byte of INPUT_STR)
                    ;          INPUT_STR = The bytes to write to file
                    ;                 Successful write, Carry Flag = 0
                    ;                        AX has Number actually written
                    ;               Unsuccessful write, Carry Flag = 1
                    ;                        AX has error number
                    ;
011C                WRITEO:
011C  8B DF                      MOV      BX,DI                ; File handle
011E  8D 16 0089 R               LEA      DX,INPUT_STR[2]
0122  8A 0E 0088 R               MOV      CL,INPUT_STR[1]    ; Number of bytes to read
0126  B4 40                      MOV      AH,40h               ; Write function number
0128  CD 21                      INT      21h
012A  8B C8                      MOV      CX,AX                ; Number actually written
                    ;
                    ; If an error on read Carry Flag is set
                    ;
012C  0F 83 0136 R               JNC      DISPLAYO
0130  E8 0000 E                  CALL     EXTERROR             ; Get error & print message
0133  EB 1F 90                   JMP      ENDHERE
                    ;
                    ; Now close the file so that end-of-file (EOF) is correct
                    ;          BX still contains the file handle
                    ;          If successful, Carry Flag = 0
                    ;          unsuccessful, Carry Flag = 1, AX holds error code
                    ;
0136                DISPLAYO:
0136  8D 16 0033 R               LEA      DX,CLOSEFILE        ; Output close file message
013A  B4 09                      MOV      AH,9
013C  CD 21                      INT      21h
                    ;
013E  B4 3E                      MOV      AH,3Eh               ; Close file function
0140  CD 21                      INT      21h
                    ;
0142  0F 83 014C R               JNC      DISPLAY1
0146  E8 0000 E                  CALL     EXTERROR             ; Get error & print messages
0149  EB 09 90                   JMP      ENDHERE
                    ;
014C                DISPLAY1:
014C  8D 16 00B1 R               LEA      DX,CR_LF            ; Put out one last CR/LF
0150  B4 09                      MOV      AH,9                 ; for prettier screen format
0152  CD 21                      INT      21h
                    ;
                    ;
0154                ENDHERE:
0154  B4 4C                      MOV      AH,4Ch               ; Standard Ending
0156  CD 21                      INT      21h
0158                CODE         ENDS
                                 END      IOWRITE
```

9
Algorithms

An *algorithm* is a prescribed set of well-defined rules or processes for the solution of a problem in a finite number of steps. For instance, a transfer algorithm is a specific algorithm design used in a demand-fetching system to determine the order in which segments demanded by concurrent processes transfer from storage to internal memory.

An object is said to be *recursive* if it is defined in terms of itself. Recursion is encountered not only in mathematics, but in daily life; for instance, product advertising often shows a picture that includes a picture of itself. Recursion is particularly powerful in mathematical definitions.

The power of recursion lies in the possibility of defining an infinite set of objects by a finite statement. Recursive algorithms are used when the problem to be solved (or the function to be computed, or the data structure to be processed) is already defined in recursive terms. This does not mean that recursive definitions guarantee that a recursive algorithm is the best way to solve the problem. Often, it is plain that recursion can be replaced by simple iteration within the main program.

The best tool for expressing recursive programs is the *procedure* (or *subroutine*). This tool allows a statement to be given a name by which this code can be invoked. If a procedure (X) contains an explicit reference to itself, it is said to be directly recursive. If X contains reference to another procedure (Y) that contains a reference to X, then X is said to be indirectly recursive.

Searching

Searching is one of the most frequent operations in computer programming. There are several basic searching variations, and each has many algorithms developed for it (and proponents who swear that their way is best). The basic assumption in searching a group of data is that the group is finite; that is, it has a fixed number within the group. The task is to locate the element of the group that is equal to a given search argument, or to determine that the match does not exist within the given group.

Linear search

When no further information is given about a group of data, the obvious approach is to proceed sequentially through the group (array)—to increase (in steps) the size of the selection where the desired element is known not to exist. This approach is called *linear search*. There are two conditions that end a linear search: the element is found, or the entire array has been scanned and no match was found.

Termination of linear searches is eventually guaranteed because in each step the index increases by one and therefore reaches the limit after a finite number of steps. Each step requires the incrementing of the index and the evaluation of whether or not the search element matches the array element. A linear search might be the only way to locate an element in an unsorted array; that is, in a group that isn't ordered in a known manner. In this book, we haven't demonstrated a linear search for a couple of reasons. First, it's easy to do (so you can do it on your own). Second, we feel that it is worth the time and resources to order an array prior to searching.

A binary search program

A search for a particular element in an array or a table can be considerably faster if the elements are already ordered (sorted). In this case, the common method is to repeatedly halve the interval where the desired element must be. This is called a *binary search*. In each repetition, the inspected interval between the indices is bisected to give a point where it is assumed the match will be made. If a match is not made, the half of the interval that probably contains the desired element becomes the interval to check. The number of required comparisons is therefore at most $\log_2(N)$, where N is the total number of elements in the array. Figure 9-1 illustrates this binary search technique.

The goal of binary searching is to eliminate, in each step, as many elements as possible from further searches no matter what the outcome of the comparison is. The optimal solution is to choose the middle element because this eliminates half the array (the search value either matches the middle, or is larger or smaller than the middle).

BNSEARCH (Program 9-1) implements the standard binary search algorithm. While the shell sort routine was built for variable-length string, BNSEARCH and QSORT are for fixed-length data. In BNSEARCH, BX points to an array description. SI points to an array of index elements that provide a set of ordered pointers to the keys to be searched. DI points to the key to locate.

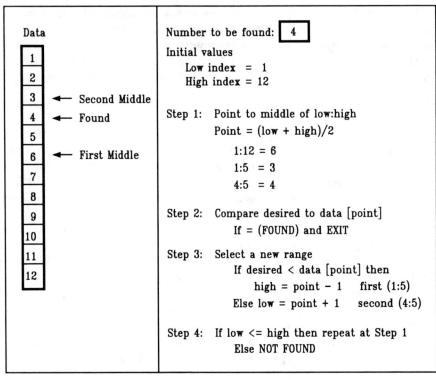

9-1 Binary search technique.

The binary search algorithm searches an ordered array. The initial partition has 1 as its left index and the maximum as its right index. The algorithm computes the index of the center of the partition (left plus right divided by 2). The center is compared to the target. If the target is equal to the center, the match is found. If the target is greater, a new left limit is set as center + 1; otherwise, a new right limit is set as center – 1. If the indices cross, there is no match in the array; otherwise, we repeat the process. At the end, ES:DI points to the record located.

KEYCOMP is a routine within BNSEARCH that compares the source key to the desired key. This routine assumes that the desired key is pointed to by DS:BP, and is of a fixed length. (This is common in the data processing industry. For example, employee records can be indexed by Social Security Number or company employee number.) The index of the comparison element is in AX, so the comparison is always A(SI(AX)):*desired*. This comparison routine is specifically for testing and demonstrating the algorithm. The location of the key in a record is not necessarily at the beginning. The length is not always 11. Keys are not always character strings, either; numbers (both floating-point and binary) are also popular. AX indexes the desired element on input. ES:DI points to the desired element on exit and the flags reflect the result of the key comparison.

ARRANDXP is a procedure that provides a method for computing a usable array element address, which is required for accessing elements of large arrays (greater than 64K) in a USE16 task. It is a modification of the full routine. AX has the index of the array element (1 . . . LAST) desired. BX has the segment array pointer. The DS array is assumed to be of the form built by the ARRABLDP.ASM routine (see Program 9-10). AX is decremented to get a zero base and DX is zeroed. DXAX is divided by the number of elements per segment. The quotient is multiplied by 2 and used to select the ES value. The remainder multiplied by the element size becomes the DI value. At output, if the element is found, DI has the displacement to the record. AX has the segment register value.

Buffers

When data are transferred to or from a secondary storage device, the individual bits are transferred as a stream. Because each secondary device imposes timing constraints on the transmission, gaps of time is left between the data transmitted and the data that will follow later. To achieve a high density of data (which leads to faster throughput), the number of time gaps ought to be kept small. To keep them as small as possible, data to be transferred are buffered. That is, they are collected in an intermediate storage area, called a *buffer*, and transferred when a sufficient amount of data is accumulated.

Think of a buffer as a logical device inserted between other devices or program elements to match peripheral speeds, to prevent mixed interactions, to supply additional drive or relay capability, or to simply modify the rate of information flow. While data are being buffered, the processor can do other things.

A simple buffer, therefore, is a technique for obtaining simultaneous performance of input/output operations and computing. A buffer is associated with only one input or output file (or data set) for the duration of the activity on that file (or data set). For example, a data communications buffer enables devices to operate at different speeds independent of communications line speeds.

A buffer acts as a first-in-first-out (FIFO) queue. If it is declared as an array, two index variables (for example, in and out) mark the positions of the next location to be written into and to be read from.

Memory buffers, as used in the programs in this book and with MS-DOS interrupts, are storage devices that allow input and output of character strings. For most MS-DOS interrupts, input buffers have two auxiliary bytes at the front of the buffer. You store the first byte, byte 0, which is the total number of bytes possible, in the buffer. MS-DOS stores the second byte, byte 1, which is the actual number of characters entered. For instance, Interrupt 21 Function 0A requires this type of memory buffer. Several of the procedures for code conversion (see chapter 7) use memory buffers, but generally without the two auxiliary bytes because they aren't input buffers.

A note about the counts in memory buffers is in order here. If, for instance, you wish to input 10 characters, your buffer must be defined with 13 bytes. The first two bytes are the auxiliary bytes; the next ten are the entered characters. The final byte is for the 0D carriage return.

A buffer handling program

There are many instances throughout the various programs and procedures in this book that show how to handle memory buffers for input and output. BUFFER (Program 9-2) gives a stand-alone example of an input buffer filled by using Interrupt 21 Function 0A. It also proves to be of secondary interest. We wanted to convert the binary bytes to printable hex in order to display how the memory buffer changes depending on your input, so we coded BUFFER to call CODEBTHX (described and listed in chapter 7). What turned out was that BUFFER now gives you a quick hex translation of your keyboard characters, along with a demonstration of memory buffers. A sample run of BUFFER is shown in Fig. 9-2.

Circular buffers

Buffers (such as keyboard buffers) allow you to read and write to them independently. Circular buffering easily allows you to put in and take out

```
C:\ASM>BUFFER

 Type up to ten characters > 1234567890

 Here is the memory buffer >0B 0A 31 32 33 34 35 36 37 38 39 30 0D

C:\ASM>BUFFER

 Type up to ten characters > ABC

 Here is the memory buffer >0B 03 41 42 43 0D 00 00 00 00 00 00 00

C:\ASM>BUFFER

 Type up to ten characters > $%&

 Here is the memory buffer >0B 03 24 25 26 0D 00 00 00 00 00 00 00

C:\ASM>
```

9-2 Sample run of BUFFER program.

keys. At any point, one of the 16 words (in the keyboard buffer) is at a place called the *head*, which is the position that the next character will be read from. The *tail* is the position that the next character can be written to. When keys are typed in, the tail advances. When you read one, the head advances. When either comes to the end of their 16-word queue, they wrap around to the beginning again. Two bytes in the BIOS data area hold the current addresses of the head and tail.

When everything has been read, the head catches up with the tail and the two are at the same address, which means that the buffer is empty. On the other hand, if the tail comes around and catches the head, the buffer is full.

The keyboard buffer, by the way, holds only 15 bytes before it is filled. The reason is that the tail word is where the next character goes. If the tail is looped around right behind the head with 15 characters input, the next character coming in would overwrite the head. Because an overlap signals an empty buffer, BIOS doesn't allow 16 characters in or it wouldn't know if the buffer is full or empty.

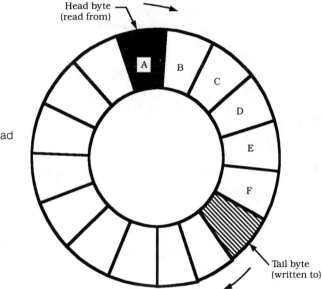

9-3 Circular buffer with head and tail.

Clearing buffers

Application programs meant for end users should clear the keyboard buffer before prompting for input, eliminating any inadvertent keystrokes that might be waiting in the buffer. The keyboard buffer holds up to 15 keystrokes, whether they are one-byte ASCII codes or two-byte extended codes. There are instances where you want to flush the buffer, such as when there is an unexpected or critical prompt the user might not have expected.

Interrupt 21 Function 0C clears the keyboard buffer and then performs one of the other keyboard input functions (01, 06, 07, 08, or 0A). If AL contains 0A, DS:DX must point to the buffer in which MS-DOS is to place the string read from the keyboard. Move 0C into AH and the other function into AL. With early versions of MS-DOS, Function 0C emptied the type-ahead buffer before executing the input function specified in AL. With versions 2.0 and later, if input has been redirected to a file, Function 0C does nothing before carrying out the input function specified in AL. If input is not redirected, the type-ahead buffer is flushed.

With a function number other than 01, 06, 07, 08, or 0A in AL, Function 0C simply flushes the standard-input buffer and returns control to the calling program. Because the buffer is flushed before the input function is carried out, any Ctrl+C (Break) character pending in the buffer is discarded. If subsequent input is a Ctrl+C, Interrupt 23 (Ctrl+C handler address) is called.

Buffer allocation

BUFFDRV (Program 9-24) tests the buffer allocate, return, and threshold procedures. The program gets the threshold value and the reset value. They are edited to ensure reasonability and then are used to build the threshold structure.

BUFF486 (Program 9-22) provides a contention-free, push-down stack manager. Its two entry points use the CMPXCHG instruction for stack management. BUFF386 (Program 9-23) has no compare-and-exchange instruction, so the buffer pool is protected with a spin lock. The lock word is presumed to follow the stack pointer in memory. THRESH (Program 9-25) has as its purpose the implementation of a resetting single-shot warning mechanism. A count, such as a running count of available buffers, can be used to provide a warning when it matches a value either as it increases or decreases.

Encryption

The need for security measures to protect computer data was recognized from the beginnings of computer usage. Security was accomplished in early batch-operated computers, which were made to perform one job completely before going to the next. Security was merely adapted from techniques used in the protection of manual handling of assets. Problems arose when technical advances allowed the sharing of resources by more than one job at a time and when storage media (such as diskettes) became extremely easy to transport.

Computers are being used for more purposes where the possibilities for unauthorized or malicious acts could result in serious losses. Money in electronic form and data records representing valuable property are being moved from vaults to computers at a rapid rate, resulting in computers becoming the new vaults.

Computer security has several dimensions. It consists of physical, personnel, operational, data, program, and hardware protection. Security functions are avoidance, deterrence, prevention, detection, recovery, and correction, which are areas beyond the scope of this book. This section directs attention to data protection.

While an ideal protection of data is available with the use of data encryption techniques, the administration of encryption keys remains a problem. That is, a programmer might come up with an encryption technique but someone in the company must know it and decide to implement it. If that key is not kept secure, then the encryption is simply an exercise. Again, this issue is outside the scope of this book, where we show one method of encrypting data.

ENCRYPT (Program 9-3) uses a simple Caesar cipher, which simply adds one to the character. Thus, A becomes B, B becomes C, and so on. Decryption is the same operation in reverse, which subtracts 1 from the character.

Another simple approach is the straight exchange. There, you set up an exchange table with the left half of the table holding all the characters and the right half of the table holding their replacement values. For instance, you might say that every A is exchanged with an X, every B is exchanged with a slash (/), and so on.

While these appear simplistic, they often serve the purpose of protecting data from the casual hacker or a deliberately malicious employee. There are other more complex methods that can be studied by programmers who must code more tightly secure programs.

ENCRYPT uses Interrupt 21 Function 0A to capture an input string into a memory buffer and display it prior to encryption. It uses the Caesar cipher to encrypt the input characters and then displays the encrypted characters. The characters are decrypted and displayed.

Hashing schemes

Hashing describes a general class of operations that transform one or more fields (usually a key) into a different and more compact arrangement. The justification for hashing derives from being able to convert naturally occurring, ill-structured, scattered key fields into compact, easily manipulated fields—usually some numeric, computer-oriented field such as a word or doubleword, or a computer memory address, to facilitate subsequent references.

The transformation from the "natural" field to the hash address is a one-way process; however, the natural field cannot be decoded or reconstructed from the hash. The hashed field also might not necessarily represent only one unique natural field, because many natural fields could hash to the same value. Ideally, the hashing scheme would convert the original keys to transformed keys with no duplicates. While schemes can be constructed to minimize collisions, or a *hash clash*, their possibility cannot be completely eliminated and the original key should be stored along with the newly computed hash value.

One simple hashing scheme is the division-remainder method. Here, you choose a number close to the number of table positions needed. Use that number as a divisor to extract a quotient and a remainder from the dividend (which is the original key). The remainder so obtained is the transformed key.

Other schemes are *folding* and *digit rearrangement*. Folding consists of splitting the original key into two or more parts, then adding the parts together or (sometimes) using the exclusive OR operator. This sum, or some part of it, is then used as the transformed key. For example, using the key of 11,5234,9999, split and add 11 + 5234 + 9999 to get 15244. Discard the high-order digit of 1 to obtain the four-digit transformed key of 5244.

Digit rearrangement consists simply of selecting and shifting digits of the original key. For example, an original key of 123456 could be transformed to a four-digit key of 5432 by selecting digit positions 2 through 5 and reversing their order.

A hashing driver

HASHDRV (Program 9-4) demonstrates the hashing routine that is coded in the HASHING program. Strings to hash are entered in response to a query. The strings are passed to HASHING and then the returned hashed answer is printed.

A hashing program

HASHING (Program 9-5) is a procedure called by HASHDRV, which gives an example of a simple hashing routine. The method used is typical of many hashing algorithms. Perform some operation on the key to form it into a number within the range of a set of indices. As explained above, hash totals can be duplicated. There is no attempt in this example to avoid the duplication, which you would want to take care of in your main-line program.

ES:DI points to an ASCIIZ string to be hashed and CX has the maximum length of the strings to be hashed. The string is obtained from HASHDRV. The first two bytes and the last byte of the string are combined to form a word that is multiplied by the length. The result is divided by 8 and ANDed against 511 to form the hash value. AX returns a hashed value in the range 0–511, which represents the string.

Sorting

Sorting is generally understood to be the process of rearranging a given set of objects in a specific order (usually ascending or descending). The purpose of sorting is to expedite the later search for members of the sorted set. (See the binary search description and program in this chapter.) As such, sorting is an almost universally performed, fundamental activity. It's estimated that sorting occupies about 25 percent of all computer time. Objects are sorted in telephone books, tables of contents, dictionaries, warehouse inventories—and so on, wherever objects must be searched and retrieved.

There aren't many techniques that do not occur somewhere in connection with sorting algorithms. In particular, sorting is an ideal subject with which to demonstrate a great diversity of algorithms, all having the same purpose and many being optimal in some sense, and most having advantages over others. The primary requirement for sorting is an economical use of available storage.

There are several factors that influence the effectiveness of a sorting algorithm, which is why there is no best sorting algorithm for all situations. Some of the factors are:

- The number of records to be sorted.
- Whether or not all records fit into available internal memory.
- The degree to which the records are already sorted.
- The type of storage media on which the records are sorted.
- The complexity and storage requirements of the sorting algorithm.

Sorting methods generally are classified into two categories: arrays and files. The two classes are often called internal and external sorting because arrays are stored in the fast, high-speed, random-access internal store of computers, while files are located on the slower, but more spacious external stores, such as disks.

The importance of this internal/external distinction is obvious from an example of sorting a deck of cards. Structuring the cards as an array corresponds to laying them out in front of the sorter so that each card is visible and individually accessible. Structuring them as a file implies that from each pile only the card on the top is visible. Such a restriction has serious consequences on the sorting method to be used, but is unavoidable if the number of cards to be laid out is larger than the available table.

As previously stated, the major requirement for sorting arrays is an economical use of available storage. This implies that the permutation of items that brings the array contents into order is performed in situ, and that methods that transport items from an input array to a result array are intrinsically of minor interest.

Efficiency is obtained by counting the numbers of needed comparisons and moves (transportation) of items. These numbers are a function of the total number of items to be sorted. Sorting methods in situ are classified into three principal categories: sorting by insertion, sorting by selection, and sorting by exchange.

Sorting by straight insertion is widely used by card players. The items (cards) are conceptually divided into a destination sequence and a source sequence. In each step, the Xth element of the source is picked and transferred into the destination sequence by inserting it at the appropriate place. Sorting by selection is based on the following principles: first, select the item with the least key value; second, exchange it with the first item; finally, repeat these operations until only one item, the largest, is left. Straight selection considers all items in the source array to find the one with the least key and to be deposited as the one next item of the destination sequence.

Sorting by straight exchange is based on the principle of comparing and exchanging pairs of adjacent items until all items are sorted. As with the previous methods of sorting, we make repeated passes over the array, each time sifting the least item of the remaining set to the left end of the array. If we view the array in a vertical instead of horizontal position, the items can be bubbles in water with weights according to their keys. Each pass over the array results in the ascension of a bubble to its appropriate level of weight. This method is widely known as the *bubble sort*. It is also the slowest and will not be shown in this book as there are many examples already existing. We do show two of the fastest: the shell sort (for variable-length records), and the quicksort (for fixed-length records).

The sorting driver program

The sorting driver, SORTDRV (Program 9-6), demonstrates the binary search and the QSORT (Quicksort) routines. The driver has a pre-built test case in it. It builds an array of items that are created in such a fashion that they go across a pseudo-segment boundary. The routine that locates records in multiple segments gets exercised without having to build a truly multiple-segment database.

SORTDRV points to the array descriptor, builds the segment-pointer portion of a standard-array descriptor, points to the array descriptor and calls QSORT. When QSORT returns, the standard array and the sorted array are both printed. The reason SORTDRV can do this is that SORTDRV uses the indirect pointers returned from QSORT.

After that, SORTDRV loops asking for entry of keys. It then uses a binary-search routine to locate the desired target within the sorted list. Try SORTDRV and experiment with it.

Shell sort

Shell sort, SHELLSRT (Program 9-7), sorts variable-length strings. SHELLSRT is a more compact implementation than QSORT, but is not as fast. It does not show evidence of degenerate cases, which Quicksort algorithms can have. SHELLSRT uses the STRZCOMP (see chapter 6) routine because of the ASCIIZ strings. SHELLSRT is a "straight vanilla" algorithm.

DS:BX points to an array of displacements into a string area. All strings are assumed to be standard ASCIIZ strings. CX holds the count of strings to sort. A distance of CX/2 is used for the first pass of compares. Elements of the array are compared and exchanged if the value of the lower indexed element is greater than the higher. When all pairs of the given distance have been compared, the distance is halved and the process is repeated until the distance is zero.

On output, SHELLSRT returns an array (of displacements into the string area) that is in alphabetic sequence.

Quicksort

Quicksort (invented by C.A.R. Hoare) is based on exchanges preferably being performed over large distances in order to be most effective. Assume N items are given in reverse order of their keys. It is possible to sort them by performing only N/2 exchanges, first taking the leftmost and the rightmost and gradually progressing inward from both sides. Naturally, this is possible only if we know that their order is exactly inverse.

The Quicksort algorithm is as follows: Pick any item at random and call it X. Scan the array from the left until an item of greater value than X is found. Then scan from the right until an item of less value than X is found. Now exchange the two items and continue this scan and swap process until the two scans meet somewhere in the middle of the array. The result is that the array is now partitioned into a left part with keys less than (or equal to) X and a right part with keys greater than (or equal to) X.

After partitioning the array, apply the same process to both partitions, then to the partitions of the partitions and so on, until every partition consists of a single item only.

To do a Quicksort, we first select a bound X, which sweeps the entire array. Therefore, exactly N comparisons are performed. With a fixed bound X, the expected number of exchange operations is equal to the number of elements in the left part of the partition, namely N – 1, multiplied by the probability that such an element reached its place by an exchange.

The crucial step is the selection of the comparand X. Hoare suggests that the choice of X be made at random, or by selecting it as the median of a small sample of, say, three keys. (This is the method we used in our implementation of Quicksort.) The median of N items is defined as that item which is less than or equal to half of the N items and which is larger than or equal to the other half of the N items. For example, the median of the string of numbers [16 12 99 95 18 87 10] is 18. The problem of finding the median is customarily connected with that of sorting because the obvious method of determining the median is to sort the N items and then to pick the item in the middle. But partitioning yields a potentially much faster way of finding the median.

Sorting is not useful if the data does not fit into a computer's main storage, but it is if some of the data comes from an external file. In this case, we describe the data as a sequential file whose characteristic is that at each moment one and only one component is directly accessible. This is a severe restriction compared to the possibilities offered by the array structure, and therefore different sorting techniques have to be used. The most important one is sorting by merging.

Merging (or collating) means combining two or more ordered sequences into a single, ordered sequence by repeated selection among

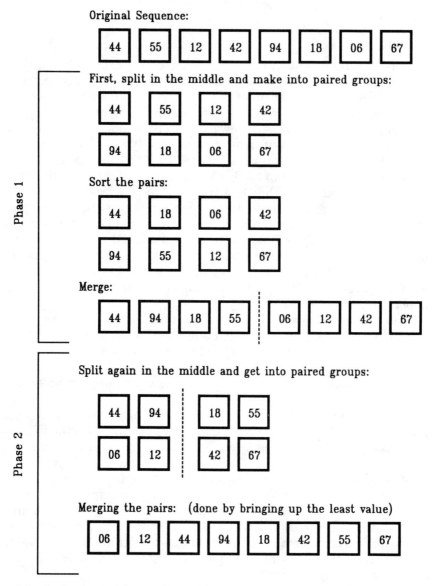

9-4 Sorting by straight merging.

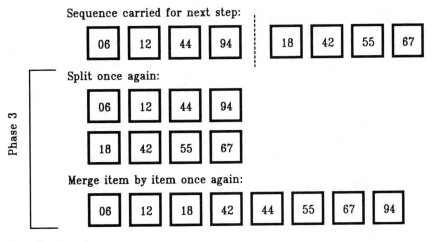

Sequence carried for next step:

| 06 | 12 | 44 | 94 | 18 | 42 | 55 | 67 |

Phase 3

Split once again:

| 06 | 12 | 44 | 94 |

| 18 | 42 | 55 | 67 |

Merge item by item once again:

| 06 | 12 | 18 | 42 | 44 | 55 | 67 | 94 |

9-4 Continued.

the currently accessible components. Merging is a much simpler operation than sorting, and it is used as an auxiliary operation in the more complex process of sequential sorting. One way of sorting on the basis of merging is called *straight merging*. Straight merging works by first splitting the sequence A into two halves called B and C. Then B and C are merged by combining single items into ordered pairs. Steps one and two are repeated, this time merging ordered pairs into ordered quadruples. The previous steps are repeated yet again, merging quadruples into octets. The process continues doing this, each time doubling the lengths of the merged sequences, until the entire sequence is ordered.

Each operation that treats the entire set of data once is called a *phase*, and the smallest subprocess that by repetition constitutes the sort process is called a *pass* or *stage*. Figure 9-4 shows an example of this sorting by straight merging.

QSORT (Program 9-8) supplies an implementation of the Quicksort algorithm, which is one of the fastest of the minimum-core sorts. It can degenerate to a slow sort, however, depending on how the partitions are decided upon. This implementation attempts to avoid that by taking any partition that is at size 4 or greater and taking the median of the left, center, and right key as a comparison value as a pivot point. If the partition is 3 or less, the median-taking operation simply sorts the partition so you don't have to worry about it. Care is taken to stack the largest of the partitions and sort the shortest of the partitions.

QSORT uses the comparison of a fixed-length key; it assumes a fixed-length record in its index calculations but not in the elementary algorithm of the sort. QSORT could be modified fairly easily to work off the same type of array that the shell sort (SHELLSRT) algorithm does.

QSORT provides an example of the 80486 Scale Index Byte type of addressing (see appendix C) in the way QSORT uses the indirect array. Notice the way it exchanges the index values.

DS:BX points to a standard-array descriptor. DS:SI points to an index array. The index array is initialized with sequential index values. This indirection is done because exchanging index values is faster than exchanging records that might be very large. The Quicksort algorithm is then applied using the indirection of the index array. On output, the index array contains pointers to records with ascending key values. Neither the array descriptor nor the record array is changed.

The way QSORT is implemented uses the 80486's stack instead of an array. This is a non-recursive implementation, but it uses the natural stacking of the 80486—as opposed to separate arrays for indices in the stack partition.

In QSORT, there are two comparison routines and a procedure to compute a usable array element address. The first, COMPARE, compares two keys together (needed for getting the median key value of the keys) with a compare of the pivot element, PIVOTC. The pivot element never changes during the partitioning operation.

The sort operates by splitting a large partition into two partitions, one having nothing but key values less than or equal to the pivot key and the other having keys larger than the pivot key. The pivot compare doesn't have to compute the index of the pivot, so it gets away "cheaper" that way. COMPARE, PIVOTC, and ARRANDXP are explained more fully in the next three paragraphs.

COMPARE compares the key in the record at SI(AX) to the key in the record at this location:

[SI(CX) key (SI(AX)) − key(SI(CX))]

It returns with the flags set. The usage is such that a call to COMPARE is followed by a conditional jump using the flag settings. The key as used in the demo program is a Social Security Number with dashes, 000-00-0000, for instance. This is the first field in the record.

PIVOTC compares to the pivot element. It's similar to the COMPARE, but assumes that the segment and offset for the pivot are set in ES:DI. Thus, the comparison is always A(SI(AX)):pivot.

ARRANDXP computes a usable array element address. This is required for accessing elements of large arrays (over 64K) in a USE16 task. It is a modification of the full routine described later in this chapter. AX has the index of the array element (1 . . LAST) desired and BX has the segment array pointer. The DS array is assumed to be of the form built by the ARRABLDP.ASM routine. AX is decremented to get a zero base and DX is zeroed. DX − AX is divided by the number of elements per segment. The quotient is multiplied by 2 and used to select the ES value. The remainder is multiplied by the element size and becomes the SI value. On return, SI has the displacement to the record and AX has the segment register value.

One additional thing that QSORT makes use of is one of the 80486 segment registers, GS. It turns out that a third segment base (GS) made it much easier.

Array manipulation and indexing

The array is probably the most widely known data structure. An array consists of a series of items arranged in a meaningful pattern. The array is also a random-access structure; all components can be selected at random and are equally accessible. In order to point to an individual component, the name of the entire structure is augmented by an index selecting the component, as shown in Fig. 9-5.

The handy thing about an index is that it can be computed—a general index expression can be substituted in place of an index constant. This

Visual Concept of an Array:

Columns =	1	2	3	4	5
Rows = 1	1,1	1,2	1,3	1,4	1,5
2	2,1	2,2	2,3	2,4	2,5
3	3,1	3,2	3,3	3,4	3,5
4	4,1	4,2	4,3	4,4	4,5

This same array, stored with a row-major method:

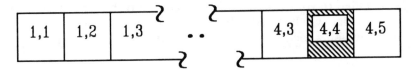

Now the array is stored in a column-major method:

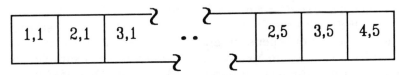

9-5 Conceptual image versus actual storage of an array.

expression is evaluated and the result identifies (points to) the selected component. This generality not only provides a powerful programming facility, but at the same time it also gives rise to one of the most frequently encountered mistakes: the resulting computation is outside the interval specified as the range of indices of the array, in which case you get a BOUNDS exception. Furthermore, when you calculate indices you have to know a basic fact: Is the array stored by rows or columns? For instance, the array position 4,4 (stored in a row-major method) will be at a different location in memory than the same 4,4 that's stored in a column-major method.

The common way of operating with arrays, particularly large ones, is to selectively update single components of the array rather than to construct entirely new structured values. Although selective updating causes only a single component value to change, from a conceptual point of view we regard the entire composite value as having changed, too.

We have provided some routines in this section to take care of a problem that OS/2 does not solve. That is, OS/2 requires that you run in a USE16 partition, which keeps you from using the extended addressing capabilities and the large segment size of the 80486. The build routine gets from MS-DOS or OS/2 blocks of memory that are nearly a full segment in size and builds a table of segment descriptors for building the arrays.

An array driver program

An array driver program, ARRADRV (Program 9-9), drives the array building and indexing procedures. You are prompted for an element size and a number of elements. The program then calls ARRABLDP to get the memory and fill in the ARRADESC structure. The structure is displayed in hex. The program then prompts for element numbers to locate; it displays the resulting segment and displacement into that segment in hex.

Note: Under MS-DOS using Microsoft's linker, you must link with the option /CP:*nnnn*, where *nnnn* is the maximum number of paragraphs to be allocated to your program. If it is less than the size of the program, the program size will be used. This option overrides the default memory allocation, which allocates all free memory to your program.

Building an array larger than 64K

ARRABLDP (Program 9-10) provides a means to build an array that exceeds the size of a single segment (64K). BX points to the structure ARRADESC with the fields *ndxmax* and *elesize* set. First, the maximum number of elements per segment is computed. The size to get is computed (the MS-DOS Allocate Memory call is used in the example, so the size is rounded up to the nearest paragraph). The number of segments to get is computed, and we loop getting them until we either have them all or an error is returned.

The field *elepseg* is set and the DS array is filled in with segment descriptors for each section of the array. If an error occurs, the Carry Flag (CF) is set.

The ARRANDXP companion routine (Program 9-11) provides a way to compute an array element address. This is useful for accessing elements of large arrays and is an 80286 protected-mode routine. It is also usable in real mode on all 8086-family processors, and is usable on the 80486 in protected mode for USE16 tasks. (USE32 tasks, with 32-bit displacements available, normally get a segment of the array size and index it directly.) ARRANDXP uses the previously established array of segment descriptor values (as created by ARRABLDP) in computing the actual segment and offset of an individual record.

Both routines assume a fixed-length record. They provide a way around the annoying protected mode problem of overrunning segment boundaries.

Computing a usable 80486 array element address

ARRANDXR (Program 9-12) assumes you've obtained a large block of memory over a segment in size and that you have a segment beginning address. Given an index value, ARRANDXR returns to you a new segment pointer and a displacement into that segment, which allows you to access the entire record without quietly wrapping around the original segment. The 80486 won't allow this wrap-around in protected mode (neither will the 80286 or the 80386), but in real mode, the segments wrap—which can be very surprising if you aren't expecting it.

AX has the index of the array element (1 . . LAST), BX has the DS value for element 1. CX has the element size in bytes and DX has the offset of element 1. The element index is converted into a byte offset into the array [(index − 1) × size]. The array offset is added to the result and the carry (if any) is propagated to DX. This gives you the byte offset from the array's segment descriptor. The lower bits of the result form the element's offset in SI. The total offset is divided by 16 and added to the segment's descriptor to form the descriptor for ES. We used shifts instead of a divide for speed (taking about a third of the time). On return, ES has the segment descriptor and SI the offset (015) of addressing the desired element.

Miscellaneous routines

The following routines do a number of things. Let's take a few examples as to why these routines might be useful. For instance, if you're designing large programs and/or large databases, you might need to know your configuration (or the configuration of your end user, which can be vastly different from the system on which you designed your code). Second, if you move data from one storage medium to another, you'll need to know if your destination drive has sufficient free space to contain the new data. Finally, you might be designing a graphics package where you want the screen display to pause to allow your user to see and understand what's happening.

Determining host system configuration

For many systems, the amount of memory on the system board and the number of peripherals are encoded in two bytes stored at address 410 hex in the BIOS data area. You can find out what it says by either reading the two bytes directly or by using BIOS Interrupt 11. In most systems, INT 11 returns the information in the AX register. Figure 9-6 identifies the bits. When you purchase your system, you should receive material that tells you what your BIOS interrupts do and how they interact.

FIND__CFG (Program 9-13) does several things. First it uses INT 21 Function 2A to get the date, which it prints after using CODEBAS (see chapter 7) to convert the binary characters to printable ASCII. Then it uses INT 11 (equipment determination), which returns bits in the AX register.

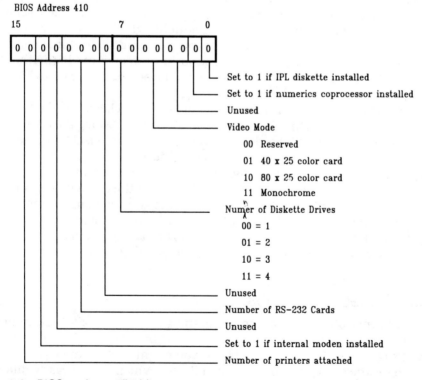

9-6   BIOS equipment list bits.

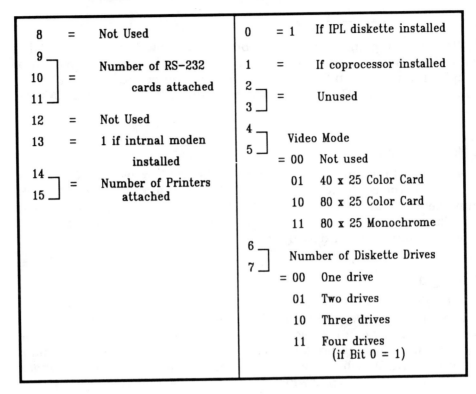

9-7 AX register bits after INT 11.

Those bits are broken down as shown in Fig. 9-7. FIND_CFG uses Interrupt 21 Function 19 to find the default drive, which it prints. One of the things you can examine is how FIND_CFG sets up arrays of fixed-length messages and uses bits to index into the correct messages.

Note that FIND_CFG also uses INT 21 Function 2A to get the date and calls CODEBAS to turn the binary digits into printable ASCII. FIND_CFG also uses INT 21 Function 19 to find out the default drive.

Free bytes on a disk drive

GET_FREE (Program 9-14) asks which drive (and gives you a choice of three) that it is to check for available space. Once you input the drive number, it calls CODEASB to convert the typed ASCII into binary. It then uses INT 21 Function 36, which returns number of sectors per cluster, the number of bytes per sector, and the number of available clusters. Multiply those values together and you have (in binary) the number of free bytes.

GET_FREE then uses CODEBAS to convert the binary to printable ASCII and prints the results to the screen. After assembly, GET_FREE was linked with CODEASB and CODEBAS.

Checking for a coprocessor

FIND_COP (Program 9-15) was run on an 80386 system built especially for us. The engineers installed an 80287 numeric coprocessor. There are a couple of ways you can find out if a numerics coprocessor is installed on your system. FIND_CFG does it one way, while FIND_COP uses INT 21 Function 14.

Determining the DOS version

FIND_VER (Program 9-16) determines the version of MS-DOS that's installed on the computer. Interrupt 21 Function 30 returns the MS-DOS number. The major version of the number (e.g., the 3 of 3.10) returns in AL. The minor version (e.g., the 10 of 3.10) returns in AH. Note that this function of Interrupt 21 destroys registers BX and CX.

Making a program wait

The PAUSE procedure (Program 9-17) provides a means of pausing from 0.02 seconds to 59.99 seconds. The system clock does not increment smoothly but in "clumps," so the granularity within PAUSE is not to the hundredths. A calling program passes parameters of seconds and hundredths to PAUSE, which edits them for conformance to the value range.

When you call this procedure, store the number of seconds to delay in DH and the number of hundredths to DL. The seconds and hundredths are edited for conformance with their value range (059 in DH, and 099 in DL, with DX less than 1). If invalid, the Carry Flag is set and the procedure returns. If valid, the procedure delays for the desired length of time and returns with Carry Flag = 0.

A driver for the PAUSE program

CHKPAUSE (Program 9-18) provides a simple visual check of the PAUSE routine. It displays a tick, calls PAUSE for a 0.5 second delay, then flips to tock. It repeats this 200 times.

Finding a computer's name

Most PCs currently on the market identify themselves in a one-byte identification in location F000:FFFE, the penultimate location in regular memory. PCNAME (Program 9-19) reads that location and indexes into an array that converts the answer into the name. The array is set up to contain:

- FF = Original PC
- FE = PC XT
- FD = PC Jr.
- FC = PC AT

When the program assembles, the data segment is set into DS, the data segment pointer register. The location 0F000 is moved into BX and from there to DS, which changes the data segment pointer to F000. Then the offset is loaded into BX and the contents of that address moved into AL.

A random number generator

RANDNUM (Program 9-20) generates a random number between 0 and 1. The program gets the time of day and uses the hundredths of a second as a key. It then rotates the answer three times (an arbitrary design decision). Then it calls CODEBAS (see chapter 7) to turn the resultant binary into a printable ASCII.

Calculating square roots

The following procedure calculates the square root by following Newton's Method, which says that if A is an approximation for the square root of a number N, then $A1 = (N/A + A)/2$ is a better guess. To get the first approximation, the routine uses $(N/200) + 2$, where N is the contents of DX:AX and the value 200 is arbitrary. To get the next approximation, the program divides N by the first and averages the two. For the third, it divides N by the second approximation and averages again. This repeats until it finds two that are identical (or differ only by 1, whether positive or negative).

After input of the number (any number up to 9,999,999), it is multiplied by 100 to get some decimal precision. On return, DS:BX holds the square root. The routine hard codes a single decimal figure and prints the figure with the decimal point.

Program 9-1   BNSEARCH

Microsoft (R) Macro Assembler Version 5.00

```
                              PAGE    55,132
                              .386
0000                   code   SEGMENT para 'CODE' USE16 PUBLIC
                              ASSUME  CS:code, DS:code, SS:code
                       ;
                       ; Name;    BNSEARCH
                       ;
                       ; Purpose: The following procedure implements the binary search
                       ;          algorithm.
                       ;
                       ;
                       ;
```

```
                    ; Inputs:   BX points to an array description.  SI points to an array
                    ;           of index elements which provide a set of ordered pointers
                    ;           to the keys to be searched.  DI points to the key to locate.
                    ;
                    ; Process: The binary search algorithm searches an ordered array.
                    ;           The initial partition has 1 as its left index and the
                    ;           maximum as its right index.  The algorithm computes the
                    ;           index of the center of the partition as (left+right)/2.
                    ;           The center is compared to the target.  If the target is
                    ;           equal to the center, we have found our match.  If the
                    ;           target is greater, a new left limit is set as center+1
                    ;           otherwise a new right limit is set as center-1.  If the
                    ;           indices cross there is no match in the array, otherwise
                    ;           we repeat.
                    ;
                    ; Output:   ES:DI will point to the record located and the zero flag
                    ;           will be set if the record was located.
                    ;
                    ;
                    ;
                    ;
                         arradesc  STRUC
0000  0000             ndxmax    dw        0           ; Maximum element index
0002  0000             elesize   dw        0           ; Size of an element
0004  0000             elepseg   dw        0           ; Elements per segment
0006  0000             elesegs   dw        0           ; First element of the DS
                    ;                                      array.  Further elements
                    ;                                      follow sequentially.
0008                   arradesc  ENDS
                    ;
                    ;
                    ;
                         PUBLIC    Bnsearch            ; Make the name usable
0000                   Bnsearch  PROC
0000  66| 52            push      EDX                  ; Save entry registers
0002  66| 51            push      ECX
0004  66| 50            push      EAX
0006  66| 56            push      ESI
0008  66| 55            push      EBP
000A  66| B8 0000FFFF    mov      EAX,0000ffffh        ; Get mask
0010  66| 23 F0          and      ESI,EAX              ; and ensure high bytes clear
0013  66| 23 F8          and      EDI,EAX
0016  66| 8B EF          mov      EBP,EDI              ; Save search target's loc.
0019  66| 23 D8          and      EBX,EAX
001C  66| 23 C8          and      ECX,EAX
001F  66| 23 D0          and      EDX,EAX
0022  8B 0F              mov      CX, [BX].ndxmax      ; Get rightmost index
0024  BA 0001            mov      DX,1                 ; and leftmost.
0027               center:
0027  8B C2              mov      AX,DX                ; Prepare to get center
0029  03 C1              add      AX,CX                ; Left + right
002B  D1 E8              shr      AX,1                 ; div 2 gives the center
002D  E8 0050 R          call     Keycomp              ; Compare to the desired key
0030  0F 84 0045 R       je       Alldone             ; We have it
0034  0F 82 003E R       jb       toolow              ; Our
0038  8B D0              mov      DX,AX                ; Set left to center
003A  42                 inc      DX                  ; and add one.
003B  EB 04 90           jmp      checkend            ; See if we are done.
003E               toolow:
003E  8B C8              mov      CX,AX                ; set right to center
0040  49                 dec      CX                  ; less one.
0041               checkend:
0041  3B D1              cmp      DX,CX                ; Check if we have a miss
0043  76 E2              jna      center              ; if not - look again.
                    ;
                    ; We fall through with zero not set.  If we branch - it is set.
```

```
                                    ;
0045                                Alldone:
0045  66| 5D                                pop      EBP
0047  66| 5E                                pop      ESI
0049  66| 58                                pop      EAX
004B  66| 59                                pop      ECX
004D  66| 5A                                pop      EDX
004F  C3                                    ret                        ; and return.

                                    ;
                                    ; Compare to the desired key.  This assumes that the desired key is
                                    ; pointed to by DS:BP.  The index of the comparison element is in AX
                                    ; so the comparison is always A(SI(AX)):desired.
                                    ;
                                    ; This comparison routine is particularized for purposes of testing
                                    ; and demonstrating the algorithm.  The location of the key in a
                                    ; record is not necessarily at the beginning.  The length is not
                                    ; always 11.  Keys are not always character strings either, numbers
                                    ; both floating point and binary, are popular too.
                                    ;
                                    ; AX indexes the desired element on input.
                                    ; ES:DI points to the desired element on exit, the flags reflect the
                                    ; result of the key comparison.
                                    ;
0050                                Keycomp    PROC
0050  56                                   push     SI                 ; Save registers used
0051  50                                   push     AX
0052  51                                   push     CX
0053  48                                   dec      AX                 ; Get indices on zero base.
0054  67| 8B 0446                          mov      AX,WORD PTR [ESI+EAX*2] ; Get indirect index AX
0058  E8 006A R                            call     arrandxp           ; Get the record location AX
005B  57                                   push     DI                 ; First save the record's disp.
                                                                       ; Add key's displacement to DI
005C  8E C0                                mov      ES,AX              ; Set the base
005E  8B F5                                mov      SI,BP              ; Get key displacement in SI
0060  B9 000B                              mov      CX,11              ; Set count to compare
                                                                       ; This would also change.
0063  F3/ A6                               repz cmpsb                  ; Compare,
                                                                       ; (for character strings)
0065  5F                                   pop      DI                 ; Restore record's displacement
0066  59                                   pop      CX                 ; restore registers,
0067  58                                   pop      AX
0068  5E                                   pop      SI
0069  C3                                   ret                         ; and return.
006A                                Keycomp    ENDP
                                    ;
                                    ;
                                    ; Purpose: The following procedure provides a method for computing
                                    ;          a usable array element address.  This is required for
                                    ;          accessing elements of large arrays (over 64k bytes in
                                    ;          size) in a USE16 task.  It is a modification of the full
                                    ;          routine.
                                    ;
                                    ; Inputs:  AX has the index of the array element (1 .. LAST) desired.
                                    ;          BX has the segment array pointer.
                                    ;
                                    ;          The DS array is assumed to be of the form built by the
                                    ;          ARRABLDP.ASM routine.
                                    ;
                                    ; Process: AX is decremented to get a zero base and DX is zeroed.
                                    ;          DX-AX is divided by the number of elements per segment.
                                    ;          The quotient is multiplied by 2 and used to select the
                                    ;          ES value.  The remainder multiplied by the element size
                                    ;          becomes the DI value.
                                    ;
                                    ; Output:  DI has the displacement to the record.  AX has the segment
                                    ;          register value.
                                    ;
```

Program 9-1 Continued.

```
006A                      Arrandxp  PROC
006A  52                            push    DX              ; Save entry registers
006B  51                            push    CX
006C  53                            push    BX
006D  48                            dec     AX              ; Get index based on zero
006E  2B D2                         sub     DX,DX           ; Clear upper word of dividend
0070  F7 77 04                      div     [BX].elepseg    ; Divide by elements / segment
0073  8B C8                         mov     CX,AX           ; Save the quotient
0075  8B C2                         mov     AX,DX           ; Position the remainder
0077  F7 67 02                      mul     [BX].elesize    ; Get the element's offset
007A  8B F8                         mov     DI,AX           ; Into DI
007C  03 D9                         add     BX,CX           ; Add the quotient to BX
007E  03 D9                         add     BX,CX           ; twice to get the displacement
0080  8B 47 06                      mov     AX,[BX].elesegs ; of the descriptor.
0083  5B                            pop     BX              ; Restore the entry registers
0084  59                            pop     CX
0085  5A                            pop     DX
0086  C3                            ret                     ; and return.
0087                      Arrandxp  ENDP

0087                      Bnsearch  ENDP
0087                      code      ENDS
                                    END
```

Program 9-2   BUFFER

```
                          PAGE    55,132
                          .386
                          EXTRN   CODEBTHX:PROC
0000              STACK   SEGMENT 'STACK' STACK
0000  0064[              DW      100 DUP(?)
        ????
                  ]

00C8              STACK   ENDS

0000              CODE    SEGMENT para 'CODE' PUBLIC USE16
                          ASSUME  CS:CODE, DS:CODE, SS:STACK
                  ;
                  ; Name:       BUFFER
                  ;
                  ; Purpose:    This program gives a graphic demonstration of what a
                  ;             memory buffer looks like once it has been loaded with
                  ;             data.
                  ;
                  ; Inputs:     A string of characters is entered via the keyboard.
                  ;
                  ; Process:    A memory buffer is established.  Interrupt 21 Function
                  ;             0A (buffered keyboard entry) is used to capture the
                  ;             input into a memory buffer called INPUT_STR.  Then
                  ;             CODEBTHX is called to transform the binary memory into
                  ;             printable hex.
                  ;
                  ;             A note on the counts.  If you store 10 (meaning you want
                  ;             10 characters), you can only type 9 before the beep, since
                  ;             your count includes the 0D carriage return.  The count
                  ;             that DOS puts in does NOT count the 0D.  Therefore, if you
                  ;             want 10 characters in, your buffer must be 13 to hold the
                  ;             two auxiliary bytes and the carriage return along with your
                  ;             10 characters.
                  ;
                  ; Outputs:    A message and the contents of the buffer.
                  ;
                  ;
0000              BUFFER:
```

264   Algorithms

```
0000    8C C8                           MOV     AX,CS           ; Prepare to set DS
0002    8E D8                           MOV     DS,AX           ;   and set it.
0004    EB 52 90                        JMP     BEGINHERE
                            ;
0007    000D [             INPUT_STR    DB      13 DUP (?)
            ??
                        ]

0014    0A 0D 20 54 79 70 65  PROMPT    DB      0Ah,0Dh,' Type up to ten characters > $'
        20 75 70 20 74 6F 20
        74 65 6E 20 63 68 61
        72 61 63 74 65 72 73
        20 3E 20 24
0034    0A 0D 20 48 65 72 65  HEADER    DB      0Ah,0Dh,' Here is the memory buffer >$'
        20 69 73 20 74 68 65
        20 6D 65 6D 6F 72 79
        20 62 75 66 66 65 72
        20 3E 24
0053    0A 0D 24           CR_LF        DB      0Ah,0Dh,'$'
0056    20 24             BLANK         DB      ' $'
                            ;
0058                       BEGINHERE:
                            ;
0058    8D 16 0014 R                     LEA     DX,PROMPT       ; Print the prompt
005C    B4 09                            MOV     AH,9h
005E    CD 21                            INT     21h
0060    C6 06 0007 R 0B                  MOV     INPUT_STR,11    ; Max 10 chars input (see Prolog)
0065    8D 16 0007 R                     LEA     DX,INPUT_STR    ; Point at buffer
0069    B4 0A                            MOV     AH,0Ah          ; Buffered keyboard input
006B    CD 21                            INT     21h
                            ;
006D    8D 16 0053 R                     LEA     DX,CR_LF        ; Space up a line
0071    B4 09                            MOV     AH,9
0073    CD 21                            INT     21h
                            ;
                            ;       Convert the binary bytes to printable hex by calling CODEHXTB.
                            ;       CODEHXTB requires:
                            ;       AL = the byte to be converted
                            ;       If successful, Carry Flag = 0
                            ;               AH = Left nibble
                            ;               AL = Right nibble
                            ;       If not, Carry Flag = 1
                            ;
0075    8D 16 0034 R                     LEA     DX,HEADER       ; Print the header
0079    B4 09                            MOV     AH,9
007B    CD 21                            INT     21h
                            ;
007D    2B C0                            SUB     AX,AX           ; Clear out AX
007F    2B C9                            SUB     CX,CX           ; Also CX
0081    BF 0000                          MOV     DI,0            ; Index through INPUT_STR
0084                       CONVERT:
0084    8A 85 0007 R                     MOV     AL,BYTE PTR INPUT_STR[DI]
0088    E8 0000 E                        CALL    CODEBTHX        ; Convert to printable hex
                            ;
008B    2B D2                            SUB     DX,DX           ; Clear out DX
008D    8B D8                            MOV     BX,AX           ; Save the byte, AX used to print
008F    8A D7                            MOV     DL,BH           ; Left nibble
0091    B4 02                            MOV     AH,2            ; Print it
0093    CD 21                            INT     21h
0095    8A D3                            MOV     DL,BL           ; Right nibble
0097    CD 21                            INT     21h             ; Print it
0099    8D 16 0056 R                     LEA     DX,BLANK        ; Print a space between bytes
009D    B4 09                            MOV     AH,9
009F    CD 21                            INT     21h
00A1    47                               INC     DI              ; Go to next byte
00A2    83 FF 0D                         CMP     DI,13           ; Done?
00A5    0F 84 00AB R                     JE      ENDHERE         ; Yes, go end program
00A9    EB D9                            JMP     CONVERT
                            ;
```

Program 9-2 Continued.

```
00AB                          ENDHERE:
00AB  8D 16 0053 R                      LEA     DX,CR_LF        ; Space up one line
00AF  B4 09                             MOV     AH,9
00B1  CD 21                             INT     21h
                              ;
00B3  B4 4C                             MOV     AH,4Ch          ; Standard Ending
00B5  CD 21                             INT     21h
00B7                          CODE      ENDS
                                        END     BUFFER
```

Program 9-3 ENCRYPT

Microsoft (R) Macro Assembler Version 5.00

```
                              PAGE    55,132
                              .386
                              EXTRN   CODEBTHX:PROC
0000                          STACK   SEGMENT 'STACK' STACK

0000  0064[                           DW      100 DUP(?)
         ????
                       ]

00C8                          STACK   ENDS
0000                          CODE    SEGMENT para 'CODE' PUBLIC USE16
                                      ASSUME  CS:CODE, DS:CODE, SS:STACK
                              ;
                              ; Name:     ENCRYPT
                              ;
                              ; Purpose:  This program takes an input string and uses a Caesar
                              ;           Cipher (add 1) to encrypt the input characters. Then it
                              ;           gives a graphic demonstration of what the characters
                              ;           looks like once they have been changed.
                              ;
                              ;           Then the characters are decrypted (subtract 1) and
                              ;           displayed.
                              ;
                              ; Inputs:   A string of characters is entered via the keyboard.
                              ;
                              ; Process:  A memory buffer is established. Interrupt 21 Function
                              ;           0A (buffered keyboard entry) is used to capture the
                              ;           input into a memory buffer called INPUT_STR. The
                              ;           characters are encrypted. Then CODEBTHX is called to
                              ;           transform the binary memory into printable hex.
                              ;
                              ;           A note on the counts. If you store 10 (meaning you want
                              ;           10 characters), you can only type 9 before the beep, since
                              ;           your count includes the 0D carriage return. The count
                              ;           that DOS puts in does NOT count the 0D. Therefore, if you
                              ;           want 10 characters in, your buffer must be 13 to hold the
                              ;           two auxiliary bytes and the carriage return along with your
                              ;           10 characters.
                              ;
                              ; Outputs:  A message and the contents of the buffer.
                              ;
0000                          ENCRYPT:
0000  8C C8                             MOV     AX,CS           ; Prepare to set DS
0002  8E D8                             MOV     DS,AX           ;   and set it.
0004  E9 0099 R                         JMP     BEGINHERE
                              ;
0007  000D[                   INPUT_STR DB      13 DUP (?)
         ??
                       ]
```

```
0014  0A 0D 20 54 79 70 65   PROMPT      DB      0Ah,0Dh,' Type up to ten characters > $'
      20 75 70 20 74 6F 20
      74 65 6E 20 63 68 61
      72 61 63 74 65 72 73
      20 3E 20 24
0034  0A 0D 20 50 72 69 6F   HEADER0     DB      0Ah,0Dh,' Prior to encryption       > $'
      72 20 74 6F 20 65 6E
      63 72 79 70 74 69 6F
      6E 20 20 20 20 20 20
      20 3E 20 24
0054  0A 0D 20 54 68 65 20   HEADER1     DB      0Ah,0Dh,' The encrypted characters  > $'
      65 6E 63 72 79 70 74
      65 64 20 63 68 61 72
      61 63 74 65 72 73 20
      20 3E 20 24
0074  0A 0D 20 54 68 65 20   HEADER2     DB      0Ah,0Dh,' The decrypted characters  > $'
      64 65 63 72 79 70 74
      65 64 20 63 68 61 72
      61 63 74 65 72 73 20
      20 3E 20 24
0094  0A 0D 24              CR_LF       DB      0Ah,0Dh,'$'
0097  20 24                BLANK       DB      ' $'
                           ;
0099                       BEGINHERE:
                           ;
0099  8D 16 0014 R                     LEA     DX,PROMPT       ; Print the prompt
009D  B4 09                            MOV     AH,9h
009F  CD 21                            INT     21h
00A1  C6 06 0007 R 0B                  MOV     INPUT_STR,11    ; Max 10 chars input (see Prolog)
00A6  8D 16 0007 R                     LEA     DX,INPUT_STR    ; Point at buffer
00AA  B4 0A                            MOV     AH,0Ah          ; Buffered keyboard input
00AC  CD 21                            INT     21h
                           ;
00AE  8D 16 0094 R                     LEA     DX,CR_LF        ; Space up a line
00B2  B4 09                            MOV     AH,9
00B4  CD 21                            INT     21h
                           ;
00B6  8D 16 0034 R                     LEA     DX,HEADER0      ; Print the header
00BA  B4 09                            MOV     AH,9
00BC  CD 21                            INT     21h
00BE  E8 0106 R                        CALL    PRINT           ; Internal procedure
                           ;
                           ; Encrypt the characters by adding a binary 1 to them
                           ;
00C1  2B C9                            SUB     CX,CX
00C3  8A 0E 0008 R                     MOV     CL,BYTE PTR INPUT_STR[1] ; Number of chars entered
00C7  8D 3E 0007 R                     LEA     DI,INPUT_STR    ; Point at the first character
00CB  83 C7 02                         ADD     DI,2            ; Skip the two aux bytes
00CE                       ENCRY:
00CE  8A 05                            MOV     AL,BYTE PTR [DI]
00D0  04 01                            ADD     AL,1
00D2  88 05                            MOV     BYTE PTR [DI],AL
00D4  47                               INC     DI
00D5  E2 F7                            LOOP    ENCRY
                           ;
00D7  8D 16 0054 R                     LEA     DX,HEADER1      ; Print the header
00DB  B4 09                            MOV     AH,9
00DD  CD 21                            INT     21h
                           ;
00DF  E8 0106 R                        CALL    PRINT
                           ;
                           ; Decrypt the characters by subtracting a binary 1 to them
                           ;
00E2  2B C9                            SUB     CX,CX
00E4  8A 0E 0008 R                     MOV     CL,BYTE PTR INPUT_STR[1] ; Number of chars entered
00E8  8D 3E 0007 R                     LEA     DI,INPUT_STR    ; Point at the first character
00EC  83 C7 02                         ADD     DI,2            ; Skip the two aux bytes
```

```
00EF                          DECRY:
00EF   8A 05                            MOV     AL,BYTE PTR [DI]
00F1   2C 01                            SUB     AL,1
00F3   88 05                            MOV     BYTE PTR [DI],AL
00F5   47                               INC     DI
00F6   E2 F7                            LOOP    DECRY
                              ;
00F8   8D 16 0074 R                     LEA     DX,HEADER2      ; Print the header
00FC   B4 09                            MOV     AH,9
00FE   CD 21                            INT     21h
                              ;
0100   E8 0106 R                        CALL    PRINT
0103   EB 2D 90                         JMP     ENDHERE
                              ;
                              ;   Convert the binary bytes to printable hex by calling CODEHXTB.
                              ;   CODEHXTB requires:
                              ;   AL = the byte to be converted
                              ;   If successful, Carry Flag = 0
                              ;                  AH = Left nibble
                              ;                  AL = Right nibble
                              ;   If not, Carry Flag = 1
                              ;
0106                          PRINT     PROC
0106   2B C0                            SUB     AX,AX           ; Clear out AX
0108   2B C9                            SUB     CX,CX
010A   8A 0E 0008 R                     MOV     CL,BYTE PTR INPUT_STR[1]
010E   BF 0002                          MOV     DI,2            ; Index through INPUT_STR
0111                          PRINT0:
0111   8A 85 0007 R                     MOV     AL,BYTE PTR INPUT_STR[DI]
0115   E8 0000 E                        CALL    CODEBTHX        ; Convert to printable hex
                              ;
0118   2B D2                            SUB     DX,DX           ; Clear out DX
011A   8B D8                            MOV     BX,AX           ; Save the byte, AX used to print
011C   8A D7                            MOV     DL,BH           ; Left nibble
011E   B4 02                            MOV     AH,2            ; Print it
0120   CD 21                            INT     21h
0122   8A D3                            MOV     DL,BL           ; Right nibble
0124   CD 21                            INT     21h             ; Print it
0126   8D 16 0097 R                     LEA     DX,BLANK        ; Print a space between bytes
012A   B4 09                            MOV     AH,9
012C   CD 21                            INT     21h
012E   47                               INC     DI              ; Go to next byte
012F   E2 E0                            LOOP    PRINT0
                              ;
0131   C3                               RET
0132                          PRINT     ENDP
                              ;
0132                          ENDHERE:
0132   8D 16 0094 R                     LEA     DX,CR_LF        ; Space up one line
0136   B4 09                            MOV     AH,9
0138   CD 21                            INT     21h
                              ;
013A   B4 4C                            MOV     AH,4Ch          ; Standard Ending
013C   CD 21                            INT     21h
013E                          CODE      ENDS
                                        END     ENCRYPT
```

Program 9-4 HASHDRV

Microsoft (R) Macro Assembler Version 5.00

```
                          .386
                      ;
                      ; Name:    HASHDRV
                      ;
                      ; Purpose: This program demonstrates the hashing routine.
                      ;
                      ; Inputs:  Strings to hash are entered in response to the query.
                      ;
                      ; Process: The program requests a string to hash, passes it to
                      ;          the hashing routine and displays the resulting number.
                      ;
                      ; Outputs: The hash index is displayed.
                      ;
                      ;
                      ; Declare the routines we are going to use
                      ;
                              EXTRN    HASHING:PROC
                              EXTRN    CODEBAS:PROC

0000                  stack   SEGMENT para 'STACK' STACK
0000  0100[                   dq       256 DUP(?)
      ??????????????
      ?
                 ]

0800                  stack   ENDS
0000                  data    SEGMENT para
0000  0100[           string  db       256 DUP(?)              ; String scratch area
      ??
                 ]

0100  0A 0A 0D 45 6E 74 65     query   db       10,10,13,"Enter a string to hash: $"
      72 20 61 20 73 74 72
      69 6E 67 20 74 6F 20
      68 61 73 68 3A 20 24
011C  0A 0D 49 74 20 68 61     result  db       10,13,"It hashes to index $"
      73 68 65 73 20 74 6F
      20 69 6E 64 65 78 20
      24
0132                  data    ENDS
0000                  code    SEGMENT para 'CODE' USE16 PUBLIC
                              ASSUME   CS:code, DS:data
                      ;
                      ; Set up the environment
                      ;
0000                  Begin:
0000  B8 ---- R               mov      AX,data            ; Get data segment pointer
0003  8E D8                    mov      DS,AX              ; into DS,
0005  8E C0                    mov      ES,AX              ; and ES.
0007  2B F6                    sub      SI,SI              ; Clear indices
0009  2B FF                    sub      DI,DI
000B                  gethash:
000B  8D 16 0100 R             lea      DX,query           ; Get the string to hash
000F  E8 0040 R                call     getinp             ; From the keyboard
0012  E3 26                    jcxz     Exit               ; Empty string exits
0014  8B FB                    mov      DI,BX              ; Set the pointer
0016  B9 0064                  mov      CX,100             ; and an arbitrary length
0019  E8 0000 E                call     Hashing            ; Get a hash value
001C  66| 98                   cwde                        ; as a double word
001E  8D 3E 0000 R             lea      DI,string          ;
0022  E8 0000 E                call     Codebas            ; and convert it
0025  8D 16 011C R             lea      DX,result          ; point to header
0029  B4 09                    mov      AH,9
002B  CD 21                    int      21h                ; and put it out
002D  B4 02                    mov      AH,2
002F                  outnbr:
002F  8A 15                    mov      DL, BYTE PTR [DI]   ; get number
0031  47                       inc      DI
```

```
0032  0A D2                              or      DL,DL               ; are we at end?
0034  74 D5                              jz      gethash             ; Yes - try again
0036  CD 21                              int     21h
0038  EB F5                              jmp     outnbr              ; do another digit
003A                          Exit:
003A  B0 00                              mov     AL,0                ; Set return code
003C  B4 4C                              mov     AH,04ch             ; Set good-by
003E  CD 21                              int     21h                 ; Return to the system
                              ;
                              ; Read a string in response to a prompt
                              ; The prompt must be in DX.  The string will be returned in string.
                              ;
0040                          getinp  PROC
0040  50                              push    AX                  ; Save registers
0041  56                              push    SI
0042  B4 09                           mov     AH,9                ; and dos request
0044  CD 21                           int     21h                 ; put out the string
0046  8D 16 0000 R                    lea     DX,string           ; point to input area
004A  C6 06 0000 R FE                 mov     string,254          ; Set max length in
004F  B4 0A                           mov     AH,10               ; Ask for read of string
0051  CD 21                           int     21h                 ; from DOS.
0053  8D 1E 0002 R                    lea     BX,string+2         ; Point to just read data
0057  8A 0E 0001 R                    mov     CL,string+1         ; Get length read
005B  B5 00                           mov     CH,0                ; as a word.
005D  8B F1                           mov     SI,CX               ; Set length
005F  C6 84 0002 R 00                 mov     string+2[SI],0      ; and make an asciiz string.
0064  5E                              pop     SI
0065  58                              pop     AX                  ; Restore registers
0066  C3                              ret                         ; and return.
0067                          getinp  ENDP

0067                          code    ENDS
                                      END     Begin
```

```
                                      .386
0000                          code    SEGMENT para 'CODE' USE16 PUBLIC
                                      ASSUME  CS:code, DS:code, SS:code
                              ;
                              ; Name;  HASHING
                              ;
                              ; Purpose: The following procedure provides an instance of a hashing
                              ;          algorithm.
                              ;
                              ; Inputs:  ES:DI points to an asciiz string to be hashed.
                              ;          CX has the maximum length of strings to be hashed.
                              ;
                              ; Process: The string length is obtained.  The first two bytes
                              ;          and the last byte of the string are combined to form
                              ;          a word which is then multiplied by the length.  The result,
                              ;          divided by 8, is ANDed against 511 to form the hash value.
                              ;
                              ; Output:  AX returns a hashed value in the range 0-511 which
                              ;          represents the string.
                              ;
                              ; Note:    The method used here is typical of many hashing algorithms.
                              ;          Perform some operation on the key to form it into a number
                              ;          within the range of a set of indices.  Not shown here is
                              ;          the method used to handle items which hash to the same
                              ;          number.  Linked lists which are then searched sequentially
                              ;          can be headed by an index word at the hash index are one
                              ;          method.
                              ;
                                      PUBLIC  Hashing             ; Make the name usable
```

```
                                        EXTRN    STRZLNG:PROC
0000                       Hashing      PROC
0000    52                              push     DX                       ; Save entry registers
0001    51                              push     CX
0002    53                              push     BX
0003    E8 0000 E                       call     Strzlng                  ; Get the string's length.
0006    0F 83 000C R                    jnc      hashln                   ; If not oversize, use length
000A    8B C1                           mov      AX,CX                    ; Else use maximum.
000C                       hashln:
000C    0B C0                           or       AX,AX                    ; Zero length strings
000E    0F 84 0026 R                    jz       hashexit                 ; return a zero hash value.
0012    8B D8                           mov      BX,AX                    ; Save the length
0014    26: 8B 05                       mov      AX,ES:[DI]               ; Get the first two chars
0017    4B                              dec      BX                       ;
0018    26: 32 21                       xor      AH,BYTE PTR ES:[BX+DI] ; Fold in the last
001B    43                              inc      BX                       ; Get length back
001C    F7 E3                           mul      BX                       ;
001E    03 C2                           add      AX,DX
0020    C1 E8 03                        shr      AX,3                     ; and divide by 8
0023    25 01FF                         and      AX,01ffh                 ; Truncate to 0-511
0026                       hashexit:
0026    5B                              pop      BX
0027    59                              pop      CX
0028    5A                              pop      DX
0029    C3                              ret                               ; and return.
002A                       Hashing      ENDP
002A                       code         ENDS
                                        END
```

Program 9-6 SORTDRV

Microsoft (R) Macro Assembler Version 5.00

```
                                  PAGE     55,132
                                  .386

                       ;
                       ; Name:     SORTDRV
                       ;
                       ; Purpose: This program demonstrates the Quicksort and Binary search
                       ;          routines.
                       ;
                       ; Inputs:  The program has the array to be sorted within itself.
                       ;          Search arguments are prompted for.
                       ;
                       ; Process: We first set up a 'standard' array description used for
                       ;          arrays of fixed length records which contain too many
                       ;          elements to fit within a single 64K segment. We break
                       ;          our array artificially to test the ability of the sort
                       ;          and search to cross segment bounds. We then call the
                       ;          qsort routine and print both the original and ordered
                       ;          arrays. We then loop getting search targets, searching
                       ;          for them and reporting the results until a null target
                       ;          is entered.
                       ;
                       ; Outputs: All outputs are displayed.
                       ;
                       ;
                       ; Declare the routines we are going to use
                       ;
                                  EXTRN    BNSEARCH:PROC
                                  EXTRN    QSORT:PROC

0000                   stack      SEGMENT  para 'STACK' STACK
0000    0100[          dq         256 DUP(?)
```

Program 9-6 Continued.
```
                 ???????????????
                 ?
                                        ]

0800                            stack   ENDS
0000                            data    SEGMENT para
0000   0100[                    string  db      256 DUP(?)              ; String scratch area
         ??
                                        ]

0100   0A 0D 45 6E 74 65 72     query   db      10,13,"Enter an SSN to find: $"
       20 61 6E 20 53 53 4E
       20 74 6F 20 66 69 6E
       64 3A 20 24
0119   0A 0D 46 20 4F 20 55     found   db      10,13,"F O U N D  I T!! $"
       20 4E 20 44 20 20 49
       20 54 21 21 20 24
012D   0A 0D 4E 6F 74 20 74     notfound db     10,13,"Not there. $"
       68 65 72 65 2E 20 24
013B   0A 0D 24                 newline db      10,13,"$"
013E   20 20 20 20 20 20 24     spaces  db      "      $"
0145   90                               ALIGN   WORD
0146   0014                     arradesc dw     20                     ; Small test case
0148   000C                     elesize  dw     12                     ; Size
014A   0010                     elepseg  dw     16                     ; Count
014C   0000                     elesegs  dw     0                      ; filled in
014E   0000                              dw     0
0150   0014[                    indirect dw     20 DUP(?)              ; indirect array for sort
         ????
                                        ]

0178   90 90 90 90 90 90 90              ALIGN   16
       90
0180   30 39 39 2D 31 32 2D     sortit  db      "099-12-3452$"         ; 1
       33 34 35 32 24
018C   33 30 30 2D 32 32 2D             db      "300-22-3452$"         ; 2
       33 34 35 32 24
0198   33 30 30 2D 31 32 2D             db      "300-12-3452$"         ; 3
       33 34 35 32 24
01A4   32 30 30 2D 31 32 2D             db      "200-12-3452$"         ; 4
       33 34 35 32 24
01B0   33 31 30 2D 31 32 2D             db      "310-12-3452$"         ; 5
       33 34 35 32 24
01BC   33 30 31 2D 31 32 2D             db      "301-12-3452$"         ; 6
       33 34 35 32 24
01C8   30 31 30 2D 31 32 2D             db      "010-12-3452$"         ; 7
       33 34 35 32 24
01D4   33 31 31 2D 31 32 2D             db      "311-12-3452$"         ; 8
       33 34 35 32 24
01E0   30 32 30 2D 31 32 2D             db      "020-12-3452$"         ; 9
       33 34 35 32 24
01EC   32 30 30 2D 31 32 2D             db      "200-12-3451$"         ; 10
       33 34 35 31 24
01F8   32 31 30 2D 31 32 2D             db      "210-12-3452$"         ; 11
       33 34 35 32 24
0204   30 30 30 2D 31 32 2D             db      "000-12-3452$"         ; 12
       33 34 35 32 24
0210   34 30 30 2D 31 32 2D             db      "400-12-3452$"         ; 13
       33 34 35 32 24
021C   33 35 30 2D 31 32 2D             db      "350-12-3452$"         ; 14
       33 34 35 32 24
0228   32 32 30 2D 31 32 2D             db      "220-12-3452$"         ; 15
       33 34 35 32 24
0234   39 39 30 2D 31 32 2D             db      "990-12-3452$"         ; 16
       33 34 35 32 24
0240   39 30 30 2D 31 32 2D     sortit0 db      "900-12-3452$"         ; 17
       33 34 35 32 24
```

```
024C  30 35 30 2D 31 32 2D        db      "050-12-3452$"      ; 18
      33 34 35 32 24
0258  30 37 30 2D 31 32 2D        db      "070-12-3452$"      ; 19
      33 34 35 32 24
0264  31 30 30 2D 31 32 2D        db      "100-12-3452$"      ; 20
      33 34 35 32 24
0270  37 30 30 2D 31 32 2D        db      "700-12-3452$"      ; 21
      33 34 35 32 24
027C                      data    ENDS
0000                      code    SEGMENT para 'CODE' USE16 PUBLIC
                                  ASSUME  CS:code, DS:data
                          ;
                          ; Set up the environment
                          ;
0000                      Begin:
0000  B8 ---- R                   mov     AX,data             ; Get data segment pointer
0003  8E D8                       mov     DS,AX               ; into DS,
0005  8E C0                       mov     ES,AX               ; and ES.
0007  2B F6                       sub     SI,SI               ; Clear indices
0009  2B FF                       sub     DI,DI
000B  8D 1E 0146 R                lea     BX,arradesc         ; point to array descriptor
000F  8D 36 0150 R                lea     SI,indirect         ; and to indirect array
0013  8D 0E 0180 R                lea     CX,sortit           ; point to data to sort
0017  C1 E9 04                    shr     CX,4                ; make into a descriptor
001A  03 C8                       add     CX,AX               ;
001C  89 0E 014C R                mov     elesegs,CX          ; For the table
0020  8D 0E 0240 R                lea     CX,sortit0          ; Get second segment
0024  C1 E9 04                    shr     CX,4                ; as a descriptor
0027  03 C8                       add     CX,AX               ; in
0029  89 0E 014E R                mov     elesegs+2,CX        ; table
002D  E8 0000 E                   call    qsort               ; call the sort
0030  8B 0E 0146 R                mov     CX,arradesc         ; get the count to print
0034  8D 1E 0180 R                lea     BX,sortit           ; point to the data
0038  B4 09                       mov     AH,9                ; set DOS code
                          ;
                          ; Print the original and sorted arrays
                          ;
003A                      printit:
003A  8D 16 013B R                lea     DX,newline          ; Point to new line
003E  CD 21                       int     21h
0040  8B D3                       mov     DX,BX               ; point to key
0042  CD 21                       int     21h                 ; write it
0044  8D 16 013E R                lea     DX,spaces           ; and some white space
0048  CD 21                       int     21h
004A  03 1E 0148 R                add     BX,elesize          ; Step to next
004E  8B 04                       mov     AX,WORD PTR[SI]     ; Get index value
0050  48                          dec     AX                  ; based on zero
0051  F7 26 0148 R                mul     elesize             ; times size.
0055  83 C6 02                    add     SI,2                ; Next entry
0058  8D 16 0180 R                lea     DX,sortit           ;
005C  03 D0                       add     DX,AX               ; Get displacement of entry
005E  B4 09                       mov     AH,9                ; Set code
0060  CD 21                       int     21h                 ; and print it
0062  E2 D6                       loop    printit             ;
                          ;
                          ; Use the binary search routine to locate various keys.
                          ;
0064                      nextsch:
0064  8D 16 0100 R                lea     DX,query            ; point to query
0068  E8 0097 R                   call    getinp              ; and get a search target
006B  E3 24                       jcxz    Exit                ; A null response quits.
006D  83 F9 0B                    cmp     CX,11               ; Check size
0070  75 F2                       jne     nextsch             ; If not right - loop
0072  8B FB                       mov     DI,BX               ; Set pointer of target,
0074  8D 1E 0146 R                lea     BX,arradesc         ; point to array descriptor,
0078  8D 36 0150 R                lea     SI,indirect         ; and to indirect array.
007C  E8 0000 E                   call    Bnsearch            ; Try to locate it
007F  8D 16 0119 R                lea     DX,found            ; assume we did
```

Program 9-6 Continued.

```
0083  0F 84 008B R                    je    putout          ; We did.
0087  8D 16 012D R                    lea   DX,notfound     ; not
008B                        putout:
008B  B4 09                           mov   AH,9            ; Set DOS code
008D  CD 21                           int   21h             ; and put message out.
008F  EB D3                           jmp   nextsch         ; and try again.

0091                        Exit:
0091  B0 00                           mov   AL,0            ; Set return code
0093  B4 4C                           mov   AH,04ch         ; Set good-by
0095  CD 21                           int   21h             ; Return to the system
                            ;
                            ; Read a string in response to a prompt
                            ; The prompt must be in DX.  The string will be returned in string.
                            ;
0097                        getinp  PROC
0097  50                            push  AX              ; Save registers
0098  56                            push  SI
0099  B4 09                         mov   AH,9            ; and dos request
009B  CD 21                         int   21h             ; put out the string
009D  8D 16 0000 R                  lea   DX,string       ; point to input area
00A1  C6 06 0000 R FE               mov   string,254      ; Set max length in
00A6  B4 0A                         mov   AH,10           ; Ask for read of string
00A8  CD 21                         int   21h             ; from DOS.
00AA  8D 1E 0002 R                  lea   BX,string+2     ; Point to just read data
00AE  8A 0E 0001 R                  mov   CL,string+1     ; Get length read
00B2  B5 00                         mov   CH,0            ; as a word.
00B4  8B F1                         mov   SI,CX           ; Set length
00B6  C6 84 0002 R 00               mov   string+2[SI],0  ; and make an asciiz string.
00BB  5E                            pop   SI
00BC  58                            pop   AX              ; Restore registers
00BD  C3                            ret                   ; and return.
00BE                        getinp  ENDP

00BE                        code    ENDS
                                    END   Begin
```

Program 9-7 SHELLSRT

Microsoft (R) Macro Assembler Version 5.00

```
                        PAGE    55,132
                        .386
0000                    code    SEGMENT  para 'CODE' USE16 PUBLIC
                                ASSUME   CS:code, DS:code, SS:code
                        ;
                        ; Name;    SHELLSRT
                        ;
                        ; Purpose: The following procedure implements the shellsort algorithm.
                        ;
                        ;
                        ;
                        ; Inputs:  DS:BX points to an array of displacements into a string
                        ;          area.  All strings are assumed to be standard asciiz
                        ;          strings.  CX holds the count of strings to sort.
                        ;
                        ; Process: A distance of CX/2 is used for the first pass of compares.
                        ;          Elements of the array are compared and exchanged if the
                        ;          value of the lower indexed element is greater than the
                        ;          higher.  When all pairs of the given distance have been
                        ;          compared, the distance is halved and the process is
                        ;          repeated until the distance is zero.
                        ;
                        ;
```

```
                              ; Output: The output is an array of displacements into the string
                              ;          area which is in alphabetic sequence.
                              ;
                              ;
                              ;
                              ;
                                      EXTRN    STRZCOMP:PROC
                                      PUBLIC   Shellsrt                 ; Make the name usable
0000                          Shellsrt PROC
0000  52                              push     DX                      ; Save entry registers
0001  51                              push     CX
0002  53                              push     BX
0003  50                              push     AX
0004  56                              push     SI
0005  57                              push     DI
0006  55                              push     BP
0007  8B E9                          mov      BP,CX                    ; Save limit value
                              ;
                              ; This loop computer closer and closer distances to compare at.
                              ;        i.e. for 15 items we compare 7, 3, and 1 apart.
                              ;
0009                          nextdist:
0009  D1 E9                          shr      CX,1                     ; Get the next distance
000B  0F 84 0052 R                   jz       sortdone                 ; If at zero - we are done.
000F  8B D5                          mov      DX,BP                    ; get original top
0011  2B D1                          sub      DX,CX                    ; less our new distance.
0013  B8 0001                        mov      AX,1                     ; j=1 to limit
                              ;
                              ; This loop steps us up the array from 1 to our limit comparing items
                              ; which are 'distance' apart.  i.e. for our distance of 7 we compare
                              ;        1:8, 2:9, 3:10, 4:11 ... 8:15.  for the 3 distance we compare
                              ;        1:4, 2:5, 3:6, 4:7 ... 12:15, for the 1 distance we compare
                              ;        1:2, 2:3, 3:4, 4:5 ... 14:15 which completes the sort.
                              ;
0016                          nextj:
0016  50                              push     AX                      ; save J and init I
                              ;
                              ; This loop compares and if an out of sequence condition is found,
                              ; steps back down the array to force the out of sequence item as far
                              ; to the left as possible.  i.e if we find an out of sequence in our
                              ; 3 distance at 4:7, we ensure that the 1:4 is in sequence after
                              ; we exchange 4 and 7.
                              ;
0017                          nexti:
0017  8B F0                          mov      SI,AX
0019  8B F8                          mov      DI,AX
001B  03 F1                          add      SI,CX                    ; Get I+distance
001D  4E                             dec      SI
001E  4F                             dec      DI                       ; zero base for indexed loads
001F  03 FF                          add      DI,DI
0021  03 F6                          add      SI,SI
0023  8B 30                          mov      SI,WORD PTR DS:[BX+SI]    ; Load string displacements
0025  8B 39                          mov      DI,WORD PTR DS:[BX+DI]
0027  E8 0000 E                      call     Strzcomp                 ; compare the strings
002A  0F 83 004A R                   jnb      inseq                    ; If in sequence - skip
002E  48                             dec      AX                       ; Get zero base
002F  96                             xchg     AX,SI
0030  03 F6                          add      SI,SI                    ; Get as index
0032  89 00                          mov      WORD PTR DS:[BX+SI],AX    ; exchange the string
0034  D1 EE                          shr      SI,1
0036  8B C6                          mov      AX,SI
0038  40                             inc      AX
0039  8B F0                          mov      SI,AX
003B  03 F1                          add      SI,CX
003D  4E                             dec      SI
003E  03 F6                          add      SI,SI
0040  89 38                          mov      WORD PTR DS:[BX+SI],DI    ; displacements
0042  2B C1                          sub      AX,CX                    ; next to compare
0044  0F 88 004A R                   js       inseq                    ; If negative - out
```

Program 9-7 Continued.

```
0048  75 CD                            jnz      nexti         ; If positive - check again
004A                     inseq:
004A  58                               pop      AX            ; Get j back
004B  40                               inc      AX            ; add 1
004C  3B D0                            cmp      DX,AX         ; Are we at our limit
004E  73 C6                            jnb      nextj         ; No - loop again
0050  EB B7                            jmp      nextdist      ; loop until distance = 0
0052                     sortdone:
0052  5D                               pop      BP            ; Restore the entry registers
0053  5F                               pop      DI
0054  5E                               pop      SI
0055  58                               pop      AX
0056  5B                               pop      BX
0057  59                               pop      CX
0058  5A                               pop      DX
0059  C3                               ret                    ; and return.
005A             Shellsrt              ENDP
005A             code                  ENDS
                                       END
```

Program 9-8 QSORT

```
                              .386
0000             code      SEGMENT    para 'CODE' USE16 PUBLIC
                           ASSUME     CS:code, DS:code, SS:code
                 ;
                 ; Name;     QSORT
                 ;
                 ; Purpose: The following procedure provides an implementation of the
                 ;          quicksort algorithm.
                 ;
                 ; Inputs:  DS:BX points to a standard array descriptor.
                 ;          DS:SI points to an index array
                 ;
                 ; Process: The index array is initialized with sequential index
                 ;          values.  This indirection is done for two reasons:
                 ;          1. Exchanging index values is faster than exchanging
                 ;             records (which may be very large).
                 ;          2. Often we don't want to change the original order
                 ;             we only want a differently ordered set of pointers.
                 ;          The quicksort algorithm is then applied using the
                 ;          indirection of the index array.
                 ;
                 ; Output:  The index array will contain pointers to records with
                 ;          ascending key values.  Neither the array descriptor nor
                 ;          the record array is changed.
                 ;
                 arradesc  STRUC
0000  0000       ndxmax    dw         0                 ; Maximum element index
0002  0000       elesize   dw         0                 ; Size of an element
0004  0000       elepseg   dw         0                 ; Elements per segment
0006  0000       elesegs   dw         0                 ; First element of the DS
                 ;                                        array.  Further elements
                 ;                                        follow sequentially.
0008             arradesc  ENDS
                 ;
                 ;
=                left      EQU        WORD PTR SS:[BP-1] ; Save area for working left
=                right     EQU        WORD PTR SS:[BP-3] ; and right of partition.
                 ;
                           PUBLIC     Qsort
0000             Qsort     PROC
0000  66| 52               push       EDX               ; Save entry registers
0002  66| 51               push       ECX
0004  66| 53               push       EBX
0006  66| 50               push       EAX
```

```
0008   66| 56               push    ESI
000A   66| 57               push    EDI
000C   06                   push    ES
000D   0F A0                push    FS
000F   0F A8                push    GS
0011   C8 0008 00           enter   8,0              ; Get some work area
0015   8C D8                mov     AX,DS            ; Move DS to GS for use.
0017   8E E8                mov     GS,AX            ; We will need ES and DS
0019   8E C0                mov     ES,AX            ; for comparisons later.
001B   66| B8 0000FFFF      mov     EAX,0000ffffh    ; Get mask
0021   66| 23 F0            and     ESI,EAX          ; and ensure high bytes clear
0024   66| 23 F8            and     EDI,EAX
0027   66| 23 D8            and     EBX,EAX
002A   66| 23 C8            and     ECX,EAX
002D   66| 23 D0            and     EDX,EAX
                          ;
                          ; Form the index array as pointed to by DS:SI.
                          ;
0030   8B FE                mov     DI,SI            ; Set pointer
0032   B8 0001              mov     AX,1             ; Set initial index value
0035   FC                   cld                      ; and set direction to up.
0036                formit:
0036   AB                   stosw                    ; store index value
0037   40                   inc     AX               ; step the index
0038   3B 07                cmp     AX,ndxmax.[BX]   ; are we done?
003A   76 FA                jna     formit           ; No - go back for next.
003C   2B C0                sub     AX,AX            ; Set stopper on stack
003E   50                   push    AX               ; left index
003F   50                   push    AX               ; and right for a partition.
0040   40                   inc     AX               ; get a 1
0041   8B 0F                mov     CX,ndxmax.[BX]   ; and the top
0043   EB 03 90             jmp     qbegin           ; Go
                          ;
                          ; Unstack a new partition, the previous is in order.
                          ;
0046                unstack:
0046   59                   pop     CX               ; Get right index
0047   58                   pop     AX               ; and left.


                          ;
                          ; Start a new partitioning process.
                          ;
                          ; We have a left and right index in AX and CX respectively.  We first
                          ; check for the completion condition - 0,0.
                          ;
0048                qbegin:
0048   50                   push    AX               ; save our left in case
0049   0B C1                or      AX,CX            ; we are not done.
004B   58                   pop     AX
004C   0F 84 0127 R         jz      alldone          ; We have unstacked our stop.
                          ;
                          ; If our partition is of size 3 or less, we just sort it without
                          ; partitioning.
                          ;
0050   8B D1                mov     DX,CX            ; Copy for our test
0052   2B D0                sub     DX,AX            ; Check distance
0054   74 F0                jz      unstack          ; Single element is in order.
                          ;
                          ; We can have a partition of size 2, or more.
                          ;
0056   E8 013E R            call    compare          ; check a(l) to a(r)
0059   0F 86 0070 R         jna     order1           ; In order - could be done.
005D   48                   dec     AX               ; down 1 to get zero base
005E   49                   dec     CX
005F   65: 67| 8B 3C46      mov     DI,GS:[ESI+EAX*2] ; Get the value from AX's
0064   65: 67| 87 3C4E      xchg    DI,GS:[ESI+ECX*2] ; exchange with CX's location
0069   65: 67| 89 3C46      mov     GS:[ESI+EAX*2],DI ; and complete the exchange
006E   40                   inc     AX
```

```
006F   41                            inc     CX              ; and back up
0070                         order1:
0070   4A                            dec     DX              ; See if we had a length of 2.
0071   74 D3                         jz      unstack         ; We did - our 2 sort did it.
0073   8B D1                         mov     DX,CX           ; Save right pointer.
0075   03 C8                         add     CX,AX           ; point to center element.
0077   D1 E9                         shr     CX,1
0079   E8 013E R                     call    compare         ; check a(l) to a(c)
007C   0F 86 0093 R                  jna     order2          ; In order leaves 1 pair
0080   48                            dec     AX              ; down 1 to get zero base
0081   49                            dec     CX
0082   65: 67| 8B 3C46               mov     DI,GS:[ESI+EAX*2] ; Get the value
0087   65: 67| 87 3C4E               xchg    DI,GS:[ESI+ECX*2] ; into CX's location
008C   65: 67| 89 3C46               mov     GS:[ESI+EAX*2],DI ; and complete the exchange
0091   40                            inc     AX
0092   41                            inc     CX              ; and back up
                             ;
                             ; We have the lowest in the first element now.  We may have to
                             ; reverse the second and third before we are done.
                             ;
0093                         order2:
0093   92                            xchg    AX,DX           ; Save left pointer and get rt
0094   91                            xchg    AX,CX           ; point to second element.
0095   E8 013E R                     call    compare         ; check a(c) to a(r)
0098   0F 86 00AF R                  jna     order3          ; If in order - OK as is.
009C   48                            dec     AX              ; down 1 to get zero base
009D   49                            dec     CX
009E   65: 67| 8B 3C46               mov     DI,GS:[ESI+EAX*2] ; Get the value
00A3   65: 67| 87 3C4E               xchg    DI,GS:[ESI+ECX*2] ; into CX's location
00A8   65: 67| 89 3C46               mov     GS:[ESI+EAX*2],DI ; and complete the exchange
00AD   40                            inc     AX
00AE   41                            inc     CX              ; and back up
                             ;
                             ; If our partition was of size 3, it is now sorted.
                             ; If more, we have the left, center, and right in order.
                             ;
00AF                         order3:
00AF   92                            xchg    AX,DX           ; Get left in AX, center DX.
00B0   2B C8                         sub     CX,AX           ; Get count between l and r.
00B2   83 F9 02                      cmp     CX,2            ; Is partition in order?
00B5   74 8F                         je      unstack         ; If size is 3, it is.
00B7   03 C8                         add     CX,AX           ; Get right pointer back.
                             ;
                             ; We have a partition of 4 or more elements.  We choose the median
                             ; of the left, center or right elements as our pivot point.  Since
                             ; we have them sorted, the center is the median.
                             ;
                             ; Our pivot element is pointed to by DX.
                             ;
00B9   4A                            dec     DX              ; down 1 to get zero base
                             ;
                             ; Now set the pivot element as our comparand in ES,DI.
                             ;
00BA   50                            push    AX              ; Save registers used
00BB   56                            push    SI
00BC   65: 67| 8B 0456               mov     AX,GS:[ESI+EDX*2] ; Get the element's pointer
00C1   E8 017F R                     call    arrandxp        ; Get pivot set into
00C4   8E C0                         mov     ES,AX
00C6   8B FE                         mov     DI,SI           ; ES:DI for all pivot compares
00C8   5E                            pop     SI
00C9   58                            pop     AX              ; Restore the registers
                             ;
                             ; We have set a pivot point and fixed it in ES:DI.
                             ;
00CA   89 46 FF                      mov     left,AX         ; Save left and
00CD   89 4E FD                      mov     right,CX        ; right beginning pointers.
```

```
                        ;
                        ; Partition for higher elements
                        ;
00D0                    nextright:
00D0    91                      xchg    AX,CX                   ; Get working right in AX
00D1                    workright:
00D1    48                      dec     AX                      ; step down 1
00D2    E8 0165 R               call    pivotc                  ; compare a(SI(AX)):pivot
00D5    77 FA                   ja      workright               ; if above - loop
                        ;
                        ; We have come down until we got an element <= to our pivot.
                        ;
                        ; Now go up from the left until we get an element >= to our pivot.
                        ;
00D7    91                      xchg    AX,CX                   ; Get working left in AX
00D8                    workleft:
00D8    40                      inc     AX                      ; step it by one
00D9    E8 0165 R               call    pivotc                  ; compare a(SI(AX)):pivot
00DC    72 FA                   jb      workleft                ; if under - loop
                        ;
                        ; If our pointers have crossed, we are done.  Otherwise we swap
                        ; our out of order items and continue.
                        ;
00DE    3B C1                   cmp     AX,CX                   ; check if we crossed
00E0    0F 87 00FB R            ja      crossed                 ; if we did - partition done
00E4    74 EA                   je      nextright               ; If equal don't exchange
00E6    48                      dec     AX                      ; down 1 to get zero base
00E7    49                      dec     CX
00E8    65: 67| 8B 1446         mov     DX,GS:[ESI+EAX*2]       ; Get the value
00ED    65: 67| 87 144E         xchg    DX,GS:[ESI+ECX*2]       ; into CX's location
00F2    65: 67| 89 1446         mov     GS:[ESI+EAX*2],DX       ; and complete the exchange
00F7    40                      inc     AX
00F8    41                      inc     CX                      ; and back up
00F9    EB D5                   jmp     nextright               ; and continue
                        ;
                        ; We have two partitions, left to AX and CX to right.
                        ;
                        ; We stack the largest partition and sort the smallest.
                        ;
00FB                    crossed:
00FB    41                      inc     CX                      ; up for right and
00FC    48                      dec     AX                      ; down for left
00FD    50                      push    AX                      ; Save left
00FE    8B 56 FD                mov     DX,right                ; Get right boundary
0101    2B D1                   sub     DX,CX                   ; And the size of the part
0103    2B 46 FF                sub     AX,left                 ; get the size of the left
0106    3B C2                   cmp     AX,DX                   ; check relative sizes
0108    0F 82 011A R            jb      bigright                ; Right is larger
                        ;
                        ; The left partition is larger than the right - We stack the left
                        ; then sort the right.  This minimizes the size of the stack.
                        ;
010C    8B 46 FF                mov     AX,left                 ; Get left index
010F    5A                      pop     DX                      ; Get the right index
0110    50                      push    AX                      ; Stack left index then
0111    52                      push    DX                      ; the right (we pop rt,lft)
0112    8B C1                   mov     AX,CX                   ; CX becomes the new left
0114    8B 4E FD                mov     CX,right                ; with old right the right.
0117    E9 0048 R               jmp     qbegin                  ; Go back and repartition
                        ;
                        ; The right partition is larger than the left - We stack the right
                        ; then sort the left.
                        ;
011A                    bigright:
011A    58                      pop     AX                      ; Get left off the stack
011B    51                      push    CX                      ; CX is the left
011C    FF 76 FD                push    right                   ; and right is still right
011F    8B C8                   mov     CX,AX                   ; New partition is left
```

Program 9-8 Continued.

```
0121   8B 46 FF                    mov     AX,left           ; to AX.
0124   E9 0048 R                   jmp     qbegin            ; Go back and repartition.
0127                     alldone:
0127   C9                          leave
0128   8C E8                       mov     AX,GS             ; Restore normal DS
012A   8E D8                       mov     DS,AX
012C   0F A9                       pop     GS                ; and the entry registers.
012E   0F A1                       pop     FS
0130   07                          pop     ES
0131   66| 5F                      pop     EDI
0133   66| 5E                      pop     ESI
0135   66| 58                      pop     EAX
0137   66| 5B                      pop     EBX
0139   66| 59                      pop     ECX
013B   66| 5A                      pop     EDX
013D   C3                          ret                       ; and return.
                     ;
                     ; Compare routine: (Replace with whatever is needed for your sort).
                     ;                  Compares the key in the record at SI(AX) to the key
                     ;                  in the record at SI(CX) key(SI(AX)) - key(SI(CX)).
                     ;                  It returns with the flags set. The usage is such
                     ;                  that a call to compare is followed by a conditional
                     ;                  jump using the flag settings.
                     ;                  The key as used in the demo program is a Social
                     ;                  Security number with dashes, 000-00-0000 for
                     ;                  instance. The key is the first field in the record.
                     ;
013E                     Compare     PROC
013E   60                          pusha                     ; Save the registers
013F   56                          push    SI                ; We need SI later
0140   48                          dec     AX                ; Get indices on zero base.
0141   65: 67| 8B 0446             mov     AX,GS:[ESI+EAX*2] ; Get indirect index for AX
0146   E8 017F R                   call    arrandxp          ; Get the record location AX
0149   8E D8                       mov     DS,AX             ; Set the base
014B   8B FE                       mov     DI,SI             ; and index
014D   5E                          pop     SI                ; For the indirect index load
014E   8B C1                       mov     AX,CX             ; Set the next record
0150   48                          dec     AX                ; Zero base
0151   65: 67| 8B 0446             mov     AX,GS:[ESI+EAX*2] ; Get indirect index for CX
0156   E8 017F R                   call    arrandxp          ; and the record location.
0159   87 FE                       xchg    DI,SI             ; Fix indices
015B   8E C0                       mov     ES,AX             ; and get next base
015D   B9 000B                     mov     CX,11             ; Set count to compare
0160   FC                          cld                       ; and direction to up
0161   F3/ A6                      repz cmpsb                 ; Compare,
0163   61                          popa                      ; restore registers,
0164   C3                          ret                       ; and return.
0165                     Compare     ENDP
                     ;
                     ; Compare to pivot element. Similar to the above but assumes that
                     ; the segment and offset for the pivot are set in ES:DI. Thus
                     ; the comparison is always A(SI(AX)):pivot.
                     ;
0165                     Pivotc      PROC
0165   57                          push    DI                ; Save registers used
0166   56                          push    SI
0167   50                          push    AX
0168   51                          push    CX
0169   48                          dec     AX                ; Get indices on zero base.
016A   65: 67| 8B 0446             mov     AX,GS:[ESI+EAX*2] ; Get indirect index for AX
016F   E8 017F R                   call    arrandxp          ; Get the record location AX
0172   8E D8                       mov     DS,AX             ; Set the base
0174   B9 000B                     mov     CX,11             ; Set count to compare
0177   FC                          cld                       ; and direction to up
0178   F3/ A6                      repz cmpsb                 ; Compare,
017A   59                          pop     CX                ; restore registers,
017B   58                          pop     AX
```

```
017C  5E                          pop    SI
017D  5F                          pop    DI
017E  C3                          ret                              ; and return.
017F                       Pivotc ENDP
                           ;
                           ;
                           ; Purpose: The following procedure provides a method for computing
                           ;          a usable array element address.  This is required for
                           ;          accessing elements of large arrays (over 64k bytes in
                           ;          size) in a USE16 task.  It is a modification of the full
                           ;          routine.
                           ;
                           ; Inputs:  AX has the index of the array element (1 .. LAST) desired.
                           ;          BX has the segment array pointer.
                           ;
                           ;          The DS array is assumed to be of the form built by the
                           ;          ARRABLDP.ASM routine.
                           ;
                           ; Process: AX is decremented to get a zero base and DX is zeroed.
                           ;          DX-AX is divided by the number of elements per segment.
                           ;          The quotient is multiplied by 2 and used to select the
                           ;          ES value.  The remainder multiplied by the element size
                           ;          becomes the SI value.
                           ;
                           ; Output:  SI has the displacement to the record.  AX has the segment
                           ;          register value.
                           ;
017F                       Arrandxp PROC
017F  52                          push   DX                        ; Save entry registers
0180  51                          push   CX
0181  53                          push   BX
0182  48                          dec    AX                        ; Get index based on zero
0183  2B D2                       sub    DX,DX                     ; Clear upper word of dividend
0185  65: F7 77 04                div    GS:[BX].elepseg           ; Divide by elements / segment
0189  8B C8                       mov    CX,AX                     ; Save the quotient
018B  8B C2                       mov    AX,DX                     ; Position the remainder
018D  65: F7 67 02                mul    GS:[BX].elesize           ; Get the element's offset
0191  8B F0                       mov    SI,AX                     ; Into SI
0193  03 D9                       add    BX,CX                     ; Add the quotient to BX
0195  03 D9                       add    BX,CX                     ; twice to get the displacement
0197  65: 8B 47 06                mov    AX,GS:[BX].elesegs        ; of the descriptor.
019B  5B                          pop    BX                        ; Restore the entry registers
019C  59                          pop    CX
019D  5A                          pop    DX
019E  C3                          ret                              ; and return.
019F                       Arrandxp ENDP

019F                       Qsort  ENDP
019F                       code   ENDS
                                  END
```

Program 9-9 ARRADRV

Microsoft (R) Macro Assembler Version 5.00

```
                              PAGE     55,132
                              .386
                           ;
                           ; Name:    ARRADRV
                           ;
                           ; Purpose: This program tests the array building and indexing
                           ;          procedures.
                           ;
                           ; Inputs:  The user is prompted for an element size and a number of
                           ;          elements.
```

Miscellaneous routines   281

Program 9-9 Continued.

```
                            ;
                            ; Process: The program gets the element size and the number of
                            ;          elements to build.  It then calls Arrabldp to get the
                            ;          memory and fill in the arradesc structure.  The structure
                            ;          is displayed in hex.  The program then prompts for element
                            ;          numbers to locate and displays the resulting segment and
                            ;          displacement in hex.  (The tester then hand verifies the
                            ;          result.)
                            ;
                            ; Outputs: The desired output is the confidence that the build and
                            ;          index routines are correct.
                            ;
                            ;
                            ;
                            ; Note:    Under MS-DOS using the Microsoft linker you must link
                            ;          with the option /CP:nnnn. This option overrides the defaul
                            ;          memory allocation which allocates all free memory to your
                            ;          program.  nnnn is the maximum number of paragraphs to be
                            ;          allocated to your program.  If it is less than the size of
                            ;          the program the program size is used.
                            ;
                            ;
                            ;
                            ;
                            ; Declare the common structure
                            ;
                            arradesc  STRUC
0000  0000                 ndxmax    dw      0                    ; Maximum element index
0002  0000                 elesize   dw      0                    ; Size of an element
0004  0000                 elepseg   dw      0                    ; Elements per segment
0006  0000                 elesegs   dw      0                    ; First element of the DS
                            ;                                       array.  Further elements
                            ;                                       are assumed to follow
                            ;                                       sequentially.
0008                       arradesc  ENDS

                                      EXTRN   ARRABLDP:PROC
                                      EXTRN   ARRANDXP:PROC

                                      EXTRN   CODEASB:PROC
                                      EXTRN   CODEBTHX:PROC
                                      EXTRN   CODEBAS:PROC

0000                       stack     SEGMENT para 'STACK' STACK
0000  0100[                          dq      256 DUP(?)
      ??????????????????
      ?
                    ]

0800                       stack     ENDS
0000                       data      SEGMENT para
0000  0100[                string    db      256 DUP(?)           ; String scratch area
      ??
                    ]

0100  0A 0D 45 6E 74 65 72 query1    db      10,13,"Enter the size of an element: $"
      20 74 68 65 20 73 69
      7A 65 20 6F 66 20 61
      6E 20 65 6C 65 6D 65
      6E 74 3A 20 24
0121  0A 0D 45 6E 74 65 72 query2    db      10,13,"Enter the number of elements: $"
      20 74 68 65 20 6E 75
      6D 62 65 72 20 6F 66
      20 65 6C 65 6D 65 6E
      74 73 3A 20 24
0142  0A 0D 45 6E 74 65 72 query3    db      10,13,"Enter an index to locate: $"
```

```
            20 61 6E 20 69 6E 64
            65 78 20 74 6F 20 6C
            6F 63 61 74 65 3A 20
            24
015F  0A 0D 41 72 72 61 79    deschead    db      10,13,"Array descriptor: $"
            20 64 65 73 63 72 69
            70 74 6F 72 3A 20 24
0174  0A 0D 49 6E 64 65 78    indxhead    db      10,13,"Index gives       $"
            20 67 69 76 65 73 20
            20 20 20 20 20 20 24

                               ;
                               ;
                               ;
0189  90 90 90                            ALIGN   4
018C  0000                 desc          arradesc <>                  ; Build the descriptor
018E  0000
0190  0000
0192  0000

0194  0014[                              dw      20 DUP(0)            ; Save room for segment values
         0000
                    ]

01BC                         data          ENDS

0000                         code          SEGMENT para 'CODE' USE16 PUBLIC
                                           ASSUME  CS:code, DS:data
                               ;
                               ; Set up the environment
                               ;
0000                         Begin:
0000  B8 ---- R                            mov     AX,data             ; Get data segment pointer
0003  8E D8                                mov     DS,AX               ; into DS,
0005  8E C0                                mov     ES,AX               ; and ES.
0007  2B F6                                sub     SI,SI               ; Clear indices
0009  2B FF                                sub     DI,DI
000B                         getsize:
000B  8D 16 0100 R                         lea     DX,query1           ; Get the size
000F  E8 0107 R                            call    getinp
0012  E3 7F                                jcxz    exit                ; Quit if null
0014  E8 00E9 R                            call    getnbr              ; convert the number
0017  72 F2                                jc      getsize             ; an error goes back
0019  A3 018E R                            mov     desc.elesize,AX     ; set the size
001C                         getcount:
001C  8D 16 0121 R                         lea     DX,query2           ; Prompt for number to build
0020  E8 0107 R                            call    getinp
0023  E3 F7                                jcxz    getcount            ; must have an input
0025  E8 00E9 R                            call    getnbr              ; convert the number
0028  72 F2                                jc      getcount            ; again if bad
002A  A3 018C R                            mov     desc.ndxmax,AX      ; Set the maximum
002D  8D 1E 018C R                         lea     BX,desc             ; Point to array descriptor
0031  E8 0000 E                            call    Arrabldp            ; and fill it in
0034  72 D5                                jc      getsize             ; If an error - try again

                               ;
                               ; Dump the array descriptor just built.
                               ;
0036  8D 16 015F R                         lea     DX,deschead         ; Point to header
003A  B4 09                                mov     AH,9
003C  CD 21                                int     21h                 ; and put it out
003E  A1 018C R                            mov     AX,desc.ndxmax      ; Get number
0041  8B D0                                mov     DX,AX               ; Save it
0043  E8 0099 R                            call    prtax               ; and print it
0046  A1 018E R                            mov     AX,desc.elesize     ; size
0049  E8 0099 R                            call    prtax               ; prints too
004C  A1 0190 R                            mov     AX,desc.elepseg     ; elements/segment
004F  8B C8                                mov     CX,AX               ; Save it too
0051  E8 0099 R                            call    prtax               ; Print as well
0054  8D 1E 0192 R                         lea     BX,desc.elesegs     ; Point to segment list
```

Program 9-9 Continued.

```
0058                            nextseg:
0058  8B 07                             mov     AX,WORD PTR [BX]    ; Get the next segment
005A  E8 00BC R                         call    prtaxhx             ; Dump it
005D  83 C3 02                          add     BX,2                ; step pointer
0060  2B D1                             sub     DX,CX               ; count out this group
0062  0F 84 0068 R                      jz      nextindex           ; Ended even
0066  79 F0                             jns     nextseg             ; loop till all out
0068                            nextindex:
0068  8D 16 0142 R                      lea     DX,query3           ; get an index value
006C  E8 0107 R                         call    getinp              ; and get it
006F  E3 9A                             jcxz    getsize             ; go try a new config
0071  E8 00E9 R                         call    getnbr              ; convert the index
0074  72 F2                             jc      nextindex           ; loop if bad
0076  8D 16 0174 R                      lea     DX,indxhead         ; point to header
007A  50                                push    AX                  ; save number
007B  B4 09                             mov     AH,9
007D  CD 21                             int     21h
007F  58                                pop     AX
0080  8D 1E 018C R                      lea     BX,desc             ; point to descriptor
0084  E8 0000 E                         call    Arrandxp            ; Get the seg:offset
0087  72 DF                             jc      nextindex           ; loop if bad
0089  E8 00BC R                         call    prtaxhx             ; Do the segment value
008C  8B C6                             mov     AX,SI               ; Get displacement
008E  E8 00BC R                         call    prtaxhx             ; and print it
0091  EB D5                             jmp     nextindex           ; loop on index gets

0093                            Exit:
0093  B0 00                             mov     AL,0                ; Set return code
0095  B4 4C                             mov     AH,04ch             ; Set good-by
0097  CD 21                             int     21h                 ; Return to the system
                                ;
                                ; Print the number in AX
                                ;
0099                            prtax   PROC
0099  60                                pusha                       ; save everything
009A  66| 98                            cwde                        ; As a 32 bit integer
009C  8D 3E 0000 R                      lea     DI,string           ; Point to output area
00A0  E8 0000 E                         call    Codebas             ; Convert it
00A3  B4 02                             mov     AH,2
00A5                            numbout:
00A5  8A 15                             mov     DL,BYTE PTR [DI]    ; Get a byte
00A7  0A D2                             or      DL,DL               ; at end?
00A9  0F 84 00B2 R                      jz      numbout0            ; Yes
00AD  CD 21                             int     21h                 ; print it
00AF  47                                inc     DI                  ; point to next
00B0  EB F3                             jmp     numbout             ; and loop
00B2                            numbout0:
00B2  B2 2C                             mov     DL,','              ; follow with comma
00B4  CD 21                             int     21h
00B6  B2 20                             mov     DL,' '              ; and a space
00B8  CD 21                             int     21h
00BA  61                                popa                        ; restore
00BB  C3                                ret
00BC                            prtax   ENDP
                                ;
                                ; Print the number in AX in hex.
                                ;
00BC                            prtaxhx PROC
00BC  60                                pusha
00BD  50                                push    AX                  ; save the number
00BE  8A C4                             mov     AL,AH               ; Position high byte
00C0  E8 0000 E                         call    Codebthx            ; and convert it
00C3  8A D4                             mov     DL,AH               ; Set high byte
00C5  8A C8                             mov     CL,AL               ; save low
00C7  B4 02                             mov     AH,2
00C9  CD 21                             int     21h                 ; Put it out
```

```
00CB  8A D1                       mov      DL,CL              ; and low byte
00CD  CD 21                       int      21h
00CF  58                          pop      AX                 ; Get low byte
00D0  E8 0000 E                   call     Codebthx           ; Hex it
00D3  8A D4                       mov      DL,AH
00D5  8A C8                       mov      CL,AL              ; save low
00D7  B4 02                       mov      AH,2
00D9  CD 21                       int      21h                ; print it
00DB  8A D1                       mov      DL,CL              ; and low byte
00DD  CD 21                       int      21h
00DF  B2 3A                       mov      DL,':'             ; follow with colon
00E1  CD 21                       int      21h
00E3  B2 20                       mov      DL,' '             ; and a space
00E5  CD 21                       int      21h
00E7  61                          popa
00E8  C3                          ret
00E9              prtaxhx         ENDP
                                ;
                                ; Convert the number just obtained
                                ;
00E9              getnbr          PROC
00E9  8B F3                       mov      SI,BX              ; set input pointer
00EB  E8 0000 E                   call     codeasb            ; Convert to binary
00EE  0F 82 0105 R                jc       badnbr             ; Overflow is too much
00F2  66| 0B C0                   or       EAX,EAX            ; check for a zero size
00F5  0F 84 0105 R                jz       badnbr             ; that is bad too
00F9  66| 3D 00008000             cmp      EAX,08000h         ; Over 32K in size
00FF  0F 83 0105 R                jnb      badnbr             ; if so - too big
0103  F8                          clc
0104  C3                          ret                         ; return ok
0105              badnbr:
0105  F9                          stc                         ; flag error
0106  C3                          ret
0107              getnbr          ENDP
                                ;
                                ; Read a string in response to a prompt
                                ; The prompt must be in DX.  The string will be returned in string.
                                ;
0107              getinp          PROC
0107  50                          push     AX                 ; Save registers
0108  56                          push     SI
0109  B4 09                       mov      AH,9               ; and dos request
010B  CD 21                       int      21h                ; put out the string
010D  8D 16 0000 R                lea      DX,string          ; point to input area
0111  C6 06 0000 R FE             mov      string,254         ; Set max length in
0116  B4 0A                       mov      AH,10              ; Ask for read of string
0118  CD 21                       int      21h                ; from DOS.
011A  8D 1E 0002 R                lea      BX,string+2        ; Point to just read data
011E  8A 0E 0001 R                mov      CL,string+1        ; Get length read
0122  B5 00                       mov      CH,0               ; as a word.
0124  8B F1                       mov      SI,CX              ; Set length
0126  C6 84 0002 R 00             mov      string+2[SI],0     ; and make an ASCIIZ string.
012B  5E                          pop      SI
012C  58                          pop      AX                 ; Restore registers
012D  C3                          ret                         ; and return.
012E              getinp          ENDP

012E              code            ENDS
                                  END      Begin
```

Program 9-10 ARRABLDP

```
                                PAGE       55,132
                                .386
0000            code            SEGMENT    para 'CODE' PUBLIC USE16
                                ASSUME     CS:code, DS:code, SS:code
```

Program 9-10 Continued.

```
                        ; Name:     ARRABLDP
                        ;
                        ; Purpose: The following procedure provides the means to build an
                        ;          array which exceeds the size of a single segment (64K).
                        ;          This is needed for MS-DOS and OS/2 even on the 80386.
                        ;
                        ; Inputs:   BX points to the structure ARRADESC with the fields
                        ;           ndxmax and elesize set.
                        ;
                        ; Process: First, the maximum number of elements per segment is
                        ;          computed.
                        ;
                        ;          The size to get is computed (the MS-DOS Allocate memory
                        ;          call is used as an example so the size is rounded up to
                        ;          the nearest paragraph).
                        ;
                        ;          The number of segments to get is computed and we loop
                        ;          getting them until we either have them all or an error
                        ;          is returned.
                        ;
                        ;          We set our return conditions and return.
                        ;
                        ; Output:  The field elepseg is set and the DS array is filled in
                        ;          with segment descriptors for each section of the array
                        ;          if no error occurred - in this case carry is reset on
                        ;          return.
                        ;
                        ;          If an error occurs we return all sections which we were
                        ;          successful in obtaining.  The return will have carry set.
                        ;
                        ; Note:    Under MS-DOS using the Microsoft linker you must link
                        ;          with the option /CP:nnnn. This option overrides the default
                        ;          memory allocation which allocates all free memory to your
                        ;          program.  nnnn is the maximum number of paragraphs to be
                        ;          allocated to your program.  If it is less than the size of
                        ;          the program the program size is used.
                        ;
                        arradesc  STRUC
0000  0000              ndxmax    dw      0              ; Maximum element index
0002  0000              elesize   dw      0              ; Size of an element
0004  0000              elepseg   dw      0              ; Elements per segment
0006  0000              elesegs   dw      0              ; First element of the DS
                        ;                                  array.  Further elements
                        ;                                  follow sequentially.
0008            arradesc  ENDS
                        ;
                        ;
                                  PUBLIC  Arrabldp
                        ;
0000            Arrabldp  PROC
0000  52                  push    DX             ; Save entry registers
0001  51                  push    CX
0002  56                  push    SI
0003  50                  push    AX
0004  2B C0               sub     AX,AX          ; Prepare low part of dividend
0006  BA 0001             mov     DX,1           ; and get double word 64K
0009  F7 77 02            div     [BX].elesize   ; Divide by element size
000C  89 47 04            mov     [BX].elepseg,AX ; Set the number in a segment
                        ;                          (except the last)
000F  F7 67 02            mul     [BX].elesize   ; Get the size to ask for
0012  05 000F             add     AX,15          ; Round up to paragraph bound
```

```
0015    83 D2 00              adc      DX,0                ; Propagate carry if any
0018    0F AC D0 04           shrd     AX,DX,4             ; and divide by 16 (para size)
001C    8B C8                 mov      CX,AX               ; Set size for loop
001E    8B 07                 mov      AX,[BX].ndxmax      ; Get count of elements.
0020    2B D2                 sub      DX,DX               ; Clear upper word.
0022    03 47 04              add      AX,[BX].elepseg     ; round up to get enough
0025    48                    dec      AX                  ; but not one too many.
0026    F7 77 04              div      [BX].elepseg        ; AX now has count for loop.
0029    91                    xchg     AX,CX               ; Flip size and count.
                              ;
                              ; We now loop ndmax/elepseg times getting AX paragraphs at a time.
                              ;
002A    8B F3                 mov      SI,BX               ; copy working pointer
002C    53                    push     BX                  ; and save it too.
002D            memget:
002D    50                    push     AX                  ; save size (used by call)
002E    8B D8                 mov      BX,AX               ; Set paragraph count to get.
0030    B4 48                 mov      AH,048h             ; Set MS-DOS request code.
0032    CD 21                 int      21h                 ; Try to get memory.
0034    0F 82 0048 R          jc       memerror            ; MS-DOS returned an error.
0038    89 44 06              mov      [SI].elesegs,AX     ; Save the new segment.
003B    83 C6 02              add      SI,2                ; and step to next
003E    58                    pop      AX                  ; Get our size back
003F    E2 EC                 loop     memget              ; and get as many as we need.
0041    5B                    pop      BX                  ; clear stack
0042    F8                    clc                          ; and carry.
0043            memexit:
0043    58                    pop      AX                  ; Restore the entry registers
0044    5E                    pop      SI
0045    59                    pop      CX
0046    5A                    pop      DX
0047    C3                    ret                          ; and return.
                              ;
                              ; An error was returned by MS-DOS on our memory request!
                              ; If it is an out of memory condition, we will return all that we
                              ; got prior to returning with carry set.
                              ;
0048            memerror:
0048    3C 08                 cmp      AL,8                ; Is it an out condition
004A    58                    pop      AX                  ; Clean stack
004B    5B                    pop      BX                  ; Get back the base
004C    0F 85 0064 R          jne      nogive              ; No - don't try returns.

0050            giveloop:
0050    3B DE                 cmp      BX,SI               ; Are we at the base?
0052    0F 84 0064 R          je       nogive              ; Yes - we are done.
0056    83 EE 02              sub      SI,2                ; Back down one segment.
0059    8B 44 06              mov      AX,[SI].elesegs     ; Get the segment address
005C    8E C0                 mov      ES,AX               ; positioned for MS-DOS.
005E    B4 49                 mov      AH,049h             ; Set code for return.
0060    CD 21                 int      21h                 ; and return it.
0062    73 EC                 jnc      giveloop            ; If we fouled up - quit.
0064            nogive:
0064    F9                    stc                          ; set carry for exit
0065    EB DC                 jmp      memexit             ; and do it


0067            Arrabldp      ENDP
0067            code          ENDS
                              END
```

Program 9-11 ARRANDXP

Microsoft (R) Macro Assembler Version 5.00

```
                              PAGE      55,132
                              .386
0000                    code  SEGMENT   para 'CODE' PUBLIC USE16
                              ASSUME    CS:code, DS:code, SS:code
                        ; Name:    ARRANDXP
                        ;
                        ;
                        ; Purpose: The following procedure provides a method for computing
                        ;          a usable array element address.  This is useful for
                        ;          accessing elements of large arrays (over 64k bytes in
                        ;          size).  This is an 80286 protected mode routine.  It is
                        ;          also usable in real mode on all 8086 family processors.
                        ;          It is usable on the 80386 in protected mode for 'Use 16'
                        ;          tasks ('Use 32'tasks, with 32 bit displacements available
                        ;          would normally get a segment of the array size and index
                        ;          it directly.)
                        ;
                        ;
                        ; Inputs:  AX has the index of the array element (1 .. LAST) desired.
                        ;          BX has the DS array pointer.
                        ;
                        ;          The DS array is assumed to be of the form built by the
                        ;          ARRABLDP.ASM routine.  (See the structure arradesc below.)
                        ;
                        ; Process: The value in AX is checked against the maximum index value
                        ;          and carry is returned if AX is bad.
                        ;          AX is decremented to get a zero base and DX is zeroed.
                        ;          DX-AX is divided by the number of elements per segment.
                        ;          The quotient is multiplied by 2 and used to select the
                        ;          ES value.  The remainder multiplied by the element size
                        ;          becomes the SI value.
                        ;          Carry is reset and we return.
                        ;
                        ; Output:  The ES - SI registers will address the desired element if
                        ;          carry is reset (AX was ok).  AX has the segment value.
                        ;          ES - SI are unchanged if carry is set (AX was out of
                        ;          bounds).
                        ;
                        ;
                        ;
                        arradesc  STRUC
0000  0000              ndxmax    dw      0               ; Maximum element index
0002  0000              elesize   dw      0               ; Size of an element
0004  0000              elepseg   dw      0               ; Elements per segment
0006  0000              elesegs   dw      0               ; First element of the DS
                        ;                                   array.  Further elements
                        ;                                   are assumed to follow
                        ;                                   sequentially.
0008                    arradesc  ENDS
                        ;
                        ;
                                  PUBLIC  Arrandxp
                        ;
0000                    Arrandxp  PROC
0000  3D 0001                     cmp     AX,1            ; Check low bound for AX
0003  0F 8C 000D R                jl      axisbad         ; If low to 1 it's bad
0007  3B 07                       cmp     AX,[BX].ndxmax  ; Check validity of index
0009  0F 8E 000F R                jng     axisok          ; If index is ok continue
000D                    axisbad:
000D  F9                          stc                     ; Signal the error AX too big
000E  C3                          ret                     ; Return with carry set
000F                    axisok:
```

```
000F  52                      push     DX              ; Save entry registers
0010  51                      push     CX
0011  53                      push     BX
0012  48                      dec      AX              ; Get index based on zero
0013  2B D2                   sub      DX,DX           ; Clear upper word of dividend
0015  F7 77 04                div      [BX].elepseg    ; Divide by elements / segment
0018  8B C8                   mov      CX,AX           ; Save the quotient
001A  8B C2                   mov      AX,DX           ; Position the remainder
001C  F7 67 02               mul      [BX].elesize    ; Get the element's offset
001F  8B F0                   mov      SI,AX           ; Into SI
0021  03 D9                   add      BX,CX           ; Add the quotient to BX
0023  03 D9                   add      BX,CX           ; twice to get the displacement
0025  8B 47 06                mov      AX,[BX].elesegs ; of the descriptor.
0028  8E C0                   mov      ES,AX           ; We need to set it.
002A  F8                      clc                      ; Clear the carry
002B  5B                      pop      BX              ; Restore the entry registers
002C  59                      pop      CX
002D  5A                      pop      DX
002E  C3                      ret                      ; and return.
002F          Arrandxp        ENDP
002F          code            ENDS
                              END
```

Program 9-12   ARRANDXR

```
                        PAGE     55,132
                        .386
0000            code    SEGMENT  para 'CODE' PUBLIC USE16
                        ASSUME   CS:code, DS:code, SS:code

                ; Name:    ARRANDXR
                ;
                ;
                ;
                ; Purpose: The following procedure provides a method for computing a
                ;          usable array element address. This is useful for accessing
                ;          elements of large arrays (over 64k bytes in size).
                ;          This is an 8088/8086 (or real mode 80286/80386) routine.
                ;
                ;
                ; Inputs:  AX has the index of the array element (1 .. LAST).
                ;          BX has the DS value for element 1.
                ;          CX has the element size in bytes.
                ;          DX has the offset of element 1.
                ;
                ; Process: The element index is converted into a byte offset into the
                ;          array [(index-1)*size].  The array offset is added to the
                ;          result and the carry (if any) is propagated to DX.  This
                ;          gives us the byte offset from the array's segment
                ;          descriptor.  The low 4 bits of the result form the
                ;          element's offset in SI.  The total offset divided by 16
                ;          is added to the segment's descriptor to form the
                ;          descriptor for ES.  Shifts were used instead of a divide
                ;          for speed (about 1/3 the time).
                ;
                ; Output:  ES will have a segment descriptor and SI will contain
                ;          an offset of 0-15 addressing the desired element.
                ;
                ;
                ;
                        PUBLIC   Arrandxr
                ;
0000            Arrandxr PROC
0000  52                 push     DX              ; Save entry registers
0001  51                 push     CX
0002  53                 push     BX
0003  50                 push     AX
0004  8B F2              mov      SI,DX           ; Position the offset
```

```
0006  48                          dec     AX                  ; Get index based on zero
0007  F7 E1                       mul     CX                  ; Get the offset increment
0009  03 C6                       add     AX,SI               ; Then the total increment
000B  0F 83 0010 R                jnc     Ncfirst             ; If no carry - skip
000F  42                          inc     DX                  ; passing the carry into DX
0010                      Ncfirst:
0010  8B F0                       mov     SI,AX               ; Set the offset in SI and
0012  83 E6 0F                    and     SI,000Fh            ; leave only the low 4 bits.
0015  B9 0004                     mov     CX,4                ; Get the shift count.
0018  D2 E2                       shl     DL,CL               ; Get overflow into top nibble.
001A  D3 E8                       shr     AX,CL               ; Get segment value in AX.
001C  02 E2                       add     AH,DL               ; With the top 4 bits from DX
001E  03 C3                       add     AX,BX               ; Add the segment value.
0020  8E C0                       mov     ES,AX               ; Place the value in ES.
0022  58                          pop     AX                  ; Restore the entry registers
0023  5B                          pop     BX
0024  59                          pop     CX
0025  5A                          pop     DX
0026  C3                          ret                         ; and return.
0027              Arrandxr        ENDP
0027              code            ENDS
                                  END
```

Program 9-13 FIND__CFG

Microsoft (R) Macro Assembler Version 5.00

```
                            PAGE    55,132
                            .386
                            .287
                            EXTRN   CODEBAS:PROC
0000              STACK     SEGMENT 'STACK' STACK
0000  00C8[                 DW      200 DUP(?)
        ????
                    ]

0190              STACK     ENDS
0000              CODE      SEGMENT para 'CODE' PUBLIC USE16
                            ASSUME  CS:CODE, DS:CODE, SS:STACK
                  ;
                  ; Name:         FIND_CFG
                  ;
                  ; Purpose:      This program does several things:
                  ;               1. Shows how to get the date and print it, calling
                  ;                     CODEBAS to turn the binary return from INT 21
                  ;                     Function 2A into printable ASCII.
                  ;               2. Finds and prints the system configuration, using
                  ;                     INT 11.
                  ;               3. Shows the default drive, using INT 21 Function 19.
                  ;               4. Shows how to index into a fixed-length array to
                  ;                     find a message to print.
                  ;
                  ; Inputs:       None
                  ;
                  ; Process:      Use INT 11 which moves 16 bits into AX.  (Those
                  ;               bits are defined in Chapter 14, and Appendix
                  ;               6.)  "0D" is a carriage return.  "0A" is a line
                  ;               feed.  Note that all character strings that print
                  ;               using function 9 of INT 21 must end with a "$".
                  ;               Note the character strings that have sub-divisions
                  ;               below them.  The sub-divisions are built all the same
                  ;               length so that the values in AX will act as indices
                  ;               into character string arrays.
```

```
;
; Outputs:          AX register holds the configuration data
;                   There will also be printed output, depending on what
;                   system configuration is used.  The date will print, as
;                   does the default drive.
;
; NOTE:             Some ROM BIOSs return nothing on an Interrupt 11.  Be
;                   sure to check register AX after INT 11 to see what your
;                   system returns.  When you purchase your system, you
;                   should get material that describes supported BIOS
;                   calls.
;
0000                              FIND_CFG:
0000  8C C8                               MOV     AX,CS            ; Prepare to set DS
0002  8E D8                               MOV     DS,AX            ;   and set it.
0004  8E C0                               MOV     ES,AX
0006  E9 0230 R                           JMP     BEGINHERE

0009  0A 0D 54 68 69 73 20     HEADING    DB      0Ah,0Dh,'This system has the following: $'
      73 79 73 74 65 6D 20
      68 61 73 20 74 68 65
      20 66 6F 6C 6C 6F 77
      69 6E 67 3A 20 24
002B  0A 0D 20 4E 6F 74 20     VIDEO      DB  0Ah,0Dh,' Not Used-Video    $'
      55 73 65 64 2D 56 69
      64 65 6F 20 20 20 20
      24
0041  0A 0D 20 34 30 20 78                DB  0Ah,0Dh,' 40 x 25 Color Card$'
      20 32 35 20 43 6F 6C
      6F 72 20 43 61 72 64
      24
0057  0A 0D 20 38 30 20 78                DB  0Ah,0Dh,' 80 x 25 Color Card$'
      20 32 35 20 43 6F 6C
      6F 72 20 43 61 72 64
      24
006D  0A 0D 20 38 30 20 78                DB  0Ah,0Dh,' 80 x 25 Monochrome$'
      20 32 35 20 4D 6F 6E
      6F 63 68 72 6F 6D 65
      24
0083  0A 0D 20 4F 6E 65 20     DRIVES     DB  0Ah,0Dh,' One drive    $'
      64 72 69 76 65 20 20
      20 24
0093  0A 0D 20 54 77 6F 20                DB  0Ah,0Dh,' Two drives   $'
      64 72 69 76 65 73 20
      20 24
00A3  0A 0D 20 54 68 72 65                DB  0Ah,0Dh,' Three drives$'
      65 20 64 72 69 76 65
      73 24
00B3  0A 0D 20 46 6F 75 72                DB  0Ah,0Dh,' Four drives $'
      20 64 72 69 76 65 73
      20 24
00C3  20 52 53 32 33 32 20     RS232      DB  ' RS232 Cards$'
      43 61 72 64 73 24
00D0  0A 0D 20 41 6E 20 49     YESMODEM   DB  0Ah,0Dh,' An Internal Modem$'
      6E 74 65 72 6E 61 6C
      20 4D 6F 64 65 6D 24
00E5  0A 0D 20 4E 6F 20 49     NOMODEM    DB  0Ah,0Dh,' No Internal Modem$'
      6E 74 65 72 6E 61 6C
      20 4D 6F 64 65 6D 24
00FA  20 50 72 69 6E 74 65 72  PRINTERS   DB  ' Printers $'
      72 73 20 24
0105  20 24                    BLANK      DB  ' $'
0107  0A 0D 24                 CR_LF      DB  0Ah,0Dh,'$'
010A  0A 0D 20 54 68 65 72     NO_PROCESSR DB 0Ah,0Dh,' There is no Coprocessor installed',0Ah,0Dh,'$'
      65 20 69 73 20 6E 6F
      20 43 6F 70 72 6F 63
      65 73 73 6F 72 20 69
      6E 73 74 61 6C 6C 65
```

```
           64 0A 0D 24
0131   0A 0D 20 54 68 65 72    YES_PROCESR DB   0Ah,0Dh,' There is a Coprocessor installed',0Ah,0Dh,'$'
           65 20 69 73 20 61 20
           43 6F 70 72 6F 63 65
           73 73 6F 72 20 69 6E
           73 74 61 6C 6C 65 64
           0A 0D 24
0157   0A 0D 20 41 6E 20 49    IPLYES      DB   10,13,' An IPL diskette is installed.$'
           50 4C 20 64 69 73 6B
           65 74 74 65 20 69 73
           20 69 6E 73 74 61 6C
           6C 65 64 2E 24
0178   0A 0D 20 41 6E 20 49    IPLNO       DB   10,13,' An IPL diskette is not installed.$'
           50 4C 20 64 69 73 6B
           65 74 74 65 20 69 73
           20 6E 6F 74 20 69 6E
           73 74 61 6C 6C 65 64
           2E 24
019D   0A 0D 44 61 74 65 20    DATE        DB   0Ah,0Dh,'Date = $'
           3D 20 24
01A7   000A[                   DATE1       DB   10 DUP (?)
           ??
                          ]

01B1   0000                    CWORD       DW   0
01B3   0A 0D 20 54 68 65 20    DEFAULT     DB   0Ah,0Dh,' The default drive is A      $'
           64 65 66 61 75 6C 74
           20 64 72 69 76 65 20
           69 73 20 41 20 20 20
           20 20 24
01D2   0A 0D 20 54 68 65 20                DB   0Ah,0Dh,' The default drive is B      $'
           64 65 66 61 75 6C 74
           20 64 72 69 76 65 20
           69 73 20 42 20 20 20
           20 20 24
01F1   0A 0D 20 54 68 65 20                DB   0Ah,0Dh,' The default drive is C      $'
           64 65 66 61 75 6C 74
           20 64 72 69 76 65 20
           69 73 20 43 20 20 20
           20 20 24
0210   0A 0D 20 54 68 65 20                DB   0Ah,0Dh,' The default is not A,B, or C$'
           64 65 66 61 75 6C 74
           20 69 73 20 6E 6F 74
           20 41 2C 42 2C 20 6F
           72 20 43 24
                                ;
0230                           BEGINHERE:
                                ;        Date = CX=Year, DH=Month Number, DL=Day of Month,
0230   8D 16 019D R                        LEA   DX,DATE         ; Date header
0234   B4 09                               MOV   AH,9
0236   CD 21                               INT   21h
0238   B4 2A                               MOV   AH,2Ah          ; Get date
023A   CD 21                               INT   21h
023C   8B EA                               MOV   BP,DX           ; Save month/day
                                ;
                                ;        CODEBAS
                                ;        EAX - Contains the word to be converted
                                ;        DI - Contains the pointer to converted data, on return
                                ;
023E   8D 3E 01A7 R                        LEA   DI,DATE1        ; String for converted data
0242   66| 2B C0                           SUB   EAX,EAX
0245   8A C6                               MOV   AL,DH           ; Month
0247   E8 0000 E                           CALL  CODEBAS
                                ;
024A                           MONTH:
024A   8A 15                               MOV   DL,BYTE PTR [DI]
```

```
024C  0A D2                        OR    DL,DL
024E  0F 84 0259 R                 JE    SLASH0          ; Done with string?
0252  B4 02                        MOV   AH,2            ; Print Month
0254  CD 21                        INT   21h
0256  47                           INC   DI              ; Go to next byte
0257  EB F1                        JMP   MONTH
                         ;
0259                     SLASH0:
0259  2B D2                        SUB   DX,DX
025B  B2 2F                        MOV   DL,2Fh          ; Slash (/)
025D  B4 02                        MOV   AH,2
025F  CD 21                        INT   21h
                         ;
0261  66| 2B C0                    SUB   EAX,EAX         ; Zero out EAX
0264  8D 3E 01A7 R                 LEA   DI,DATE1
0268  8B D5                        MOV   DX,BP           ; Restore Month/Day
026A  8A C2                        MOV   AL,DL           ; Day
026C  E8 0000 E                    CALL  CODEBAS
                         ;
026F                     DAY:
026F  8A 15                        MOV   DL,BYTE PTR [DI]
0271  0A D2                        OR    DL,DL
0273  0F 84 027E R                 JE    SLASH1
0277  B4 02                        MOV   AH,2            ; Print Day
0279  CD 21                        INT   21h
027B  47                           INC   DI              ; Go to next byte
027C  EB F1                        JMP   DAY
                         ;
027E                     SLASH1:
027E  B2 2F                        MOV   DL,2Fh          ; Slash (/)
0280  B4 02                        MOV   AH,2
0282  CD 21                        INT   21h
                         ;
0284  8D 3E 01A7 R                 LEA   DI,DATE1
0288  8B C1                        MOV   AX,CX           ; Year
028A  E8 0000 E                    CALL  CODEBAS
028D  83 C7 02                     ADD   DI,2            ; Skip first two digits
0290                     YEAR:
0290  8A 15                        MOV   DL,BYTE PTR [DI]
0292  0A D2                        OR    DL,DL
0294  0F 84 029F R                 JE    SYSTEM
0298  B4 02                        MOV   AH,2
029A  CD 21                        INT   21h
029C  47                           INC   DI              ; Go to next digit
029D  EB F1                        JMP   YEAR
                         ;
029F                     SYSTEM:
029F  8D 16 0009 R                 LEA   DX,HEADING      ; Print the Heading
02A3  B4 09                        MOV   AH,9h
02A5  CD 21                        INT   21h
02A7  CD 11                        INT   11h             ; Get equipment information
02A9  50                           PUSH  AX              ; Save the info
02AA  2B D2                        SUB   DX,DX
                         ;
                         ; Do number of installed Drives
                         ;
02AC  C0 E8 06                     SHR   AL,6            ; Leave only # of drives
02AF  8D 16 0083 R                 LEA   DX,DRIVES       ; The beginning of this array
02B3  B1 10                        MOV   CL,16           ; Each array element is 16 bytes
02B5  F6 E1                        MUL   CL              ; This multiplies AL by 16
02B7  03 D0                        ADD   DX,AX           ; Now has the array start point
02B9  B4 09                        MOV   AH,9h           ; Ready to print drives
02BB  CD 21                        INT   21h
                         ;
                         ; Now do Video Mode
                         ;
02BD  2B D2                        SUB   DX,DX
02BF  58                           POP   AX              ; Retrieve the original info
```

Program 9-13 Continued.

```
02C0  50                          PUSH    AX                    ; Keep info unchanged
02C1  8D 16 002B R                LEA     DX,VIDEO              ; Beginning array point
02C5  C0 EC 02                    SHL     AL,2                 ; Get rid of top 2 bits
02C8  C0 E8 06                    SHR     AL,6                 ; Now Video mode=AL
02CB  B1 16                       MOV     CL,22                ; Each entry 22 bytes long
02CD  F6 E1                       MUL     CL                   ; Multiply value in AL by 22
02CF  03 D0                       ADD     DX,AX                ; Point at right array element
02D1  B4 09                       MOV     AH,9h                ; Print
02D3  CD 21                       INT     21h

                            ;
                            ; Number of RS232 Cards
                            ;
02D5  8D 16 0107 R                LEA     DX,CR_LF
02D9  B4 09                       MOV     AH,9h
02DB  CD 21                       INT     21h
02DD  8D 16 0105 R                LEA     DX,BLANK             ; Print a blank, to line up output
02E1  B4 09                       MOV     AH,9h
02E3  CD 21                       INT     21h
02E5  58                          POP     AX                   ; Go get that info again
02E6  50                          PUSH    AX                   ; Save info
02E7  C0 E4 04                    SHL     AH,4                 ; Get rid of top 4 bits
02EA  C0 EC 05                    SHR     AH,5
02ED  80 C4 30                    ADD     AH,30h               ; Make it printable
02F0  8A D4                       MOV     DL,AH                ; Put it where INT knows to print
02F2  B4 02                       MOV     AH,2h                ; Get ready to print RS232 #
02F4  CD 21                       INT     21h
02F6  8D 16 00C3 R                LEA     DX,RS232             ; Print 'RS232'
02FA  B4 09                       MOV     AH,9h
02FC  CD 21                       INT     21h

                            ;
                            ; Internal Modem present?
                            ;
02FE  58                          POP     AX                   ; Go retrieve info
02FF  50                          PUSH    AX                   ; Save one more time
0300  A9 2000                     TEST    AX,0010000000000000B ; Is there an internal?
0303  0F 84 030E R                JE      NONE
0307  8D 16 00D0 R                LEA     DX,YESMODEM          ; Print that there IS a modem
030B  EB 05 90                    JMP     NEXTOPTN
030E              NONE:
030E  8D 16 00E5 R                LEA     DX,NOMODEM           ; Print that there is NOT
0312              NEXTOPTN:
0312  B4 09                       MOV     AH,9h
0314  CD 21                       INT     21h

                            ;
                            ; Number of Printers Attached
                            ;
0316  8D 16 0107 R                LEA     DX,CR_LF
031A  B4 09                       MOV     AH,9
031C  CD 21                       INT     21h
031E  8D 16 0105 R                LEA     DX,BLANK             ; Print a blank, to line up output
0322  B4 09                       MOV     AH,9h
0324  CD 21                       INT     21h
0326  58                          POP     AX                   ; Get info again.
0327  50                          PUSH    AX
0328  C0 EC 06                    SHR     AH,6                 ; Printers in last two bits
032B  80 C4 30                    ADD     AH,30h               ; Make it printable
032E  8A D4                       MOV     DL,AH
0330  B4 02                       MOV     AH,2h                ; Print # of printers
0332  CD 21                       INT     21h
0334  8D 16 00FA R                LEA     DX,PRINTERS          ; Now print 'Printers'
0338  B4 09                       MOV     AH,9h
033A  CD 21                       INT     21h

                            ;
                            ; Now see if there is a math coprocessor
                            ;
```

```
033C  58                              POP     AX
033D  50                              PUSH    AX
033E  A9 0002                         TEST    AX,0000000000000010B  ;Is there one?
0341  0F 84 034C R                    JZ      NO_PROC          ; No
                            ;
0345                        INSTALLED:
0345  8D 16 0131 R                    LEA     DX,YES_PROCESR    ; Load offset to Message
0349  EB 05 90                        JMP     PRNTMSG          ; Exit this procedure
034C                        NO_PROC:
034C  8D 16 010A R                    LEA     DX,NO_PROCESSR    ; Load offset to Message
0350                        PRNTMSG:
0350  B4 09                           MOV     AH,9h            ; Get ready to print msg
0352  CD 21                           INT     21h              ; Print message

                            ;
                            ; Find default drive
                            ;      After INT 21 Function 19, AL holds the current disk, where
                            ;      0=A, 1=B, 2=C, and so on.
                            ;
0354  B4 19                           MOV     AH,19h
0356  CD 21                           INT     21h
0358  B1 1F                           MOV     CL,31            ; Each array element 31 bytes
035A  F6 E1                           MUL     CL               ; Multiply value in AL by 21
035C  8D 16 01B3 R                    LEA     DX,DEFAULT
0360  03 D0                           ADD     DX,AX            ; Point at right array element
0362  B4 09                           MOV     AH,9h            ; Get ready to print RAM #
0364  CD 21                           INT     21h
                            ;
                            ; Default disk the IPL disk?
                            ;
0366  58                              POP     AX               ; Retrieve again
0367  A9 0001                         TEST    AX,0000000000000001B ; Check the bit
036A  8D 16 0157 R                    LEA     DX,IPLYES        ; assume it is on
036E  0F 85 0376 R                    JNZ     GOODGUESS        ; It was
0372  8D 16 0178 R                    LEA     DX,IPLNO         ; oh well,
0376                        GOODGUESS:
0376  B4 09                           MOV     AH,9h            ; Get ready to print MSG
0378  CD 21                           INT     21h
                            ;
                            ; End of Program - Wrap-Up
                            ;
037A                        ENDHERE:
037A  B4 4C                           MOV     AH,4Ch           ; Standard Ending
037C  CD 21                           INT     21h
037E                        CODE    ENDS
                                      END     FIND_CFG
```

Program 9-14 GET__FREE

Microsoft (R) Macro Assembler Version 5.00


```
                                      PAGE    55,132
                                      .386
                                      EXTRN   CODEASB:PROC
                                      EXTRN   CODEBAS:PROC
0000                        STACK   SEGMENT 'STACK' STACK
0000  0064[                          DW      100 DUP(?)
         ????
                    ]

00C8                        STACK   ENDS
0000                        CODE    SEGMENT para 'CODE' PUBLIC USE16
                                      ASSUME  CS:CODE, DS:CODE, SS:STACK
                            ;
                            ; Name:       GET_FREE
```

Program 9-14 Continued.

```
                                      ;  Purpose:        This program checks whichever disk number is
                                      ;                  entered and checks how many free bytes are
                                      ;                  available.
                                      ;
                                      ;  Inputs:         Disk drive number, per menu.
                                      ;
                                      ;  Process:
                                      ;
                                      ;  Outputs:        A message with the number of free bytes.
                                      ;
0000                                  GET_FREE:
0000  8C C8                                           MOV      AX,CS              ; Prepare to set DS
0002  8E D8                                           MOV      DS,AX              ;    and set it.
0004  8E C0                                           MOV      ES,AX
0006  E9 00B3 R                                       JMP      BEGINHERE
                                      ;
0009  0A 0D 44 72 69 76 65           DRIVE_ERR        DB       0Ah,0Dh,'Drive is invalid.$'
      20 69 73 20 69 6E 76
      61 6C 69 64 2E 24
001D  0A 0D 59 6F 75 72 20           DRIVE_MENU       DB       0Ah,0Dh,'Your choices are:'
      63 68 6F 69 63 65 73
      20 61 72 65 3A
0030  0A 0D 20 20 30 20 3D                            DB       0Ah,0Dh,'  0 = Default'
      20 44 65 66 61 75 6C
      74
003F  0A 0D 20 20 31 20 3D                            DB       0Ah,0Dh,'  1 = A'
      20 41
0048  0A 0D 20 20 32 20 3D                            DB       0Ah,0Dh,'  2 = B'
      20 42
0051  0A 0D 20 20 33 20 3D                            DB       0Ah,0Dh,'  3 = C'
      20 43
005A  0A 0D 20 20 34 20 3D                            DB       0Ah,0Dh,'  4 = D'
      20 44
0063  0A 0D 45 6E 74 65 72                            DB       0Ah,0Dh,'Enter Drive (0, - 4) > $'
      20 44 72 69 76 65 20
      28 30 2C 20 2D 20 34
      29 20 3E 20 24
007D  0004[                          DRIVE_NO         DB       4 DUP(?)
        ??
                      ]
0081  0A 0D 54 68 65 20 64           FREE_SPACE       DB       0Ah,0Dh,'The drive has $'
      72 69 76 65 20 68 61
      73 20 24
0092  20 62 79 74 65 73 20           BYTE_FREE        DB       ' bytes free.$'
      66 72 65 65 2E 24
009F  0014[                          NO_BYTES         DB       20 DUP(?)
        ??
                      ]


                                      ;
00B3                                  BEGINHERE:
00B3  C6 06 007D R 04                                 MOV      DRIVE_NO,4         ; Max one character entered
00B8  8D 16 001D R                                    LEA      DX,DRIVE_MENU      ; First print choices header
00BC  B4 09                                           MOV      AH,9
00BE  CD 21                                           INT      21h
                                      ;
00C0  8D 16 007D R                                    LEA      DX,DRIVE_NO        ; Now get choice number
00C4  B4 0A                                           MOV      AH,0Ah
00C6  CD 21                                           INT      21h

                                      ;  CODEASB:
                                      ;       SI = String to be converted
                                      ;       CX = Count of digits to be converted
                                      ;       If Carry Flag = 0, successful
                                      ;               AX contains the result
                                      ;       If Carry Flag = 1, unsuccessful
```

```
                            ;              AX is 0
                            ;
00C8  8D 36 007D R              LEA     SI,DRIVE_NO      ; Load input buffer into SI
00CC  83 C6 02                  ADD     SI,2             ; Skip the first two bytes
00CF  2B C9                     SUB     CX,CX
00D1  8A 0E 007E R              MOV     CL,DRIVE_NO[1]   ; Count actually entered
00D5  E8 0000 E                 CALL    CODEASB
00D8  0F 82 00F0 R              JC      ERROR0           ; Is Carry Flag set?
00DC  3D 0005                   CMP     AX,5             ; Too high a number?
00DF  0F 8D 00F0 R              JGE     ERROR0

00E3                       GETSPACE:
00E3  8A D0                     MOV     DL,AL            ; Drive Number (0,1,2,3,4)
00E5  B4 36                     MOV     AH,36h           ; Free disk space
00E7  CD 21                     INT     21h
                            ;
                            ; AX = FFFF if drive number is invalid
                            ;    = Number of sectors per cluster
                            ; BX = Number of available clusters
                            ; CX = Bytes per sector
                            ;
00E9  3D 0FFF                   CMP     AX,0FFFh         ; Was drive invalid?
00EC  0F 85 00FB R              JNE     FREE0            ; No, go calculate
00F0                       ERROR0:
00F0  8D 16 0009 R              LEA     DX,DRIVE_ERR     ; Entry error
00F4  B4 09                     MOV     AH,9
00F6  CD 21                     INT     21h
00F8  EB 41 90                  JMP     ENDHERE
                            ;
00FB                       FREE0:
00FB  66| 25 0000FFFF           AND     EAX,0000FFFFh    ; Ensure top half is clear
0101  66| 81 E3 0000FFFF        AND     EBX,0000FFFFh
0108  66| 81 E1 0000FFFF        AND     ECX,0000FFFFh
010F  66| F7 E1                 MUL     ECX              ; Mul bytes x sectors=bytes/cluster
0112  66| F7 E3                 MUL     EBX              ; Mul by avail clusters
                            ;
                            ; CODEBAS
                            ;     AX = Number to be converted
                            ;     DI = Pointer to char string returned
                            ;
0115  8D 3E 009F R              LEA     DI,NO_BYTES      ; Space for returned char str
0119  E8 0000 E                 CALL    CODEBAS
011C  8D 16 0081 R              LEA     DX,FREE_SPACE    ; Print Header
0120  B4 09                     MOV     AH,9
0122  CD 21                     INT     21H
0124                       FREE1:
0124  8A 15                     MOV     DL,BYTE PTR [DI]
0126  0A D2                     OR      DL,DL
0128  0F 84 0133 R              JE      LASTMSG
012C  B4 02                     MOV     AH,2
012E  CD 21                     INT     21h
0130  47                        INC     DI
0131  EB F1                     JMP     FREE1
                            ;
0133                       LASTMSG:
0133  8D 16 0092 R              LEA     DX,BYTE_FREE     ; Print last word.
0137  B4 09                     MOV     AH,9
0139  CD 21                     INT     21h
013B                       ENDHERE:
013B  B4 4C                     MOV     AH,4Ch           ; Standard Ending
013D  CD 21                     INT     21h
013F                  CODE     ENDS
                               END      GET_FREE
```

Program 9-15 FIND_COP

```
                              PAGE    55,132
                              .386
0000                  STACK   SEGMENT 'STACK' STACK
0000  0064[           DW      100 DUP(?)
      ????
                  ]

00C8                  STACK   ENDS
0000                  CODE    SEGMENT para 'CODE' PUBLIC USE16
                              ASSUME  CS:CODE, DS:CODE, SS:STACK
                      ;
                      ; Purpose:        This macro finds out whether or not the
                      ;                 numeric coprocessor is installed.
                      ;
                      ; Inputs:         Move 14h into Register AL
                      ;
                      ; Process:        Function 14h determines if the numeric
                      ;                 coprocessor is installed.  Move 14h into
                      ;                 AL and test if AL=10B.
                      ;
                      ; Outputs:        A message whether or not a coprocessor is
                      ;                 installed
                      ;
0000                  FIND_COP:
0000  8C C8                   MOV     AX,CS           ; Prepare to set DS
0002  8E D8                   MOV     DS,AX           ;    and set it.
0004  EB 48 90                JMP     BEGINHERE
0007  54 68 65 72 65 20 69   NO_PROCESSR  DB  'There is no coprocessor installed',0Ah,0Dh,'$'
      73 20 6E 6F 20 63 6F
      70 72 6F 63 65 73 73
      6F 72 20 69 6E 73 74
      61 6C 6C 65 64 0A 0D
      24
002B  54 68 65 72 65 20 69   YES_PROCESR  DB  'There is a coprocessor installed',0Ah,0Dh,'$'
      73 20 61 20 63 6F 70
      72 6F 63 65 73 73 6F
      72 20 69 6E 73 74 61
      6C 6C 65 64 0A 0D 24

004E                  BEGINHERE:
004E  B0 14                   MOV     AL,14h          ; Move function 14h into AL
0050  E6 70                   OUT     70h,AL          ; Send the register request
0052  E4 71                   IN      AL,71h          ; Read the register
0054  A8 02                   TEST    AL,10b          ; Is bit 1 set?
0056  0F 84 0061 R            JZ      NO_PROC         ; Send message if not installed
005A                  INSTALLED:
005A  8D 16 002B R            LEA     DX,YES_PROCESR  ; Load offset to Message
005E  EB 06 90                JMP     PRNTMSG         ; Exit this procedure
0061                  NO_PROC:
0061  50                      PUSH    AX
0062  8D 16 0007 R            LEA     DX,NO_PROCESSR  ; Load offset to Message
0066                  PRNTMSG:
0066  B4 09                   MOV     AH,9h           ; Get ready to print msg
0068  CD 21                   INT     21h             ; Print message
006A  58                      POP     AX
006B                  EXITHERE:
006B  B4 4C                   MOV     AH,4Ch          ; Standard Ending
006D  CD 21                   INT     21h
006F                  CODE    ENDS
                              END     FIND_COP
```

Program 9-16 FIND_VER

Microsoft (R) Macro Assembler Version 5.00

```
                              PAGE    55,132
                              .386
0000                  STACK   SEGMENT 'STACK' STACK
0000  0064[           DW      100 DUP(?)
        ????
                  ]

00C8                  STACK   ENDS
0000                  CODE    SEGMENT para 'CODE' PUBLIC USE16
                              ASSUME  CS:CODE, DS:CODE, SS:STACK
                      ;
                      ; Purpose:      This program finds which version of DOS
                      ;               is installed on a computer.
                      ;
                      ; Inputs:       Move 30h into AH
                      ;
                      ; Process:      Function 30h of INT 21 returns the DOS number.
                      ;               The major version number (for example, the "3"
                      ;               of 3.10) returns in AL.  The minor version number
                      ;               (the ".10" of 3.10) returns in AH.  Interrupt 21
                      ;               destroys registers BX and CS.
                      ;
                      ; Outputs:      Major version in AL, minor in AH.
                      ;
0000                  FIND_VER:
0000  8C C8                   MOV     AX,CS           ; Prepare to set DS
0002  8E D8                   MOV     DS,AX           ;   and set it.
0004  EB 18 90                JMP     BEGINHERE
0007  59 6F 75 72 20 44 4F    Version_no  DB  'Your DOS version is $'
      53 20 76 65 72 73 69
      6F 6E 20 69 73 20 24
001C  2E 24           Period  DB      '.$'
001E                  BEGINHERE:
001E  8D 16 0007 R            LEA     DX,Version_no   ; Load offset to message
0022  B4 09                   MOV     AH,9h           ; Get ready to print the string
0024  CD 21                   INT     21h             ; Print it
0026  B4 30                   MOV     AH,30h          ; Move function 30 into AH
0028  CD 21                   INT     21h             ; This gets the DOS version
002A  50                      PUSH    AX              ; Save Version Number
002B  8A D0                   MOV     DL,AL           ; Move Major Version Number
002D  80 C2 30                ADD     DL,30h          ; Make high order 0011/0100
0030  B4 02                   MOV     AH,2h           ; Get ready to print version
0032  CD 21                   INT     21h             ; Print major version
0034  8D 16 001C R            LEA     DX,Period       ; Now print the "."
0038  B4 09                   MOV     AH,9h
003A  CD 21                   INT     21h
003C  58                      POP     AX              ; Retrieve the Major/Minor
003D  C1 E8 08                SHR     AX,8            ; Move minor version
0040  50                      PUSH    AX              ;   and save it
0041  8B D0                   MOV     DX,AX           ; Save only minor version now
0043  80 C2 10                ADD     DL,16
0046  C0 EA 04                SHR     DL,4            ; Want high-order of two digits
0049  80 C2 30                ADD     DL,30h          ; Make it printable
004C  B4 02                   MOV     AH,2h
004E  CD 21                   INT     21h
0050  58                      POP     AX              ; Now get low order number
0051  8B D0                   MOV     DX,AX
0053  C0 E2 07                SHL     DL,7
0056  C0 EA 07                SHR     DL,7
0059  80 C2 30                ADD     DL,30h          ; Make it printable
005C  B4 02                   MOV     AH,2h
005E  CD 21                   INT     21h
0060                  ENDHERE:
```

Program 9-16 Continued.

```
0060  B4 4C                          MOV    AH,4Ch        ; Standard Ending
0062  CD 21                          INT    21h
0064                    CODE         ENDS
                                     END    FIND_VER
```

Program 9-17 PAUSE

```
                                     PAGE      55,132
                                     .386
0000                    code         SEGMENT   para 'CODE' USE16 PUBLIC
                                     ASSUME    CS:code, DS:code, SS:code
                        ;
                        ; Name;     PAUSE
                        ;
                        ; Purpose: The following procedure provides a means of pausing
                        ;          for a time span of from .02 seconds to 59.99 seconds.
                        ;          The clock does not increment smoothly so the granularity
                        ;          is not to the hundredth.
                        ;
                        ;
                        ; Inputs:  DH should contain the number of seconds to delay.
                        ;          DL should contain the number of hundredths to delay.
                        ;
                        ; Process: The seconds and hundredths are edited for conformance
                        ;          with their value range. (DH 0-59, DL 0-99 and DX >1)
                        ;          If invalid, carry is set and the procedure returns.
                        ;          The target time is computed as current time + ss.hh.
                        ;          We then loop, getting and checking the current time
                        ;          until we get a time greater than our target.
                        ;
                        ; Output:  The output is simply the delay in time.  Carry is set
                        ;          if the input values were bad and reset otherwise.
                        ;
                        ; Note:    The complete time is compared because the clock does
                        ;          not update 'smoothly' (which would allow us to check
                        ;          only the seconds and hundredths).
                        ;
                        ;
                                     PUBLIC  Pause           ; Make the name usable
0000                    Pause        PROC
0000  52                             push    DX              ; Save entry registers
0001  51                             push    CX
0002  53                             push    BX
0003  50                             push    AX
0004  56                             push    SI
0005  83 FA 02                       cmp     DX,2            ; Check for minimum wait
0008  0F 82 0098 R                   jb      badwait         ; If < 2 it is bad
000C  80 FA 64                       cmp     DL,100          ; Is hundredths 0-99
000F  0F 83 0098 R                   jnb     badwait         ; If not - bad
0013  80 FE 3C                       cmp     DH,60           ; Is seconds 0-59
0016  0F 83 0098 R                   jnb     badwait         ; If not - bad
001A  8B DA                          mov     BX,DX           ; Save for computation
                        ;
                        ; Pause procedure, first compute the time to stop the loop.
                        ;
001C  B4 2C                          mov     AH,2ch          ; Get the Time of Day
001E  CD 21                          int     21h
0020  02 DA                          add     BL,DL           ; Add the current time (.01s)
0022  80 FB 64                       cmp     BL,100          ; Flow over the max hundredths?
0025  0F 82 002E R                   jb      notover         ; No overflow
0029  80 EB 64                       sub     BL,100          ; Get back to less than a sec
002C  FE C7                          inc     BH              ; Step the seconds figure
002E                    notover:
002E  02 FE                          add     BH,DH           ; add current seconds
```

```
0030   80 FF 3C              cmp     BH,60           ; Flow over a minute?
0033   OF 82 0051 R          jb      notovers        ; No
0037   80 EF 3C              sub     BH,60           ; If so, bring down to range.
003A   FE C1                 inc     CL              ; add to minutes
003C   80 F9 3C              cmp     CL,60           ; Overflow into hours?
003F   OF 82 0051 R          jb      notovers        ; No - don't change
0043   80 E9 3C              sub     CL,60           ; Back to minutes
0046   FE C5                 inc     CH              ; Roll to the hour
0048   80 FD 18              cmp     CH,24
004B   OF 82 0051 R          jb      notovers        ; Not across midnight
004F   2A ED                 sub     CH,CH           ; We are at hour zero
0051          notovers:
0051   8B F3                 mov     SI,BX           ; Save low order times
0053   8B D9                 mov     BX,CX           ; Get target time hh:mm
0055          gethour:
0055   CD 21                 int     21h             ; get next time
0057   3A FD                 cmp     BH,CH           ; check the hour
0059   OF 84 007B R          je      getmin          ; we are there.
005D   OF 82 006D R          jb      chkmid          ; If hour is high loop
       ;
       ; New hour is < target - if 0:23 we rolled over midnight
       ;
0061   80 FF 17              cmp     BH,23           ; Is target 2300
0064   75 EF                 jne     gethour         ; If not - not there yet
0066   OA ED                 or      CH,CH           ; Is new 0000 (2200)
0068   75 EB                 jne     gethour         ; No - let hour roll over
006A   EB 25 90              jmp     passed          ; Yes - we went across
       ;
       ; Target hour is < new hour - if 0:23 wait for midnight
       ;
006D          chkmid:
006D   OA FF                 or      BH,BH           ; Across midnight
006F   OF 85 0091 R          jnz     passed          ; if not - time is expired.
0073   80 FD 17              cmp     CH,23           ; Waiting for midnight?
0076   74 DD                 je      gethour         ; Yes - delay some more.
0078   EB 17 90              jmp     passed          ; No ( 0:1) time expired
       ;
       ; The hour is equal
       ;
007B          getmin:
007B   3A D9                 cmp     BL,CL           ; Check for minute
007D   OF 82 0091 R          jb      passed          ; If target is low - done
0081   77 D2                 ja      gethour         ; If not there - loop
0083   8B CE                 mov     CX,SI           ; Get low order times
0085   3A EE                 cmp     CH,DH           ; At a second yet?
0087   77 CC                 ja      gethour         ; No - get another time
0089   OF 82 0091 R          jb      passed          ; beyond - we get out.
008D   3A CA                 cmp     CL,DL           ; Check hundredths
008F   77 C4                 ja      gethour         ; If low, branch
0091          passed:
0091   F8                    clc                     ; reset carry
0092          exit:
0092   5E                    pop     SI
0093   58                    pop     AX              ; Restore the entry registers
0094   5B                    pop     BX
0095   59                    pop     CX
0096   5A                    pop     DX
0097   C3                    ret                     ; and return
0098          badwait:
0098   F9                    stc                     ; set carry
0099   EB F7                 jmp     exit            ; and return
009B          Pause   ENDP
009B          code    ENDS
                      END
```

Program 9-18 CHKPAUSE

```
                                      .386
                            ; Name:    CHKPAUSE
                            ;
                            ; Purpose: This program provides a simple visual check of the pause
                            ;          routine.
                            ;
                            ; Inputs:  Nothing.
                            ;
                            ; Process: Display tick, call pause for .5 sec delay then flip to
                            ;          tock.  Repeat 200 times.
                            ;
                            ; Outputs: A tick TOCK display for 100 seconds.
                            ;
                            ; Declare the routines we are going to use
                                      EXTRN    Pause:PROC
                            ;
0000                        stack     SEGMENT para 'STACK' STACK
0000   0100[                          dq       256 DUP(?)
        ??????????????????
        ?
                       ]

0800                        stack     ENDS
0000                        data      SEGMENT para
0000   0D 74 69 63 6B 24    tick      db       13,"tick$"
0006   0D 54 4F 43 4B 24    tock      db       13,"TOCK$"
000C                        data      ENDS
0000                        code      SEGMENT para 'CODE' USE16 PUBLIC
                                      ASSUME   CS:code, DS:data
                            ;
                            ; Set up the environment
                            ;
0000                        Begin:
0000   B8 ---- R                      mov      AX,data         ; Get data segment pointer
0003   8E D8                          mov      DS,AX           ; into DS,
0005   8E C0                          mov      ES,AX           ; and ES.
0007   2B F6                          sub      SI,SI           ; Clear indices
0009   2B FF                          sub      DI,DI
000B   8D 3E 0000 R                   lea      DI,tick
000F   8D 36 0006 R                   lea      SI,tock
0013   B9 00C8                        mov      CX,200
0016                        looph:
0016   87 F7                          xchg     SI,DI           ; Flip them
0018   8B D6                          mov      DX,SI
001A   B4 09                          mov      AH,9
001C   CD 21                          int      21h             ; display tick or TOCK
001E   BA 0032                        mov      DX,50           ; Set half second
0021   E8 0000 E                      call     Pause           ; Wait .5 seconds
0024   E2 F0                          loop     looph           ; Do it again
0026   B0 00                          mov      AL,0            ; Set return code
0028   B4 4C                          mov      AH,04ch         ; Set good-by
002A   CD 21                          int      21h             ; Return to the system
002C                        code      ENDS
                                      END      begin
```

Program 9-19 PCNAME

```
Microsoft (R) Macro Assembler Version 5.00




                                      PAGE     55,132
                                      .386
0000                        STACK     SEGMENT 'STACK' STACK
0000   0064[                          DW       100 DUP(?)
```

```
                ????
                              ]

00C8                          STACK   ENDS
0000                          CODE    SEGMENT para 'CODE' PUBLIC USE16
                                      ASSUME  CS:CODE, DS:CODE, SS:STACK
                              ;
                              ; Name:       PCNAME
                              ;
                              ; Purpose:    For most PCs currently in the market, this will get
                              ;             the "name" of the PC.  PCs often identify themselves
                              ;             in a one-byte ID in F000:FFFE, the next to the last
                              ;             location in regular memory.
                              ;
                              ; Inputs:     Nothing
                              ;
                              ; Process:    When the program assembles, the data segment is set.
                              ;             Then the location 0F000h is moved into BX and from
                              ;             there into DS, changing the pointer of the data
                              ;             segment to F000.  Then the offset is loaded into BX
                              ;             and the contents of that address moved into AL.
                              ;
                              ; Outputs:    Message with the name of the computer.
                              ;
                              ; Note:       FF - Original PC
                              ;             FE - PC XT
                              ;             FD - PC Jr
                              ;             FC - PC AT
                              ;
0000                          PCNAME:
0000  8C C8                           MOV     AX,CS           ; Prepare to set DS
0002  8E D8                           MOV     DS,AX           ;   and set it.
0004  EB 54 90                        JMP     BEGINHERE
                              ;
0007  0A 0D 20 43 6F 6D 70    HEADER  DB      0Ah,0Dh,' Computer:  $'
      75 74 65 72 3A 20 20
      24
0016  20 20 20 20 20 20 20    PCTYPE  DB      '              $'
      20 20 20 20 20 24
0023  20 50 43 20 41 54 20            DB      ' PC AT      $'
      20 20 20 20 20 24
0030  20 50 43 20 4A 72 20            DB      ' PC Jr      $'
      20 20 20 20 20 24
003D  20 50 43 20 58 54 20            DB      ' PC XT      $'
      20 20 20 20 20 24
004A  20 4F 72 69 67 69 6E            DB      ' Original PC$'
      61 6C 20 50 43 24
0057  0D 0A 24               CR_LF    DB      0Dh,0Ah,'$'
                              ;
005A                         BEGINHERE:
005A  BB F000                         MOV     BX,0F000h
005D  8E DB                           MOV     DS,BX
005F  BB FFFE                         MOV     BX,0FFFEh
0062  8A 07                           MOV     AL,[BX]
                              ;
0064  8C CA                           MOV     DX,CS           ; Restore data segment
0066  8E DA                           MOV     DS,DX
0068  8B F0                           MOV     SI,AX           ; Save AL value
006A  8D 16 0007 R                    LEA     DX,HEADER       ; Print header
006E  B4 09                           MOV     AH,9
0070  CD 21                           INT     21h
0072  8D 16 0016 R                    LEA     DX,PCTYPE       ; Print header
0076  8B C6                           MOV     AX,SI           ; Restore value into AX
0078  B4 00                           MOV     AH,0            ; Clear AH
007A  2C F0                           SUB     AL,0F0h         ; Remove top nibble
007C  2C 0B                           SUB     AL,11           ; Make answer 1,2,3 or 4
007E  2B C9                           SUB     CX,CX
0080  B1 0D                           MOV     CL,13
```

```
0082  F6 E1                      MUL      CL            ; Each string is 13 bytes
0084  02 D0                      ADD      DL,AL         ; Index into PCTYPE array
0086  B4 09                      MOV      AH,9
0088  CD 21                      INT      21h
008A  8D 16 0057 R               LEA      DX,CR_LF      ; Space up a line
008E  B4 09                      MOV      AH,9
0090  CD 21                      INT      21h
0092              ENDHERE:
0092  B4 4C                      MOV      AH,4Ch        ; Standard Ending
0094  CD 21                      INT      21h
0096              CODE           ENDS
                                 END      PCNAME
```

Program 9-20 RANDNUM

Microsoft (R) Macro Assembler Version 5.00

```
                             PAGE     55,132
                             .386
                             EXTRN    CODEBAS:PROC
0000             STACK       SEGMENT  'STACK' STACK
0000  0064[                  DW       100 DUP(?)
        ????
                      ]

00C8             STACK       ENDS
0000             CODE        SEGMENT  para 'CODE' PUBLIC USE16
                             ASSUME   CS:CODE, DS:CODE, SS:STACK
                 ;
                 ; Name:     RANDNUM
                 ;
                 ; Purpose:  This program generates pseudo-random numbers.  The
                 ;           assumed decimal point is on the left of the answer.
                 ;
                 ; Inputs:   None
                 ;
                 ; Process:  The program gets the time of day and uses the
                 ;           hundredths of a second as a key.  It then rotates
                 ;           the answer three times (arbitrary number).  Then it
                 ;           calls CODEBAS to turn the resultant binary into a
                 ;           printable ASCII.
                 ;
                 ; Outputs:  A message with the generated number.  When it is printed,
                 ;           a decimal point is printed first, to "force" the answer to
                 ;           be between 0 and 1.
                 ;
0000             RANDNUM:
0000  8C C8                  MOV      AX,CS         ; Prepare to set DS
0002  8E D8                  MOV      DS,AX         ;    and set it.
0004  8E C0                  MOV      ES,AX
0006  EB 3E 90               JMP      BEGINHERE
                 ;
0009  0A 0D 20 59 6F 75 72   RANDOM      DB     0Ah,0Dh,' Your random number is > $'
      20 72 61 6E 64 6F 6D
      20 6E 75 6D 62 65 72
      20 69 73 20 3E 20 24
0025  000A[                  OUTPUT_ST   DB     10 DUP (?)
        ??
                      ]

002F  0A 0D 20 45 72 72 6F   CODE_ERR    DB     0Ah,0Dh,' Error in number.$'
      72 20 69 6E 20 6E 75
```

```
              6D 62 65 72 2E 24
0043    0A 0D 24                          CR_LF       DB      0Ah,0Dh,'$'
        ;
0046                                       BEGINHERE:
0046    2B C9                                          SUB     CX,CX           ; Empty CX
0048    B4 2C                                          MOV     AH,2Ch          ; Get time
004A    CD 21                                          INT     21h
        ;
        ; DL now has hundredths of a second
        ;
004C    8A CA                                          MOV     CL,DL
004E    C1 C9 03                                       ROR     CX,3
        ;
        ; Convert result to printable ASCII with CODEBAS
        ;       AX = Word to be converted
        ;       DI = Points to char string for converted returned value
        ;       If successful, Carry Flag = 0
        ;       If not, Carry Flag = 1
        ;
0051    8D 3E 0025 R                                    LEA     DI,OUTPUT_ST
0055    66| 2B C0                                       SUB     EAX,EAX
0058    8A C1                                          MOV     AL,CL           ; Move random number into DL
005A    E8 0000 E                                      CALL    CODEBAS
005D    0F 83 006C R                                   JNC     PRINTO
        ;
        ; Error in CODEBAS result
        ;
0061    8D 16 002F R                                    LEA     DX,CODE_ERR
0065    B4 09                                          MOV     AH,9
0067    CD 21                                          INT     21h
0069    EB 1E 90                                       JMP     ENDHERE
        ;
        ; Print answer
        ;
006C                                       PRINTO:
006C    8D 16 0009 R                                    LEA     DX,RANDOM       ; Print the header
0070    B4 09                                          MOV     AH,9
0072    CD 21                                          INT     21h
0074    BA 002E                                        MOV     DX,2Eh          ; Decimal point (period)
0077    B4 02                                          MOV     AH,2            ; Print the decimal point
0079    CD 21                                          INT     21h
007B    2B D2                                          SUB     DX,DX           ; Clear out DX
007D    8A 15                                          MOV     DL,BYTE PTR [DI] ; Move the byte into DL
007F    0A D2                                          OR      DL,DL           ; Is it hex 00 ?
0081    0F 84 0089 R                                   JE      ENDHERE         ; Yes, go end
0085    B4 02                                          MOV     AH,2            ; Print a single character
0087    CD 21                                          INT     21h
        ;
0089                                       ENDHERE:
0089    8D 16 0043 R                                    LEA     DX,CR_LF        ; Space down one space
008D    B4 09                                          MOV     AH,9
008F    CD 21                                          INT     21h
        ;
0091    B4 4C                                          MOV     AH,4Ch          ; Standard Ending
0093    CD 21                                          INT     21h
0095                                       CODE        ENDS
                                                        END     RANDNUM
```

Program 9-21 SQRT

Microsoft (R) Macro Assembler Version 5.00

PAGE   55,132
.386

Program 9-21 Continued.

```
                              ; Name:        SQRT
                              ;
                              ; Purpose:     This procedure finds the square root of integers of
                              ;              up to five digits.
                              ;
                              ; Inputs:      The original number is requested to be input from
                              ;              the keyboard.
                              ;
                              ; Process:     The procedure calculates the square root by
                              ;              following Newton's Method, which says that if A
                              ;              is an approximation for the square root of a
                              ;              number N, then A1=(N/a + A)2 is a better
                              ;              approximation.  To get to the first approximation,
                              ;              the routine uses (N/200)+2 (where N is the contents
                              ;              of DX:AX and the value 200 is arbitrary.  To get the
                              ;              next approximation, it divides N by the first and
                              ;              averages the two.  For the third, it divides N by
                              ;              the second approximation and averages again.  It
                              ;              repeats until it finds two approximations that are
                              ;              identical (or differ only by 1, whether positive or
                              ;              negative).
                              ;
                              ; Outputs:     Register BX holds the square root.
                              ;
                                       EXTRN    CODEASB:PROC
                                       EXTRN    CODEBAS:PROC
                                       EXTRN    STRZLNG:PROC
0000                          STACK   SEGMENT  'STACK' STACK
0000  0064[                           DW       100 DUP(?)
         ????
                      ]

00C8                          STACK   ENDS
0000                          DATA    SEGMENT para
                              ;
0000  0014[                   INPUT_STR     DB       20 DUP (?)
         ??
                      ]

0014  0014[                   OUTPUT_ST     DB       20 DUP (?)
         ??
                      ]

0028  0A 0D 20 49 6E 70 75    PROMPT        DB       0Ah,0Dh,' Input an integer (0 to end) > $'
      74 20 61 6E 20 69 6E
      74 65 67 65 72 20 28
      30 20 74 6F 20 65 6E
      64 29 20 3E 20 24
004A  0A 0D 20 54 68 65 20    HEADER        DB       0Ah,0Dh,' The answer (to one decimal) > $'
      61 6E 73 77 65 72 20
      28 74 6F 20 6F 6E 65
      20 64 65 63 69 6D 61
      6C 29 20 3E 20 24
006C  0A 0D 20 49 6E 63 6F    BADNUM        DB       0Ah,0Dh,' Incorrect number.  Re-enter.$'
      72 72 65 63 74 20 6E
      75 6D 62 65 72 2E 20
      20 52 65 2D 65 6E 74
      65 72 2E 24
008C  0A 0D 20 53 51 52 54    BADRTN        DB       0Ah,0Dh,' SQRT number incorrect.$'
      20 6E 75 6D 62 65 72
      20 69 6E 63 6F 72 72
      65 63 74 2E 24
00A6  20 24                   BLANK         DB       ' $'
00A8  0A 0D 24                CR_LF         DB       0Ah,0Dh,'$'
00AB                          DATA    ENDS
0000                          CODE    SEGMENT para 'CODE' PUBLIC
```

306   Algorithms

```
                                    ASSUME   CS:CODE, DS:DATA, SS:STACK
0000                            DO_SQRT:
0000  66| B8 ---- R                         MOV      AX,DATA          ; Prepare to set DS
0004  66| 8E D8                             MOV      DS,AX            ;   and set it.
0007  66| 8E C0                             MOV      ES,AX
                                ;
                                ; Get the input number
                                ;
000A                            BEGINHERE:
000A  8D 15 00000028 R                      LEA      DX,PROMPT        ; Print the prompt
0010  B4 09                                 MOV      AH,9h
0012  CD 21                                 INT      21h
0014  C6 05 00000000 R 08                   MOV      INPUT_STR,8      ; Max 8 characters
001B  8D 15 00000000 R                      LEA      DX,INPUT_STR     ; Point at buffer
0021  B4 0A                                 MOV      AH,0Ah           ; Buffered keyboard input
0023  CD 21                                 INT      21h
                                ;
                                ; Allow only ten digits input
                                ;
0025  8A 0D 00000001 R                      MOV      CL,BYTE PTR INPUT_STR[1]
002B  80 F9 0A                              CMP      CL,10
002E  0F 8F 0000004E R                      JG       ERR0
                                ;
                                ; Now convert the ASCII input to a binary number by calling
                                ;       CODEASB.  For CODEASB,
                                ;       SI points to the string to be converted
                                ;       CX is the count of characters
                                ;       If successful, Carry Flag = 0, AX holds returned number
                                ;       If not, Carry Flag = 1
                                ;
0034                            CONVERT:
0034  66| 2B C9                             SUB      CX,CX            ; Be sure CX is empty
0037  8D 35 00000002 R                      LEA      SI,INPUT_STR+2   ; This holds the input number
003D  8A 0D 00000001 R                      MOV      CL,INPUT_STR[1]  ; Count of bytes
0043  E8 00000000 E                         CALL     CODEASB          ; Convert to binary
0048  0F 83 0000006F R                      JNC      BEGIN
                                ;
                                ; Error - bad number
                                ;
004E                            ERR0:
004E  8D 15 0000006C R                      LEA      DX,BADNUM        ; Print error
0054  EB 09 90 90 90                        JMP      ERR2
0059                            ERR1:
0059  8D 15 0000008C R                      LEA      DX,BADRTN
005F                            ERR2:
005F  B4 09                                 MOV      AH,9
0061  CD 21                                 INT      21h
0063  8D 15 000000A8 R                      LEA      DX,CR_LF         ; Go get next number
0069  B4 09                                 MOV      AH,9
006B  CD 21                                 INT      21h
006D  EB 9B                                 JMP      BEGINHERE
                                ;
006F                            BEGIN:
006F  0B C0                                 OR       EAX,EAX          ; Any number?
0071  0F 84 000000FE R                      JZ       ENDHERE          ; Yes, go end the program
                                ;
0077  B9 00000064                           MOV      ECX,100          ; Multiply by 100 for greater
007C  F7 E1                                 MUL      ECX              ;   precision
                                ;
007E                            NEXTNUM:
007E  52                                    PUSH     EDX              ; Save the number
007F  50                                    PUSH     EAX
0080  66| 8B EC                             MOV      BP,SP            ; Point to it in stack
0083  BB 000000C8                           MOV      EBX,200          ; First approximation
0088  F7 F3                                 DIV      EBX              ; Divide source by 200
008A  83 C0 02                              ADD      EAX,2
008D                            AGAIN:
008D  8B D8                                 MOV      EBX,EAX          ; Save this guess/approximation
```

Program 9-21 Continued.

```
008F   67| 8B 56 04                     MOV    EDX,[BP+4]       ; Get source number again
0093   67| 8B 46 00                     MOV    EAX,[BP]
0097   F7 F3                            DIV    EBX              ; Divide by last approx.
0099   66| 2B D2                        SUB    DX,DX            ; First could need DX because
                                                               ;   of scaling by 100.
009C   03 C3                            ADD    EAX,EBX          ; Average last two approx
009E   D1 E8                            SHR    EAX,1

                                  ;
00A0   2B D8                            SUB    EBX,EAX          ; Check for difference of 1
00A2   0F 84 000000B3 R                 JE     FINISHED         ; Zero, go exit
00A8   0F 89 000000B0 R                 JNS    FINISHEDQ
00AE   F7 DB                            NEG    EBX              ; Get absolute value
00B0                             FINISHEDQ:
00B0   4B                               DEC    EBX              ; Was diff 1?
00B1   75 DA                            JNZ    AGAIN

                                  ;
                                  ;    When finished, convert the binary back to ASCII by calling
                                  ;    CODEBAS.  CODEBAS requires:
                                  ;    EAX = the word to be converted (it holds square root now)
                                  ;    DI points to the character string to store the answer
                                  ;    If successful, Carry Flag = 0
                                  ;    If not, Carry Flag = 1
                                  ;
00B3                             FINISHED:
00B3   5B                               POP    EBX              ; Clear the stack.
00B4   5B                               POP    EBX
00B5   8D 3D 00000014 R                 LEA    DI,OUTPUT_ST
00BB   E8 00000000 E                    CALL   CODEBAS
00C0   72 8C                            JC     ERRO

                                  ;
                                  ; Print the result
                                  ;    To decide where to put decimal on output, find the length
                                  ;    of the answer, call STRZLNG
                                  ;    STRZLNG: ES:DI - Address of ASCIIZ string
                                  ;             Note: in this case DI already holds the correct start
                                  ;                   of the string, so do not reset it.
                                  ;             CX - Maximum length to examine
                                  ;             If successful, Carry Flag=0, AX = count of bytes in
                                  ;                   the string excluding the terminating null
                                  ;             If not, Carry Flag = 1, AX returned equal to CX
                                  ;
00C2   66| B9 000A                      MOV    CX,10            ; Max length of string
00C6   E8 00000000 E                    CALL   STRZLNG          ; Find length of the string
00CB   0F 83 000000D3 R                 JNC    PRNTO
00D1   EB 86                            JMP    ERR1
00D3                             PRNTO:
00D3   66| 8B F0                        MOV    SI,AX            ; Save the length
00D6   8D 15 0000004A R                 LEA    DX,HEADER
00DC   B4 09                            MOV    AH,9h
00DE   CD 21                            INT    21h
00E0   66| 2B D2                        SUB    DX,DX
00E3   66| 8B CE                        MOV    CX,SI            ; Put length in loop register
00E6   66| 49                           DEC    CX               ; Back up 1 count, then loop
00E8   B4 02                            MOV    AH,2             ; Print a character
00EA                             PRNT1:
00EA   67| 8A 15                        MOV    DL,BYTE PTR [DI] ; Print each digit
00ED   CD 21                            INT    21h
00EF   66| 47                           INC    DI
00F1   E2 F7                            LOOP   PRNT1

                                  ;
00F3   B2 2E                            MOV    DL,2Eh           ; Decimal point
00F5   B4 02                            MOV    AH,2
00F7   CD 21                            INT    21h
00F9   67| 8A 15                        MOV    DL,BYTE PTR [DI] ; Now print last digit
00FC   CD 21                            INT    21h
```

```
                              ;
00FE                          ENDHERE:
00FE  8D 15 000000A8 R                        LEA     DX,CR_LF        ; Space up one line
0104  B4 09                                   MOV     AH,9
0106  CD 21                                   INT     21h
                              ;
0108  B4 4C                                   MOV     AH,4Ch          ; Standard Ending
010A  CD 21                                   INT     21h
010C                          CODE            ENDS
                                              END     DO_SQRT
```

Program 9-22   BUFF486

```
1
2                                 .486
3                             ;
4                             ; Name:       BUFF486
5                             ;
6                             ; Purpose:    This program provides a contention free push-down stack
7                             ;             manager.  Its two entry points (getbuf and putbuf) use
8                             ;             the 80486 cmpxchg instruction to proper stack management
9                             ;             in a general multiprocessing or multiprogramming
10                            ;             environment.
11                            ;
12                            ; Inputs:     Both entries work off the buffer stack which is pointed
13                            ;             to by DS:SI.  The stack is assumed to be totally within a 64K
14                            ;             segment. NOTE: The 16 bit restriction can easily be removed
15                            ;             by simply using the 32 bit register set (i.e. replace AX with
16                            ;             EAX, etc.) in these routines.
17                            ;
18                            ;             getbuf requires no input from the caller (except SI).
19                            ;
20                            ;             putbuf assumes the address (offset) of the buffer being
21                            ;             returned is in AX.
22                            ;
23                            ; Process:    The buffer pool is a simple push down stack.  No assumption
24                            ;             is made about the buffer size or the location of the
25                            ;             pointer within it.  The pointers are assumed to point to
26                            ;             the next pointer location and in the example are at the
27                            ;             beginning of the buffer.  The end of stack indicator is
28                            ;             a next pointer of zero.
29                            ;
30                            ;                getbuf loads the next buffer pointer and checks if it is
31                            ;             end of stack.  If not, the pointer is used to get the next
32                            ;             address.  If it was zero, zero is used as the next address.
33                            ;             The next address conditionally replaces the top of stack
34                            ;             using the cmpxchg instruction.  If an access conflict
35                            ;             occurs the process is repeated. Note: Even when the empty
36                            ;             stack indication is initially obtained, the cmpxchg is
37                            ;             executed - a return could occur between the fetch and the cmpxchg.
38                            ;
```

```
39                           ;           putbuf receives the address of the buffer being returned.
40                           ;           It moves the top of stack pointer to the address word of the
41                           ;           buffer and then conditionally replaces the top of stack
42                           ;           address with the new buffer pointer.  If an access conflict
43                           ;           is detected the process is repeated.
44                           ;
45                           ;
46                           ; Outputs:  getbuf returns the buffer address in AX.  Additionally,
47                           ;           the condition code is set zero if the end of chain address
48                           ;           is returned.  Non-zero is returned otherwise.
49                           ;           NOTE: it is the responsibility of the caller to handle the
50                           ;           out of buffers condition.
51                           ;
52                           ;           putbuf returns a condition code of zero if the buffer's
53                           ;           return corrects an out of buffers condition.  A non-zero
54                           ;           condition code is returned otherwise.
55                           ;
56                           ;
57                           ; This macro corrects for an error in Turbo Assembler.  The opcode for
58                           ; cmpxchg was copied from the Intel manual which was wrong.  The proper
59                           ; opcode is 0FB0 for byte operands and 0FB1 for word/dword operands.
60                           ;
61                           cmpxchgf  MACRO loc,reg
62                                     LOCAL orgto,orgfro
63                           orgto:
64                                     cmpxchg loc,reg
65                           orgfro:
66                                     nop
67                                     org    orgto+1
68                                     db     0b1h
69                                     org    orgfro
70                                     ENDM
71
72
73      0000                 code      SEGMENT    para 'CODE' USE16 PUBLIC
74
75                                     ASSUME     CS:code
76
77                                     PUBLIC  getbuf,putbuf
78                           ;
79      0000                 getbuf    PROC
80      0000  53                       push  BX
81      0001  8B 04                    mov   AX,[SI]        ; Get next buffer address
82      0003                 g_again:
83      0003  8B D8                    mov   BX,AX          ; Copy in case it's empty
84      0005  23 C0                    and   AX,AX          ; Check for end of chain
85      0007  74 02                    jz    SHORT g_empty ;
```

```
86      0009   8B 1F                    mov    BX,[BX]      ; Get pointer to next
87      000B              g_empty:
88      000B   F0>                      lock                ; Lock may hang some single processor systems
89                                      cmpxchgf [SI],BX ; Do interlocked pop (conditional)
90      000C              ??0000:
91      000C   0F A7 1C                 cmpxchg [SI],BX
92      000F              ??0001:
93      000F   90                       nop
94      000D   B1                       db     0b1h
95
96      000F   75 F2                    jnz    g_again      ; loop if changed (AX is set)
97      0011   5B                       pop    BX
98      0012   23 C0                    and    AX,AX        ; Set z flag
99      0014   C3                       ret
100     0015              getbuf    ENDP
101
102     0015              putbuf    PROC
103     0015   53                       push   BX
104     0016   8B D8                    mov    BX,AX        ; save returned address
105     0018   8B 04                    mov    AX,[SI]      ; Get next buffer address
106     001A              p_again:
107     001A   89 07                    mov    [BX],AX      ; push old top of stack address
108     001C   F0>                      lock                ; Lock may hang some single processor systems
109                                     cmpxchgf [SI],BX ; Put returnee as top (conditional)
110     001D              ??0002:
111     001D   0F A7 1C                 cmpxchg [SI],BX
112     0020              ??0003:
113     0020   90                       nop
114     001E   B1                       db     0b1h
115     0020   75 F8                    jnz    p_again      ; loop if changed (new AX is set)
116
117     0022   5B                       pop    BX
118     0023   23 C0                    and    AX,AX        ; set z flag
119     0025   C3                       ret
120     0026              putbuf    ENDP
121
122     0026              code      ENDS
123
124                                 END
```

Symbol Name	Type	Value	Cref (defined at #)
??0000	Near	CODE:000C	#90 94
??0001	Near	CODE:000F	#92 95
??0002	Near	CODE:001D	#110 114
??0003	Near	CODE:0020	#112 115
??DATE	Text	"02/22/92"	
??FILENAME	Text	"buff486 "	
??TIME	Text	"10:21:18"	

Program 9-22   Continued.

??VERSION	Number	0202	
@CPU	Text	0D1FH	#2
@CURSEG	Text	CODE	#73
@FILENAME	Text	BUFF486	
@WORDSIZE	Text	2	#2 #73
GETBUF	Near	CODE:0000	77 #79
G_AGAIN	Near	CODE:0003	#82 96
G_EMPTY	Near	CODE:000B	85 #87
PUTBUF	Near	CODE:0015	77 #102
P_AGAIN	Near	CODE:001A	#106 115

Macro Name	Cref (defined at #)
CMPXCHGF	#61 89 109

Groups & Segments	Bit Size Align	Combine Class	Cref (defined at #)
CODE	16 0026 Para	Public CODE	#73 75

Program 9-23   BUFF386

```
 1
 2                              .386
 3                      ;
 4                      ; Name:        BUFF386
 5                      ;
 6                      ; Purpose:     This program provides a protected push-down stack
 7                      ;              manager.  Its two entry points (getbuf and putbuf) use a
 8                      ;              spin lock to protect against conflicts in a general
 9                      ;              multiprocessing or multiprogramming environment.
10                      ;
11                      ; Inputs:   Both entries work off the buffer stack which is pointed to
12                      ;           by DS:SI at entry to the routines.  The word at DS:SI is the
13                      ;           stack and is followed by an access lock word.
14                      ;
15                      ;              getbuf requires no input from the caller.
16                      ;              putbuf assumes the address (offset) of the buffer being
17                      ;           returned is in AX.
18                      ;
19                      ; Process:  The buffer pool is a simple push down stack.  No assumption
20                      ;           is made about the buffer size or the location of the
21                      ;           pointer within it.  The pointers are assumed to point to
22                      ;           the next pointer location and in the example are at the
23                      ;           beginning of the buffer.  The end of stack indicator is
24                      ;           a next pointer of zero.
25                      ;
26                      ;              The 80386 has no compare and exchange instruction so the
```

```
27                          ;       buffer pool is protected with a spin lock.  The lock word is
28                          ;       presumed to follow the stack pointer in memory.
29                          ;
30                          ;           getbuf first calls the lock manager to serialize access
31                          ;       to the buffer pool.  It then loads the next buffer pointer
32                          ;       and checks if it is end of stack.  If not, the pointer is used
33                          ;       to get the next address for the top of the stack.  If it is
34                          ;       the end of stack, (a zero pointer), no change is made to the
35                          ;       stack.  Otherwise, the next address becomes the top of stack.
36                          ;       The lock is then released.
37                          ;
38                          ;           putbuf receives the address of the buffer being returned.
39                          ;       Prior to use of the buffer pool, the lock manager is called to
40                          ;       serialize access to the pool.
41                          ;       It moves the top of stack pointer to the first word of the
42                          ;       buffer and then replaces the top of stack address with the
43                          ;       new buffer pointer.  The lock is then freed,
44                          ;
45                          ;           set_lock provides a simple spin lock mechanism.  The pool
46                          ;       is available when the lock word is zero and is in use
47                          ;       otherwise.  This locking method is subject to endless looping
48                          ;       if resource conflicts are not carefully monitored.
49                          ;
50                          ;
51                          ; Outputs:      getbuf returns the buffer address in AX.  Additionally,
52                          ;           the condition code is set zero if the end of chain address
53                          ;           is returned.   Non-zero is returned otherwise.
54                          ;               NOTE: it is the responsibility of the caller to handle the
55                          ;           out of buffers condition.
56                          ;
57                          ;               putbuf returns a condition code of zero if the buffer's
58                          ;           return corrects an out of buffers condition.  A non-zero
59                          ;           condition code is returned otherwise.
60
61                          ;
62
63      0000            code        SEGMENT    para 'CODE' USE16 PUBLIC
64
65                          ASSUME    CS:code
66
67
68                          PUBLIC  getbuf,putbuf
69                          ;
70      0000            getbuf    PROC NEAR
71      0000  53            push  BX
72
73      0001  E8 002E         call  set_lock      ; Gain access to the buffer pool
74
```

Program 9-23 Continued.

```
75    0004  8B 04              mov    AX,[SI]         ; Get next buffer address
76    0006  8B D8              mov    BX,AX           ; Copy in case it's empty
77    0008  23 C0              and    AX,AX           ; Check for end of chain
78    000A  74 06              jz     SHORT g_empty   ; Don't change if empty
79    000C  8B 07              mov    AX,[BX]         ; Get pointer to next
80    000E  89 04              mov    [SI],AX         ; Set new top of chain
81    0010  8B C3              mov    AX,BX           ; position buffer pointer
82    0012               g_empty:
83
84    0012  2B DB              sub    BX,BX           ; Get available flag
85    0014  F0>               lock
86    0015  87 5C 02          xchg   [SI+2],BX        ; Clear the pool-in-use flag
87
88    0018  5B                pop    BX
89    0019  23 C0             and    AX,AX            ; Set z flag
90    001B  C3                ret
91    001C         getbuf     ENDP
92
93    001C         putbuf     PROC   NEAR
94    001C  53                push   BX               ; save one scratch register
95
96    001D  E8 0012           call   set_lock         ; lock the buffer pool
97
98    0020  8B D8             mov    BX,AX            ; save returned address
99    0022  8B 04             mov    AX,[SI]          ; Get next buffer address
100   0024  89 07             mov    [BX],AX          ; push old top of stack address on new
101   0026  89 1C             mov    [SI],BX          ; and set the new as top of stack.
102
103   0028  2B DB             sub    BX,BX            ; Get available flag
104   002A  F0>               lock
105   002B  87 5C 02          xchg   [SI+2],BX        ; Clear the pool-in-use flag
106
107   002E  5B                pop    BX
108   002F  23 C0             and    AX,AX            ; set z flag if we cleared empty
109   0031  C3                ret
110   0032         putbuf     ENDP
111              ;
112              ; Busy wait/set of spin lock
113              ;
114   0032         set_lock   PROC
115   0032  50                push   AX               ; Save a work register
116   0033  B8 FFFF           mov    AX,-1            ; Set the busy indicator
117   0036         spin:
118   0036  F0>               lock
119   0037  87 44 02          xchg   AX,[SI+2]        ; Protected set and fetch
120   003A  0B C0             or     AX,AX            ; Was lock set?
121   003C  75 F8             jnz    spin             ; yes - wait for free lock
```

```
122    003E   58                              pop     AX              ; restore register
123    003F   C3                              ret
124    0040                    set_lock  ENDP
125
126    0040                              ENDS
127                                      END
```

Symbol Name	Type	Value	Cref (defined at #)
??DATE	Text	"03/01/92"	
??FILENAME	Text	"buff386 "	
??TIME	Text	"22:33:51"	
??VERSION	Number	0202	
aCPU	Text	0D0FH	#2
aCURSEG	Text	CODE	#63
aFILENAME	Text	BUFF386	
aWORDSIZE	Text	2	#2 #63
GETBUF	Near	CODE:0000	68 #70
G_EMPTY	Near	CODE:0012	78 #82
PUTBUF	Near	CODE:001C	68 #93
SET_LOCK	Near	CODE:0032	73 96 #114
SPIN	Near	CODE:0036	#117 121

Groups & Segments	Bit Size Align	Combine Class	Cref (defined at #)
CODE	16 0040 Para	Public CODE	#63 65

Program 9-24 BUFFDRV

```
1
2                              .486
3                    ;
4                    ; Name:    BUFFDRV
5                    ;
6                    ; Purpose: This program tests the buffer allocate, return and
7                    ;          threshold procedures.
8                    ;
9                    ; Inputs:  The user is prompted for a threshold and a reset value.
10                   ;
11                   ; Process: The program gets the threshold value and the reset value.
12                   ;          These are edited to ensure that 0< threshold < reset < 10
13                   ;          (the number of buffers in the example).  They are used to
14                   ;          build the threshold structure.  The driver then gets buffers,
15                   ;          saving their addresses until the pool is exhausted.  As each
16                   ;          buffer is obtained a call is made to the threshold routine
17                   ;          and when the threshold is signalled a message is produced.
18                   ;          The buffers are then returned, a call to the threshold
19                   ;          routine is made and when the reset is signalled, a message is
```

```
20                           ;              produced.
21                           ;
22                           ; Outputs: The desired output is the confidence that the allocate and
23                           ;              return routines and the threshold monitor routine are
24                           ;              correct.  (The maintainance of the linked list should be
25                           ;              verified using debug to inspect the the address values.)
26                           ;
27                           ;
28                           ;
29                           ; Note:        It is beyond the scope of this program to verify that the
30                           ;              buffer routines are proof against multiprogramming and multi-
31                           ;              processing.  The interested reader may wish to develope such
32                           ;              a test.  (The most obvious involves inserting one time
33                           ;              recursive calls in the allocation or return routines.)
34                           ;
35                           ;
36                           ;
37                           ;
38                           ;
39
40
41
42    0000                          stackt      SEGMENT para 'STACK' STACK USE16
43    0000 0100*                    +           dq      256 DUP(?)
44         (??????????????????)
45    0800                          stackt      ENDS
46
47    0000                          data        SEGMENT para USE16
48
49
50
51                           ;
52                           ;
53                           ; Declare the common threshold control structure
54                           ;
55 00000000                 TCONTROL    STRUC
56 00000000  01*(????)       COUNT       DW      ?                    ; The count being monitored
57 00000002  01*(????)       LIMIT       DW      ?                    ; The warning level
58 00000004  01*(????)       OK_NOW      DW      ?                    ; The reset value
59 00000006  01*(????)       SEMA        DW      ?                    ; The semaphore
60 00000008                 TCONTROL    ENDS
61
62
63                           ;
64                           ; Then an instantiation of it
65                           ;
66 0000  000A 0000 0000 0000  my          TCONTROL <10,0,0,0>          ; Build the descriptor
```

```
67
68
69                                          ;
70      0008   000Cr 0000              STACKP        DW      BUFF01,0         ; Simple pointer and lock
71                                          ;
72                                          ;
73                                          ;
74                                          ;
75      000C   0022r                  BUFF01        DW      BUFF02           ; Point to next pointer
76      000E   14*(??)                              DB      20 DUP(?)        ; Some buffer space
77      0022   0038r                  BUFF02        DW      BUFF03           ; Point to next pointer
78      0024   14*(??)                              DB      20 DUP(?)        ; Some buffer space
79      0038   004Er                  BUFF03        DW      BUFF04           ; Point to next pointer
80      003A   14*(??)                              DB      20 DUP(?)        ; Some buffer space
81      004E   0064r                  BUFF04        DW      BUFF05           ; Point to next pointer
82      0050   14*(??)                              DB      20 DUP(?)        ; Some buffer space
83      0064   007Ar                  BUFF05        DW      BUFF06           ; Point to next pointer
84      0066   14*(??)                              DB      20 DUP(?)        ; Some buffer space
85      007A   0090r                  BUFF06        DW      BUFF07           ; Point to next pointer
86      007C   14*(??)                              DB      20 DUP(?)        ; Some buffer space
87      0090   00A6r                  BUFF07        DW      BUFF08           ; Point to next pointer
88      0092   14*(??)                              DB      20 DUP(?)        ; Some buffer space
89      00A6   00BCr                  BUFF08        DW      BUFF09           ; Point to next pointer
90      00A8   14*(??)                              DB      20 DUP(?)        ; Some buffer space
91      00BC   00D2r                  BUFF09        DW      BUFF10           ; Point to next pointer
92      00BE   14*(??)                              DB      20 DUP(?)        ; Some buffer space
93      00D2   0000                   BUFF10        DW      0                ; Last buffer in chain
94      00D4   14*(??)                              DB      20 DUP(?)        ; Some buffer space
95
96                                          ;
97                                          ; Define messages
98                                          ;
99      00E8   0100*(??)              string        db      256 DUP(?)           ; String scratch area
100     01E8   0A 0D 45 6E 74 65 72+  query1        db      10,13,'Enter the threshold value (0<t<10): $'
101            20 74 68 65 20 74 68+
102            72 65 73 68 6F 6C 64+
103            20 76 61 6C 75 65 20+
104            28 30 3C 74 3C 31 30+
105            29 3A 20 24
106     020F   0A 0D 45 6E 74 65 72+  query2        db      10,13,'Enter the reset value (t<r<10): $'
107            20 74 68 65 20 72 65+
108            73 65 74 20 76 61 6C+
109            75 65 20 28 74 3C 72+
110            3C 31 30 29 3A 20 24
111     0232   0A 0D 54 68 72 65 73+  limbad        db      10,13,'Threshold is not in range - retry.',10,13,'$'
112            68 6F 6C 64 20 69 73+
113            20 6E 6F 74 20 69 6E+
114            20 72 61 6E 67 65 20+
```

```
115            2D 20 72 65 74 72 79+
116            2E 0A 0D 24
117    0259    0A 0D 52 65 73 65 74+   rsetbad    db    10,13,'Reset value is not in range - retry.',10,13,'$'
118            20 76 61 6C 75 65 20+
119            69 73 20 6E 6F 74 20+
120            69 6E 20 72 61 6E 67+
121            65 20 2D 20 72 65 74+
122            72 79 2E 0A 0D 24
123    0282    0A 0D 54 68 72 65 73+   contrl     db    10,13,'Threshold controls (c,t,r,f): $'
124            68 6F 6C 64 20 63 6F+
125            6E 74 72 6F 6C 73 20+
126            28 63 2C 74 2C 72 2C+
127            66 29 3A 20 24
128    02A3    0A 0D 42 75 66 66 65+   bchain     db    10,13,'Buffer chain is (head buf buf ...'
129            72 20 63 68 61 69 6E+
130            20 69 73 20 28 68 65+
131            61 64 20 62 75 66 20+
132            62 75 66 20 2E 2E 2E
133    02C6    62 75 66 20 30 29 3A+              db    'buf 0):',10,13,'$'
134            0A 0D 24
135    02D0    0A 0D 57 61 72 6E 69+   warnmsg    db    10,13,'Warning level indicated.$'
136            6E 67 20 6C 65 76 65+
137            6C 20 69 6E 64 69 63+
138            61 74 65 64 2E 24
139    02EB    0A 0D 52 65 73 65 74+   resetmsg   db    10,13,'Reset of warning level indicated.$'
140            20 6F 66 20 77 61 72+
141            6E 69 6E 67 20 6C 65+
142            76 65 6C 20 69 6E 64+
143            69 63 61 74 65 64 2E+
144            24
145    030F    0A 0D 41 6C 6C 20 62+   chnend     db    10,13,'All buffers allocated.$'
146            75 66 66 65 72 73 20+
147            61 6C 6C 6F 63 61 74+
148            65 64 2E 24
149    0328    0A 0D 41 6C 6C 20 62+   chnback    db    10,13,'All buffers returned.$'
150            75 66 66 65 72 73 20+
151            72 65 74 75 72 6E 65+
152            64 2E 24
153    0340    0A 0D 2A 2A 2A 2A 20+   chnerror   db    10,13,'**** ERROR **** chain too long!$'
154            45 52 52 4F 52 20 2A+
155            2A 2A 2A 20 63 68 61+
156            69 6E 20 74 6F 6F 20+
157            6C 6F 6E 67 21 24
158    0362    0A 0D 2A 2A 2A 2A 20+   chnaddr    db    10,13,'**** ERROR **** link out of chain!$'
159            45 52 52 4F 52 20 2A+
160            2A 2A 2A 20 6C 69 6E+
161            6B 20 6F 75 74 20 6F+
```

```
162        66 20 63 68 61 69 6E+
163        21 24
164
165  0387                   data      ENDS
166  0000                   code      SEGMENT   para 'CODE' USE16 PUBLIC
167
168                         ;
169                         ; Declare the routines we are going to use
170                         ;
171
172
173                              EXTRN    GETBUF: NEAR
174                              EXTRN    PUTBUF:  NEAR
175                              EXTRN    THRESHU: NEAR
176                              EXTRN    THRESHD: NEAR
177
178
179                              EXTRN    CODEASB: NEAR
180                              EXTRN    CODEBTHX: NEAR
181                              EXTRN    CODEBAS: NEAR
182
183
184                              ASSUME   CS:code, DS:data
185                         ;
186                         ; Set up the environment
187                         ;
188  0000            Begin:
189  0000  B8 0000s            mov      AX,data            ; Get data segment pointer
190  0003  8E D8               mov      DS,AX              ; into DS,
191  0005  8E C0               mov      ES,AX              ; and ES.
192  0007  2B F6               sub      SI,SI              ; Clear indices
193  0009  2B FF               sub      DI,DI
194  000B            getlimit:
195  000B  BA 01E8r            lea      DX,query1          ; Get the limit value
196  000E  E8 01BB             call     getinp
197  0011  0B C9               or       CX,CX              ; check presence of string
198  0013  0F 84 00B6          jz       exit               ; Quit if null
199  0017  E8 019E             call     getnbr             ; convert the number
200  001A  72 EF               jc       getlimit           ; an error goes back
201  001C  A3 0002r            mov      my.LIMIT,AX        ; set the limit
202  001F  3D 0000             cmp      AX,0               ; Check if within lower bound
203  0022  0F 96 C5            setbe    CH                 ; Remember the result
204  0025  3D 0009             cmp      AX,9               ; Check if limit is too high
205  0028  0F 9F C1            setg     CL                 ; and remember result
206  002B  0A CD               or       CL,CH              ; Was either result bad?
207  002D  74 09               jz       SHORT getreset     ; If neither was bad, get reset
208                         ;
209                         ; Print the error message
```

Program 9-24 Continued.

```
210                             ;
211   002F  BA 0232r              lea     DX,limbad        ; Point to message
212   0032  B4 09                 mov     AH,9
213   0034  CD 21                 int     21h              ; and put it out
214   0036  EB D3                 jmp     getlimit         ; Then try again
215
216   0038              getreset:
217   0038  BA 020Fr              lea     DX,query2        ; Get the reset value
218   003B  E8 018E               call    getinp
219   003E  E3 F8                 jcxz    getreset         ; try again if null
220   0040  E8 0175               call    getnbr           ; convert the number
221   0043  72 F3                 jc      getreset         ; an error goes back
222   0045  A3 0004r              mov     my.OK_NOW,AX     ; set the limit
223   0048  3B 06 0002r           cmp     AX,my.LIMIT      ; Check if not over threshold
224   004C  0F 96 C5              setbe   CH               ; Remember the result
225   004F  3D 000A               cmp     AX,10            ; Check if reset is too high
226   0052  0F 97 C1              seta    CL               ; and remember result
227   0055  0A CD                 or      CL,CH            ; Was either result bad?
228   0057  74 09                 jz      SHORT wearego    ; If neither was bad, we are go
229                             ;
230                             ; Print the error message
231                             ;
232   0059  BA 0259r              lea     DX,rsetbad       ; Point to message
233   005C  B4 09                 mov     AH,9
234   005E  CD 21                 int     21h              ; and put it out
235   0060  EB A9                 jmp     getlimit         ; Then try again
236
237   0062              wearego:
238   0062  E8 00BB               call    prtctl           ; display completed threshold
239   0065  E8 006B               call    prtbchn          ; and initial buffer chain
240
241                             ;
242                             ; We now get buffers until an end of stack condition (0 return)
243                             ; Each buffer obtained is counted out with the threshold routine
244                             ; and the threshold control is displayed when the return code indicates
245                             ; an event (along with the event).
246                             ;
247   0068  B8 0000               mov     AX,0             ; Get an end of stack flag
248   006B  50                    push    AX               ; and save it
249
250   006C              getagain:
251   006C  BE 0008r              lea     SI,STACKP        ; Set buffer pool control
252   006F  E8 0000e              call    GETBUF           ; and get a buffer
253   0072  74 1F 90 90           jz      allgone          ; done if empty pool
254   0076  50                    push    AX               ; save the buffer's address
255   0077  BB 0000r              lea     BX,my            ; Point to control
256   007A  E8 0000e              call    THRESHD          ; Count down one buffer
```

```
257    007D   75 12              jnz     SHORT noaction    ; If no action needed - continue
258    007F   BA 02D0r           lea     DX,warnmsg        ; Assume warning
259    0082   73 03              jnc     SHORT warning     ; jump if right
260    0084   BA 02EBr           lea     DX,resetmsg       ; Need a reset notice??????
261    0087              warning:
262    0087   B4 09              mov     AH,9
263    0089   CD 21              int     21h               ; so put it out
264    008B   E8 0092            call    prtctl            ; then the area
265    008E   E8 0042            call    prtbchn           ; and the buffer chain
266    0091              noaction:
267    0091   EB D9              jmp     getagain          ; then back to get another
268                      ;
269                      ; All buffers are allocated - now we loop giving them back
270                      ;
271    0093              allgone:
272    0093   BA 030Fr           lea     DX,chnend         ; Point to text
273    0096   B4 09              mov     AH,9
274    0098   CD 21              int     21h               ; and display it
275    009A   58                 pop     AX                ; Get buffer addr from stack
276    009B              putagain:
277    009B   BE 0008r           lea     SI,STACKP         ; Set buffer pool control
278    009E   E8 0000e           call    PUTBUF            ; and put a buffer
279    00A1   BB 0000r           lea     BX,my             ; Point to control
280    00A4   E8 0000e           call    THRESHU           ; Count up one buffer
281    00A7   75 12              jnz     SHORT noact2      ; If no action needed - continue
282    00A9   BA 02D0r           lea     DX,warnmsg        ; Assume warning
283    00AC   73 03              jnc     SHORT warning2    ; jump if right ???????
284    00AE   BA 02EBr           lea     DX,resetmsg       ; Need a reset notice
285    00B1              warning2:
286    00B1   B4 09              mov     AH,9
287    00B3   CD 21              int     21h               ; so put it out
288    00B5   E8 0068            call    prtctl            ; then the area
289    00B8   E8 0018            call    prtbchn           ; and the buffer chain
290    00BB              noact2:
291    00BB   58                 pop     AX                ; Get buffer address
292    00BC   0B C0              or      AX,AX             ; are we at our stopper
293    00BE   75 DB              jnz     putagain          ; No - then back to put another
294                      ;
295                      ; All buffers are returned - We do one last dump and are done
296                      ;
297
298    00C0   BA 0328r           lea     DX,chnback        ; Tell watcher we are done
299    00C3   B4 09              mov     AH,9
300    00C5   CD 21              int     21h               ; so put it out
301    00C7   E8 0056            call    prtctl            ; then the control
302    00CA   E8 0006            call    prtbchn           ; and the buffer chain
303
304
305
```

Program 9-24 Continued.

```
306    00CD                          Exit:
307    00CD  B0 00                            mov     AL,0           ; Set return code
308    00CF  B4 4C                            mov     AH,04ch        ; Set good-by
309    00D1  CD 21                            int     21h            ; Return to the system
310                                  ;
311                                  ; Dump the chain of available buffers
312                                  ;
313    00D3                          prtbchn   PROC
314    00D3  60                                pusha                  ; save everything
315    00D4  BA 02A3r                          lea     DX,bchain      ; Point to text
316    00D7  B4 09                             mov     AH,9
317    00D9  CD 21                             int     21h            ; and display it
318    00DB  A1 0008r                          mov     AX,STACKP      ; Get stack pointer
319    00DE  E8 00B2                           call    prtaxhx        ; in hex
320    00E1  E8 0091                           call    prtcolon       ; and follow with a colon
321    00E4  0B C0                             or      AX,AX          ; Check if end of chain
322    00E6  74 33                             jz      SHORT chn_done ; and exit if it is
323    00E8  B9 000A                           mov     CX,10          ; Set maximum count of buffers
324    00EB                          chn_next:
325    00EB  3D 000Cr                          cmp     AX,OFFSET BUFF01 ; Check to first buffer
326    00EE  72 1E                             jb      SHORT bad_addr  ; if below - error
327    00F0  3D 00D2r                          cmp     AX,OFFSET BUFF10 ; Check to last buffer
328    00F3  77 19                             ja      SHORT bad_addr  ; if above - error
329    00F5  8B D8                             mov     BX,AX          ; Copy for load
330    00F7  8B 07                             mov     AX,word ptr[BX] ; and load next in chain ptr
331    00F9  E8 0097                           call    prtaxhx        ; dump pointer
332    00FC  0B C0                             or      AX,AX          ; Check if end of chain
333    00FE  74 1B                             jz      SHORT chn_done ; and exit if it is
334    0100  E8 0063                           call    prtcomma       ; follow with comma
335    0103  E2 E6                             loop    chn_next       ; loop to display next
336                                  ;
337                                  ; We have an error - either there are more than 10 buffers or
338                                  ; the chain has been wiped out in some way.  In either case the
339                                  ; program quits with an error code (10).
340                                  ;
341    0105  BA 0340r                          lea     DX,chnerror    ; Point to text
342    0108  B4 09                             mov     AH,9
343    010A  CD 21                             int     21h            ; and display it
344    010C  EB 07                             jmp     SHORT ch_err_x ; and quit
345    010E                          bad_addr:
346    010E  BA 0362r                          lea     DX,chnaddr     ; Point to text
347    0111  B4 09                             mov     AH,9
348    0113  CD 21                             int     21h            ; and display it
349    0115                          ch_err_x:
350    0115  B0 0A                             mov     AL,10          ; Set return code
351    0117  B4 4C                             mov     AH,04ch        ; Set good-by
352    0119  CD 21                             int     21h            ; Return to the system
```

```
353                            ;
354                            ; The expected exit - we dump to end of chain and quit
355                            ;
356    011B            chn_done:
357    011B  E8 0066                 call    prtlfcr         ; go to next line
358    011E  61                      popa                    ; restore
359    011F  C3                      ret                     ; and return
360    0120            prtbchn     ENDP
361
362                            ;
363                            ; Display the threshold control values
364                            ;
365    0120            prtctl      PROC
366    0120  60                      pusha                   ; save everything
367    0121  BA 0282r                lea     DX,contrl       ; Point to text
368    0124  B4 09                   mov     AH,9
369    0126  CD 21                   int     21h             ; and display it
370    0128  A1 0000r                mov     AX,my.COUNT     ; Get count
371    012B  E8 0020                 call    prtax           ; and display it
372    012E  E8 0035                 call    prtcomma        ; with comma and space
373    0131  A1 0002r                mov     AX,my.LIMIT     ; Get limit
374    0134  E8 0017                 call    prtax           ; and display it
375    0137  E8 002C                 call    prtcomma        ; with comma and space
376    013A  A1 0004r                mov     AX,my.OK_NOW    ; Get reset
377    013D  E8 000E                 call    prtax           ; and display it
378    0140  E8 0023                 call    prtcomma        ; with comma and space
379    0143  A1 0006r                mov     AX,my.SEMA      ; Get semaphore
380    0146  E8 004A                 call    prtaxhx         ; in hex
381    0149  E8 0038                 call    prtlfcr         ; go to next line
382    014C  61                      popa
383    014D  C3                      ret
384    014E            prtctl      ENDP
385
386                            ;
387                            ; Print the number in AX
388                            ;
389    014E            prtax       PROC
390    014E  60                      pusha                   ; save everything
391    014F  66| 98                  cwde                    ; As a 32 bit integer
392    0151  BF 00E8r                lea     DI,string       ; Point to output area
393    0154  E8 0000e                call    Codebas         ; Convert it
394    0157  B4 02                   mov     AH,2
395    0159            numbout:
396    0159  8A 15                   mov     DL,BYTE PTR [DI] ; Get a byte
397    015B  0A D2                   or      DL,DL           ; at end?
398    015D  74 05                   jz      SHORT numbout0  ; Yes
399    015F  CD 21                   int     21h             ; print it
400    0161  47                      inc     DI              ; point to next
```

```
401    0162   EB F5                          jmp      numbout        ; and loop
402    0164                          numbout0:
403    0164   61                             popa                    ; restore
404    0165   C3                             ret
405    0166                          prtax    ENDP
406                                  ;
407                                  ; Print a comma and space
408                                  ;
409    0166                          prtcomma PROC
410    0166   50                             push     AX             ; save everything
411    0167   52                             push     DX             ; we use
412    0168   B4 02                          mov      AH,2
413    016A   B2 2C                          mov      DL,','          ; follow with comma
414    016C   CD 21                          int      21h
415    016E   B2 20                          mov      DL,' '          ; and a space
416    0170   CD 21                          int      21h
417    0172   5A                             pop      DX
418    0173   58                             pop      AX             ; restore
419    0174   C3                             ret
420    0175                          prtcomma ENDP
421                                  ;
422                                  ; Print a colon and space
423                                  ;
424    0175                          prtcolon PROC
425    0175   50                             push     AX             ; save everything
426    0176   52                             push     DX             ; we use
427    0177   B4 02                          mov      AH,2
428    0179   B2 3A                          mov      DL,':'          ; follow with colon
429    017B   CD 21                          int      21h
430    017D   B2 20                          mov      DL,' '          ; and a space
431    017F   CD 21                          int      21h
432    0181   5A                             pop      DX
433    0182   58                             pop      AX             ; restore
434    0183   C3                             ret
435    0184                          prtcolon ENDP
436                                  ;
437                                  ; Print a line feed and carriage return
438                                  ;
439    0184                          prtlfcr  PROC
440    0184   50                             push     AX             ; save everything
441    0185   52                             push     DX             ; we use
442    0186   B4 02                          mov      AH,2
443    0188   B2 0A                          mov      DL,10           ; follow with line feed
444    018A   CD 21                          int      21h
445    018C   B2 0D                          mov      DL,13           ; and a carriage return
446    018E   CD 21                          int      21h
447    0190   5A                             pop      DX
```

Black Bond Books

CANADIANA ...

NATIONAL and REGIONAL

Historical, Pictorial plus our particular interest in B.C.

Gift Books to Paperbacks

DON'T FORGET ... We **ALWAYS** make a determined effort to find that special book.

Black Bond Books

- WILLOWBROOK MALL
  LANGLEY
  533-7577

- HANEY PLACE MALL
  MAPLE RIDGE
  463-8624

- LANGLEY MALL
  530-6757

- SCOTTSDALE MALL
  591-8757

- WEST OAKS MALL
  CLEARBROOK
  859-7701

- SURREY PLACE
  583-1282

- CITY SQUARE MALL
  12th & CAMBIE
  872-5554

- WAREHOUSE STORE
  WHITE ROCK
  (Open To The Public)
  #14 - 15531 - 24th Avenue

Fax 536-3551
Order Line 536-4444

```
448   0191  58                              pop    AX              ; restore
449   0192  C3                              ret
450   0193                  prtlfcr         ENDP
451                         ;
452                         ; Print the number in AX in hex.
453                         ;
454   0193                  prtaxhx         PROC
455   0193  60                              pusha
456   0194  50                              push   AX              ; save the number
457   0195  8A C4                           mov    AL,AH           ; Position high byte
458   0197  E8 0000e                        call   Codebthx        ; and convert it
459   019A  8A D4                           mov    DL,AH           ; Set high byte
460   019C  8A C8                           mov    CL,AL           ; save low
461   019E  B4 02                           mov    AH,2
462   01A0  CD 21                           int    21h             ; Put it out
463   01A2  8A D1                           mov    DL,CL           ; and low byte
464   01A4  CD 21                           int    21h
465   01A6  58                              pop    AX              ; Get low byte
466   01A7  E8 0000e                        call   Codebthx        ; Hex it
467   01AA  8A D4                           mov    DL,AH
468   01AC  8A C8                           mov    CL,AL           ; save low
469   01AE  B4 02                           mov    AH,2
470   01B0  CD 21                           int    21h             ; print it
471   01B2  8A D1                           mov    DL,CL           ; and low byte
472   01B4  CD 21                           int    21h
473   01B6  61                              popa
474   01B7  C3                              ret
475   01B8                  prtaxhx         ENDP
476                         ;
477                         ; Convert the number just obtained
478                         ;
479   01B8                  getnbr          PROC
480   01B8  8B F3                           mov    SI,BX           ; set input pointer
481   01BA  E8 0000e                        call   codeasb         ; Convert to binary
482   01BD  72 0B 90 90                     jc     badnbr          ; Overflow is too much
483   01C1  3D 000A                         cmp    AX,10           ; Over 10 is too large
484   01C4  73 04 90 90                     jnb    badnbr          ; if so - too big
485   01C8  F8                              clc
486   01C9  C3                              ret                    ; return ok
487   01CA                  badnbr:
488   01CA  F9                              stc                    ; flag error
489   01CB  C3                              ret
490   01CC                  getnbr          ENDP
491                         ;
492                         ; Read a string in response to a prompt
493                         ; The prompt must be in DX.  The string will be returned in string.
494                         ;
495   01CC                  getinp          PROC
```

Program 9-24 Continued.

```
496   01CC  50                            push    AX                    ; Save registers
497   01CD  56                            push    SI
498   01CE  B4 09                         mov     AH,9                  ; and dos request
499   01D0  CD 21                         int     21h                   ; put out the string
500   01D2  BA 00E8r                      lea     DX,string             ; point to input area
501   01D5  C6 06 00E8r FE                mov     string,254            ; Set max length in
502   01DA  B4 0A                         mov     AH,10                 ; Ask for read of string
503   01DC  CD 21                         int     21h                   ; from DOS.
504   01DE  BB 00EAr                      lea     BX,string+2           ; Point to just read data
505   01E1  8A 0E 00E9r                   mov     CL,string+1           ; Get length read
506   01E5  B5 00                         mov     CH,0                  ; as a word.
507   01E7  8B F1                         mov     SI,CX                 ; Set length
508   01E9  C6 84 00EAr 00                mov     string+2[SI],0        ; and make an ascii string.
509   01EE  5E                            pop     SI
510   01EF  58                            pop     AX                    ; Restore registers
511   01F0  C3                            ret                           ; and return.
512   01F1             getinp   ENDP
513
514
515   01F1             code     ENDS
516                             END     Begin
```

Symbol Name	Type	Value	Cref (defined at #)
??DATE	Text	"02/22/92"	
??FILENAME	Text	"buffdrv "	
??TIME	Text	"10:52:06"	
??VERSION	Number	0202	
@CPU	Text	0D1FH	#2
@CURSEG	Text	CODE	#42 #47 #166
@FILENAME	Text	BUFFDRV	
@WORDSIZE	Text	2	#2 #42 #47 #166
ALLGONE	Near	CODE:0093	253 #271
BADNBR	Near	CODE:01CA	482 484 #487
BAD_ADDR	Near	CODE:010E	326 328 #345
BCHAIN	Byte	DATA:02A3	#128 315
BEGIN	Near	CODE:0000	#188 516
BUFF01	Word	DATA:000C	70 #75 325
BUFF02	Word	DATA:0022	75 #77
BUFF03	Word	DATA:0038	77 #79
BUFF04	Word	DATA:004E	79 #81
BUFF05	Word	DATA:0064	81 #83
BUFF06	Word	DATA:007A	83 #85
BUFF07	Word	DATA:0090	85 #87
BUFF08	Word	DATA:00A6	87 #89
BUFF09	Word	DATA:00BC	89 #91
BUFF10	Word	DATA:00D2	91 #93 327

CHNADDR	Byte	DATA:0362		#158	346							
CHNBACK	Byte	DATA:0328		#149	298							
CHNEND	Byte	DATA:030F		#145	272							
CHNERROR	Byte	DATA:0340		#153	341							
CHN_DONE	Near	CODE:011B		322	333	#356						
CHN_NEXT	Near	CODE:00EB		#324	335							
CH_ERR_X	Near	CODE:0115		344	#349							
CODEASB	Near	CODE:----	Extern	#179	481							
CODEBAS	Near	CODE:----	Extern	#181	393							
CODEBTHX	Near	CODE:----	Extern	#180	458	466						
CONTRL	Byte	DATA:0282		#123	367							
EXIT	Near	CODE:00CD		198	#306							
GETAGAIN	Near	CODE:006C		#250	267							
GETBUF	Near	CODE:----	Extern	#173	252							
GETINP	Near	CODE:01CC		196	218	#495						
GETLIMIT	Near	CODE:000B		#194	200	214	235					
GETNBR	Near	CODE:01B8		199	220	#479						
GETRESET	Near	CODE:0038		207	#216	219	221					
LIMBAD	Byte	DATA:0232		#111	211							
MY	Struct	DATA:0000	TCONTROL	#66	201	222	223	255	279	370	373	376	379
NOACT2	Near	CODE:00BB		281	#290							
NOACTION	Near	CODE:0091		257	#266							
NUMBOUT	Near	CODE:0159		#395	401							
NUMBOUT0	Near	CODE:0164		398	#402							
PRTAX	Near	CODE:014E		371	374	377	#389					
PRTAXHX	Near	CODE:0193		319	331	380	#454					
PRTBCHN	Near	CODE:00D3		239	265	289	302	#313				
PRTCOLON	Near	CODE:0175		320	#424							
PRTCOMMA	Near	CODE:0166		334	372	375	378	#409				
PRTCTL	Near	CODE:0120		238	264	288	301	#365				
PRTLFCR	Near	CODE:0184		357	381	#439						
PUTAGAIN	Near	CODE:009B		#276	293							
PUTBUF	Near	CODE:----	Extern	#174	278							
QUERY1	Byte	DATA:01E8		#100	195							
QUERY2	Byte	DATA:020F		#106	217							
RESETMSG	Byte	DATA:02EB		#139	260	284						
RSETBAD	Byte	DATA:0259		#117	232							
STACKP	Word	DATA:0008		#70	251	277	318					
STRING	Byte	DATA:00E8		#99	392	500	501	504	505	508		
THRESHD	Near	CODE:----	Extern	#176	256							
THRESHU	Near	CODE:----	Extern	#175	280							
WARNING	Near	CODE:0087		259	#261							
WARNING2	Near	CODE:00B1		283	#285							
WARNMSG	Byte	DATA:02D0		#135	258	282						
WEAREGO	Near	CODE:0062		228	#237							

Structure Name	Type	Offset		Cref (defined at #)
TCONTROL				#55 66

Program 9-24 Continued.

COUNT	Word	0000	
LIMIT	Word	0002	
OK_NOW	Word	0004	
SEMA	Word	0006	

Groups & Segments	Bit Size	Align	Combine	Class	Cref (defined at #)		
CODE	16 01F1	Para	Public	CODE	#166	184	
DATA	16 0387	Para	none		#47	184	189
STACKT	16 0800	Para	Stack	STACK	#42		

Program 9-25 THRESH

```
 1
 2
 3                              .486
 4                      ;
 5                      ; Name:    THRESHU, THRESHD
 6                      ;
 7                      ; Purpose: THRESH has as its purpose the implementation of a
 8                      ;          resetting single shot warning mechanism.
 9                      ;
10                      ;          A count, such as a running count of available buffers,
11                      ;          can be used to provide a warning when it matches a value
12                      ;          either as it increases or decreases.  To be effective,
13                      ;          however, the warning should be given once when the level
14                      ;          is reached.  To avoid multiple warnings, a semaphore is
15                      ;          used and the warning is issued only if the semaphore is
16                      ;          reset.  The semaphore is reset when the count  returns
17                      ;          to the comfort level.  i.e. If a buffer pool consists of
18                      ;          100 buffers, a warning might be issued when only 25
19                      ;          remain.  The semaphore might be reset when 50 buffers
20                      ;          are available.
21                      ;
22                      ;          Note that multiple warning points can be implemented for
23                      ;          a single count to provide various levels of urgency.
24                      ;
25                      ;          Also note that this routine is not protected against
26                      ;          multiprogramming or multiprocessor conflicts.  To do so,
27                      ;          a spin (or other) lock for the TCONTROL structure would be
28                      ;          necessary.
29                      ;
30                      ;
31                      ; Inputs:  [BX] points to a threshold data structure which is defined
32                      ;          as TCONTROL.
33                      ;
```

```
34                      ; Process: The count is incremented or decremented and checked against
35                      ;          the threshold.  If it passed the threshold and if the
36                      ;          semaphore is not set, the semaphore is set and a warn CC is
37                      ;          returned.  Otherwise, the comfort level is checked, and if
38                      ;          it was passed, the semaphore is reset.  A no-warn CC is
39                      ;          returned.
40                      ;
41                      ;
42                      ; Output: The CC is set Z if a warning is needed or if the reset value
43                      ;          is encountered while a warning is outstanding and NZ otherwise.
44                      ;          The carry flag is set if the reset value is encountered
45                      ;          and is reset otherwise.  Thus, a NZ return indicates no
46                      ;          special processing is needed and carry is used to distinguish
47                      ;          which action to take if it is.
48
49                      ;          The count is adjusted and the semaphore is set/reset as
50                      ;          necessary.
51                      ;
52                      ;
53      0000            code      SEGMENT para 'CODE' USE16 PUBLIC
54
55 00000000            TCONTROL  STRUC
56 00000000 01*(????)  COUNT     DW      ?              ; The count being monitored
57 00000002 01*(????)  LIMIT     DW      ?              ; The warning level
58 00000004 01*(????)  OK_NOW    DW      ?              ; The reset value
59 00000006 01*(????)  SEMA      DW      ?              ; The semaphore
60 00000008            TCONTROL  ENDS
61
62                      ;
63
64                                PUBLIC  THRESHU,THRESHD      ; Make the names usable
65
66                                ASSUME  CS:code
67
68      0000            THRESHU   PROC
69      0000 50                   push    AX             ; Save registers used
70      0001 51                   push    CX
71      0002 B8 0001              mov     AX,1           ; Set to count up
72      0005 EB 05                jmp     SHORT UP_DOWN  ; and join routine
73
74      0007            THRESHD:
75      0007 50                   push    AX             ; Save registers used
76      0008 51                   push    CX
77      0009 B8 FFFF              mov     AX,-1          ; Set to count down
78
79      000C            UP_DOWN:
80      000C 8B 4F 06             mov     CX,[BX.SEMA]   ; Get semaphore value
81      000F 0F C1 07             xadd    [BX.COUNT],AX  ; Add but get previous count
```

Program 9-25 Continued.

```
82
83    0012  OB C9                          or      CX,CX                ; Is the semaphore set
84    0014  75 OE                          jnz     SHORT AT_RESET       ; Yes - check if reset reached
85
86    0016  3B 47 02                       cmp     AX,[BX.LIMIT]        ; Did we cross warning level
87    0019  75 16                          jne     SHORT GET_OUT        ; If not - done
88
89    001B  C7 47 06 FFFF                  mov     [BX.SEMA],-1          ; Set the semaphore
90    0020  OB C9                          or      CX,CX                ; Check its previous value
91                                                                      ; This sets CC for warn/no-warn
92    0022  EB OD                          jmp     SHORT GET_OUT        ; So just exit
93
94
95    0024             AT_RESET:
96    0024  3B 47 04                       cmp     AX,[BX.OK_NOW]       ; Did we cross the ok level
97    0027  75 08                          jne     SHORT GET_OUT        ; No - just exit (CC is no-warn)
98    0029  C7 47 06 0000                  mov     [BX.SEMA],0          ; Clear the semaphore
99    002E  F9                             stc                          ; with carry set (reset done)
100                                                                     ; Z was set by the compare
101   002F  EB 01                          jmp     SHORT GET_OUT2       ; Skip clear of carry
102
103   0031             GET_OUT:
104   0031  F8                             clc                          ; No carry if not reset
105   0032             GET_OUT2:
106   0032  59                             pop     CX                   ; Restore registers used
107   0033  58                             pop     AX
108   0034  C3                             ret                          ; and return.
109
110   0035             THRESHU  ENDP
111   0035             code     ENDS
112                             END
```

Symbol Name	Type	Value	Cref (defined at #)			
??DATE	Text	"02/16/92"				
??FILENAME	Text	"thresh "				
??TIME	Text	"10:41:04"				
??VERSION	Number	0202				
@CPU	Text	OD1FH	#3			
@CURSEG	Text	CODE	#53			
@FILENAME	Text	THRESH				
@WORDSIZE	Text	2	#3	#53		
AT_RESET	Near	CODE:0024	84	#95		
GET_OUT	Near	CODE:0031	87	92	97	#103
GET_OUT2	Near	CODE:0032	101	#105		
THRESHD	Near	CODE:0007	64	#74		

```
THRESHU                    Near   CODE:0000              64  #68
UP_DOWN                    Near   CODE:000C              72  #79


Structure Name             Type   Offset                Cref (defined at #)


TCONTROL                                                 #55
  COUNT                    Word   0000
  LIMIT                    Word   0002
  OK_NOW                   Word   0004
  SEMA                     Word   0006


Groups & Segments          Bit Size Align  Combine Class  Cref (defined at #)


CODE                       16  0035 Para    Public  CODE  #53  66
```

10
Graphics

Graphics have been going through major changes. Graphics color standards are solidifying around the various cards that implement IBM's Video Graphics Array (VGA). VGA supports 640×480 for 16 colors in graphics mode and 720×400 for 15 colors in text mode. The standards are static only at the lower densities. Further, the super VGA cards tend to push the envelope with resolution and features about as fast as relatively inexpensive monitors become available.

Monochrome mode

In monochrome mode, the Hercules monochrome adapter card has become a widely accepted standard. A *monochrome adapter card* is a printed circuit board installed inside the main computer cabinet where it works with the monochrome display unit. Most monochrome adapters produce a textual display of 80 characters horizontally and 25 lines vertically, for a total of 2000 characters. The screen requires 4000 bytes (because two bytes are required for each character), so most monochrome adapter cards contain 4K (4096 bytes) of memory. Table 10-1 is an overview of the specifics of monochrome adapters. The graphics tools in this chapter are designed for a monochrome monitor, using a Hercules (or compatible) graphics card.

Of the two bytes reserved for each character, each 16-bit location in screen memory uses the first byte (the even address) for the character to be displayed. The second byte (the odd address) describes the attribute of the character. There are four attributes (i.e., ways a character can be displayed): normal, bright, reverse-video (a dark character on a lighted back-

Table 10-1   CGA graphics and adapter overview.

Mode	Text/ graphics	Horizontal resolution	Vertical resolution	Char per row	Number of rows
Low—resolution Text	Text	40	25	40	25
High—resolution Text	Text	80	25	80	25
Medium—resolution Text	Graphics	320	200	40	25
High—resolution	Graphics	640	200	80	25

ground), and bright on a reverse-video field. You can make characters blink or not and you can underline them whether they are blinking or not.

The lowest three bits of the attribute byte turn on the foreground. The next bit controls brightness. The next three control the background. The high-order bit controls blinking. Figure 10-1 shows the breakdown of the bits and a binary breakdown of how they work.

The character matrix

Each of the characters on the video display is formed within a matrix, often 9-dots wide by 14-dots tall, although most characters do not use the entire 9×14 matrix. For example, a capital letter might occupy a 7×9 matrix that sits inside the total matrix; this keeps space between the characters when they are printed, so they don't run into each other. The smaller 7×9 matrix does not include the leftmost and rightmost columns of the larger matrix. It also does not include the upper two rows and the bottom three rows of the larger matrix. This means there will be at least two dot positions horizontally and five dot positions vertically between capital letters.

Most of the lowercase characters fit with the 7×9 matrix also. Characters with descenders (like g and q) drop two rows below, reaching the next-to-bottom row of the full matrix.

There are some symbols, like the caret (^), that reach the top row. There also are some special symbols for drawing single and double lines and corners, as shown in Fig. 10-2, and detailed in appendix D. Some of the special characters reach the bottom row, the top, the leftmost column, or the rightmost. There are also block characters that fill the entire matrix.

The symbols in Fig. 10-2 are ASCII-format codes in the range from 179 to 218 and were designed for the extended character set, used on IBM and compatible computers. They do not appear in numeric order; they are grouped logically for easy use and lookup. You can produce these symbols directly on your screen: press the Alt key and type the corresponding three-digit ASCII code.

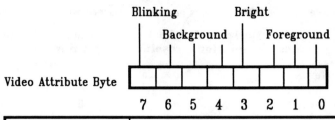

Type	Bit Pattern								Hex
Normal Character	0	0	0	0	0	1	1	1	7
Bright, Normal Char	0	0	0	0	1	1	1	1	F
Reverse Video Char	0	1	1	1	0	0	0	0	70
Bright Character, Reverse Video Background	0	1	1	1	1	0	0	0	78
No Character	0	0	0	0	0	0	0	0	0

Foreground	Background	Normal	Underline	Blinking	Blinking Underline
Normal	Dark	7	1	87	81
Bright	Dark	F	9	8F	89
Dark	Normal	70		F0	
Bright	Normal	78		F8	
Dark	Dark	0			

10-1   Video attribute bytes.

The special characters were designed to fit together to make larger figures, such as frames, underlines, and boxes. For each symbol, the patterns are set up within their matrix and all protruding lines extend all the way to the edges (using all the columns). This allows continuity of lines from one character to the next.

Bit shifting

Bit shifting for graphics requires some thought. Many devices, such as display devices, fetch one byte at a time from memory. To do animation, you might want to shift data in consecutive memory locations, but the hardware doesn't allow you to do it as you might think. Figure 10-3 shows how bytes are stored in a register and in memory. (Note that the bytes are reversed.) If you do a shift left (SHL) of three bits, note what happens.

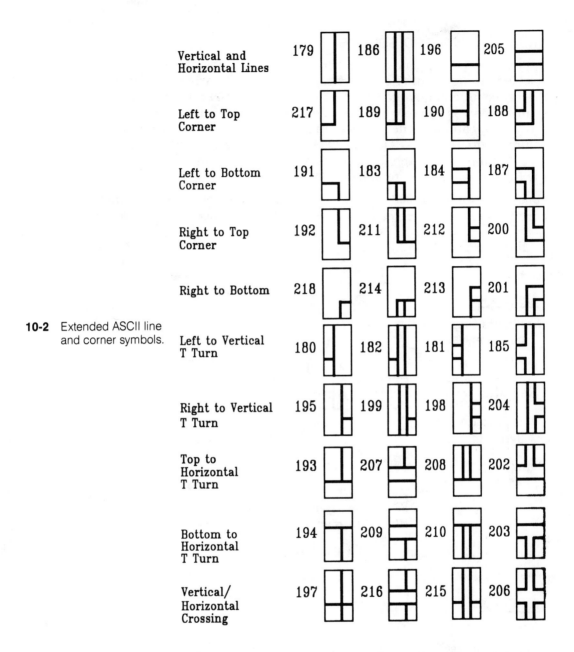

10-2 Extended ASCII line and corner symbols.

Vertical and Horizontal Lines	179		186		196		205
Left to Top Corner	217		189		190		188
Left to Bottom Corner	191		183		184		187
Right to Top Corner	192		211		212		200
Right to Bottom	218		214		213		201
Left to Vertical T Turn	180		182		181		185
Right to Vertical T Turn	195		199		198		204
Top to Horizontal T Turn	193		207		208		202
Bottom to Horizontal T Turn	194		209		210		203
Vertical/ Horizontal Crossing	197		216		215		206

Pixels that appear adjacent on a screen might not be adjacent in memory. If you want bit 7 of byte 1 to shift to bit 0 of byte 0, you are forced to use bit shifts into and out of the CF. You can't do it as a word shift. In a register, bit 0 of byte 1 actually is adjacent to bit 7 of byte 0 because of how the 80486 treats words. They are stored in reverse by registers. (This can't be said too often, because it is one of the most common sources of errors in programming the 80486, particular in assembler.)

ROM BIOS video services

Interrupt 10 (see appendix E) performs a variety of operations that can be selected through a function number; Fig. 10-4 summarizes the functions. Select the function by placing the number in the AH register. When you want to address any row or column of the screen, remember that the top row is row 0 and that the left column is column 0. Rows run from 0 to 24; columns run from 0 to 79 for the 80-column mode, and from 0 to 39 for the 40-column mode. In the following function descriptions, remember that the function numbers are in hex.

Function 0: set video mode   Most computer systems can use both mono-chrome and graphic screens. Because this book concentrates on mono-

Data: 3 3 3 4

	3 3	3 4
Memory	0011 0011	0011 1000

Bit Position   7   0 7   0
Byte Address   0   1

	3 4	3 3
Register	0011 0100	0011 0011

Bit Position   7   0 7   0
Byte Address   1   0

Doing a SHIFT in memory gives the same result as a:

```
MOV     to register
SHIFT   Register
MOV     to memory
```

10-3 Examples of SHIFT on memory and register.

Note: A SHL 3 was done to get "98A1" from "3343".

	9 8	A 1
Memory	1001 1000	1010 0001

Bit Position   7   0 7   0
Byte Address   0   1

	A 1	9 8
Register	1010 0001	1001 1000

Bit Position   7   0 7   0
Byte Address   1   0

Register AH	Function	Input	Output
0	Set Video Mode	AL = Mode	
1	Change Cursor Size	CH = Starting Scan Line CL = Ending Scan Line	
2	Change Cursor Position	BH = Page DH = Row DL = Column	
3	Find Cursor Position	BH = Page	BH = Page DH = Row DL = Column CH = Cursor Start Scan Line CL = Cursor Stop Scan Line
5	Select Video Page	AL = Page Number	
6	Scroll Up	AL = Lines Up CL = Left Column CH = Top Row DL = Right Column DH = Bottom Row BH = VIdeo Attribute	
7	Scroll Down	AL = Lines Down CL = Left Column CH = Top Row DL = Right Column DH = Bottom Row BH = VIdeo Attribute	
8	Read Character and Attribute	BH = Page	AL = Character AH = Attribute
9	Write Character and Attribute	AL = Character BL = Attribute BH = Page CX = Copies to Write	
A	Write Character	AL = Character BL = Attribute BH = Page CX = Copies to Write	
F	Find Video Mode		AL = Mode AH = Screen Width BH = Page

10-4 ROM BIOS video services.

chrome examples, the video mode will always be 7. If you have a graphics screen, you can switch to any of the seven graphics modes (06). To change from one mode to another, place the new mode in register AL and function number 0 in register AH. Then issue Interrupt 10. This clears the screen, even if the new video mode is the same as the previous. (To avoid clearing the screen, set bit 7 of AL.)

Function 1: change cursor size   The cursor shows where the next character will appear. Characters use a dot matrix (8×13 for monochrome and 5×7 for graphics). Initially, the cursor is formed from the bottom two rows of the matrix, rows 11 and 12 for the monochrome screen and rows 6 and 7 for the graphics screen.

To change the cursor size, put the starting row in register CH and the ending row in register CL. Set register AH to 1 and issue Interrupt 10.

Function 2: change cursor position   You can change the cursor position by putting the page number (monochrome has one page, graphics has four) in the BH register, the new row number in the DH register, and the new column number in the DL register. Then place function number 2 in the AH register and issue Interrupt 10.

Function 3: find cursor position   To find where your cursor is, put the page number in the BH register, function number 3 in the AH register, and issue Interrupt 10. On return, the DH register has the row and the DL register has the column of the cursor position. Also, the cursor shape is identified; the CH register has the beginning row and CL has the ending row.

Function 5: select video page   The monochrome monitor has only one page, so normally the page number is 0. If you have a graphics monitor, you can have four pages in the 80-column mode and eight in the 40-column mode. If you want to change pages, put the page number in AL, function number 5 in AH, and then issue Interrupt 10.

Function 6: scroll up   You can scroll either the entire screen or a portion of it. To scroll up, place the number of lines to scroll (0 to 24) in the AL register, the left column number in CL, the upper row in CH, the right column in DL, and the lower row number in DH. If you want to clear the entire screen, place a 0 in AL. Also, as the text scrolls up, blank lines fill in below. The video attribute for the blank lines is placed in BH: 0 for blanks and 70 for reverse video. Set AH to 6 and issue Interrupt 10.

Function 7: scroll down   Scroll down is the opposite of scroll up, the only difference being what you see on the monitor. With this function, the lines go downward instead of upward.

Function 8: read character and attribute   If you want to know what attribute the character at the cursor position has, set BH to the display page (0 for monochrome, 04 for 80-column graphics, 07 for 40-column), AH to 8, and issue Interrupt 10. The character value in ASCII returns in AL and its attribute in AH.

Function 9: write character and attribute   Place the character you want to write in the AL register and its desired attribute in BL. The page number is placed in BH and the number of characters to write goes in CX. Set AH to 9 and issue Interrupt 10. Because the cursor does not move after the character is written, you must move it with Function 2 after each write operation.

Function 0A: write character   Function 0A is like Function 9, except that you do not also write the character attribute. Set the AH register to 0A and issue Interrupt 10.

Function 0F: find video mode   To find out what video mode you have, set the AH register to 0F and issue Interrupt 10. The video mode is returned in register AL, the video page in BH, and the screen width (40 or 80) in AH.

Elementary graphics routines

Many of the elementary text mode graphics routines have been combined into one program. Examples of clearing the screen, locating the cursor at a specific spot, drawing a line (vertical and horizontal) and scrolling are all in GRAPH_IT.

A text-mode graphics program

GRAPH_IT (Program 10-1) performs several functions. First, it draws horizontal and vertical lines to divide the full screen into five sections. A point at the line crossing is plotted and a graphic (+) is printed there. The line-drawing functions are procedures within the program; parameters of beginning locations, width, and depth are passed.

Second, GRAPH_IT uses a box-drawing procedure (also coded inside GRAPH_IT) to draw individual boxes (windows) within the four squares of the screen. Inside each of those four windows, additional features are shown. Figure 10-5 shows what the final screen looks like.

In window 1, four smaller boxes are drawn and then filled in. The fill-in procedure shows you how to fill a rectangular area on the screen. In window 2, horizontal and vertical lines are drawn, using the same procedure that drew the original lines dividing the full screen. Window 3 shows how to draw a checkerboard pattern. That section of GRAPH_IT code illustrates how to swap beginning columns for printing alternating patterns. Window 4 displays scrolling within a smaller window (instead of the entire screen).

A graphics-mode driver

GRAFDRV (Program 10-2) exercises 16 graphics routines that work in graphics mode. The graphics package is a good start for learning to program for Hercules and Hercules-compatible monochrome graphics cards. The package uses direct I/O to the 6845 controller chip. The chip accepts

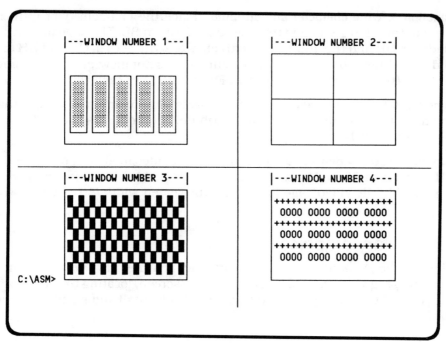

10-5 GRAPH__IT example.

only 8-bit-wide I/O, so the routines do not demonstrate the full power of the 80486.

The package consists of a driver (which exercises and tests the package routines) and a set of routines that are explained in the following paragraphs. One comment, though; this set of packages is almost impossible to step through with a debug package because the debug packages make assumptions about the state of the screen that this package invalidates. This situation caused us some extra work during debugging, as it will when you begin to explore the graphics mode.

GRAFCLS: clear the screen   No input is required. The state of the graphics adapter is tested to determine the clearing size and value. The buffer is cleared. The output is a clear buffer.

GRAFOFF: leave graphics mode   The page is cleared with an STOSD, which is more than twice as fast as an 80286 could do it. If the adapter is in text mode, nothing happens. If it is in graphics mode, here's what happens: The display is turned off, the 6845 controller is loaded with the text mode parameters, the screen is cleared, and the display is turned back on. The mode flag is set to text.

GRAFON: enter graphics mode and clear first page   Again this is done more than twice as fast as you could do it on an 80286, because of the 32-bit STOSD instruction.

GRAFBXY: locate a dot This procedure returns the byte offset and the bit mask for the bit X,Y. BX holds the horizontal displacement of the bit (0 – 719) X. AX had the vertical displacement of the bit (0 – 347) Y. The procedure computes the proper byte displacement for a Hercules compatible monochrome graphics adapter. The buffer displacement is:

8192h × (Y MOD 4) + 90 × INT(Y/4) + INT(X/8)

Bit number is 7 – (X MOD 8). BX has the displacement into the graphics page (0000 – 7FFF). AH has the mask for setting the bit off (AND), AL has the mask for setting the bit on (OR). Carry will be reset (set to 0) if X,Y was valid for conversion. If an invalid X,Y coordinate is detected, Carry is set and the return is immediate; no registers are changed in this case.

GRAFSET: set a dot This procedure sets the screen bit for the pixel given in BX and AX. BX has the horizontal displacement of the bit (0 – 719) X, and AX has the vertical displacement of the bit (0 – 347) Y. GRAFSET uses GRAFBXY to locate the bit to set, and then sets it. If the location is valid, the bit is set to 1 and Carry is reset (CF = 0) on return. The location (GRAFXVAL,GRAFYVAL) will set in this case. If the position is invalid, CF = 1 on return.

GRAFRSET: reset a dot GRAFRSET resets the screen bit for the pixel given in BX and AX. It uses GRAFBXY to locate the bit to reset and resets it. BX has the horizontal displacement of the bit (0 – 719) X and AX has the vertical displacement of the bit (0 – 347) Y. If the location is valid, the bit is set to 0 and Carry is reset (CF = 0) on return. The location (GRAFXVAL,GRAFYVAL) will set in this case. If the position is invalid, CF = 1 on return.

GRAFLINE: draw a line GRAFLINE draws or erases a line between the (GRAFXVAL,GRAFYVAL) point and the (BX,AX) point. BX has the horizontal displacement of the bit (0 – 719) X, and AX has the vertical displacement of the bit (0 – 347) Y. CL is zero for an erase and non-zero for a draw. GRAFLINE computes the factors for forming the line in terms of a step value for X and Y (+ 1) and a direction. The line is either drawn or erased and Carry is reset (CF = 0) if the endpoints are valid. The point (GRAFXVAL, GRAFYVAL) will be set to the (BX,AX) values at the end. If the endpoint is invalid, return is made with CF = 1 and no changes made.

GRAFLOC: return location of last dot GRAFLOC returns the location of the last pixel modified. The procedure loads the values of GRAFXVAL and GRAFYVAL into BX and AX. BX has the horizontal displacement of the bit (0 – 719) X, and AX has the vertical displacement of the bit (0 – 347) Y.

GRAFCLOC: return last character's location GRAFCLOC returns the values MONOROW in BH, and MONOCOL in BL.

GRAFBIT: return state of pixel GRAFBIT sets the condition code to the pixel given in BX and AX. BX has the horizontal displacement of the bit (0 – 719) X and AX has the vertical displacement of the bit (0 – 347) Y. The procedure uses GRAFBXY to locate the bit and copies it into the condition code.

GRAFTXT: mimic Interrupt 21 Function 9 GRAFTXT displays text until it encounters an embedded "$" character. It honors backspace, line feed, and carriage returns. DX points to the text location.

GRAFDRV memory locations Listed below are several labeled memory locations used by GRAFDRV:

> GRAFMODE: A byte flag 00 = OFF, 01 = ON
> GRAFXVAL: A word that has the last X
> GRAFYVAL: A word that has the last Y
> MONOROW: A word that has the last row
> MONOCOL: A word that has the last column

Character output in graphics mode

GRAFCHR (Program 10-3) provides a character output in graphics mode. The upper left graphic point of the character is computed (note that Hercules graphics font characters are 9 horizontal and 14 vertical positions in size, i.e., 80×24 with 12 positions vertical unused at the bottom of the screen). The character set resides in the font table portion of the program; the set we created is similar to the IBM standard font, but is not exactly the same. The 14 lines of the character are placed into the graphics buffer. The registers are restored and CF is set if there's a problem. If set, no change in the display is made.

To save a lot of space in the book, only a representative sample of the characters is included to illustrate the definition technique; you should define at least the lower 128 characters in ascending numerical order from 0 through 7Fh. In the listing area that defines the character set, you'll notice the character "C" to the right of the byte location and to the left of the DW. That indicates that this file/procedure/code was included during assembly from a separate .asm file. (Our complete GRAFDRV font is available on the optional diskette for this book.)

GRAFTYPE (Program 10-4) identifies the graphic adapter present in a system. The standard BIOS extension for an advanced graphic adapter is checked.

Program 10-1 GRAPH__IT

```
Microsoft (R) Macro Assembler Version 5.00


                                      PAGE    55,132
                                      .386
                                      EXTRN   PAUSE:PROC
0000                          STACK   SEGMENT 'STACK' STACK
0000   0064 [                         DW      100 DUP(?)
         ????
                        ]
```

```
00C8                            STACK   ENDS
0000                            CODE    SEGMENT para 'CODE' PUBLIC USE16
                                        ASSUME  CS:CODE, DS:CODE, SS:STACK

                                ;
                                ; Name:          GRAPH_IT
                                ;
                                ; Purpose:       This program does some simple graphics as a
                                ;                demonstration of screen handling, scrolling,
                                ;                line drawing, cursor positioning, and waiting for
                                ;                a while (pausing).
                                ;
                                ;                We wanted to slow the graphics down so each action is
                                ;                visible.  A procedure called PAUSE pauses for a time
                                ;                span from .02 seconds to 59.99 seconds.  PAUSE is
                                ;                described in Chapter 9 of "80386 Assembly Language
                                ;                Toolkit."
                                ;
                                ; Inputs:        ASCII strings are input with DB statements.
                                ;
                                ; Process:       The screen is cleared, lines are drawn vertically
                                ;                and horizontally, and then graphics are drawn in
                                ;                each section of the screen.  The pause was decided to
                                ;                be 1 second.  1 is stored in BH, 0 in BL for the call
                                ;                to PAUSE.  BX is then PUSHed and POPed when needed.
                                ;
                                ; Outputs:       Screen images.
                                ;
                                ; NOTE:          Parameters to be passed are kept in memory variables
                                ;                for easier code reading.  But in loops, the memory
                                ;                variables are moved into registers to keep from
                                ;                making multiple memory references.
                                ;
0000                            GRAPH_IT:
0000  8C C8                             MOV     AX,CS           ; Prepare to set DS
0002  8E D8                             MOV     DS,AX           ;   and set it.
0004  E9 00B1 R                         JMP     BEGINHERE
0007  2B 2B 2B 2B 2B 2B 2B      PLUS    DB      '+++++++++++++++++++++$'
      2B 2B 2B 2B 2B 2B 2B
      2B 2B 2B 2B 2B 2B 2B
      24
001D  20 30 30 30 30 20 30      ZEROS   DB      ' 0000 0000 0000 0000 $'
      30 30 30 20 30 30 30
      30 20 30 30 30 30 20
      24
0033  B3 24                     VERT_LINE   DB  '|$'
0035  C4 24                     HORIZ_LINE  DB  '-$'
0037  C5 24                     CROSS       DB  '+$'
0039  7C 2D 2D 2D 57 49 4E      LABEL_1     DB  '|---WINDOW NUMBER 1---|$'
      44 4F 57 20 4E 55 4D
      42 45 52 20 31 2D 2D
      2D 7C 24
0051  7C 2D 2D 2D 57 49 4E      LABEL_2     DB  '|---WINDOW NUMBER 2---|$'
      44 4F 57 20 4E 55 4D
      42 45 52 20 32 2D 2D
      2D 7C 24
0069  7C 2D 2D 2D 57 49 4E      LABEL_3     DB  '|---WINDOW NUMBER 3---|$'
      44 4F 57 20 4E 55 4D
      42 45 52 20 33 2D 2D
      2D 7C 24
0081  7C 2D 2D 2D 57 49 4E      LABEL_4     DB  '|---WINDOW NUMBER 4---|$'
      44 4F 57 20 4E 55 4D
      42 45 52 20 34 2D 2D
      2D 7C 24
0099  BF 24                     RT_CORNER    DB  '┐$'
009B  D9 24                     RB_CORNER    DB  '┘$'
009D  DA 24                     LT_CORNER    DB  '┌$'
009F  C0 24                     LB_CORNER    DB  '└$'
00A1  C3 24                     LEFT_CONNECT DB  '├$'
```

```
00A3  B4 24              RIGHT_CONNECT    DB      '┤$'
00A5  C2 24              TOP_CONNECT      DB      '┬$'
00A7  C1 24              BOTTOM_CONNECT   DB      '┴$'
00A9  B1 24              SHADE            DB      '▒$'
                         ;
                         ; Parameters to pass to box drawing procedure
                         ;
00AB  00                 LT_ROW           DB      0
00AC  00                 L_COLUMN         DB      0
00AD  00                 R_COLUMN         DB      0
00AE  00                 LB_ROW           DB      0
00AF  00                 WIDE             DB      0
00B0  00                 HEIGHT           DB      0
                         ;
                         ; This first routine clears the screen
                         ;
00B1                     BEGINHERE:
00B1  B4 0F                      MOV     AH,15           ; Read the video mode
00B3  CD 10                      INT     10h
00B5  B4 00                      MOV     AH,0            ; Set the mode
00B7  CD 10                      INT     10h
00B9  B6 01                      MOV     DH,1            ; 1 second wait
00BB  B2 00                      MOV     DL,0            ; No hundredths
00BD  52                         PUSH    DX              ; Save DX on the stack
                         ;
                         ; Draw a horizontal line
                         ;
00BE  5A                         POP     DX              ; Retrieve DX
00BF  E8 0000 E                  CALL    PAUSE           ; Wait
00C2  52                         PUSH    DX              ; Save it again
00C3  C6 06 00AB R 0B            MOV     LT_ROW,11       ; Define on which row to draw
00C8  C6 06 00AC R 00            MOV     L_COLUMN,0      ; Where to start
00CD  C6 06 00AF R 4F            MOV     WIDE,79         ; How long to draw it
00D2  E8 043A R                  CALL    DRAW_HORIZ
                         ;
                         ; Now draw a vertical line
                         ;
00D5  5A                         POP     DX              ; Retrieve DX
00D6  E8 0000 E                  CALL    PAUSE           ; Wait
00D9  52                         PUSH    DX              ; Save it again
00DA  C6 06 00AB R 00            MOV     LT_ROW,0        ; Start at top of screen
00DF  C6 06 00AC R 27            MOV     L_COLUMN,39     ; Draw in middle
00E4  C6 06 00B0 R 18            MOV     HEIGHT,24
00E9  E8 045F R                  CALL    DRAW_VERT
                         ;
                         ; Put a "+" where the lines cross
                         ;
00EC  5A                         POP     DX              ; Retrieve DX
00ED  E8 0000 E                  CALL    PAUSE           ; Wait
00F0  52                         PUSH    DX              ; Save it again
00F1  B6 0B                      MOV     DH,11           ; Move cursor to row 12
00F3  B2 27                      MOV     DL,39           ; Column 0
00F5  B4 02                      MOV     AH,2            ; Position the cursor
00F7  CD 10                      INT     10h
00F9  8D 16 0037 R               LEA     DX,CROSS        ; Print the "+"
00FD  B4 09                      MOV     AH,9
00FF  CD 21                      INT     21h
                         ;
                         ; Draw a box in window 1
                         ;
0101  5A                         POP     DX              ; Retrieve DX
0102  E8 0000 E                  CALL    PAUSE           ; Wait
0105  52                         PUSH    DX              ; Save it again
0106  C6 06 00AB R 01            MOV     LT_ROW,1        ; Left,top row is 2
010B  C6 06 00AC R 08            MOV     L_COLUMN,8      ; Left column = 9
```

```
0110  C6 06 00AD R 1E              MOV     R_COLUMN,30      ; Right column = 31
0115  C6 06 00AF R 15              MOV     WIDE,21
011A  C6 06 00B0 R 07              MOV     HEIGHT,7
011F  E8 048A R                    CALL    DRAW_BOX
                        ;
                        ; Labeling Window 1
                        ;
0122  5A                           POP     DX               ; Retrieve DX
0123  E8 0000 E                    CALL    PAUSE            ; Wait
0126  52                           PUSH    DX               ; Save it again
0127  C6 06 00AB R 00              MOV     LT_ROW,0         ; Move cursor to row 1
012C  C6 06 00AC R 08              MOV     L_COLUMN,8       ; Column 9
0131  8D 0E 0039 R                 LEA     CX,LABEL_1       ; Address of Label
0135  E8 0523 R                    CALL    DRAW_LABEL
                        ; Draw Cards inside Window 1
                        ;
0138  5A                           POP     DX               ; Retrieve DX
0139  E8 0000 E                    CALL    PAUSE            ; Wait
013C  52                           PUSH    DX               ; Save it again
013D  C6 06 00AB R 03              MOV     LT_ROW,3         ; Card 1
0142  C6 06 00AC R 09              MOV     L_COLUMN,9
0147  C6 06 00AD R 0C              MOV     R_COLUMN,12
014C  C6 06 00AF R 02              MOV     WIDE,2
0151  C6 06 00B0 R 04              MOV     HEIGHT,4
0156  E8 048A R                    CALL    DRAW_BOX
                        ;
0159  5A                           POP     DX               ; Retrieve DX
015A  E8 0000 E                    CALL    PAUSE            ; Wait
015D  52                           PUSH    DX               ; Save it again
015E  C6 06 00AB R 03              MOV     LT_ROW,3         ; Card 2
0163  C6 06 00AC R 0D              MOV     L_COLUMN,13
0168  C6 06 00AD R 10              MOV     R_COLUMN,16
016D  C6 06 00AF R 02              MOV     WIDE,2
0172  C6 06 00B0 R 04              MOV     HEIGHT,4
0177  E8 048A R                    CALL    DRAW_BOX
                        ;
017A  5A                           POP     DX               ; Retrieve DX
017B  E8 0000 E                    CALL    PAUSE            ; Wait
017E  52                           PUSH    DX               ; Save it again
017F  C6 06 00AB R 03              MOV     LT_ROW,3         ; Card 3
0184  C6 06 00AC R 11              MOV     L_COLUMN,17
0189  C6 06 00AD R 14              MOV     R_COLUMN,20
018E  C6 06 00AF R 02              MOV     WIDE,2
0193  C6 06 00B0 R 04              MOV     HEIGHT,4
0198  E8 048A R                    CALL    DRAW_BOX
                        ;
019B  5A                           POP     DX               ; Retrieve DX
019C  E8 0000 E                    CALL    PAUSE            ; Wait
019F  52                           PUSH    DX               ; Save it again
01A0  C6 06 00AB R 03              MOV     LT_ROW,3         ; Card 4
01A5  C6 06 00AC R 15              MOV     L_COLUMN,21
01AA  C6 06 00AD R 18              MOV     R_COLUMN,24
01AF  C6 06 00AF R 02              MOV     WIDE,2
01B4  C6 06 00B0 R 04              MOV     HEIGHT,4
01B9  E8 048A R                    CALL    DRAW_BOX
                        ;
01BC  5A                           POP     DX               ; Retrieve DX
01BD  E8 0000 E                    CALL    PAUSE            ; Wait
01C0  52                           PUSH    DX               ; Save it again
01C1  C6 06 00AB R 03              MOV     LT_ROW,3         ; Card 5
01C6  C6 06 00AC R 19              MOV     L_COLUMN,25
01CB  C6 06 00AD R 1C              MOV     R_COLUMN,28
01D0  C6 06 00AF R 02              MOV     WIDE,2
01D5  C6 06 00B0 R 04              MOV     HEIGHT,4
01DA  E8 048A R                    CALL    DRAW_BOX
                        ;
                        ; Shade in the boxes
```

```
                              ;
01DD  5A                      POP    DX              ; Retrieve DX
01DE  E8 0000 E               CALL   PAUSE           ; Wait
01E1  52                      PUSH   DX              ; Save it again
01E2  C6 06 00AB R 04         MOV    LT_ROW,4        ; Card 1
01E7  C6 06 00AC R 0A         MOV    L_COLUMN,10
01EC  C6 06 00AF R 02         MOV    WIDE,2
01F1  C6 06 00B0 R 04         MOV    HEIGHT,4
01F6  8D 0E 00A9 R            LEA    CX,SHADE
01FA  E8 0538 R               CALL   FILL_REC
                              ;
01FD  5A                      POP    DX              ; Retrieve DX
01FE  E8 0000 E               CALL   PAUSE           ; Wait
0201  52                      PUSH   DX              ; Save it again
0202  C6 06 00AB R 04         MOV    LT_ROW,4        ; Card 2
0207  C6 06 00AC R 0E         MOV    L_COLUMN,14
020C  C6 06 00AF R 02         MOV    WIDE,2
0211  C6 06 00B0 R 04         MOV    HEIGHT,4
0216  8D 0E 00A9 R            LEA    CX,SHADE
021A  E8 0538 R               CALL   FILL_REC
                              ;
021D  5A                      POP    DX              ; Retrieve DX
021E  E8 0000 E               CALL   PAUSE           ; Wait
0221  52                      PUSH   DX              ; Save it again
0222  C6 06 00AB R 04         MOV    LT_ROW,4        ; Card 3
0227  C6 06 00AC R 12         MOV    L_COLUMN,18
022C  C6 06 00AF R 02         MOV    WIDE,2
0231  C6 06 00B0 R 04         MOV    HEIGHT,4
0236  8D 0E 00A9 R            LEA    CX,SHADE
023A  E8 0538 R               CALL   FILL_REC
                              ;
023D  5A                      POP    DX              ; Retrieve DX
023E  E8 0000 E               CALL   PAUSE           ; Wait
0241  52                      PUSH   DX              ; Save it again
0242  C6 06 00AB R 04         MOV    LT_ROW,4        ; Card 4
0247  C6 06 00AC R 16         MOV    L_COLUMN,22
024C  C6 06 00AF R 02         MOV    WIDE,2
0251  C6 06 00B0 R 04         MOV    HEIGHT,4
0256  8D 0E 00A9 R            LEA    CX,SHADE
025A  E8 0538 R               CALL   FILL_REC
                              ;
025D  5A                      POP    DX              ; Retrieve DX
025E  E8 0000 E               CALL   PAUSE           ; Wait
0261  52                      PUSH   DX              ; Save it again
0262  C6 06 00AB R 04         MOV    LT_ROW,4        ; Card 5
0267  C6 06 00AC R 1A         MOV    L_COLUMN,26
026C  C6 06 00AF R 02         MOV    WIDE,2
0271  C6 06 00B0 R 04         MOV    HEIGHT,4
0276  8D 0E 00A9 R            LEA    CX,SHADE
027A  E8 0538 R               CALL   FILL_REC
                              ;
                              ;
                              ; Draw a box in window 2
                              ;
027D  5A                      POP    DX              ; Retrieve DX
027E  E8 0000 E               CALL   PAUSE           ; Wait
0281  52                      PUSH   DX              ; Save it again
0282  C6 06 00AB R 01         MOV    LT_ROW,1        ; Left,top row is 2
0287  C6 06 00AC R 2D         MOV    L_COLUMN,45     ; Left column = 46
028C  C6 06 00AD R 43         MOV    R_COLUMN,67     ; Right column = 68
0291  C6 06 00AF R 15         MOV    WIDE,21
0296  C6 06 00B0 R 07         MOV    HEIGHT,7
029B  E8 048A R               CALL   DRAW_BOX
                              ;
                              ; Divide Window 2 into 4 boxes
                              ;
```

```
029E  5A                      POP     DX                  ; Retrieve DX
029F  E8 0000 E               CALL    PAUSE               ; Wait
02A2  52                      PUSH    DX                  ; Save it again
02A3  B6 05                   MOV     DH,5                ; Row 6
02A5  B2 2D                   MOV     DL,45               ; Column 45
02A7  B4 02                   MOV     AH,2                ; Position cursor
02A9  CD 10                   INT     10h
02AB  8D 16 00A1 R            LEA     DX,LEFT_CONNECT     ; Print the left-side connector
02AF  B4 09                   MOV     AH,9
02B1  CD 21                   INT     21h
                      ;            Draw horizontal line in window 2
02B3  5A                      POP     DX                  ; Retrieve DX
02B4  E8 0000 E               CALL    PAUSE               ; Wait
02B7  52                      PUSH    DX                  ; Save it again
02B8  C6 06 00AB R 05         MOV     LT_ROW,5            ; Row 6
02BD  C6 06 00AC R 2E         MOV     L_COLUMN,46         ; Column 47
02C2  C6 06 00AF R 15         MOV     WIDE,21
02C7  E8 043A R               CALL    DRAW_HORIZ
                      ;
02CA  5A                      POP     DX                  ; Retrieve DX
02CB  E8 0000 E               CALL    PAUSE               ; Wait
02CE  52                      PUSH    DX                  ; Save it again
02CF  8D 16 00A3 R            LEA     DX,RIGHT_CONNECT    ; Print the right-side connector
02D3  B4 09                   MOV     AH,9
02D5  CD 21                   INT     21h
                      ;            Draw vertical line in window 2
02D7  5A                      POP     DX                  ; Retrieve DX
02D8  E8 0000 E               CALL    PAUSE               ; Wait
02DB  52                      PUSH    DX                  ; Save it again
02DC  B6 01                   MOV     DH,1                ; Draw top connector
02DE  B2 38                   MOV     DL,56
02E0  B4 02                   MOV     AH,2
02E2  CD 10                   INT     10h
02E4  8D 16 00A5 R            LEA     DX,TOP_CONNECT
02E8  B4 09                   MOV     AH,9
02EA  CD 21                   INT     21H
                      ;
02EC  5A                      POP     DX                  ; Retrieve DX
02ED  E8 0000 E               CALL    PAUSE               ; Wait
02F0  52                      PUSH    DX                  ; Save it again
02F1  C6 06 00AB R 02         MOV     LT_ROW,2            ; Start at row 2 for vert line
02F6  C6 06 00AC R 38         MOV     L_COLUMN,56         ; Draw at column 56
02FB  C6 06 00B0 R 07         MOV     HEIGHT,7
0300  E8 045F R               CALL    DRAW_VERT
                      ;
0303  5A                      POP     DX                  ; Retrieve DX
0304  E8 0000 E               CALL    PAUSE               ; Wait
0307  52                      PUSH    DX                  ; Save it again
0308  8A 16 00AC R            MOV     DL,L_COLUMN         ; Position cursor at bottom of box
030C  B6 09                   MOV     DH,9
030E  B4 02                   MOV     AH,2
0310  CD 10                   INT     10h
0312  8D 16 00A7 R            LEA     DX,BOTTOM_CONNECT   ; Draw the bottom connector
0316  B4 09                   MOV     AH,9
0318  CD 21                   INT     21h
                      ;
                      ; Put a "+" where the lines cross
                      ;
031A  5A                      POP     DX                  ; Retrieve DX
031B  E8 0000 E               CALL    PAUSE               ; Wait
031E  52                      PUSH    DX                  ; Save it again
031F  B6 05                   MOV     DH,5                ; Move cursor to row 6
0321  B2 38                   MOV     DL,56               ; Column 56
0323  B4 02                   MOV     AH,2                ; Position the cursor
0325  CD 10                   INT     10h
0327  8D 16 0037 R            LEA     DX,CROSS            ; Print the "+"
032B  B4 09                   MOV     AH,9
032D  CD 21                   INT     21h
```

```
                                ;
                                ; Label Window 2
                                ;
032F  5A                                POP     DX              ; Retrieve DX
0330  E8 0000 E                         CALL    PAUSE           ; Wait
0333  52                                PUSH    DX              ; Save it again
0334  C6 06 00AB R 00                   MOV     LT_ROW,0        ; Row 1
0339  C6 06 00AC R 2D                   MOV     L_COLUMN,45     ; Column 46
033E  8D 0E 0051 R                      LEA     CX,LABEL_2
0342  E8 0523 R                         CALL    DRAW_LABEL

                                ;
                                ; Draw a box in window 3
                                ;
0345  5A                                POP     DX              ; Retrieve DX
0346  E8 0000 E                         CALL    PAUSE           ; Wait
0349  52                                PUSH    DX              ; Save it again
034A  C6 06 00AB R 0D                   MOV     LT_ROW,13       ; Left,top row is 14
034F  C6 06 00AC R 08                   MOV     L_COLUMN,8      ; Left column = 9
0354  C6 06 00AD R 1E                   MOV     R_COLUMN,30     ; Right column = 31
0359  C6 06 00AF R 15                   MOV     WIDE,21
035E  C6 06 00B0 R 07                   MOV     HEIGHT,7
0363  E8 048A R                         CALL    DRAW_BOX

                                ;
                                ; Labeling Window 3
                                ;
0366  5A                                POP     DX              ; Retrieve DX
0367  E8 0000 E                         CALL    PAUSE           ; Wait
036A  52                                PUSH    DX              ; Save it again
036B  C6 06 00AB R 0C                   MOV     LT_ROW,12       ; Move cursor to row 13
0370  C6 06 00AC R 08                   MOV     L_COLUMN,8      ; Column 9
0375  8D 0E 0069 R                      LEA     CX,LABEL_3      ; Address of Label
0379  E8 0523 R                         CALL    DRAW_LABEL

                                ;
                                ;     Now draw a checkerboard in Window 3
                                ;
                                ;     The ASCII character is from the IBM-US Extended
                                ;     ASCII.
                                ;
                                ;     DX = Row/column for cursor positioning
                                ;     SI = Hex ASCII character
                                ;     BP = Even row column starting position
                                ;     DI = Odd row column starting position
                                ;
037C  5A                                POP     DX              ; Retrieve DX
037D  E8 0000 E                         CALL    PAUSE           ; Wait
0380  52                                PUSH    DX              ; Save it again
0381  2B ED                             SUB     BP,BP           ; Zero BP
0383  2B FF                             SUB     DI,DI           ; Zero DI
0385  BE 00DB                           MOV     SI,219          ; Blackouts (in hex=DB)
0388  B1 0A                             MOV     CL,10
038A  8B E9                             MOV     BP,CX           ; column 10
038C  B1 09                             MOV     CL,9
038E  8B F9                             MOV     DI,CX           ; column 9,10
0390  2B DB                             SUB     BX,BX           ; Make sure this is zero
0392  B6 0E                             MOV     DH,14           ; Row 15
0394                          CHECKER0:
0394  8B CF                             MOV     CX,DI           ; First time 9, second 10
0396  8A D1                             MOV     DL,CL           ; Column to begin in
0398  B4 02                             MOV     AH,2            ; Position cursor
039A  CD 10                             INT     10h
                                ;
039C                          CHECKER1:
039C  87 D6                             XCHG    DX,SI           ; Swap row/col with char string
039E  B4 02                             MOV     AH,2
03A0  CD 21                             INT     21H
```

```
03A2  87 F2                          XCHG    SI,DX           ; Swap back, now row/col in DX
03A4  80 C2 02                       ADD     DL,2            ; Skip a space & position cursor
03A7  CD 10                          INT     10h
03A9  80 FA 1E                       CMP     DL,30           ; All the way across?
03AC  7C EE                          JL      CHECKER1
                            ;
03AE  8B C2                          MOV     AX,DX           ; Save row/column
03B0  5A                             POP     DX              ; Get time to pause
03B1  E8 0000 E                      CALL    PAUSE
03B4  52                             PUSH    DX              ; Save time again
03B5  8B D0                          MOV     DX,AX           ; Retrieve row/column
03B7  87 EF                          XCHG    BP,DI           ; Swap which col to start on
03B9  FE C6                          INC     DH              ; Go to next row
03BB  80 FE 15                       CMP     DH,21           ; Done?
03BE  75 D4                          JNE     CHECKER0
                            ;
                            ; Draw a box in window 4
                            ;
03C0  5A                             POP     DX              ; Retrieve DX
03C1  E8 0000 E                      CALL    PAUSE           ; Wait
03C4  52                             PUSH    DX              ; Save it again
03C5  C6 06 00AB R 0D                MOV     LT_ROW,13       ; Left,top row is 14
03CA  C6 06 00AC R 2D                MOV     L_COLUMN,45     ; Left column = 46
03CF  C6 06 00AD R 43                MOV     R_COLUMN,67     ; Right column = 68
03D4  C6 06 00AF R 15                MOV     WIDE,21
03D9  C6 06 00B0 R 07                MOV     HEIGHT,7
03DE  E8 048A R                      CALL    DRAW_BOX
                            ;
                            ; Labeling Window 4
                            ;
03E1  5A                             POP     DX              ; Retrieve DX
03E2  E8 0000 E                      CALL    PAUSE           ; Wait
03E5  52                             PUSH    DX              ; Save it again
03E6  C6 06 00AB R 0C                MOV     LT_ROW,12       ; Move cursor to row 13
03EB  C6 06 00AC R 2D                MOV     L_COLUMN,45     ; Column 46
03F0  8D 0E 0081 R                   LEA     CX,LABEL_4      ; Address of Label
03F4  E8 0523 R                      CALL    DRAW_LABEL
                            ;
                            ; Scroll in window 4
                            ;
                            ;       AL = Number of lines blanked at bottom
                            ;       CH,CL = Upper left row/column of area to scroll
                            ;       DH,DL = Lower right row/column of area to scroll
                            ;       BH = Attribute used on blank line
                            ;       BP = Number of times to loop through scroll routine
                            ;
                            ;       Position cursor first, with DH,DL being position
                            ;       Then write a line of characters
                            ;
03F7  5A                             POP     DX              ; Retrieve DX
03F8  E8 0000 E                      CALL    PAUSE           ; Wait
03FB  52                             PUSH    DX              ; Save it again
03FC  8D 36 0007 R                   LEA     SI,PLUS         ; Address of Plus char string
0400  8D 3E 001D R                   LEA     DI,ZEROS        ; Address of Zero char string
0404  BD 0008                        MOV     BP,8            ; Number of times to loop
0407  2B DB                          SUB     BX,BX           ; Make sure this is zero
0409                        SCROLL0:
0409  B6 14                          MOV     DH,20           ; Position of bottom left corner
040B  B2 2E                          MOV     DL,46           ;   of window 4
040D  B4 02                          MOV     AH,2            ; Set cursor position
040F  CD 10                          INT     10h
                            ;
0411  87 D6                          XCHG    DX,SI           ; Swap row/col with char str addr
0413  B4 09                          MOV     AH,9
0415  CD 21                          INT     21h             ; Print char string
0417  87 D6                          XCHG    DX,SI           ; Swap back
0419  87 F7                          XCHG    SI,DI           ; This will print other string next
```

```
                                ;
041B 5A                                         POP    DX              ; Retrieve DX
041C E8 0000 E                                  CALL   PAUSE           ; Wait
041F 52                                         PUSH   DX              ; Save it again
0420 B5 0E                                       MOV    CH,14           ; Row 15 - Top row of scroll
0422 B1 2E                                       MOV    CL,46           ; Column 46 - Top column
0424 B6 14                                       MOV    DH,20           ; Row 21 - Bottom row of scroll
0426 B2 42                                       MOV    DL,66           ; Column 66 - Bottom column
0428 BB 0000                                     MOV    BX,0
                                ;
042B B4 06                                       MOV    AH,6            ; Now scroll
042D B0 01                                       MOV    AL,1            ; Scroll 1 line
042F CD 10                                       INT    10h
0431 4D                                          DEC    BP
0432 83 FD 00                                    CMP    BP,0            ; Through with this?
0435 75 D2                                       JNE    SCROLL0
                                ;
0437 E9 0572 R                                   JMP    ENDHERE         ; Go around PAUSE code
                                ;
                                ; Draw a horizontal line
                                ;
                                ;               DX - Row/column to move cursor
                                ;                         Also for address of horizontal line character
                                ;               DI - Width
                                ;
043A                  DRAW_HORIZ        PROC
043A 60                                          PUSHA                  ; Save all registers
043B B6 00                                       MOV    DH,0
043D 8A 16 00AF R                                MOV    DL,WIDE         ; Move memory reference to reg
0441 8B FA                                       MOV    DI,DX           ; Save width in DX
                                ;
0443 8A 36 00AB R                                MOV    DH,LT_ROW       ; Move cursor to row
0447 8A 16 00AC R                                MOV    DL,L_COLUMN     ; Column to begin drawing
044B B4 02                                       MOV    AH,2            ; Position the cursor
044D CD 10                                       INT    10h
                                ;
044F 8D 16 0035 R                                LEA    DX,HORIZ_LINE
0453 B4 09                                       MOV    AH,9            ; Get ready to print
0455                  LINE:
0455 CD 21                                       INT    21h
0457 4F                                          DEC    DI
0458 83 FF 00                                    CMP    DI,0            ; Print it enough times?
045B 75 F8                                       JNE    LINE
                                ;
045D 61                                          POPA
045E C3                                          RET
045F                  DRAW_HORIZ        ENDP
                                ;
                                ;
                                ; Draw a Vertical Line Procedure
                                ;
                                ;               SI - Address of vertical line character
                                ;               DI - Height
                                ;               DX - Row/column to move cursor
                                ;
045F                  DRAW_VERT         PROC
045F 60                                          PUSHA                  ; Save all registers
                                ;
0460 8D 36 0033 R                                LEA    SI,VERT_LINE    ; Save address of char string
0464 8A 16 00B0 R                                MOV    DL,HEIGHT
0468 B6 00                                       MOV    DH,0
046A 8B FA                                       MOV    DI,DX           ; Save height
046C 8A 36 00AB R                                MOV    DH,LT_ROW       ; Beginning row
0470 8A 16 00AC R                                MOV    DL,L_COLUMN
                                ;
0474                  LINE2:
```

```
0474  B4 02                                MOV     AH,2
0476  CD 10                                INT     10h              ; Position the cursor
0478  87 D6                                XCHG    DX,SI            ; Swap row/col with char addr
047A  B4 09                                MOV     AH,9             ; Get ready to print '|'
047C  CD 21                                INT     21h
047E  87 D6                                XCHG    DX,SI            ; Swap them back
                          ;
0480  FE C6                                INC     DH               ; Increment row number
0482  4F                                   DEC     DI               ; Printed it enough times?
0483  83 FF 00                             CMP     DI,0             ; The right number of times?
0486  75 EC                                JNE     LINE2

0488  61                                   POPA                     ; Retrieve all registers
0489  C3                                   RET
048A              DRAW_VERT                ENDP
                          ;
                          ;
                          ; Draw a box procedure
                          ;
                          ;              DX - Row/column to move cursor
                          ;                     Also used for address of characters
                          ;              CX - Width (CL) for drawing top
                          ;
048A              DRAW_BOX                 PROC
048A  60                                   PUSHA                    ; Save entry registers
                          ;
048B  8A 36 00AB R                         MOV     DH,LT_ROW        ; Move cursor to top row
048F  8A 16 00AC R                         MOV     DL,L_COLUMN      ; Left Column
0493  B4 02                                MOV     AH,2
0495  CD 10                                INT     10h
                          ;
0497  8D 16 009D R                         LEA     DX,LT_CORNER     ; Print top/left corner
049B  B4 09                                MOV     AH,9
049D  CD 21                                INT     21h
049F  8A 0E 00AF R                         MOV     CL,WIDE          ; However wide box is
04A3  8D 16 0035 R                         LEA     DX,HORIZ_LINE    ; Addr of horiz line character
04A7  B4 09                                MOV     AH,9
04A9              BOX_TOP:
04A9  CD 21                                INT     21h
04AB  FE C9                                DEC     CL
04AD  80 F9 00                             CMP     CL,0
04B0  75 F7                                JNE     BOX_TOP
                          ;
04B2  8D 16 0099 R                         LEA     DX,RT_CORNER     ; Print right/top corner
04B6  B4 09                                MOV     AH,9
04B8  CD 21                                INT     21H
                          ;
                          ; Draw both sides at once
                          ;
                          ;              CX - Left column(CH), Right column (CL)
                          ;              SI - Address of vertical line character
                          ;              DI - Height
                          ;
04BA  8D 36 0033 R                         LEA     SI,VERT_LINE     ; Addr of vertical line char
04BE  8A 2E 00AC R                         MOV     CH,L_COLUMN
04C2  8A 0E 00AD R                         MOV     CL,R_COLUMN
04C6  B6 00                                MOV     DH,0
04C8  8A 16 00B0 R                         MOV     DL,HEIGHT        ; Save height
04CC  8B FA                                MOV     DI,DX
04CE  8A 36 00AB R                         MOV     DH,LT_ROW        ; Move cursor to left top row
04D2  FE C6                                INC     DH               ; Go to next row
04D4              SIDE:
04D4  8A D5                                MOV     DL,CH            ; Adjust to left column
04D6  B4 02                                MOV     AH,2             ; Position cursor
04D8  CD 10                                INT     10h
04DA  87 F2                                XCHG    SI,DX            ; Swap row/col with char str addr
04DC  B4 09                                MOV     AH,9             ; Draw left side
04DE  CD 21                                INT     21h
04E0  87 F2                                XCHG    SI,DX            ; Swap back
```

```
                              ;
04E2  8A D1                        MOV    DL,CL          ; Right Column, Same Row
04E4  B4 02                        MOV    AH,2           ; Position cursor
04E6  CD 10                        INT    10h
04E8  87 F2                        XCHG   SI,DX          ; Swap row/col & char addr string
04EA  B4 09                        MOV    AH,9           ; Draw right side
04EC  CD 21                        INT    21h
04EE  87 F2                        XCHG   SI,DX          ; Swap back
04F0  FE C6                        INC    DH             ; New row
04F2  4F                           DEC    DI
04F3  83 FF 00                     CMP    DI,0           ; Is it the right height?
04F6  75 DC                        JNE    SIDE           ; No, go draw another line

04F8  8A D5                        MOV    DL,CH          ; Now have row/column of bottom
04FA  B4 02                        MOV    AH,2           ; Position cursor
04FC  CD 10                        INT    10h
04FE  8D 16 009F R                 LEA    DX,LB_CORNER   ; Print left/bottom corner
0502  B4 09                        MOV    AH,9
0504  CD 21                        INT    21h
                              ;
0506  8A 0E 00AF R                 MOV    CL,WIDE
050A  8D 16 0035 R                 LEA    DX,HORIZ_LINE  ; Now draw the bottom line
050E  B4 09                        MOV    AH,9
0510                         BOX_BOTTOM:
0510  CD 21                        INT    21h
0512  FE C9                        DEC    CL
0514  80 F9 00                     CMP    CL,0
0517  75 F7                        JNE    BOX_BOTTOM
                              ;
0519  8D 16 009B R                 LEA    DX,RB_CORNER   ; Print right/bottom corner
051D  B4 09                        MOV    AH,9
051F  CD 21                        INT    21h
0521  61                           POPA                  ; Retrieve all registers
0522  C3                           RET
0523                         DRAW_BOX              ENDP
                              ;
                              ;
                              ; Position Cursor and Draw a Label
                              ;
                              ;            DX - Row/column to move cursor
                              ;            CX - Address of label
                              ;
0523                         DRAW_LABEL    PROC
0523  60                           PUSHA                 ; Save registers
                              ;
0524  8A 36 00AB R                 MOV    DH,LT_ROW      ; Row
0528  8A 16 00AC R                 MOV    DL,L_COLUMN    ; Column
052C  B4 02                        MOV    AH,2
052E  CD 10                        INT    10h
                              ;
0530  8B D1                        MOV    DX,CX          ; Address of label
0532  B4 09                        MOV    AH,9
0534  CD 21                        INT    21h
                              ;
0536  61                           POPA                  ; Retrieve registers
0537  C3                           RET
0538                         DRAW_LABEL    ENDP
                              ;
                              ;
                              ;   Fill a rectangular space
                              ;            SI - Fill character address
                              ;            DI - Height
                              ;            BP - Width
                              ;            CX - Brings in fill char address, used in PROC
                              ;                    as a counter
                              ;            DX - Row/column to move cursor
                              ;
```

```
0538                     ;
0538                     FILL_REC    PROC
0538  60                             PUSHA                       ; Save entry registers
                         ;
0539  8B F1                          MOV      SI,CX              ; Addr of Fill character
053B  2B C9                          SUB      CX,CX              ; Zero CX
053D  8A 0E 00B0 R                   MOV      CL,HEIGHT          ; Save height
0541  8B F9                          MOV      DI,CX
0543  8A 0E 00AF R                   MOV      CL,WIDE            ; Save width
0547  8B E9                          MOV      BP,CX
0549  8A 36 00AB R                   MOV      DH,LT_ROW          ; Row to begin fill
054D  8A 16 00AC R                   MOV      DL,L_COLUMN        ; Column to begin fill
0551                     FILL0:
0551  B4 02                          MOV      AH,2               ; Position cursor
0553  CD 10                          INT      10h
                         ;
0555  87 F2                          XCHG     SI,DX              ; Swap row/col with fill char addr
0557  8B CD                          MOV      CX,BP              ; Save width
0559  B4 09                          MOV      AH,9
055B                     FILL1:
055B  CD 21                          INT      21h
055D  FE C9                          DEC      CL
055F  80 F9 00                       CMP      CL,0
0562  75 F7                          JNE      FILL1
                         ; Now go to next row
0564  87 F2                          XCHG     SI,DX              ; Swap back
0566  8B CD                          MOV      CX,BP              ; Restore width
0568  FE C6                          INC      DH                 ; Go to next row
056A  4F                             DEC      DI                 ; Printed enough?
056B  83 FF 00                       CMP      DI,0
056E  75 E1                          JNE      FILL0
                         ;
0570  61                             POPA                        ; Restore registers
0571  C3                             RET
0572                     FILL_REC    ENDP
                         ;
                         ;
0572                     ENDHERE:
0572  B4 4C                          MOV      AH,4Ch             ; Standard ending
0574  CD 21                          INT      21h
0576                     CODE        ENDS
                                     END      GRAPH_IT
```

Program 10-2 GRAFDRV

```
1                                            .386
2                        ;
3                        ; Name:    GRAFDRV
4                        ;
5                        ; Purpose: This program exercises the graphics package.
6                        ;
7                        ; Inputs:  Permission to start is prompted for, as is permission to
8                        ;          end.  Anything entered is ok.
9                        ;
10                       ; Process: This driver prompts, then enters graphics mode.  The
11                       ;          supplied font is displayed and the program pauses for 5
12                       ;          seconds.  A diagonal line is drawn bit by bit and the
13                       ;          program pauses.  A horizontal line is drawn, a pause,
14                       ;          and the rest of a box is formed.  The box is erased in
15                       ;          the same manner.  We then test an on and off pixel and
16                       ;          use the text display to print the result.
```

Program 10-2 Continued.

```
17                            ;          We then exit the graphic mode and prompt for permission
18                            ;          to quit.
19                            ;
20                            ; Outputs: All output is displayed.
21                            ;
22                            ; Note:    This is a difficult package to debug.  The error routine
23                            ;          must exit graphic mode in order to permit a debug package
24                            ;          an intelligible display.  Individual routines were tested
25                            ;          with graphics mode off to eliminate stack problems which
26                            ;          cause entry into never never land.
27                            ;
28
29
30    0000                    stackt   SEGMENT para 'STACK' STACK USE16
31    0000  0100*        +     dq       256 DUP(?)
32          (??????????????????)
33    0800                    stackt   ENDS
34
35    0000                    data     SEGMENT para USE16
36    0000  0100*(??)         string   db       256 DUP(?)           ; String scratch area
37    0100  0A 0A 0D 41 64 61 70+  queryb   db       10,10,13,"Adaptor type is "
38          74 6F 72 20 74 79 70+
39          65 20 69 73 20
40    0113  00000000          detect   dd       0                    ; Type as decoded
41    0117  0A 0D 4A 75 73 74 20+      db       10,13,"Just Enter to quit, any key (then Enter)"
42          45 6E 74 65 72 20 74+
43          6F 20 71 75 69 74 2C+
44          20 61 6E 79 20 6B 65+
45          79 20 28 74 68 65 6E+
46          20 45 6E 74 65 72 29
47    0141  20 74 6F 20 62 65 67+      db       " to begin: $"
48          69 6E 3A 20 24
49    014D  0A 0A 0D 45 6E 74 65+  querye   db       10,10,13,"Enter anything to end: $"
50          72 20 61 6E 79 74 68+
51          69 6E 67 20 74 6F 20+
52          65 6E 64 3A 20 24
53    0168  0A 0A 0A 0D 4F 6E 20+  bitonms  db       10,10,10,13,"On test ok.  $"
54          74 65 73 74 20 6F 6B+
55          2E 20 20 24
56    017A  4F 66 66 20 74 65 73+  bitoffms db       "Off test ok.  $"
57          74 20 6F 68 2E 20 20+
58          24
59    0189  0A 0D 45 6E 64 65 64+  errmsg   db       10,13,"Ended with error! $"
60          20 77 69 74 68 20 65+
61          72 72 6F 72 21 20 24
62    019E  55 6E 6B 2E 43 47 41+  types    db       "Unk.","CGA ","EGA ","Err.","VGA "
63          20 45 47 41 20 45 72+
```

```
64              72 2E 56 47 41 20
65   01B2                            data      ENDS
66
67   0000                            code      SEGMENT para 'CODE' USE16 PUBLIC
68
69                                   ;
70                                   ; Declare the routines we are going to use
71                                   ;
72                                             EXTRN     PAUSE:PROC
73                                             EXTRN     GRAFTYPE:PROC
74                                             EXTRN     GRAFON:PROC
75                                             EXTRN     GRAFOFF:PROC
76                                             EXTRN     GRAFCHR:PROC
77                                             EXTRN     GRAFCLS:PROC
78                                             EXTRN     GRAFSET:PROC
79                                             EXTRN     GRAFRSET:PROC
80                                             EXTRN     GRAFLINE:PROC
81                                             EXTRN     GRAFBIT:PROC
82                                             EXTRN     GRAFLOC:PROC
83                                             EXTRN     GRAFCLOC:PROC
84                                             EXTRN     GRAFTXT:PROC
85                                             EXTRN     CODEBAS:PROC
86
87         = 0000                    typ_unk   EQU       0             ; Simple tests can't tell
88         = 0008                    typ_vga   EQU       8             ; Best possible type
89         = 0004                    typ_ega   EQU       4             ; Not too bad
90         = 0002                    typ_cga   EQU       2             ; Yeeech
91
92                                             ASSUME    CS:code, DS:data
93                                   ;
94                                   ; Set up the environment
95                                   ;
96   0000                            Begin:
97   0000  B8 0000s                            mov       AX,data       ; Get data segment pointer
98   0003  8E D8                               mov       DS,AX         ; into DS,
99   0005  8E C0                               mov       ES,AX         ; and ES.
100  0007  2B F6                               sub       SI,SI         ; Clear indices
101  0009  2B FF                               sub       DI,DI
102  000B  E8 0000e                            call      graftype      ; Get adaptor type
103  000E  D1 E0                               shl       AX,1
104  0010  8B D8                               mov       BX,AX         ; as mult of 4 for index
105  0012  66| 8B 87 019Er                     mov       EAX,DWORD PTR types[BX] ; and fetch the text
106  0017  66| A3 0113r                        mov       detect,EAX    ;
107  001B  BA 0100r                            lea       DX,queryb     ; Put out start msg
108  001E  E8 00F2                             call      getinp
109  0021  0B C9                               or        CX,CX         ; check length and
110  0023  0F 84 00D7                          jz        exit          ; Get out if just enter
111                                  ;
```

```
112                                              ; set graphic mode on
113                                              ;
114     0027  E8 0000e               call     Grafon         ; Set it on
115     002A  B9 0050                mov      CX,80          ; Prepare char set line 1
116     002D  2A C0                  sub      AL,AL          ; starting character
117     002F  2B DB                  sub      BX,BX          ; Col 0 row 0
118     0031                first80:
119     0031  E8 0000e               call     grafchr        ; put out a char
120     0034  0F 82 00CC             jc       charerr        ; error routine if bad
121     0038  FE C7                  inc      BH
122     003A  FE C0                  inc      AL
123     003C  E2 F3                  loop     first80        ; Do 0-79
124     003E  FE C3                  inc      BL             ; next row
125     0040  B9 0050                mov      CX,80          ; all of it
126     0043  2A FF                  sub      BH,BH          ; With col 0 as start
127     0045                second80:
128     0045  E8 0000e               call     grafchr        ; Put character out
129     0048  0F 82 00B8             jc       charerr        ; If error - quit
130     004C  FE C7                  inc      BH             ; Step horizontal loc
131     004E  FE C0                  inc      AL             ; and character
132     0050  E2 F3                  loop     second80       ; do 80-159 (check folding
133     0052  BA 0500                mov      DX,500h        ; Delay five seconds
134     0055  E8 0000e               call     pause
135                                              ;
136                                              ; The character set is now displayed - set some points below it
137                                              ;
138     0058  2B DB                  sub      BX,BX          ; start at left margin
139     005A  B8 0046                mov      AX,70          ; and fifth char row
140     005D  B9 0032                mov      CX,50
141     0060                points1:
142     0060  E8 0000e               call     grafset        ; Set the point
143     0063  0F 82 009D             jc       pointerr       ; If error - quit
144     0067  40                     inc      AX
145     0068  43                     inc      BX             ; diag.
146     0069  E2 F5                  loop     points1
147     006B  BA 0500                mov      DX,500h        ; wait for half a sec
148     006E  E8 0000e               call     pause
149     0071  48                     dec      AX             ; to draw a line horizontal
150     0072  81 C3 012C             add      BX,300         ; to the last bit set
151     0076  B1 01                  mov      CL,1           ; set to draw
152     0078  E8 0000e               call     grafline       ;
153     007B  BA 0500                mov      DX,500h        ; wait half a second
154     007E  E8 0000e               call     pause
155
156     0081  05 00C8                add      AX,200         ; Go down
157     0084  E8 0000e               call     grafline       ;
158     0087  81 EB 012C             sub      BX,300         ; to the left
```

```
159    008B    E8 0000e           call      grafline
160    008E    2D 00C8            sub       AX,200          ; and join the box
161    0091    E8 0000e           call      grafline
162    0094    BA 0500            mov       DX,500h         ; Wait 5 seconds
163    0097    E8 0000e           call      pause
164
165    009A    81 C3 012C         add       BX,300          ; to the last bit set
166    009E    B1 00              mov       CL,0            ; set to erase
167    00A0    E8 0000e           call      grafline        ;
168    00A3    BA 0500            mov       DX,500h         ; wait half a second
169    00A6    E8 0000e           call      pause
170    00A9    05 00C8            add       AX,200          ; Go down
171    00AC    E8 0000e           call      grafline        ;
172    00AF    81 EB 012C         sub       BX,300          ; to the left
173    00B3    E8 0000e           call      grafline
174    00B6    2D 00C8            sub       AX,200          ; and join the box
175    00B9    E8 0000e           call      grafline
176    00BC    BA 0500            mov       DX,500h         ; Wait 5 seconds
177    00BF    E8 0000e           call      pause
178
179    00C2    B8 0046            mov       AX,70           ; To first bit vert
180    00C5    2B DB              sub       BX,BX           ; Horizontal at left margin
181    00C7    E8 0000e           call      grafbit
182    00CA    72 38 90 90        jc        charerr         ; Can't be bad!
183    00CE    74 34 90 90        jz        charerr         ; This should not be
184    00D2    BA 0168r           lea       DX,bitonms      ; point to message
185    00D5    E8 0000e           call      Graftxt         ; and display it
186    00D8    B8 0046            mov       AX,70           ;
187    00DB    BB 0001            mov       BX,1            ; One to the right
188    00DE    E8 0000e           call      grafbit         ; test it
189    00E1    72 21 90 90        jc        charerr         ; Location is ok
190    00E5    75 1D 90 90        jnz       charerr         ; Error if not off
191    00E9    BA 017Ar           lea       DX,bitoffms     ; Point to message
192    00EC    E8 0000e           call      graftxt         ; and write it
193    00EF    BA 0500            mov       DX,500h         ; wait 5 seconds
194    00F2    E8 0000e           call      pause           ;
195
196
197
198    00F5    E8 0000e           call      grafoff         ; Back into char mode
199    00F8    BA 014Dr           lea       DX,querye       ; Ask permission
200    00FB    E8 0015            call      getinp          ; to quit
201    00FE            Exit:
202    00FE    B0 00              mov       AL,0            ; Set return code
203    0100    B4 4C              mov       AH,04ch         ; Set good-by
204    0102    CD 21              int       21h             ; Return to the system
205    0104            charerr:
206    0104            pointerr:
```

```
207    0104  60                              pusha                          ; save on the stack all
208    0105  0E                              push    CS
209    0106  1E                              push    DS
210    0107  06                              push    ES
211    0108  E8 0000e                        call    Grafoff
212    010B  BA 0189r                        lea     DX,errmsg              ; indicate error
213    010E  E8 0002                         call    getinp
214    0111  EB EB                           jmp     exit                  ; breakpoint here
215                          ;
216                          ; Read a string in response to a prompt
217                          ; The prompt must be in DX.  The string will be returned in string.
218                          ;
219    0113              getinp  PROC
220    0113  50                              push    AX                    ; Save registers
221    0114  56                              push    SI
222    0115  B4 09                           mov     AH,9                  ; and dos request
223    0117  CD 21                           int     21h                   ; put out the string
224    0119  BA 0000r                        lea     DX,string             ; point to input area
225    011C  C6 06 0000r FE                  mov     string,254            ; Set max length in
226    0121  B4 0A                           mov     AH,10                 ; Ask for read of string
227    0123  CD 21                           int     21h                   ; from DOS.
228    0125  BB 0002r                        lea     BX,string+2           ; Point to just read data
229    0128  8A 0E 0001r                     mov     CL,string+1           ; Get length read
230    012C  B5 00                           mov     CH,0                  ; as a word.
231    012E  8B F1                           mov     SI,CX                 ; Set length
232    0130  C6 84 0002r 00                  mov     string+2[SI],0        ; and make an asciiz string.
233    0135  5E                              pop     SI
234    0136  58                              pop     AX                    ; Restore registers
235    0137  C3                              ret                           ; and return.
236    0138              getinp  ENDP
237
238    0138          code    ENDS
239                          END     Begin
```

Symbol Name	Type	Value	Cref (defined at #)
??DATE	Text	"03/01/92"	
??FILENAME	Text	"grafdrv "	
??TIME	Text	"10:33:58"	
??VERSION	Number	0202	
aCPU	Text	0D0FH	#1
aCURSEG	Text	CODE	#30 #35 #67
aFILENAME	Text	GRAFDRV	
aWORDSIZE	Text	2	#1 #30 #35 #67
BEGIN	Near	CODE:0000	#96 239
BITOFFMS	Byte	DATA:017A	#56 191
BITONMS	Byte	DATA:0168	#53 184

CHARERR	Near	CODE:0104	120	129	182	183	189	190	#205			
CODEBAS	Near	CODE:---- Extern	#85									
DETECT	Dword	DATA:0113	#40	106								
ERRMSG	Byte	DATA:0189	#59	212								
EXIT	Near	CODE:00FE	110	#201	214							
FIRST80	Near	CODE:0031	#118	123								
GETINP	Near	CODE:0113	108	200	213	#219						
GRAFBIT	Near	CODE:---- Extern	#81	181	188							
GRAFCHR	Near	CODE:---- Extern	#76	119	128							
GRAFCLOC	Near	CODE:---- Extern	#83									
GRAFCLS	Near	CODE:---- Extern	#77									
GRAFLINE	Near	CODE:---- Extern	#80	152	157	159	161	167	171	173	175	
GRAFLOC	Near	CODE:---- Extern	#82									
GRAFOFF	Near	CODE:---- Extern	#75	198	211							
GRAFON	Near	CODE:---- Extern	#74	114								
GRAFRSET	Near	CODE:---- Extern	#79									
GRAFSET	Near	CODE:---- Extern	#78	142								
GRAFTXT	Near	CODE:---- Extern	#84	185	192							
GRAFTYPE	Near	CODE:---- Extern	#73	102								
PAUSE	Near	CODE:---- Extern	#72	134	148	154	163	169	177	194		
POINTERR	Near	CODE:0104	143	#206								
POINTS1	Near	CODE:0060	#141	146								
QUERYB	Byte	DATA:0100	#37	107								
QUERYE	Byte	DATA:014D	#49	199								
SECOND80	Near	CODE:0045	#127	132								
STRING	Byte	DATA:0000	#36	224	225	228	229	232				
TYPES	Byte	DATA:019E	#62	105								
TYP_CGA	Number	0002	#90									
TYP_EGA	Number	0004	#89									
TYP_UNK	Number	0000	#87									
TYP_VGA	Number	0008	#88									

Groups & Segments	Bit	Size	Align	Combine	Class	Cref (defined at #)
CODE	16	0138	Para	Public	CODE	#67 92
DATA	16	01B2	Para	none		#35 92 97
STACKT	16	0800	Para	Stack	STACK	#30

Program 10-3 GRAFCHR

```
                              PAGE      55,132
                              .386
0000                 code     SEGMENT   para 'CODE' PUBLIC USE16
                              ASSUME    CS:code, DS:code, SS:code

                     ;
                     ; Name:    GRAFCHR
                     ;
                     ; Purpose: The following procedure provides a character output in
                     ;          graphics mode.
                     ;
                     ;
```

```
;  Inputs:    AL contains the character to put out.
;             BH contains the horizontal position (0-79).
;             BL contains the vertical position (0-23).
;
;  Process:   The position is checked and if invalid, return is made
;             with carry set.
;             The upper left graphic point of the character is computed.
;             (Characters are 9 horizontal and 14 vertical positions in
;                size.  i.e. 80 x 24 with 12 positions vertical unused at
;                the bottom of the screen.)
;             The character is located in the font table and the 14
;             lines of the character are placed into the graphics
;             buffer.  The registers are restored, carry is reset and we
;             return.
;
;  Output:    The carry flag indicates the result - if set, no change to
;             the display was made.  If reset, the character is set in
;             the display buffer.
;
;
;
;
;

                           PUBLIC  Grafchr
                           EXTRN   Grafbxy:PROC

0000                Grafchr   PROC
0000  24 7F                   and     AL,127          ; Force into our 128 cset.
0002  80 FB 17                cmp     BL,23           ; Check the vertical position.
0005  0F 8F 0010 R            jg      error           ; If over - out with carry
0009  80 FF 4F                cmp     BH,79           ; Check the horizontal position
000C  0F 8E 0012 R            jng     posok           ; We are go!
0010                error:
0010  F9                      stc                     ; signal the error
0011  C3                      ret                     ; and go back
0012                posok:
0012  57                      push    DI              ; Save entry registers
0013  56                      push    SI
0014  55                      push    BP
0015  52                      push    DX
0016  51                      push    CX
0017  53                      push    BX
0018  50                      push    AX
0019  06                      push    ES
001A  B1 1C                   mov     CL,28           ; char * 2 * 14
001C  F6 E1                   mul     CL              ; for font index.
001E  8D 36 00B2 R            lea     SI,CS:font      ; Font address plus
0022  03 F0                   add     SI,AX           ; index gives source.
0024  B0 0E                   mov     AL,14           ; Get multiplier of 14
0026  F6 E3                   mul     BL              ; Times bit's vertical
0028  8B D0                   mov     DX,AX           ; Save for Grafbxy call

002A  8D 2E 008A R            lea     BP,CS:stepyv    ; Get offset of y step value
002E  25 0003                 and     AX,3            ; Bit position (Y) mod 4
0031  03 E8                   add     BP,AX           ; Added to y step value
0033  03 E8                   add     BP,AX           ; twice for word index.

0035  B0 09                   mov     AL,9            ; Get horizontal as position
0037  F6 E7                   mul     BH              ; times 9
0039  8B D8                   mov     BX,AX           ; to get horizontal displ.
003B  8A C8                   mov     CL,AL           ; Save the bit number
003D  8B C2                   mov     AX,DX           ; Set vertical

003F  E8 0000 E               call    Grafbxy         ; Get the starting bit's byte
                    ;                                 (Ignore the bit masks)
0042  B5 0E                   mov     CH,14           ; Get the repeat count
0044  80 E1 07                and     CL,7            ; Get Herc style bit number
```

```
0047  F6 D9                         neg     CL               ; as negative then
0049  80 C1 07                      add     CL,7             ; convert to rotate count
004C  BA 03BA                       mov     DX,03bah         ; Get vid status I/O address
004F                        nexty:
004F  26: 8B 07                     mov     AX,ES:[BX]       ; Grab a word
0052  86 E0                         xchg    AH,AL            ; Get positioned as in memory
0054  D3 C8                         ror     AX,CL            ; Position in bits 8-0.
0056  25 FE00                       and     AX,0FE00h        ; Set all to zeros
0059  2E: 0B 04                     or      AX,CS:[SI]       ; Set on a font row
005C  83 C6 02                      add     SI,2             ; Step to next row
005F  D3 C0                         rol     AX,CL            ; Get bits repositioned
0061  86 E0                         xchg    AH,AL            ; Position for their return.
0063  51                            push    CX               ; Save a work register
0064  8B C8                         mov     CX,AX            ; because I/O uses AL.
                              ;
                              ; First we wait for a non vertical retrace state.  When we get one,
                              ; we then wait for a change back to vertical retrace.  This allows
                              ; us to store into video memory without conflicting with video fetch
                              ; (which causes 'snow').
                              ;
0066                        waitnon:
0066  EC                            in      AL,DX            ; Get status from adapter
0067  24 01                         and     AL,1             ; and check if in vertical retrace.
0069  75 FB                         jnz     waitnon          ; it is on - so loop
006B                        waiton:
006B  EC                            in      AL,DX            ; Check status
006C  24 01                         and     AL,1             ; for retrace bit
006E  74 FB                         jz      waiton           ; Wait for it to reappear

0070  26: 89 0F                     mov     ES:[BX],CX       ; return to vid buffer
0073  59                            pop     CX               ; restore our work register

0074  83 C5 02                      add     BP,2             ; Step to next value
0077  2E: 03 5E 00                  add     BX,CS:[BP]       ; for Y.
007B  FE CD                         dec     CH               ; count how many rows
007D  75 D0                         jnz     nexty            ; if not done, do another
007F  07                            pop     ES
0080  58                            pop     AX               ; Restore the entry registers
0081  5B                            pop     BX
0082  59                            pop     CX
0083  5A                            pop     DX
0084  5D                            pop     BP
0085  5E                            pop     SI
0086  5F                            pop     DI
0087  F8                            clc                      ; indicate no error
0088  C3                            ret                      ; and return.
                              ;
                              ; Stepping values for the 14 rows
0089  90                            EVEN
008A  0005[                 stepyv  dw      5 dup(-24486,8192,8192,8192)
      A05A
      2000
      2000
      2000
               ]

                              ;
                                    EVEN                     ; Get word alignment
                                    INCLUDE grafont0.asm     ; Bring the font in
                            C ;
                            C ; Here begins the character font definition table.
                            C ; Only a selected sampling is shown, to illustrate the technique.
                            C ; Set to 1 those bits corresponding to the pixels you want lighted
                            C ; within the 9 x 14 character cell.
                            C ;
00B2  0000                  C font  dw      000000000b       ; First line of each cell
00B4  0000                  C       dw      000000000b       ; is normally zero.
```

```
00B6  0000                    C         dw    000000000b    ; First char is ASCII 0 (NUL).
00B8  0000                    C         dw    000000000b    ;
00BA  0000                    C         dw    000000000b    ;
00BC  0000                    C         dw    000000000b    ;
00BE  0000                    C         dw    000000000b    ;
00C0  0000                    C         dw    000000000b    ;
00C2  0000                    C         dw    000000000b    ;
00C4  0000                    C         dw    000000000b    ;
00C6  0000                    C         dw    000000000b    ;
00C8  0000                    C         dw    000000000b    ;
00CA  0000                    C         dw    000000000b    ;
00CC  0000                    C         dw    000000000b    ;
                              C    ;
00CE  0000                    C         dw    000000000b    ; The character ☺ (01h)
00D0  0000                    C         dw    000000000b    ;
00D2  0000                    C         dw    000000000b    ;
00D4  007C                    C         dw    001111100b    ;
00D6  0082                    C         dw    010000010b    ;
00D8  0082                    C         dw    010000010b    ;
00DA  00AA                    C         dw    010101010b    ;
00DC  0092                    C         dw    010010010b    ;
00DE  0082                    C         dw    010000010b    ;
00E0  007C                    C         dw    001111100b    ;
00E2  0000                    C         dw    000000000b    ;
00E4  0000                    C         dw    000000000b    ;
00E6  0000                    C         dw    000000000b    ;
00E8  0000                    C         dw    000000000b    ;
                              C    ;
00EA  0000                    C         dw    000000000b    ; The character ● (02h)
00EC  0000                    C         dw    000000000b    ;
00EE  0000                    C         dw    000000000b    ;
00F0  007C                    C         dw    001111100b    ;
00F2  00FE                    C         dw    011111110b    ;
00F4  00FE                    C         dw    011111110b    ;
00F6  00FE                    C         dw    011111110b    ;
00F8  00D6                    C         dw    011010110b    ;
00FA  00EE                    C         dw    011101110b    ;
00FC  007C                    C         dw    001111100b    ;
00FE  0000                    C         dw    000000000b    ;
0100  0000                    C         dw    000000000b    ;
0102  0000                    C         dw    000000000b    ;
0104  0000                    C         dw    000000000b    ;
                              C    ;
0106  0000                    C         dw    000000000b    ; The character ♥ (03h)
0108  0000                    C         dw    000000000b    ;
010A  0000                    C         dw    000000000b    ;
010C  006C                    C         dw    001101100b    ;
010E  00FE                    C         dw    011111110b    ;
0110  00FE                    C         dw    011111110b    ;
0112  007C                    C         dw    001111100b    ;
0114  0038                    C         dw    000111000b    ;
0116  0010                    C         dw    000010000b    ;
0118  0000                    C         dw    000000000b    ;
011A  0000                    C         dw    000000000b    ;
011C  0000                    C         dw    000000000b    ;
011E  0000                    C         dw    000000000b    ;
0120  0000                    C         dw    000000000b    ;

                                  .
                                  .
                                  .

                              C  ; Beginning of standard set of printable characters
                              C  ;
0432  0000                    C         dw    000000000b    ; The space character (20h)
0434  0000                    C         dw    000000000b    ;
```

```
0436    0000                C           dw      000000000b      ;
0438    0000                C           dw      000000000b      ;
043A    0000                C           dw      000000000b      ;
043C    0000                C           dw      000000000b      ;
043E    0000                C           dw      000000000b      ;
0440    0000                C           dw      000000000b      ;
0442    0000                C           dw      000000000b      ;
0444    0000                C           dw      000000000b      ;
0446    0000                C           dw      000000000b      ;
0448    0000                C           dw      000000000b      ;
044A    0000                C           dw      000000000b      ;
044C    0000                C           dw      000000000b      ;
                            C   ;
044E    0000                C           dw      000000000b      ; The character ! (21h)
0450    0018                C           dw      000011000b      ;
0452    003C                C           dw      000111100b      ;
0454    003C                C           dw      000111100b      ;
0456    003C                C           dw      000111100b      ;
0458    003C                C           dw      000111100b      ;
045A    0018                C           dw      000011000b      ;
045C    0000                C           dw      000000000b      ;
045E    0018                C           dw      000011000b      ;
0460    0018                C           dw      000011000b      ;
0462    0000                C           dw      000000000b      ;
0464    0000                C           dw      000000000b      ;
0466    0000                C           dw      000000000b      ;
0468    0000                C           dw      000000000b      ;
                                                .
                                                .
                                                .
                            C   ; Beginning of numeric characters 0-9
                            C   ;
05F2    0000                C           dw      000000000b      ; The character 0 (30h)
05F4    007C                C           dw      001111100b      ;
05F6    0082                C           dw      010000010b      ;
05F8    0086                C           dw      010000110b      ;
05FA    008A                C           dw      010001010b      ;
05FC    0092                C           dw      010010010b      ;
05FE    00A2                C           dw      010100010b      ;
0600    00C2                C           dw      011000010b      ;
0602    0082                C           dw      010000010b      ;
0604    007C                C           dw      001111100b      ;
0606    0000                C           dw      000000000b      ;
0608    0000                C           dw      000000000b      ;
060A    0000                C           dw      000000000b      ;
060C    0000                C           dw      000000000b      ;
                            C   ;
060E    0000                C           dw      000000000b      ; The character 1 (31h)
0610    0010                C           dw      000010000b      ;
0612    0030                C           dw      000110000b      ;
0614    0050                C           dw      001010000b      ;
0616    0010                C           dw      000010000b      ;
0618    0010                C           dw      000010000b      ;
061A    0010                C           dw      000010000b      ;
061C    0010                C           dw      000010000b      ;
061E    0010                C           dw      000010000b      ;
0620    007C                C           dw      001111100b      ;
0622    0000                C           dw      000000000b      ;
0624    0000                C           dw      000000000b      ;
0626    0000                C           dw      000000000b      ;
0628    0000                C           dw      000000000b      ;
                                                .
                                                .
                                                .
                            C   ; Beginning of uppercase alphabetic characters
                            C   ;
07CE    0000                C           dw      000000000b      ; The character A (41h)
```

```
07D0   0000                C           dw       000000000b      ;
07D2   0010                C           dw       000010000b      ;
07D4   0028                C           dw       000101000b      ;
07D6   0044                C           dw       001000100b      ;
07D8   0082                C           dw       010000010b      ;
07DA   0082                C           dw       010000010b      ;
07DC   00FE                C           dw       011111110b      ;
07DE   0082                C           dw       010000010b      ;
07E0   0082                C           dw       010000010b      ;
07E2   0082                C           dw       010000010b      ;
07E4   0000                C           dw       000000000b      ;
07E6   0000                C           dw       000000000b      ;
07E8   0000                C           dw       000000000b      ;
                           C    ;
07EA   0000                C           dw       000000000b      ; The character B (42h)
07EC   0000                C           dw       000000000b      ;
07EE   00FC                C           dw       011111100b      ;
07F0   0042                C           dw       001000010b      ;
07F2   0042                C           dw       001000010b      ;
07F4   0042                C           dw       001000010b      ;
07F6   007C                C           dw       001111100b      ;
07F8   0042                C           dw       001000010b      ;
07FA   0042                C           dw       001000010b      ;
07FC   0042                C           dw       001000010b      ;
07FE   00FC                C           dw       011111100b      ;
0800   0000                C           dw       000000000b      ;
0802   0000                C           dw       000000000b      ;
0804   0000                C           dw       000000000b      ;
```

```
                           C    ; Beginning of lowercase alphabetics
                           C    ;
0B4E   0000                C           dw       000000000b      ; The character a (61h)
0B50   0000                C           dw       000000000b      ;
0B52   0000                C           dw       000000000b      ;
0B54   0000                C           dw       000000000b      ;
0B56   0000                C           dw       000000000b      ;
0B58   0038                C           dw       000111000b      ;
0B5A   0004                C           dw       000000100b      ;
0B5C   003C                C           dw       000111100b      ;
0B5E   0044                C           dw       001000100b      ;
0B60   0044                C           dw       001000100b      ;
0B62   001A                C           dw       000011010b      ;
0B64   0000                C           dw       000000000b      ;
0B66   0000                C           dw       000000000b      ;
0B68   0000                C           dw       000000000b      ;
                           C    ;
0B6A   0000                C           dw       000000000b      ; The character b (62h)
0B6C   0000                C           dw       000000000b      ;
0B6E   0060                C           dw       001100000b      ;
0B70   0020                C           dw       000100000b      ;
0B72   0020                C           dw       000100000b      ;
0B74   0020                C           dw       000100000b      ;
0B76   0030                C           dw       000110000b      ;
0B78   002C                C           dw       000101100b      ;
0B7A   0022                C           dw       000100010b      ;
0B7C   0022                C           dw       000100010b      ;
0B7E   006C                C           dw       001101100b      ;
0B80   0000                C           dw       000000000b      ;
0B82   0000                C           dw       000000000b      ;
0B84   0000                C           dw       000000000b      ;
```

```
0DD2  0000          C        dw    000000000b    ; The character x (78h)
0DD4  0000          C        dw    000000000b    ;
0DD6  0000          C        dw    000000000b    ;
0DD8  0000          C        dw    000000000b    ;
0DDA  0000          C        dw    000000000b    ;
0DDC  0042          C        dw    001000010b    ;
0DDE  0024          C        dw    000100100b    ;
0DE0  0018          C        dw    000011000b    ;
0DE2  0018          C        dw    000011000b    ;
0DE4  0024          C        dw    000100100b    ;
0DE6  0042          C        dw    001000010b    ;
0DE8  0C00          C        dw    000000000b    ;
0DEA  0000          C        dw    000000000b    ;
0DEC  0000          C        dw    000000000b    ;
                    C    ;
0DEE  0000          C        dw    000000000b    ; The character y (79h)
0DF0  0000          C        dw    000000000b    ;
0DF2  0000          C        dw    000000000b    ;
0DF4  0000          C        dw    000000000b    ;
0DF6  0000          C        dw    000000000b    ;
0DF8  0044          C        dw    001000100b    ;
0DFA  0044          C        dw    001000100b    ;
0DFC  0044          C        dw    001000100b    ;
0DFE  0044          C        dw    001000100b    ;
0E00  003C          C        dw    000111100b    ;
0E02  0004          C        dw    000000100b    ;
0E04  0008          C        dw    000001000b    ;
0E06  0030          C        dw    000110000b    ;
0E08  0000          C        dw    000000000b    ;
                    C    ;
0E0A  0000          C        dw    000000000b    ; The character z (7Ah)
0E0C  0000          C        dw    000000000b    ;
0E0E  0000          C        dw    000000000b    ;
0E10  0000          C        dw    000000000b    ;
0E12  0000          C        dw    000000000b    ;
0E14  0000          C        dw    000000000b    ;
0E16  007C          C        dw    001111100b    ;
0E18  0044          C        dw    001000100b    ;
0E1A  0008          C        dw    000001000b    ;
0E1C  0010          C        dw    000010000b    ;
0E1E  0024          C        dw    000100100b    ;
0E20  007C          C        dw    001111100b    ;
0E22  0000          C        dw    000000000b    ;
0E24  0000          C        dw    000000000b    ;
                    C    ;
0E26  0000          C        dw    000000000b    ; The character ( (7Bh)
0E28  0000          C        dw    000000000b    ;
0E2A  0030          C        dw    000110000b    ;
0E2C  0040          C        dw    001000000b    ;
0E2E  0040          C        dw    001000000b    ;
0E30  0040          C        dw    001000000b    ;
0E32  0080          C        dw    010000000b    ;
0E34  0040          C        dw    001000000b    ;
0E36  0040          C        dw    001000000b    ;
0E38  0040          C        dw    001000000b    ;
0E3A  0030          C        dw    000110000b    ;
0E3C  0000          C        dw    000000000b    ;
0E3E  0000          C        dw    000000000b    ;
0E40  0000          C        dw    000000000b    ;
                    C    ;
0E42  0000          C        dw    000000000b    ; The character | (7Ch)
0E44  0000          C        dw    000000000b    ;
0E46  0010          C        dw    000010000b    ;
0E48  0010          C        dw    000010000b    ;
0E4A  0010          C        dw    000010000b    ;
0E4C  0010          C        dw    000010000b    ;
0E4E  0000          C        dw    000000000b    ;
```

```
0E50  0010              C         dw    000010000b    ;
0E52  0010              C         dw    000010000b    ;
0E54  0010              C         dw    000010000b    ;
0E56  0010              C         dw    000010000b    ;
0E58  0000              C         dw    000000000b    ;
0E5A  0000              C         dw    000000000b    ;
0E5C  0000              C         dw    000000000b    ;
                       C  ;
0E5E  0000              C         dw    000000000b    ; The character } (7Dh)
0E60  0000              C         dw    000000000b    ;
0E62  0018              C         dw    000011000b    ;
0E64  0004              C         dw    000000100b    ;
0E66  0004              C         dw    000000100b    ;
0E68  0004              C         dw    000000100b    ;
0E6A  0002              C         dw    000000010b    ;
0E6C  0004              C         dw    000000100b    ;
0E6E  0004              C         dw    000000100b    ;
0E70  0004              C         dw    000000100b    ;
0E72  0018              C         dw    000011000b    ;
0E74  0000              C         dw    000000000b    ;
0E76  0000              C         dw    000000000b    ;
0E78  0000              C         dw    000000000b    ;
                       C  ;
0E7A  0000              C         dw    000000000b    ; The character ˜ (7Eh)
0E7C  0000              C         dw    000000000b    ;
0E7E  0014              C         dw    000010100b    ;
0E80  0028              C         dw    000101000b    ;
0E82  0000              C         dw    000000000b    ;
0E84  0000              C         dw    000000000b    ;
0E86  0000              C         dw    000000000b    ;
0E88  0000              C         dw    000000000b    ;
0E8A  0000              C         dw    000000000b    ;
0E8C  0000              C         dw    000000000b    ;
0E8E  0000              C         dw    000000000b    ;
0E90  0000              C         dw    000000000b    ;
0E92  0000              C         dw    000000000b    ;
0E94  0000              C         dw    000000000b    ;
                       C  ;
0E96  0000              C         dw    000000000b    ; The character ■ (7Fh)
0E98  0000              C         dw    000000000b    ;
0E9A  00FE              C         dw    011111110b    ;
0E9C  00FE              C         dw    011111110b    ;
0E9E  00FE              C         dw    011111110b    ;
0EA0  00FE              C         dw    011111110b    ;
0EA2  00FE              C         dw    011111110b    ;
0EA4  00FE              C         dw    011111110b    ;
0EA6  00FE              C         dw    011111110b    ;
0EA8  00FE              C         dw    011111110b    ;
0EAA  00FE              C         dw    011111110b    ;
0EAC  0000              C         dw    000000000b    ;
0EAE  0000              C         dw    000000000b    ;
0EB0  0000              C         dw    000000000b    ;
                       C
                          ;
0EB2              Grafchr    ENDP
0EB2              code       ENDS
                             END
```

Program 10-4 GRAFTYPE

```
 1                                      .386
 2
 3   0000                     data      SEGMENT para 'DATA' USE16
 4   0000  0100*(00)          vga_work  db      256 DUP(0)
 5   0100                     data      ENDS
 6
 7
 8   0000                     code      SEGMENT para 'CODE' PUBLIC USE16
 9
10                                      ASSUME  CS:code, DS:data, SS:code
11
12                            ; Name:    Graftype
13                            ;
14                            ; Purpose: The following procedure attempts to identify the graphic
15                            ;          adapter present in the system.
16                            ;
17                            ; Inputs:  No input is required.
18                            ;
19                            ; Process: The 'standard' BIOS extension for an advanced graphic
20                            ;          adaptor is checked for at C000:0000.  If located, the
21                            ;          is in text mode, the display is turned off, the graphic
22                            ;          controller is loaded with the parameters for graphic display
23                            ;          mode, the screen is cleared, and graphic mode is set.
24                            ;
25                            ; Output:  The mode is changed and the screen is cleared.
26                            ;
27
28                                      PUBLIC  Graftype
29
30         = 0000            typ_unk    EQU     0                       ; Simple tests can't tell
31         = 0008            typ_vga    EQU     8                       ; Best possible type
32         = 0004            typ_ega    EQU     4                       ; Not too bad
33         = 0002            typ_cga    EQU     2                       ; Yeeech
34
35   0000                    Graftype   PROC
36   0000  06                           push    ES                     ; Save registers
37   0001  1E                           push    DS
38   0002  53                           push    BX
39   0003  52                           push    DX
40   0004  57                           push    DI
41   0005  BB 0000s                     mov     BX,data                ; Get para of data segment
42   0008  BA 0000                      mov     DX,typ_unk             ; Set 'I don't know'
43   000B  B8 C000                      mov     AX,0C000h              ; Get segment address
44   000E  8E C0                        mov     ES,AX                  ; into ES
45   0010  26: A1 0000                  mov     AX,ES:0                ; load the word
46   0014  3D AA55                      cmp     AX,0AA55h              ; check if it is proper
47   0017  75 34                        jne     SHORT exit             ; and exit 'unknown' if not
```

Program 10-4 Continued.

```
48    0019  B8 1B00            mov     AX,1B00h        ; Set ah,al for bios call
49    001C  8E C3              mov     ES,BX           ; Set destination
50    001E  8E DB              mov     DS,BX           ; and normal reference
51    0020  2B DB              sub     BX,BX           ; set zeros in BX
52    0022  BF 0000r           lea     DI,vga_work     ; and DI to work area
53    0025  CD 10              int     10h             ; Call bios display facilities
54    0027  3C 1B              cmp     AL,1bh          ; was data returned?
55    0029  75 22              jne     SHORT exit      ; No - assume non E/VGA
56    002B  C4 3E 0000r        les     DI,DWORD PTR vga_work ;
57    002F  66| 26: 8B 05      mov     EAX,ES:[DI]     ; Get the characteristics
58                             ;
59                             ; The first 3 bytes are flags identifying the capabilities of the
60                             ; card.  0 has CGA bits, 1 has EGA and PC-jr Bits and 2 has
61                             ; bits 0 EGA, 1 MGCA, and 2,3 VGA.
62                             ;
63    0033  0A C0              or      AL,AL           ; Are CGA bits on?
64    0035  74 16              jz      SHORT exit      ; If not - get out
65    0037  BA 0002            mov     DX,typ_cga      ; try least useful
66    003A  66| C1 E8 08       shr     EAX,8           ; position others
67    003E  A8 E0              test    AL,0E0h         ; Check the EGA bits
68    0040  74 0B              jz      SHORT exit      ; if none - it's CGA
69    0042  BA 0004            mov     DX,typ_ega      ; We have at least EGA
70    0045  F6 C4 0C           test    AH,0Ch          ; Either VGA bit on
71    0048  74 03              jz      SHORT exit      ; no - it's EGA
72    004A  BA 0008            mov     DX,typ_vga      ; Set VGA as type
73
74    004D               exit:
75    004D  8B C2              mov     AX,DX           ; Set return type
76    004F  5F                 pop     DI              ; Restore saved registers
77    0050  5A                 pop     DX
78    0051  5B                 pop     BX
79    0052  1F                 pop     DS
80    0053  07                 pop     ES
81    0054  C3                 ret
82    0055           Graftype  ENDP
83    0055           code      ENDS
84                             END
```

Symbol Name	Type	Value	Cref (defined at #)
??DATE	Text	"03/01/92"	
??FILENAME	Text	"graftype"	
??TIME	Text	"19:38:28"	
??VERSION	Number	0202	
@CPU	Text	0D0FH	#1
@CURSEG	Text	CODE	#3 #8

```
@FILENAME              Text    GRAFTYPE
@WORDSIZE              Text    2                           #1  #3  #8
EXIT                   Near    CODE:004D                   47  55  64  68  71  #74
GRAFTYPE               Near    CODE:0000                   28  #35
TYP_CGA               Number  0002                         #33  65
TYP_EGA               Number  0004                         #32  69
TYP_UNK               Number  0000                         #30  42
TYP_VGA               Number  0008                         #31  72
VGA_WORK               Byte    DATA:0000                   #4  52  56


Groups & Segments      Bit Size Align  Combine Class       Cref (defined at #)


CODE                   16  0055 Para   Public  CODE        #8  10  10
DATA                   16  0100 Para   none    DATA        #3  10  41
```

A

80486 architecture overview

The 80486 features multitasking, on-chip memory management, virtual memory with paging, software protection, and large address space. Compatibility with earlier Intel chips (8086 through 80386) is preserved through the instruction set, register handling, and bus sizing. This appendix gives an overview of the 80486 architecture; for more complete information, see *80486: A Programming and Design Handbook*.

The 80486 is designed for applications requiring high performance and is optimized for multitasking. The 32-bit registers support 32-bit addresses and data types. Instruction pipelining and on-chip address translation ensure execution at sustained rates of between 3 and 4 million instructions per second (MIPS).

80486 consists of nine elements: a bus interface, cache, instruction pre-fetch, instruction decode, control, integer and datapath, floating-point unit (FPU), segmentation, and paging. See Fig. A-1 for a graphic view of the nine units of the 80486.

Signals from outside the 80486 come through the bus interface unit. Inside, the bus unit and cache unit pass addresses through a 32-bit bidirectional bus. Data are passed from the cache to the bus unit on the 32-bit data bidirectional bus. The cache and instruction pre-fetch units simultaneously receive instruction pre-fetches from the bus unit over a shared 32-bit data bus, also used by the cache to receive operands and other types of data. Instructions in the cache can be used by the instruction pre-fetch unit, which contains a 32-byte queue of instructions waiting to be executed.

When internal data requests can be satisfied from cache, cycles on the external bus are avoided, increasing throughput. The instruction decode unit translates instructions into low-level control signals and microcode

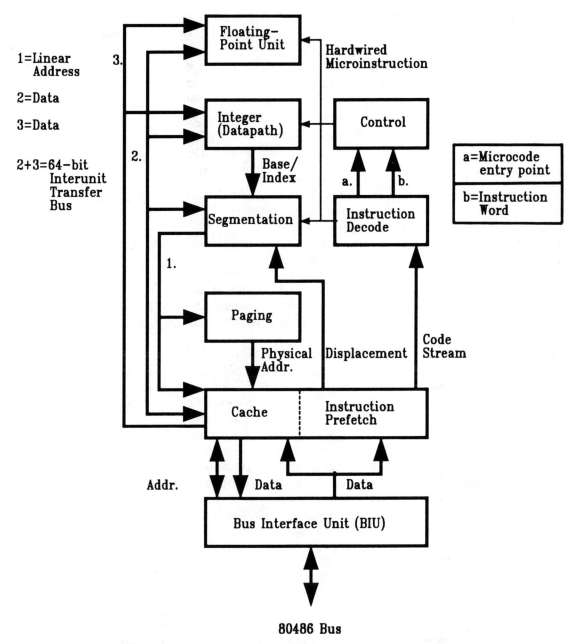

A-1 Basic units of the 80486.

entry points. The control unit executes microcode and controls the integer, floating-point, and segmentation units. Computation results are placed in internal registers in the integer or floating-point units, or in cache.

Cache shares two 32-bit data buses with the segmentation, integer, and floating-point units. You can use these buses together as a 64-bit interunit transfer bus.

The segmentation and paging units perform address generation. The segmentation unit translates logical addresses and passes them to the paging and cache units on a 32-bit linear address bus. The paging unit translates the linear addresses into physical addresses, which are then passed to the cache on a 20-bit bus.

Definitions

The following are definitions for terms you will need to know for this architecture overview. For other terms, see the glossary:

descriptor   A descriptor is a specific data structure used to define the characteristics of a program element. For example, descriptors describe a data record, a segment, or a task.

flag   A flag is an indicator whose state is used to inform a later section of a program that a condition has occurred. The condition is identified with the flag and designated by the state of the flag; that is, the flag is either set or not set.

gate   A gate is a logic design that allows only certain processes to pass through it. The 80486 provides protection for control transfers among executable segments at differing privilege levels by use of gate descriptors, of which there are four: Call gates, Trap gates, Interrupt gates, and Task gates.

linear address space   An address indicates the location of a register, a particular place in storage, or some other data source or destination. In the 80486, the memory's linear address space runs from byte 0 to 4Gb. A linear address points to a particular byte within this space. Figure A-2 outlines the linear address translation process.

logical address   First, there is no conceptual parallel from linear address space to the space used by logical addressing. A logical address consists of a selector and offset. The selector points to some segment descriptor (part of which is that segment's linear base address). The offset tells how far into the segment the required byte is. Figure A-3 depicts physical address translation.

microcode   A list of small program steps; also a set of control functions performed by the instruction decoding and executing logic of a computer system. It is code that lies below the level of assembly language.

paging   Paging refers to a procedure that transmits the consecutive bytes called a page between locations, such as between disk storage and memory. A paging function simplifies the operating system swapping algorithms because it provides a uniform mechanism for managing the physical structure of memory.

physical address   The address that actually selects the memory where a

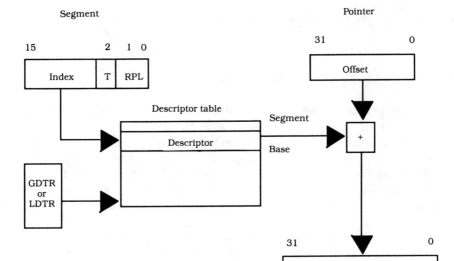

A-2 Linear address translation.

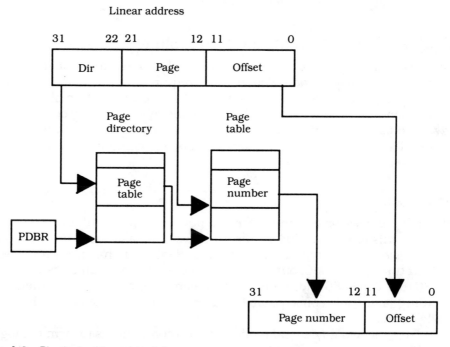

A-3 Physical address translation.

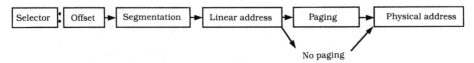

A-4 Virtual to physical address translation.

required byte is located. In the 80486, linear and physical addresses differ only when paging is in effect (see Fig. A-4).

segment Beginning with the 8086, Intel introduced the concept of segments, which were defined as units of contiguous (adjacent) address space. In the 8086, this space had a maximum of 64K or 65536 bytes. In the 80486, that limitation no longer applies and programmers can now view segments as one-dimensional subspaces, each with some specified length up to 4Gb.

table A table is a collection or ordering of data laid out in rows and columns for reference, or which is stored as an array. Elements of a table can be obtained by direct calculation from a known selector or base address.

task A task is a basic, unique function of a program or system. It can be one instance of the execution of a program. Tasks are also referred to as processes.

Task State Segment (TSS) A TSS is a data structure delineated and pointed to by a descriptor, wherein the (interrupted) state of a task is stored. Systems software creates the TSSs and places the initial information in them, such as correct stack pointers for interrupt handlers.

Real- and protected-mode architecture

The 80486 has two modes of operation: real address mode (called *real mode*), and *protected mode*. Real mode is required primarily to set up the processor for protected-mode operation and to allow execution of software for previous chip generations. Protected mode provides access to the advanced paging, memory management, and privilege capabilities of the 80486. These design features allow object-code compatibility with previous Intel chip generations.

Real mode

When the processor is either reset or powered up, it initializes in real mode. In this mode, the 80486 operates as a very fast 8086, but with 32-bit extensions, if the programmer desires. Real mode has the same base architecture as the 8086, but also allows access to the 32-bit register set of the 80486. The 8086 addressing mechanism, memory size, and interrupt handling (and their consequent limitations) are all identical to the real mode on the 80486.

Like protected mode, real mode uses two components to form the logical address. A 16-bit selector is used to determine the linear base address of a segment. The base address is then used as the 32-bit physical address. The difference between the two modes lies in how the base address is calculated.

Relocatability is a property of programs or data such that they can be located in different places in memory at different times without requiring modification to system or application software. Segment relocation is done in the 80486 real mode as it is in the 8086. The 16-bit value in a segment selector is shifted left by four bits (multiplied by 16) to form the 20-bit base address of a segment. The effective address is extended with four high-order zeros (to give a 20-bit value) and added to the base to form a linear address. This linear address is equivalent to the physical address because paging is not used in real-address mode.

Interrupts and exceptions are breaks in the normal flow of a system or routine. Interrupts and exceptions in 80486 real-address mode work exactly as they do on the 8086. (See chapter 9 for a list of the interrupts recognized by the 80486.) In real mode, the Interrupt Descriptor Table (IDT) is an 8086 real interrupt vector table, starting at real zero and extending through real 1024 (4 bytes per interrupt with 256 possible entries).

The only way to leave real-address mode is to switch explicitly to protected mode. The 80486 enters the protected mode when a Move to Control Register Zero (MOV to CR0) instruction sets the protection enable (PE) bit in CR0. For compatibility with the 80286, the Load Machine Status Word (LMSW) instruction can also be used to set the PE bit.

The processor reenters real-address mode if software clears the PE bit in CR0 with a MOV to CR0 instruction.

Protected mode

The complete capabilities of the 80486 are available when it operates in protected mode. Software can perform a task switch to enter tasks designated as virtual 8086 mode tasks. Each such task behaves with 8086 semantics (the relationship between symbols and their intended meanings independent of their interpretation devices). This allows 8086 software—an application program or an entire operating system—to execute on the 80486. At the same time, the virtual 8086 tasks are isolated and protected from one another and from the host 80486 operating system.

In protected mode, the 16-bit selector is used to specify an index into an operating system-defined table that contains the 32-bit base address of a given segment. The physical address is formed by adding the base address obtained from the table to the offset.

In general, programs designed for the 80386 will execute without modification on the 80486. Also, the 80486 supports the descriptors used by the 80286 as long as the Intel-reserved word (the last word) of the 80286 descriptor is zero. See chapter 3 for additional tips to keep in mind when programming on the 80486.

Registers

The 80486 registers are a superset of the previous 8086, 80186, 80286, and 80386 registers. All the previous generations' 8- and 16-bit registers are contained within the 32-bit architecture. Register contents (flags and bits) are shown in appendix C.

General registers

The eight general-purpose registers are 32-bits long and hold addresses or data. They support data operands of 1, 8, 16, 32, and 64 bits (which require two registers) and bit fields of 1 to 32 bits, in addition to address operands of 16 and 32 bits. The 32-bit registers are named EAX, EBX, ECX, EDX, ESI, EDI, EBP, and ESP.

The least significant 16 bits of the registers can be accessed separately by using the 16-bit names of the registers: AX, BX, CX, DX, SI, DI, BP, and SP. Eight-bit operations can individually access the low byte (bits 0 – 7) and the high byte (bits 8 – 15) of the general registers AX, BX, CX, and DX. The low bytes are named AL, BL, CL, and DL, respectively, while the high bytes are named AH, BH, CH, and DH. Again, this selection is done by using the register names. If one of the 8-bit registers is accessed, the contents of the remaining 24 bits are undisturbed.

Segment registers

The 80486 architecture includes six directly accessible segment-selector registers, which contain values that point to the segments. These selector values can be loaded while a program executes and also are task-specific, which means that the segment registers are automatically reloaded upon a task switch operation. Six 16-bit segment registers hold the segment selector values that identify the currently addressable memory segments. The registers are:

Code Segment (CS) register   The CS points to the segment that contains the currently executing sequence of instructions. The 80486 fetches all instructions from this segment, using as an offset the contents of the instruction pointer. CS is changed as the result of intersegment control-transfer instructions, and interrupts and exceptions. The CS cannot be explicitly loaded (see the programs in this book). Values are loaded into a general register and then the contents of that register can be MOVed to CS.

Stack Segment (SS) register   Subroutine calls, parameters, and procedure-activation records usually require a region of memory that is allocated for a stack. All stack operations use SS to locate that stack. Unlike the CS register, the SS register can be loaded explicitly by program instructions.

Data Segment registers (DS, ES, FS, GS)   The next four registers are data segment registers, each of which is addressable by the currently executing program. Having access to four separate data areas aids program efficiency by allowing them to access different types of data structures. These four registers can be changed under program control.

To use the data segment registers, the 80486 associates a base address with each segment selected. To address a data unit within a segment, a 32-bit offset is added to the segment's base address. Once a segment is selected (by loading the segment selector into a segment register), a data-manipulation instruction needs only to specify the offset.

Segmented memory management registers

Segmented memory management registers are also known as System Address Registers. Four registers locate the data structures that control segmented memory management. These registers are defined to reference the tables or segments supported by the 80286 through 80486 protection model. The addresses of these tables and segments are stored in special System Address and System Segment Registers.

Global Descriptor Table Register (GDTR)   The GDTR holds the 32-bit linear base address and the 16-bit limit of the Global Descriptor Table.

Local Descriptor Table Register (LDTR)   This register holds the 16-bit selector for the Local Descriptor Table. Because the LDT is a task-specific segment, it's defined by selector values stored in the system segment registers.

Interrupt Descriptor Table Register (IDTR)   The IDTR points to a table of entry points for interrupt handlers (the IDT). The register holds the 32-bit linear base address and the 16-bit limit of the Interrupt Descriptor Table.

Task Register (TR)   This register points to the information needed by the processor to define the current task. The register holds the 16-bit selector for the Task State Segment descriptor. Because the TSS segment is task-specific, it is defined by selector values stored in the system segment registers. Figure A-5 shows how TR assists in linking TSSs.

Processor control registers

Two registers control the operation of the 80486 processor: the System Flags Register and the Instruction Pointer Register.

System Flags Register (EFLAGS)   The EFLAGS register controls I/O, maskable interrupts, debugging, task switching, and enabling of virtual 8086 execution in a protected, multitasking environment; it does all this in addition to providing status flags that represent the result of instruction execution. The low 16 bits (0 – 15) of EFLAGS contain the 80286 16-bit status or flag register named FLAGS, which is most useful when executing 8086 and 80286 code. See appendix B for a detailed format of the EFLAGS register.

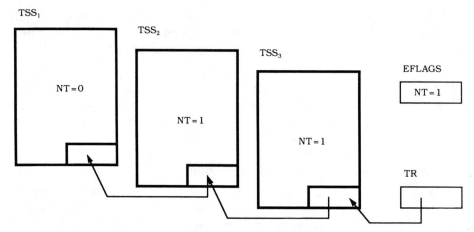

A-5 Control Register formats. (Zero entries indicate Intel reserved bits; do not define.)

Instruction Pointer Register (EIP) The Extended Instruction Pointer (EIP) is a 32-bit register. EIP contains the offset address of the next sequential instruction to be executed. This offset is relative to the start (or base address) of the current code segment. The EIP is not directly visible to programmers, but is controlled explicitly by control-transfer instructions, interrupts, and exceptions.

The low-order 16 bits of EIP are named IP and can be used by the processor as a unit. This feature is useful when executing instructions designed for the 8086 and 80286 processors, which only have an IP.

Control registers

The 80486 has three 32-bit control registers, CR0, CR2, and CR3 (CR1 is reserved by Intel). These registers hold machine states or global statuses. A global status is one that can be accessed by (or that controls) any of the logical units of the system. Along with the System Address Registers, these registers hold machine-state information that affects all tasks in the system. Load and store instructions have been defined to access the control registers. Figure A-6 shows Control Register formats.

Control registers are accessible to systems programmers only via variants of the MOV instruction, which allows them to be loaded from or stored in general registers.

CR0 This register contains flags that control or indicate conditions that apply to the system as a whole, not to an individual task. The low-order 15 bits of this register is the Machine Status Word (MSW), bits 0 – 15, for compatibility with 80286 protected mode.

CR1 As noted earlier, this register is reserved for future Intel processors.

CR2 The CR2 register is used for handling page faults when the PG bit in

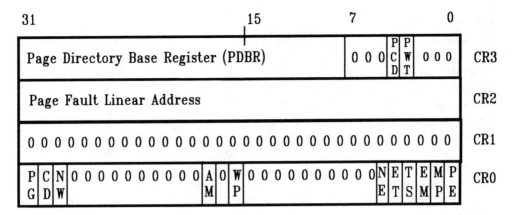

A-6 Task State Segment (TSS). (Zero entries indicate Intel reserved bits; do not define.)

CR0 is set. The 80486 stores in CR2 the linear address that triggers the fault. The error code pushed onto the page fault handler's stack when it is invoked provides additional status information on this page fault.

CR3 This register is used when PG is set in CR0. CR3 enables the processor to locate the page table directory for the current task. This register contains the physical base address of the page directory table. The 80486 page directory table is always page-aligned (4K-aligned). The lowest 12 bits of CR3 are ignored when written and they store as undefined. A task switch through a TSS that changes the value in CR3 (or as an explicit load to CR3) invalidates all cached page table entries in the paging unit cache. Note that if the value in CR3 does not change during the task switch, the cached page table entries are not flushed.

Debug registers

A breakpoint allows you to set a specific condition at a particular linear address that causes program execution to jump into the exception handler. The 80486 supports four simultaneous breakpoint conditions, which allows you to set up to four locations in a program for which the 80486 will jump to the exception handler. To support the four breakpoints, additional registers are added to the 80486. These registers can only be read or written at privilege level 0; any attempted access at other levels raises an invalid opcode exception.

These six programmer-accessible debug registers (DR0–DR3, DR6, and DR7) bring advanced debugging abilities to the 80486. These debugging abilities include data breakpoints and the ability to set instruction breakpoints without modifying code segments. Debug Registers DR0–DR3 specify the four linear breakpoints. DR4 and DR5 are reserved by Intel for future development. DR6 displays the current state of the breakpoints, and DR7 is used to set the breakpoints.

Test registers

Two test registers are used to control the testing of the Content Address-able Memories (RAM/CAM) in the translation lookaside buffer (TLB), which is the cache used for storing information from page tables. TR6 is the command test register and TR7 is the data register that contains the data of the TLB test. (Data registers TR0 – TR5 do not exist.) See appendix B for a detailed format of the test registers.

These registers are accessed by variants of the MOV instruction, which is defined in both real-address mode and protected mode. In the protected mode, the MOV instruction that accesses them can be executed only at privilege level 0. Any attempt to read from or write to either of the test registers when executing in any other privilege level causes a general protection exception.

Translation Lookaside Buffer (TLB)

The Translation Lookaside Buffer (TLB) is a cache used for translating lin-ear addresses to physical addresses. *Warning:* The TLB testing mecha-nism is unique to the 80486 and might not be continued in the same way in future processors. Software that uses this mechanism as it currently is might be incompatible with future processors.

The TLB is a four-way, set-associative memory. A *set* is a collection of elements that have some feature in common or which bear a certain rela-tion to one another. In the TLB, there are three:

1. Content-Addressable Memory (CAM). CAM holds 32 linear ad-dresses and associated tag bits, which are used for data protection and cache implementation.
2. Random Access Memory (RAM). RAM holds the upper 20 bits of the 32 physical addresses that correspond to the linear addresses in the CAM.
3. Logic implements the four-way cache and includes a 3-bit pseudo-LRU pointer that decides which of the four sets into which a new entry is directed during a write to the TLB.

Addresses and commands are written to the TLB through the com-mand register, while data is read from or written to the TLB through the data register. TR6 is the command register for TLB accesses while TR7 is used as the data register.

Segmentation

Segmentation organizes virtual memory as a collection of variable-sized units, called segments. The 80486 supports a wide range of segmentation strategies; each uses a two-part virtual address: a segment part and an off-set part. Segments form the basis of the virtual-to-linear address translation mechanism. Each segment is defined by three parameters, two of which relate virtual addresses given by offsets within the segment to linear addresses. Those three parameters are:

1. *Base address*. This is the starting address of the segment in the linear address space. The base address is the linear address corresponding to the virtual address at offset 0 within the segment.
2. *Limit*. This is the largest offset that can be used with the segment in a virtual address and defines the size of the segment.
3. *Attributes*. These indicate segment characteristics such as whether the segment can be read from, written to, or executed as a program, the privilege level of the segment, and so on.

Address space comes as one or more segments, any size from 1 byte to 4Gb. Each segment can be protected individually by privilege levels and selectively shared between tasks.

Segment descriptor tables

The Global Descriptor Table (GDT) and the Local Descriptor Table (LDT) are special segments that contain the segment descriptor tables. The hardware maintains the descriptor tables and references them by memory-management mechanisms. These segments should be stored in protected memory, accessible only by operating system software, to prevent application software from modifying the address translation information.

The virtual-address space divides into two equal halves, one half mapped by the GDT and the other half by the LDT. The total virtual-address space consists of 2^{14} segments. A segment descriptor is located by indicating a descriptor table (either the GDT or the LDT) along with a descriptor number within the indicated table.

Segment selectors

Segment selectors identify a segment and can be thought of as the segment's name. A selector is a 16-bit pointer that, when loaded into a register or used with certain instructions, selects certain descriptors; that is, a selector names a segment by locating the descriptor for the segment. In a logical address, the selector portion identifies an individual descriptor by first specifying the descriptor table and then indexing to the descriptor within that table.

Segment descriptors

Descriptors are those objects to which the segment selectors point. They are 8-byte quantities that contain attributes about a given linear address space (that is, about a segment). These attributes include the segment 32-bit base linear address; the segment's 30-bit length and granularity, the protection level; read, write, or execute privileges; the default size of the operands (16- or 32-bit); and the type of segment.

All descriptor attribute information is contained in 12 bits of the segment descriptor. All segments on the 80486 have three attribute fields in common: the Present (P) bit, the Descriptor Privilege Level (DPL) bits, and the Segment Descriptor (S) bit.

Segment descriptors are stored in either a Global Descriptor Table (GDT) or Local Descriptor Table (LDT). These descriptor tables are stored in special segments maintained by the operating system and referenced by memory management hardware. The 80486 locates the GDT and the current LDT in protected memory by means of the GDTR and LDTR registers.

A segment descriptor provides the 80486 with the data it needs to map a logical address into a linear address. These descriptors are not created by programs, but by compilers, linkers, loaders, or the operating system.

Interrupts and exceptions

Both hardware- and software-generated interrupts alter the programmed execution of the 80486. (A description of the 80486 interrupts is given in chapter 5.) A hardware-generated interrupt occurs in response to an active input on one of two 80486 interrupt inputs: NMI, which is nonmaskable, or INTR, which is maskable.

The NMI input signals a catastrophic event such as an imminent power loss, a memory error, or a bus parity error. The NMI causes the 80486 to execute the service routine that corresponds to location 2 in the IDT. The processor does not service subsequent NMI requests until the current one has been serviced.

Entry point descriptors to the service routines or the interrupt tasks are stored in memory in the Interrupt Descriptor Table (IDT). The IDT associates each interrupt or exception identifier with a descriptor for the instructions that service the associated event. The IDT is an array of 8-byte descriptors and can hold up to 256 identifiers. To locate the correct descriptor, the processor multiplies the identifier by eight.

Exceptions are classified as faults, aborts, or traps, depending on the way they are reported and also whether restart of the instruction that caused the exception is supported. Aborts are used to report severe errors such as illegal, inconsistent values in system tables, or hardware errors. An abort allows neither the restart of the program that caused the exception nor the identification of the precise location of the instruction causing the exception. Faults are exceptions that are either detected before the instruction begins to execute or during execution. A trap is reported at the instruction boundary immediately after the instruction in which the exception was detected.

Memory organization

Segmentation is the division of memory into logical blocks for use by a computer. In the 80486, memory is organized into one or more variable-length segments, from 1 byte up to 4Gb in size. Every task in the 80486 can have up to 16,381 segments (each up to 4Gb in length), which provides 64 terabytes of virtual memory. Any given location of the linear address space (a segment of the physical memory) has several attributes associated with it: size, location, type (stack, code, or data), and protection characteristics.

80486 physical memory organizes into a sequence of 8-bit bytes. Each byte has a unique address that ranges from 0 to $2^{32} - 1$, or 4Gb. The three distinct address spaces are: physical, logical, and linear.

Physical addresses are the actual addresses used to select the physical memory chips that contain the data. A logical address consists of a segment selector and an offset into that segment. A linear address is the address formed by adding the offset to the base address of the segment.

Paging

Paging is useful in multitasking operating systems. Paging operates underneath segmentation to complete the virtual-to-physical address translation process. Segmentation translates virtual addresses to linear addresses. Paging translates the linear address put out by segmentation to physical addresses.

In the 80486, paging operates only in protected mode and provides a means of managing the very large segments that the 80486 supports. Paging divides programs into uniformly sized pages—unlike segmentation, which modularizes programs and data into variable-length segments. In a real sense, paging operates beneath segmentation; that is, the paging mechanism translates the protected linear address, which comes from the segmentation unit, into a physical address.

The paging mechanism is enabled by the PG bit in CR0. IF PG = 1, paging is enabled and linear addresses are translated to physical addresses. If PG = 0, paging is disabled and the linear addresses generated by the segmentation mechanism are used directly as physical addresses (see Fig. A-4).

The paging-translation function is described by a memory-resident table called the *page table*, which is stored in the physical address space and can be thought of as a simple array of 230 physical addresses. The linear-to-physical mapping function is simply an array lookup. Each page table entry is 32 bits in size.

80486 cache memory

Cache memory is a mechanism interposed in the memory hierarchy between main memory and the processor to improve effective memory transfer rates and to raise processor speeds. The cache anticipates the likely use (by the CPU) of data in main storage by organizing a copy of the data in cache memory. The cache also includes data in adjacent blocks to the actual data needed; it is likely that the adjacent data will be requested next. This principle is called locality of reference.

The 80486 has an 8K on-chip internal cache, organized as 128 sets of four 16-byte (128 bit) entries. Each entry contains 128 bits of data with tag information. The line size (the unit of transfer) between the cache and Dynamic Random Access Memory (DRAM) is 128 bits. The tag field uniquely identifies a 16-byte location in main memory.

Privilege and protection

The concept of privilege is central to the 80486. As applied to procedures, privilege is the degree to which the procedure can be trusted not to make a mistake that might affect other procedures or data. Applied to data, privilege is the degree of protection that a data structure should have from less-trusted procedures. Privilege is implemented by assigning a value (from 0 to 3) to key objects that are recognized by the processor. This value is called the *privilege level*. Value 0 is the greatest privilege level and 3 is the lowest privilege level.

There are two broad classes of protection supported by the 80486. The first is the ability to separate tasks completely by giving each task a different virtual address space; this is accomplished by giving each task a different virtual-to-physical address translation map. The other protection mechanism operates within a task to protect operating system memory segments and special processor registers from access by application programs. The key items the processor recognizes are:

- Descriptor Privilege Level (DPL). Descriptors contain a field called the DPL. This is the least privilege that a task must have to access the descriptor.
- Requester's Privilege Level (RPL). The RPL represents the privilege level requested by the procedure that originate a selector.
- Current Privilege Level (CPL). The CPL is equal to the segment DPL of the code segment which the processor is currently executing. CPL changes when control transfers to segments with differing DPLs.

Multitasking

To switch tasks efficiently, the 80486 uses special high-speed hardware. Only a single instruction or interrupt keys the processor to do a switch. Running at 16 MHz, the 80486 can save the state of one task (all registers), load the state of another task, and resume execution in less than 16 microseconds. The 80486 uses no special instructions to control multitasking. Instead, it interprets ordinary control-transfer instructions when they refer to the special data structures.

Task State Segment (TSS)

Task State Segment, or TSS, is a data structure (a special segment) that holds the state of a task's virtual processor. The TSS for the active task is addressed by the TR register. The 80486 schedules and executes tasks based on a priority set by the operating system. To switch tasks, the operating system issues a JMP or CALL instruction whose operand is a selector for the TSS or the task gate of the new task. Figure A-7 shows the TSS.

To resume execution of the old task, the operating system issues a JMP instruction to the old task's TSS. The privilege level at which execution restarts in the incoming task is not restricted by the privilege level of the outgoing task. The tasks are isolated by their separate address spaces and TSSs, and privilege access rules are used to prevent improper access to a TSS.

The TSS link field is at offset 0 in the TSS and it is a 32-bit field with a selector in the low-order 16 bits. This link field is used in conjunction with the NT bit in the EFLAGS register to link the TSSs for task suspended by CALL instructions or interrupts. Figure A-8 shows how TSSs are linked.

Also in the TSS is an I/O Permission Bitmap that defines what addresses in the 64K I/O space can be accessed by programs executing at any privilege level. A 64K bit string is stored in the current TSS, each bit corresponding to a single, byte-wide I/O address. Bit 0 corresponds to I/O address 0, bit 1 to I/O address 1, and so on. A 0 stored in the bitmap indicates that the corresponding I/O address is accessible to programs at any privilege level. A 1 indicates that the I/O address is only accessible to programs at IOPL, or an inner level. An exception is raised if a program attempts to access an I/O address corresponding to a 1 in the bitmap while executing at an outer level relative to IOPL.

The T bit in the TSS causes the debug handler to be invoked whenever a task switch through this TSS occurs. This provides a convenient way for the debugger to monitor the activities of certain tasks. The BT bit of DR6 notes that this condition was detected. There is no specific enable bit for this condition in DR7.

Bus interfacing

The 80486 features 32-bit-wide internal and external data paths and eight general-purpose 32-bit registers. The processor communicates with external memory, I/O, and other devices through a parallel bus interface. This interface consists of a bidirectional data bus, a separate address bus, five bus status pins, and three bus control pins.

Each bus cycle is made up of at least two states. Each of the states requires a clock cycle. The maximum data transfer rate for a bus operation is determined by the 80486 internal clock, and is normally 32 bits for every two CLK cycles. That works out to 32Mb per second for a 16-MHz

31	23	16	15	7	0	
I/O Permission Bitmap Base			0 0 0 0 0 0 0 0 0 0 0 0 0 0 0 T			64
0 0 0 0 0 0 0 0 0 0 0 0 0 0 0 0			Local Descriptor Table (LDT)			
0 0 0 0 0 0 0 0 0 0 0 0 0 0 0 0			GS			
0 0 0 0 0 0 0 0 0 0 0 0 0 0 0 0			FS			
0 0 0 0 0 0 0 0 0 0 0 0 0 0 0 0			DS			
0 0 0 0 0 0 0 0 0 0 0 0 0 0 0 0			SS			
0 0 0 0 0 0 0 0 0 0 0 0 0 0 0 0			CS			
0 0 0 0 0 0 0 0 0 0 0 0 0 0 0 0			ES			48
EDI						
ESI						
EBP						
ESP						
EBX						
EDX						
ECX						2C
EAX						
EFLAGS						
EIP						
(Reserved)						
0 0 0 0 0 0 0 0 0 0 0 0 0 0 0 0			SS2			18
ESP2						
0 0 0 0 0 0 0 0 0 0 0 0 0 0 0 0			SS1			
ESP1						0C
0 0 0 0 0 0 0 0 0 0 0 0 0 0 0 0			SS0			
ESP0						
0 0 0 0 0 0 0 0 0 0 0 0 0 0 0 0			Back Link to Previous TSS			0

Note: Zeros indicate Intel reserved bits.

A-7 Linked TSSs.

clock. However, in burst mode, the rate can be 5 clocks for 4 words, which is 52.8Mb per second.

The 80486 offers both pipelined and nonpipelined bus cycles. When pipelining is selected, the 80486 overlaps bus cycles which allows longer access times. Because cache memory can be accessed without wait states,

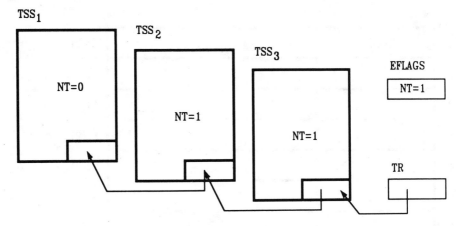

A-8 80387 accumulator stack registers.

nonpipelined cycles are often preferred. Using nonpipelined cycles minimizes latency between the processor requesting information from the outside world and data becoming available at the 80486 pins.

Floating-Point Unit

The 80486 Floating-Point Unit (FPU) numerical registers consist of: (1) eight individually-addressable 80-bit registers, which are organized as a register stack; (2) three error pointers, which are two 16-bit registers that contain selectors for the last instruction and operation, two 32-bit registers that contain offsets for the last instruction and operand, and one 11-bit register that contains the opcode of the last non-control FPU instructions; and (3) three 16-bit registers that contain the FPU control word, the FPU status, and the tag word.

FPU register stack

The register stack is an array of eight physical registers, with a separate 3-bit field that identifies the current stack top, as shown in Fig. A-9. A 3-bit field (named TOP) in the status word contains the absolute register number of the current top of the accumulator stack, ST. After a PUSH, the previous ST becomes ST(1), and all the stacked accumulators have their ST-relative names incremented by 1.

Tag-Word register

The 16-bit Tag-Word register, as shown in Fig. A-10, contains eight 2-bit fields, one for each of the eight floating-point registers. The TAG fields indicate whether the corresponding register holds a valid, zero, special floating-point number, or is empty. To avoid the need to rotate the tag word as the

	79 78	64 63	0	
0	S	Exponent	Significand	ST(7)
1				ST
2				ST(1)
3				ST(2)
4				ST(3)
5				ST(4)
6				ST(5)
7				ST(6)

TOP ← 001b

If TOP (in the Status Word) = 001b, then ST is at the second register, or register 1. After a PUSH, TOP increments by 1 and all the registers have their values incremented also. The increments and decrements ignore wrap-around. If TOP = 000b, a PUSH decrements TOP to 111b and stores the new value in register 7.

A-9 Tag Word register.

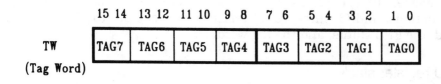

15 14	13 12	11 10	9 8	7 6	5 4	3 2	1 0
TAG7	TAG6	TAG5	TAG4	TAG3	TAG2	TAG1	TAG0

TW
(Tag Word)

Tag Field Encoding

TAG	Meaning
00	Valid
01	Zero
10	Special – Infinity, NaN, Denormal
11	Empty

A-10 Control Word register.

accumulator stack is pushed and popped, the fields in the TAG word correspond to the physical registers, rather than being relative to the stack top.

Control Word register

The Control Word register contains three fields, all under program control:

1. Bits 0–5 contain the exception masks for each of the six floating-point exception conditions recognized by the 80486.
2. Bits 8 and 9 specify Precision Control, PC. The results of floating-point arithmetic are rounded to one of the precision levels as shown in Fig. A-11, before they are stored in the destination.
3. Bits 10 and 11 are for Rounding Control, RC. There are four rounding modes, as shown in Fig. A-11.

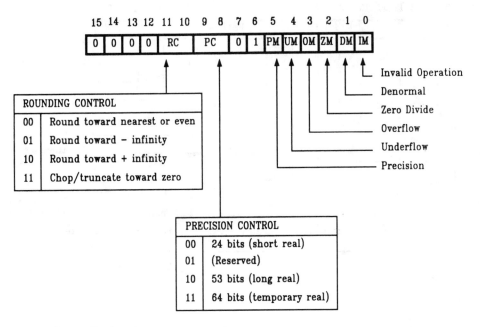

A-11 Status Word register.

Status Word register

The 16-bit FPU Status Word register reflects the overall state of the FPU. These bits can be tested under program control, using FSTSW/FNSTSW, FSTENV/FNSTENV, and FSTSW AS/FNSTSW AX. Figure A-12 shows the format of the Status Word register. The fields are:

- Bits 0–5 are set if an exception is detected and are sticky bits; that is, the processor sets them and they must be explicitly reset under program control. Bits 0–5 indicate whether the FPU has detected one of six possible exception conditions.

- Bit 6, Stack Fault (SF), is set if an invalid operation exception is due to overflow or underflow of the register stack. Otherwise, it is reset. When SF = 1, bit 9 = 1 if the stack overflowed, or bit 9 = 0, if underflowed.
- Bit 15 (B Bit) is for 8087 compatibility. It is tied to Bit 7 (ES), the error summary status.
- Bits 8 (C0), 9 (C1), 10 (C2), and 14 (C3) are Condition Code flags. These flags are set depending on the floating-point operations. They can be moved to the lower 8 bits of the EFLAGS register.
- Bits 11–13, TOP. This field indicates which of the seven accumulator registers is the top of the stack.

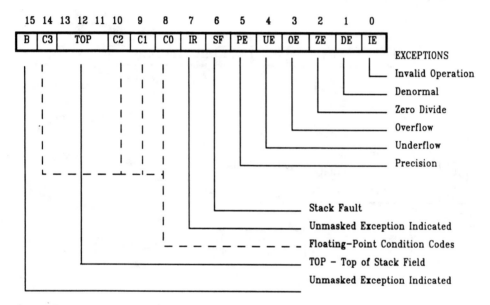

A-12 Error pointer registers.

Error Pointer registers

There are three 32-bit Error Pointer registers that hold pointers to the last instruction executed and that instruction's data, as shown in Fig. A-13. These registers are useful in analyzing and reporting exceptions that occur during floating-point instruction execution.

Precision control

You can calculate with 64, 53, or 24 bits of precision in the significand, depending on how you set the precision control (PC) field of the Control

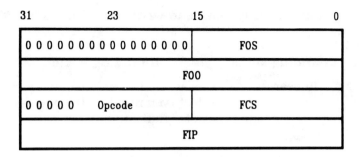

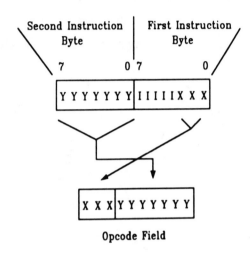

Opcode Field

A-13 Error pointer registers.

Word. The default setting is 64 bits. The other settings are required by the IEEE standard. If you specify lesser precision, the advantages of the extended format's extended fraction length are nullified. When you specify reduced precision, the rounding of the fractional value clears the unused bits on the right to zeros. Precision Control affects only FADD, FSUB, FMUL, FDIV, and FSQRT.

Rounding control

The 80486 uses three extra bits (the guard, round, and sticky bits) to allow it to round numbers in accord with the infinitely precise true results of a computation. These bits are not usable by programmers.

Rounding occurs when the format of the destination cannot exactly represent the exact result. The FPU has four rounding modes, selectable by the RC field in the control word. The FPU determines the two numbers that most closely bracket the result, then rounds according to the mode selected in the RC field. Rounding introduces an error in a result which is less than one unit in the last place to which the result is rounded. The rounding modes are:

RC Field	Rounding Mode	Rounding Action
00	To nearest	Closer to b of a or c; if equally close, select even number, the one whose least significant bit is zero
01	Down	a
10	Up	c
Chop	(toward 0)	Smaller in magnitude of a or c

Note: a < b < c. a and c are successive representable numbers. b is not representable.

B
80486 registers, flags, and bits

The register set available to programmers consists of eight, 32-bit general-purpose registers (EAX, EBX, ECX, EDX, ESP, EBP, ESI, and EDI); 32-bit status registers (EIP and EFLAGS); 16-bit segment-pointer registers (ES, CS, SS, DS, FS, and GS); 32-bit test registers (TR6 and TR7); and the 32-bit debug registers (DR0, DR1, DR2, DR3, DR6 and DR7). Not discussed are the general registers (whose contents depend on program need) and the EIP (because the contents of an instruction pointer depend on the location of the next line of code).

The first section of this appendix shows the location of the flags in the various registers that contain flags and bits that control your use of the 80486. The second section lists the FPU registers. The third section alphabetically lists the 80486 registers. The fourth section gives an alphabetical list of all flags used in and with the 80486. In the following descriptions, the term set means set to 1, and reset means clear to zero.

System Flags register (EFLAGS)

The 32-bit EFLAGS contains status flag and control flag bits. The program sets the control bits to control the operation of certain functions of the 80486. The 80486 sets the status bits, which are then tested by the program after arithmetic operations to check for special conditions. Bits 31–19, 15, 5, 3, and 1 are Intel reserved. See Fig. B-1.

Alignment Check (AC) bit 18   The AC bit, along with the AM bit in the CR0 register, enables alignment checking in memory references. An alignment check is run when a reference is made to an unaligned operand, such as a

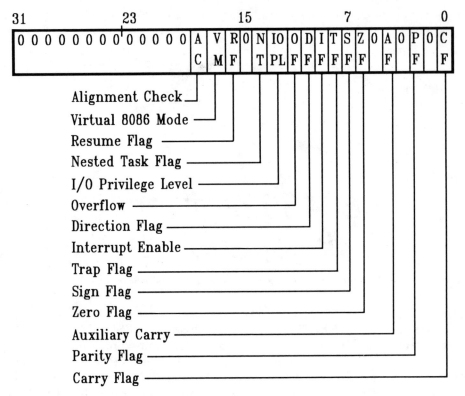

B-1 EFLAGS register. (Zero entries indicate Intel reserved bits; do not define.)

word at an odd byte address or a doubleword at an address that is not an integral multiple of four.

Virtual 8086 Mode (VM) bit 17 The VM bit provides Virtual 8086 Mode within the protected mode. If set while the processor is in protected mode, the 80486 switches to Virtual 8086 Mode operation. The VM flag can be set only two ways: in protected mode by the IRET instruction and only if Current Privilege Level (CPL) is 0; and by task switches at any privilege level.

Resume Flag (RF) bit 16 This flag temporarily disables debug exceptions (breaks to normal program flow) so that an instruction can be restarted after a debug exception without immediately causing another debug exception.

Nested Task (NT) bit 14 The 80486 uses this flag to control chaining of interrupted and CALLed tasks. A CALL transfers the program-execution sequence on a temporary basis to a subroutine or subprogram. On termination of that subroutine, execution is resumed at the instruction following the CALL. NT influences the operation of the IRET instruction.

Input/Output Privilege Level (IOPL) bits 13 – 12   This 2-bit field applies to protected mode. IOPL shows the highest CPL value permitted to execute I/O instructions without generating an exception 13 fault or consulting the I/O Permission Bitmap. It also shows the highest CPL value that allows change of the INTR Enable Flag (IF) bit when new values are popped into the EFLAGS register.

Overflow Flag (OF) bit 11   OF is set if the operation resulted in carry/borrow into the sign bit (high-order bit) of the result but did not result in a carry/borrow out of the high-order bit, or vice versa.

Direction Flag (DP) bit 10   DF defines whether the ESI and/or EDI registers are to decrement or increment during string operations. If DF = 0, the registers increment; if DF = 1, they decrement.

Interrupt-Enable (IF) bit 9   Setting IF allows the CPU to recognize external (maskable) interrupt requests. Clearing this bit disables these interrupts. IF has no effect on either nonmaskable external interrupts or exceptions.

Trap Flag (TF) bit 8   Setting TF puts the processor into single-step mode for debugging. The CPU automatically generates an Exception 1 after each instruction, which allows a program to be inspected as it executes each instruction. When TF is reset, Exception 1 traps occur only as a function of the breakpoint addresses loaded into debug registers DR0DR3. Further information is given in an upcoming discussion of the debug registers.

Sign Flag (SF) bit 7   SF is set if the high-order bit of the result is set; otherwise it is reset. For 8-, 16-, and 32-bit operations, SF reflects the state of bit 7, 15, and 31, respectively.

Zero Flag (ZF) bit 6   ZF is set if all bits of the result are 0. Otherwise, it is reset.

Auxiliary Carry Flag (AF) bit 4   This flag is used to simplify the addition and subtraction of packed BCD quantities. Regardless of the operand length (8, 16, or 32 bits), AF is set if the operation resulted in a borrow into bit 3 (which is a subtraction) or a carry out of bit 3 (which is an addition). Otherwise, AF is reset. Remember that BCD uses bits 0 – 3 to represent decimal digits.

Parity Flag (PR) bit 2   PF is set if the low-order eight bits of the operation contain an even number of 1's (even parity). PF is reset if the low-order eight bits have odd parity. PF is a function of only the low-order bits, regardless of operand size.

Carry Flag (CF) bit 0   CF is set if the operation resulted in a carry out of the high-order bit (an addition), or a borrow into the high-order bit (a subtraction). Otherwise CF is reset. For 8- , 16-, or 32-bit operations, CF is set according to the carry/borrow at bit 7, 15, or 31, respectively.

Control register flags

There are four 32-bit control registers: CR0, CR1, CR2 and CR3. CR1 is reserved for future processors and is undefined for the 80486. If you use an instruction that codes CR1 as the register, you'll get an invalid opcode exception. These control registers can be loaded and stored only by programs executing at privilege level 0, by using special forms of the MOV instructions.

Control register CR0

CR0 contains bits that enable and disable paging and protection, and bits that control the operation of the floating-point arithmetic. Bits 28 – 19, 17, and 15 – 6 are reserved and must be loaded with zeros.

The PE bit (bit 0) and the PG bit (bit 31) control the operation of the segmentation and paging mechanisms. Table B-1 shows processor modes with PG and PE, and Fig. B-2 shows control register formats.

Table B-1   Processor modes with PG and PE.

PG	PE	Execution mode
0	0	Real mode
0	1	Protected mode, paging disabled
1	0	Illegal combination, do not use
1	1	Protected mode, paging enabled

Paging (PG) bit 31   PG indicates whether the 80486 uses page tables to translate linear addresses into physical addresses. If PG = 1, paging is enabled; if PG = 0, paging is disabled and the linear addresses produced by the segmentation mechanism are passed through as physical addresses.

Cache Disable (CD) bit 30   CD enables the internal cache when clear and disables the cache when set. When set, cache misses do not cause cache line fills. Be certain to flush cache to completely disable cache, because cache hits are not disabled.

Not Write-through (NW) bit 29   When reset, NW enables write-throughs and cache invalidation cycles; when set, it disables invalidation cycles and write-throughs that hit in the cache. Note that disabling write-throughs can allow stale data to appear in the cache.

Alignment Mask (AM) bit 18   When set, AM allows alignment checking; when reset, it disables alignment checking. Alignment checking is done only when three conditions occur at once: AM is set; AC is set; and CPL is 3 (user mode).

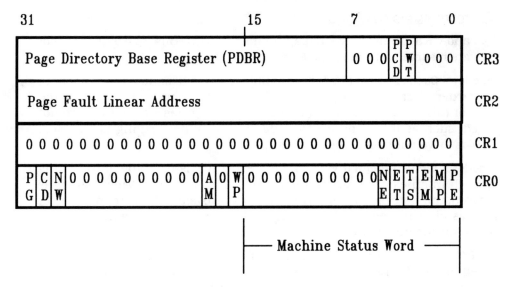

B-2 Control Register formats.

Extension Type (ET) bit 4   ET indicates the type of coprocessor present in the system, either an 80287 or 80387.

Write Protect (WP) bit 16   When set, WP write-protects user-level pages against any supervisor-mode access. If reset, WP allows read-only user-level pages to be written by a supervisor process. You might use this bit for implementing copy-on-write when creating a new process (forking), which is used by some operating systems, such as UNIX.

Numeric Error (NE) bit 5   When set, NE enables the mechanism for reporting floating-point errors. When reset (and the IGNNE# input is active), numeric errors cause the processor to stop and wait for an interrupt.

Task Switched (TS) bit 3   The processor sets TS with every task switch. It also tests TS when it interprets floating-point instructions. Loading into the CR0 register can reset TS. Also the CLTS instruction specifically resets the TS.

Emulation (EM) bit 2   When either EM or TS are set, execution of WAIT (or numeric instructions) generates the coprocessor-not-available exception. You can set EM to cause exception 7 on any WAIT or numeric instruction.

Math Present (MP) bit 1   On the 80286 and 80386, MP controls the function of the WAIT instruction, which is used to coordinate a coprocessor. When running programs on the 80486, set this bit to 1.

Protection Enable (PE) bit 0   If PE = 1, the 80486 operates with segmentation mechanism enabled. When PE = 1, the segmentation is turned off and the processor operates in real mode as an 8086.

Control registers CR2 and CR3

CR2 and CR3 are used by the paging mechanism. Bits $11-5$ and $2-0$ of CR3 are reserved and must be loaded with zeros.

Page-level Cache Disable (PCD) bit 4 of CR3   PCD is used to control caching in an external cache on a cycle-by-cycle basis. When paging is enabled, the state of this bit is driven on the PCD pin during bus cycles that are not paged, such as interrupt acknowledge cycles. When paging is disabled, PWT is driven during all bus cycles.

Page-level Write-Through (PWT) bit 3 of CR3   PWT is used to control write-through in an external cache on a cycle-by-cycle basis. When paging is enabled, the state of PWT is driven during bus cycles which are not paged, such as interrupt acknowledge cycles. When paging is disabled, PWT is driven during all bus cycles.

CR2 is used to report error information when a page exception is raised. In bits $3-12$, the 80486 stores the linear address that caused the exception into CR2 when reporting a page exception.

In bits $31-12$, CR3 contains the physical address of the page containing the first level of the page table, the directory. The directory is page-aligned, so only the top 20 bits are significant. The bottom 11 bits are reserved for use in future processors. Be sure to load zeros into them when loading a new value into CR3.

Test registers TR6 and TR7

Two test registers, TR6 and TR7, control the testing of the RAM/CAM in the translation lookaside buffer (TLB), the cache used for storing information from page tables. TR6 is the command test register and TR7 is the data register that contains the data of the TLB test. These two registers are diagramed in Fig. B-3. (Note also that TR0 through TR5 do not exist.)

Linear address bits 31 – 12 of TR6   On a TLB write, a TLB entry is allocated to this linear address. The rest of the TLB entry is set depending on the value of TR7 and the value just written into TR6. On a TLB lookup, the TLB is interrogated per this value. If one and only one TLB entry matches, the rest of the fields of TR6 and TR7 are set from the matching TLB entry.

Valid data (V) bit 11 of TR6   The TLB uses the V bit to identify entries that contain valid data. Valid means a successful translation has been made. Entries in the TLB that have not been assigned values have 0 in the valid bit. All valid bits can be cleared by writing to CR03.

Dirty (D) and (D#) bits 10 and 9 of TR6   Bit 10 indicates that the entry has been changed and bit 9 is its complement for/from the TLB entry.

User accessible (U) and (U#) bits 8 and 7 of TR6   Bit 8 is the User accessible bit and bit 7 is its complement for/from the TLB entry.

	11	7	4	0	
Physical Address	P C D / P W T	L R U 0 0	P L / REP	0 0	TR7
Linear Address	V D D# U U# W W#	0 0 0 0	C		TR6

B-3 Test Registers TR6 and TR7. (Zero entries indicate Intel reserved bits; do not define.)

TR7	PCD	= Page–level Cache Disable
	PWT	= Page–level Write–through
	LRU	= Pseudo–LRU cache replacement algorithm
	PL	= Lookup was a HIT=1, MISS=0
	REP	= Block where tag was found, if HT=1, Undefined if HT=0.

TR6	V	= Valid bit
	D/D#	= Dirty bit
	U/U#	= User bit
	W/W#	= Read/Write bit
	C	= Command bit

Writable (W) and (W#) bits 6 and 5 of TR6 Bit 6 is the Writable bit and bit 5 is its complement for/from the TLB entry.

Command (C) bit 0 of TR6 There are two TLB testing commands: write entries into the TLB, and perform TLB lookups. To write into the TLB entry, move a doubleword into TR6, which contains a 0 in the C bit. To cause a lookup, move a doubleword into TR6 that contains a 1 in this bit. Note that TLB operations are triggered by writing to TR6.

Physical address bits 31 – 12 of TR7 These 20 bits are the data field of the TLB. On a write to TLB, the TLB entry allocated to the linear address in TR6 is set to this value. On a TLB lookup, if PL is set, the data field (physical address) from the TLB is read out to this field. If PL bit is not set, this field is undefined.

Page-level Cache Disable (PCD) bit 11 of TR7 This bit corresponds to the

PCD (bit 4) of CR03. See the Control register section in this appendix for additional information.

Page-level Write-Through (PWT) bit 10 of TR7   This bit corresponds to PWT (Bit 3) of CR03. See the Control register section in this appendix for additional information.

LRU bits 9 – 7 of TR7   On a TLB read, the LRU corresponds to the bits used in the pseudo-LRU cache replacement algorithm. The reported states are the values of these bits before the TLB lookup. Note that TLB lookups that results and TLB writes can change these bits.

Pseudo-LRU (PL) bit 4 of TR7   For a TLB write, PL = 1 causes the REP field of TR7 to be used for selecting which of four blocks of the TLB entry is loaded. If PL = 0, the internal pointer of the paging unit is used to select the block. The internal pointer is driven by the pseudo-LRU cache replacement algorithm. On a TLB lookup, PL = 1 means the read was a hit; PL = 0 means a miss.

REP bits 3 and 2   For a TLB write, one of four associative blocks of the TLB is to be written—these bits indicate which blocks will be written. For a TLB read, if PL is set, REP shows in which of the four associative blocks the tag was found. If PL is not set on a TLB read, REP is undefined.

Debug registers

The six programmer-accessible debug registers (DR0 – DR3, DR6 and DR7) bring advanced debugging to the 80486, including breakpoints and the ability to set instruction breakpoints without modifying code segments. Registers DR0 – DR3 specify the four linear breakpoints. DR4 and DR5 are reserved for future Intel developments. DR6 displays the current state of the breakpoints and DR7 is used to set the breakpoints. Figure B-4 shows the debug register formats.

Debug register DR6

The bit assignments for debug register DR6 are described as follows.

BT bit 15   The BT bit indicates that the cause for the debug exception was a task switch into a task where the debug trap bit in the TSS is enabled.

BS bit 14   This bit is set if a single-step exception occurs. The single-step condition is enabled by the TF bit in the EFLAGS register. The BS bit is set only if a single-step trap actually occurs, not if a single-step condition (enabled or not) was detected.

BD bit 13   The BD bit is set at an instruction boundary if the next instruction reads or writes to one of the eight debug registers (debug register pro-

```
31                                                                      0
┌─────────────────────────────────────────────────────────────────────┐
│                    Breakpoint 0 Linear Address                        │  DR0
├─────────────────────────────────────────────────────────────────────┤
│                    Breakpoint 1 Linear Address                        │  DR1
├─────────────────────────────────────────────────────────────────────┤
│                    Breakpoint 2 Linear Address                        │  DR2
├─────────────────────────────────────────────────────────────────────┤
│                    Breakpoint 3 Linear Address                        │  DR3
├─────────────────────────────────────────────────────────────────────┤
│                            Reserved                                   │  DR4
├─────────────────────────────────────────────────────────────────────┤
│                            Reserved                                   │  DR5
├───────────────────────────────┬──┬──┬──┬──────────────────┬──┬──┬──┬─┤
│ 0000 0000 0000 0000           │BT│BS│BD│ 000 0 0 0 0 0 0   │B3│B2│B1│B0│ DR6
├───────────┬───────────┬───────┴──┴──┴──┴──┬───┬──┬──┬──┬──┬─┴──┴──┴──┴─┤
│LEN RWE 3  │LEN RWE 2  │LEN RWE 1 │LEN RWE 0│000│000│GE│LE│G3│L3│G2│L2│G1│L1│G0│L0│ DR7
└───────────┴───────────┴──────────┴─────────┴───────────────────────────┘
31              23              15              7                       0
```

B-4 Debug Register formats.

tection). BD is set whenever a read or write to the debug registers is about to occur.

B0, B1, B2, and B3 bits 3 – 0   These bits indicate that the breakpoint condition specified by the corresponding breakpoint linear address register was detected.

Debug register DR7

LEN   The four 2-bit LEN fields indicate the length of the breakpoint for each of the four breakpoint registers. The encoding is:

00	One-byte length
01	Two-byte length
10	Reserved
11	Four-byte length

RWE   The four 2-bit RWE fields indicate the type of access that causes a breakpoint exception to be raised. The encoding is:

00	Instruction execution only
01	Data writes only
10	Reserved
11	Data reads or writes

GE/LE These bits indicate the exact data breakpoints (global and local, respectively). If GE or LE is set, the 80486 slows execution such that data breakpoints are reported on exactly the instruction that causes them. If these bits are not set, the 80486 might get slightly ahead of the reporting of the breakpoint conditions on instructions that perform data writes near the end of their execution.

L0 – L3 and G0 – G3 bits 70 The L0–L3 and G0–G3 bits are the local and global enable signals for the four debug breakpoint registers. If either the local or global enable is set, the breakpoint specified by the corresponding breakpoint register DRn is enabled.

Selector flags

Figure B-5 shows the Selector format. In a general selector, the fields are as described below.

Index These bits (1 – 53) select one of up to 8192 descriptors in a descriptor table. The 80486 multiplies this index value by eight (the length of a descriptor) and then adds the result to the base address of the descriptor table. This accesses the correct entry in the table.

Table Indicator (TI) This bit specifies the descriptor table to which the selector refers: a 0 points to the GDT (Global Descriptor Table) and a 1 indicates the current Local Descriptor Table (LDT).

Requested Privilege Level (RPL) Bits 1 and 0 are used by the system protection mechanism. See chapter 6 for more on protection and privilege.

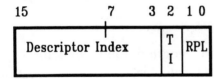

```
15              7     3 2 1 0
┌─────────────────────┬───┬────┐
│                     │ T │    │
│  Descriptor Index   │   │RPL │
│                     │ I │    │
└─────────────────────┴───┴────┘
```

RPL = Requestor Privilege Level
      00= Most privileged
      11= Least privileged

B-5 Selector format.

TI   = Identifies the Descriptor Table which
        contains the descriptor of the segment
        TI = 0, Descriptor is in the GDT
        TI = 1, Descriptor is in the LDT

Descriptor Index = The index within the GDT or
        LDT where the segment descriptor is

Segment descriptor flags/fields

The segment descriptor flags/fields shown in Fig. B-6 are:

BASE   This defines the location of the segment within the 4Gb linear address space. The 80486 concatenates the three fragments of the base address to form a single 32-bit value.

LIMIT   This field defines the size of the segment. The 80486 links the two parts of the LIMIT field to form a 20-bit result. The processor then interprets the LIMIT field in one of two ways, depending on the setting of the Granularity bit:

1. In units of one byte, to define a LIMIT of up to 1Mb.
2. In units of 4K (one page), to define a LIMIT of up to 4Gb. The LIMIT is shifted left by 12 bits when loaded, and low-order one-bits are inserted.

Granularity bit   This bit specifies the units with which the LIMIT field is interpreted. When G = 0, LIMIT is interpreted as units of one byte. If G = 1, LIMIT is interpreted in units of 4K.

S bit   The Segment bit determines if a given segment is a system segment (S = 0), or a code or data segment (S = 1).

TYPE   This differentiates among various types of descriptors. Code and data descriptors split TYPE into a 3-bit TYPE and 1-bit of Accessed Flag. System segments use the following set of values in TYPE:

0 = Invalid	8 = Invalid
1 = Available 286 TSS	9 = Available 486 TSS
2 = LDT	A = Intel reserved
3 = Busy 286 TSS	B = Busy 486 TSS
4 = 286 Call Gate	C = 486 Call Gate
5 = Task Gate	D = Intel reserved
6 = 286 Interrupt Gate	E = 486 Interrupt Gate
7 = 286 Trap Gate	F = 486 Trap Gate

Descriptor Privilege Level (DPL)   This is used by the protection mechanism.

Segment-Present bit   If this bit holds a 0, the descriptor is not valid for use in address translation. The 80486 signals an exception when a selector for the descriptor is loaded into a segment register.

Accessed bit   The 80486 sets this bit when the segment is accessed in data and code descriptors. Operating systems that implement virtual memory at the segment level can monitor the frequency of segment usage by periodically testing and clearing this bit.

Data Segment Descriptor

| 31 | | | | | | 15 | | | 7 | | 0 |

Base 31..24	G	B	0	A V L	Limit 19..16	P	DPL	TYPE 1 0 E W A	Base 23..16
Segment Base 15..0					Segment Limit 15..0				

Executable Segment Descriptor

| 31 | | | | | | 15 | | | 7 | | 0 |

Base 31..24	G	D	0	A V L	Limit 19..16	P	DPL	TYPE 1 1 C R A	Base 23..16
Segment Base 15..0					Segment Limit 15..0				

System Segment Descriptor

| 31 | | | | | | 15 | | | 7 | | 0 |

Base 31..24	G	X	0	A V L	Limit 19..16	P	DPL	0	TYPE	Base 23..16
Segment Base 15..0					Segment Limit 15..0					

A	Accessed	E	Expand Down
AVL	Available	G	Granularity
B	Big	P	Segment Present
C	Conforming	R	Readable
D	Default	W	Writeable
DPL	Descriptor Privilege Level		

B-6 Descriptor format.

FPU registers

The 80486 FPU registers appears as a set of additional registers, data types, and instructions.

FPU Status Word

The FPU Status Word is a 16-bit register that reflects the overall state of the FPU. See Fig. B-7.

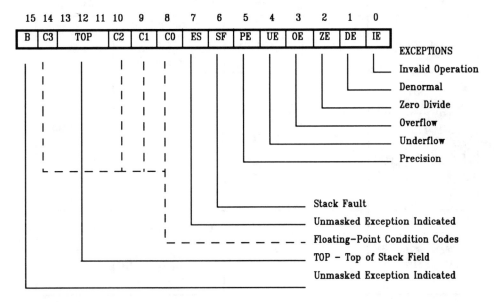

B-7 FPU Status Word.

Busy (B) bit 15   B is included for 8087 compatibility only. It reflects the contents of ES (Bit 7), see below.

Condition Code (C3), (C2), (C1), and (C0) bits 14, 10, 9, and 8   These bits are updated to reflect the outcome of arithmetic operations. The condition code bits are summarized in Fig. B-8. Use these bits for conditional branching. FSTSW AX stores the FPU Status Word directly into AX. SAHF copies the bits to 80486 flag bits to simplify branching. C0 = CF; C1 = No flag assigned; C2 = PF; and C3 = ZF.

Top of Stack TOS bits 13 – 11   TOP points to the FPU register that is the current Top of Stack.

Exception Status (ES) bit 7.   ES is set if any unmasked exception bits are set, and is reset otherwise.

Bits 5 through 0 indicate whether the FPU has detected any of six possible exception conditions. See Fig. B-7 for the condition codes.

Instruction	C0	C3	C2	C1
FCOM, FCOMP, FCOMPP, FTST, FUCOM, FUCOMP, FUCOMPP, FICOM, FICOMP	Result of comparison		Operand is not comparable	Zero or 0/U#
FXAM	Operand Class			Sign or 0/U#
FPREM, FRREM1	Q2	Q1	0 - reduction complete 1 - reduction incomplete	Q1 or 0/U#
FIST, FBSTP, FRNDINT, FST, FSTP, FADD, FMUL, FIDIV, FDIVR, FSUB, FSUBR, FSCALE, FSQRT, FPATAN, F2XM1, FYL2X, FYL2XP1	Undefined			Roundup or 0/U#
FPTAN, FSIN, FCOS, FSINCOS	Undefined		0 - reduction complete 1 - reduction incomplete	Roundup or 0/U# (Undefined if C2=1)
FCHS, FABS, FXCH, FINCSTP, FDECSTP, Constant Loads, FXTRACT, FLD, FILD, FBLD, FSTP (ext. real)	Undefined			Zero or 0/U#
FLDENV, FRSTOR	Each bit loaded from memory			
FLDCW, FSTENV, FSTCW, FSTSW, FCLEX	Undefined			
FINIT, FSAVE	Zero	Zero	Zero	Zero

B-8 Interpretation of condition codes.

FPU control word

Figure B-9 illustrates the FPU control word. Rounding control, bits 11 and 10, provide for the common round-to-nearest mode, as well as directed rounding and true chop. Rounding control affects only the arithmetic instructions.

Precision control, bits 9 and 8, are used if you want precision less than the default 64-bit precision. These bits affect the results of only five instructions: ADD, SUB(R), MUL, DIV(R), and SQRT. Bits 15 – 12, 7, and 6 are reserved.

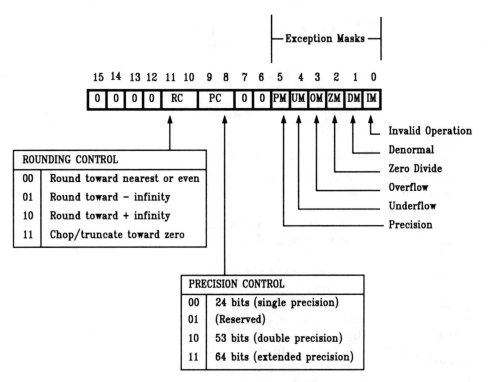

B-9 FPU Control Word register.

FPU Tag Word

The FPU Tag Word indicates the contents of each register in the FPU register stack. The FPU uses it to determine empty and non-empty register locations. Use the current TOP pointer stored in the FPU Status Word to associate the tag values with the relative stack registers, ST(0) through ST(7). Figure B-10 illustrates the FPU Tab Word format.

```
         15 14  13 12  11 10  9  8   7  6   5  4   3  2   1  0
       ┌──────┬──────┬──────┬──────┬──────┬──────┬──────┬──────┐
  TW   │ TAG7 │ TAG6 │ TAG5 │ TAG4 │ TAG3 │ TAG2 │ TAG1 │ TAG0 │
       └──────┴──────┴──────┴──────┴──────┴──────┴──────┴──────┘
(Tag Word)
```

TAG Meaning

00   Valid

01   Zero

10   Special – Unsupported, Infinity, NaN,
              or Denormal

11   Empty

B-10 Tag Word format.

Alphabetic listing of registers

The registers described in preceding sections are listed as follows in alphabetical order.

AH	High-order byte of AX register
AL	Low-order byte of AX register
AX	16-bit register, part of EAX
BH	High-order byte of BX register
BL	Low-order byte of BX register
BP	16-bit register, part of EBP
BX	16-bit register, part of EBX
CH	High-order byte of CX register
CL	Low-order byte of CX register
CR0	Control register, low order 16 bits is MSW
CR1	Control register, reserved
CR2	Page fault linear address register
CR3	Page directory base address
CX	16-bit register, part of ECX
DH	High-order byte of DX register
DI	16-bit register, part of EDI
DL	Low-order byte of DX register
DR0	Debug register, linear breakpoint address 0
DR1	Debug register, linear breakpoint address 1
DR2	Debug register, linear breakpoint address 2
DR3	Debug register, linear breakpoint address 3
DR4	Debug register, Intel reserved

DR5	Debug register, Intel reserved	
DR6	Debug register, breakpoint status	
DR7	Debug register, breakpoint control	
DS	Data Segment register	
DX	16-bit register, part of EDX	
EAX	General 32-bit register	
EBP	General 32-bit register, stack-frame base pointer	
EBX	General 32-bit register	
ECX	General 32-bit register	
EDI	General 32-bit register	
EDX	General 32-bit register	
EFLAGS	Flags register	
EIP	Instruction Pointer	
ES	Data segment register	
ESI	General 32-bit register	
ESP	Stack Pointer register	
FLAGS	The low-order 16 bits of EFLAGS	
FS	Data segment register	
GDT	Global Descriptor Table	
GS	Data segment register	
IDT	Interrupt Descriptor Table	
IP	Instruction Pointer, low-order 16 bits of EIP	
LDT	Local Descriptor Table	
SI	16-bit register, part of ESI	
SP	16-bit register, part of ESP	
SS	Stack Segment register	
TR6	Test register for page cache, test control	
TR7	Test register for page cache, test status	
TSS	Task State Segment	

Alphabetic listing of flags and bits

The following is a list of the flags used in the 80486 and its environs, along with which register they're in. Note that if the bit is in the EFLAGS register, it is commonly called a flag; otherwise it's called a bit.

Bit/Flag	Location	Description
A	Bit 5 of Page Table entry	Accessed
AC	Bit 18 of EFLAGS	Alignment Check
AF	Bit 4 of EFLAGS	Auxiliary carry
AM	Bit 18 of CR0	Alignment Mask
B0 – B3	Bits 0 to 3 of DR6	Breakpoint conditions detected
BD	Bit 13 of DR6	If instruction reads or writes to debug registers
BS	Bit 14 of DR6	Single-step exception

Bit/Flag	Location	Description
BT	Bit 15 of DR6	Cause for debug exception
CD	Bit 30 of CR0	Cache Disable
CF	Bit 0 of EFLAGS	Carry Flag
D	Bit 6 of Page Table entry	Dirty
DF	Bit 10 of EFLAGS	Direction Flag
EM	Bit 2 of CR0	Emulation
ET	Bit 4 of CR0	Processor Extension Type
GD	Bit 13 of DR7	Enable debug register protection
GE/LE	Bits 0 to 7 of DR7	Global or local data breakpoints
IF	Bit 9 of EFLAGS	Interrupt enable
IOPL	Bit 13/12 of EFLAGS	I/O Privilege Level
L0–L3/		
G0–G3	Bits 0 through 7 of DR7	Local or global enable signals
MP	Bit 1 of CR0	Math Present
NE	Bit 5 of CR0	Numeric Error
NT	Bit 14 of EFLAGS	Nested Task flag
NW	Bit 29 of CR0	Not Write-Through
OF	Bit 11 of EFLAGS	Overflow
P	Bit 0 of Page Table entry	Present
PCD	Bit 4 of CR3	Page-level Cache Disable
PDBR	Bits 31-12	Page Directory Base Register
PE	Bit 0 of CR0	Protection Enable
PF	Bit 2 of EFLAGS	Parity Flag
PG	Bit 31 of CR0	Paging enable
PWT	Bit 3 of CR3	Page-level Write-Through
R/W	Bit 1 of Page Table entry	Read/Write
RF	Bit 16 of EFLAGS	Resume Flag
SF	Bit 7 of EFLAGS	Sign Flag
TF	Bit 8 of EFLAGS	Trap Flag
TS	Bit 3 of CR0	Task Switched
U/S	Bit 2 of Page Table entry	User/Supervisor
VM	Bit 17 of EFLAGS	Virtual 8086 Mode
WP	Bit 16 of CR0	Write Protect
ZF	Bit 6 of EFLAGS	Zero Flag

C

The 80486 instruction set

The 80486 instruction set is a superset of previous generations' instructions, with additional instructions for specific 80486 uses. The instruction set is listed in this appendix in alphabetic order by mnemonic. Along with each instruction, the forms are given for each operand combination, including the object code that is produced, the operands required, and a description of the instruction.

Instruction formats

80486 instructions are made up of various elements and have various formats. Of the elements described as follows, only one (the opcode) is always present in each individual instruction. The others might or might not be present, depending on the operation involved and the location and type of the operands.

Instructions are made up of optional instruction prefixes; one or two primary opcode bytes; possibly an address specifier that consists of the Mod R/M byte and the Scale Index Base byte; a displacement (if required); and an immediate data field (if required). All the instruction encodings are subsets of the general instruction format shown in Fig. C-1. The elements of an instruction, in their order of occurrence, are as follows:

Prefixes A prefix consists of one or more bytes preceding an instruction that modify the operation of that instruction. There are four types of prefixes:

1. Repeat is used with a string instruction to cause the instruction to act on each element of the string.

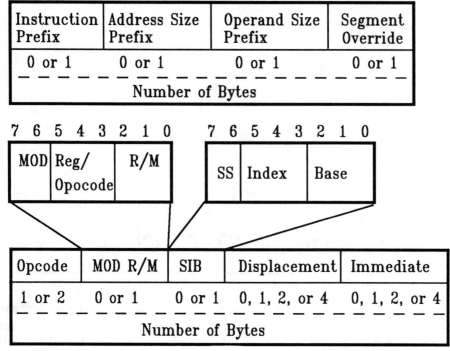

Instruction Prefix	Address Size Prefix	Operand Size Prefix	Segment Override
0 or 1	0 or 1	0 or 1	0 or 1

Number of Bytes

Opcode	MOD R/M	SIB	Displacement	Immediate
1 or 2	0 or 1	0 or 1	0, 1, 2, or 4	0, 1, 2, or 4

Number of Bytes

C-1 General instruction format.

2. Operand Size switches between 32-bit and 16-bit operands.
3. Address Size switches between 32-bit and 16-bit address generation.
4. Segment Override explicitly specifies which segment register an instruction should use. This overrides the default segment-register selection generally used by the 80486 for that instruction.

Opcode This specifies the operation performed by the instruction. Some operations have several opcodes, each specifying a different variant of the operation.

Register Specifier The instruction can specify one or two register operands. Register specifiers might occur in either the same byte as the opcode, or in the same byte as the addressing-mode specifier.

Addressing-Mode Specifier When present, this element specifies whether an operand is a register or a memory location. If it's in memory, this specifies whether a displacement, an index register, a base register, and scaling is to be used.

MOD R/M and Scale Index Base (SIB) bytes Most instructions that can refer to an operand in memory have an addressing-form byte following the primary opcode byte(s). This byte specifies the address form to be used. Some encodings of the MOD R/M byte indicate a second addressing byte, the Scale Index Base (SIB) byte. The MOD R/M and SIB bytes contain the following information:

- The indexing type or register number to be used in the instructions.
- The register to be used, or more information to select the instruction.
- The base, index, and scale information.

The MOD R/M byte contains these three fields:

- MOD (bits 7 and 6) occupies the two most significant bits of the byte. They combine with the R/M field to form 32 possible values: eight registers and 24 indexing modes.
- REG (bits 5, 4, and 3) specify either a register number or three more bits of opcode information. The meaning of REG is specified by the first (opcode) byte of the instruction.
- R/M (bits 2, 1, and 0) can specify a register as the location of an operand, or it can form part of the addressing-mode encoding in combination with the MOD field as described above.

The SIB byte includes these three fields:

1. SS (bits 7 and 6) specifies the scale factor.
2. INDEX (bits 5, 4, and 3) specifies the register number of the index register.
3. BASE (bits 2, 1, and 0) specifies the register number of the base register.

Encoding of 32-bit address mode   Register modifiers for address computation are all 32-bit registers (EAX, for example). Address computation without SIB byte includes the following: a MOD of 00, which specifies address computation of DS:[r/m], which specifies a register as follows:

000	DS:[EAX]
001	DS:[ECX]
010	DS:[EDX]
011	DS:[EBX]
100	SIB Present
101	DS:*32-bit displacement*
110	DS:[ESI]
111	DS:[EDI]

Thus, the effective address is DS:*32-bit modifier* from register or memory. A MOD of 01 adds an 8-bit displacement to the preceding, so that these *r/m* values are of the following form:

000	DS:[EAX + *8-bit displacement*]
100	SIB Present
101	SS:[EBP + *8-bit displacement*]

A MOD of 10 adds a 32-bit displacement. An *r/m* of 000 is DS:[EAX-+ *displacement*]:

000	DS:[EAX + *32-bit displacement*]
100	SIB Present
101	SS:[EBP + *32-bit displacement*]

MOD 11 specifies a register in the *r/m* with the following equivalences:

000	AL or EAX
001	CL or ECX
010	DL or EDX
011	BL or EBX
100	AH or ESP
101	CH or EBP
110	DH or ESI
111	BH or EDI

The register selected depends on whether an 8-bit operation or a 32-bit operation is specified in the W bit. The MOD value indicates the length of the displacement field to address:

00	No displacement, except for base 101
01	8-bit displacement
10	32-bit displacement

Therefore the SIB modifies the computed address:

DS:[*base + scaled index + displacement*]

except for the base where the base is ESP or EBP and then the logical substitution of SS: is made for the segment, instead of DS:.

Where an SIB is present, *r/m* = 100 for MOD = 00, 01, or 10, the address computation is done using a combination of the following:

- A 32-bit scaled index value is computed as index $* 2^{scale}$ where *scale* is the first two bits of the SIB byte and is specified by its binary value. The index register is specified as an index of:

000	EAX
001	ECX

010	EDX
011	EBX
100	no index value, scale must be 0
101	EBP
110	ESI
111	EDI

- If the byte is laid out, the bits appear as SSIIIBBB, where SS is the scale, III is the index, and BBB is the base. The base is selected as follows:

000	EAX
001	ECX
010	EDX
011	EBX
100	ESP
101	Special (a 32-bit displacement if MOD is 00 and the EBP register otherwise)
110	ESI
111	EDI

Displacement   When the addressing-mode specifier indicates that a displacement will be used to compute the address of an operand, the displacement is encoded in the instruction. A displacement is a signed integer of 8, 16, or 32 bits. The 8-bit form is used in the common case when the displacement is sufficiently small.

Immediate operand   When present, this element provides the value of an operand of the instruction. Immediate operands might be 8-, 16-, or 32-bits wide. In cases where an 8-bit immediate operand is combined in some way with a 16- or 32-bit operand, the processor automatically extends the size of the 8-bit operand, taking into account the sign.

Description notations

The following explains the notational conventions and abbreviations used when illustrating the instruction set: +rb, +rw, +rd. A register code, 0–7, is added to the hexadecimal byte given at the left of the plus sign, in order to form a single opcode byte. The codes are:

rb	rw	rd
AL =0	AX =0	EAX =0
CL =1	CX =1	ECX =1
DL =2	DX =2	EDX =2
BL =3	BX =3	EBX =3
AH =4	SP =4	ESP =4

rb	rw	rd
CH = 5	BP = 5	EBP = 5
DH = 6	SI = 6	ESI = 6
BH = 7	DI = 7	EDI = 7

/digit   The digit is generally between 0 and 7. It indicates that the MOD R/M byte of the instruction uses only *r/m* operand. The reg field contains the digit that provides an extension to the instruction's opcode.

/r   This shows that the instruction's MOD R/M byte contains both a register operand and an *r/m* operand.

cb, cw, cd, cp   A 1-byte (*cb*), 2-byte (*cw*), 4-byte (*cd*), or a 6-byte (*cp*) value that follows the opcode is used to specify a code offset and possibly a new value for the code segment register.

ib, iw, id   A 1-byte (*ib*), 2-byte (*iw*), or 4-byte (*id*) immediate operand to the instruction that follows the opcode, MOD R/M bytes or scale-indexing bytes. The opcode determines if the operand is a signed value. Note that all words and doublewords are given with the low-order byte first.

imm8   An immediate byte value. *imm8* is a signed number between − 128 and + 127, inclusive. For those instructions where *imm8* combines with a word or doubleword operand, the immediate value is sign-extended to form a word or doubleword. The upper byte of the word/doubleword is filled with the topmost bit of the immediate value.

imm16   An immediate word value. It is used for instructions whose operand-size attribute is 16 bits. Inclusive, this number runs from − 32,768 to + 32,767.

imm32   An immediate doubleword. The imm32 abbreviation is used for instructions whose operand-size attribute is 32 bits. The range of numbers is inclusive from − 2,147,483,648 to + 2,147,483,647.

m8   A memory byte addressed by DS:SI or ES:DI.

m16   A memory word addressed by DS:SI or ES:DI.

m32   A memory doubleword addressed by DS:SI or ES:DI.

moffs8, moffs16, moff232   A memory offset. A simple memory variable of type BYTE, WORD, or DWORD, used by some variants of the MOV instruction. The actual address is given by a simple offset relative to the segment base. The number shows with the *moffs* indicates its size, which is determined by the address-size attribute of the instruction. No MOD R/M byte is used in the instruction.

ptr16:16, ptr16:32   FAR pointer. Typically it is in a code segment different from that of the instruction. The notation 16:16 shows that the pointer value has two parts. The value to the left of the colon is the offset within the destination segment. The value to the right of the colon is a 16-bit selector or value destined for the code segment register. When the instruction's operand has a size attribute of 16, use 16:16. For the 32-bit attribute, use 16:32.

r8 One of the byte registers AL, CL, DL, BL, AH, CH, DH, or BH.

r16 One of the word registers AX, CS, DX, BX, SP, BP, SI, or DI.

r32 One of the doubleword registers EAX, ECX, EDX, EBX, ESP, EBP, ESI, or EDI.

rel8 A relative address in the range from 128 bytes before the end of the instruction to 127 bytes after the instruction's end.

rel16, rel32 A relative address within the same code segment as the instruction assembled: *rel16* is applied to instructions whose operand-size attribute is 16 bits, while *rel32* is applied to the instructions with a 32-bit operand-size attribute.

r/m8 A one-byte operand. It is either the contents of a byte from memory or from a byte register—AL, BL, CL, DL, AH, BH, CH, or DH.

r/m16 A word register or memory operand. It is used for instructions whose operand-size attribute is 16 bits. The contents of memory are found at the address provided by the effective address computation. The word registers are: AX, BX, CX, DX, SP, BP, SI, and DI.

r/m32 A doubleword register or memory operand. It is used for instructions whose operand-size attribute is 32 bits. The contents of memory are found at the address provided by the effective address computation. The doubleword registers are: EAX, EBX, ECX, EDX, ESP, EBP, ESI, and EDI.

rrr When *rrr* appears in the binary equivalent column, it appears as the last three digits of the binary figure and indicates a particular register is referenced. The *rrr* translates to the following:

$$
\begin{array}{ll}
000 = AX/EAX & 100 = SP/ESP \\
001 = CX/ECX & 101 = BP/EBP \\
010 = DX/EDX & 110 = SI/ESI \\
011 = BX/EBX & 111 = DI/EDI
\end{array}
$$

Sreg A segment register. The segment register bit assignments are ES = 0, CS = 1, SS = 2, DS = 3, FS = 4, and GS = 5.

Description of modifiers and specifications

In the figures that illustrate each instruction, there are some extensions that show modifiers, register specifications, and register/memory specifications. The notation *mm 00 r/m* specifies memory and *mm 11 r/m* specifies *rrr*. A further explanation of how those interact with the opcode follows, *disp8* is an 8-byte displacement, *disp16* is a 16-byte displacement, and *disp32* is a 32-byte displacement.

8-bit modifiers

rrr	8-bit registers	16- or 32-bit registers
000	AL	AX,EAX
001	CL	CX,ECX
010	DL	DX,EDX
011	BL	BX,EBX
100	AH	SP,ESP
101	CH	BC,EBP
110	DH	SI,ESI
111	BH	DI,EDI

16-bit modifiers

r/m or mm	00	01	10	11
000	[BX + SI]	+ *disp8*	+*disp16*	*rrr*
001	[BX + DI]			
010	[BP + SI]			
011	[BP + DI]			
100	[SI]			
101	[DI]			
110	*disp16*	[BP]+*disp8*	[BP] +*disp16*	[BP] +*disp16*
111	[BX]	+*disp8*	+*disp16*	

32-bit modifiers

r/m and mm	00	01	10	11
000	[EAX]	+*disp8*	+disp32	rrr
001	[ECX]	+*disp8*		
010	[EDX]	+*disp8*		
011	[EBX]	+*disp8*		
100	SIB Follows			
101	*disp32*	[EBC]+ +*disp8*	[EBP]+*disp32*	
110	[ESI]	[EBC]+*disp8*		
111	[EDI]			

Scaled Index Byte (SIB)

In the following coding scheme, SS = the scale factor.

SS		
	00	Times 1
	01	Times 2

| | 10 | Times 4 |
| | 11 | Times 8 |

Index	**Base**
000 EAX	000 EAX
001 ECX	001 ECX
010 EDX	010 EDX
011 EBX	011 EBX
100 None	100 ESP
101 EBP	101 Special
110 ESI	110 ESI
111 EDI	111 EDI

AAA ASCII adjust after addition

INSTRUCTION	OPCODE	BINARY
AAA	37	00110111

Purpose: AAA changes the contents of register AL to a valid unpacked decimal number and zeros the top 4 bits. AAA follows the addition of two unpacked decimal operands in AL, but it can be used for other BCD conversions also. If a decimal carry results from the addition, or the contents of the lower nibble of AL are greater than 9, then AL is incremented by 6, AH incremented by 1, and CF and AF set to 1. If no decimal carry occurred, AH is unchanged, CF and AF set to 0, and the lower 4 bits of AL are unchanged. Whether or not a decimal carry occurred, the upper 4 bits of AL are cleared.

AAD ASCII adjust register AX before division

INSTRUCTION	OPCODE	BINARY
AAD	D5 0A	11010101 00001010

Purpose: AAD modifies the numerator in AH and AL, to prepare for the division of two valid unpacked decimal operands so that the quotient produced by the division will be a valid unpacked decimal number. AH should contain the high-order digit and AL the low-order digit. AAD adjusts the value and places the result in AL. AH will contain zero.

AAM   ASCII adjust AX register after multiplication

INSTRUCTION	OPCODE	BINARY
AAM	D4 0A	11010100 00001010

Purpose: Two BCD digits multiplied together might produce an invalid BCD result. AAM corrects the result of a multiplication of two valid unpacked decimal numbers back into a pair of digits in AH and AL. AAM follows the multiplication of two decimal numbers to produce a valid result. The high-order digit is left in AH, the low-order in AL.

AAS   ASCII adjust AL register after subtraction

INSTRUCTION	OPCODE	BINARY
AAS	3F	00111111

Purpose: AAS changes the contents of register AL to a valid unpacked decimal number and zeros the top 4 bits. AAS follows the subtraction of one unpacked decimal operand from another in AL. If a decimal borrow results from the subtraction, then AL is decremented by 6, AH is decremented by 1, and the CF and AF flags are set. If no decimal carry occurred, AH is unchanged, CF and AF are set to 0, and the lower 4 bits of AL are unchanged. Whether a decimal carry occurred or not, the upper 4 bits of AL are cleared.

ADC   Add integers with carry

INSTRUCTION	OPCODE	BINARY
ADC AL,imm8	14 ib	00010100
ADC AX,imm16	15 iw	00010100
ADC EAX,imm32	15 id	00010101
ADC r/m8,imm8	90 /2 ib	00010000 mm 010 r/m
ADC r/m16,imm16	90 /2 /w	10010000 mm 010 r/m
ADC r/m32,imm32	91 /2 id	10010001 mm 010 r/m
ADC r/m16,imm8	93 /2 ib	10010011 mm rrr r/m
ADC r/m32,imm8	93 /2 ib	10010011 mm rrr r/m
ADC r/m8,r8	10 /r	00010000 mm rrr r/m
ADC r/m16,r16	11 /r	00010001 mm rrr r/m

INSTRUCTION	OPCODE	BINARY
ADC r/m32,r32	11 /r	00010001 mm rrr r/m
ADC r8,r/m8	12 /r	00010010 mm rrr r/m
ADC r16,r/m16	13 /r	00010011 mm rrr r/m
ADC r32,r/m32	13 /r	00010011 mm rrr r/m

Purpose: ADC sums the operands, adds one if CF is set and replaces the destination operand with the result. If CF is cleared, ADC does the same operation as the ADD instruction. An ADD followed by multiple ADC instructions can be used to add numbers longer than 32 bits.

ADD   Add integers

INSTRUCTION	OPCODE	BINARY
ADD AL,imm8	04 ib	00000100
ADD AX,imm16	05 /w	00000101
ADD EAX,imm32	05 id	00000101
ADD r/m8,imm8	80 /0 ib	10000000 mm 000 r/m
ADD r/m16,imm16	81 /0 iw	10000001 mm 000 r/m
ADD r/m32,imm32	81 /0 id	10000001 mm 000 r/m
ADD r/m16,imm8	83 /0 ib	10000011 mm 000 r/m
ADD r/m32,imm8	83 /0 ib	10000011 mm 000 r/m
ADD r/m8,r8	00 /r	00000000 mm rrr r/m
ADD r/m16,r16	01 /r	00000001 mm rrr r/m
ADD r/m32,r32	01 /r	00000001 mm rrr r/m
ADD r8,r/m8	02 /r	00000010 mm rrr r/m
ADD r16,r/m16	03 /r	00000011 mm rrr r/m
ADD r32,r/m32	03 /r	00000011 mm rrr r/m

Purpose: ADD replaces the destination operation with the sum of the source and destination operands. It sets CF if there is an overflow.

AND   Logical AND

INSTRUCTION	OPCODE	BINARY
AND AL,imm8	24 ib	00100100
AND AX,imm16	25 iw	00100101
AND EAX,imm32	25 id	00100101
AND r/m8,imm8	A0 /4 ib	10100000 mm 100 r/m
AND r/m16,imm16	A1 /4 iw	10100001 mm 100 r/m
AND r/m32,imm32	A1 /4 ib	10100001 mm 100 r/m

AND r/m16,imm8	A3 /4 ib	10100011 mm 100 r/m
AND r/m32,imm8	A3 /4 ib	10100011 mm 100 r/m
AND r/m8,r8	20 /r	00100000 mm rrr r/m
AND r/m16,r16	21 /r	00100001 mm rrr r/m
AND r/m32,r32	21 /r	00100001 mm rrr r/m
AND r8,r/m8	22 /r	00100010 mm rrr r/m
AND r16,r/m16	23 /r	00100011 mm rrr r/m
AND r32,r/m32	23 /r	00100011 mm rrr r/m

Purpose: AND is used to ensure that user-specified bits are off, e.g., the parity bit in an ASCII input stream from a terminal. When AND is used in conjunction with a compare, AND makes certain that the specified bits are on. In use, AND is executed prior to the compare. Both AND and the compare use known masks.

ARPL   Adjust requester privilege level of selector

INSTRUCTION	OPCODE	BINARY
ARPL r/m16,r16	63 /r	01100011 mm rrr r/m

Purpose: ARPL is used by systems software to guarantee that selector parameters to a subroutine do not request more privilege than allowed to the caller. ARPL has two operands. The first is a 16-bit word register or memory variable that contains the value of the selector. The second operand is generally a register that contains the caller's CS selector value.

ARPL checks that the requested privilege level (RPL) of the first operand against the RPL of the second. The RPL is specified in the least significant bits of each operand. If RPL of the first operand is less than that of the second, the Zero Flag (ZF) is set to 1.

BOUND   Check array index against bounds

INSTRUCTION	OPCODE	BINARY
BOUND r16,m16&16	62 /r	01100010 mm rrr r/m
BOUND r32,m32&32	62 /r	01100010 mm rrr r/m

Purpose: BOUND verifies that the signed value contained in the specified register lies within specified limits. Interrupt 5 occurs if the value in the register is less than the lower bound or greater than the upper bound. The upper and lower limit values might each be a word or a doubleword.

The block of memory that specifies the lower and upper limits of an array might typically reside just before the array itself. This makes the array bounds accessible at a constant offset from the beginning of the array. Because the address of the array is already present in a register, this avoids extra calculations to obtain the effective address of the array bounds.

BOUND includes two operands. The first specifies the register being tested. The second contains the effective address of the two signed BOUND limit values. BOUND assumes that the upper limit and the lower limit are in adjacent memory locations. These limit values cannot be register operands. If they are, an invalid opcode exception occurs.

BSF — Bit scan forward

INSTRUCTION	OPCODE	BINARY
BSF r16,r/m16	OF BC	00001111 10111100 mm rrr r/m
BSF r32,r/m32	OF BC	00001111 10111100 mm rrr r/m

Purpose: This instruction scans a word or doubleword (from the least significant bit to the most significant bit) for a one-bit and stores the number of the first set bit into a register. The bit string being scanned might be either in a register or in memory. ZF is set if the entire word is 0; that is, no set bits are found. ZF is cleared if a one-bit is found. Note: If no set bit is found, the value of the destination register is undefined.

This instruction is new with the 80486. It is useful for scanning allocation bitmaps for an allocatable or free bit. Returning the number of the bit provides the relative number of the item within the word being examined.

BSR — Bit scan reverse

INSTRUCTION	OPCODE	BINARY
BSR r16,r/m16	OF BD	00001111 10111101 mm rrr r/m
BSR r32,r/m32	OF BD	00001111 10111101 mm rrr r/m

Purpose: This instruction scans a word or doubleword (from the most significant bit to the least significant bit) for a one-bit and stores the index of the first set bit into a register. The bit string being scanned might be either in a register or in memory. ZF is set if the entire word is 0; that is, no set bits are found. ZF is cleared if a one-bit is found. This is a new instruction with the 80486.

Note: If no set bit is found, the value of the destination register is undefined.

BSWAP   Byte swap

INSTRUCTION	OPCODE	BINARY
BSWAP	OF C8 /r	00001111 11001000

Purpose: BSWAP reverses the byte order of a 32-bit register; this converts a value in little/bit endian form to big/little endian form. When used with 16-bit operand sizes, the result in the destination register is unidentified.

Note: This instruction is new to the 80486.

BT   Bit test

INSTRUCTION	OPCODE	BINARY
BT r/m16,r16	OF A3	00001111 10100011 mm rrr r/m
BT r/m32,r32	OF A3	00001111 10100011 mm rrr r/m
BT r/m16,imm8	OF BA /r ib	00001111 10111010 mm 100 r/m
BT r/m32,imm8	OF BA /r ib	00001111 10111010 mm 100 r/m

Purpose: BT is a means of determining whether or not a bit in a bitmap is set. BT sets CF to the same value as the bit being tested. This instruction is new with the 80486. It is recommended not to use BT to reference memory-mapped I/O registers directly. Use MOV to load from or store to the memory-mapped device registers and then use the register form of BT.

BTC   Bit test and complement

INSTRUCTION	OPCODE	BINARY
BTC r/m16,r16	OF BB	00001111 10111011 mm rrr r/m
BTC r/m32,r32	OF BB	00001111 10111011 mm rrr r/m
BTC r/m16,imm8	OF BA /7 ib	00001111 10111010 mm 111 r/m
BTC r/m32,imm8	OF BA /7 ib	00001111 10111010 mm 111 r/m

Purpose: BTC tests a specific bit, copies that bit to CF, and inverts the original bit (e.g., if the bit was a 1, it's changed to a 0 and CF is set to 1). This instruction is new with the 80486. It is recommended not to use BTC to directly reference memory-mapped I/O registers. Use MOV to load from or store to the memory-mapped device registers and then use the register form of BTC.

BTR — Bit test and reset

INSTRUCTION	OPCODE	BINARY
BTR r/m16,r16	0F B3	00001111 10100011 mm rrr r/m
BTR r/m32,r32	0F B3	00001111 10100011 mm rrr r/m
BTR r/m16,imm8	0F BA /6 ib	00001111 10111010 mm 101 r/m
BTR r/m32,imm8	0F BA /6 ib	00001111 10111010 mm 101 r/m

Purpose: BTR saves the value of the [bit in the base (first operand) and the bit offset (in the second operand)] into the CF flag and then stores 0 in the bit. The index of the selected bit can be given by the immediate constant in the instruction or by a value in a general register; only an 8-bit immediate value is used in the instruction. The operand is taken modulo 32, which means that the range of the immediate bit offset is 0..31.

In real address mode, interrupt 13 occurs if any part of the operand lies outside of the effective address space from 0 to 0FFFF.

BTS — Bit test and set

INSTRUCTION	OPCODE	BINARY
BTS r/m16,r16	0F AB	00001111 10101011 mm rrr r/m
BTS r/m32,r32	0F AB	00001111 10101011 mm rrr r/m
BTS r/m16,imm8	0F BA /5 ib	00001111 10111010 mm 101 r/m
BTS r/m32,imm8	0F BA /5 ib	00001111 10111010 mm 101 r/m

Purpose: BTS tests a specific bit, copies that bit to CF, and sets the original bit to 1. This instruction is new with the 80486. It is recommended not to use BTC to reference memory-mapped I/O registers directly. Use MOV to load from or store to the memory-mapped device registers and then use the register form of BTS.

CALL   Call a procedure

INSTRUCTION	OPCODE	BINARY
CALL rel16	E8 cw	11101000
CALL r/m16	FF /2	11111111 mm 010 r/m
CALL ptr16:16	9A cd	10011010
CALL m16:16	FF /3	11111111 mm 011 r/m
CALL rel32	E8 cd	11101000
CALL r/m32	FF /2	11111111 mm 010 r/m
CALL ptr16:32	9A cp	10011010
CALL ptr32:32	9A cp	10011010
CALL m16:32	FF /3	11111111 mm 011 r/m

Purpose: CALL transfers control from one code segment location to another. These locations can be within the same code segment (near) or in different ones (far). Prior to actual transfer, CALL saves on the stack, the address of the instruction following the CALL, and the current value of EIP.

CALL instructions have relative, direct, and indirect versions. Indirect instructions specify an absolute address in one of two ways: (1) the 80486 can obtain the destination address from a memory operand specified in the instruction; or (2) the program CALLs a location specified by a general register (EAX, EDX, ECX, EBX, EBP, ESI, or EDI).

CBW   Convert byte to word
CWDE   Convert word to doubleword

INSTRUCTION	OPCODE	BINARY
CBW	98	10011000
CWDE	99	10011001

Purpose: These instructions extend the sign bit into the top portion of the larger register so that arithmetic operations can occur with correct results. The value of bit 7 of AX or bit 15 of EAX is placed in every bit of AH or the upper 16 bits of EAX.

CLC   Clear carry flag (CF)

INSTRUCTION	OPCODE	BINARY
CLC	F8	11111000

Purpose: This instruction sets the CF to zero. No other flags are affected.

CLD — Clear direction flag (DF)

INSTRUCTION	OPCODE	BINARY
CLD	FC	11111100

Purpose: CLD sets DF to 0. No other flags are affected. By setting DF to 0, DF now signals the automatic indexing feature to increment the index registers ESI and EDI. Automatic indexing is used by string instructions.

CLI — Clear interrupt flag (IF)

INSTRUCTION	OPCODE	BINARY
CLI	FA	11111010

Purpose: If the current privilege level is at least as privileged as the IOPL, CLI sets the interrupt flag (IF) to 0. No other flags are affected. An exception is raised if the program does not have the correct I/O privilege.

Note: External interrupts are ignored at the end of CLI until the interrupt flag is set.

CLTS — Clear task-switched flag in CR0

INSTRUCTION	OPCODE	BINARY
CLTS	0F 06	00001111 00000110

Purpose: CLTS sets the Task Switched (TS bit in CR0) to 0. TS is set to 1 by the 80486 at each occurrence of a task switch. If a task switch has occurred and the new task attempts to use the processor extension:

- Every execution of an ESC instruction is trapped if the TS flag is set.
- Execution of a WAIT instruction is trapped if the MP flag and the TS flag are both set.

Note: CLTS is used in systems programming. It is a privileged instruction, running at privilege level zero only.

CMC Complement carry flag (CF)

INSTRUCTION	OPCODE	BINARY
CMC	F5	11110101

Purpose: CMC reverses the value of the carry flag, e.g., CF becomes a 0 if it was a 1. No other flags are affected.

CMP Compare

INSTRUCTION	OPCODE	BINARY
CMP AL,imm8	3C ib	00111100
CMP AX,imm16	3D iw	00111101
CMP EAX,imm32	3D id	00111101
CMP r/m8,imm8	80 /7 ib	10000000 mm 111 r/m
CMP r/m16,imm16	81 /7 iw	10000001 mm 111 r/m
CMP r/m32,imm32	81 /7 id	10000001 mm 111 r/m
CMP r/m16,imm8	83 /7 ib	10000011 mm 111 r/m
CMP r/m32,imm8	83 /7 ib	10000011 mm 111 r/m
CMP r/m8,r8	38 /r	00111000 mm rrr r/m
CMP r/m16,r16	39 /r	00111001 mm rrr r/m
CMP r/m32,r32	39 /r	00111001 mm rrr r/m
CMP r8,m8	3A /r	00111010 mm rrr r/m
CMP r16,r/m16	3B /r	00111011 mm rrr r/m
CMP r32,r/m32	3B /r	00111011 mm rrr r/m

Purpose: CMP subtracts the source operand from the destination operand but does not store the result. Only the flags are changed. That is, CMP updates OF, SF, ZF, AF, PF, and CF, but does not alter the source or destination operands.

CMPS Compare string operands
CMPSB Compare string byte
CMPSW Compare string word
CMPSD Compare string doubleword

INSTRUCTION	OPCODE	BINARY
CMPS m8,m8	A6	10100110

```
CMPS m16,m16    A7      10100111
CMPS m32,m32    A7      10100111
```

Note: CMPSB is a common assembler mnemonic for CMPS m8,m8.
CMPSW is a common mnemonic for CMPS m16,m16.
CMPSD is a common mnemonic for CMPS m32,m32.

Purpose: These instructions operate on strings rather than on logical or numeric values. They operate on one element of a string, which might be a byte, a word, or a doubleword. The string elements are addressed by the registers ESI and EDI. After each string operation, ESI and/or EDI are automatically updated to point to the next element of the string. If DF = 0, the index registers are incremented. If DF = 1, they are decremented. The amount incremented or decremented is 1, 2, or 4, depending on the size of the string element.

CMPS subtracts the destination string element (at ES:EDI) from the source string element (at DS:ESI). It then updates the flags AF, SF, PF, CF, and OF. If the string elements are equal, ZF = 1. Otherwise, ZF = 0. If DF = 0, the 80486 increments the memory pointers ESI and EDI for two strings. The segment register used for the source address can be changed with a segment register override prefix. The destination segment register cannot be overridden.

The assembler always translates CMPS into one of the other types. CMPSB compares bytes. CMPSW compares words. CMPSD compares doublewords.

If the REPE or REPNE prefix modifies this instruction, the 80486 compares the value of the destination string element to the value of the source string element, stepping SI and DI in the direction indicated by the DF, by the indicated size, until either the REPE/REPNE condition is false or ECX counts to zero.

CMPXCHG Compare and exchange

INSTRUCTION	OPCODE	BINARY
CMPXCHG r/m8,r8	0F B0 /r	00001111 10110000
CMPXCHG r/m16,r16	0F B1 /r	00001111 10110001
CMPSCHG r/m32,r32	0F B1 /r	00001111 10110001

Purpose: CMPXCHG compares the accumulator (AL, AX, or EAX) with the destination. If they compare equal, the source operand is loaded into the destination and ZF is set. If they do not compare equal, the destination is loaded into the accumulator and ZF is reset (to 0).

CMPSCHG can be used with a LOCK prefix. To simplify the interface to the processor bus, the destination operand receives a write cycle without regard to the result of the comparison. Note that the 80486 never produces a locked read without also producing a locked write.

The AF, CF, OF, PF, and SF flags are affected as if a CMP instruction has been executed with a destination and the accumulator as operands. ZF is set if the destination and the accumulator are equal; otherwise it is reset.

CWD	Convert word to doubleword
CDQ	Convert doubleword to quadword
CWDE	Convert word to doubleword extended

INSTRUCTION	OPCODE	BINARY
CW	99	10011001
CDQ	99	10011001

Note: CDQ is for 32-bit mode.

Purpose: CWD doubles the size of the source operand. CWD extends the sign of the word in register AX throughout register DX. CWD can be used to produce a doubleword dividend from a word before a word division.

CWDE extends the sign of the word in register AX throughout EAX. CDQ extends the sign of the doubleword in EAX throughout EDX. CDQ can be used to produce a quadword dividend from a doubleword before doubleword division.

| DAA | Decimal adjust AL register after addition |

INSTRUCTION	OPCODE	BINARY
DAA	27	00100111

Purpose: DAA adjusts the result of adding two valid packed decimal operands in AL. DAA must always follow the addition of two pairs of packed decimal numbers (one digit in each half-byte) to obtain a pair of valid packed decimal digits as results.

If the low nibble of AL is greater than 9, AF is set and 6 added to AL. Otherwise AF is reset. If the high nibble is greater than 9h or the CF flag is set, then add 60h to AL and set CF. Otherwise, CF is reset.

DAS — Decimal adjust AL register after subtraction

INSTRUCTION	OPCODE	BINARY
DAA	27	00100111
DAS	2F	00101111

Purpose: DAS adjusts the result of subtracting two valid packed decimal operands in AL. DAS follows subtraction of one pair of packed decimal numbers (one digit in each half-byte) from another to obtain a pair of valid packed decimal digits as results. If the low nibble of AL is greater than 9 or if AF is set, then AL has 6 subtracted from it and AF is set. Otherwise, AF is reset. If the high nibble of AL is greater than 9h or the CF bit is set, then AL has 60h subtracted from it and CF is set. Otherwise, CF is reset.

DEC — Decrement by 1

INSTRUCTION	OPCODE	BINARY
DEC r/m8	FE /1	11111110 mm 001 r/m
DEC r/m16	FF /1	11111111 mm 001 r/m
DEC r/m32	FF /1	11111111 mm 001 r/m
DEC r16	48+rw	01001rrr
DEC r32	48+rw	01001rrr

Purpose: DEC subtracts 1 from the destination operand and replaces the result into the destination operand. DEC does not update CF. Use SUB with an operand of 1 if a Carry Flag update is desired.

DIV — Unsigned integer divide

INSTRUCTION	OPCODE	BINARY
DIV AL,r/m8	F6 /6	11110110 mm 110 r/m
DIV AX,r/m16	F7 /6	11110111 mm 110 r/m
DIV EAX,r/m32	F7 /6	11110111 mm 110 r/m

Purpose: DIV divides an unsigned number in the accumulator by the source operand. The dividend (which is the accumulator) is twice the size of the divisor (which is the source operand); the dividend is AX, DX:AX, or EDX:EAX, for divisors of 8, 16, or 32 bits. The quotient and the remainder have the same size as the divisor. The quotient is placed in AL, AX, or EAX for 8-, 16-, or 32-bit operands, respectively. The remainder is in AH, DX, or EDX. Registers and operands of DIV are summarized in Table C-1. A divisor of 0 or a quotient too large for the designated register causes an 80486 interrupt 0.

Note: Non-integer quotients are truncated to integers. The remainder is always less than the divisor. For unsigned byte division, the largest quotient is 255. For unsigned word division, the largest quotient is 65,535. For unsigned doubleword division, the largest quotient is $2^{32} - 1$.

Table C-1 Summary of registers and operands for DIV.

Length of operand 1	Dividend	Divisor	Quotient	Remainder
8	AX	Operand 1	AL	AH
16	DS:AX	Operand 1	AX	DX
32	EDX:EAX	Operand 1	EAX	EDX

ENTER   Make stack frame for procedure parameter

INSTRUCTION	OPCODE	BINARY
ENTER imm16,0	C8 iw 00	11001000
ENTER imm16,1	C8 /2 01	11001000
ENTER imm16,imm8	C8 iw ib	11001000

Purpose: ENTER creates a stack frame that can be used to implement the rules of block-structured high-level languages. A LEAVE instruction at the end of the procedure complements the ENTER.

ENTER has two parameters. The first specifies the number of bytes of dynamic storage to be allocated on the stack for the routine being entered. The second parameter, 0–31, corresponds to the lexical nesting level of the routine. This level determines how many sets of stack frame pointers the CPU copies into the new stack frame from the proceeding frame. This list of stack frames is often called the display. Lexical level has no relationship to either the protection levels or to the I/O privilege level.

ENTER creates the new display for a procedure. Then it allocates the dynamic storage space for that procedure by decrementing ESP by the number of bytes specified in the first parameter. This new value of ESP serves as the starting point for all PUSH and POP operations within that procedure.

ENTER can be used either nested or non-nested. If the lexical level is 0, the non-nested form is used. The main procedure operates at the highest logical level, level 1. The first procedure it calls operates at the next deeper level, level 2. And so on. A level 2 procedure can access the variables in the main program because a program operating at a higher logical level (calling a program at a lower level) requires that the called procedure have access to the variables of the calling program.

A procedure calling another procedure at the same level implies that they are parallel procedures and should not have access to the variables of the calling program. The new stack frame does not include the pointer for addressing the calling procedure's stack frame. ENTER treats a re-entrant procedure as a procedure calling another procedure at the same level.

F2XM1   Computer $2^x - 1$

INSTRUCTION   OPCODE   BINARY

F2XM1   09 F0   00001001 11110000

Purpose: The item in the top of stack is ST in the computation of $2^{ST} - 1$. The result of this computation replaces the initial ST. The input operand range is $-1 < ST < 1$. If the operand is out of this range, the results are undefined.

F2XM1 is designed to produce a very accurate result even when the operand is close to zero. Larger errors are incurred for operands with magnitudes very close to 1. In real mode, interrupt 7 occurs if either EM or TS in CR0 is set.

FABS   Absolute value

INSTRUCTION   OPCODE   BINARY

FABS   D9 E1   11011001 11100001

Purpose: The top stack element is changed to its absolute value. The top stack element is always positive, following the FABS instruction execution.

FADD	Real addition
FIADD	Integer addition
FADDP	Real addition and POP

INSTRUCTION	OPCODE	BINARY
FADD m32real	D8 /0	11011000
FADD m64real	DC /0	11011100
FADD ST,ST(n)	D8 C0+i	11011000 11000000
FADD ST(n),ST	DC C0+i	11011100 11000000
FADDP ST(n),ST	DE C0+i	11011110 11000000
FADD	DE C1	11011110 11000001
FIADD m32int	DA /0	11011010
FiADD m16int	DE /0	11011110

Purpose: The explicitly defined or implicitly specified floating-point operands are added, with the result being stored in the first operand. The destination (or first) operand in all cases is the stack top, except the two-operand form where the destination can be ST(n), where n is the accumulator in the stack with reference to the top of stack. If the source operand is in memory, it is automatically converted to the extended-real format.

Note: An FADDP or FADD without operands causes the stack to be popped. Thus FADD with no operands is synonymous with FADDP ST(1),ST.

| FBLD | BCD load |

INSTRUCTION	OPCODE	BINARY
FBLD m80dec	D8 /4	11011000

Purpose: The 10-byte packed BCD memory operand pointed to by m80 is converted to a temporary real value and PUSHed onto the top of the stack. The conversion is always exact. The BCD digits are assumed to be in the range 0h to 9h. An attempt to load invalid BCD digits puts an undefined temporary real value into ST.

| FBSTP | BCD store and POP |

INSTRUCTION	OPCODE	BINARY
FBSTP m80dec	DF /6	11011111

Purpose: The stack top is converted to a BCD number, which is then stored into memory and then the stack is popped. ST is rounded to an integer according to the RC field in the Control Word.

In real mode, interrupt 13 occurs if any part of the operand lies outside the effective address space from 0 to 0FFFFFh. Interrupt 7 occurs if either DM or TS in CR0 is set.

FCHS   Change sign

INSTRUCTION	OPCODE	BINARY
FCHS	D9 E0	11011001 11100000

Purpose: The sign at the top of stack element is inverted; the operation changes a negative value with a positive one, and vice versa.

In real mode, interrupt 7 occurs if either EM or TS in CR0 is set.

FCLEX   Clear exceptions
FNCLEX

INSTRUCTION	OPCODE	BINARY
FCLEX	9B DB E2	10011011 11011011 11100010
FNCLEX	DB E2	11011011 11100010

Purpose: These instructions clear all exceptions and the busy bit of the FPU Status Word. FCLEX checks for unmasked floating-point error conditions, while FNCLEX does not.

FCOM   Compare real
FCOMP   Compare real and POP
FCOMPP Compare real and POP twice

INSTRUCTION	OPCODE	BINARY
FCOM m32real	D8 /2	11011000
FCOM m64real	DC /2	11011100
FCOM ST(i)	D8 D0+i	11011000 11010000
FCOM	D8 D1	11011000 11010001

```
FCOMP  m32real   D8 /3      11011000
FCOMP  m64real   DC /3      11011100
FCOMP  ST(i)     D8 D8+i    11011000 11011000
FCOMP            D8 D9      11011000 11011001
FCOMPP           DE D9      11011110 11011001
```

Purpose: The given operand is compared with the top of stack, which can be a register or a single- or double-real operand. If no operand is encoded, ST is compared to ST(1). Following the instruction, the condition codes are set according to the table shown in Fig. A-11.

If the opcode was FCOMPP, the operand compared against the top of stack is ST(1)—the first below the top of stack. If the operand was FCOMP, the stack is popped once after comparison. Unordered comparison occurs if either of the two operands are NaNs. The sign of zero is ignored in comparisons.

FCOM generates an invalid operation exception if either operand is a quiet NaN. Usually, operations with quiet NaNs do not cause operation exceptions.

FCOS   Cosine

INSTRUCTION	OPCODE	BINARY
FCOS	D9 FF	11011001 11111111

Purpose: The cosine of ST (top of stack) is computed. After the computation, the stack top is set to the cosine of ST and 1.0 is PUSHed onto the stack. The input operand to FCOS must be in the range of absolute 0 to 2^{63}. If the source operand is within this range, C2 is set to 0 (see the section on the Status Word for the location of C2). Otherwise, C2 is set to 1, ST is left intact, and the stack-top pointer is unchanged.

FDECSTP Decrement stack pointer

INSTRUCTION	OPCODE	BINARY
FDECSTP	D9 F6	11011001 11110110

Purpose: One is subtracted from the stack-top pointer TOP in the FPU Status Word. See the section on Status Word in appendix B for the location of TOP. The effect of FDECSTP is to rotate the stack; it does not alter register tags or contents, nor does it transfer data.

FDIV   Real division
FIDIV   Integer divide
FDIVP   Real divide and POP

INSTRUCTION	OPCODE	BINARY	
FDIV m32real	D8 /6	11011000	
FDIV m64real	DC /6	11011100	
FDIV ST,ST(n)	D8 F0+i	11011000	11110000
FDIV ST(n),ST	DC F8+i	11011100	11111000
FDIVP ST(n),ST	DE F8+i	11011110	11111000
FDIV	DE F9	11011110	11111001
FIDIV m32int	DA /6	11011010	
FIDIV m16int	DE /6	11011110	

Purpose: The instructions divide the top of stack by the other oper-
and and then returns the quotient to the destination. If the source operand
is in memory, it is automatically converted to the extended-real format.

Performance of these instructions depend on the PC field in the FPU
Control Word. If PC specifies a precision of 53 bits, the instruction executes in 62 clocks; if precision is 24 bits, it executes in only 35 clocks.

FDIVR   Reverse divide
FIDIVR   Integer reverse divide
FDIVRP   Real divide reverse and POP

INSTRUCTION	OPCODE	BINARY	
FDIVR m32real	D8 /7	11011000	
FDIVR m64real	DC /7	11011100	
FDIVR ST,ST(n)	D8 F8+i	11011000	11111000
FDIVR ST(n),ST	DC F0+i	11011100	11110000
FIDIVRP ST(n),ST	DE F0+i	11011110	11110000
FDIVR	DE F1	11011110	11110001
FIDIVR m32int	DA /7	11011010	
FIDIVR m16int	DE /7	11011110	

Purpose: The instructions divide the other operand by the stack top
and returns the quotient to the destination. If the source operand is in
memory, it is automatically converted to extended-real.

Performance of these instructions depend on the PC field of the FPU
Control Word. If PC specifies a precision of 53 bits, the reverse divisions
will execute in 62 clocks; if it's 24 bits, the instructions will take 35 clocks.

FFREE Free floating-point register

INSTRUCTION	OPCODE	BINARY
FFREEST(n)	DD C0+i	11011101 11000000

Purpose: The tag-word bits associated with the specified register are set to 11b, which indicates that the specified stack element is changed to empty. Neither the floating-point stack nor the floating-point stack pointer are modified. The tag word describes the physical stack registers and FFREE gives an accumulator stack reference that is relative to the stack top.

FICOM Integer compare
FICOMP Integer compare and POP

INSTRUCTION	OPCODE	BINARY
FICOM m16real	DE /2	11011110
FICOM m32real	DA /2	11011010
FICOMP m16int	DE /3	11011110
FICOMP m32int	DA /3	11101010

Purpose: These instructions compare the stack top to the source. Following the instruction, the condition codes reflect the relation between ST and the source. The memory operand is converted to extended-real before the comparison is performed.

If either operand is a NaN or is undefined, or if a stack fault occurs, the invalid-operation exception is raised and the condition bits are set to "unordered."

FILD Integer load

INSTRUCTION	OPCODE	BINARY
FILD m16int	DF /0	11011111
FILD m32int	DB /0	11011011
FILD m64int	DF /5	11011111

Purpose: The memory word, short, or long integer specified by the first operand, is read from memory and converted into extended-real format. The stack is pushed and the number is placed in the new top of stack. The source is loaded without rounding error. ST(7) must be empty to avoid causing an invalid-operation exception.

FINCSTP   Increment stack-top pointer

INSTRUCTION	OPCODE	BINARY
FINCST	D9 F7	11011001 11110111

Purpose: This instruction allows direct control of the stack pointer. One is added to the stack pointer in the Status Word (see the section on the Status Word Register for the location of the pointer). The tag word (TW) and the contents of the floating-point stack are not updated. If FINCSTP is executed when the stack-top pointer (TOP) is 7, ST becomes 0. Popping an element off the stack causes the stack pointer to be incremented.

FINIT   Initialize processor
FNINIT

INSTRUCTION	OPCODE	BINARY
FINIT	DB E3	11011011 11100011
FNINIT	DB E3	11011011 11100011

Purpose: These instructions set all the control-word, status-word, and tag-word registers to their default values. The FPU Control Word is set to 037Fh (round to nearest, all exceptions masked, 64-bit precision). The FPU Status Word is cleared (no exception flags set, stack register R0=stack-top). The stack registers are all tagged as empty. The error pointers (both instruction and data) are cleared.

FINIT checks for unmasked floating-point error conditions before performing the initialization; FNINIT does not. Both FINIT and FNINIT leave the FPU in the same state as that which results from a hardware RESET. On the 80486 (unlike the 80386), FINIT and FNINIT clear the error pointers.

FIST   Integer store
FISTP   Integer store and POP

INSTRUCTION	OPCODE	BINARY
FIST m16int	DF /2	11011111
FIST m32int	DB /2	11011011
FISTP m16int	DF /3	11011111
FISTP m32int	DB /3	11011011
FISTP m64int	DF /7	11011111

Purpose: The stack top is rounded to a signed integer according to the RC field of the FPU Control Word; the instruction then transfers the result to the destination. ST remains unchanged.

If the value is too large to represent as an integer, an I exception is raised. The masked response is to write the most negative integer to memory.

FLD   Real load

INSTRUCTION	OPCODE	BINARY
FLD m32real	D9 /0	11011001
FLD m64real	DD /0	11011101
FLD m80real	DB /5	11011011
FLD ST(n)	D9 C0+i	11011001 11000000

Purpose: The source operand is pushed onto the top of the stack. If the operand is a single- or double-real, it is converted to a extended-real format before being pushed onto the stack. Loading an extended-real operand does not require conversion, so the I and D exceptions will not occur in this case.

FLDx   Load constant

INSTRUCTION	OPCODE	BINARY
FLD1	D9 E8	11011001 11101000
FLDL2T	D9 E9	11011001 11101001
FLDL2E	D9 EA	11011001 11101010
FLDPI	D9 EB	11011001 11101011
FLDLG2	D9 EC	11011001 11101100

```
FLDLN2      D9 ED   11011001  11101101
FLDZ        D9 EE   11011001  11101110
```

Purpose: The constant value that is specified by the instruction itself is pushed onto the stack and becomes the new top of stack. FLD is 1.0. FLDL2E is $\log_2 e$. FLDL2T is $\log_2 10$. FLDLG2 is $\log_{10} 2$. FLDLN2 is $\log_e 2$. FLDPI is the value of π. FLDZ is 0.0.

FLDCW   Load control word

INSTRUCTION	OPCODE	BINARY
FLDCW m16	D9 /5	11011001

Purpose: This instruction loads the Control Word (CW) with the value found in m16. An exception is flagged if any of the exception flags in SW are unmasked by the new Control Word. FLDCW is generally used to set up or change the FPU mode of operation.

If an exception bit in SW is set, loading a new Control Word that unmasks that exception results in a floating-point error condition. When changing modes, clear any pending exceptions before loading the new Control Word.

FLDENV   Load FPU environment

INSTRUCTION	OPCODE	BINARY
FLDENV m14/28byte	D9 /4	11011001

Purpose: This instruction loads the FPU environment from the given memory area (which should have been set up by a FSTENV or FNSTENV). This environment consists of the tag-word register, the Status Word, and the Control Word, along with the error-pointer registers of the most recent floating-point instruction executed. Note that the error-pointer registers contain information on the most recent opcode and the data referenced. If the environment image contains an unmasked exception, loading it results in a floating-point error.

The USE attribute of the current code segment determines the operand size: the 14-byte operand applies to a USE16 segment, and the 28-byte operand applies to a USE32 segment.

FMUL	Real multiply
FIMUL	Integer multiply
FMULP	Real multiply and POP

INSTRUCTION	OPCODE	BINARY	
FMUL m32real	D8 /1	11011000	
FMUL m64real	DC /1	11011100	
FMUL ST,ST(n)	D8 C8+i	11011000	11001000
FMUL ST(n),ST	DC C8+i	11011100	11001000
FMULP ST(n),ST	DE C8+i	11011110	11001000
FMUL	DE C9	11011110	11001001
FIMUL m32int	DA /1	11011010	
FIMUL m64int	DE /1	11011110	

Purpose: The specified operands are multiplied, with the result being stored in the first operand, which is the destination. The destination is the top of stack in all cases except the two-operand form, where the destination can be ST(n). If the source operand is in memory, it is automatically converted to extended-real format.

If the first operand is a memory operand, it is automatically converted to real format before any operations are performed on it. An FMUL without operands causes the stack to be popped, which makes it synonymous with FMULP ST(1),ST.

| FNOP | No operation |

INSTRUCTION	OPCODE	BINARY
FNOP	D9 D0	11011001 11010000

Purpose: FNOP performs no operation and affects nothing except the instruction pointer.

| FPATAN | Partial arctangent |

INSTRUCTION	OPCODE	BINARY
FPATAN	D9 F3	11011001 11110011

Purpose: The arctangent of ST(1)/ST is computed and the computed value is returned in radians and stored to ST(1). The result has the same sign as the operand from ST(1), and a magnitude less than π. There is no restriction on the range of arguments that FPATAN accepts.

FPREM   Partial remainder

INSTRUCTION	OPCODE	BINARY
FPREM	D9 F8	11011001 11111000

Purpose: FPREM computes the partial remainder of ST/ST(1). The remainder is computed by a series of successive scaled subtractions, so the remainder produced is exact, with no precision error possible. If the operands differ greatly in magnitude, this series of subtractions can take a very long time.

FPREM is not the remainder operation specified in IEEE Std 754; use FPREM1 to get that remainder. FPREM is supported for downward compatibility with the 8087 and 80287.

If FPREM produces a remainder that is less than the modulus, the function is complete and the C2 flag is cleared; otherwise C2 is set, and the result in ST is called the *partial remainder*. The exponent of the partial remainder is less than the exponent of the original dividend by at least 32. Software can re-execute the instruction (using the partial remainder in ST as the dividend) until C2 is cleared. A higher-priority interrupt routine that needs the FPU can force a context switch between the instructions in the remainder loop.

FPREM1   Partial remainder (IEEE Std. 754)

INSTRUCTION	OPCODE	BINARY
FPREM1	D9 F5	11011001 11110101

Purpose: FPREM1 computes the partial remainder of ST/ST(1). It is for the purpose of IEEE compatibility. The remainder is computed by a series of successive scaled subtractions, so the remainder is exact with no precision error. When the operands differ greatly in magnitude, these subtractions can take a very long time. To prevent severe degradation of interrupt latency, the instruction only partially computes the remainder. A software loop is required to complete the reduction.

FPREM1 reduces a magnitude difference up to 264 in one execution. If the reduction is complete, condition code 2 is set to 0 and condition codes

0, 3, and 1 (in that order) reflect the three least significant bits of the quotient. If the reduction is incomplete, C2 is set to 1. (See appendix B on the Control Word for the location of the condition codes.)

FPTAN   Partial tangent

INSTRUCTION	OPCODE	BINARY
FPTAN	D9 F2	11011001 11110010

Purpose: The tangent of ST is computed. After the computation, the stack top is set to the tangent of ST and 1.0 PUSHed onto the FPU stack. If the operand is outside the acceptable range, C2 is set and ST remains unchanged. The programmer must reduce the operand to an absolute value smaller than 2^{63} by subtracting an appropriate integer multiple of 2π.

FPTAN pushes a 1.0 into the FPU stack after computing the tan(ST) to maintain compatibility with the 8087 and 80287 coprocessors; it also simplifies the calculation of other trigonometric functions. For instance, the cotangent (the reciprocal of the tangent) can be computed by executing FDIVR after FPTAN.

Note: ST(7) must be empty to avoid an invalid-operation exception. Also note that the 80486 checks for interrupts while performing this instruction; FPTAN will be aborted to service an interrupt.

FRNDINT Round to integer

INSTRUCTION	OPCODE	BINARY
FRNDINT	D9 FC	11011001 11111100

Purpose: FRNDINT rounds the top of stack element to an integer. The rounding obeys the RC setting found in the Control Word (see appendix B on the Control Word for the location of RC). The four rounding modes are: 00 = nearest, 01 = minus infinity, 10 = plus infinity, and 11 = chop.

FRSTOR Restore state

INSTRUCTION	OPCODE	BINARY
FRSTOR m94/108byte	DB /4	11011011

Purpose: This instruction reloads the complete state of the FPU from a 108-byte location given by the source operand. The FPU environment consists of a the FPU Control Word, Status Word, Tag Word, and error pointers (both instruction and data). The stack registers, beginning with ST and ending with ST(7), are in the 80 bytes that immediately follow the environment image. If the state image contains an unmasked exception, loading it results in a floating-point error.

The environment layout in memory depends on both the operand size and the current operating mode of the 80486. The USE attribute of the current code segment determines the operand size: the 14-byte operand applies to a USE16 segment, and the 28-byte operand to a USE32 segment.

FSAVE   Save FPU state
FNSAVE

INSTRUCTION	OPCODE	BINARY
FSAVE m94/108bytes	9B DD /6	10011011 11011101
FNSAVE m94/108bytes	DD /6	11011101

Purpose: These instructions store the complete state of the FPU into a memory location specified by the operand. This environment consists of the FPU Control Word, the Status Word, and the Tag-Word registers, the error-pointer registers, and the complete floating-point stack (eight 80-bit registers).

The environment layout in memory depends on both the operand size and the current operating mode of the 80486. The USE attribute of the current code segment determines the operand size: the 14-byte operand applies to a USE16 segment, and the 28-byte operand to a USE32 segment.

FSAVE and FNSAVE do not store the FPU state until all FPU activity completes. That means that the same image reflects the FPU state after any previously decoded instruction has been executed.

FSCALE   Power of Two scaling

INSTRUCTION	OPCODE	BINARY
FSCALE	D9 FD	11011001 11111101

Purpose: FSCALE interprets the value in ST(1) as an integer and adds this integer to the exponent of ST. This means that FSCALE provides rapid multiplication or division by integral powers of 2.

There is no limit on the range of the scale factor in ST(1). If the value is not integral, FSCALE uses the nearest integer that is smaller in magnitude; that is, it chops the value toward 0. If the resulting integer is zero, the value in ST is not changed.

FSIN   Sine

INSTRUCTION	OPCODE	BINARY
FSIN	D9 FE	11011001 11111110

Purpose: FSIN computes the sine of STf and places the result in ST. Expressed in radians, ST must lie in the range of absolute 0 to 2^{63}. If the operand is outside the acceptable range, C2 is set and ST remains unchanged. The programmer must reduce the operand to an absolute value smaller than 2^{63} by subtracting an appropriate integer multiple of 2π. The 80486 periodically checks for interrupts while performing FSIN; the instruction will be aborted to service an interrupt.

FSINCOS Sine and cosine

INSTRUCTION	OPCODE	BINARY
FSINCOS	D9 FB	10111001 11111011

Purpose: FSINCOS computes both the sine and cosine of ST. After the computation is completed, the stack top is set to the sine of ST and the cosine is pushed onto the stack. ST must be in the range of absolute 0 to 2^{63}. If it is, C2 is set to 0. Otherwise, C2 is set to 1 and ST and TOP are unchanged.

Note: It is faster to execute FSINCOS than to execute both FSIN and FCOS. Also note that the 80486 periodically checks for interrupts while performing FSINCOS; the instruction will be aborted to service an interrupt.

FSQRT   Square root

INSTRUCTION	OPCODE	BINARY
FSQRT	D9 FA	11011001 11111010

Purpose: The top of the stack is replaced with the square root of the top of the stack.

FST   Store real

INSTRUCTION	OPCODE	BINARY	
FST m32real	D9 /2	11011001	
FST m64real	DD /2	11011101	
FST ST(n)	DD D0+i	11011101	11010000
FSTP m32real	D9 /3	11011001	
FSTP m64real	DD /3	11011101	
FSTP m80real	DB /7	11011011	
FSTP ST(n)	DD D8+i	11011101	11011000

Purpose: The top of stack is stored in the destination, which can be another register or a single- or double-real memory operand. FSTP copies and then POPs ST; it accepts extended-real memory operands as well as types accepted by FST. The invalid-operation exception is not raised when the destination is a non-empty stack element.

If the top of stack is a single- or double-real, the top of stack is first converted according to RC in the Control Word, and the exponent is converted to the width and bias of the destination format. The overflow and underflow conditions are checked for as well.

If the top of stack is a NaN or an infinity, the stack-top exponent and significand are chopped rather than rounded to fit the destination. Also, the exponent is not converted; it too is chopped on the right. These operations preserve the value's itentity as infinity or NaN (exponent all ones).

FSTCW   Store FPU control word
FNSTCW

INSTRUCTION	OPCODE	BINARY	
FSTCW m16	9B D9 /7	10011011	11011001
FNSTCW m16	D9 /7	11011001	

Purpose: These instructions store the FPU Control Word into a t-byte memory location. FSTCW checks for unmasked floating-point exceptions before storing the word; FNSTCW does not.

FSTENV   Store FPU environment
FNSTENV

INSTRUCTION	OPCODE	BINARY
FSTENV m14/28byte	9B D9 /6	10011011 11011001
FNSTENV m14/28byte	D9 /6	11011001

Purpose: These instructions store the FPU environment to the given memory location. This environment consists of the FPU Control Word, the Status Word, the Tag-Word register, and the error pointers of the most recent floating-point instruction executed. FSTENV checks for unmasked floating-point errors before storing the FPU environment; FNSTENV does not.

Exception handlers often use these instructions to have access to the FPU error pointers. After saving the environment, the instructions set all the exception masks in the FPU Control Word; this prevents floating-point errors from interrupting an exception handler.

FSTENV and FNSTENV do not store the environment until all FPU activity completes. That means that the saved environment reflects the FPU state after any previously decoded instruction has been executed.

FSTSW   Store Status Word
FNSTSW

INSTRUCTION	OPCODE	BINARY
FSTSW m2byte	9B DF /7	10011011 11011111
FSTSW	9B DF E0	10011011 11011111 11100000
FNSTSW m2byte	DF /7	11011111
FNSTSW AX	DF E0	11011111 11100000

Purpose: These instructions write the current of the FPU Status Word to the destination, which can be either a two-byte location in memory or the AX register. FNSTSW checks for unmasked floating-point errors before storing the Status Word; FNSTSW does not. When FNSTSW AX is executed, AX is updated before the 80486 executes any further instructions. The Status Word stored is that from the completion of the prior ESC.

FSUB   Real subtraction
FISUB   Integer subtraction
FSUBP   Real subtraction and POP

INSTRUCTION	OPCODE	BINARY	
FSUB m32real	D8 /4	11011000	
FSUB m64real	DC /4	11011100	
FSUB ST,ST(n)	D8 E0+i	11011000	11100000
FSUB ST(n),ST	DC E8+i	11011100	11101000
FSUBP ST(n),ST	DE E8+i	11011110	11101000
FSUB	DE E9	11011110	11101001
FISUB m32int	DA /4	11011010	
FISUB m16int	DE /4	11011110	

Purpose: The operand is subtracted from the stack top, with the result being stored in the first operand, the destination. The destination is the stack top in all cases, except the two-operand form where the destination can be ST(n). If the first operand is a memory operand, it is automatically converted to extended-real format before any operations are performed with it. An FSUB without operands causes the stack to be popped, which makes it synonymous with FSUBP ST(1),ST.

FSUBR   Real reverse subtract
FISUBR   Integer reverse subtract
FSUBRP   Real reverse subtract with POP

INSTRUCTION	OPCODE	BINARY	
FSUBR m32real	D8 /5	11011000	
FSUBR m64real	DC /5	11011100	
FSUBR ST,ST(n)	D8 E8+i	11011000	11101000
FSUBR ST(n),ST	DC E0+i	11011100	11100000
FSUBRP ST(n),ST	DE E0+i	11011110	11100000
FSUBR	DE E1	11011110	11100001
FISUBR m32int	DA /5	11011010	
FISUBR m16int	DE /5	11011110	

Purpose: The stack top is subtracted from the other operand and the difference returned to the destination (the first operand). The destination is the stack top in all cases except the two-operand form where the destination can be ST(n). If the first operand is a memory operand, it is automatically converted to extended-real format before any operations are performed with it. An FSUBR without operands causes the stack to be popped, which makes it synonymous with FSUBRP ST(1),ST.

FTST   Test

INSTRUCTION	OPCODE	BINARY
FTST	D9 E4	11011001 11100100

Purpose: The stack top is numerically compared against 0. The condition code bits in the Status Word are set according to those shown in Table C-2.

Invalid-operation is raised if ST is a NaN or if a stack fault occurs; the condition bits are set to "unordered." The sign of zero is ignored in comparisons.

Table C-2   Test condition codes.

Operation	C3	C2	C0
ST > 0.0	0	0	0
ST < 0.0	0	0	1
ST = 0.0	1	0	0
Unordered	1	1	1

FUCOM   Unordered compare
FUCOMP   Unordered compare with POP
FUCOMPP   Unordered compare and POP twice

INSTRUCTION	OPCODE	BINARY
FUCOM ST(n)	DD E0+i	11011101 11100000
FUCOM	DD E1	11011101 11100001
FUCOMP ST(n)	DD E8	11011101 11101000
FUCOMP	DD E9	11011101 11101001
FUCOMPP	DA E9	11011010 11101001

Purpose: The source (which must be a register) is compared with the top of the stack. If no operand is coded, ST is compared with ST(1). The condition codes are set as shown in Table C-3.

If the opcode was FUCOMPP, the operand compared against the top of stack is ST(1) and the stack popped twice. If the operand was FUCOMP, the stack is popped once. If either of the operands is a NaN or if a stack fault occurs, the invalid-operation occurs and the condition bits are set to "unordered." The sign of zero is ignored in the comparisons.

Table C-3   Unordered compare condition codes.

Operation	C3	C2	C0
ST > Operand 1	0	0	0
ST < Operand 1	0	0	1
ST = Operand 1	1	0	0
Unordered	1	1	1

FWAIT   Wait

INSTRUCTION	OPCODE	BINARY
FWAIT	9B	10011011

Purpose: This instruction causes the 80486 to check for pending unmasked numeric exceptions before proceeding. FWAIT is not actually an ESC instruction, but an alternate mnemonic for WAIT.

If you code FWAIT after an ESC, this ensures that any unmasked floating-point exception that the instruction might cause is handled before the 80486 has a chance to modify the instruction's results.

FXAM   Examine

INSTRUCTION	OPCODE	BINARY
FXAM	D9 E5	11011001 11100101

Table C-4   Examine compare codes.

ST Value	C3	C2	C1	C0
+ Unsupported	0	0	0	0
+ NaN	0	0	0	1
− Unsupported	0	0	1	0
− NaN	0	0	1	1
+ Normal	0	1	0	0
+ Infinity	0	1	0	1
− Normal	0	1	1	0
− Infinity	0	1	1	1
+ 0	1	0	0	0
+ Empty	1	0	0	1
− 0	1	0	1	0
− Empty	1	0	1	1
+ Denormal	1	1	0	0
+ Empty	1	1	0	1
− Denormal	1	1	1	0
− Empty	1	1	1	1

Purpose: The stack top is examined. The condition codes of the Status Word are modified according to Table C-4. The unsupported entry in the table refers to any pseudo-NaN, pseudo-infinity, or pseudo-zero.

FXCH   Exchange register contents

INSTRUCTION	OPCODE	BINARY	
FXCH ST(n)	D9 C8+i	11011001	11001000
FXCH	D9 C9	11011001	11001001

Purpose: FXCH swaps the contents of the destination and stack-top.

If a destination is not coded, ST(1) is used. These instructions provide a convenient way to use the various instructions that operate only on the top of stack, such as FSQRT and FSIN.

FXTRACT Extract exponent and significand

INSTRUCTION   OPCODE   BINARY

FXTRACT   D9 F4   11011001 11110100

Purpose: FXTRACT splits the value in ST into its exponent and significand. The significand and sign are pushed onto the stack, as the new top-of-stack. Thus, the original stack top is decomposed into a true exponent, ST(1), and a significand, ST. The significand has an exponent of zero.

If the operand is zero, ST(1)—the exponent—is set to negative infinity and ST—the significand—is set to 0 with the same sign as the original stack top. If the operand was infinity, the ST(1) exponent is positive infinity and the ST significand is infinity with the sign of the original stack top.

FYL2X   Compute Y × log$_2$X

INSTRUCTION   OPCODE   BINARY

FYL2X   D9 F1   11011001 11110001

Purpose: FYL2X computes the base-2 logarithm of ST; it then multiplies the logarithm by ST(1) and returns the resulting value to ST(1). It then POPs ST. The operand in ST cannot be negative. The 80486 periodically checks interrupts while executing this instruction, which will be aborted so the 80486 can service the interrupt.

FYL2XP1 Compute Y × log$_2$ (X + 1)

INSTRUCTION   OPCODE   BINARY

FYL2XP1   D9 F9   11011001 11111001

Purpose: FYL2XP1 computes the base-2 logarithm of (ST + 1.0); it then multiplies the logarithm by ST(1) and returns the resulting value to ST(1). It then POPs ST. ST must be in the range shown in Fig. C-2. The

$- (1 - \sqrt{2}/2)$ to $+ (1 - \sqrt{2}/2)$

80486 periodically checks for interrupts while executing this instruction; it will abort the instruction to service the interrupt.

HLT Halt

INSTRUCTION	OPCODE	BINARY
HLT	F4	11110100

Purpose: HLT stops the execution of all instructions and places the 80486 in a halt state. An NMI, reset, or an enabled interrupt will resume execution. A HLT would normally be the last instruction in a sequence that shuts down the system, such as for a checkpoint after a power failure is detected.

IDIV Signed divide

INSTRUCTION	OPCODE	BINARY
IDIV r/m8	F6 /7	11110110 mm 111 r/m
IDIV AX,r/m16	F7 /7	11110111 mm 111 r/m
IDIV EAX,r/m32	F7 /7	11110111 mm 111 r/m

Purpose: IDIV does signed division. The dividend, quotient, and remainder are implicitly allocated to fixed registers (see Table C-5), while only the divisor is given as an explicit r/m operand. The divisor determines which registers are to be used. Table C-5 shows which registers to use for IDIV. Non-integral quotients are truncated toward zero. Remainders are

Table C-5   IDIV registers.

Size	Divisor	Quotient	Remainder	Dividend
Byte	r/m 8	AL	AH	AX
Word	r/m 16	AX	DX	DX:AX
Dword	r/m 32	EAX	EDX	EDX:EAX

always the same sign as the dividend and always have less magnitude than the divisor.

An interrupt 0 is taken if a zero divisor or a quotient too large for the destination register is generated. If a divide by zero occurs, the quotient and remainder are undefined.

IMUL	Signed integer multiply

INSTRUCTION	OPCODE	BINARY
IMUL r/m8	F6 /5	11110110 mm 101 r/m
IMUL r/m16	F7 /5	11110111 mm 101 r/m
IMUL r/m32	F7 /5	11110111 mm 101 r/m
IMUL r16,r/m16	OF AF /r	00001111 10101111 mm rrr r/m
IMUL r32,r/m32	OF AF /r	00001111 10101111 mm rrr r/m
IMUL r16,r/m16,imm8	6B /r ib	01101011 mm rrr r/m
IMUL r32,r/m32,imm8	6B /r ib	01101011 mm rrr r/m
IMUL r16,imm8	6B /r ib	01101011 mm rrr r/m
IMUL r32,imm8	6B /r ib	01101011 mm rrr r/m
IMUL r16,r/m16,imm16	69 /r iw	01101001 mm rrr r/m
IMUL r32,r/m32,imm32	69 /r id	01101001 mm rrr r/m
IMUL r16,imm16	69 /r iw	01101001 mm rrr r/m
IMUL r32,imm32	69 /r id	01101001 mm rrr r/m

Purpose: IMUL performs a signed multiplication operation. This instruction has three variations. In the one-operand form, the operand might be a byte, word, or doubleword located in memory or in a general register. IMUL uses EAX and EDX as implicit operands in the same way that MUL does.

In a two-operand form, one of the source operands can be in any general register while the other can be either in memory or in a general register. The product replaces the general-register operand. If the result is within the range of the first operand, CF and OF are zero. Otherwise, CF and OF are set to 1.

In a three-operand form, two operands are source and one is destination. One of the source operands is an immediate value stored in the instruction. The second can be in memory or in any general register. The product can be stored in any general register. The immediate operand is treated as signed. If the immediate operand is a byte, the processor automatically sign-extends it to the size of the second operand before doing the multiplication. If the result is within the range of the first operand, CF and OF are zero. Otherwise, CF and OF are set to 1.

IN — Input from port

INSTRUCTION	OPCODE	BINARY
IN AL,imm8	E4 ib	11100100
IN AX,imm8	E5 ib	11100101
IN EAX,imm8	E5 ib	11100101
IN AL,DX	EC	11101100
IN AX,DX	ED	11101101
IN EAX,DX	ED	11101101

Purpose: IN brings a byte, word, or dword from a specified port and stores it in register AL, AX, or EAX, respectively. The port is specified by the second operand and is in the range of 0 to 64K – 1. The port is accessed by using an immediate operand or by placing its number into the DX register and using an IN instruction with DX as the second parameter. The immediate byte allows ports 0–255 to be accessed, in which case the upper bits of the port are always 0. The register form (DX) allows for the full range to be used. An exception occurs if the current task has insufficient privilege for the I/O.

INC — Increment by 1

INSTRUCTION	OPCODE	BINARY			
INC r/m8	FE /0	11111110	mm	000	r/m
INC r/m1	FF /0	11111111	mm	000	r/m
INC r/m3	FF /0	11111111	mm	000	r/m
INC r16	40+rw	01000000	rrr		
INC r32	40+rd	01000000	rrr		

Purpose: INC adds 1 to the destination operand, but (unlike ADD) INC does not affect CF. Other flags are set according to the result. Use ADD with an operand of 1 if the CF update is desired.

INS	Input string from port
INSB	Input byte
INSW	Input word
INSD	Input doubleword

INSTRUCTION	OPCODE	BINARY
INS r/m8,DX	6C	01101100
INS r/m16,DX	6D	01101101
INS r/m32,DX	6D	01101101

Note: INSB is a common assembler mnemonic for INS r/m8,DX
INSW is a common assembler mnemonic for INS r/m16,DX
INSD is a common assembler mnemonic for INS r/m32,DX

Purpose: These instructions allow a read from a specified device into memory (ES:EDI), the input device being specified in the DX register. After the transfer is made, EDI is updated to point to the next string location, depending on how DF is set. If DF = 0, EDI increments by 1, 2, or 4. If DF = 1, EDI decrements by 1, 2, or 4. The data is read into the segment specified by ES and no segment override is possible. INS does not allow port number specification as an immediate value. The port must be addressed through DX.

These instructions normally use a REP prefix, to indicate the reading of the number of bytes as specified in CX. An exception is raised if the current task has insufficient privilege to perform I/O.

INT	Call to interrupt procedure
INTO	Interrupt on overflow

INSTRUCTION	OPCODE	BINARY
INT 3	CC	11001100
INT imm8	CD ib	11001101
INTO	CE	11001110

Purpose: INT transfers control from one code segment location to another. These locations can be within the same code segment (near) or in different code segments (far). INT is a software-generated interrupt that allows a programmer to transfer control to an interrupt service routine from within a program.

When any of the INTs are used, the flags register, the code segment registers, and the instruction pointer is pushed onto the stack. When CS is PUSHed onto the stack, a full 32-bit word is PUSHed. This keeps the stack aligned, which improves the 80486 performance.

INT n activates the interrupt service that corresponds to the number coded in the instruction. INT can specify any interrupt type. Note that Interrupts 031 are reserved by Intel. INT n returns control at the end of the service routine with an IRET.

INTO invokes Interrupt 4 if the Overflow Flag (OF) is set and Interrupt 4 is reserved for this purpose. OF is set by several arithmetic, logical, and string instructions.

INT 3 is a single-byte form (the breakpoint instruction), which is useful for debugging.

INVD   Invalidate cache

INSTRUCTION   OPCODE   BINARY

INVD   0F 08   00001111 00001000

Purpose: This instruction causes the internal cache to be flushed, and a special-function bus cycle issued that indicates that external caches should also be flushed. Any data held in write-back external cache is discarded. Note that this instruction is not supported on any predecessor processors (8086 through 80386) and the instruction can change in future Intel processors.

INVLPG   Invalidate TLB entry

INSTRUCTION   OPCODE   BINARY

INVLGP m   0F 01 /7   00001111 00000001

Purpose: INVLPG is used to invalidate a single entry in the TLB, the cache used for page table entries. If the TLB entry maps to the address of the memory operand, that TLB entry is marked invalid. Note that this instruction is not supported on any predecessor processors (8086 through 80386) and the instruction might change in future Intel processors.

IRET	Return from interrupt
IRETD	Return from interrupt (32-bit mode)

INSTRUCTION	OPCODE	BINARY
IRET	CF	11001111
IRETD	CF	11001111

Purpose: IRET returns control to an interrupted procedure. If the NT flag is cleared, IRET returns from an interrupt procedure without a task switch. The code returned to must be equally or less privileged than the interrupt routine. If the destination code is less privileged, IRET also pops the stack pointer and SS from the stack. If the NT flag is set, IRET reverses the operation of a CALL or INT that caused the task switch. The updated state of the task executing the IRET is saved in its TSS. If the task is reentered later, the code that follows the IRET instruction is executed.

In real address mode, IRET POPs the flags register, the code segment register, and the instruction pointer from the stack. In protected mode, IRET depends on the setting of the Nested Task (NT) bit in the flag register. When the new flag image is popped from the stack, the IOPL bits in the flag register are changed only when CPL equals 0.

The registers are PUSHed onto the stack by the interrupt mechanism. When CS is popped, the full 32-bit word is popped for stack alignment and the upper 16 bits are discarded. Stack alignment improves 80486 performance.

Note: In the case of IRET, the flags register is FLAGS. If IRETD is used, then it's the EFLAGS register.

JMP	Jump
Jcc	Jump on condition code

INSTRUCTION	OPCODE	BINARY
JA rel8	77 cb	01110111
JAE rel8	73 cb	01110011
JB rel8	72 cb	01110010
JBE rel8	76 cb	01110110
JC rel8	72 cb	01110010
JCXZ rel8	E3 cb	11100011
JECXZ rel8	E3 cb	11100011
JE rel8	74 cb	01110100
JZ rel8	74 cb	01110100

JG rel8	7F cb	01111111
JGE rel8	7D cb	01111101
JL rel8	7C cb	01111100
JLE rel8	7E cb	01111110
JNA rel8	76 cb	01110110
JNAE rel8	72 cb	01110010
JNB rel8	73 cb	01110011
JNBE rel8	77 cb	01110111
JNC rel8	73 cb	01110011
JNE rel8	75 cb	01110101
JNG rel8	7E cb	01111110
JNGE rel8	7C cb	01111100
JNL rel8	7D cb	01111101
JNLE rel8	7F cb	01111111
JNO rel8	71 cb	01110001
JNP rel8	7B cb	01111011
JNS rel8	79 cb	01111001
JNZ rel8	75 cb	01110101
JO rel8	70 cb	01110000
JP rel8	7A cb	01111010
JPE rel8	7A cb	01111010
JPO rel8	7B cb	01111011
JS rel8	78 cb	01111000
JZ rel8	74 cb	01110100
JA rel16/32	0F 87 cw/cd	00001111 10000111
JAE rel16/32	0F 83 cw/cd	00001111 10000011
JB rel16/32	0F 82 cw/cd	00001111 10000010
JBE rel16/32	0F 86 cw/cd	00001111 10000110
JC rel16/32	0F 82 cw/cd	00001111 10000010
JE rel16/32	0F 84 cw/cd	00001111 10000100
JZ rel16/32	0F 84 cw/cd	00001111 10000100
JG rel16/32	0F 8F cw/cd	00001111 10001111
JGE rel16/32	0F 8D cw/cd	00001111 10001101
JL rel16/32	0F 8C cw/cd	00001111 10001100
JLE rel16/32	0F 8E cw/cd	00001111 10001110
JNA rel16/32	0F 86 cw/cd	00001111 10000110
JNAE rel16/32	0F 82 cw/cd	00001111 10000010
JNB rel16/32	0F 83 cw/cd	00001111 10000011
JNBE rel16/32	0F 87 cw/cd	00001111 10000111
JNC rel16/32	0F 83 cw/cd	00001111 10000011
JNE rel16/32	0F 85 cw/cd	00001111 10000101
JNG rel16/32	0F 8E cw/cd	00001111 10001110
JNGE rel16/32	0F 8C cw/cd	00001111 10001100
JNL rel16/32	0F 8D cw/cd	00001111 10001101

JNLE rel16/32	OF 8F cw/cd	00001111 10001111
JNO rel16/32	OF 81 cw/cd	00001111 10000001
JNP rel16/32	OF 8B cw/cd	00001111 10001011
JNS rel16/32	OF 89 cw/cd	00001111 10001001
JNZ rel16/32	OF 85 cw/cd	00001111 10000101
JO rel16/32	OF 80 cw/cd	00001111 10000000
JP rel16/32	OF 8A cw/cd	00001111 10001010
JPE rel16/32	OF 8A cw/cd	00001111 10001010
JPO rel16/32	OF 8B cw/cd	00001111 10001011
JS rel16/32	OF 88 cw/cd	00001111 10001000
JZ rel16/32	OF 84 cw/cd	00001111 10000100

Purpose: JMP transfers control from one code segment location to another. The Jcc jumps depend on the flags, as shown at the end of the next two paragraphs. These locations can be within the same code segment (near) or in different code segments (far). JMP unconditionally transfers control to the target location and is a one-way transfer. JMP does not save a return address on the stack as CALL does.

JMP's implementation varies depending on whether the address is directly specified within the instruction or indirectly through a register or memory. A direct JMP includes the destination address as part of the instruction. An indirect JMP gets the destination address through a register or a pointer variable. An indirect JMP specifies an absolute address by one of the following ways: (1) a register modifies the address of the memory pointer to select a destination address; (2) the program can JMP to a location specified by a general register (EAX, EDX, ECX, EBX, EBP, ESI, or EDI)—the 80486 moves this 32-bit value into EIP and resumes execution; or (3) the 80486 obtains the destination address from a memory operand specified in the instruction.

The following Jcc conditional transfer instructions might or might not transfer control, depending on the state of the flags when the instruction executes. The flags are assumed to have been set in some meaningful way by preceding instruction(s).

JA/JNBE	Above, not below nor equal	lCF = 0, ZF = 0
JAE/JNB	Above or equal, not below	CF = 0
JB/JNAE	Below, not above nor equal	CF = 1
JBE/JNA	Below or equal, not above	CF = 1, ZF = 1
JC	Carry	CF = 1
JE/JZ	Equal, zero	ZF = 1
JNC	Not carry	CF = 0
JNE/JNZ	Not equal, not zero	ZF = 0
JNP/JPO	Not parity, parity odd	PF = 0
JP/JPE	Parity, parity even	PF = 1

The following Jcc instructions are signed control transfers:

JG/JNLE	Greater, not less nor equal	ZF = 0, SF = OF
JGE/JNL	Greater or equal, not less	SF = OF
JL/JNGE	Less, not greater nor equal	SF = OF
JLE/JNG	Less or equal, not greater	SF = OF, ZF = 1
JNO	Not overflow	OF = 0
JNS	Not sign	SF = 0
JO	Overflow	OF = 1

JCXZ (Jump if ECX is zero) branches to the label specified in the instruction if it finds a value of 0 in the ECX register. JCXZ is useful in that sometimes it is desirable to design a loop that executes zero times if the count variable in ECX is initialized to zero. When used with repeated string scan and compare instructions, JCXZ determines whether the repetitions ended due to a zero in ECX or to satisfaction of the scan or compare conditions.

LAHF   Load flags into AH register

INSTRUCTION	OPCODE	BINARY
LAHF	9F	10011111

Purpose: Though specific instructions exist to alter CF and DF, there is no direct way of altering the other applications-oriented flags. The flag-transfer instructions (LAHF and SAHF) allow a program to alter the other flag bits with the bit-manipulation instructions after transferring these flags to the stack or the AH register.

LAHF copies SF, ZF, AF, PF, and CF to AH bits 7, 6, 4, 2, and 0, respectively. The contents of the remaining bits (5, 3, and 1) are undefined. The flags remain unaffected (see Fig. C-3).

```
7 6 5 4 3 2 1 0
┌─────────────────┐
│ S Z   A   P   C │
│ F F 0 F 0 F 1 F │
└─────────────────┘
```
C-3   Low byte of the Flags register.

LAR   Load access rights byte

INSTRUCTION	OPCODE	BINARY
LAR r16,r/m16	OF 02 /r	00001111 00000010 mm rrr r/m
LAR r32,r/m32	OF 02 /r	00001111 00000010 mm rrr r/m

Purpose: LAR reads a segment descriptor and puts the Granularity (bit 23), Programmer Available (bit 20), Present (bit 15), DPL (bit 14), Type (bit 9-11), and Accessed (bit 8) into a 32-bit register, the first operand. If you specify a 16-bit register as the first operand, the Granularity and Programmer Available bits are not moved.

The segment attribute field is simply the high-order four bytes of the descriptor ANDed with 00FxFF00h, where x indicates that bits 16 through 19 are undefined in the value loaded by LAR.

Table C-6   Valid special segment and gate descriptor types.

Type	Name
0	Undefined, invalid
1	Available 80286 TSS
2	Local Descriptor Table
3	Busy 80286 TSS
4	80286 Call Gate
5	80286/80386 Task Gate
6	80286 Interrupt Gate
7	80286 Trap Gate
8	Undefined, invalid
9	Available 80386 TSS
A	Undefined, invalid
B	Busy 80386 TSS
C	80386 Call Gate
D	Undefined, invalid
E	80386 Interrupt Gate
F	80386 Trap Gate

Note: The only valid special segment and gate descriptor types are shown in Table C-6. The descriptor specified by the selector in the first operand must be within the descriptor table limits, have a valid Type field, and be accessible at both CPL and RPL of the selector in the second operand compared to DPL. If so, ZF is set to 1 and the segment attributes are loaded to operand 1. If not, ZF is set to zero and the first operand is unmodified.

LEA — Load effective address

INSTRUCTION	OPCODE	BINARY
LEA r16,m	8D /r	10001101 mm rrr r/m
LEA r32,m	8D /r	10001101 mm rrr r/m

Purpose: LEA transfers the offset of the source operand, rather than its value, to the destination operand. The source operand must be a memory operand. The destination operand must be a general register. LEA is particularly useful for initializing registers before the execution of the string primitives or the XLAT.

LEAVE — High-level procedure exit

INSTRUCTION	OPCODE	BINARY
LEAVE	C9	11001001

Purpose: LEAVE reverses the action of a previous ENTER. LEAVE does not use any operands. LEAVE copies EBP to ESP to release all stack space allocated to the procedure by the most recent ENTER. Then LEAVE POPs the old value of EBP from the stack. A subsequent RET can then remove any arguments that were pushed on the stack by the calling program for use by the called procedure.

LGDT — Load global descriptor table register
LIDT — Load interrupt descriptor table register

INSTRUCTION	OPCODE	BINARY
LGDT m16&32	0F 01 /2	00001111 00000001 mm 010 r/m
LIDT m16&32	0F 01 /3	00001111 00000001 mm 011 r/m

Purpose: LGDT loads the global descriptor table (GDT) register. LGDT loads the global descriptor table (GDTR) from the 48-bit pseudo-descriptor given in the instruction. This 48-bit group has two components—the limit and the base. The 16-bit limit is stored at the low word and the 32-bit base at the high dword.

LIDT tells the hardware where to go in case of interrupts. LIDT loads the interrupt descriptor table (IDTR) from the 48-bit pseudo-descriptor given in the instruction. This 48-bits has two components—the limit and the base. The 16-bit limit is stored at the low word and the 32-bit base at the high dword.

Both GDT and IDT are loaded at system reset (initialization of the operating system), which is usually at the beginning of the work session.

LGS	Load full pointer
LSS	Load pointer using SS
LDS	Load pointer using DS
LES	Load pointer using ES
LFS	Load pointer using FS

INSTRUCTION	OPCODE	BINARY
LDS r16,m16:16	C5 /r	11000101 mm rrr r/m
LDS r32,m16:32	C5 /r	11000101 mm rrr r/m
LSS r16,m16:16	0F B2 /r	00001111 10110010 mm rrr r/m
LSS r32,m16:32	0F B2 /r	00001111 10110010 mm rrr r/m
LES r16,m16:16	C4 /r	11000100 mm rrr r/m
LES r32,m16:32	C4 /r	11000100 mm rrr r/m
LFS r16,m16:16	0F B4 /r	00001111 10110100 mm rrr r/m
LFS r32,m16:32	0F B4 /r	00001111 10110100 mm rrr r/m
LGS r16,m16:16	0F B5 /r	00001111 10110101 mm rrr r/m
LGS r32,m16:32	0F B5 /r	00001111 10110101 mm rrr r/m

Purpose: The data pointer instructions load a pointer that consists of a segment selector and an offset into a segment register and a general register.

LDS transfers a pointer variable from the source operand to DS and the destination register. The source operand must be a memory operand. The destination operand must be a general register. DS receives the segment-selector of the pointer. The destination register receives the offset part of the pointer, which points to a specific location within the segment. The other instructions use the various registers, as noted in the instruction mnemonic.

LSS is particularly important because it allows the two registers that identify the stack (SS:ESP) to be changed in one operation that cannot be interrupted.

LLDT — Load Local Descriptor Table Register (LDTR)

INSTRUCTION	OPCODE	BINARY
LLDT r/m16	OF 00 /2	00001111 00000000 mm 010 r/m

Purpose: The Local Descriptor Table (LDT) is loaded whenever a task or major subsystem gains or regains control of the system. LLDT loads the Local Descriptor Table Register (LDTR). The operand (memory or register) should hold a selector to the GDT. The descriptor registers are not affected and the LDT field in the task state segment does not change. The first operand might be a null selector, which causes the LDT to be marked invalid. Loading a selector naming an LDT segment raises a segment load exception if LDTR contains a null selector.

LMSW — Load Machine Status Word (MSW)

INSTRUCTION	OPCODE	BINARY
LMSW r/m16	OF 01 /6	00001111 00000001 mm 110 r/m

Purpose: LMSW loads the MSW into CR0 from the source as specified in the first operand. LMSW can be used to switch to Protected Mode, by setting the PE bit to 1. If so, the instruction queue must be flushed and LMSW followed by an intra-segment jump instruction. LMSW will not switch back to Real Address Mode; that is, you cannot alter the PE bit to zero with an LMSW.

For compatibility with the 80286, the ET bit of MSW is not altered by the LMSW instruction. ET is the processor Extension Type.

LOCK — Assert LOCK# signal prefix

INSTRUCTION	OPCODE	BINARY
LOCK	F0	11110000

Purpose: LOCK asserts a hold on shared memory so that the 80486 has exclusive use of it during the instruction that immediately follows the LOCK. LOCK's integrity is not affected by memory field alignment. LOCK will only work with:

BT, BTC, BTR, BTS	memory, reg/imm
ADD, ADC, AND, OR, SBB, SUB, XOR	memory, reg/imm
DEC, INC, NEG, NOT	memory
XCHG	reg, memory or memory, reg

An undefined opcode trap is generated if LOCK is used with any instruction not listed here. Note that XCHG always asserts LOCK# whether or not it has the LOCK prefix.

Note: LOCK is not assured if another 80486 is concurrently executing an instruction that has any of the following characteristics. If it:

1. Is not one of the instructions in the list above.
2. Is not preceded by a LOCK prefix.
3. It specifies a memory operand that does not exactly overlap the destination operand. LOCK is not guaranteed for partial overlap, even if one memory is contained wholly within the other.

LODS	Load string operand
LODSB	Load byte
LODSW	Load word
LODSD	Load doubleword

INSTRUCTION	OPCODE	BINARY
LODS m8	AC	10101100
LODS m16	AD	10101101
LODS m32	AD	10101101

Purpose: These instructions operate on strings rather than on logical or numeric values. They operate on one element of a string, which can be a byte, a word, or a doubleword. The string elements are addressed by the DS (default) and ESI registers. After each string operation, ESI is automatically updated to point to the next element of the string. If DF = 0, the index register increments. If DF = 1, it decrements, the amount of either being 1, 2, or 4, depending on the size of the string element.

LODS places the source string element at ESI into AL for byte strings, AX for word strings, and in EAX for doubleword strings. LODS increments or decrements ESI according to DF.

The operand specifies the length of the operand, e.g., AH specifies 8 bits, AX 16, and EAX 32. The actual transfer is always done with the address specified in ESI. A segment override prefix can be specified in the operand, which is applied to [ESI].

LOOP	Loop control while ECX counter not zero
LOOPcond	
LOOPE	Loop while equal
LOOPZ	Loop while zero
LOOPNE	Loop while not equal
LOOPNZ	Loop while not zero

INSTRUCTION	OPCODE	BINARY
LOOP rel8	E2 cb	11100010
LOOPE rel8	E1 cb	11100001
LOOPNE rel8	E1 cb	11100001

Note: LOOPZ is an alternate mnemonic for LOOPE rel8
        LOOPNZ is an alternate mnemonic for LOOPNE rel8

Purpose: The LOOP instructions are conditional jumps that use a value stored in ECX to specify the number of times a section of software will loop to a label. All LOOPs automatically decrement ECX and terminate when ECX = 0. LOOP is placed at the bottom of the loop and the label at the top.

LOOP first decrements ECX before testing ECX for the branch condition. If ECX is not zero, the program branches to the target label specified in the instruction. If ECX = 0, control transfers to the instruction immediately following the LOOP. ECX decrements without affecting any of the flags.

LOOPE and LOOPZ are synonymous for the same instruction. These instructions decrement ECX before testing ECX and ZF for branch condition. If ECX is non-zero and ZF = 1, the program branches to the target label as specified in the instruction. If LOOPE or LOOPZ finds ECX = 0 or ZF = 0, control transfers to the instruction immediately following the LOOPE or LOOPZ.

LOOPNE and LOOPNZ are synonymous for the same instruction. These instructions decrement ECX before testing ECX or ZF for branch conditions. If ECX is non-zero and ZF = 0, the program branches to the target label specified by the instruction. If ECX = 0 or ZF = 1, control transfers to the instruction immediately following LOOPNE or LOOPNZ.

LSL   Load segment limit

INSTRUCTION	OPCODE	BINARY
LSL r16,r/m16	0F 03 /r	00001111 00000011 mm rrr r/m
LSL r32,r/m32	0F 03 /r	00001111 00000011 mm rrr r/m

Purpose: LSL loads a user-specified register with a segment limit from the descriptor for the segment specified by the selector in the second operand. If the source selector is visible at the CPL and the descriptor is a type accepted by LSL (see Table C-7), LSL sets ZF to 1; otherwise, LSL sets ZF to 0 and keeps the destination register unchanged. The 32-bit forms of LSL store the 32-bit granular limit in the 16-bit destination register.

Note that this segment limit is a byte-granular value. If the descriptor uses a page-granular (the G bit = 1) segment limit, LSL translates that value to a byte limit (shifts it left 12 bits and fills the low 12 bits with 1s) and then loads it into the destination register.

Table C-7   Valid system segments and gates for LSL.

Type	Name
0	Undefined, invalid
1	Available 80286 TSS
2	Local Descriptor Table
3	Busy 80286 TSS
4	80286 Call Gate
5	80286/80386 Task Gate
6	80286 Interrupt Gate
7	80286 Trap Gate
8	Undefined, invalid
9	Available 80386 TSS
A	Undefined, invalid
B	Busy 80386 TSS
C	80386 Call Gate
D	Undefined, invalid
E	80386 Interrupt Gate
F	80386 Trap Gate

LTR   Load task register

INSTRUCTION	OPCODE	BINARY
LTR r/m16	OF 00 /3	00001111 00000000 mm 011 r/m

Purpose: The first operand of LTR specifies the source register or memory location that contains information for the task register. LTR loads data from that location into the task register. The loaded TSS is marked busy; however, a task switch does not occur. The given selector must point to a GDT entry that is of the descriptor type TSS. If this is the case, the Task Register is loaded.

MOV   Move data

INSTRUCTION	OPCODE	BINARY
MOV r/m8,r8	88 /r	10001000 mm rrr r/m
MOV r/m16,r16	89 /r	10001001 mm rrr r/m
MOV r/m32,r32	89 /r	10001001 mm rrr r/m
MOV r8,r/m8	8A /r	10001010 mm rrr r/m
MOV r16,r/m16	8B /r	10001011 mm rrr r/m
MOV r32,r/m32	8B /r	10001011 mm rrr r/m
MOV r/m16,sreg	8C /r	10001100 mm rrr r/m
MOV Sreg,r/m16	8D /r	10001101 mm rrr r/m
MOV AL,moffs8	A0	10100000
MOV AX,moffs16	A1	10100001
MOV EAX,moffs32	A1	10100001
MOV moffs8,AL	A2	10100010
MOV moffs16,AX	A3	10100011
MOV moffs32,EAX	A3	10100011
MOV reg8,imm8	B0+rb	10110rrr
MOV reg16,imm16	B8+rw	10111rrr
MOV reg32,imm32	B8+rd	10111rrr
MOV r/m8,imm8	C6	11000110 mm rrr r/m
MOV r/m16,imm16	C7	11000111 mm rrr r/m
MOV r/m32,imm32	C7	11000111 mm rrr r/m

Purpose: MOV transfers a byte, word, or doubleword from the source operand to the destination operand. MOV is useful for transferring data along these paths:

- Immediate data to a memory location

- Immediate data to a register
- Between general registers
- To a register from memory
- To memory from a register

There are some variations of MOV that operate on segment registers, which is how the segment registers are initialized in programs in this book.

Note: MOV cannot move from memory to memory or from segment register to segment register. Memory to memory can be done with the string move instruction MOVS.

MOV   Move to/from special registers

INSTRUCTION	OPCODE	BINARY
MOV r32,CR0/CR2/CR3	0F 20 /r	00001111 00100000 mm ccc r/m
MOV CR0/CR2/CR3,r32	0F 22 /r	00001111 00100010 mm ccc r/m
MOV r32,TR6/TR7	0F 24 /r	00001111 00100100 mm + + +r/m
MOV TR6/TR7,r32	0F 26 /r	00001111 00100110 mm + + +r/m
MOV r32,DR0-3/6/7	0F 21 /r	00001111 00100001 mm ddd r/m
MOV DR03/6/7,r32	0F 23 /r	00001111 00100011

Purpose: These forms of MOV load or store special registers to or from a general register. They are particularly designed for the Control Registers (CR0, CR2, CR3), Test Registers (TR6 and TR7), and the Debug Registers (DR0, DR1, DR2, DR3, DR6, and DR7).

MOVS   Move data from string to string
MOVSB   Move string byte
MOVSW   Move string word
MOVSD   Move string doubleword

INSTRUCTION	OPCODE	BINARY
MOVS m8,m8	A4	10100100
MOVS m16,m16	A5	10100101
MOVS m32,m32	A5	10100101

Note: MOVSB is a common assembler mnemonic for MOVS m8,m8
MOVSW is a common assembler mnemonic for MOVS m16,m16
MOVSD is a common assembler mnemonic for MOVS m32,m32

Purpose: These instructions operate on strings rather than on logical or numeric values. They operate on one element of a string addressed by [ESI] (which can be a byte, a word, or a doubleword) and move it to the area addressed by ES:[EDI]. After each string operation, ESI and/or EDI are automatically updated to point to the next element of the string. If the direction (DF) is 0, the index registers increment, and if DF = 1, they decrement, the amount of either being 1, 2, or 4, depending on the size of the string element.

When prefixed by REP, MOVS operates as a memory-to-memory block transfer and repeats for the number of times of the value stored in ECX. To set this up, the program must first initialize ECX and the register pairs ESI and EDI. ECX specifies the number of bytes, words or doublewords in the block. If the direction flag (DF) is 0, the program must point ESI to the first element of the source string and point EDI to the destination address for the first element. If DF = 1, the program points these two registers to the last element of the source string and to the destination address for the last element, respectively.

MOVSX   Move with sign extension

INSTRUCTION	OPCODE	BINARY
MOVSX r16,r/m8	OF BE /r	00001111 10111110 mm rrr r/m
MOVSX r32,r/m8	OF BE /r	00001111 10111110 mm rrr r/m
MOVSX r32,r/m16	OF BF /r	00001111 10111111 mm rrr r/m

Purpose: MOVSX sign-extends an 8-bit value to a 16-bit value and an 8-bit or 16-bit value to 32-bit value. If both operands are words, a normal move occurs.

MOVZX   Move with zero extension

INSTRUCTION	OPCODE	BINARY
MOVZX r16,r/m88	OF B6 /r	00001111 10110110 mm rrr r/m
MOVZX r32,r/m8	OF B6 /r	00001111 10110110 mm rrr r/m
MOVZX r32,r/m16	OF B7 /r	00001111 10110111 mm rrr r/m

Purpose: MOVZX extends an 8-bit value to a 16-bit value and an 8- or 16-bit value to 32-bit value by padding with high-order zeros. If both operands are words, a normal move occurs.

MUL   Unsigned integer multiply of AL, AX, or EAX

INSTRUCTION	OPCODE	BINARY
MUL AL,r/m8	F6 /4	11110110 mm 100 r/m
MUL AX,r/m16	F7 /4	11110111 mm 100 r/m
MUL EAX,r/m32	F7 /4	11110111 mm 100 r/m

Purpose: MUL multiplies the numbers in the source operand and the accumulator. If the source is a byte, the 80486 multiplies it by the contents of AL and returns the double-length result in AH and AL. If the source operand is a word, the 80486 multiplies it by the contents of AX and returns the double-length result to DX and AX. If the source is a doubleword, the processor multiplies it by the contents of EAX and returns the 64-bit result in EDX and EAX. MUL sets CF and OF to zero, if AH, DX, or EDX is all zeros for 8-, 16-, or 32-bit operations. Otherwise CF and OF are set to 1.

NEG   Negate (two's complement)

INSTRUCTION	OPCODE	BINARY
NEG r/m8	F6 /3	11110110 mm 011 r/m
NEG r/m16	F7 /3	11110111 mm 011 r/m
NEG r/m32	F7 /3	11110111 mm 011 r/m

Purpose: NEG subtracts a signed integer operand from zero. Its effect is to make a positive into a negative or vice versa. That is, NEG forms a two's complement of a given operand, which is subtracted from zero. The result is placed in the operand. CF is set to 1 except when the operand prior to the NEG was zero.

NOP   No operation

INSTRUCTION	OPCODE	BINARY
NOP	90	10010000

Purpose: NOP occupies a byte of storage. It affects nothing but the instruction pointer, EIP. NOP is useful for providing space in fixing up branch addresses, i.e., the address might require an 8- or 16-bit displacement—if 16 bits are reserved, an 8-bit displacement and a NOP can be used to fill the 16 bits.

NOT — Negate (one's complement)

INSTRUCTION	OPCODE	BINARY
NOT r/m8	F6 /2	11110110 mm 010 r/m
NOT r/m16	F7 /2	11110111 mm 010 r/m
NOT r/m32	F7 /2	11110111 mm 010 r/m

Purpose: NOT inverts the bits in the specified operand to form a one's complement of the operand. NOT is a unary operation (refers to an arithmetic operator having only one term) that uses a single operand in a register or memory. The result is stored in the operand. NOT has no effect on flags.

OR — Logical inclusive OR

INSTRUCTION	OPCODE	BINARY
OR AL,imm8	0C ib	00001100
OR AX,imm16	0D iw	00001101
OR EAX,imm32	0D id	00001101
OR r/m8,imm8	80 /1 ib	10000000 mm 001 r/m
OR r/m16,imm16	81 /1 iw	10000001 mm 001 r/m
OR r/m32,imm32	81 /1 id	10000001 mm 001 r/m
OR r/m16,imm8	83 /1 ib	10000011 mm 001 r/m
OR r/m32,imm8	83 /1 ib	10000011 mm 001 r/m
OR r/m8,r8	08 /r	00001000 mm 001 r/m
OR r/m16,r16	09 /r	00001001 mm 001 r/m
OR r/m32,r32	09 /r	00001001 mm 001 r/m
OR r8,r/m8	0A /r	00001010 mm rrr r/m
OR r16,r/m16	0B /r	00001011 mm rrr r/m
OR r32,r/m32	0B /r	00001011 mm rrr r/m

Purpose: OR compares its two operands and computes the following: if each corresponding bit in the operands are zeros, the result is a zero; otherwise, the result is a 1, and the result is stored in the operand.

Operand 1	0 0 1 1
Operand 2	0 1 1 0
Result	0 1 1 1

OUT   Output to port

INSTRUCTION	OPCODE	BINARY
OUT imm8,AL	E6 ib	11100110
OUT imm8,AX	E7 ib	11100111
OUT imm8,EAX	E7 ib	11100111
OUT DX,AL	EE	11101110
OUT DX,AX	EF	11101111
OUT DX,EAX	EF	11101111

Purpose: OUT transfers data from a register to an output port. The source is a register (AL, AX, or EAX) and is given as the second operand. The output port is specified in the first operand. To output data to any port from 0 to 65536, the port number is placed in the DX register. OUT is then used with DX as the first operand. If the instruction contains an 8-bit port ID, the value is zero-extended to 16 bits in DX. If the immediate 8 is used, only ports from 0 to 255 are valid. In this case, the upper bits of the port address are zero.

Note: I/O ports 00F8 through 00FF are reserved by Intel.

OUTS   Output string to port
OUTSB   Output byte
OUTSW   Output word
OUTSD   Output doubleword

INSTRUCTION	OPCODE	BINARY
OUTS DX,r/m8	6E	01101110
OUTS DX,r/m16	6F	01101111
OUTS DX,r/m32	6F	01101111

Note: OUTSB is a common assembler mnemonic for OUTS DX,r/m8
OUTSW is a common assembler mnemonic for OUTS DX,r/m16
OUTSD is a common assembler mnemonic for OUTS DX,r/m32

Purpose: OUTS operates much like OUT, in that it transfers data (memory byte, word, or doubleword) at the source-index register to the output port addressed by the DX register. After the data transfer, the source-index register (SI or ESI, see following) is advanced; that is, it either increments or decrements. If the DF is 0 (CLD was executed), the index increments. If DF is 1 (STD was executed), it decrements. The amount that either changes depends on the size of the output: a 1 if it is a byte, a 2 if a word, or 4 if a doubleword.

The source data address is determined by the contents of a source-index register. The correct index value must be loaded into either SI or ESI before executing these instructions. SI is used for the source-index register if the address size attribute for these instructions is 16 bits. Otherwise, ESI is used and the address size attribute is 32 bits.

The port must be addressed through the DX register value. OUTS does not allow specification of the port number as an immediate value.

OUTS can be preceded by the REP prefix. In this case, ECX bytes, words, or dwords are transferred.

POP — Pop a word from the stack

INSTRUCTION	OPCODE	BINARY
POP m16	8F /0	10001111 mm 000 r/m
POP m32	8F /0	10111111 mm 000 r/m
POP r16	58 + rw	01011rrr
POP r32	58 + rd	01011rrr
POP DS	1F	00011111
POP ES	07	00000111
POP SS	17	00010111
POP FS	OF A1	00001111 10100001
POP GS	OF A9	00001111 10101001

Purpose: POP transfers the word or doubleword at the current top of stack (indicated by SS:ESP) to the destination operand. It then increments SS:ESP to point to the new top of stack. Care should be taken when popping 16-bit operands, to avoid misaligning the stack, which causes performance degradation.

POPA — POP all registers
POPAD — POP all registers (32-bit mode)

INSTRUCTION	OPCODE	BINARY
POPA	61	01100001
POPAD	61	01100001

Purpose: POPA restores the eight general-purpose registers saved on the stack by PUSHA. It discards the saved value of ESP. The order in which the registers are popped is: DI, SI, BP, SP, BX, DX, CX, and AX for POPA, or EDI, ESI, EBP, ESP, EBX, EDX, ECX, and EAX for POPAD.

POPF — POP stack into FLAGS or EFLAGS
POPFD — POP stack (32-bit mode)

INSTRUCTION	OPCODE	BINARY
POPF	9D	10011101
POPFD	9D	10011101

Purpose: POPF transfers specific bits from the word at the top of stack into the low-order byte of EFLAGS. Then POPF increments ESP by 2. POPFD transfers the 16 or 32 bits and increments ESP by 4. The RF and VM flags are not changed by either POPF or POPFD.

PUSHF and POPF are useful for storing the flags in memory where they can be examined and modified. They are useful also for preserving the state of the flags register while executing a procedure.

The IOPL flag will be altered only if the CPL is 0. If not 0, IOPL is not altered and no exception results. If CPL is as privileged or more privileged than the current IOPL, the interrupt enable flag, IF is altered. If not, IF is unchanged and no exception results.

PUSH — Push operand to the stack

INSTRUCTION	OPCODE	BINARY
PUSH m16	FF /6	11111111 mm 110 r/m
PUSH m32	FF /6	11111111 mm 110 r/m
PUSH r16	50+/r	01010rrr
PUSH r32	50+/r	01010rrr
PUSH imm8	6A	01101010
PUSH imm16	68	01101000
PUSH imm32	68	01101000
PUSH CS	0E	00001110
PUSH SS	16	00010110
PUSH DS	1E	00011110
PUSH ES	06	00000110
PUSH FS	0F A0	00001111 10100000
PUSH GS	0F A8	00001111 10101000

Purpose: PUSH decrements the stack pointer (ESP) then transfers the source operand to the TOS indicated by ESP. PUSH is often used to place parameters on the stack before calling a procedure. It is also the means of storing temporary variables on the stack. PUSH operates on memory operands, register operands (including segment registers) and immediate operands.

Immediate data is always considered to be 32 bits in size, although it can be encoded in the instruction as an 8-bit immediate.

Be careful when pushing 16-bit operands to avoid misaligning the stack, which causes performance degradation.

PUSHA
PUSHAD   Push all general registers

INSTRUCTION	OPCODE	BINARY
PUSHA	60	01100000
PUSHAD	60	01100000

Purpose: PUSHA saves the contents of the eight general-purpose registers on the stack. PUSHA eliminates the need for eight consecutive PUSH instructions. The order of the registers PUSHed is: AX, CX, DX, BX, SP, BP, SI and DI for word, or EAX, ECX, EDX, EBX, ESP, EBP, ESI and EDI for dword. Note that the value PUSHed for SP or ESP is the original value. The order of the registers PUSHed is correct for a subsequent POPA.

PUSHF   Push flags register EFLAGS onto the stack PUSHFD

INSTRUCTION	OPCODE	BINARY
PUSHF	9C	10011100
PUSHFD	9C	10011100

Purpose: PUSHF decrements ESP by two and then transfers the low-order word of EFLAGS to the word at the top of stack pointed to by ESP. PUSHFD decrements ESP by 4 and then transfers both words of the EFLAGS to the top of stack pointed to by ESP. Note the VM and RF flags are not moved.

PUSHF and POPF are useful for storing the flags in memory, where they can be examined and modified. They are useful also for preserving the state of the flags register while executing a procedure.

RCL Rotate left through carry (uses CF)
RCR Rotate right through carry (uses CF)
ROL Rotate left (wrap bits around)
ROR Rotate right (wrap bits around)

INSTRUCTION	OPCODE	BINARY
RCL r/m8,1	D0 /2	11010000 mm 010 r/m
RCL r/m8,CL	D2 /2	11010010 mm 010 r/m
RCL r/m8,imm8	C0 /2 ib	11000000 mm 010 r/m
RCL r/m16,1	D1 /2	11010001 mm 010 r/m
RCL r/m16,CL	D3 /2	11010011 mm 010 r/m
RCL r/m16,imm8	C1 /2 ib	11000001 mm 010 r/m
RCL r/m32,1	D1 /2	11010001 mm 010 r/m
RCL r/m32,CL	D3 /2	11010011 mm 010 r/m
RCL r/m32,imm8	C1 /2 ib	11000001 mm 010 r/m
RCR r/m8,1	D0 /3	11010000 mm 011 r/m
RCR r/m8,CL	D2 /3	11010010 mm 011 r/m
RCR r/m8,imm8	C0 /3 ib	11000000 mm 011 r/m
RCR r/m16,1	D1 /3	11010001 mm 011 r/m
RCR r/m16,CL	D3 /3	11010011 mm 011 r/m
RCR r/m16,imm8	C1 /3 ib	11000001 mm 011 r/m
RCR r/m32,1	D1 /3	11010001 mm 011 r/m
RCR r/m32,CL	D3 /3	11010011 mm 011 r/m
RCR r/m32,imm8	C1 /3 ib	11000001 mm 011 r/m
ROL r/m8,1	D0 /0	11010000 mm 000 r/m
ROL r/m8,CL	D2 /0	11010010 mm 000 r/m
ROL r/m8,imm8	C0 /0 ib	11000000 mm 000 r/m
ROL r/m16,1	D1 /0	11010001 mm 000 r/m
ROL r/m16,CL	D3 /0	11010011 mm 000 r/m
ROL r/m16,imm8	C1 /0 ib	11000001 mm 000 r/m
ROL r/m32,1	D1 /0	11010001 mm 000 r/m
ROL r/m32,CL	D3 /0	11010011 mm 000 r/m
ROL r/m32,imm8	C1 /0 ib	11000001 mm 000 r/m
ROR r/m8,1	C0 /1	11000000 mm 001 r/m
ROR r/m8,CL	D2 /1	11010010 mm 001 r/m
ROR r/m8,imm8	C0 /1 ib	11000000 mm 001 r/m
ROR r/m16,1	D1 /1	11010001 mm 001 r/m
ROR r/m16,CL	D3 /1	11010011 mm 001 r/m
ROR r/m16,imm8	C1 /1 ib	11000001 mm 001 r/m
ROR r/m32,1	D1 /1	11010001 mm 001 r/m
ROR r/m32,CL	D3 /1	11010011 mm 001 r/m
ROR r/m32,imm8	C1 /1 ib	11000001 mm 001 r/m

Purpose: Rotate instructions allow bits in bytes, words and doublewords to be rotated. Bits rotated out of an operand are not lost as in a shift but are circled back into the other end of the operand. Rotates affect only the carry and overflow flags. CF can act as an extension of the operand in two of the rotate instructions. This allows a bit to be isolated and then tested by a conditional jump instruction (JC or JNC). CF always contains the value of the last bit rotated out, even if the instruction does not use this bit as an extension of the rotated operand.

In single-bit rotates, OF is set if the operation changes the high-order (sign) bit of the destination operand. If the sign bit retains its original value, OF is cleared. On multibit rotates, the value of OF is always undefined.

RCL rotates bits in the byte, word, or doubleword destination operand left by one or by the number of bits specified in the count operand. RCL differs from ROL in that it treats CF as a high-order one-bit extension of the destination operand. Each high-order bit that exits from the left side of the operand moves to CF before it returns to the operand as the low-order bit on the next rotation cycle.

RCR rotates bits in the byte, word, or doubleword destination right by one or by the number of bits specified in the count operand. RCR differs from ROR in that it treats CF as a low-order one-bit extension of the destination operand. Each low-order bit that exits from the right side of the operand moves to CF before it returns to the operand as the high-order bit on the next rotation cycle.

ROL rotates the byte, word, or doubleword destination operand left by one or by the number of bits specified in the count operand, ECX. For each rotation specified, the high-order bit that exits from the left of the operand returns at the right to become the new low-order bit of the operand. If the ROL count is 1, the overflow flag (OF) is set to 0 if the CF (after the ROL) equals the high bit of the resultant operand. Otherwise, OF is set to 1. If ROL is not 1, OF is undefined. ROL with a 0 count does not affect OF or CF.

ROR rotates the byte, word, or doubleword destination operand right by one or by the number of bits specified in the count operand. For each rotation, the low-order bit that exits from the right of the operand returns at the left to become the new high-order bit of the operand. If the ROR count is 1, the OF is set to 0 if the top two bits of the resultant operand are equal. Otherwise, OF = 1. If the ROR count is not 1, OF is undefined. Rotates with a zero count do not alter OF or CF.

Note: Rotates with a count equal to 0 do not alter CF. Also, RCL or RCR of 32 or 33 bits (for dwords) cannot be done, because only a count of 0 to 31 is valid.

REP	Repeat following string operation
REPE	Repeat while equal
REPZ	Repeat while zero
REPNE	Repeat while not equal
REPNZ	Repeat while not zero

INSTRUCTION	OPCODE	BINARY
REP INS r/m8,DX	F3 6C	11110011 01101100
REP INS r/m16,DX	F3 6D	11110011 01101101
REP INS r/m32,DX	F3 6D	11110011 01101101
REP MOVS m8,m8	F3 A4	11110011 10100100
REP MOVS m16,m16	F3 A5	11110011 10100101
REP MOVS m32,m32	F3 A5	11110011 10100101
REP OUTS DX,r/m8	F3 6E	11110011 01101110
REP OUTS DX,r/m16	F3 6F	11110011 01101111
REP OUTS DX,r/m32	F3 6F	11110011 01101111
REP STOS m8	F3 AA	11110011 10101010
REP STOS m16	F3 AB	11110011 10101011
REP STOS m32	F3 AB	11110011 10101011
REPE CMPS m8,m8	F3 A6	11110011 10100110
REPE CMPS m16,m16	F3 A7	11110011 10100111
REPE CMPS m32,m32	F3 A7	11110011 10100111
REPE SCAS m8	F3 AE	11110011 10101110
REPE SCAS m16	F3 AF	11110011 10101111
REPE SCAS m32	F3 AF	11110011 10101111
REPNE CMPS m8,m8	F2 A6	11110010 10100110
REPNE CMPS m16,m16	F2 A7	11110010 10100111
REPNE CMPS m32,m32	F2 A7	11110010 10100111
REPNE SCAS m8F2	AE	11110010 10101110
REPNE SCAS m16F2	AF	11110010 10101111
REPNE SCAS m32F2	AF	11110010 10101111

Purpose: The REP prefixes specify repeated operation of a string, which enables the 80486 to process strings much faster than with a regular software loop. When a string operation has one of these repeat prefixes, the operation is executed repeatedly for ECX times. Each time, the operation uses a different element of the string. The repetition ends when one of the conditions specified by the prefix is satisfied.

At the repetition of the instruction, the string operation can be suspended temporarily to handle an external interrupt or exception. After that interrupt has been handled, the string operation begins where it left off.

REPE repeats ECX times or until ZF becomes zero. REPZ is synonymous with REPE. REPNE repeats ECX times, or until ZF becomes 1. REPNZ is synonymous with REPNE.

RET   Return from procedure

INSTRUCTION	OPCODE	BINARY
RET	C3	11000011
RET imm16	CA /w	11001010

Purpose: RET ends the execution of a CALLed procedure and transfers control through the back-link on the top of the stack, which is the EIP value. The back-link points to the program that originally invoked the procedure. RET restores the value of EIP that was saved on the stack by the previous CALL instruction.

RET can optionally specify an immediate operand. By adding this constant to the new top-of-stack pointer, RET removes any arguments that the CALLing program pushed onto the stack before the CALL executed.

SAHF   Store AH into flags register

INSTRUCTION	OPCODE	BINARY
SAHF	9E	10011110

Purpose: Though specific instructions exist to alter CF and DF, there is no direct way of altering the other applications-oriented flags. The flag transfer instructions (LAHF and SAHF) allow a program to alter the other flag bits with the bit manipulation instructions after transferring these flags to the stack or the AH register. Then SAHF stores the contents of AH to the low byte of EFLAGS.

Shift instructions

INSTRUCTION	OPCODE	BINARY
SAL r/m8,1	D0 /4	11010000 mm 100 r/m
SAL r/m8,CL	D2 /4	11010010 mm 100 r/m
SAL r/m8,imm8	C0 /4 ib	11000000 mm 100 r/m
SAL r/m16,1	D1 /4	11010001 mm 100 r/m
SAL r/m16,CL	D3 /4	11010011 mm 100 r/m
SAL r/m16,imm8	C1 /4 ib	11000001 mm 100 r/m
SAL r/m32,1	D1 /4	11000001 mm 100 r/m
SAL r/m32,CL	D3 /4	11010011 mm 100 r/m
SAL r/m32,imm8	C1 /4 ib	11000001 mm 100 r/m
SAR r/m8,1	D0 /7	11010000 mm 111 r/m
SAR r/m8,CL	D2 /7	11000010 mm 111 r/m
SAR r/m8,imm8	C0 /7 ib	11000000 mm 111 r/m
SAR r/m16,1	C1 /7	11000001 mm 111 r/m
SAR r/m16,CL	D3 /7	11010011 mm 111 r/m
SAR r/m16,imm8	C1 /7 ib	11000001 mm 111 r/m
SAR r/m32,1	D1 /7	11010001 mm 111 r/m
SAR r/m32,CL	D3 /7	11010011 mm 111 r/m
SAR r/m32,imm8	C1 /7 ib	11000001 mm 111 r/m
SHR r/m8,1	D0 /5	11010000 mm 101 r/m
SHR r/m8,CL	C2 /5	11000010 mm 101 r/m
SHR r/m8,imm8	C0 /5 ib	11000000 mm 101 r/m
SHR r/m16,1	D1 /5	11010001 mm 101 r/m
SHR r/m16,CL	D3 /5	11010011 mm 101 r/m
SHR r/m16,imm8	C1 /5 ib	11000001 mm 101 r/m
SHR r/m32,1	D1 /5	11010001 mm 101 r/m
SHR r/m32,CL	D3 /5	11010011 mm 101 r/m
SHR r/m32,imm8	C1 /5 ib	11000001 mm 101 r/m

Note: SHL is an alternate assembler opcode for SAL.

Purpose: The bits in bytes, words, and doublewords can be shifted logically or arithmetically. Bits can be shifted up to 31 places, depending on a specified count in ECX. Shift instructions specify the count in one of three ways: (1) implicitly by specifying the count as a single shift; (2) specifying the count as an immediate value; or (3) specifying the count as the value contained in ECX. The result is stored back into the first operand.

The shift instructions provide a convenient way to do multiplication or division by binary. The division of signed numbers by shifting right is not the same kind of division performed by IDIV.

CF always contains the value of the last bit shifted out of the destination operand. In a single-bit shift, OF is set if the value of the high-order (sign) bit was changed by the operation. If the sign bit was not changed, OF is cleared. After a multibit shift, the contents of OF is always undefined.

SAL shifts the destination byte, word, or doubleword operand left by one or by the number of bits specified in the count register. The processor shifts zeros in from the right (low-order) side of the operand as bits exit from the left (high-order) side. If the shift count is 1, OF is set to 0 if the CF after the shift equals the high bit of the first operand. Otherwise, OF = 1. If the shift count is not 1, OF is undefined.

SAR shifts the destination byte, word, or doubleword operand to the right by one or by the number of bits specified in the count operand. The processor preserves the sign of the operand by shifting in zeros on the left (high-order) side if the value is positive or by shifting by ones if the value is negative. If the shift count is 1, OF is set to 0. Otherwise, it is unchanged. Another way to think of SAR is that operand 1 is being divided by 2, shift-count times. The divide rounds to negative infinity (which is different than IDIV) for negative numbers. Shifts of zero do not alter any flags.

SHL is a synonym for SAL.

SHR shifts the destination byte, word, or doubleword operand right by one or by the number of bits specified in the count operand. The processor shifts zeros in from the left (high-order) side of the operand as bits exit from the right (low-order) side.

SBB   Subtract integers with borrow

INSTRUCTION	OPCODE	BINARY
SBB AL,imm8	1C ib	00011100
SBB AX,imm16	1D iw	00011101
SBB EAX,imm32	1D id	00011101
SBB r/m8,imm8	80 /3 ib	10000000 mm 011 r/m
SBB r/m16,imm16	81 /3 iw	10000001 mm 011 r/m
SBB r/m32,imm32	81 /3 id	10000001 mm 011 r/m
SBB r/m16,imm8	83 /3 ib	10000011 mm 011 r/m
SBB r/m32,imm8	83 /3 ib	10000011 mm 011 r/m
SBB r/m8,r8	18 /r	00011000 mm rrr r/m
SBB r/m16,r16	19 /r	00011001 mm rrr r/m
SBB r/m32,r32	19 /r	00011001 mm rrr r/m
SBB r8,r/m8	1A /r	00011010 mm rrr r/m

```
SBB r16,r/m16        1B /r     00011011 mm rrr r/m
SBB r32,r/m32        1B /r     00011011 mm rrr r/m
```

Purpose: SBB subtracts the source operand from the destination operand and then returns the results to the destination operand. It subtracts 1 if CF is set. If CF is cleared, SBB performs the same operation as does SUB. SUB followed by multiple SBB instructions can be used to subtract numbers longer than 32 bits.

SCAS	Compare string data
SCASB	Compare byte
SCASW	Compare word
SCASD	Compare doubleword

INSTRUCTION	OPCODE	BINARY
SCAS m8	AE	10101110
SCAS m16	AF	10101111
SCAS m32	AF	10101111

Note: SCASB is a common assembler mnemonic for SCAS m8
        SCASW is a common assembler mnemonic for SCAS m16
        SCASD is a common assembler mnemonic for SCAS m32

Purpose: These instructions operate on strings rather than on logical or numeric values. They operate on one element of a string, which can be a byte, a word, or a doubleword. SCAS subtracts ES:[EDI] from AL, AX, or EAX (for byte, word, or dword) operations. The result of the subtraction is not stored; only the flags are changed. After each string operation, EDI is updated to point to the next element of the string. If DF is 0, the index register increments. If DF = 1, it decrements, with the amount either changes being 1, 2, or 4, depending on the size of the string element.

If the values are equal, the ZF is set to 1. Otherwise, ZF = 0. If DF = 0, the 80486 increments the memory pointer (EDI) for the string. The destination segment register (ES) cannot be overridden.

SCAS might be preceded by REPE (REPZ) or REPNE (REPNZ). If preceded by REPE, SCAS is repeated while ECX is not 0 and the string elements are equal to AL, AX, or EAX (ZF = 1). If preceded by REPNE, SCAS is repeated while ECX is not 0 and the string element is not equal to AL, AX, or EAX (ZF = 0). In this way, SCAS is useful to find the first mismatch (REPE) or match (REPNE) to AL, AX or EAX in the string if they exist.

The specification of mem is used by the assembler to determine the length of the operation only. The string is always taken from ES:[EDI]. No segment override is possible for SCAS.

SETcc   Set byte on condition code

INSTRUCTION	OPCODE	BINARY
SETA r/m8	OF 97	00001111 10010111 mm rrr r/m
SETAE r/m8	OF 93	00001111 10010011 mm rrr r/m
SETB r/m8	OF 92	00001111 10010010 mm rrr r/m
SETBE r/m8	OF 96	00001111 10010110 mm rrr r/m
SETC r/m8	OF 92	00001111 10010010 mm rrr r/m
SETE r/m8	OF 94	00001111 10010100 mm rrr r/m
SETG r/m8	OF 9F	00001111 10011111 mm rrr r/m
SETGE r/m8	OF 9D	00001111 10011101 mm rrr r/m
SETL r/m8	OF 9C	00001111 10011100 mm rrr r/m
SETLE r/m8	OF 9E	00001111 10011110 mm rrr r/m
SETNA r/m8	OF 96	00001111 10010110 mm rrr r/m
SETNAE r/m8	OF 92	00001111 10010010 mm rrr r/m
SETNB r/m8	OF 93	00001111 10010011 mm rrr r/m
SETNBE r/m8	OF 97	00001111 10010111 mm rrr r/m
SETNC r/m8	OF 93	00001111 10010011 mm rrr r/m
SETNE r/m8	OF 95	00001111 10010101 mm rrr r/m
SETNG r/m8	OF 9E	00001111 10011110 mm rrr r/m
SETNGE r/m8	OF 9C	00001111 10011100 mm rrr r/m
SETNL r/m8	OF 9D	00001111 10011101 mm rrr r/m
SETNLE r/m8	OF 9F	00001111 10011111 mm rrr r/m
SETNO r/m8	OF 91	00001111 10010001 mm rrr r/m
SETNP r/m8	OF 9B	00001111 10011011 mm rrr r/m
SETNS r/m8	OF 99	00001111 10011001 mm rrr r/m
SETNZ r/m8	OF 95	00001111 10010101 mm rrr r/m
SETO r/m8	OF 90	00001111 10010000 mm rrr r/m
SETP r/m8	OF 9A	00001111 10011010 mm rrr r/m
SETPE r/m8	OF 9A	00001111 10011010 mm rrr r/m
SETPO r/m8	OF 9B	00001111 10011011 mm rrr r/m
SETS r/m8	OF 98	00001111 10011000 mm rrrr/m
SETZ r/m8	OF 94	00001111 10010100 mm rrr r/m

Purpose: SETcc sets a byte to 0 or 1 depending on any of the conditions defined by the status flags, shown immediately following. The byte can be in memory or can be a 1-byte general register. SETcc sets the byte to 1 if the condition *cc* is true; otherwise, it sets the byte to 1. The condition codes are:

SETB/SETNAE/SET	CCF = 1
SETBE/SETNA	CF = 1, ZF = 1
SETE/SETZ	ZF = 1
SETL/SETNGE	SF = OF

SETLE/SETNG	SF = OF, ZF = 1
SETNB/SETAE/SETN	CCF = 0
SETNBE/SETA	CF = 0, ZF = 1
SETNE/SETNZ	ZF = 0
SETNL/SETGE	SF = OF
SETNLE/SETG	ZF = 0, SF = OF
SETNO	OF = 0
SETNP/SETPO	PF = 0
SETNS	SF = 0
SETO	OF = 1
SETP/SETPE	PF = 1
SETS	SF = 1

SGDT Store Global Descriptor Table
SIDT Store Interrupt Descriptor Table

INSTRUCTION	OPCODE	BINARY
SGDT m	0F 01 /0	00001111 00000001 mm 000 r/m
SIDT m	0F 01 /1	00001111 00000001 mm 001 r/m

Purpose: These instructions copy the contents of the Global Descriptor Table (GDT) register or the Interrupt Descriptor table (IDT) register the 6 bytes (48 bits) indicated by the operand. The 16-bit forms of the SGDT/SIDT instructions are compatible with the 80286, but only if the value in the upper 8 bits is not referenced. The 80286 stores 1s in these bits while the 80386 and 80486 stores 0s.

The 16-bit limit is stored in the low word and the 32-bit Base is stored in the high dword.

SHLD Double-precision shift left
SHRD Double-precision shift right

INSTRUCTION	OPCODE	BINARY
SHLD r/m16,r16,imm8	0F A4	00001111 10100100 mm rrr r/m
SHLD r/m32,r32,imm8	0F A4	00001111 10100100 mm rrr r/m
SHLD r/m16,r16,CL	0F A5	00001111 10100101 mm rrr r/m
SHLD r/m32,r32,CL	0F A5	00001111 10100101 mm rrr r/m
SHRD r/m16,r16,imm8	0F AC	00001111 10101100 mm rrr r/m
SHRD r/m32,r32,imm8	0F AC	00001111 10101100 mm rrr r/m

SHRD r/m16,r16,CL	OF AD	00001111 10101101 mm rrr r/m
SHRD r/m32,r32,CL	OF AD	00001111 10101101 mm rrr r/m

Purpose: SHLD and SHRD provide the basic operations needed to implement operations on long unaligned bit strings. The double shifts either (1) take two word operands as input, producing a one-word output, or (2) take two doubleword operands as input, producing a doubleword output. The result is stored back in the first operand.

One of the two input operands might be in either a general register or in memory; the other can only be in a general register. The results replace the memory or register operand. The number of bits to be shifted is specified either in the CL register or in an immediate byte of the instruction. This count is masked to 5 bits—thus, shifts of 0 to 31 bits are performed. CF is set to the value of the last bit shifted out of the destination operand. SF, ZF, and PF are set according to the value of the result. OF and AF are left undefined.

If the count is 0, the instructions are equivalent to a NOP and do not alter the flags. If the shift count is greater than the operand length, the flags and the result in the first operand are undefined.

SLDT   Store local descriptor table register

INSTRUCTION	OPCODE	BINARY
SLDT r/m16	OF 00 /0	00001111 00000000 mm 000 r/m

Purpose: The LDT is pointed to by a selector that resides in the LDT Register. SLDT stores the LDTR in the register or memory location indicated by the effective address operand.

Note: The operand-size attribute has no effect on the operation of SLDT.

SMSW   Store Machine Status Word

INSTRUCTION	OPCODE	BINARY
SMSW r/m16	OF 01 /4	00001111 00000001 mm 100 r/m

Purpose: The Machine Status Word is part of CR0. SMSW stores this word in the 2-byte register or memory location indicated by the effective address operand. SMSW provides compatibility with the 80286. 80486 programs should use MOV CR0.

STC — Set Carry Flag (CF)

INSTRUCTION	OPCODE	BINARY
STC	F9	11111001

Purpose: STC sets the Carry Flag (CF) to 1.

STD — Set Direction Flag (DF)

INSTRUCTION	OPCODE	BINARY
STD	FD	11111101

Purpose: STD sets the Direction Flag (DF) to 1. This causes all subsequent string operations to decrement the index register(s) SI (or ESI) and DI (or EDI).

STI — Set Interrupt Flag (IF)

INSTRUCTION	OPCODE	BINARY
STI	FB	11111011

Purpose: STI sets the Interrupt Flag (IF) to 1. After executing the next operation, the 80486 responds to external interrupts—if the next instruction allows the interrupt flag to remain enabled. However, if external interrupts are disabled, code STI, RET (such as at the end of a subroutine) and RET is allowed to execute before external interrupts are recognized. Also, if external interrupts are disabled, and STI, CLI are coded, the interrupts are not recognized because CLI clears the interrupt flag during its execution.

If the current task has insufficient privilege to alter IF, an undefined opcode fault is generated.

STOS	Store string data	
STOSB	Store byte	
STOSW	Store word	
STOSD	Store doubleword	

INSTRUCTION	OPCODE	BINARY
STOS m8	AA	10101010
STOSB	AA	10101010
STOS m16	AB	10101011
STOSW	AB	10101011
STOS m32	AB	10101011
STOSD	AB	10101011

Purpose: These instructions operate on strings rather than on logical or numeric values. They operate on one element of a string, which can be a byte, a word, or a doubleword. The string elements are transferred from AL, AX, or EAX into ES:[EDI]. After each string operation, EDI is automatically updated to point to the next element of the string. If DF = 0, the index registers increment. If DF = 1, they decrement. The amount of either being 1, 2, or 4, depending on the size of the string element.

STOS can be preceded by a REP prefix. This allows a string to be filled with the contents of AL, AX or EAX.

STR   Store task register

INSTRUCTION	OPCODE	BINARY
STR r/m16	0F 00 /1	00001111 00000000 mm 001 r/m

Purpose: STR copies the contents of the Task Register to the 2-byte register or memory location specified in the first operand. The operand-size attribute has no effect on STR.

SUB   Subtract integers

INSTRUCTION	OPCODE	BINARY
SUB AL,imm8	2C ib	00101100
SUB AX,imm16	2D iw	00101101

SUB EAX,imm32	2D id	00101101
SUB r/m8,imm8	80 /5 ib	10000000 mm 101 r/m
SUB r/m16,imm16	81 /5 iw	10000001 mm 101 r/m
SUB r/m32,imm32	81 /5 id	10000001 mm 101 r/m
SUB r/m16,imm8	83 /5 ib	10000011 mm 101 r/m
SUB r/m32,imm8	83 /5 ib	10000011 mm 101 r/m
SUB r/m8,r8	28 /r	00101000 mm rrr r/m
SUB r/m16,r16	29 /r	00101001 mm rrr r/m
SUB r/m32,r32	29 /r	00101001 mm rrr r/m
SUB r8,r/m8	2A /r	00101010 mm rrr r/m
SUB r16,r/m16	2B /r	00101011 mm rrr r/m
SUB r32,r/m32	2B /r	00101011 mm rrr r/m

Purpose: SUB subtracts the source operand from the destination operand and then replaces the destination operand with the result. If a borrow is required, CF is set. The operands can be signed or unsigned bytes, words, or doublewords.

TEST   Logical compare

INSTRUCTION	OPCODE	BINARY
TEST AL,imm8	A8 ib	10101000
TEST AX,imm16	A9 iw	10101001
TEST EAX,imm32	A9 id	10101001
TEST r/m8,imm8	F6 /0 ib	11110110 mm 000 r/m
TEST r/m16,imm16	F7 /0 iw	11110111 mm 000 r/m
TEST r/m32,imm32	F7 /0 id	11110111 mm 000 r/m
TEST r/m8,r8	84 /r	10000100 mm rrr r/m
TEST r/m16,r16	85 /r	10000101 mm rrr r/m
TEST r/m32,r32	85 /r	10000101 mm rrr r/m

Purpose: TEST ANDs two operands. It then clears OF and CF, leaves AF undefined, and updates SF, ZF, and PF. The flags can be tested by conditional control-transfer instructions or by the byte-set-on-condition instructions.

The difference between TEST and AND is that TEST does not store the result in the first operand. TEST differs from BT (Bit Test) in that TEST tests the value of multiple bits in one operation, while BT tests a single bit.

VERR Verify a segment for reading
VERW Verify a segment for writing

INSTRUCTION	OPCODE	BINARY
VERR r/m16	OF 00 /4	00001111 00000000 mm 100 r/m
VERW r/m16	OF 00 /5	00001111 00000000 mm 101 r/m

Purpose: These instructions verify whether a segment noted by the selector is reachable with the CPL and if the segment is readable. If the segment is accessible, ZF is set to 1; if not, ZF is set to 0. The validation performed is the same as if the segment were loaded into DS, ES, FS or GS and the indicated read was performed.

Because ZF receives the result of the validation, the selector's value does not result in a protection exception. This allows software to anticipate possible segment access problems.

WAIT

INSTRUCTION	OPCODE	BINARY
WAIT	9B	10011011

Purpose: WAIT causes the 80486 to check for pending unmasked numeric exceptions before proceeding. Coding WAIT after ESC ensures that any unmasked floating-point exceptions are handled before the 80486 has a chance to modify WAIT's results. FWAIT is an alternate mnemonic for WAIT.

WBINVD Write-back and invalidate cache

INSTRUCTION	OPCODE	BINARY
WBINVD	OF 09	00001111 00001001

Purpose: WBINVD causes internal cache to be flushed; a special-function bus cycle is issued which indicates that external cache should write-back its contents to main memory. Then another special-function bus cycle follows, which directs the external cache to flush itself. Note that WBINVD is implementation-dependent; future Intel processors might not implement the instruction in the same way, or at all. The instruction is not implemented on earlier processors (8086 through 80386).

XADD   Exchange and add

INSTRUCTION	OPCODE	BINARY
XADD r/m8,r8	0F C0 /r	00001111 11000000
XADD r/m16,r16	0F C1 /r	00001111 11000001
XADD r/m32,r32	0F C1 /r	00001111 11000001

Purpose: XADD loads the destination into the source, and then loads the sum of the destination and the source into the destination. This instruction is new to the 80486.

XADD can be used with a LOCK prefix.

XCHG   Exchange register/memory with register

INSTRUCTION	OPCODE	BINARY
XCHG AX,r16	90+r	10010rrr
XCHG r16,AX	90+r	10010rrr
XCHG EAX,r32	90+r	10010rrr
XCHG r32,EAX	90+r	10010rrr
XCHG r/m8,r8	86 /r	10000110 mm rrr r/m
XCHG r8,r/m8	86 /r	10000110 mm rrr r/m
XCHG r/m16,r16	87 /r	10000111 mm rrr r/m
XCHG r16,r/m16	87 /r	10000111 mm rrr r/m
XCHG r/m32,r32	87 /r	10000111 mm rrr r/m
XCHG r32,r/m32	87 /r	10000111 mm rrr r/m

Note that XCHG, AX,AX is a NOP.

Purpose: XCHG swaps the contents of two operands and takes the place of three MOV instructions. It does not require a temporary location to save the contents of one operand while loading the other. XCHG is useful for implementing semaphores or similar data structures for process synchronization.

If one of the operands is memory, the bus transfer is always performed as if a LOCK prefix is given, even if LOCK was not specified.

XLAT
XLATB
Table lookup-translation

INSTRUCTION	OPCODE	BINARY
XLAT m8	D7	11010111

Purpose: XLAT is useful for translating from one coding system to another, such as from EBCDIC to ASCII. The translate table can be up to 256-bytes long. The value placed in AL serves as an index to the location of the corresponding translation value.

XLAT replaces a byte in AL with a byte from a user-coded translation table at [EBX + AL]. AL is always an unsigned value. When XLAT is executed, AL should have the unsigned index to the table addressed by EBX. XLAT changes the contents of AL from the table index to the table entry. EBX is unchanged.

The table is always based at [EBX], regardless of the m8. However, m8 does allow a segment override to be specified rather than the default DS:[EBX].

XOR
Logical, exclusive OR

INSTRUCTION	OPCODE	BINARY
XOR AL,imm8	34 ib	00110100
XOR AX,imm16	35 iw	00110101
XOR EAX,imm32	35 id	00110101
XOR r/m8,imm8	80 /6 ib	10000000 mm 110 r/m
XOR r/m16,imm16	81 /6 iw	10000001 mm 110 r/m
XOR r/m32,imm32	81 /6 id	10000001 mm 110 r/m
XOR r/m16,imm8	83 /6 ib	10000011 mm 110 r/m
XOR r/m32,imm8	83 /6 ib	10000011 mm 110 r/m
XOR r/m8,r8	30 /r	00110000 mm rrr r/m
XOR r/m16,r16	31 /r	00110001 mm rrr r/m
XOR r/m32,r32	31 /r	00110001 mm rrr r/m
XOR r8,r/m8	32 /r	00110010 mm rrr r/m
XOR r16,r/m16	33 /r	00110011 mm rrr r/m
XOR r32,r/m32	33 /r	00110011 mm rrr r/m

Purpose: XOR compares the bits in its two operands and stores the result into the first operand. Each bit of the result is 1 if the corresponding bits in the operands are different. Each bit is 0 if the corresponding bits are the same. The result replaces the first operand.

```
Operand 1   1 1 0 0 0 1
Operand 2   0 0 1 1 0 1
Result      1 1 1 1 0 0
```

D
ASCII characters and keyboard codes

There are certain conventions in the use of keyboard keys that should be followed to make software more user-friendly; that is, users could move from one software package to another without having to relearn some basic conventions. The following conventions are recommended, but realize that even the largest software companies violate them:

Backspace   Removes the character to the left of the cursor, moves the cursor to that position, and shifts left all that follows.

Shift – Tab   Jumps the cursor left when struck.

Ctrl – Tab   Moves the cursor left or right by one word. Alternatively, scrolls the screen horizontally one tab-width to the left or right.

Ctrl – End   Deletes all text from the cursor to the end of the line.

Ctrl – Home   Clears the screen and positions the cursor at the top left.

Ctrl – PgDn   Deletes all text from the cursor to the bottom of the screen.

Del   Removes the character under the cursor and moves all that follows one space left.

End   Moves the cursor to the end of the line, or alternatively, to the end of the document.

Esc   Exits from a program or program routine.

Home   In text, moves the cursor to the start of a line, or alternatively, to the start of the document. In menus, Home switches to the topmost menu.

Ins   Toggles in and out of a mode where text is inserted in the midst of other text.

PgUp   Scrolls backward one screen, less 1 line.

PgDn   Scrolls forward one screen, less 1 line.

Scroll Lock Toggles the cursor keys in and out of a state where they scroll the screen rather than move the cursor.

Tab Jumps the cursor to the next tab position.

In addition to the 128 standard ASCII codes shown in Fig. D-1, there are codes called *box graphic* codes. These codes can be accessed by giving your program the hex number associated with the graphic. As shown in Fig. D-2, these codes are easy to use to draw a series of complex boxes or other maze-type figures.

IBM PC keyboard scan codes

The keys on the IBM PC keyboard have assigned numbers, called *scan codes*. When you press a key, the system converts the scan code to ASCII

Low 4 Bits	High 3 Bits							
	000	001	010	011	100	101	110	111
0000	NUL	DLE	SP	0	@	P	`	p
0001	SOH	DC1	!	1	A	Q	a	q
0010	STX	DC2	"	2	B	R	b	r
0011	ETX	DC3	#	3	C	S	c	s
0100	EOT	DC4	$	4	D	T	d	t
0101	ENQ	NAK	%	5	E	U	e	u
0110	ACK	SYN	&	6	F	V	f	v
0111	BEL	ETB	'	7	G	W	g	w
1000	BS	CAN	(	8	H	X	h	x
1001	HT	EM	)	9	I	Y	i	y
1010	LF	SUB	*	:	J	Z	j	z
1011	VT	ESC	+	;	K	[	k	{
1100	FF	FS	,	<	L	\	l		
1101	CR	GS	–	=	M	]	m	}
1110	SO	RS	.	>	N	^	n	~
1111	SI	US	/	?	O	–	o	DEL

D-1 Standard ASCII codes.

Where:

NUL	Null	DLE	Data Link Escape
SOH	Start of Heading	DC1	Device Control 1
STX	Start of Text	DC2	Device Control 2
ETX	End of Text	DC3	Device Control 3
EOT	End of Transmission	DC4	Device Control 4
ENQ	Enquiry	NAK	Negative Acknowledge
ACK	Acknowledge	SYN	Synchronous Idle
BEL	Audible Bell	ETB	End of Transmission Block
BS	Backspace	EM	End of Medium
HT	Horizontal Tab	SUB	Substitute
LF	Line Feed	ESC	Escape
VT	Vertical Tab	FS	File Separator
FF	Form Feed	GS	Group Separator
CR	Carriage Return	RS	Record Separator
SO	Shift Out	US	Unit Separator
SI	Shift In	DEL	Delete

(if it can) and sends the result to the keyboard buffer. However, certain keystrokes and combinations cannot be represented in ASCII. For these keystrokes and combinations, two bytes are sent. The first byte is a 0 and the second is the extended code shown in Fig. D-3.

IBM PC AT keyboard scan codes

The 80286 PC AT keyboard has keyboard scan numbers that range from 1 to A6. The numbers begin with the numeric and alphabetic characters, continue with function keys, and finish with cursor keys. When you press one of the keys, the keyboard sends the scan code (also called the *make* code) to the computer. When that key is released, the scan code +80 is sent (called the *break* code). The scan codes are shown in Fig. D-3.

Normally, BIOS translations of the keyboard scan codes are sufficient. If you intercept Interrupt 9h, however, you'll need to handle the make and break interrupts, and translate scan codes as your application requires.

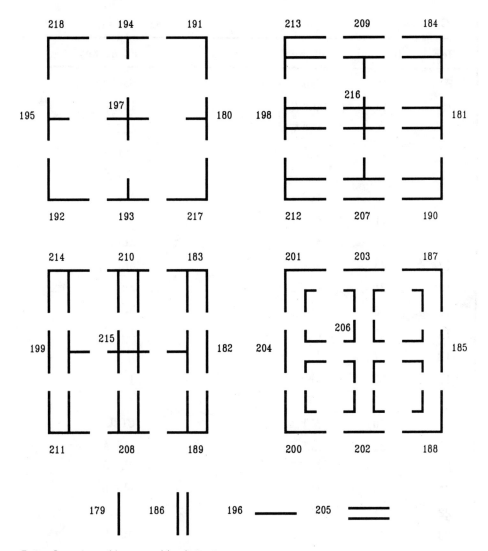

D-2 Overview of box graphic characters.

Hex	Decimal	PC Key	PC AT Key
1	1	ESC	Tilde ~
2–B	2–11	1–9, 0	1–9, 0
C	12	Minus, Underline	Minus, Underline
D	13	Equal, Plus	Equal, Plus
E	14	Backspace	Blackslash \, Vertical Bar |

D-3 IBM PC and PC AT keyboard scan codes.

Hex	Decimal	PC Key	PC AT Key
F	15	Tab	Backspace
10	16	ALT Q	Tab
11	17	ALT W	ALT Q
12	18	ALT E	ALT W
13	19	ALT R	ALT E
14	20	ALT T	ALT R
15	21	ALT Y	ALT T
16	22	ALT U	ALT Y
17	23	ALT I	ALT U
18	24	ALT O	ALT I
19	25	ALT P	ALT O
1A	26	[	ALT P
1B	27	]	[
1C	28	ENTER	]
1D	29	CTRL	
1E	30	ALT A	CTRL
1F	31	ALT S	ALT A
20	32	ALT D	ALT S
21	33	ALT F	ALT D
22	34	ALT G	ALT F
23	35	ALT H	ALT G
24	36	ALT J	ALT H
25	37	ALT K	ALT H
26	38	ALT L	ALT J
27	39	Semicolon, Colon	ALT L
28	40	Quote	Semicolon, Colon
29	41	Tilde ~	Quote
2A	42	Left Shift	
2B	43	Blackslash \, Vertical Bar |	ENTER
2C	44	ALT Z	Left Shift

Hex	Decimal	PC Key	PC AT Key
2D	45	ALT X	
2E	46	ALT C	ALT Z
2F	47	ALT V	ALT X
30	48	ALT B	ALT C
31	49	ALT N	ALT V
32	50	ALT M	ALT B
33	51	Comma	ALT N
34	52	Period	ALT M
35	53	Slash /, Question Mark ?	Comma
36	54	Right Shift	Period
37	55	Asterisk *, PrtSc	Slash /, Question Mark ?
38	56	ALT	
39	57	Space Bar	Right Shift
3A	58	Caps Lock	ALT
3B	59	F1	
3C	60	F2	
3D	61	F3	Space Bar
3E	62	F4	
3F	63	F5	
40	64	F6	Caps Lock
41	65	F7	F2
42	66	F8	F4
43	67	F9	F6
44	68	F10	F8
45	69	Num Lock	F10
46	70	Scroll Lock, BREAK	F1
47	71	Home	F3
48	72	Up Arrow	F5
49	73	PgUp	F7
4A	74	Minus (Far Left)	F9
4B	75	Left Arrow	

Hex	Decimal	PC Key	PC AT Key
4C	76	Keypad 5	
4D	77	Right Arrow	
4E	78		
4F	79	End	
50	80	Down Arrow	
51	81	PgDn	
52	82	Insert	
53	83	Delete	
5A	90		Escape
5B	91		Home
5C	92		Left Arrow
5D	93		End
5F	95		Num Lock
60	96		Up Arrow
61	97		Keypad 5
62	98		Down Arrow
63	99		Insert
64	100		Scroll Lock
65	101		PgUp
66	102		Right Arrow
67	103		PgDn
68	104		Delete
69	105		Sys
6A	106		Asterisk, PrSc
6B	107		Minus
6C	108		Plus

E
Overview of BIOS/MS-DOS interrupts and calls

A full list of BIOS and MS-DOS interrupts is described later in this appendix. Because it is often necessary to find a function because of a task you're programming, an effective way to get an overview of the very useful Interrupt 21 is to look at a list of the INT 21 functions grouped by the type of task each performs.

Interrupt 21 function summary
Character input

01	Character input with echo
03	Auxiliary input
06	Direct console I/O
07	Unfiltered character input without echo
08	Character input without echo
0A	Buffered keyboard input
0B	Check keyboard status
0C	Flush buffer, read keyboard

Character output

02	Character output
04	Auxiliary output
05	Print character
05	Direct console I/O
09	Display string (that ends with "$")

Disk management

OD   Disk reset
OE   Select disk
19   Get current disk
1B   Get default drive data
1C   Get drive data
2E   Set/reset verify flag
36   Get disk free space
54   Get verify flag

File management

OF   Open file with FCB
10   Close file with FCB
11   Find first file
12   Find next file
13   Delete file
16   Create file with FCB
17   Rename file
1A   Get DTA address
23   Get file size
2F   Get DTA address
3C   Create file with handle
3D   Open file with handle
3E   Close file
41   Delete file
43   Get/set file attributes
45   Duplicate file handle
46   Force duplicate file handle
4E   Find first file
4F   Find next file
56   Rename file
57   Get/Set Date/Time of file
5A   Create temporary file
5B   Create new file
5C   Lock/Unlock file region

Information management

14   Sequential read
15   Sequential write
21   Random read
22   Random write
24   Set relative record
27   Random block read

28	Random block write
3F	Read file or device
40	Write file or device
42	Move file pointer

Directory management

39	Create directory
3A	Remove directory
3B	Change current directory
47	Get current directory

Process management

00	Terminate process
31	Terminate and stay resident
4B	Load and execute program (EXEC)
4C	Terminate process with return code
4D	Get return code of child process
59	Get extended error information

Memory management

48	Allocate memory block
49	Free memory block
4A	Resize memory block
58	Get/Set allocation strategy

Miscellaneous system management

25	Set interrupt vector
26	Create new program segment prefix
29	Parse file name
2A	Get date
2B	Set date
2C	Get time
2D	Set time
30	Get MS-DOS version number
33	Get/set Ctrl+C check flag
35	Get interrupt vector
38	Get/set current country
44	IOCTL
5E	Network Machine Name/Printer setup
5F	Get/Make assign list entry
62	Get program segment prefix address

General BIOS interrupts

BIOS means *Basic I/O System*. It does just what the name implies—handles the system's input and output while keeping track of the equipment connected to the system.

BIOS is updated by the manufacturer as often (or perhaps more so) than DOS, which means that some of the information in this appendix will change at some point in time. However, MS-DOS and BIOS designers seem to be keeping the basic user interfaces the same, which is good news, even if the underlying code changes.

Interrupt 0: divide by zero

If the processor executes a divide by 0, INT 0 is called, which generally stops program execution.

Interrupt 1: single step

INT 1 single-steps through code, a necessity for debugging a program. There is a call to INT 1 between each line of program code.

Interrupt 2: nonmaskable interrupt (NMI)

INT 2 is a hardware interrupt that cannot be blocked off by using either STI or CLI. INT 2 executes when called.

Interrupt 3: breakpoint

INT 3 is another important debug interrupt. In fact, the programs DEBUG and SYMDEB use INT 3 with the GO command. For instance, if you want to execute code to a particular address and then stop, DEBUG and SYMDEB insert INT 3 into the code at that point and give control to the program. When the INT 3 is reached, the debugger takes control again.

Interrupt 4: overflow

If there is an overflow condition, INT 4 is called. Generally, no action is called for and BIOS returns.

Interrupt 5: print screen

The PrtSc key uses INT 5 to print the screen. Your program can do the same by simply calling this interrupt.

Interrupt 6 and 7: reserved

As with undefined bits in registers, you can use these interrupts for your own uses, but it's highly recommended that you do not because future development will cause you to go back and reprogram.

Interrupt 8: time of day

INT 8 updates the computer's internal clock. It does this as many times a second as the internal clock runs. This interrupt calls Timer Tick Interrupt INT. We recommend that you actually use INT 1C if you have to write a handler that interacts with the clock.

Interrupt 9: keyboard input

Each time you press a keyboard key, INT 9 is generated. The waiting keystroke is read from the keyboard port, processed, and stored in the keyboard buffer (if required). INT 9 does a lot of work, so we recommend that you allow INT 9 to do its job and read from the keyboard buffer (if anything is stored there).

Interrupt 0a: reserved

The same caveat is stressed here. You can use this if you are willing to invest future time to go back and rewrite when BIOS finally uses this interrupt.

Interrupts 0b through 0f: end-of-interrupt routines

These interrupts point to the BIOS routine End-of-Interrupt (D_EOI) routine. D_EOI simply resets the interrupt handler at port 20h and return.

BIOS Interrupt 10: screen/character handling

BIOS INT 10 includes a whole collection of routines that use AH as input with various quantities as output. Each of the functions have an Input and Output notation. Input values are always in AH. In the notation below, B&W means black and white on a graphics screen and does not refer to a monochrome screen.

INT 10 Function 00: set screen mode

This function of INT 10 establishes the video operating mode of the computer.

    Input: AH = 00
                  AL = mode:

                    00   16-shade gray text, 40×25; EGA: 64-color

01	16/8-color text, 40×25; EGA: 64-color
02	16-shade gray text, 80×25; EGA: 64-color
03	16/8-color text, 80×25; EGA: 64-color
04	4-color graphics, 320×200
05	4-shade gray graphics, 320×200
06	2-shade gray graphics, 640×200
07	Monochrome text, 80×25
08	16-color graphics, 160×200
09	16-color graphics, 320×200
0A	4-color graphics, 640×200
0B	Reserved
0C	Reserved
0D	16-color graphics, 320×200
0E	16-color graphics, 640×200
0F	Monochrome graphics, 640×350
10	16/64-color graphics, 640×350

INT 10 Function 01: set cursor type

INT 10 Function 1 allows you to change the appearance of the cursor. The cursor on a monochrome screen is 14-lines tall (0–13) and on a graphics screen is 8-lines tall (0–7). You put the starting line of the cursor matrix in CH and the ending line in CL. For instance, if you want the cursor to be only 1-line tall, store 0C in CH and 0D in CL before you issue INT 10. If you want the cursor to be at both the top and bottom, use the wrap-around feature: store 0D in CH and 00 in CL. You can't stop the cursor from blinking—that's set in hardware—but you can redesign or eliminate it.

Input: AH = 01
CH = Starting scan line
CL = Ending scan line

Note: CH < CL gives normal one-part cursor, CH > CL gives two-part cursor, and CH = 20 gives no cursor.

INT 10 Function 02: set cursor position

This function changes the position of the cursor. Store the row number in DH and the column in DL, remembering that 0,0 is the upper left corner of your screen. If you're using a graphics screen with a possibility of 4 pages, put the page number in BH. If you're using a monochrome display, store a 0 in BH.

Input: AH = 02
BH = Display page number (0 in graphics)
DH = Row number
DL = Column number

INT 10 Function 03: find cursor position

This function allows you to find where your cursor is, remembering that 0,0 is the upper left corner of the screen. If you're using a graphics screen with 4 pages, put the page number into BH. If you're using monochrome, store a 0 in BH. Function 3 of INT 10 returns the row number in DH, the column number in DL, the cursor mode in CH,CL (where the matrix starting line is in CL and the ending line is in CH).

Input: AH = 03
                BH = Display page number
Output: CH = Matrix ending line
                CL = Matrix starting line
                DH = Row number
                DL = Column number

INT 10 Function 04: read light pen position

This function returns the light pen position. (Remember that 0,0 is the upper left corner of the screen.)

Input: AH = 04
Output: AH = 00 Light pen switch not set
                AL = 01 Then:
                DH = Row of light pen position
                DL = Column of light pen position
                CH = Pixel line (vertical row) 0 – 199
                CX = Pixel line number (for some EGA modes)
                BX = Pixel column (horizontal column) 0 – 319,639

INT 10 Function 05: set active display page

By using INT 10 Function 05, you can move between the various pages in text mode on graphics monitors. Note that if you are doing graphics on the graphics monitor, only one page (page 0) is available for your use. On monochrome monitors, you only have page 0.

Input: AH = 05
                AL = Page number:
                        0 – 7 Screen modes 0 and 1 = 40-column text modes
                        0 – 3 Screen modes 2 and 3 = 80-column text modes

    Note: Each page = 2K in 40-column text mode, 4K in 80-column text mode.

INT 10 Function 06: scroll active page up

INT 10 Function 06 is useful when you have fill-in-the-blank applications where you selectively clear parts of the screen (see Fig. E-1). It's also useful for scrolling windows.

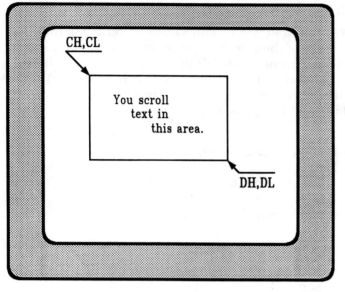

E-1 Example of scrolling selectively.

Input: AH = 06
AL = Number of lines blanked at bottom of the screen (00 blanks entire screen)
BH = Display attribute used on blank lines
CH = Upper left row of area to scroll
CL = Upper left column of area to scroll
DH = Lower right row of area to scroll
DL = Lower right column of area to scroll

INT 10 Function 07: scroll active page down

This function is the inverse of Function 06.

Input: AH = 07
AL = Number of lines blanked at top of screen (00 blanks entire screen)
BH = Display attribute used on blank lines
CH = Upper left row of area to scroll
CL = Upper left column of area to scroll
DH = Lower right row of area to scroll
DL = Lower right column of area to scroll

INT 10 Function 08:
read attribute and character at cursor position

This function returns the character byte and the following attribute byte for the current cursor position.

Input: AH = 08

BH = Display page number (for text mode only)

Output: If text mode:

AL = Character read (in ASCII)

AH = Attribute of character (alphanumerics only)

If graphics mode:

AL = ASCII character (00 if unmatched)

INT 10 Function 09:
write attribute and character at cursor position

Function 09 of INT 10 is the same as Function 8, except that it's a write operation.

Input: AH = 09

AL = ASCII character to write

BH = Display page number (graphics 1 – 4, monochrome = 0)

BL = Text attribute (Alpha mode); color of foreground (graphics mode)

CX = Number of times to write characters (must be > 0)

Note: Function 09 modifies AL, even though this is undocumented. AL returns with the last character in the character string, hex 24, a ($).

INT 10 Function 0A:
write character only at cursor position

This function writes only the specified character, which assumes whatever attribute happens to be current.

Input: AH = 0A

AL = ASCII character to write

BH = Display page number (graphics 14, monochrome = 0)

BL = Graphics foreground color (unused in text modes)

CX = Number of times to write character (must be > 0)

INT 10 Function 0B: select color palette

This function selects one of two color palettes.

Input: AH = 0B

BH = Palette color ID

BL = Background color (if BH = 0)

= Palette number (if BH = 1)

0 – Green/Red/Yellow

1 – Cyan/Magenta/White

INT 10 Function 0C: write dot

Note that in this function, instead of using DX for row/column, the column number is in CX.

Input: AH = 0C
             AL = Color attribute of pixel (0 – 3)
             CX = Pixel column number (0 – 319,639)
             DX = Pixel raster line number (0 – 199)

INT 10 Function 0D: read pixel dot

In this function, if bit 7 of AL is 1, then the color value is XORed with the current value of the dot. Position 0,0 is the upper left corner of the screen.

Input: AH = 0D
Output: AL = Pixel color attribute
             DX = Pixel row number (0 – 199)
             CX = Pixel column number (0 – 319,639)

INT 10 Function 0E: teletype write to active page

The cursor position is advanced. Beep, backspace, linefeed, and carriage return are active and all other characters are displayed.

Input: AH = 0E
             AL = ASCII character
             BH = Display page number
             BL = Foreground color in graphics mode (unused in text mode)

INT 10 Function 0F: return video state

This function returns the current values of the video state.

Input: AH = 0F
Output: AH = Characters per line (20, 40, or 80)
             AL = Current video mode

00	16-shade gray text, 40×25; EGA: 64-color
01	16/8-color text, 40×25; EGA: 64-color
02	16-shade gray text, 80×25; EGA: 64-color
03	16/8-color text, 80×25; EGA: 64-color
04	4-color graphics, 320×200
05	4-shade gray graphics, 320×200
06	2-shade gray graphics, 640×200
07	Monochrome text, 80×25
08	16-color graphics, 160×200
09	16-color graphics, 320×200
0A	4-color graphics, 640×200

	0B	Reserved
	0C	Reserved
	0D	16-color graphics, 320×200
	0E	16-color graphics, 640×200
	0F	Monochrome graphics, 640×350
	10	16/64-color graphics, 640×350

BH = Active display page

INT 10 Function 13: write character string

This function contains an implicit loop that iterates the same number of times as there are characters in the string.

Input: AH = 13
AL = Subfunction number
     00   String shares attribute in BL, cursor unchanged
     01   String shares attribute in BL, cursor advanced
     02   Each character has attribute, cursor unchanged
     03   Each character has attribute, cursor advanced
BH = Active display page
BL = String attribute (for AL=00 or 01 only)
CX = Length of character string
DH = Starting row number
DL = Starting column number
ES:BP = Address of string to be displayed

Note: For AL = 00 or 01, string=(char,char, . . .)
For AL = 02 or 03, string=(char,attr,char,attr, . . .)
For AL = 01 or 03, cursor position set to location following last character output.

BIOS Interrupt 11: equipment determination

This interrupt tells you most of the equipment that is installed in or on your computer. Look at the program FIND_CFG in chapter 9 to see how INT 11 can be used.

Input: AH   = 11
Output: AX Bits =
           0 = 1 if IPL diskette installed
           1 = 1 if numerics coprocessor here
         2,3 = Unused
         4,5 = Video mode
          00 = Reserved
          01 = 40×25 color card
          10 = 80×25 color card
          11 = 80×25 monochrome
         6,7 = Number of diskette drives

```
              00 = 1
              01 = 2
              10 = 3
              11 = 4
               8 = Unused
        9,10,11 = Number of RS-232 cards
             12 = Unused
             13 = If internal modem installed
          14,15 = Number of printers attached
```

Interrupt 12: determine memory size

INT 12 checks the size of installed memory as set by the internal DIP switches.

> **Input:** AH = 12
> **Output:** AX = Number of contiguous 1K memory blocks

BIOS Interrupt 13: disk I/O

INT 13 is used as the fundamental channel to most disk activities in most IBM PCs and clones. INT 13 works for both hard disk drives and floppy disk drives. Different drive numbers are used to distinguish between the two. For floppy drives, the numbers 0–3 are used, while hard disks use 80–87 (remember: all numbers are hex, unless stated specifically that they are not). Note that floppy disks support only functions 00 through 05 of INT 13. Hard drives support all INT 13 functions.

INT 13 Function 00: reset disk

INT 13, Function 00, is a hard reset to the disk controller to restore things to boot status. If there is an error using this function, CF is set and AH will contain the error code. The disk error codes are shown in Fig. E-2.

> **Input:** AH = 00
> AL = Drive number
>   00–07 Floppy disk
>   80–FF Fixed disk
> **Output:** Carry Flag = 0 (AL=0) successful
> Carry Flag = 1 (AL error code)

INT 13 Function 01: read status of last operation

If the function does not go to correct completion, an error code is stored into AL. See Fig. E-2 for a list of error codes and their meanings.

> **Input:** AH = 01
> **Output:** AH = Disk status (00 if successful)

Input	
AH = Function Number of INT 13	

Output

AL = Disk Error Code

00	No error
01	Bad command passed to controller
02	Address mark not found
03	Diskette is write–protected
04	Sector not found
05	Reset failed
06	Floppy Disk Removed
07	Drive parameters wrong
08	DMA Overflow
09	DMA across segment end
0A	Bad sector flag
0B	Bad track flag seen
10	Data error
11	Data is error–corrected
20	Controller failure
40	Seek operation failed
80	No response from disk , Time out
AA	Drive not ready
BB	Undefined error
E0	Status Error
0FF	Sense operation failed

E-2 Disk error codes. (All codes are in hexadecimal.)

INT 13 Function 02: read sectors into memory

As with function 00 and 01, if this function is not successful, AH contains an error code. See Fig. E-2 for a list of the error codes and their meanings. For hard disks, the drive number in DL can range from 80 to 87.

Input: AH = 02
AL = number of sectors to read
Floppies 1 – 8
Hard disk 1 – 80
Hard disk read/write long 1 – 79
CH = cylinder or track (floppy disk) number
CL = Sector number
DH = Head number
DL = Drive number
ES:BX = Buffer address
Output: Carry Flag = 0 (AL = 0) successful
Carry Flag = 1 (AL contains error code)

INT 13 Function 03: write sectors to disk

As with functions 00 through 02, if this function is not successful, AH contains an error code. See Fig. E-2 for a list of the error codes and their meanings. For hard disks, the drive number in DL can range from 80 to 87.

Input: AH = 03
AL = Number of sectors to write
Floppy diskettes = 1 – 8
Hard disks = 1 – 80
Hard disks read/write long = 1 – 79
CH = Cylinder or track (floppy) number
CL = Sector number
DH = Head number
DL = Drive number
ES:BX = Address of buffer for reads/writes
Output: Carry Flag = 0 (AL = 00) successful
Carry Flag = 1 (AL has error code)

INT 13 Function 04: verify sectors

As with functions 00 through 03, if this function is not successful, AH contains an error code. See Fig. E-2 for a list of the error codes and their meanings. For hard disks, the drive number in DL can range from 80 to 87.

Input: AH = 04
AL = number of sectors to verify
Floppy diskettes = 1 – 8
Hard disks = 180
Hard disks read/write long = 1 – 79
CH = Cylinder (hard drive) or track (floppy) number
CL = Sector number
DH = Head number
DL = Drive number

Output: Carry Flag = 0 (AL = 00) successful
Carry Flag = 1 (AL has error code)

INT 13 Functions 05, 06, and 07: formatting

Function 05 is supported only by floppy diskettes. Functions 06 and 07 work only on hard disks. As with functions 00 through 04, if this function is not successful, AH contains an error code. See Fig. E-2 for a list of the error codes and their meanings. For hard disks, the drive number in DL can range from 80 to 87.

Input: AH = 05 Format desired track
AH = 06 Format desired track and set bad sector flags
AH = 07 Format the desired disk starting at the indicated track
CH = Cylinder (hard drive) or track (floppy) number
DH = Head number
DL = Drive number (80 – 87 only allowed for hard disks)
ES:BX = 4-byte address field entries, 1 per sector
byte 0: Cylinder number
byte 1: Head number
byte 2: Sector number
byte 3: Sector-size code
00 = 128 bytes/sector
01 = 256 bytes/sector
02 = 512 bytes/sector
03 = 1024 bytes/sector
Output: Carry Flag = 0 (AL = 0) successful
Carry Flag = 1 (AL has error code)

INT 13 Function 08: return drive parameters

Function 08 of INT 13 works only on hard disks.

Input: AH = 08
DL = Drive number
Output: AH = 00
BH = 00
BL = Drive type
CH = Low-order 8 bits of 10-bit maximum number of cylinders
CL = Bits 7 and 6: high-order 2 bits of 10-bit maximum number of cylinders
Bits 5 – 0: maximum number of sectors/track
DH = Maximum value for head number

DL   = Number of drives attached to the controller
ES:DI = Address of floppy-disk drive parameter table

INT 13 Function 09: initialize drive

Function 09 is used by BIOS to initialize the drive and to point INT 41 to the drive's parameter block.

Input: AH = 09

INT 13 Functions 0A and 0B: Read/write long sectors

As with most INT 13 functions, if function 0A/0B is not successful, AL will contain an error code. See Fig. E-2 for a list of the error codes and their meanings. For hard disks, the drive number in DL can range from 80 to 87. Function 0A is for Read and 0B is for Write. This function is for hard disks only.

Input: AH = 0A,0B
              AL = Number of sectors to read
                          Floppy diskettes 1 – 8
                          Hard disk 1 – 80
                          Hard disk read/write long 179
              CH = Cylinder or track (floppy disk) number
              CL = Sector number
              DH = Head number
              DL = Drive number
          ES:BX = Buffer address
Output: Carry Flag = 0 (AL=0) successful
              Carry Flag = 1 (AL has error code)

INT 13 Function 0C: seek

As with most INT 13 functions, if function 0C is not successful, AL will contain an error code. See Fig. E-2 for a list of the error codes and their meanings. This function is for hard disks only, and the drive number in DL can range from 80 to 87.

Input: AH = 0C
              AL = Number of sectors to read
                          Floppy diskettes 1 – 8
                          Hard disk 1 – 80
                          Hard disk read/write long 179
              CH = Cylinder or track (floppy disk) number
              CL = Sector number
              DH = Head number
              DL = Drive number
          ES:BX = Buffer address

Output: Carry Flag = 0 (AL=0) successful
Carry Flag = 1 (AL has error code)

INT 13 Function 0D: alternate disk reset

This alternate disk reset is used only for hard disk drives. Function 0 also works to reset diskettes as well.

Input: AH = 0D
DL = Drive number

INT 13 Function 0E and 0F: read/write sector buffer

As with most INT 13 functions, if function 0D is not successful, AH contains an error code. See Fig. E-2 for a list of the error codes and their meanings. For hard disks, the drive number in DL can range from 80 to 87. Function 0E is for Read and 0F is for Write. This function is only for hard disks.

Input: AH = 0E,0F
DH = Head number
DL = Drive number (80 – 87 allowed)
CH = Cylinder number
CL = Sector number
ES:BX = Address of buffer for reads/writes
Output: Carry Flag = 0 (AL=0) successful
Carry Flag = 1 (AL has error code)

INT 13 Function 10: test drive ready

Function 10 of INT 13 tests whether or not a hard disk is ready for a read or write.

INT 13 Function 11: recalibrate hard drive

As with most INT 13 functions, if Function 11 is not successful, AH contains an error code. See Fig. E-2 for a list of the error codes and their meanings. For hard disks, the drive number in DL can range from 80 to 87. This function is only for hard disks.

Input: AH = 11
DL = Drive number (80 – 87 allowed)
Output: Carry Flag = 0 (AL=0) successful
Carry Flag = 1 (AL has error code)

INT 13 Functions 12 and 13: diagnostic services

As with most INT 13 functions, if Function 13 is not successful, AH contains an error code. See Fig. E-2 for a list of the error codes and their meanings. For hard disks, the drive number in DL can range from 80 to 87. This function is only for hard disks.

> **Input:** AH = 12 RAM diagnostics
> AH = 13 drive diagnostics
> AH = 14 controller diagnostics
> DL = Drive number (80 – 87 allowed)
> **Output:** Carry Flag = 0 (AL = 0) successful
> Carry Flag = 1 (AL has error code)

INT 13 Function 14: controller diagnostic

As with other INT 13 functions, if Function 14 is not successful, AH contains an error code. See Table E-1 for a list of status codes and their meanings.

> **Input:** AH = 14
> **Output:** AH = Status

INT 13 Function 15: get disk type

As with other INT 13 functions, if Function 15 is not successful, AH contains an error code. See Table E-1 for a list of status codes and their meanings.

> **Input:** AH = 15
> DL = Drive number
> **Output:** AH = Disk drive code:
> 00 = No drive present
> 01 = Cannot sense when floppy is changed
> 02 = Can sense when floppy is changed
> 03 = Fixed disk, also CX:DX = Number of sectors

INT 13 Function 16:
check for change of floppy disk status

As with other INT 13 functions, if Function 16 is not successful, AH contains an error code. See Table E-1 for a list of status codes and their meanings.

> **Input:** AH = 16
> DL = Number of drive to check
> **Output:** AH = 00 = No change
> 06 = Floppy disk change

INT 13 Function 17: set disk type

As with other INT 13 functions, if Function 17 is not successful, AH contains an error code. See Table E-1 for a list of status codes and their meanings.

Input: AH = 17
          AL = Floppy-diskette type code
          DL = Drive number

Interrupt 14: port usage

INT 14's various functions initialize RS-232C ports, send characters to them, receive characters from them, or return the status of the port.

INT 14 Function 00: initialize RS-232 port

This function configures the RS-232 port for one of eight baud rates and sets up the other parameters necessary for correct data transmission. There must be an installed RS-232 card in your system before this function works.

Input: AH = 00
          AL =
                Bits 0,1 = Character length
                      00 = Unused
                      01 = Unused
                      10 = 7 bits
                      11 = 8 bits
                   2 = Stop bits
                      0 = 1 stop bit
                      1 = 2 stop bits
                 3,4 = Parity
                      00 = None
                      01 = Odd
                      10 = None
                      11 = Even
               5,6,7 = Baud rate
                      000 = 110 baud
                      001 = 150 baud
                      010 = 300 baud
                      011 = 600 baud
                      100 = 1200 baud
                      101 = 2400 baud
                      110 = 4800 baud
                      111 = 9600 baud
          DX = Serial port number (0 = first port)

INT 14 Function 01: send one character

INT 14 Function 01 allows you to send data over your system's serial port. You load the character to send in AL, store 1 in AH, and call INT 14. AH holds the status on return. See Table E-1 for a list of the status and error codes and their meanings.

Return value	Meaning
8000	Time out
4000	Transfer shift register empty
2000	Transfer holding register empty
1000	Break detect
0800	Framing error
0400	Parity error
0200	Overrun error
0100	Data ready
0080	Received line signal detect
0040	Ring indicator
0020	Data set ready
0010	Clear to send
0008	Delta receive line signal detect
0004	Trailing edge ring detector
0002	Delta data set ready
0001	Delta clear to send

Input: AH = 01
AL = Character to send
DX = Serial port number (0 = first port)
Output: AX = Status (see Table E-1)

INT 14 Function 02: receive character

Function 02 allows you to read a character from the RS-232 port. AH holds the status on return. See Table E-1 for a list of the status and error codes and their meanings.

Input: AH = 02
DX = Serial port number (0 = first)
Output: AH = Status (see Table E-1)
If successful, AL holds the character

INT 14 Function 03: return status

Function 03 gives you the status of an RS-232 port. The status returns in AH. For a list of the status and error codes, see Table E-1.

Input: AH = 03

DX = Serial port number (0 = first)

Output: AH = Status

Interrupt 15: cassette I/O

INT 15 is the only BIOS support for cassettes, because they are rarely used. They can supply a large amount of storage and accurate, rapid back-ups are coming into the market.

Input: AH = 00 Turn cassette motor on

= 01 Turn cassette motor off

= 02 Read one or more 256-byte blocks

Store data at ES:BX

CX = Count of bytes to read

On return, DX holds number of bytes read

ES:BX points to one byte past the last read

= 03 Write one or more 256 byte blocks from ES:BX.

CX = Count of bytes to write

On return, CX = 00 ES:BX points to location following last byte written

Output: DX = Number of bytes actually read

Carry Flag = 1, if error

If set, AH = 01 CRC error

= 02 Data transitions lost

= 03 No data found

Interrupt 16: keyboard services

INT 16 handles keyboard input. AL will contain the ASCII code on return. However, if the key pressed was in the extended code, AH will contain the scan code.

INT 16 Function 00: read key from keyboard

Function 00 waits until a character is read; it then removes the character from the keyboard buffer.

Input: AH = 00

Output: If standard ASCII:

AH = Standard keyboard scan code

AL = ASCII code

If extended ASCII:

AH = Extended ASCII code

AL = 00

INT 16 Function 01: check if key ready to be read

This function returns immediately and does not remove the character from the keyboard buffer.

Input: AH = 01
Output: ZF = 0
            ZF = 1 Buffer is empty
            If standard ASCII:
                  AH = Standard keyboard scan code
                  AL = ASCII code
            If extended ASCII:
                  AH = Extended ASCII code
                  AL = 00

INT 16 Function 02: get shift status

This function returns the status of the various shift keys. There can be multiple shifts active at the same time.

Input: AH = 02
Output: AL = Shift status
            01 = Right shift active
            02 = Left shift active
            04 = Ctrl active
            08 = Alt active
            10 = Scroll Lock active
            20 = Num Lock active
            40 = Caps Lock active
            80 = Insert state active

Interrupt 17: printer services

INT 17 Function 00: send byte to printer

INT 17 Function 00 is how BIOS talks to your printer. Set DX to the printer number you will print on (numbers range from 0–2 and correspond to printer cards). Generally you'll choose 0. To print a character, store it in AL, set AH to 0, and issue INT 17.

Input: AH = 00
            AL = Character to be printed
            DX = Printer number (0, 1, 2)
Output: AH = Printer status (see Table E-2)

INT 17 Function 01: initialize printer port

INT 17 Function 01 resets the printer and prepares it for output. On return, AH holds the printer's status as shown in Table E-2. If you select a printer you don't have, you get a time-out for status.

Table E-2   Printer status codes.

Return value	Meaning
80	Printer not busy
40	Printer Acknowledgement
20	Out of paper
10	Printer selected
08	I/O Error
04	Unused
02	Unused
01	Time out

Note: Multiple states can be active

simultaneously

Input: AH = 01
DX = Printer number (0, 1, 2)
Output: AH = Printer status

INT 17 Function 02: read printer status into AH

In case your program seems to be having problems sending information to the printer, you can check on its status. See Table E-2 for a list of the status codes that will return in AH.

Input: AH = 02
DX = Printer number (0, 1, 2)
Output: AH = Status

Interrupt 18: resident BASIC

INT 18 starts ROM-resident BASIC.

Interrupt 19: bootstrap (warm start)

INT 19 loads the boot record from disk, if there is one. If not, ROM-resident BASIC is executed.

Interrupt 1A: time of day

Your system's clock increments at a vast rate, depending on the clock rate, measured in megahertz. The functions of INT 1A work with the clock.

INT 1A Function 00: read time of day

Function 00 of Interrupt 1A reads the time of day from the system clock.

Input: AH = 00
Output: AL = 0 if timer has not passed 24 hours since last read
CX = High word of timer count
DX = Low word of timer count

INT 1A Function 01: set time of day

Function 01 sets the time of day.

Input: AH = 01
CX = High word of timer count
DX = Low word of timer count

INT 1A Function 02: read real-time clock

Function 02 returns the number of hours, minutes, and seconds since the last system reset.

Input: AH = 02
Output: CF = 0 Clock running
= 1 Clock stopped
CH = Hours in BCD
CL = Minutes in BCD
DH = Seconds in BCD
Note: See the procedures in chapter 4 (BCDUNPK) to get digits into AH,AL.

INT 1A Function 03: set real-time clock

See procedures in chapter 4 on how to pack BCD values before calling this function.

Input: AH = 03
CH = Hours in BCD
CL = Minutes in BCD
DH = Seconds in BCD
DL = 00 Standard Time
01 Daylight saving time

INT 1A Function 04: read date from real-time clock

See procedures in chapter 4 on how to unpack BCD.

Input: AH = 04
Output: CF = 0 Clock running
= 1 Clock stopped
CH = Century in BCD
CL = Year in BCD

DH = Month in BCD
DL = Day in BCD

INT 1A Function 05: set date in real-time clock

Before calling this function, see procedures in chapter 4 on how to pack BCD.

Input: AH = 05
CH = Century in BCD
CL = Year in BCD
DH = Month in BCD
DL = Day in BCD

INT 1A Function 06: set alarm

See procedures in chapter 4 on how to pack BCD.

Input: AH = 06
CH = Hours in BCD
CL = Minutes in BCD
DH = Seconds in BCD
Output: CF = 0 Operation successful
= 1 Alarm already set or clock stopped

INT 1A Function 07: reset alarm (turn alarm off)

This function cancels the activity of Function 6.

Input: AH = 07

Other BIOS interrupts
Interrupt 1B: keyboard break address

INT 1B holds the address that control will be transferred to if your program is broken with a Break. You can write your own Break handler by intercepting and redirecting this interrupt. This is useful when you don't want the program interrupted while running.

Interrupt 1C: timer tick interrupt

INT 1C is called by INT 8. Originally, INT 1C points only to an IRET instruction, which can be redirected to another location at your option.

Interrupt 1D: video parameter tables

INT 1D points to the address of the video controller parameter tables.

Interrupt 1E: diskette parameters

INT 1E is like INT 1D, in that it points to a parameter table, the Diskette Base Table, which is 11-bytes long. Because it's in ROM, you can't change it. However, DOS also stores it in low memory, at 0000:0078, which you can change. See Fig. E-3 for the table format. It is recommended, however, that you do not change the values.

```
DOS Memory 0000:0078
─────────────────────────────────────────────────────────────
   Byte 0,1    Contain step rate time and head load/unload times
        2      The time it takes diskette motors to turn off
                  after an operation
        3      Number of bytes per sector
        4      Number of sectors per track
    5,6,7      These bytes are concerned with the layout of the
                  disk sectors
        8      Fill byte – The byte used to fill newly formatted
                  disk sectors
        9      Head settle time – the time given for the diskette
                  head to come to rest after it has shot into
                  position over the track
       10      Diskette motor start and warm–up time.
```

E-3 Diskette base table. (It is recommended that you do not change these values.)

Interrupt 1F: graphics character definitions

INT 1F points to a table in memory that allows you to define the top 128 ASCII characters in high-resolution graphics mode for graphics screens only. The table is a list of 128 characters, with 8 bytes each, for 1,024 total bytes.

About MS-DOS interrupts

Many operating systems are disk-based and offer interactive operation to users. MS-DOS offers many special features in tightly coded system interrupts. These interrupts allow multitasking and pipeline processing, both of which keep a processor busy instead of waiting for work. This business allows more processes to flow through a computer, which means that more tasks are accomplished in a shorter period of time.

The MS-DOS interrupts, 20F0, are usable by systems programmers.

Interrupt 20: terminate

At the end of user programs, INT 20 terminates the program and gives control back to MS-DOS.

Interrupt 21: service interrupts

INT 21 is a power-packed interrupt, with a great number of subfunctions. To call one of its functions, load the function number into AH (and any other register values as shown in each of the functions) and issue INT 21. As throughout this book, all numbers are hexadecimal unless specifically stated otherwise.

INT 21 Function 0: program terminate

This function of INT 21 is exactly the same as INT 20. It ends your program and returns control to MS-DOS.

Input: AH = 0

INT 21 Function 1: keyboard input

With this function, any key you press (that has a graphic) is echoed to the display screen. When you use Function 1, processing stops until a key is pressed; that is, it waits for input. If the corresponding character is ASCII, it prints it on the screen. The tab character is automatically expanded to the end of the next 8-column field by adding spaces. Holding the Ctrl key and pressing Break terminates operation.

If the pressed key corresponds to an extended code, the AL register contains a 0. Then you must execute this function again to get the code. If the second value is less than 84, it represents the scan code of the pressed key. For example, a value of 30 means that the Alt key and the letter A were pressed. Values above 83 are more difficult to decode but are shown in appendix D. Input can be read from another device or disk file by redirection of the standard input.

Input: AH = 1
Output: AL = ASCII code of struck key

INT 21 Function 2: character output on screen

This function displays the character contained in the DL register onto the screen. It is useful for writing a single character (use Function 9 for a string). Function 2 is useful for displaying the dollar sign ($), because Function 9 uses $ as the end-of-string character. The Backspace key moves the cursor to the left, but does not erase the character printed there.

The output can be sent to another device or disk file by redirecting the standard output.

> **Input:**   AH = 2
> DL = ASCII character

INT 21 Function 3: standard auxiliary device input

This function reads a character from the standard auxiliary device, generally the serial port, defined as AUX or COM1. However, you can change the standard auxiliary port to COM2. Function 3 waits until a byte is available.

> **Input:**   AH = 3
> **Output:** Character in AL

INT 21 Function 4: standard auxiliary device output

Function 4 sends the byte in register DL to the auxiliary port AUX or COM1.

> **Input:**   AH = 4
> DL = The character to output

INT 21 Function 5: printer output

This function sends the character in register DL to the standard printer port, PRN or LPT1. As with Function 4, the byte to be written to the printer is passed in DL. You could also use INT 17 for this purpose.

> **Input:**   AH = 5
> DL = The character to output

INT 21 Function 6: console input/output

Function 6 can perform both input and output; it can also determine the input status. It does not wait for input. Also, the input character is not automatically displayed and Ctrl-Break does not terminate the operation.

> **Input:**   AH = 6
> **Output:** If DL = FF AL holds the character if one is ready
>   DL < FF Type ASCII code in DL out

INT 21 Function 7: console input without echo

INT 21 Function 7, like Function 1, waits for keyboard entry. If an ASCII character is entered, the ASCII value is returned in the AL register. The IBM graphics characters can be entered by holding the Alt key and typing the decimal value on the number keypad. If an extended character (such as a function key) is entered, a 0 is stored in AL. This function must then be called a second time to determine the character. Unlike Function 1, Function 7 does not display the input character. Also, Ctrl + Break does not terminate the process.

Input: AH = 7
Output: AL = ASCII code of struck key

INT 21 Function 8: console input without echo, but with break check

Function 8 waits for a character and terminates when Ctrl + Break is pressed. The input character is not displayed and tab characters are not expanded.

Input: AH = 8
Output: AL = ASCII code of struck key

INT 21 Function 9: string print

INT 21 Function 9 is useful for printing a string of characters on the screen. Function 9 is easy to use. To do so, place the string somewhere in memory and terminate it with a dollar sign ($), which means that you cannot include a dollar sign as part of the string (use Function 2 to print a $). The address of the string is placed in the DS:DX registers.

Input: AH   = 9
        DS:DX = Address of the string that ends in $

INT 21 Function 0A: string input

All characters typed by the user are entered into the keyboard buffer. When the Return key is pressed, the line is stored into the input buffer.

Before you use this function, set up a buffer in memory. Remember that there are two auxiliary bytes located at the beginning of the buffer, as shown in Fig. E-4. The first byte defines the maximum length of text that can be stored in the buffer. The second byte gives the number of characters that were entered by the user. You set the value of the first byte. MS-DOS fills in the second byte after the buffer has been read. MS-DOS also adds a carriage return to the end of the input string. However, this carriage return is not included in the count that MS-DOS enters in the second byte. So, you should set the maximum size of the buffer to be one-byte larger than you need.

Input: AH   = 0A
        [DS:DX] = Length of buffer
Output: Buffer at DS:DX filled
        Echoes the typed keys

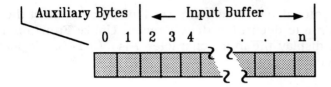

Aux byte 0 = The maximum length of the input (set by user)

1 = The number of bytes actually entered (set by DOS)

This count does NOT include the carriage return

that DOS adds to the end of the string.

E-4   Input buffer format.

INT 21 Function 0B: check input status

This function is useful for checking to see if there is any keyboard input waiting, which avoids having a program wait for something if there's no need to. On return from this function, AL contains 0 if no key has been pressed. Any other AL value indicates a character is waiting to be read— although this function does not read the character.

Input: AH = 0B
DS:DX points to an FCB
Output: AL = FF if a character is ready
AL = 0 if nothing is there to be read in

INT 21 Function 0C: clear buffer and invoke service

INT 21 Function 0C clears the keyboard buffer before it invokes a keyboard function (1, 6, 7, 8, or 0A). This is important when your user might be typing ahead (because of familiarity with your software, the user knows what question comes next and will type an answer before the question hits the screen). If your program finds an error (such as an Abort, Retry, Ignore?), you must have a correct answer to that prompt before you can allow your normal software to continue. So you flush the keyboard buffer and wait for that answer to be entered. INT 21 Function 0C also checks for Break.

Input: AH = 0C
AL = Keyboard function number

INT 21 Function 0D: disk reset

This function serves the same purpose as BIOS Interrupt 13 Function 00.

Input: AH = 0D

INT 21 Function 0E: select disk

INT 21 Function 0E is how MS-DOS selects your default disk. Whenever you type C: at a prompt, INT 21 Function 0E is called. This was one of the early MS-DOS interrupts. INT 21 Function 3B is more comprehensive; it allows you to change the current directory, including the default drives.

Input: AH = 0E
                DL = Drive number

INT 21 Function 0F: open pre-existing file

This function opens a file that you created some time in the past (it might be just before you used this function). It does not create the file for you. It uses file control blocks (FCBs), which are supported under all MS-DOS versions, although it's recommended now to use file handles because FCBs do not allow you to specify subdirectories. See Fig. E-5 for the format of an opened FCB.

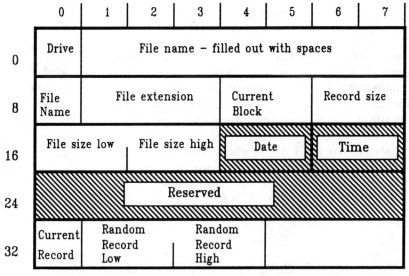

E-5 File Control Block (FCB) format for an opened file. (Shaded areas are reserved by MS-DOS.)

There is no space in the normal FCB for either the file's creation time or its attribute. You can add the attribute by using an extended FCB. The extended FCB looks the same as the FCB, with an added seven bytes at the beginning: a byte of FF, five bytes of zeros, and the attribute byte. See Table E-3 for a list of file attributes and their meanings.

Using the FCBs (instead of file handles) is somewhat awkward, so instead of continuing, we're recommending that you study your MS-DOS

Table E-3   File attribute—extended FCB.

Attribute bit	Meaning
0	Read–only
1	Hidden. Directory searches will not find.
2	System file, same attribute as IBMDOS.COM
3	Volume file, the eleven letters of the file name actually are the disk's label
4	Directory
5	Archive, this bit is checked by BACKUP to see if the file has been rewritten since last BACKUP run
6	Reserved
7	Reserved

manual carefully. There are two ways to read files, sequential and random. Sequential files need a marker between records (because MS-DOS knows that the records can be of differing lengths). If you use MS-DOS sequential read/writing functions, MS-DOS takes care of the markers. Random files, on the other hand, need records of the same size. MS-DOS defaults to a size of 128 bytes. If your record size is different, you must modify the record size in the FCB after a successful open.

Input: AH = OF
Output: AL = 0 if successful
　　　　　AL = FF if unsuccessful

INT 21 Function 10: close file

To keep your data intact, be sure to close all files before you exit your program. INT 21 Function 10 reads what's in the FCB and writes it to the directory. Its major use is to give the file a non-zero size. MS-DOS usually keeps track of file size, but you can use this function to do so.

Input: AH = 10
Output: AL = 0 if successful
　　　　　AL = FF if unsuccessful
　　　　　　　DS:DX points to an FCB.

INT 21 Function 11: search for first matching file

MS-DOS uses INT 21 Function 11 to search the disk for files. Point DX:DX at an unopened FCB and call this function. The FCB can use a ? wildcard (but not the *, which file handle functions can use). For example, if you want to find all the file names with a ".ASM" extension, you would have to fill the FCB file name with ???????? and the extension with *ASM*. The eight question marks will find any length file name, from a single character to eight. If the search finds a match, an unopened FCB (for the matching file) will be stored in the DTA. You can use this FCB for any use, just as you would any other FCB.

Input: AH = 11
Output: AL = 0 if successful
AL = FF if unsuccessful
DTA holds FCB for match
DX:DX points to an unopened FCB.

INT 21 Function 12: search for next matching file

After you find the first matching file (using INT 21 Function 11), MS-DOS fills part of the reserved areas in the FCB. This function uses that information to find the next match in the directory.

Input: AH = 12
Output: AL = 0 if successful
AL = FF if unsuccessful
DTA holds FCB for match
DX:DX points to an unopened FCB.

INT 21 Function 13: deletes files

INT 21 Function 13 simply deletes files. All you have to do is to point DS:DX at an unopened FCB and issue this interrupt and function.

Input: AH = 13
Output: AL = 0 if successful
AL = FF if unsuccessful
DTA holds FCB for match.
DX:DX points to an unopened FCB.

INT 21 Function 14: sequential read

INT 21 Function 14 reads sequential records from an opened file. You set the current block field (bytes 0C–0D in the FCB) and the current record field from 0 to 127 in byte 1F. The data read is dumped in the DTA. If you change the record length from the default 128 bytes, you get whatever your change is in the DTA. The record address increments with each read, which means that if the current record is 127, the next record will be 0.

Input: AH = 14
Output: Requested record put in DTA
        AL = 0 if successful
              1 End of file, no data in record
              2 DTA segment too small for record
              3 End of file, record padded with 0's
              Current address is incremented, current block
              and record is set in FCB, and DX:DX points
              to an opened FCB.

INT 21 Function 15: sequential write

INT 21 Function 15 writes a record from the Disk Transfer Area (DTA is always used in FCB operations) to an open file. The record address increments. Note that if your record size is significantly smaller than a sector (512 bytes), MS-DOS buffers your data and writes it only when there is enough to write, or when you end the program. (Note that this is one of the tasks that INT 20 or INT 27 takes care of for you.)

Input: AH = 15
Output: One record read from DTA and written
        AL = 0 if successful
              1 Disk full
              2 DTA segment too small for record
              Record address is incremented, current
              block and record is set in FCB, and DX:DX
              points to an opened FCB.

INT 21 Function 16: create file

INT 21 Function 16 creates a file. If a file already exists with the same name (the one you put into the FCB), that file will be opened and set to zero length—which can destroy valid data you stored there earlier, if you overwrite it by accident. If there is no identical file, a directory entry is opened for this new one. If there is no space left on your diskette or hard disk, this function returns an FF and you have to free some space.

Input: AH = 16
Output: AL = 0 if successful
              FF Directory full
              DX:DX points to an unopened FCB.

INT 21 Function 17: rename file

If you need to rename files, use this interrupt and function (it's the way MS-DOS does it). The FCB can use a "?" wildcard (but not the "*," which file handles functions can). For example, if you want to find all the file names with a ".ASM" extension, you would have to fill the FCB file name with *????????* and the extension with *ASM*. The eight question marks will find any length file name, from a single character to eight.

To use INT 21 Function 17, set up an unopened FCB for the file(s) you want to rename.

Input: AH = 17
Output: AL = 0 if successful
FF Directory full
DX:DX points to a modified FCB
For a modified FCB, the second file name
starts 6-bytes after the end of the first
file name at DS:DX + 11.

INT 21 Function 18: internal to MS-DOS

This function is used only by MS-DOS. It is here so you can see that it is used and unavailable for your use.

INT 21 Function 19: find current disk

INT 21 Function 19 is handy if you want to find out where you are.

Input: AH = 19
Output: AL = Current disk
0 = A
1 = B
2 = C
3 = D (and so on)

INT 21 Function 1A: set disk transfer area (DTA) location

MS-DOS default Disk Transfer Area (DTA) and record size in the FCB are only 128 bytes, but you might need a larger size. One area you can use for more bytes is the end of your program in memory. Be careful not to overwrite the stack that MS-DOS supplies at the top of every .COM file's segment.

Input: AH = 1A
DS:DX points to new DTA address.

INT 21 Function 1B: file allocation table (FAT) information

This function returns FAT information for the default drive.

Input: AH = 1B
Output: AL = Number of sectors/cluster

DS:DX points to the FAT byte
DX = Number of clusters
CX = Size of a sector (e.g., 512)

INT 21 Function 1C:
file allocation table (FAT) information for specified drive

After issuing this interrupt, DX holds the number of usable clusters. AL holds the number of sectors/cluster, while CX holds the size of a physical sector on the drive selected.

Input: AH = 1C
          DS:DX points to an unopened FCB.
Output: AL = Number of sectors/cluster
          DS:DX points to the FAT byte
          DX = Number of clusters
          CX = Size of a sector (e.g., 512)

INT 21 Function 1D through 20: internal to MS-DOS

These functions are used only by MS-DOS. They're here so you can see that they are used and unavailable for your use.

INT 21 Function 21: random read

To write into the DTA from a random read, set the random record field in an opened FCB. DS:DX + 21 holds the low word of the random record number and DS:DX + 23 holds the high word. When you request the read, MS-DOS sets the current block and record fields for you.

Input: AH = 21
Output: AL = 00 Successful
                01 End of file, no more data
                02 Not enough space in DTA segment
                03 End of file, partial record padded with 0's
              DS:DX points to an opened FCB
              Set FCB's Random Record field at DS:DX + 21
              and DS:DX + 23

INT 21 Function 22: random write

To use INT 21 Function 22, fill the DTA with the record you want to write. Set the random record field in the FCB. It's recommended that you double-check your record field and record number. If you use an incorrect record field, you'll overwrite something you don't want destroyed. Also, if your record number is far in excess of what is currently in your file, MS-DOS will simply extend your file the required length to stick that record at the end and fill in the intervening space (if there was garbage in storage, that's what you get in the intervening space). MS-DOS sets the current block and record fields for you.

Input: AH = 21
Output: AL = 00 Successful
                01 Disk is full
                02 Not enough space in DTA segment
                DS:DX points to an opened FCB
                Set FCB's Random Record field at DS:DX+21
                and DS:DX+23.

INT 21 Function 23: file size

If you want to know the size of a file (without having to opening it), use this function. You'll need an unopened FCB. Point DS:DX at the FCB and MS-DOS searches the current directory for a match to the file name. If it finds a match, the random record fields of the FCB will be set to the total length of the file in records—rounded up. If you set the record length to a value, the total bytes are divided by that number and the result rounded up. If you want the total size in bytes, set the record length to 1 byte. If MS-DOS does not find a match in the directory, AL returns FF.

Input: AH = 22
Output: AL = 00 Successful
              = FF No file found that matched FCB
                    Random Record Field is set to file length in
                    records, rounded up
                    DS:DX points to an unopened FCB

INT 21 Function 24: set random record field

Random Record Field is set to match Current Record and Current Block.

Input: AH = 24
                DX:DX points to an opened FCB

INT 21 Function 25: set interrupt vector

The value in DS:DX is the address. It is not a segment value (DS) and an offset (DX).

Input: AH   = 25
                AL   = Interrupt number
                DS:DX = New address

INT 21 Function 26: create a new program segment

This is an old implementation of the operation needed for creating new segments. Use Function 4B instead.

INT 21 Function 27: random block read

When you read in a random record, INT 21 Function 27 updates the random record field. When the function is finished, the random record field is set to the number of the next, unread record.

Input: AH = 27
Output: AL = 00 Successful
01 End of file, no more data
02 Not enough space in DTA segment
03 End of file, partial record padded with 0's
CX = Number of records read
Random Record Fields are set to access next record.
DS:DX points to an opened FCB. Set FCB's Random
Record field at DS:DX + 21 and DS:DX + 23.

INT 21 Function 28: random block write

If you set CX to 0 when you call this function, the fill will be set to the length given by the random record field. This might force the file to be truncated or enlarged. If it enlarges, it includes whatever garbage is in the free sectors on the disk.

Input: AH = 28
CX = Number of records to write.
0 = File is set to size indicated in Random Record field.
Output: AL = 00 Successful
01 Disk is full
02 Not enough space in DTA segment
Random Record Fields set to access next record,
DS:DX points to an opened FCB, and FCB's
Random. Record field is set at DS:DX + 21 and
DS:DX + 23.

INT 21 Function 29: parse file name

INT 21 Function 29 is useful in parsing file names from the command line. You give it the address of the command line. If it finds a file name, the function places an unopened FCB for the file at address ES:DI. If the command line does not contain a valid file name, ES:[DI + 1] will contain blanks.

Input: AH = 29
AL = Bit 0 = 1 Leading separators are scanned off command
line
1 = 1 Drive ID in final FCB will be changed only if a
drive was specified

2 = 1 File name in FCB changed only if command
line includes file name
3 = 1 File name extension in FCB will be changed
only if command line contains a file name
extension
DS:SI = Command line to parse
ES:DI = Address to put FCB
Output: DS:SI = First character after file name
ES:DI = Valid FCB

INT 21 Function 2A: get date

Input: AH = 2A
Output: CX = Year 1980 through 2099
DH = Month number, where January = 1
DL = Day of the month

INT 21 Function 2B: set date

Input: AH = 2B
CX = Year − 1980
DH = Month number, where January = 1
DL = Day of the month
Output: AL = 0 if successful
AL = FF if date not valid

INT 21 Function 2C: get time

Input: AH = 2C
Output: CH = Hours (0 – 23)
CL = Minutes (0 – 59)
DH = Seconds (0 – 59)
DL = Hundredths of seconds (0 – 99)

INT 21 Function 2D: set time

Input: AH = 2D
CH = Hours (0 – 23)
CL = Minutes (0 – 59)
DH = Seconds (0 – 59)
DL = Hundredths of seconds (0 – 99)
Output: AL = 0 if successful
AL = FF if time is invalid

INT 21 Function 2E: set or reset verify switch

INT 21 Function 2E turns verification for disk writing on or off. This helps
protect you against disk errors.

Input: AH = 2E
              AL = 0 Turn verify off
                   1 Turn verify on
              DL = 0

INT 21 Function 2F: get current DTA

This function is useful if you move the DTA location often and want to know where you are.

Input: AH   = 2F
Output: ES:BX = Current DTA address

INT 21 Function 30: get MS-DOS version number

This function lets you know what version of MS-DOS is running. AL holds the major version, the 3 in MS-DOS 3.10. AH holds the minor version, the 10 of 3.10. If AL returns a 0, you're working with an early MS-DOS, before 2.0. Program FIND_VER shows a use of this function.

Input: AH = 30
Output: AL = Major version number
            AH = Minor version number
            BX = 0
            CX = 0

INT 21 Function 31: terminate process and stay resident

This is the preferred method of installing a TSR routine. It is intended to supersede INT 27.

Input: AH = 31
              AL = Binary exit code
              DX = Size of memory request in paragraphs

INT 21 Function 32: internal to MS-DOS

This function is used only by MS-DOS. It's here so you can see that it is used and unavailable for your use.

INT 21 Function 33: control break check

MS-DOS uses this function to check if a Break is pending each time an MS-DOS function is called. Otherwise, the user might wait a long time for a Break to be noticed and processed.

Input: AH = 33
              AL = 0 to check the state of BREAK checking
                   1 to set the state of BREAK checking

               DL = 0 to turn it off
                     1 to turn it on
     Output: DL = 0 if off
                     1 if on

INT 21 Function 34: internal to MS-DOS

This function is used only by MS-DOS. It's here so you can see that it is
used and unavailable for your use.

INT 21 Function 35: get interrupt vector

This function works with Function 25, which sets vectors.

     Input: AH = 35
                   AL = Interrupt number
     Output: ES:BX = Interrupt vector

INT 21 Function 36: get free disk space

MS-DOS uses this function when it tells you how many free bytes are available on a disk. The smallest piece of the disk that is kept track of is the
cluster, so the number of bytes in a cluster multiplied by cluster number
gives the total number of bytes available. INT 21 Function 36 returns similar information as INT 21 Function 1C, except that instead of pointing at
the file allocation table (FAT) byte, BX holds the number of free clusters.

     Input: AH = 36
                   DL = Drive number
                         0 – Default
                         1 – A
                         2 – B, and so on
     Output: AX = 0FFF – Drive number is invalid.
                         Number of sectors/clusters
                   BX = Number of available clusters
                   CX = Size of a sector
                   DX = Number of clusters

INT 21 Function 37: internal to MS-DOS

This function is used only by MS-DOS. It's here so you can see that it is
used and unavailable for your use.

INT 21 Function 38: return country-dependent information

This function is valuable if you're writing or modifying international software. See Fig. E-6 for the formats of the various fields.

The 32-byte block format:	

0,1	Date/Time Format
	    0 = USA (H:M:S M/D/Y)
	    1 = Europe (H:M:S D/M/Y)
	    2 = Japan (H:M:S D:M:Y)

2	Currency symbol ASCII
3	Set to 0
4	Thousands separator ASCII
5	Set to 0
6	Decimal separator ASCII
7	Set to 0
8–31	Used internally, do not use

E-6   Country-dependent information.

Input: AH = 38
        AL = 0
   DS:DX = Address of 32-byte block
Output: Filled-in 32-byte block (see Fig. E-6)

INT 21 Function 39: create a subdirectory

The MS-DOS command MKDIR uses this function to create a subdirectory. All you have to do to create a subdirectory is to point DX:DX to a string that has the disk, path, and subdirectory information. For example, use a line in your program like:

```
MK_SUB DB C:\ASM ,O
```

A subdirectory ASM will be created. If there's one already there, or some other problem is encountered, an error returns in AH.

Input: AH = 39
Output: Carry Flag = 0 Successful
        Carry Flag = 1 AH holds error value
               = 3 Path not found
               = 5 Access denied
        DS:DX points to ASCIIZ string with directory name

INT 21 Function 3A: delete a subdirectory

INT 21 Function 3A is the companion of INT 21 Function 39. The MS-DOS command RMDIR uses this function to remove directories. Point DS:DX to a string with the disk, and path in it. Use a line in your program such as:

```
RM_DIR DB C: \ ASM ,O
```

As with the MS-DOS command, the subdirectory must be empty before you can remove it. You can use INT 21 Function 41 to delete all the files in it. If you try and delete a subdirectory that still has files, AH will return with a 5.

Input: AH = 3A
Output: Carry Flag = 0 Successful
Carry Flag = 1 AH holds error value
= 3 Path not found
= 5 Access denied
DS:DX points to ASCIIZ string with directory name

INT 21 Function 3B: change a current directory

INT 21 Function 3B allows you to change the default directory. It's useful when you're searching for files and you're not certain in which subdirectory the file exists. MS-DOS uses this function for the CD command.

Input: AH = 3B
Output: Carry Flag = 0 Successful
Carry Flag = 1 AH holds error value
= 3 Path not found
DS:DX points to ASCIIZ string with directory name

INT 21 Function 3C: create a file

INT 21 Function 3C needs a string that gives drive, directories (and any subdirectories), and file name (with any extension). Point DS:DX at the character string. You might have a string definition in your program such as:

```
MY_FILE DB C: \ ASM \ MACRO/SQRT.ASM,O
```

If that file already exists in that subdirectory, it is set to a 0 length. However, if that file exists and is marked read only, error 5 returns in AL. If this function works correctly, a 16-bit file handle returns in AX. You can use this word to refer to the file from then on; it's the file handle.

Input: AH = 3C
DS:DX pointed to ASCIIZ string with directory name
CX = File attribute
Output: Carry Flag = 0 Successful

AH = File handle

Carry Flag = 1 AL holds error value

= 3 Path not found

= 4 Too many files open

= 5 Directory full, or previous read-only file exists

INT 21 Function 3D: open a file

This function uses the file handle (see INT 21 Function 3C as to how the handle can be created). You don't need to specify if you're opening the file for sequential or random access, or specify a record size. Just give this function an ASCIIZ string with the drive, path name, and a file name. Enter the access code in AL (0, 1, or 2) which specifies how you want to work with the file. Those codes are shown below. If the Carry Flag is set, there was an error, which returns in AL.

Input: AH = 3D

AL = Access code

0 File opened for reading

1 File opened for writing

2 Filed opened for reading and writing

DS:DX pointed to ASCIIZ string with directory name

Output: Carry Flag = 0 Successful

AH = File Handle

Carry Flag = 1 AL holds error value

= 3 Path not found

= 4 Too many files open

= 5 Directory full, or previous read-only file exists

DS:DX points to ASCIIZ string with directory name

INT 21 Function 3E: close a file handle

INT 21 Function 3E needs the file handle loaded into BX. If there was an error during the close, the Carry Flag is set.

Input: AH = 3E

BX = Valid file handle

Output: Carry Flag Set, AL = 6 Invalid file handle

INT 21 Function 3F: read from a file or device

This function reads bytes from your file, not records. However many bytes you want to read, you store in CX and this function returns them to whatever location you've specified in DS:DX (but not in the disk transfer area, DTA). AX returns the number of bytes read. Because MS-DOS won't read past the end of the file, check AX to see that you got the full number of bytes expected.

```
Input:    AH = 3F
          BX = File handle
          CX = Number of bytes to read
       DS:DX = Data buffer address
Output: Carry Flag = 0 Successful
          AX = Number of bytes read
          Carry Flag = 1
          AL = 5 Access denied
             = 6 Invalid handle
```

INT 21 Function 40: write to a file or device

To use this function, load the number of bytes you want to write into DX. AX returns the number of bytes actually written. If the numbers don't match, you have an error—most likely the disk is full. Note that INT 21 Function 40 does not consider a full disk an error. Redirecting output is easy, using file handles. To change output from the screen to the printer, change the handle number from 1 to 4. One caution: If you use the keyboard as an input file, you are limited to 80 bytes, no matter what limit you've set.

```
Input:    AH = 40
          BX = File handle
          CX = Number of bytes to write
       DS:DX = Data buffer address
Output: Carry Flag = 0 Successful
          AX = Number of bytes written
          Carry Flag = 1
          AL = 5 Access denied
             = 6 Invalid handle
```

INT 21 Function 41: delete a file

In this function, you cannot use wildcards in the file names and strings that identify drive, pathname and file name are limited to 63 characters. The string can look like:

```
DEL_FILE DB C: \ ASM \ FILE.OBJ ,O
```

```
Input:    AH = 41
       DX:DX = ASCIIZ file name
Output: Carry Flag = 0 Successful
          Carry Flag = 1
          AL = 2 File not found
             = 5 Access denied
```

INT 21 Function 42: move read/write pointer

The read/write pointer is your position in a file. You can skip around in the file by moving the pointer.

Input: AH = 42
AL = Method value
0 Read/write pointer moved to CX:DX from the start of file
1 Pointer incremented CX:DX bytes
2 Pointer moved to end-of-file plus offset CX:DX
BX = File handle
CX:DX = Desired offset
Output: Carry Flag = 0
DX:AX = new pointer location
Carry Flag = 1
      AL = 1 Illegal function number
        = 6 Invalid handle

INT 21 Function 43: change a file's attribute

Table E-3 lists the possible file attributes. To summarize: 0 is normal, 1 is read-only, 2 is hidden, 4 is a system file, 8 is a volume label, 10 a subdirectory, and 20 an archive. Use INT 21 Function 43 to change the attributes when you need to.

Input: AH = 43
AL = 0 File's current attribute returned in CX
      1 File attribute changed, CX holds new attribute
DS:DX = ASCIIZ file string
Output: Carry Flag = 0 Successful
Carry Flag = 1
AL = 0, CX returns attribute
    = 2 File not found
    = 3 Path not found
    = 5 Access denied

INT 21 Function 44: input/output control

INT 21 Function 44 is used for I/O Control (IOCTL) when you set up and define your own devices. It has many, many options and cautions in its use. Because of its complexity, we recommend that you study your MS-DOS manual.

INT 21 Function 45: duplicate a file handle

Use this function if you want to refer to a file with more than one handle. This service duplicates the handle for you. When you move around in the file using one handle, the duplicate one also moves.

Input: AH = 45
BX = File handle to duplicate
Output: Carry Flag = 0
AX = New, duplicated handle
Carry Flag = 1
AL = 4 Too many files open
= 6 Invalid file handle

INT 21 Function 46: force duplication of a file handle

If you're locked into a particular file handle, this function can help. Note that handle 2 (standard error output) cannot be redirected and, if you try, your program will crash. The function does not return an error in that case.

Input: AH = 46
BS = File handle to duplicate
CX = Second file handle
Output: Carry Flag = 0 Handles refer to same stream
Carry Flag = 1
AL = 6 Invalid handle

INT 21 Function 47:
get current directory on specified drive

Note that in this function, the drive letter is not returned in the ASCIIZ string, only the directory. It returns the name of the current default directory at a location pointed to by DS:SI. To call INT 21 Function 47, point DS:SI at a 64-byte free region and store the drive number in DL.

Input: AH = 47
DL = Drive number
DS:SI = Points to 64-byte buffer
Output: Carry Flag = 0 Successful, ASCIIZ at DS:SI
Carry Flag = 1
AH = 15 Invalid drive specified

INT 21 Function 48: allocate memory

When you load a .COM file, MS-DOS gives all memory to it. When you load an .EXE file, all memory isn't always given to it (see program ARRADRV in chapter 9). You can request more memory in your program by using this function. If you ask for too much, the maximum number you will be allowed returns in BX. The trick is to request a huge number and then use whatever returns in BX as your real request.

Input: AH = 48
BX = Number of paragraphs requested

Output: Carry Flag = 0 Successful
AX:0000 = Memory block address
Carry Flag = 1
AL = 7 Memory control blocks destroyed
AL = 8 Insufficient memory, BX contains max. allowed

INT 21 Function 49: free allocated memory

This function frees memory that was allocated by Function 48. A program that loads and runs another program must first free the memory in which it is to load the second program. As a normal practice, it's not good for memory-resident programs to use these memory allocation functions, because you might just free memory that belongs to another program. MS-DOS would then crash.

Input: AH = 49
ES = Segment of block being freed
Output: Carry Flag = 0 Successful
Carry Flag = 1
AL = 7 Memory control blocks destroyed
AL = 9 Incorrect memory block address

INT 21 Function 4A: set block

INT 21 Function 4A allows you to expand or shrink memory blocks. If you're expanding, ask for a huge amount, let it come back with an error and the actual maximum allowable in BX. Then issue this again, using BX as your actual request.

Input: AH = 4A
BX = Requested size in paragraphs
ES = Segment of block to modify
Output: Carry Flag = 0 Successful
Carry Flag = 1
AL = 7 Memory blocks destroyed
= 8 Insufficient memory, BX holds max. allowed
= 9 Invalid memory block address

INT 21 Function 4B: load or execute a program (EXEC)

INT 21 Function 4B allows you to load another program and run it. The environment is a set of strings that indicate something about the PC's operating environment. For example, if you set VERIFY On, the environment will hold the string VERIFY+ON. Before loading another program into memory, you must free memory for it (with Function 4A). If you load another program and run it, control returns to the instruction after the INT 21 when the second program finishes.

Input: AH = 4B
AL = 0 Load and execute the program parameter block:
Segment address of environment (word)
Address of command to put at PSP+80 (dword)
Address of default FCB to put at PSP+5C (dword)
Address of second default FCB to put at PSP+6C (dword)
AL = 3 Load but create no PSP. Don't run (overlay).
Parameter block:
Segment address to load file at (word)
Relocation factor for image (word)
DS:DX = ASCIIZ string with drive, path name, file name
ES:BX = Parameter Block Address for AL
Output: Carry Flag = 0 Successful
Carry Flag = 1
AL = 1 Invalid function number
= 2 File not found
= 5 Access denied
= 8 Insufficient memory
= 10 Invalid environment
= 11 Invalid format

INT 21 Function 4C: exit with return code

Use INT 21 Function 4C to end your program if you want to communicate with a calling program. A program that was loaded and run can send a return code to the parent program if the parent program uses INT 21 Function 4D. So these two functions can work together.

Input: AH = 4C
AL = Binary return code

INT 21 Function 4D: get return code of subprocess

The binary return code loaded into AL (before issuing INT 21 Function 4C) can be retrieved with this call in the subprocess program. Also, AH tells you how the subprocess ended (normally, with a Break Error or with Function 31).

Input: AH = 4D
Output: AL = Binary return code from subprocess
AH = 0 if subprocess ended normally
1 if subprocess ended with Break
2 if subprocess ended with a critical device error
3 if subprocess ended with Function 31

INT 21 Function 4E: find first matching file

Point DS:DX at an ASCIIZ string that has the drive letter, path name, and wildcards. If MS-DOS finds the file(s), the DTA is filled with 43 bytes of information as shown in Fig. E-7.

```
┌─────────────────────────────────────────────────────┐
│                                                       │
│   Disk Transfer Area – First 43 bytes                 │
│                                                       │
├───────────────────────────────────────────────────────┤
│                                                       │
│       0–20   Reserved                                 │
│         21   Found Attribute                          │
│      22–23   File's Time                              │
│      24–25   File's Date                              │
│      26–27   Size – Low word                          │
│      28–29   Size – High word                         │
│      30–42   Name and extension of found file         │
│                 in ASCIIZ form                        │
│                                                       │
└───────────────────────────────────────────────────────┘
```

E-7 DTA information from INT 21 Function 4E. Note that there is no path name or drive returned.

Because the file name is returned without drive or path name, you'll have to construct your own if you want to do anything with the file.

Input: AH = 4E
CX = Attribute to match
DS:DX = ASCIIZ file string
Output: Carry Flag = 0 DTA filled with:
21 reserved bytes
1 byte Found Attribute
2 bytes File's Time
2 bytes File's Date
2 bytes Low Word – Size
2 bytes High Word – Size
13 bytes Name and extension of found file in ASCIIZ form (no pathname)
Carry Flag = 1
AL = 2 No match found
18 No more files

INT 21 Function 4F: find next matching file

Use INT 21 Function 4D before using this function. This function finds all subsequent matches to a file name, but only after the first one has been found. The 21 reserved bytes (as shown in Fig. E-7) in the DTA that MS-DOS used contain information that this function requires.

Input: AH = 4F
Output: Carry Flag = 0 DTA filled with information (see Fig. E-7)
           Carry Flag = 1
           AL = 18 No more files

INT 21 Function 50-53: internal to MS-DOS

These functions are used only by MS-DOS. They're listed here so you can see that they are used and unavailable for your use.

INT 21 Function 54: get/verify state

INT 21 Function 54 checks to see if disk writes are being verified or not. If so, AL returns 1. If not, AL returns 0. Verify can be turned on and off with Function 2E.

Input: AH = 54
Output: AL = 0 Verify is Off
             1 Verify is On

INT 21 Function 55: internal to MS-DOS

This function is used only by MS-DOS. It's here so you can see that it is used and unavailable for your use.

INT 21 Function 56: rename a file

When you use this function, remember that a file cannot be sent to another drive.

Input: AH = 56
        DS:DX = ASCIIZ file string to be renamed
        ES:DI = ASCIIZ file string that holds the new name
Output: Carry Flag = 0 Successful
           Carry Flag = 1
           AL = 3 Path not found
              = 5 Access denied
              = 17 Not the same device

INT 21 Function 57: get/set a file's date and time

To use this function, the file must already be open. Store the file handle in BX and load AL with a 1 or 0, depending on what you want to do. If you want to set the date and time, store the values in DX and DX first.

Input: AH = 57
                AL = 0 Get Date and Time
                AL = 1 Store Time as located in CX
                          Store Date as located in DX
                Time: $(2,045 \times hours) + (32 \times minutes) + (seconds/2)$
                Date: $512 + (Year - 1980) + (32 \times Month\ number) + Day$

Output: CX returns Time = 0
               CX returns Time
               DX returns Date
               Carry Flag = 1
               AL = 1 Invalid function number
                   = 6 Invalid handle

INT 21 Function 58: internal to MS-DOS

This function is used only by MS-DOS. It's here so you can see that it is used and unavailable for your use.

INT 21 Function 59: get extended error

This function only works with MS-DOS releases newer than 3.0. When there was an error, this function returns an extended error code and tells you where the error was physically located, plus suggests corrective action. See program EXTERROR in chapter 5.

Input: AH = 59

INT 21 Function 5A: create unique file

This function only works with MS-DOS releases newer than 3.0. This function creates a temporary file and returns a string with the file's name.

INT 21 Function 5B: create a new file

This function only works with MS-DOS releases newer than 3.0. INT 21 Function 5B will not create a file with a name that already exists.

INT 21 Function 5C: lock/unlock access to a file

This function only works with MS-DOS releases newer than 3.0. With a shared file, you can lock a certain number of bytes or a byte range.

INT 21 Function 5E00: get machine name

This function only works with MS-DOS releases newer than 3.0. Note that with this function, you must load the full word into AX. MS-DOS uses the full word to distinguish between functions, such as between Function 5E00 and 5E02. INT 21 5E00 returns an ASCIIZ string filled with the computer's name—a 15-character string that can be set in PC networks.

INT 21 Function 5E02: set printer setup

Note that with this function, you must load the full word into AX. This function works only with MS-DOS releases newer than 3.0.

INT 21 Function 5E03: get printer setup

Note that with this function, you must load the full word into AX. This function works only with MS-DOS releases newer than 3.0.

INT 21 Function 5F02: get redirection list entry

This function works only with MS-DOS releases newer than 3.0. Note that with this function, you must load the full word into AX.

INT 21 Function 5F03: redirect device

INT 21 Function 5F03 defines the current directories and redirects printer output in a PC network. Note that with this function, you must load the full word into AX. This function works only with MS-DOS releases newer than 3.0.

INT 21 Function 5F04: cancel redirection

This function cancels the action of Function 5F03. Note that with this function, you must load the full word into AX. This function works only with MS-DOS releases newer than 3.0.

INT 21 Function 62: get PSP

INT 21 Function 62 returns the PSP of the currently executing process. This function works only with MS-DOS releases newer than 3.0.

Interrupt 22: terminate address

This interrupt stores the address to which control will be transferred when your program is done. It's recommended that you let MS-DOS functions use this terminate address and not call it yourself.

Interrupt 23: control break exit address

INT 23 stores the address to which control will be transferred when you type *Break*.

Interrupt 24: critical error handler

INT 24 holds the address to which control transfers if there is a critical error, such as a seek error. You can intercept the INT 24 handler and install your own handler if you want. If the most significant bit of AH = 0, the error was a disk error; otherwise bit 7 = 1. Error codes are round in the lower four bits of DI and are shown in Table E-4. If you execute an IRET, MS-DOS takes an action based on the values in AL.

Table E-4   Critical error handler error codes.

DI Lower four bits		Meaning
0	0000	Diskette is write protected
1	0001	Unknown unit
2	0010	The requested drive is not ready
3	0011	Unknown Command
4	0100	Cyclic Redundancy Check error in the data
5	0101	Bad request structure length
6	0110	Seek error
7	0111	Media type unknown
8	1000	Sector not found
9	1001	Printer is out of paper
A	1010	Write fault
B	1011	Read fault
C	1100	General failure
D	1101	Not used
E	1110	Not used
F	1111	Invalid disk change

Interrupt 25: absolute disk read

INT 25 destroys the contents of all registers. Also, flags are PUSHed onto the stack because this INT call is returned in current flags. Error type is

Table E-5   Absolute disk-read error flags.

If carry flag (CF) = 1,

AH =		Meaning
80	10000000	Disk did not respond
40	01000000	Seek failed
20	00100000	Controller failure
10	00010000	Bad Cyclic Redundancy Check
08	00001000	DMA overrun
04	00000100	Sector not found
03	00000011	Write protect error
02	00000010	Address Mark missing
00	00000000	Bad command

returned in AH, as shown in Table E-5. After you check the current flags, be sure to POP the flags off the stack. The difference between this interrupt and the BIOS interrupts is that here you use the logical sector number. MS-DOS calculates the head number, cylinder, number, and so on (that BIOS needs) and passes the information to BIOS, which does the work.

A logical sector starts from 0 and runs (on a double-sided, nine-sector diskette) up to:

$$2 \text{ sides} \times 40 \text{ tracks} \times 9 \text{ sectors} - 1 = 719$$

BIOS does not start sectoring at 0, but at 1 (as far as we can see, the only time that counting begins at 1). For that reason, logical sector zero is track 0, head 0, sector 1. This continues until all sectors in the current track, and current head (side) are used. For example, logical sector 8 is track 0, head 0, sector 9, which means that logical sector 9 is track 0, head 1, sector 1. The values change from right to left, which says that head changes before track does.

Input: AH = 25
           AL = Drive number
           CX = Number of sectors to read
           DX = First logical sector
    DS:BX = Buffer address
Output: Carry Flag = 0 Successful
           Carry Flag = 1
           AH = See Table E-5

Interrupt 26: absolute disk write

INT 26 destroys the contents of all registers. Also, flags are PUSHed onto the stack because this INT call is returned in current flags. Error type is returned in AH, as shown in Table E-5. After you check the current flags, be sure to POP the flags off the stack. The difference between this interrupt and the BIOS interrupts is that here you use the logical sector number. MS-DOS calculates the head number, cylinder, number, and so on (that BIOS needs) and passes the information to BIOS, which does the work.

A logical sector starts from 0 and runs (on a double-sided, nine-sector diskette) up to:

$$2 \text{ sides} \times 40 \text{ tracks} \times 9 \text{ sectors} - 1 = 719$$

BIOS does not start sectoring at 0, but at 1 (as far as we can see, the only time that counting begins at 1). For that reason, logical sector zero is track 0, head 0, sector 1. This continues until all sectors in the current track, and current head (side) are used. For example, logical sector 8 is track 0, head 0, sector 9. Which means that logical sector 9 is track 0, head 1, sector 1. The values change from right to left, which says that head changes before track does.

Input: AH = 26
AL = Drive number
CX = Number of sectors to write
DX = First logical sector
DS:BX = Buffer address
Output: Carry Flag = 0 Successful
Carry Flag = 1
AH = See Table E-5

Interrupt 27: terminate and stay resident

INT 27 makes .COM files code memory-resident, but not .EXE files. If you need additional memory space, use INT 21 Function 31. To use INT 27, set DS:DX to the address at which programs can be loaded; that is, set DS:DX to the end of the program you want to keep in memory and ADD 1 to DX.

Interrupts 28 – 2E: internal to MS-DOS

These interrupts are used only by MS-DOS. They're here so you can see that they are used and unavailable for your use.

Interrupt 2F: multiplex interrupt

INT 2F sets up communication between two processes. It can also create queues. This is a complex interrupt and it's recommended that you study your MS-DOS manual carefully before you use it.

Interrupts 30 – 3F: internal to MS-DOS

These interrupts are used only by MS-DOS. They are shown here so you can see that they are used and unavailable for your use.

Interrupts 40 – 5F: reserved

These interrupts are reserved for future use only by MS-DOS. They're here so you can see that they could be used but you'd better consider them unavailable.

Interrupts 60 – 67: reserved for user software

These are specifically set aside for your use. Your programs can use them without fear of overlapping current MS-DOS implementation.

Interrupts 68 – 7F: not used

To date, these interrupts have not been used by MS-DOS software.

Interrupts 80 – 85: reserved by BASIC

BASIC compilers use these interrupts.

Interrupts 86 – F0: used by BASIC interpreter

The interpreted BASIC uses these interrupts. You can consider them usable only if you never use BASIC.

Interrupts F1 – FF: not used

To date, these interrupts have not been used by MS-DOS software.

Glossary

access To make use of a reference; that is, to execute the statement in which the reference is contained.

access byte In 80486 terms, this is a field in a descriptor that contains protection information and identifies the descriptor's type.

access time The interval between a request for data or information from the memory unit and its actual availability to the processing unit.

accumulator A register used to hold sums during arithmetic operations. In 80486 terms, this is another name for the AX register.

address Information used to identify individual storage locations or words in a memory unit.

address, absolute The fully defined address by a memory address number.

address decoder In 80486 terms, this is a circuit that converts the 80486 address into chip-select signals that are sent to the bus control logic.

address decoding Condensing an address on the bus into a single signal, which then either selects or disables a particular device.

address latch A circuit that maintains its contents for a specified period of time. Latches are used to maintain the I/O address for the duration of a bus cycle.

address, memory Every word in memory has a unique address. A word can be defined as a set of bits comprising the largest addressable unit of information in a programmable memory.

address-size prefix An instruction prefix that selects the size of address offsets; offsets can be 16- or 32-bit. The default size is specified by the D bit in the code segment for the instruction.

address space The total area accessible to a program.

address translation In 80486 terms, this is the conversion of a selector and offset into a physical address.

addressability   The characteristic of certain storage devices in which each storage area or location has a unique address. This address is then usable by the programmer to access the information stored at that location.

addressing capacity   The programming addressing range determines how large a program can be written without resorting to special external hardware and internal software techniques.

adjacency   A term used to describe modules that execute one right after the other.

aggregate   A contiguous group of statements, bounded by boundary elements.

algorithm   A strategy or plan or series of steps for the solution of a problem.

aliases   Two or more descriptors referring to the same segment.

alternate returns   A module linkage convention that allows the subordinate to return to a location other than the normal return location.

ALU   See *Arithmetic Logic Unit.*

American Standard Code for Information Interchange (ASCII)   A binary encoding scheme using seven bits to represent characters, numbers, and special symbols. ASCII was originally designed for information interchange among data processing systems, data communication systems and associated equipment.

analog computer   A specialized computer that handles data coming from sensing devices rather than data in digital form. It is usually used in special scientific applications or as a process-control device.

anticipatory loading   An automatic storage management discipline that loads modules into memory before they are invoked, based on knowledge of the hierarchy of modules in the system.

applications software   Programs written to perform particular business functions, such as inventory, payroll, or accounts receivable, as opposed to systems software that operates a computer system.

architecture   An orderly organization of subsystems to satisfy overall system objectives.

Arithmetic Logic Unit (ALU)   A unit that performs all the arithmetic and logic operations in a microprocessor.

ASCII   See *American Standard Code for Information Interchange.*

assembler   A software program that translates assembly language into binary machine language.

assembly language   A symbolic notation for writing machine instructions. The language is at a high enough level to free the programmer from working directly in machine code.

auxiliary storage   A place for the long-term storage of data. Storage of this type usually is on magnetic media, such as diskette, and has the capability of storing millions or even billions of characters. Also known as secondary storage.

balanced systems   Systems that are not input-driven or output-driven.

Such systems usually have a deep hierarchy of modules to obtain inputs and to deliver outputs.

bar   A sign that denotes the inverse, or complement, of a function. It is written as a line over the function or value.

base address   In 80486 terms, the physical address of the start of a segment.

base load   A set of modules activated by an unbroken chain of explicit commands.

base register   A register used for addressing an operand relative to an address held in the register.

BASIC   Beginner's All-purpose Symbolic Instruction Code, a programming language with a small repertoire of commands and a simple syntax.

baud   A unit of signaling speed equal to the number of discrete conditions or signal events per second.

BCD   See *Binary Coded Decimal*.

benchmark testing   The process of actually testing in terms of time, ease of operation, ability to perform the job as described and so on.

binary   A term used to describe the base-two number system.

binary coded decimal (BCD)   A coding scheme in which every decimal digit from 0 to 9 is represented by its equivalent four-bit binary number.

binary search   A method of searching an index in which the system first goes to the middle of the index to see which half of the index could contain the item wanted. Each succeeding test goes to the midpoint of the remaining part of the index that is being searched. The net effect is that a large index can be searched very quickly.

BIOS   Basic Input/Output System. The ROM-resident BIOS provides device level control of the major I/O devices in a microprocessor system unit.

bit   Binary digit, a single binary position that can exist in only one of two states: On (1) or Off (0).

bit field   A contiguous sequence of bits. A bit field can begin at any bit location of any byte and can contain up to 32 bits (in the 80486).

bit string   A contiguous sequence of bits. A bit string can begin at any bit position of any byte and (in the 80486) can contain up to $2^{32} - 1$ bits.

black box   A system (or a component) with known inputs, known outputs, and generally a known transform, but with unknown (or irrelevant) contents.

bootstrap   A technique or device designed to bring itself into a desired state by means of its own action, e.g., a machine routine whose first few instructions are sufficient to bring the rest of itself into the computer from an input device.

bottom-up testing   A testing strategy in which bottom-level modules are tested first, and then are integrated into higher-level superordinates. Usually contrasted with top-down testing.

branch The act of causing control to be shifted to another part of the program.

breakpoint An aid to program debugging in which a programmer specifies forms of memory access that generate exceptions; the exceptions invoke debugging software.

buffer Storage elements, such as registers or memory locations, for the temporary storage of information prior to its use by the intended system, such as a peripheral device.

bus A collection of signal transmission lines.

bus controller A component that produces bus commands and other useful signals by monitoring the processor's status pins.

bus cycle A single transfer of information on the bus.

bus pipelining A timing trick that allows a device to take more time than a single bus cycle to carry out a bus transaction, without slowing down the bus.

byte A collection of eight adjacent bits.

cache A buffer type of high-speed memory that is filled at medium speed from main memory. Cache memory (especially in the 80486) is the fastest portion of the overall memory that stores only the data that the processor might need in the immediate future.

cache flush An operation that marks all cache lines as invalid. The 80486 has instructions for flushing both internal and external caches.

cache line The smallest unit of storage that can be allocated in a cache. The 80486 has a line size of 128 bits.

cache miss A request for access to memory which requires actually reading main memory.

Cathode Ray Tube (CRT) A display device such as a monochrome monitor.

Central Processing Unit (CPU) The electronic device that controls all other parts of the computer system.

channel Circuitry responsible for generating memory references for use in direct memory accessing (DMA).

character This general term refers to all alphabetic characters, alphabetic punctuation marks, mathematical operators, and the coded representation of such symbols.

chop In the FPU, sets one or more low-order bits of a real number to zero, which yields the nearest representable number in the direction of zero.

clear/reset A process that sets all relevant data to binary zero.

code A set of unambiguous rules specifying the manner in which data can be represented in a discrete form. Also a computer program or part of a computer program.

code segment An address space that contains instructions; an executable segment.

coding The process of writing the computer instructions after procedural design has been carried out by a programmer, after structural design has been carried out by a designer, and after specifications have been developed by a systems analyst.

common-data environment A means of describing data such that the data can be accessed by any module in a system.

communications channels Paths over which data is moved. These paths or links are usually described in terms of their speed and capacity to carry information.

compiler A software program that translates procedure-oriented or problem-oriented instructions into machine language.

complexity of interface One of the factors influencing coupling between modules. The complexity of the interface is approximately equal to the number of different items being passed; the more items, the higher the coupling.

computer A data processor that can perform substantial computation, including numerous arithmetic operations, or logic operations, without intervention by a human operator during the run.

condition code The four bits of the FPU Status Word that indicate the results of the compare, test, examine, and remainder functions of the FPU.

conditioned transfer A jump out from the current execution sequence with the condition that control eventually will be returned to the execution sequence from which the jump was made; for example, a subroutine call.

conforming In 80486 terms, a property of a segment that indicates that each procedure in that segment will move outward to the ring of its caller when it is called.

constant A value that does not change during the execution of a program. Compare with variable.

control register In the 80486, these registers hold data of machine states of a global nature. They are called CR0, CR1, CR2, and CR3. The low-order 15 bits of CR0 are called the Machine Status Word (MSW) for 80286 compatibility with the 80486.

control structure The structure of a program defined by references that represent control transfers.

control transfers In the 80486, transfer of control is done by use of exceptions, interrupts and by the instructions CALL, JMP, INT, IRET, and RET. A near transfer goes to a place within the current code segment. Far transfers go to other segments.

control unit The electronic part of the central processing unit (CPU) that, under program direction, coordinates the action of the system hardware.

control word A 16-bit FPU register that a user can set to determine the modes of computation the FPU will use and the exception interrupts that will be enabled.

conversion Changing from one method to another.

counter A programming device used to control the number of times a process is executed.

coupling A measure of the strength of interconnection between one module and another.

CRT See *Cathode Ray Tube*.

Current Privilege Level (CPL) In the 80486, this is the privilege level of the program that currently is executing. CPL can be determined by examining the lowest 2 bits of the Code Segment (CS) register.

cylinder A group of disk tracks that are accessed at one time by a single set of read/write heads. A disk pack having 40 tracks on each disk surface would have 40 cylinders.

data A representation of facts, concepts, or instructions in a formalized manner suitable for communication, interpretation, or processing by humans or automatic means. Also, any representations such as characters to which meaning is, or might be assigned.

database An integrated source of data that is accessed by many users (or often by one user) and is controlled by a database management system.

database management system (DBMS) A package of programs designed to operate internally with a collection of computer-stored files.

data conversion The act of changing data from one form to another.

data-coupling A form of coupling caused by an intermodule connection that provides output from one module and that serves as input to another module.

data field The column or consecutive columns used to store a particular piece of information.

data file A collection of data records usually organized on a logical basis.

data item The smallest accessible element in a database.

data record A collection of data fields pertaining to a particular subject.

data segment Address space that contains data.

data-structure design Type of design strategy that derives a structural design by considering the structure of data sets associated with the problem.

debug registers In the 80486, there are six programmer-accessible registers: DR0–DR3, DR6, and DR7. DR0–DR3 specify the four linear breakpoints. DR4 and DR5 are reserved by Intel for future implementation. DR6 displays the current state of the breakpoints, and DR7 is used to set the breakpoints.

debugger A program that helps a programmer locate the source of problems found during run-time testing of a program.

debugging The act of removing errors or bugs from a computer program.

decoupling Any systematic method or technique by which modules can be made more independent.

denormal A special form of floating-point number. On the FPU, a denormal is defined as a number that has a biased exponent of zero.

descriptor In the 80486, a descriptor is an 8-byte quantity specifying an independently protected object. The descriptor for an object specifies the object's base address or the address of its entry point, in addition to protection information.

Descriptor Privilege Level (DPL) In the 80486, the DPL is a field in a descriptor that indicates how protected the descriptor is. The DPL is the least-privileged level at which a task can access a particular descriptor and access the segment associated with that descriptor.

design principles Very broad principles that generally work in the sense that they favor increasing quality for decreased development cost.

device driver A program that transforms I/O requests made in a standard, device-independent fashion into the operations necessary to make a specific piece of hardware fulfill that request.

device monitor A mechanism that allows processes to track and/or modify device data streams.

digital computer A general-purpose computer that handles data in numerical or digital form.

DIP Dual in-line package, a widely used container for an integrated circuit. DIP pins are usually in two parallel rows, are spaced on $1/10$-inch intervals, and come in different configurations ranging from a 14-pin assembly to a 40-pin configuration.

direct addressing Specifying a memory location by an address embedded in an instruction.

direct memory addressing (DMA) A technique for transferring data in or out of memory without disturbing the program being executed by the processing unit.

disjoint LDT space The LDT selectors reserved for memory objects that are shared or that can be shared among processes.

disk storage A magnetic storage device that closely resembles a phonograph record. The tracks of data are in concentric rings instead of a single spiral, however.

diskette Small, plastic disk platters used as auxiliary storage on many small computer systems.

displacement In the 80486, this is a 16-bit value specified in an instruction and used for computing address offsets.

DMA See *direct memory addressing*.

documentation The sum total of the forms, flow charts, program listings, and so on, associated with a computer program.

double extended IEEE Std 754 term for the FPU's extended format, with more exponent and significand bits than the double format and an explicit integer bit in the significand.

double format A floating-point format supported by the FPU that consists of a sign, an 11-bit biased exponent, an implicit integer bit, and a 52-bit significand, a total of 64 explicit bits.

doubleword A 32-bit quantity of memory.

driver   A primitive simulation of a superordinate module used in the bottom-up testing of a subordinate module.

dump   Recording the system's memory contents on an external medium, such as magnetic tape or printer.

dynamic recursion   A form of recursion that exists wherever a module is shared by two or more tasks that can be among active jobs at the same time. For example, it is used by routines handling different interrupts.

E notation   Also known as scientific notation, E notation is a format for the representation of numbers that are larger than six digits. The notation consists of two parts: a mantissa and an exponent.

EBCDIC   Extended Binary Coded Decimal Interchange Code.

editing   As used by a programmer, editing instructions allow the programmer to add, replace, and otherwise modify code. As done by a computer, editing allows a human to modify storage.

Effective Privilege Level (EPL)   In the 80486, the EPL is the least privilege of the RPL and DPL.

EIP   See *Instruction Pointer*.

emulation   The act of executing a program written for one computer on a different computer.

encapsulation   The principle of hiding the internal implementation of a program, function, or service so that its clients can tell what it does but not how it does it.

exception   A condition when an instruction violates the rules of normal operation. An exception generally causes an interrupt.

exception pointer   In the FPU, the indication used by exception handlers to identify the cause of an exception.

exclusion   A strategy for designing generalized systems in which the designer examines as many applications as possible, but excludes those aspects that make the application special or unique.

expand down   A property of a segment that causes the processor to check that, in all accesses to that segment, offsets are greater than the segment's limits. This is used for stack segments.

expand up   A property of a segment that causes the processor to check that all accesses to that segment are no greater than the segment's limit. Generally, all segments other than stack segments have this property.

exponent   The right-most part of a number that has been converted into E notation. This position tells the power of 10 to which the original number had to be raised in order to generate a correct mantissa.

extended cache   A cache memory provided outside of the processor chip. The 80486 has instructions and page-table entry bits which are used to control external caches from software.

far pointer   In the 80486, a 48-bit logical address of two components: a 16-bit segment selector and a 32-bit offset.

fault   An exception that is reported at the instruction boundary immediately before the instruction that generates the exception.

feasibility study A study, normally conducted at the beginning of a systems development project, to determine the likelihood that a system can, in fact, be built within the constraints of time, manpower, and budget.

field One or more contiguous bits that represent a piece of a larger item of data.

file handle A binary value that represents an open file, used in all file I/O calls.

firmware Memory chips with the software programs already built in.

fixed-point arithmetic Operations on numbers without decimal points.

flag A field in the flags register. A flag indicates the status of a previously executed instruction or controls the operation of the processor.

flag bit A single bit that indicates one of two mutually exclusive conditions or states.

flat memory organization In the 80486, an address space that consists of a single array of up to 4Gb. The 80486 maps the 4Gb flat space onto the physical address space by address translation mechanisms.

flexibility A measure of the degree to which a system, as is, can be used in a variety of ways.

Floating-Point Unit (FPU) The part of the 80486 that contains the floating-point registers and performs the operations required by floating-point instructions.

floppy disk See *diskette*.

flow charting A representation of a data processing activity by the use of special graphic symbols.

font A full assortment of one size and style of printing type.

FPU See *Floating-Point Unit*.

function In programming, a function is a prebuilt series of instructions that can be used or called by means of a single word or term. A typical function is SQRT to do square root.

function key A specific key on a keyboard that causes a receiving device to perform a certain mechanical function so that a message will be received in proper form. Also keys on keyboards that are used to query the system or have it perform certain operations.

function key, programmable By changing the keyboard-handling routine, the user can change the function of any key or symbol that will be displayed on the screen.

functional requirements A precise description of the requirements of a computer system. They include a statement of the inputs to be supplied by the user, the outputs desired by the user, the algorithms involved in any computations desired by the user, and a description of such physical constraints as response time, volumes, and so on.

gate The simplest logic circuit. In the 80486, there are four types of gates: a call gate, a trap gate, an interrupt gate, and a task gate.

GDT See *Global Descriptor Table*.

GDTR See *Global Descriptor Table Register*.

general register In the 80486, one of the 16-bit registers: AX, BX, CX, or DX.

generality A measure of the degree to which a system exhibits the properties of a general-purpose system.

generation A differentiation of the ages to which computer equipment belongs. Considerable controversy exists as to what generation we are currently in. Generally, it is agreed that we are in the last of a fourth generation and entering a fifth.

giga A prefix meaning 1 billion (10^9). Also, the power of 2 closest to 1 billion, $2^{30} = 1,073,741,824$. This latter is used when referring to computer memory (gigabyte, gigabit, and so on).

GIGO A term standing for garbage-in, garbage-out. It simply means that if incorrect data is fed into a computer, incorrect answers result.

giveaway shared memory A shared memory mechanism in which a process that already has access to the segment can grant access to another process. Processes cannot obtain access for themselves; access must be granted by another process that already has access.

Global Descriptor Table (GDT) In the 80486, a table in memory that contains descriptors for segments that are shared by all tasks.

Global Descriptor Table Register (GDTR) In the 80486, this register holds the 32-bit linear base address and the 16-bit limit of the Global Descriptor Table.

graphic display A communications terminal linked to a computer that displays data in shapes and drawings, usually a CRT.

graphics Symbols produced by a process such as handwriting or printing, synonymous with graphic symbol.

hardware The physical parts of a computer system, usually a printer, video screen device, circuit chips, and so on.

hashing routine A mathematical formula that is applied to a key field to determine where the record is stored.

heuristic A specific rule of thumb that usually works but is not guaranteed.

hexadecimal A base-16 number system, most often called hex. The hex digits are 0, 1, 2, 3, 4, 5, 6, 7, 8, 9, A ($= 10$), B ($= 11$), C ($= 12$), D ($= 13$), E ($= 14$), and F ($= 15$).

high-order position The left-most position in a string of characters.

Hollerith card The name given to the punched-card developed by Dr. Herman Hollerith. It is also commonly known as an IBM card.

identifier The name, address, label, or distinguishing index of an object in a program.

IDT See *Interrupt Descriptor Table*.

IDTR See *Interrupt Descriptor Table Register*.

IEEE Std 754 A set of formats and operations that apply to floating-point numbers. The format consists of 32-, 64-, and 80-bit operand sizes.

immediate operand In the 80486, a constant contained in an instruction and used as an operand.

impact printer Any printing mechanism that employs some hitting or striking mechanism in order to print.

incremental implementation A testing/implementation strategy for adding a new (potentially error-prone) module to a tested collection of modules, and then testing the new combination.

index A listing of the data records and the disk areas on which they are stored. Also, a number used to access a table.

index register In the 80486, one of the 16-bit registers: SI or DI. Generally, an index register holds an offset into the current data or extra segment.

indirect addressing Accessing a memory location by first fetching the desired address from some other memory location or register.

infinity A floating-point result that has greater magnitude than any integer or any real number.

initialize A programming term that refers to the act of establishing fixed values in certain areas of memory. Generally, the term refers to all the housekeeping that must be completed before the main part of the program can be executed.

input The general term used to describe the act of entering data into a data processing system, or the data being entered.

Input/Output (I/O) Pertaining to a device or to a channel that might be involved in an input process and, at a different time, in an output process. Also pertaining to a device whose parts can be performing an input process and an output process at the same time.

Instruction Pointer (IP) A register that contains the offset of the instruction currently being executed. A selector for the segment containing this instruction is stored in the CS register. In the 80486, the EIP (an extended instruction pointer) is a 32-bit register that contains the offset address of the next sequential instruction to be executed. The low-order 16 bits of the EIP are the IP.

instruction prefetch Reading instructions into the processor from sequentially higher addresses before execution.

instruction register A register that stores the current instruction being executed.

instruction set The set of all machine-language instructions that can be executed by a processor.

integer A number (positive, negative, or zero) that is finite and has no fractional parts.

interactive program A program whose function is to obey commands from a user, such as an editor or a spreadsheet program. Programs such as compilers might literally interact by asking for file names and compilation options, but they are considered non-interactive because their function is to compile a source program, not to provide answers to user-entered commands.

interface A connecting point between two systems.

intermodular connection A reference from one module to an identifier in a different module.

internal cache A cache memory on the processor chip. The 80486 has 8K of internal cache memory.

interpreter A computer program used to interpret. Also synonymous with interpretive program.

interrupt To suspend execution of the current program in order to service one or more peripheral devices. Also, a forced call, not appearing explicitly in a program, which is triggered by an exception, by a signal from a device external to the processor, or by a special interrupt instruction.

Interrupt Descriptor Table (IDT) In the 80486, this is a table in memory which is indexed by interrupt number and which contains gates to the corresponding interrupt handlers.

Interrupt Descriptor Table Register (IDTR) In the 80486, this register points to a table of entry points for interrupt handlers. The IDTR holds the 32-bit linear base address and the 16-bit limit of the IDT.

interrupt handler A procedure or task that is called in response to an interrupt.

interrupt module A module activated by an interrupt.

invalid operation The exception condition for the FPU that covers all cases not covered by other exceptions.

I/O Permissions Bit Map The mechanism that allows the 80486 to selectively trap references to specific I/O addresses. The Permissions Bit Map resides in the Task State Segment (TSS). The map is a bit vector and its size and location in the TSS are variable. The 80486 locates the map by means of the I/O Map Base field in the fixed portion of the TSS.

IP See *Instruction Pointer*.

jump An instruction that causes a transfer of control from one part of the program to another.

K Kilo, a prefix meaning one thousand (10^3). Also, the power of 2 closest to 1000, namely $2^{10} = 1024$. This latter definition is used when referring to computer memory (kilobytes).

Kb Kilobyte, a thousand bytes.

KHz Kilohertz, a unit of frequency equal to 1000 hertz.

labels Identifying statements or numbers used to describe locations. Also, a set of symbols used to identify or describe an item, record, message, or file.

LDT See *Local Descriptor Table*.

LDTR See *Local Descriptor Table Register*.

lexical Of or pertaining to the program as written, as it appears in a program listing. Also, the order in which items appear.

light pen A pen-like device used in interactive graphic units to communicate between the computer and the user.

linear address space Address space that runs from 0 bytes to the maximum physical address that a processor can address. In the 80486, the linear address space runs up to 4Gb.

local address space In the 80486, this is the collection of segments accessible through a task's LDT.

Local Descriptor Table (LDT) A table in memory that contains descriptors for segments that are private to a task.

Local Descriptor Table Register (LDTR) In the 80486, this register holds the 16-bit selector for the Local Descriptor Table.

localization A technique of decoupling affected by subdividing the data elements communicated through a common environment into a number of regions common to a smaller number of modules.

lock In a multiple processor system, this is the signal from one processor that prevents the others from accessing memory. The processor has exclusive use of the memory until it stops sending the lock signal.

logic design The design of the procedural logic within a single module.

logical address In the 80486, a logical address consists of a selector and offset. The selector points to some segment's descriptor, which includes a segment's linear base address. The offset tells how far into the segment the required byte is located.

logical device A symbolic name for a device that the user can cause to be mapped to any physical (actual) device.

logical directory A symbolic name for a directory that the user can cause to be mapped to any actual drive and directory.

long integer An integer format supported by the FPU that consists of a 64-bit two's complement quantity.

low-order position The right-most position in a string of characters.

low priority category A classification of processes that consists of processes that get CPU time only when no other thread in the other categories needs it. This category is lower in priority than the general priority category.

M Mega is 1 million (10^6). Also, the power of 2 that is closest to 1 million, $2^{20} = 1,048,576$. This latter definition is used when referring to computer memories (megabyte).

machine cycle A set period of time in which the computer can perform a specific machine operation.

machine language A language that is used directly by a machine. Also, another term for computer instruction code. At this level, instructions are usually in the form of a string of digits that have particular meaning to the internal circuitry of the computer.

Machine Status Word (MSW) A register that contains a bit for controlling the mode (real versus virtual) and bits that control the processor's execution of WAIT and ESC instructions. In the 80486, the low-order 15 bits of the Control Register Zero (CR0) are the MSW, for upward compatibility from the 80286.

macro A module whose body is effectively copied in-line during translation (compilation or assembly) as a result of being invoked by name.

macro instructions Those instructions that are so complex that a single command generates several machine-language instructions.

main memory The large memory, external to the 80486, used for holding most instruction code and data.

maintainability The extent to which a system can be easily corrected when errors are discovered during the system's productive lifetime.

mantissa The left-most part of a number that has been put into E notation. In the mantissa portion, all numbers are reduced to a single-digit whole number plus a decimal fraction.

mask bit A bit used to cover up or disable some condition.

masking A means of examining only certain bits in a word. This is usually done by ANDing the word with a mask containing 1s in the desired bit locations.

matrix printer An output device that prints each character by means of a specially placed series of dots.

memory address A value that selects one specific memory location.

memory map The list of memory locations addressed directly by the computer.

memory-mapped input/output A technique whereby a peripheral device masquerades as a memory location.

MHz Megahertz, a unit of frequency equal to one million hertz.

microprocessor A central processing unit implemented on a single chip.

microsecond One-millionth of a second.

millisecond One-thousandth of a second.

mnemonic Symbol or symbols used instead of terminology more difficult to remember. Usually, a mnemonic has two or three letters.

mode A method of operation, e.g., the binary mode. Also, one of the FPU status word fields *rounding control* and *precision control*, which programs can set, sense, save, and restore to control the execution of subsequent arithmetic operations.

modifiability The ability of a system to be changed or enhanced to meet the needs of a user during its productive lifetime.

module A contiguous sequence of program statements, bounded by boundary elements, having an aggregate identifier.

monitor A device that observes and verifies the operation of a data processing system and indicates any specific departure from the norm. Also, a television-type display such as a monochrome monitor.

MSW See *Machine Status Word*.

NaN An abbreviation of *Not a Number*, a floating-point quantity that does not represent any numeric or infinite quantity.

nano One billionth (10^{-9}).

nanosecond One-billionth of a second.

near pointer In the 80486, this is a 32-bit logical address. A near pointer is an offset within a segment.

NMI See *nonmaskable interrupt.*

nonmaskable interrupt (NMI) A signal to the processor from an external device that indicates that a problem has arisen or is imminent.

normal The representation of a number in a floating-point format in which the significand has an integer bit one (either explicit or implicit).

not present In a virtual memory, this describes a segment that is on disk but not in main memory.

null selector A selector in which all bits are 0.

object program The numeric, machine language output of an assembler.

offset A quantity specifying the position of a byte within a segment.

opcode The part of an instruction that specifies the operation to be performed, such as ADD, as opposed to the items upon which the operation is performed.

open system Hardware or software design that allows third-party additions and upgrades in the field.

operand Data operated on arithmetically or logically by a processor.

operand-size prefix An instruction prefix which selects the sizes of integer operands (which can be 8- and 16-bit, or they can be 8- and 32-bit). The default size is specified by the D bit in the descriptor for the code segment that contains the instruction.

operating system OS, the collection of programs for operating a computer.

output Pertaining to a device, process, or channel involved in an output process or to the data or states involved in an output process.

output-driven system A system in which the top-level module produces the output of the system in elementary (or raw) form.

overflow An exception which occurs when a number is too large in absolute value to be represented. Stack overflow is an exception which occurs when too much data is pushed onto a stack.

packaging The assignment of the modules of a total system into sections handled as distinct physical units for execution on a computer.

packed BCD A packed byte representation of two decimal digits, each in the range of 0 through 9. One digit is stored in each half-byte. The digit in the high-order, half-byte is the most significant.

page A set of consecutive bytes. In the 80486, pages begin on 4K boundaries. Paging divides programs into multiple uniform-sized pages that have no direct relationship to the logical structure of the program.

Page Directory Base Register (PDBR) A processor register that holds the base address of the page directory; same as the CR3 register.

page fault In the 80486, if the processor finds one of the two following conditions, it issues an Interrupt 14: (1) if the current procedure does not have enough privilege to access the indicated page; or (2) if the page-table entry or page-directory needed for the address translation has a 0 in its P (present) bit. That is, the page is not currently loaded from auxiliary storage.

page frame A 4K unit of contiguous addresses of a physical memory. The page frame address specifies the physical starting address of a page. The low-order 12 bits are always 0.

page table In the 80486, this is an array of 32-bit page specifiers. The table itself is a page, containing pointers to 4K of memory, or up to 1K 32-bit entries.

peripheral device An electronic device connected to the processor. Peripheral devices communicate to the processor by means of input and output instructions, interrupts, or memory-mapped input/output.

personal computer PC, a small home or business computer complete with a system unit, keyboard, and available with a variety of options such as monochrome monitor and dot matrix printer.

phased implementation A form of testing/implementation in which several untested modules are combined together at once, and the collection tested for correctness.

physical address A number transmitted to the memory hardware in order to specify the location of a memory access. Also, the mechanism that actually selects the memory where a required byte is located. In the 80486, the physical address differs from linear address only when paging is in effect.

pointer An entity containing or having the value of an identifier. In the 80486, this also is an address that is used by software and consists of a selector and offset. In real mode, pointers are real addresses. In virtual mode, they are virtual addresses.

pointer register In the 80486, one of the BP or BX registers. Generally, a pointer register holds an offset into the current stack segment.

port A connection to an input/output (I/O) device that can be used by input and output instructions.

portability A property of a program representing ease of movement among distinct solution environment.

precision The effective number of bits in the significand of the floating-point representation of a number.

precision control An option programmed through the FPU Control Word; it allows all FPU arithmetic to be performed with reduced precision.

prefix A byte preceding the opcode of an instruction. It specifies that the instruction should be repeated, or locked, or that an alternate segment should be used.

priority This is a precedence relationship applied to simultaneous occurrences.

privilege level A number in a predetermined range that indicates the degree of protection or degree of privilege.

processing element Any part of the task performed by a module; not only the processing accomplished by statements executed within that module, but also that which results from calls on subroutines.

program A system composed of precise, ordered statements and aggregate. Also, a series of code designed to achieve a certain result.

program counter A register in a processor that stores the address of the next instruction to be executed.

Program Status Word (PSW) A special register used to keep track of the address of the next instruction to be executed; also, often other status flags are stored in the PSW.

programmer An informal term used to describe the person who designs and writes the programming instructions to implement a module. Often, the programmer is also responsible for the structural design of the system.

protected virtual address mode A mode of operation in which the processor offers multitasking, advanced protection facilities, and virtual memory.

PSW See *Program Status Word.*

quadword A 64-bit operand.

read/write head A magnetic coil device that is capable of magnetizing or detecting magnetism on a tiny spot on the surface of a magnetic storage device.

real address In the 80486, this is an address that consists of a selector and offset in real address mode.

real address mode In the 80486, this is a mode of operation in which the processor closely mimics the behavior of a lower-level chip in the same chip family. For example, the 80486 mimics an 8086.

recursion The act of invoking a module as a subroutine of itself.

reentrant A module is reentrant if it can be activated correctly at any time, whether or not it has been suspended by a conditioned transfer or return.

register Fast, temporary-storage locations, usually in the processor itself.

reliability A measure of the quality of a program or system, sometimes expressed as mean time between failure (MTBF).

Requested Privilege Level (RPL) In the 80486, this is a field in a selector that indicates the degree of trust or privilege a program has in the selector.

RPL RPL is determined by the least two significant bits of a selector. See *Requested Privilege Level.*

scan code The first byte of a 2-byte extended ASCII code sent to a system to indicate that the next byte is from the extended ASCII character set. The second byte is the character.

scatter read Reading a block of data into noncontiguous locations in memory.

scope of control The scope of control of a module consists of the module itself and all of its subordinates.

security kernel That part of an operating system devoted to protection and security.

segment A region of memory, in a range of 1 byte to the maximum that can be handled by the processor. Also, units of contiguous address space.

segment descriptor table   A memory array of 8-byte entries that contain descriptors. An 80486 descriptor table can contain up to 8192 descriptors.

segment-override prefix   An instruction prefix which overrides the default segment selection.

segment register   In the 80486, one of the registers CS, DS, ES, or SS.

segmented memory organization   An address space that consists of up to 16,383 linear address spaces up to 4Gb each. The total space, as viewed by a program in the 80486, can be as large as 24^6 bytes (64 terabytes).

selector   In the 80486, this is a quantity that specifies a segment.

semaphore   A software flag or signal used to coordinate the activities of two or more threads, commonly used to protect a critical section.

serial printers   Devices that print one character at a time, such as a type-writer.

set-associative   A form of cache organization in which the location of a data block in main memory constrains (but does not completely determine) its location in the cache. An *n-way* set-associative cache allows data from a given address in main memory to be in cache memory in any of *n* locations.

shared memory   A memory segment that can be accessed simultaneously by more than one process.

SIB byte   A byte following an instruction opcode and modR/M bytes that is used to specify a scale factor, index, and base register.

signals   Notification mechanisms implemented in software that operate in a fashion analogous to hardware interrupts.

single stepping   Executing a program one instruction at a time and pausing after each instruction. This is a means by which programmers determine the effect of a line of code.

software   The computer programs, procedures, rules, and possibly associated documentation concerned with the operation of a data processing system.

software reliability   A measure of the quality of a program or system, sometimes expressed as mean time between failures (MTBF).

source program   The original program submitted to the computer for translation or compiling.

stack   A buffer whose information is generally accessed in a last-in-first-out (LIFO) manner.

stack fault   A special case of the invalid-operation exception, which is indicated by a 1 in the SF bit of the FPU Status Word. This condition usually results from stack underflow or overflow.

stack frame   The space used on the stack by a procedure.

stack pointer   A register that stores the memory address of the top (last-in) element of a stack in memory.

stack segment   A data segment that is used to hold a stack.

statement   A line, sentence, or other similar well-defined portion of a programming language that defines, describes, or directs one step or part of the problem, or part of the solution of the problem.

Status Word   A 16-bit FPU register that can be manually set, and which is usually controlled by side effects to FPU instructions.

string   A contiguous sequence of bytes, words, or double words. In the 80486, a string can contain from 0 bytes through $2^{32} - 1$ bytes (4Gb).

structural design   The design of the structure of a system, the specification of the pieces, and the interconnection between the pieces.

structured design   A set of guidelines and techniques that assists a systems designer in determining which modules, interconnected in which way, will best solve a well-stated problem.

structured programming   A disciplined programming technique that ensures a single entry point and a single exit point from every processing module.

subroutine   A module activated at execution time by a conditioned transfer.

swapping   Moving a segment from disk to memory (swapping in) or from memory to disk (swapping out).

system clock   The fundamental time signal in a computer. The system clock runs at twice the frequency of the 80486.

systems analyst   An informal term for a person whose job it is to analyze the user's needs, and to then derive the functional requirements of a system.

tag   The part of a cache line that holds the address information used to determine if a memory operation is a hit or a miss on that cache line.

tag word   A 16-bit FPU register that is automatically maintained by the FPU. For each space in the FPU stack, it tells if the space is occupied by a number; if so, it gives information about what kind of number.

task   A defined function that is unique within the computer.

task dispatching   Selecting a task that is not currently running and running it. This includes saving the status of the currently running task in its TSS.

Task Register (TR)   In the 80486, this register points to the information needed by the processor to define the current task.

Task State Segment (TSS)   In the 80486, a TSS is a segment that holds the contents of a task's registers when the processor is executing another task.

task switch   Switching from one task to another.

terminal failure   A software error that causes a system to completely stop functioning.

test registers   In the 80486, registers TR6 and TR7 are used to control testing of the Content Addressable Memory (CAM) in the Translation Lookaside Buffer (TLB).

testing   A process of demonstrating that a system carries out its functions as specified.

text   In ASCII and data communications, a sequence of characters treated as an entity.

text editing   The general term that covers any additions, changes, or deletions made to electronically stored material.

TLB   See *Translation Lookaside Buffer*.

TOP   The three-bit field of the Status Word that indicates which FPU register is the current top of stack.

top-down design   A design strategy in which the major functions of a system are identified, and their implementation expressed in terms of lower-level primitives. The design process is then repeated on the primitives until the designer has identified primitives of a sufficiently low level that their implementation can be expressed in terms of available program statements.

top-down testing   A testing/implementation strategy in which high-level modules are tested before low-level modules.

TR   See *Task Register*.

track   In reference to magnetic disk the term refers to the concentric rings on the disk surface on which data are recorded.

transaction   Any element of data, control, signal, event or change of state that causes, triggers, or initiates some action or sequence of actions.

transfer rate   In reference to magnetic tape or disk, this term indicates how much data can be moved from auxiliary storage to memory per second.

Translation Lookaside Buffer (TLB)   In the 80486, the TLB is a cache used for translating linear addresses to physical addresses. The TLB is a four-way, set-associative memory. The TLB testing mechanism is unique to the 80486 and might not be implemented in the same way in future Intel processors.

TSS   See *Task State Segment*.

two's complement   A method of representing integers. If the uppermost bit is 0, the number is considered positive, with the value given by the rest of the bits. If the uppermost bit is 1, the number is negative.

unconditional transfer   A transfer of control from one module to another with no tacit condition of return.

underflow   A numeric underflow is an exception that occurs when a number is too small in absolute value to be represented as a normalized floating-point number. Stack underflow is an exception that occurs when an instruction attempts to pop more data off the stack than is currently on the stack.

unpacked BCD   A representation for integers in which each decimal digit is represented by 4 bits and each byte contains only a single decimal digit.

USE16   An assembly language directive that specifies 16-bit code and data segments.

USE32   An assembly language directive that specifies 32-bit code and data segments.

user A term describing the person, persons, or organizations that expect to benefit from the development of a computer hardware or software system.

variable As opposed to a constant, a variable is a value that changes during the execution of a program.

vectored interrupt A technique of interrupt processing in which each interrupt specifies the address of the first instruction of its service routine.

video A computer display shown or displayed on a cathode ray tube monitor or display.

virtual address An address that consists of selector and offset in protected virtual address mode.

virtual memory A technique for running programs that are larger than the available physical memory. Pieces of the program are stored on disk and are moved into memory only as necessary. This movement is automatically performed by the operating system and is invisible to the program.

virtual mode See *protected virtual address mode.*

virtual storage A hardware/software technique that allows the programmer to write programs that are larger than main memory. The system automatically breaks the program into pages and brings the pages into memory when required.

virtualization The general technique of hiding a complicated actual situation behind a simple, standard interface.

wait state An extra processor cycle added to the bus cycle in order to allow for slower devices on the bus to respond.

word A machine-dependent unit of storage that is generally the width of the data bus or internal registers. In the 80486, a word is 32 bits.

word processing A system comprised of people, procedures, and automated electronic equipment to more effectively produce written communication.

write-back A form of caching in which memory writes will load only the cache memory. Data propagates to main memory when a write-back operation is invoked.

write-through An option when a file write operation is performed that specifies that the normal caching mechanism is to be sidestepped and the data to be written through to the disk surface immediately.

zero divide An exception condition in which floating-point inputs are finite, but the correct answer, even with an unlimited exponent, has infinite magnitude.

zone punch A punch in the 12, 11, or 0 row of the Hollerith card. The zone punches are usually combined with the digit punches to make alphabetic characters.

Bibliography

Brumm, Penn and Don Brumm. 1986. *80386—A programming and design handbook*. Blue Ridge Summit, Pa.: TAB Books.

Crawford, John H. and Patrick P. Gelsinger. 1987. *Programming the 80386*. San Francisco, Calif.: Sybex.

Duncan, Ray, ed. 1988. *The MS-DOS encyclopedia*. Redmond, Wash.: Microsoft Press.

Microsoft Corporation. 1985. *Microsoft macro assembler*. Redmond, Wash.: Microsoft Press.

Sedgewick, Robert. 1983. *Algorithms*. Menlo Park, Calif.: Addison-Wesley Publishing Company.

Wirth, Niklaus. 1986. *Algorithms and data structures*. Englewood Cliffs, N.J.: Prentice-Hall.

Yourdon, Edward. 1975. *Techniques of program structure and design*. Englewood Cliffs, N.J.: Prentice-Hall.

Index

A

Accessed bit (A), 403
Add Integers (ADD), 421
Add Integers with Carry (ADC),
  420-421
address
  linear, 398
  logical, 38, 372-373
  physical, 38, 42-43, 372-374,
    399
Adjust for Add (AAA), 419
Adjust for Divide (AAD), 419
Adjust for Multiply (AAM), 162,
  420
Adjust for Subtract (AAS), 420
Adjust Requester Privilege Level
  (ARPL), 422
algorithms, 240-331
  ARRABLDP, 285-287
  ARRADRV, 281-285
  ARRANDXP, 288-289
  ARRANDXR, 289-290
  array manipulation and index-
    ing, 255-257
  BNSEARCH, 261-264
  BUFF386, 312-315
  BUFF486, 309-312
  BUFFDRV, 315-328
  BUFFER, 264-266
  buffers, 243-246
  calculating square roots, 261
  checking for coprocessor, 260
  determining DOS version, 260

determining free bytes on disk
  drive, 259-260
determining host system config-
  uration, 258-259
driver for PAUSE program, 260
ENCRYPT, 266-268
encryption, 246-247
finding computer's name, 260-
  261
FIND_CFG, 290-295
FIND_COP, 298
FIND_VER, 299-300
GET_FREE, 295-297
HASHDRV, 268-270
hashing schemes, 247-248
HASHING, 270-271
making a program wait, 260
PAUSE, 300-302
PCNAME, 302-304
QSORT, 276-281
RANDNUM, 304-305
random number generator, 261
recursive, 240
searching, 240-243
SHELLSRT, 274-276
SORTDRV, 271-274
sorting, 248-255
SQRT, 305-309
THRESH, 328-331
Alignment Check (AC), 393
Alignment Mask (AM), 396
AND, 41, 116-117, 421-422
architecture

80486, 370-392
  definitions, 372-374
arithmetic, 50-86
  80486 data types, 51
  algorithms, 240-331
  BCD (*see* binary-coded deci-
    mal)
  binary, 52
  binary addition and subtraction,
    52-53
  Boolean logic, 116-117
  code conversion, 156-206
  floating-point numbers, 158-
    159
  fractions and exponents, 158
  numeric abbreviations, 51
  overflow, 50
  single and double precision
    numbers, 50
array manipulation, 255-257
  building one larger than 64K,
    256-257
  computing 80486 array ele-
    ment address, 257
  driver program, 256
ASCII
  characters and keyboard
    codes, 496-502
  converting binary code to ASCII
    and back, 162
  converting code to EBCDIC
    and back, 160-162
  converting IEEE code to ASCII

583

Compare String Byte (CMPSB), 428-429
Compare String Doubleword (CMPSD), 428-429
Compare String Word (CMPSW), 428-429
Compare and Exchange (CMPXCHG), 429-430
Condition Code, 405
conditional transfers, 8
Control Register Zero (CR0), 44
Control Word (CW), 37, 389, 407
Convert Byte to Word (CBW), 426
Convert Doubleword to Quadword (CDQ), 430
Convert Word to Doubleword (CWD), 430
Convert Word to Doubleword Extended (CWDE), 426, 430
Current Privilege Level (CPL), 384

D

Data Segment (DS/ES/FS/GS) registers, 376
databases, creating, 5-7
DEBUG, 17
debugging, 14-15
Decimal Adjust Add (DAA), 430
Decimal Adjust Subtact (DAS), 431
Decrement (DEC), 431
descriptor, 37, 372
Descriptor Privilege Level (DPL), 384, 403
descriptors, 43-44
  segment, 381-382
Direction Flag (DP), 395
Dirty (D), 398
disks, 208-210
  cylinders, 208
  directories, 209-210
  File Allocation Table (FAT), 208
  sectors, 208-209
  tracks, 208
Divide (DIV), 41, 431-432
documentation, 4
double extended, 37

E

EBCDIC, converting ASCII code to EBCDIC and back, 160-162
EFLAGS (see System Flags Register)
80486
  architecture, 370-392
  basic units of, 371
  cache memory, 383-384

computing an array element address, 257
  data handling, 156
  data types, 51, 156-158
  descriptors, 43-44
  input/output (I/O), 210-215
  instruction set, 411-495
  interrupts, 90-95
  memory, 42-43
  program instructions, 40-42
  programming tips, 36-49
  registers, 44
  software guidelines, 39-40
  string instructions, 122-123
  tasks, 45-46
  terminology, 37-39
  testing and debugging, 48
Emulation (EM), 397
encryption, 246-247
ENTER, 432-433
error return codes
  access denied, 33
  attempted to remove current directory, 33
  file not found, 33
  insufficient memory, 33
  invalid access code, 33
  invalid date, 33
  invalid drive specified, 33
  invalid environment, 33
  invalid file handle, 33
  invalid format, 33
  invalid function number, 33
  invalid memory block address, 33
  memory control blocks destroyed, 33
  no more files, 33
  not same device, 33
  path not found, 33
  too many open files, 33
Exception Status (ES), 405
exceptions, 88-89, 382 (see also interrupts)
  general protection, 94
  masked and unmasked, 90
  stack, 94
Exchange (XCHG), 493
Exchange and Add (XADD), 493
extended cache, 37
Extension Type (ET), 397

F

F2XM1, 433
FABS, 433
FADD, 434
FADDP, 434
FBLD, 434

FBSTP, 434-435
FCHS, 435
FCLEX, 435
FCOM, 435-436
FCOMP, 435-436
FCOMPP, 435-436
FCOS, 436
FDECSTP, 436
FDIV, 437
FDIVP, 437
FDIVR, 437
FDIVRP, 437
FFREE, 438
FIADD, 434
FICOM, 438
FICOMP, 438
FIDIV, 437
FIDIVR, 437
FILD, 438-439
File Allocation Table (FAT), 208
file handle, 17
file manipulation, 217-223
  checking/renaming/deleting a file, 218-219
  creating/writing/closing a file, 220-223
  I/O (see input/output)
  opening/reading an existing file, 219-220
  structure, 217
files
  merging MS-DOS, 23
  MS-DOS name extensions, 34-35
  viewing ASCII in DOS, 23
FIMUL, 442
FINCSTP, 439
FINIT, 439
first-in, first-out (FIFO), 243
FIST, 440
FISTP, 440
FISUB, 449
FISUBR, 449-450
flags, 37-38, 90, 372, 394-410
  alphabetical listing, 409-410
FLD, 440
FLDCW, 441
FLDENV, 441
FLDx, 440-441
Floating-Point Unit (FPU), 38, 387-392
  Control Word registers, 37, 389, 407
  Error Pointer registers, 390
  precision control, 390-391
  register stack, 387
  registers, 405-408
  rounding control, 391-392

Other Bestsellers of Related Interest

FOXPRO® PROGRAMMING
—2nd Edition—Les Pinter,
Foreword by Walter Kennamer,
COO, Fox Software

If you've been looking for a book that concentrates entirely on the FoxPro language and not on the product itself, then look no further! This book is a gold mine of fully-tested techniques, ready-to-run source code, and application templates to use as is or build upon in your own programs. You'll get complete programming models for creating FoxPro report generators, screens, menus, spreadsheets, multiuser interfaces, network support, and much more. 384 pages, 150 illustrations. Book No. 4057, $22.95 paperback only

CONVERTING C TO TURBO C++
—Len Dorfman

Discover how to move existing C applications into the OOP/GUI environment—often without changing a single line of code! This book explains the principles of OOP and outlines the procedures you should follow to develop commercial-quality graphical interfaces with C++. You'll develop C++ class libraries for all functions—display, window, keyboard, sound, and mouse—of software development and a complete object-oriented user interface. 352 pages, 100 illustrations. Includes 5.25″ disk. Book No. 4084, $29.95 paperback, $39.95 hardcover

VISUAL BASIC: Easy Windows™
Programming—Namir C. Shammas

Enter the exciting new world of visual object-oriented programming for the Windows environment. *Visual Basic* is chock-full of screen dumps, program listings, and illustrations to give you a clear picture of how your code should come together. You'll find yourself referring to its tables, listings, and quick-reference section long after you master Visual Basic. As a bonus, the book is packaged with a 3.5-inch disk filled with all the working Visual Basic application programs discussed in the text. 480 pages, 249 illustrations. Book No. 4086, $29.95 paperback

BUSINESS APPLICATIONS
SHAREWARE—PC-SIG, Inc.

Shareware allows you to evaluate hundreds of dollars worth of software before buying it. Once you decide, you simply register the shareware you want at a fraction of the cost of buying commercially marketed packages. This resource shows you a wide variety of these programs including: PC Payroll, Bill Power Plus, Painless Accounting, Graphtime, PC Inventory Plus, Formgen, and more. 312 pages, 81 illustrations. Book No. 3920, $29.95 paperback only

MAINTAIN AND REPAIR YOUR
COMPUTER PRINTER AND SAVE A
BUNDLE—Stephen J. Bigelow

A few basic tools are all you need to fix many of the most common printer problems quickly and easily. You may even be able to avoid printer hangups altogether by following a regular routine of cleaning, lubrication, and adjustment. Why pay a repairman a bundle when you don't need to? With this time- and money-saving book on your printer stand, repair bills will be a thing of the past! 240 pages, 160 illustrations. Book No. 3922, $16.95 paperback, $26.95 hardcover

ONLINE INFORMATION HUNTING
—Nahum Goldmann

Cut down dramatically on your time and money spent online, and increase your online productivity with this helpful book. It will give you systematic instruction on developing cost-effective research techniques for large-scale information networks. You'll also get detailed coverage of the latest online service, new hardware and software, and recent advances that have affected online research. 256 pages, 125 illustrations. Book No. 3943, $19.95 paperback. $29.95 hardcover

**BUILD YOUR OWN MACINTOSH AND
SAVE A BUNDLE—2nd Edition**—Bob Brant

Assemble an affordable Mac with inexpensive, easy-to-obtain mail-order parts. This helpful book includes all-new illustrated instructions for building the Mac Classic, Mac portable, and new 68040-based machines (LC, IIci, and Quadra 700). It also provides valuable tips for using System 7, outlines ways you can breathe new life into older Macs with a variety of upgrade options, and updates prices on all peripherals, expansion boards, and memory upgrades. 368 pages, illustrated. Book No. 4156, $19.95 paperback, $29.95 hardcover

**MACINTOSH HARD DISK
MANAGEMENT**—Bob Brant

Keep your hard drive healthy. This comprehensive guide takes a close look at the disk itself—how it works, how to keep it running properly, and how to fix it if it breaks down. In addition, you'll explore how to make the most of your Mac hard disk's storage capacity and capabilities. Several utilities, such as ADB Probe, Connectix Mode 32, RAM Check, System Picker, DisKeeper, Speedometer, and Layout, are included on an accompanying 3.5" disk! 344 pages, 150 illustrations. Book No. 4087, $29.95 paperback only

Prices Subject to Change Without Notice.

Look for These and Other TAB Books at Your Local Bookstore

To Order Call Toll Free 1-800-822-8158
(24-hour telephone service available.)

or write to TAB Books, Blue Ridge Summit, PA 17294-0840.

Title	Product No.	Quantity	Price

☐ Check or money order made payable to TAB Books

Charge my ☐ VISA ☐ MasterCard ☐ American Express

Acct. No. _____ Exp. _____

Signature: _____

Name: _____

Address: _____

City: _____

State: _____ Zip: _____

Subtotal $ _____

Postage and Handling
($3.00 in U.S., $5.00 outside U.S.) $ _____

Add applicable state and local
sales tax $ _____

TOTAL $ _____

TAB Books catalog free with purchase; otherwise send $1.00 in check or money order and receive $1.00 credit on your next purchase.

Orders outside U.S. must pay with international money order in U.S. dollars drawn on a U.S. bank.

TAB Guarantee: If for any reason you are not satisfied with the book(s) you order, simply return it (them) within 15 days and receive a full refund.   **BC**

80386/80486 Assembly Language Programming

If you're interested in using programs shown in *80306/80486 Assembly Language Programming* (TAB Book No. 4217), you might want to order the companion source code disk rather than type in all the code yourself. Aside from saving you hours at your keyboard, this disk ensures that no typos are introduced in the code itself.

Available on high density 5¼″ or 3½″ disk requiring Borland Turbo Assembler 2.0 and MS-DOS 5.0 or higher on IBM/Compatible. Send $24.95 plus $2.50 shipping and handling.

YES, I'm interested. Please send me:

_____ copies 5¼″ disk with said requirements (#6811S), $24.95 each.... $ _____

_____ copies 3½″ disk with said requirements (#6810S), $24.95 each.... $ _____

_____ TAB Books catalog (free with purchase; otherwise send $1.00 in check or money order and receive coupon worth $1.00 off your next purchase)....................................... $ _____

Shipping & Handling: $2.50 per disk in U.S. ($5.00 per disk outside U.S.) $ _____

Please add applicable state and local sales tax. $ _____

TOTAL $ _____

☐ Check or money order enclosed made payable to TAB Books

Charge my ☐ VISA ☐ MasterCard ☐ American Express

Acct No. _____ Exp. Date _____

Signature _____

Name _____

Address _____

City _____ State _____ Zip _____

TOLL-FREE ORDERING: 1-800-822-8158
(24-hour telephone service available.)

or write to TAB Books, Blue Ridge Summit, PA 17294-0840

Prices subject to change. Orders outside the U.S. must be paid in international money order in U.S. dollars drawn on a U.S. bank.

TAB-4217